The **Rough Guide** to

# Florence and Siena

written and researched by

**Jonathan Buckley and Tim Jepson**

with additional contributions by

**Charles Hebbert**

**ROUGH GUIDES**

NEW YORK • LONDON • DELHI

www.roughguides.com

# Contents

3

◄◄ The Duomo, Baptistery and Campanile, Florence ◄ A detail from Duccio's *Maestà*, Siena

## Introduction to

# Florence and Siena

**Since the early nineteenth century, Florence (Firenze in Italian) has been celebrated as the epitome of everything that is beautiful in Italian civilization: Stendhal staggered around its medieval streets in a stupor of delight, the Brownings sighed over its idyllic charms, and E.M. Forster's *A Room with a View* portrayed it as the great antidote to the bloodless sterility of Anglo-Saxon life. And for most modern visitors the first, resounding impressions of the city tend to confirm the myth. The stupendous dome of the cathedral is visible over the rooftops the moment you step out of the train station, and when you reach the Piazza del Duomo the close-up view is even more breathtaking, with the multicoloured Duomo rising behind the marble-clad Baptistery. Wander from there down towards the River Arno and the attraction still holds: beyond the Piazza della Signoria, site of the immense Palazzo Vecchio, the water is spanned by the shop-laden medieval Ponte Vecchio, with gorgeous San Miniato al Monte glistening on the hill behind it.**

It has to be said, however, that intensive exploration of the city is not always a stress-free business. The wonders of Florence are known to the whole world, which means that in high season the sheer number of tourists at the major sights is overwhelming – the Uffizi, for instance, is all but impossible to get into unless you've pre-booked your tickets many days in advance. And yet, such is the wealth of monuments

and artistic treasures here, it's impossible not to find the experience an enriching one. Tuscany was the powerhouse of what has come to be known as the Renaissance, and Florence – the region's dominant political and cultural centre – is the continent's supreme monument to European civilization's major evolutionary shift into modernity. The development of this new sensibility can be plotted stage by stage in the vast picture collection of the **Uffizi**, and charted in the sculpture of the **Bargello**, the **Museo dell'Opera del Duomo** and the guild church of **Orsanmichele**. Equally revelatory are the fabulously decorated chapels of **Santa Croce** and **Santa Maria Novella**, forerunners of such astonishing creations as Masaccio's frescoes at **Santa Maria del Carmine**, Fra' Angelico's serene paintings at **San Marco**, and Andrea del Sarto's work at **Santissima Annunziata**, to name just a few. During the fifteenth century, the likes of Brunelleschi and Alberti began to transform the cityscape of Florence, raising buildings that were to provide generations of architects with examples from which to take a lead, and still adorn the fabric of the city today. The Renaissance emphasis on harmony and rational design is expressed with unrivalled eloquence in Brunelleschi's interiors of **San**

> **Every quarter of Florence can boast a church or collection worth an extended call**

**Lorenzo**, **Santo Spirito** and the **Cappella dei Pazzi**, and in Alberti's work at Santa Maria Novella and the Palazzo Rucellai. The bizarre architecture of San Lorenzo's **Sagrestia Nuova** and the marble statuary of the **Accademia** – home of the *David* – display the full genius of **Michelangelo**, the dominant creative figure of sixteenth-century Italy. Every quarter of

5

■

## Fact file

**Tuscany** (Toscana) has a **population** of around 3.5 million, with some 370,000 in **Florence**, its capital. In recent years the population of Florence has been steadily declining (it was 450,000 in 1981), while the proportion of elderly people has increased.

Though many large factories closed in the 1970s and 1980s, the province of Florence is still the third largest **industrial centre** in Italy. Textiles, metalwork, glass, ceramics, pharmaceuticals and chemical production remain major industries in the province, while in Florence itself many long-established crafts continue to thrive, notably jewellery and gold-working, the manufacture of handmade paper, perfumery and leatherwork. Commercial research and development businesses are also important, while the University of Florence, with more than 60,000 students, is one of the largest in the world.

But **tourism** is of course the mainstay of the Florentine economy: the city attracts upwards of eight million tourists a year, more than five million of whom stay for at least one night.

**Siena** is the capital of its province (*provincia*), but is a far more modest metropolis than Florence. Its current population of around 56,000 is relatively stable (about a third of its medieval peak), and is bolstered by a student population of some 20,000. Light industry such as food processing and furniture making dots the city's immediate hinterland, but such money as is made in Siena itself revolves around service industries and – inevitably – tourism.

Florence can boast a church or collection worth an extended call, and the enormous **Palazzo Pitti** constitutes a museum district on its own: half a dozen museums are gathered here, one of them an art gallery that any city would envy.

So there are sights enough to fill a month, but to enjoy a visit fully it's best to ration yourself to a couple each day, and spend the rest of your time strolling and involving yourself in the life of the city. Though Florence might seem a little sedate on the surface, its university – and the presence of large numbers of language and art schools – guarantees a fair range of term-time diversions and **nightlife**. The city has some excellent **restaurants** and **café-bars** amid the tourist joints, as well as the biggest and liveliest **markets** in Tuscany, and plenty of browsable, high-quality **shops**.

▼ Cellini's *Perseus*, Piazza della Signoria

And there's certainly no shortage of special events – from the high-art festivities of the **Maggio Musicale** to the licensed bedlam of the **Calcio Storico**, a series of costumed football matches held in the last week of June.

More compact than Florence, and self-contained behind its old defensive walls, **Siena** is an immediately striking city: a majestic ensemble of well-preserved medieval buildings set on three ridges, affording a succession of beautiful vistas over terracotta rooftops to the bucolic Tuscan coun-

▲ Lunch at *Boccadama* restaurant, Florence

tryside beyond. In its great scallop-shaped piazza, **Il Campo**, Siena has the loveliest of all Italian public squares and in its zebra-striped Duomo, a religious focus to match. It's also a place of immediate charm: airy, easy-going and pedestrianized – where Florence is cramped, busy and traffic-ridden, despite the introduction of vehicle restrictions – and it is refreshingly untouristy away from the main sights. Perhaps most important of all, the city is host to the undisputed giant of Italian festivals, the **Palio**, an exciting and chaotic bareback horse-race around the Campo, held on July 2 and August 16.

If Florence is associated above all with the Renaissance, in Siena it's the Gothic that holds sway. The Duomo and Palazzo Pubblico are two of the purest examples of Italian Gothic, while the finest of the city's paintings – many of which are collected in the Palazzo's **Museo Civico** and the separate **Pinacoteca Nazionale** – are in the same tradition. Bearing the stamp of Byzantine, Romanesque and Gothic influences long after classical humanism had transformed Florence's art, Sienese painting of the medieval and Renaissance periods is characterized by brilliance of colour and decorative detail, as well as an almost exclusive devotion to religious subjects – principally the city's patroness, the Virgin. Its traditions were shaped by a group of artists working in the last half of the thirteenth century and the first half of the fourteenth: Duccio di Buoninsegna, Simone Martini and the brothers Ambrogio and Pietro Lorenzetti. Arguably the greatest

## Popes and Saints

Siena may have produced the most famous Tuscan saint – St Catherine, the joint patron saint of Italy – but Florence's contribution to the religious life of the nation is by no means negligible, even if none of the godlier Florentines has achieved a degree of fame to equal that of the supremely secular Niccolò Machiavelli, for example.

The city's first Christian martyr, Minias (see p.168), was beheaded here in the third century, and immediately offered incontrovertible proof of his holiness by carrying his severed head up the hill to the spot where the church dedicated to him – San Miniato – now stands. Around 345AD the boy who would grow up to become the very first bishop of Florence was baptized in the church of San Lorenzo; canonized as St Zenobius, he's commemorated by a column that stands close to the Baptistery. Frescoes in Santa Trìnita (see p.95) record the life of St Giovanni Gualberto, founder of this church and of the Vallombrosan order of Benedictines, while in the monastery of San Marco (and in paintings all over the city) you'll find images of the implacably zealous St Peter Martyr. The only Renaissance artist to have been beatified, Fra' Angelico (see p.122) was a Dominican friar at San Marco, which was later to be the base of the firebrand preacher Girolamo Savonarola (see p.122), the city's de facto ruler for a while in the 1490s. From the ranks of the Pazzi family – one

of Florence's pre-eminent clans – came St Maria Maddalena dei Pazzi (see p.151), who was famed for her wild religious visions and excesses of self-punishment; and the most eminent of all Florentine families, the Medici, raised two popes: Leo X, who was the second son of Lorenzo il Magnifico, and Clement VII, the illegitimate son of Giuliano de' Medici, Lorenzo's brother. Neither of these pontiffs, it has to be admitted, could be ranked alongside Siena's Aeneas Sylvius Piccolomini (see p.245), an eminent scholar, poet, humanist and patron of the arts who, in 1458, became Pope Pius II.

of all Siena's paintings belongs to the first of these, a magnificent Maestà housed in the **Museo dell'Opera del Duomo**. Another supreme work, the fresco cycle of Domenico di Bartolo, an artist working on the cusp of the Renaissance, fills part of **Santa Maria della Scala**, the city's hospital for some eight hundred years and now one of its premier exhibition spaces. In its sculpture, which is also well represented in the Museo dell'Opera, Siena drew mainly on foreign artists: the Florentines Donatello and

Ghiberti worked on the font in the Baptistery, while Michelangelo and Nicola and Giovanni Pisano left their mark on the Duomo.

Nightlife does not have the range or sophistication of Florence – there are only a handful of late-night bars and clubs – but the choice of **restaurants** is good, and there are plenty of backstreet places still not overwhelmed by visitors. Shopping, too, pales by comparison with the regional capital, but there are one or two food shops, in particular, of which any city would be proud.

# When to go

F lorence and Siena are often stiflingly hot in midsummer – Florence especially so, as the hills that ring the city form a natural roasting pan for the city. The combination of heat and throngs of tour groups can take a lot of the pleasure out of a visit between early June and end of August – and August, moreover, is the month when the great majority of Italians take their holidays, which means that many restaurants and bars are closed for the entire month. If possible, you should go shortly **before Easter** or **between September and mid-October**, when the weather should be fine, and you'll be able to savour the sights at your leisure. The period of maximum tranquillity is from November to March, a season which can be quite wet and misty (and sharply cold, when the *tramontana* wind comes whistling off the Apennines), but is equally likely to give you days of magical clarity.

▼ Siena's Duomo

9

◀ Piazza del Campo, Siena

If you do have to go in the summer months, make sure that you've reserved your accommodation long before your trip: Siena doesn't have a great profusion of hotels, and although Florence has scores of them it's by no means rare for every single bed in the city to be taken. The table below shows average daytime temperatures and monthly rainfall.

| | January | April | July | October |
|---|---|---|---|---|
| **Florence** | | | | |
| °C | 6 | 13 | 25 | 16 |
| °F | 42 | 55 | 77 | 60 |
| mm | 62 | 70 | 23 | 96 |
| inches | 2.5 | 3 | 1 | 4 |
| **Siena** | | | | |
| °C | 5 | 12 | 25 | 15 |
| °F | 40 | 54 | 77 | 59 |
| mm | 70 | 62 | 20 | 110 |
| inches | 3 | 2.5 | 1 | 4 |

◀ Statue in the Bóboli gardens, Florence

# 25

## things not to miss

*It's not possible to see everything that Florence and Siena have to offer in one trip – and we don't suggest you try. What follows is a selective taste of the cities' highlights: great places to visit, outstanding buildings, glorious artworks and unforgettable events. They're arranged in five colour-coded categories, which you can browse through to find the very best things to see and experience. All entries have a page reference to take you straight into the Guide, where you can find out more.*

**01** **The Uffizi** Page **77** • The galleries of the Uffizi are packed with masterpieces by Botticelli and almost every other front-rank Italian Renaissance painter.

**02** **The Campo** Page **226** • Siena's Piazza del Campo is Italy's finest square and the stage for the Palio horserace.

**04** **The Bargello** Page **136** • An astounding collection of Renaissance sculpture is the principal attraction at Florence's former prison.

**03** **The Accademia** Page **120** • Everyone comes to see *David*, but Michelangelo's unfinished *Slaves* are just as powerful.

**05** **Santa Maria della Scala** Page **249** • Swathes of Renaissance frescoes recount the myths, legends and historical episodes associated with this rambling medieval building, a place that served as Siena's main hospital for around eight hundred years.

**06** **Ponte Vecchio** Page **154** • For more than four hundred years the Ponte Vecchio has been a midstream avenue of jewellery workshops.

**07** **Wine bars** Page **201** • With some of the country's most famous vineyards on its doorstep, Florence is a great place for wine tasting.

**09** **The Museo di San Marco** Page **121** • Florence's tranquil monastery of San Marco is nowadays a museum devoted to the serene art of Fra' Angelico.

**08** **Santa Croce** Page **142** • With paintings by Giotto and a wonderful chapel by Brunelleschi, the Dominican church of Santa Croce is another essential stop on the Florentine art-circuit.

**10** **San Miniato al Monte** Page **168** • Visible all over Florence, San Miniato is as perfect inside as out.

**11 Santa Maria Novella** Page
**99** • Remarkable frescoes make the
Dominican church of Santa Maria Novella an
unforgettable Florentine experience.

**13 Piazza Santo Spirito,**
**Florence** Page **197** • Wind down
with a feast at one of Piazza Santo Spirito's
terrific restaurants.

**15 Santa Maria del Carmine**
Page **164** • If one single spot can be
said to mark the emergence of Renaissance
art, it's the Brancacci chapel in Santa Maria
del Carmine.

**12 The Duomo** Page **240** • Siena's
cathedral, with its distinctive Pisan–
Romanesque campanile, stands at one of
the city's highest points on a site previously
occupied by a Roman temple.

**14 Museo dell'Opera del**
**Duomo** Page **255** • Statues by
Giovanni Pisano removed for safekeeping
from the facade of the Duomo are just some
of the many sculptures, paintings and other
works of art in Siena's cathedral museum.

**16 La Specola** Page **162** •
Admire art in the service of science
at La Specola's incredible collection of
anatomical waxworks.

**17 Pinacoteca Nazionale** Page **268** • The Madonna and Child was the most popular subject for Sienese artists in the fourteenth and fifteenth centuries. This outstanding example is by Ambrogio Lorenzetti, an artist who died in the Black Death of 1348.

**18 The Palazzo Vecchio** Page 72 • The craggy Palazzo Vecchio was for centuries the nerve-centre of the Florentine state.

**19 Palio** See *The Siena Palio* **colour section** • The twice-yearly Palio, one of Italy's most colourful and chaotic spectacles, is simply not to be missed and well worth planning your trip around.

**20 San Lorenzo** Page **108** • The ancient church of San Lorenzo was both the parish church and the mausoleum of the Medici.

**21 Fiesole** Page **173** • For a dose of country air – and fabulous vistas – take the bus up to the hilltop town of Fiesole.

**22 Palazzo Pitti** Page **157** • Titian's *Mary Magdalene* is one of the star exhibits at the Palazzo Pitti, the largest private building in Florence.

**23 The Mercato Centrale** Page **118** • Florence's vast central market is in effect the biggest delicatessen in Italy.

**24 Museo Civico** Page **223** • The equestrian portrait of Guidoriccio da Fogliano is Siena's best-known painting, but its attribution to Simone Martini is the most contentious in Italian art history.

**25 Florence's Piazza del Duomo** Page **52** • The marble-clad Duomo, Baptistery and Campanile make the Piazza del Duomo one of Italy's most impressive public spaces.

# Basics

# Basics

# Getting there

The easiest way to get to Florence and Siena is to fly. Most visitors fly to **Pisa** (PSA), an easy train or bus journey from the airport to the centre of Florence. The smaller **Florence Perètola** (Amerigo Vespucci) airport (FLR), located on the edge of the city, is served by a small number of international flights. Bologna's Marconi airport (BLQ) is also within easy reach. Siena is around two to two and a half hours' journey by train or bus from both Pisa and Florence Perètola.

**From the UK and Ireland**, competitive prices for charter or scheduled flights outweigh the inconvenience of the long rail or bus journey. Flights **from North America and Australasia** come into Rome (or, less conveniently, Milan), from where you can move on by plane or overland; from down under, you may find it cheaper to fly to London and you get a budget onward flight from there.

Airfares depend on the **season**, with the highest being around Easter, from June to August, and from Christmas to New Year; fares drop during the "shoulder" seasons – September to October and April to May – and you'll get the best prices during the November to March low season (excluding Christmas and New Year). Note also that it is generally more expensive to fly at weekends; price ranges quoted below assume midweek travel. You can often cut costs by going through a **discount flight agent** who may also offer special student and youth fares and a range of other travel-related services such as travel insurance, rail passes, car rentals, tours and the like. Some agents specialize in **charter flights**, which may be cheaper than anything available on a scheduled flight, but departure dates are fixed and withdrawal penalties are high. You may find it cheaper to pick up a **package deal**, which takes care of flights and accommodation for an all-in price.

## Online booking agents

ⓦ **www.flyaow.com** Online air travel info and reservations site.
ⓦ **www.smilinjack.com/airlines.htm** Up-to-date list of airline websites.
ⓦ **travel.yahoo.co.uk** Good information and destination coverage.

ⓦ **www.cheaptickets.com** Discount flight specialists from the US only.
ⓦ **www.cheapflights.com** Bookings from the UK and Ireland only. Flight deals, travel agents, plus links to other travel sites.
ⓦ **www.expedia.co.uk** Discount airfares, all-airline search engine and daily deals.
ⓦ **www.flights4less.co.uk** Does just what it says on the tin.
ⓦ **www.flynow.com** Simple-to-use independent travel site offering good-value fares.
ⓦ **www.hotwire.com** Bookings from the US only. Last-minute savings of up to forty percent on regular published fares. Travellers must be at least 18 and there are no refunds, transfers or changes allowed.
ⓦ **www.lastminute.com** Bookings from the UK only. Offers good last-minute holiday package and flight-only deals.
ⓦ **www.skyauction.com** Bookings from the US only. Auctions tickets and travel packages using a "second bid" scheme.
ⓦ **www.travelocity.co.uk** Destination guides, hot Web fares and best deals for car rental, accommodation and lodging as well as fares.
ⓦ **www.travelshop.com.au** Australian website offering discounted flights, packages, insurance and online bookings.

## Packages and organized tours

Florence is a prime destination in Italian package and tour programmes, and – a definite plus – most of these holidays are sold by small, independently run travel companies. Holidays on the market mostly fall into one of the following categories (sample prices in British pounds and US dollars):

• **Flight-plus-hotel**. These deals can be excellent value, usually featuring a good three-star hotel. All-in prices for a week's bed and breakfast in Florence, for example, start at around £500/$900 per person per week, rising by about £50/$90 in high season.

• **Specialist holidays**. An increasing number of operators offer art and archeology holidays, and food and wine jaunts. Many are group tours and most don't come cheap: accommodation, food, local transport and the services of a guide are nearly always included, and a week's half-board holiday can cost £1200/$2175 or more per person.

• **Short-break deals**. Florence is a standby in major holiday companies' "Italian City Break" programmes; reckon on spending about £350–500/$620–900 per person for three nights, depending on season and the class of hotel. Always check precisely where your hotel is located: cheaper places may be some way from the city centre.

## From the UK and Ireland

**No-frills airlines in the UK** serving Pisa include Ryanair, flying from London Stansted, Glasgow and Liverpool, and easyJet from Bristol, while in summer Jet2 flies from Manchester, and Thomson from Bournemouth, Coventry and Doncaster. If you book well in advance you can sometimes find tickets for as little as £25 return for mid-week off-peak flights, though these rock-bottom prices tend to apply only to early-morning or late-evening flights. For more reasonable flight times from these budget airlines, you're looking at something in the region of £100–150 return in summer, as long as you make your reservation well in advance: prices can rise so much for last-minute bookings on no-frills airlines (ie within two weeks of departure date) that they become more expensive than their full-service rivals. You may also find **charter flight** bargains in high season: it's worth checking with a specialist agent or scouring the classified section of the weekend newspapers for last-minute deals.

Of the **full-service airlines in the UK** British Airways serves Pisa several times daily out of London Gatwick and Manchester, and Alitalia flies via Milan or Rome. A return flight with Alitalia or BA from London to Pisa in low season can cost from around £80, with prices at £150 and upwards in high season. Again, it pays to book as far in advance as possible, and to keep your eyes open for special offers, which have become more numerous in the wake of the competition from the no-frills outfits. Meridiana is currently the only airline with non-stop flights from Gatwick to Florence Perètola; their tickets tend to be more expensive – from £150 off-peak and £200 in summer.

There are also regular flights to **Bologna** Marconi airport: easyJet departs daily from London Stansted and British Airways flies from London Gatwick. This is generally a cheaper option than flying to Pisa, and because Bologna is a less popular destination you can often find seats when the Pisa flights are sold out. **Bologna** airport is a shuttle-bus ride from Bologna main train station, from where Florence is an hour's rail journey away. (Forlì airport, which Ryanair sells as Bologna, is a good deal further away and will add an extra hour on to your journey.)

**From Ireland**, Aer Lingus has three flights a week to Bologna (Marconi), and three daily flights from Dublin direct to Rome Fiumicino; Alitalia covers the same route three to five times a week. You can find return deals for around €270 if you book early, but prices are usually significantly higher (€345–400). A cheaper option would be to pick up an inexpensive Ryanair flight from Dublin or Shannon to London Stansted and catch a Pisa plane from there. Ryanair's hub at Brussels (Charleroi) is a useful alternative, linked by direct flights from Dublin (from €40) and on to Pisa for as little as €40 return if you book early.

### Airlines in the UK and Ireland

**Aer Lingus** UK ☎0845/084 4444, Ireland ☎0818/365 000, ⊛www.aerlingus.ie.
**Alitalia** UK ☎0870/544 8259, Ireland ☎01/677 5171, ⊛www.alitalia.com.
**British Airways** UK ☎0870/850 9850, Ireland ☎1800/626 747, ⊛www.ba.com.
**easyJet** UK ☎0905/821 0905 (calls charged at premium rate), ⊛www.easyjet.com.
**Jet2** UK ☎0871/226 1737, Ireland ☎0818/20001, ⊛www.jet2.com.
**Meridiana** UK ☎020/7839 2222, ⊛www.meridiana.it.
**Ryanair** UK ☎0871/246 0000, Ireland ☎0818/303 030, ⊛www.ryanair.com.
**Thomson** UK ☎0870/1900 737, Ireland ☎01/247 7723, ⊛www.thomsonfly.com.

## Flight and travel agents in the UK and Ireland

**Aran Travel International** Galway ☎091/562 595, ⓦ homepages.iol.ie/~arantvl/aranmain.htm. Good-value flights to all parts of the world.

**CIE Tours International** Dublin ☎01/703 1888, ⓦ www.cietours.ie. General flight and tour agent.

**Co-op Travel Care** UK ☎0870/112 0085, ⓦ www .travelcareonline.com. Flights and holidays.

**Flightbookers** UK ☎0870/010 7000, ⓦ www .ebookers.com, Ireland ☎01/241 5689, ⓦ www .ebookers.ie. Low fares on an extensive selection of scheduled flights.

**Joe Walsh Tours** Dublin ☎01/676 0991, ⓦ www .joewalshtours.ie. General budget fares agent.

**McCarthy's Travel** Cork ☎021/427 0127, ⓦ www.mccarthystravel.ie. General flight agent.

**Neenan Travel** Dublin ☎01/607 9900, ⓦ www .neenantrav.ie. Specialists in European city breaks.

**North South Travel** UK ☎01245/608 291, ⓦ www.northsouthtravel.co.uk. Friendly, competitive travel agency, offering discounted fares worldwide. Profits are used to support projects in the developing world, especially the promotion of sustainable tourism.

**Premier Travel** Derry ☎028/7126 3333, ⓦ www .premiertravel.uk.com. Discount flight specialists.

**STA Travel** UK ☎0870/160 0599, ⓦ www .statravel.co.uk. Worldwide specialists in low-cost flights and tours for students and under-26s, though other customers welcome.

**Top Deck** UK ☎020/8879 6789, ⓦ www .topdecktravel.co.uk. Long-established agent dealing in discount flights.

**Trailfinders** UK ☎0845/0585 858, ⓦ www .trailfinders.co.uk; Dublin ☎01/677 7888, ⓦ www .trailfinders.ie. One of the best informed and most efficient agents for independent travellers.

## General package operators in the UK

**Citalia** ☎020/8686 0677, ⓦ www.citalia.co.uk. Long-established company offering city-break packages in mid-range three-star and smarter four-star hotels.

**Crystal Premier Italy** ☎0870 888 0222, ⓦ www .crystalitaly.co.uk. Well-priced city breaks to Florence and Siena.

**Italian Expressions** ☎020/7433 2675, ⓦ www .expressionsholidays.co.uk. Good on- and off-season special offers to Florence and Siena.

**Italiatour!** ☎0870 733 3000, ⓦ www.italiatour .co.uk. Package deals, city breaks, winter sun holidays and specialist Italian-cuisine tours. Also offers tailor-made itineraries and can book local events and tours.

**Kirker Holidays** ☎0870 112 3333, ⓦ www .kirkerholidays.com. Independent operator renowned for their excellent city- and short-break deals to Tuscany.

**Sunvil Holidays** ☎020/8758 4722, ⓦ www .sunvil.co.uk. City breaks and hotel and villa packages, but especially strong on tailor-made fly-drive packages in three-to five-star hotels.

### Apartments and villas

**Carefree Italy** ☎01293/552 277, ⓦ www .carefree-italy.com. Farmhouses and villas, often in shared complexes; also has a range of small hotels and city apartments.

**Cottages to Castles** ☎01622/726 883, ⓦ www .cottagestocastles.com. Over a hundred cottages, villas and apartments around Florence and Siena, with some properties inside the cities.

**Italian Life** ☎0870/444 8811, ⓦ www.italianlife .co.uk. Large database of hundreds of properties in Tuscany, with a comprehensive online search facility to find just the right one.

## Specialist tour operators in the UK

### Art and culture holidays

**Bollini** ☎020/7602 7602, ⓦ www.bollinitravel .com. Tailor-made tours by a company specializing in Italy that can arrange private access to art collections and palazzos.

**Inscape** ☎01993/891 726, ⓦ www.inscapetours .co.uk. Florence and Siena sometimes feature on the study courses offered by this well-established company.

**JMB Travel** ☎01905/830099, ⓦ www.jmb-travel .co.uk. Specialists solely in opera holidays, with packages to Florence's major opera events and the Maggio Musicale.

**Liaisons Abroad** ☎020/7376 4020, ⓦ www .liaisonsabroad.com. Agency for tickets to major Italian opera and musical events, timed museum tickets, Siena Palio, Serie A football matches, and more.

**Light and Land** ☎01432/839111, ⓦ www .lightandland.co.uk. Week-long photographic holidays in Tuscany for camera enthusiasts of all standards. Well-scouted locations, plus time for sightseeing and relaxation: some trips led by Charlie Waite, one of Britain's most distinguished landscape photographers.

**Martin Randall** ☎020/8742 3355, ⓦ www .martinrandall.com. One of the best operators in the sector: imaginative art, music and cultural tours ranging from three to twelve nights, including Piero della Francesca, Florence & Siena and Florence Revisited (lesser-known sights and private palaces).

### Wine and cookery holidays

**Arblaster & Clarke** ☎01730/893 344, ⓦwww
.winetours.co.uk. Upmarket wine tours in Florence
and near Siena, staying at four- and five-star hotels
and with tastings at the premier estates.
**Winetrails** ☎01306/712 111, ⓦwww.winetrails
.co.uk. Exercise and indulgence combined: tours link
vineyard visits with guided walks and good food. An
independent programme is also available.

### By train from the UK and Ireland

Travelling **by train** to Italy won't save much
money. The beauty of train travel and tick-
eting, however, is that you can break your
journey en route. The eighteen-hour journey
to Florence costs around £210, but special
offers are always worth checking. Bear in
mind that going via Paris on Eurostar you
will have to lug your bags from the Gare
du Nord to the Gare de Lyon. Discounts
for under-26s and special offers are
sometimes available and advance booking
is essential. An alternative route is to
use the cross-Channel **ferry** and catch
slower trains through France and Italy but
this won't cut costs significantly and the
connecting trains from Calais to Paris are
notoriously badly timetabled: many arrive
too late for the evening train to Florence,
meaning an overnight stay in Paris. If
you're planning to include Italy as part of
a longer European trip you could invest in
a **rail pass**: the InterRail and Eurail passes
offer a month's unlimited rail travel throughout Europe but they must be bought before
leaving home.

### Train information

**Eurostar** ☎0870/160 6600, ⓦwww.eurostar.com.
**Rail Europe** UK ☎0870/584 8848, ⓦwww
.raileurope.co.uk. First stop for information on
everything to do with international train travel,
including purchase of tickets and passes.
**Trainseurope** UK ☎020/8699 3654, ⓦwww
.trainseurope.co.uk.

## From North America

There are no direct flights **from the US or
Canada** to Pisa or Florence but it's easy to
fly to Rome or Milan Malpensa (MXP) and
pick up an onward flight or train from there.
Alitalia and Delta fly the widest choice of

direct routes between the US and Italy,
with daily flights to Milan from New York,
Miami, Chicago and Boston, and to Rome
from New York. Other options to Rome
include American Airlines from Chicago,
and Alitalia and Air Canada from Toronto.
Many European carriers fly from most major
US and Canadian cities (via their capitals)
to Rome, Florence and Pisa. The cheapest
**round-trip fares** to Rome, travelling
midweek in low season, start at around
$550 from New York or C$950 from
Toronto, rising to $950/C$1300 during
the summer. Add another $100–250 for
a connecting flight from Rome or Milan to
Florence or Pisa – or there are plenty of
fast rail connections.

### Airlines in North America

**Air Canada** ☎1-888/247-2262, ⓦwww
.aircanada.com.
**Air France** US ☎1-800/237-2747, Canada
☎1-800/667-2747, ⓦwww.airfrance.com.
**Alitalia** US ☎1-800/223-5730, Canada
☎1-800/361-8336, ⓦwww.alitalia.com.
**American Airlines** ☎1-800/433-7300,
ⓦwww.aa.com.
**Austrian** ☎1-800/843-0002, ⓦwww.aua.com.
**British Airways** ☎1-800/247-9297, ⓦwww
.ba.com.
**Continental** ☎1-800/231-0856, ⓦwww
.continental.com.
**Delta** ☎1-800/241-4141, ⓦwww.delta.com.
**Iberia** ☎1-800/772-4642, ⓦwww.iberia.com.
**KLM/Northwest** ☎1-800/447-4747, ⓦwww
.klm.com.
**Lufthansa** US ☎1-800/645-3880, Canada
☎1-800/563-5954, ⓦwww.lufthansa.com.
**Swiss** ☎1-877/359-7947, ⓦwww.swiss.com.
**United** ☎1-800/538-2929, ⓦwww.united.com.
**US Airways** ☎1-800/622-1015, ⓦwww.usair
.com.
**Virgin Atlantic** ☎1-800/862-8621, ⓦwww
.virgin-atlantic.com.

### Flight and travel agents in North America

**Airtech** ☎1-877-247-8324 or 212/219-7000,
ⓦwww.airtech.com. Standby seat broker; also deals
in consolidator fares and courier flights.
**Educational Travel Center** ☎1-800/747-5551 or
608/256-5551, ⓦwww.edtrav.com. Student/youth
discount agent.

**STA Travel** US ☎1-800/329-9537, Canada ☎1-888/427-5639, ⓦwww.sta-travel.com. Worldwide specialists in independent travel; also student IDs, travel insurance, car rental, rail passes, and more.
**Student Flights** ☎1-800/255-8000 or 480/951-1177, ⓦwww.isecard.com. Student/youth fares, student IDs.
**TFI Tours International** ☎1-800/745-8000 or 212/736-1140, ⓦwww.lowestairprice.com. Consolidator.
**Travelers Advantage** ☎1-877/259-2691, ⓦwww.travelersadvantage.com. Discount travel club; annual membership fee required (currently $1 for 3 months' trial).
**Worldtek Travel** ☎1-800/243-1723, ⓦwww.worldtek.com. Discount travel agency for worldwide travel.

## Tour operators in North America

**Abercrombie & Kent** ☎1-800/323-7308, ⓦwww.abercrombiekent.com. Deluxe village-to-village hiking and biking tours, as well as rail journeys.
**Classic Journeys** ☎1-800/200-3887, ⓦwww.classicjourneys.com. Hiking and cooking tours.
**Cross-Culture** ☎1-800/491-1148 or 413/256-6303, ⓦwww.crosscultureinc.com. Small-group cultural tours to Florence and the Tuscan hill towns.
**Delta Vacations** ☎1-800/654-6559, ⓦwww.deltavacations.com. City breaks to Florence.
**Journeys International** ☎1-800/255-8735, ⓦwww.journeys-intl.com. Seven-day walking tours.
**New Frontiers** ☎1-800/677-0720 or 310/670-7318, ⓦwww.newfrontiers.com. City breaks and independent packages.
**Travel Bound** ☎1-800/456-8656, ⓦwww.booktravelbound.com. Numerous packages to Florence, including a five-night stay with tickets booked to the Uffizi and Accademia.

# From Australia and New Zealand

There are no direct flights to Italy **from Australia or New Zealand**, but plenty of airlines fly to Rome via Asian hubs. Round-trip fares from Sydney with the major airlines (Alitalia, Qantas, Japan, Singapore or Malaysian) are A$1500–1850 in low season, A$1700–2500 in high season. With the same carriers from New Zealand you can expect to pay NZ$2000 in low season, NZ$3400 in high season.

## Airlines in Australia and New Zealand

**Alitalia** Australia ☎02/9244 2445, New Zealand ☎09/308 3357.
**British Airways** Australia ☎1300/767 177, New Zealand ☎09/966 9777, ⓦwww.ba.com.
**Cathay Pacific** Australia ☎13 17 47, NZ ☎09/379 0861, ⓦwww.cathaypacific.com.
**China Airlines** Australia ☎02/9244 2121, NZ ☎09/308 3364, ⓦwww.china-airlines.com.
**Garuda** Australia ☎1300/365 330 or 02/9334 9944, New Zealand ☎09/366 1862, ⓦwww.garuda-indonesia.com.
**Japan** Australia ☎02/9272 1111, NZ ☎09/379 9906, ⓦwww.japanair.com.
**Malaysian** Australia ☎13 26 27, NZ ☎0800/777 747 or 649/379 3743, ⓦwww.malaysiaairlines.com.
**Qantas** Australia ☎13 13 13, NZ ☎09/357 8900 or 0800/808 767, ⓦwww.qantas.com.
**Singapore** Australia ☎13 10 11, NZ ☎09/379 3209, ⓦwww.singaporeair.com.
**Sri Lankan** Australia ☎02/9244 2234, NZ ☎09/308 3353, ⓦwww.srilankan.aero.
**Thai** Australia ☎1300/651 960, NZ ☎09/377 3886, ⓦwww.thaiair.com.

## Flight and travel agents in Australia and New Zealand

**Australian Pacific Touring** Australia ☎1800/675 222 or 03/9277 8555, New Zealand ☎09/279 6077, ⓦwww.aptours.com. Long-established, award-winning operator running package tours and independent travel.
**Budget Travel** NZ ☎09/366 0061 or 0800/808 040, ⓦwww.budgettravel.co.nz.
**CIT** Australia ☎02/9267 1255, ⓦwww.cittravel.com.au. Italian specialists, with packages to Florence and elsewhere.
**Flight Centre** Australia ☎13 31 33, ⓦwww.flightcentre.com.au, NZ ☎0800/243 544, ⓦwww.flightcentre.co.nz. Specializes in discount airfares and holiday packages.
**Northern Gateway** Australia ☎1800/174 800, ⓦwww.northerngateway.com.au.
**Silke's Travel** Australia ☎1800/807 860, ⓦwww.silkes.com.au. Gay and lesbian specialist travel agent.
**STA Travel** Australia ☎1300/733 035, ⓦwww.statravel.com.au, New Zealand ☎0508/782 872, ⓦwww.statravel.co.nz.
**Student Uni Travel** Australia ☎02/9232 8444. Great deals for students.
**Trailfinders** Australia ☎02/9247 7666, ⓦwww.trailfinders.com.au. One of the best informed and most efficient agents for independent travellers.

Travel.com Australia ☎02/9249 6000, ⓦwww.travel.com.au. Agent for a broad range of tour operators.

## Tour operators in Australia and NZ

Abercrombie and Kent Australia ☎02/9241 3213, NZ ☎0800/441 638, ⓦwww .abercrombiekent.com.au. Upmarket tours.

Contiki Holidays Australia ☎02/9511 2200, NZ ☎09/309 8824, ⓦwww.contiki.com. Frenetic tours for 18–35-year-old party animals.
Viatour Australia ☎02/8219 5400. Bookings for hundreds of travel suppliers.
Walkabout Gourmet Adventures Australia ☎03/5159 6556, ⓦwww.walkaboutgourmet .com. Classy food, wine and walking tours in Tuscany.

# Red tape and visas

All EU citizens can enter Italy, and stay as long as they like, simply on production of a valid passport. Citizens of the United States, Canada, Australia and New Zealand need only a valid passport, but are limited to stays of ninety days. All other nationals should consult the relevant embassies about visa requirements.

Legally, you're required to **register with the police** within three days of entering Italy, though if you're staying at a hotel this will be done for you. Some policemen are more punctilious about this than ever, though others would be astonished by any attempt to register yourself at the local police station while on holiday.

## Italian embassies and consulates abroad

Australia Embassy: 12 Grey St, Deakin, Canberra, ACT 2600 ☎02/6273 3333, ⓦwww.ambitalia.org .au. Consulates in Melbourne ☎03/9867 5744 and Sydney ☎02/9392 7900.
Canada Embassy: 275 Slater St, Ottawa, ON K1P 5H9 ☎613/232-2401, ⓦwww.italyincanada.com. Consulates in Montréal ☎514/849-8351 and Toronto ☎416/977-1566.
Ireland Embassy: 63–65 Northumberland Rd, Dublin 4 ☎01/660 1744.
New Zealand Embassy: 34–38 Grant Rd, PO Box 463, Thorndon, Wellington ☎04/473 5339, ⓦwww .italy-embassy.org.nz.
UK Embassy: 14 Three King's Yard, London W1Y 2EH ☎020/7312 2200, ⓦwww.embitaly.org.uk.

Consulates in Edinburgh ☎0131/226 3695 and Manchester ☎0161/236 9024.
USA Embassy: 3000 Whitehaven St NW, Washington DC 20008 ☎202/612-4400, ⓦwww .italyemb.org. Consulates in Chicago ☎312/467-1550, New York ☎212/737-9100 and San Francisco ☎415/292-9210.

## Embassies and consulates in Italy

Australia Embassy: Via Alessandria 215, 00198 Roma ☎06.852.721, ⓦwww.australian-embassy.it.
Canada Embassy: Via G B de Rossi 27, 00161 Roma ☎06.445.981, ⓦwww.canada.it.
Ireland Embassy: Piazza di Campitelli 3, 00186 Roma ☎06.697.9121.
New Zealand Embassy: Via Zara 28, 00198 Roma ☎06.441.7171.
UK Embassy: Via XX Settembre 80a, 00187 Roma ☎06.4220.0001, ⓦwww.britain.it. Consulate in Florence: Lungarno Corsini 2 ☎055.284.133.
US Embassy: Via V Veneto 119/a, 00187 Roma ☎06.46.741, ⓦwww.usembassy.it. Consulate in Florence: Lungarno Vespucci 38 ☎055.239.8276, ⓦwww.usis.it/florence.

# Information, websites and maps

BASICS | Information, websites and maps

Before you leave home, you might want to contact the Italian State Tourist Office (ENIT) for a selection of maps and accommodation listings – though you can usually pick up much the same information from tourist offices in Italy. Details of the tourist offices in Florence and Siena are given on p.49 and p.225 respectively.

## ENIT offices

Worldwide listing at ⓦ www.enit.it.
**Australia** Level 26, 44 Market St, Sydney, NSW 2000 ☎ 02/9962 1666, ⓔ enitour@ihug.com.au.
**Canada** 175 Bloor St E #907, South Tower, Toronto, ON M4W 3R8 ☎ 416/925-4882, ⓦ www.italiantourism.com.
**Ireland** 63 Northumberland Rd, Dublin ☎ 01/660 1744.
**New Zealand** 34 Grant Rd, Thorndon, Wellington ☎ 04/473 5339.
**UK** 1 Princes St, London W1B 2AY ☎ 020/7408 1254, ⓦ www.italiantouristboard.co.uk.
**US** 630 5th Ave #1565, New York NY 10111 ☎ 212/245-4822; 500 N Michigan Ave #2240, Chicago, IL 60611 ☎ 312/644-0996; 12400 Wilshire Blvd #550, Los Angeles, CA 90025 ☎ 310/820-1898, ⓦ www.italiantourism.com.

## Websites

The following are general websites on Tuscany and Italy. For sites specifically related to Florence and Siena see p.49 and p.225 respectively.
ⓦ **www.enit.it** Italian State Tourist Board.
ⓦ **www.turismo.toscana.it** Official website of the Tuscan tourist board.
ⓦ **www.itwg.com** Italy's reliable and comprehensive tourist Web guide, with up-to-date travel information.
ⓦ **www.zoomata.com** New ezine with loads of information about Italy today.
ⓦ **www.terraditoscana.com** Well-designed, informative site covering every aspect of Tuscany from walking and sleeping to wild flowers and local cuisine.
ⓦ **www.camping.it** Details of virtually every campsite in Italy.
ⓦ **www.museionline.it** Links to museums and exhibition sites.
ⓦ **www.tuscanydirect.it** Hundreds of links

to Tuscany Web pages, plus general tourist information.
ⓦ **www.internettrain.it** Chain of cybercafés, present in major cities.
ⓦ **www.lega-calcio.it** Up-to-date news on Italian league football.
ⓦ **www.meteo.it** Italian weather forecast.
ⓦ **www.paginegialle.it** Italian *Yellow Pages*.

## Maps

Our **maps** should be fine for most purposes, and the tourist offices in Florence and Siena hand out free maps as well. More detailed maps are produced by a multitude of companies, notably Italy's leading street-plan publisher LAC (Litografia Artistica Cartografica), and the TCI (Touring Club Italiano), who also produce the country's best road maps. Combining the two cities on one sheet, the *Rough Guide Map: Florence and Siena* has the additional benefit of being printed on waterproof, crease-resistant paper.

## Map outlets

### UK and Ireland

**Stanfords** 12–14 Long Acre, London WC2E 9LP ☎ 020/7836 1321, ⓦ www.stanfords.co.uk.
**Blackwell's Map and Travel Shop** 50 Broad St, Oxford OX1 3BQ ☎ 01865/793 550, ⓦ maps.blackwell.co.uk; see website for branches all over the UK.
**Easons** 40 Lower O'Connell St, Dublin 1 ☎ 01/858 3881, ⓦ www.eason.ie.
**Map Shop** 30a Belvoir St, Leicester LE1 6QH ☎ 0116/247 1400, ⓦ www.mapshopleicester.co.uk.

### North America

**Elliot Bay Book Company** 101 S Main St, Seattle, WA 98104 ☎ 1-800/962-5311, ⓦ www.elliotbaybook.com.
**Globe Corner** 28 Church St, Cambridge, MA 02138 ☎ 1-800/358-6013, ⓦ www.globecorner.com.

Map Link 30 S La Patera Lane, Unit 5, Santa Barbara, CA 93117 ☎805/692-6777 or 1-800/962-1394, ⓦwww.maplink.com.
Rand McNally US ☎1-800/333-0136, ⓦwww.randmcnally.com.
World of Maps 1235 Wellington St, Ottawa, ON K1Y 3A3 ☎1-800/214-8524, ⓦwww.worldofmaps.com.

### Australia and NZ

Mapland 372 Little Bourke St, Melbourne, VIC 3000 ☎03/9670 4383, ⓦwww.mapland.com.au.
Map Shop 6–10 Peel St, Adelaide, SA 5000 ☎08/8231 2033, ⓦwww.mapshop.net.au.

Map World (Australia) 371 Pitt St, Sydney ☎02/9261 3601, ⓦwww.mapworld.net.au. Also at 900 Hay St, Perth ☎08/9322 5733, Jolimont Centre, Canberra ☎02/6230 4097 and 1981 Logan Road, Brisbane ☎07/3349 6633.
Map World (New Zealand) 173 Gloucester St, Christchurch ☎0800/627 967, ⓦwww.mapworld.co.nz.
Perth Map Centre 1/884 Hay St, Perth, WA 6000 ☎08/9322 5733, ⓦwww.perthmap.com.au.
Specialty Maps 46 Albert St, Auckland 1001 ☎09/307 2217, ⓦwww.ubdonline.co.nz/maps.

# Insurance and health

**Even though EU health care privileges apply in Italy, you'd do well to take out an insurance policy before travelling to cover against theft, loss, illness or injury.**

Before paying for a new policy, however, it's worth checking whether you're already covered: some all-risks home insurance policies may cover your possessions when overseas, and many private medical schemes include cover when abroad. In Canada, provincial health plans usually provide partial cover for medical mishaps overseas, while holders of official student/teacher/youth cards in Canada and the US are entitled to meagre accident coverage and hospital in-patient benefits. Students will often find that their student health coverage extends during the vacations and for one term beyond the date of last enrolment.

After exhausting the possibilities above, you might want to contact a specialist **travel insurance** company, or consider Rough

### Rough Guides travel insurance

Rough Guides has teamed up with Columbus Direct to offer you travel insurance that can be tailored to suit your needs.

Readers can choose from many different travel-insurance products, including a low-cost backpacker option for long stays; a short-break option for city getaways; a typical holiday package option; and many others. There are also annual multi-trip policies for those who travel regularly, with variable levels of cover available. Different sports and activities (trekking, skiing etc) can be covered if required on most policies.

Rough Guides travel insurance is available to the residents of 36 different countries with different language options to choose from via our website – ⓦwww.roughguidesinsurance.com – where you can also purchase the insurance.

Alternatively, UK residents should call ☎0800/083 9507, US citizens ☎1-800/749-4922 and Australians ☎1 300/669 999. All other nationalities should call ☎+44 870 890 2843.

Guides' own travel insurance deal (see box). A typical travel insurance policy usually provides cover for the loss of baggage, tickets and – up to a certain limit – cash or cheques, as well as cancellation or curtailment of your journey. Most exclude so-called dangerous sports unless an extra premium is paid: in Italy this can mean scuba-diving, windsurfing or trekking. If you do take medical coverage, ascertain whether benefits will be paid as treatment proceeds or only after you return home, and whether there is a 24-hour medical emergency number. When securing baggage cover, make sure that the per-article limit – typically under £500 – will cover your most valuable possession. If you need to make a claim, you should keep receipts for medicines and medical treatment, and in the event you have anything stolen, you must obtain an official statement from the police (either *polizia* or *carabinieri*).

## Health

If you're arriving in Italy from elsewhere in Europe, North America or Australasia, you don't need any jabs. Citizens of all EU countries are entitled to emergency medical care under the same terms as the residents of the country. For British citizens, this used to mean presenting a stamped E111 form, but in late 2005, this was phased out and replaced by the new **European Health Insurance Card (EHIC)**, valid for five years. As with the E111, this can be applied for, free of charge, at UK post offices. The latest information is available online at ⓦ www.doh .gov.uk/traveladvice. Note, however, that the EHIC won't cover the full cost of major treatment, making travel insurance essential. You normally have to pay the full cost of emergency treatment upfront – which never comes cheap – and claim it back when you get home (minus a small excess); make very sure you hang onto full doctors' reports, signed prescription details and all receipts to back up your claim.

An Italian **pharmacist** (*farmacia*) is well qualified to give advice on minor ailments and to dispense prescriptions; there's generally one open all night in the bigger towns and cities. They work on a rota system, and the address of the one currently open is posted on any *farmacia* door. If you require a **doctor** (*médico*), ask for help in the first instance at your hotel or the local tourist office. Alternatively look in the *Yellow Pages* (*Pagine Gialle*): some larger towns have English-speaking doctors specifically earmarked to help visitors. Follow a similar procedure if you have dental problems. Keep all receipts for treatment or medicines for later insurance claims.

If you are taken **seriously ill** or involved in an **accident**, go to the *Pronto Soccorso* (Casualty/A&E) section of the nearest hospital; in a real emergency, phone ☎113 and ask for *ospedale* or *ambulanza*. Major train stations and airports often have first-aid facilities with qualified doctors on hand.

**Mosquitoes** (*zanzare*) can be a nuisance between June and September; most supermarkets and pharmacies sell sprays, mosquito coils and after-bite cream.

# Costs, money and banks

The days are long gone when Italy was a relatively inexpensive country to visit: the glut of visitors and rounding-up effect of the euro's introduction have conspired to increase prices. Accommodation rates in particular have soared.

Italy is one of twelve European Union countries whose currency is the **euro** (€), composed of 100 cents. There are **notes** of €500, €200, €100, €50, €20, €10 and €5, each a different colour, and **coins** of €2, €1, 50c, 20c, 10c, 5c, 2c and 1c. Coins in the Eurozone (Austria, Belgium, Finland, France, Germany, Greece, Ireland, Italy, Luxembourg, the Netherlands, Portugal and Spain) have a common design on one face, but different country-specific designs on the other; regardless of the design, all are legal tender throughout. At the time of writing, the **exchange rate** was roughly €1.42 to the pound, €0.73 to the US dollar, €0.60 to the Canadian dollar, €0.56 to the Australian dollar and €0.53 to the New Zealand dollar.

An increasing number of tourist centres have automatic money-changing machines (notes only). Otherwise the place to change money or travellers' cheques is at a **bank**, though the process can sometimes be excruciatingly slow. There are a few banking chains that you'll find nationwide – Banca Nazionale del Lavoro, Banca d'Italia and Cassa di Risparmio – as well as regional chains like the Monte dei Paschi di Siena. For details on banks and banking hours in Florence and Siena see p.218 and p.309 respectively. Outside banking hours you can change money at larger hotels or any bureau de change (*cambio*).

## Travellers' cheques, credit and debit cards

Although it's a good idea to have some cash when you first arrive, it's safer to bring your money in the form of **travellers' cheques**, available from any bank or post office in the UK, and from most banks elsewhere, in various brands: American Express ⓦ www.american express.com, Thomas Cook ⓦ www.thomas cook.com or Visa ⓦ www.visa.com. The usual

fee for travellers' cheque sales is one or two percent, though this fee may be waived if you buy the cheques through a bank where you have an account. It pays to get a selection of denominations. Make sure you keep the purchase agreement and a record of cheque serial numbers safe and separate from the cheques themselves. In the event that cheques are lost or stolen, the issuing company will expect you to report the loss forthwith to their office in Italy; most companies claim to replace lost or stolen cheques within 24 hours. You'll usually pay a small commission when you **exchange** sterling or dollar travellers' cheques – again around one percent of the amount changed, although some banks will make a standard charge per cheque regardless of its denomination. You shouldn't have to pay this commission in Italy if you are using euro travellers' cheques.

**Credit and debit cards** can be used either in an ATM (*bancomat*) or over the counter. MasterCard, Visa and American Express are accepted in most larger city stores, hotels and restaurants, but some petrol stations and smaller establishments may be reluctant to accept plastic: cash still reigns supreme in much of Italy, so check first before embarking on a big meal out. ATMs are found in even small towns, and most accept all major cards, with a minimum withdrawal of €50 and a maximum of €250 per day.

**Visa TravelMoney** (see ⓦ www.visa .com) combines the security of travellers' cheques with the convenience of plastic. It's a disposable debit card, charged up before you leave home with whatever amount you like, separate from your normal banking or credit accounts. You can then access these dedicated travel funds from any ATM that accepts Visa worldwide, with a PIN that you select yourself. Citicorp, and Thomas Cook/ Interpayment outlets sell the card worldwide (see the website). When your money runs out, you just throw the card away. Since you can buy up to nine cards to access the same funds – useful for families travelling together – it's recommended that you buy at least one extra card as a back-up in case your first is lost or stolen. The 24-hour Visa customer service line from Italy is ☎800.819.014.

## Average costs

Most **basics** are inexpensive: delicious picnic meals can be put together for under £5/$9, and a pizza or plate of pasta in a cheap pizzeria or trattoria will come to around £6/$10 on average. However, in most restaurants in Florence and Siena you'll be lucky to get away with paying €30 a head for a three-course meal with wine. **Public transport** is good value: the train journey from Florence to Siena (97km) costs around £7/$12 for a second-class return. Wine is cheap, but other **drinks** are not: soft drinks and coffee cost around the same as in Britain, and a pint of beer can be as much as £4/$7. Accommodation in Florence and Siena is expensive, with **room rates** starting at around £50/$90 for a double room in a one-star hotel.

Overall, an average minimum daily budget for a couple staying in one-star hotels and eating one modest-priced meal out a day, would be in the region of £60/$110 per person. If you want to allow yourself the occasional extravagance or an intensive bout of museum-visiting, then you'll need £70/$120 per day – and in view of the disproportionate cost of single hotel rooms, a person travelling alone can expect this figure to increase by about twenty-five percent.

**Youth/student ID cards** soon pay for themselves in savings, principally on international air, rail and bus fares, local transport, accommodation, entertainment, admission to larger museums and attractions, and some food outlets and courses. Full-time students are eligible for the *International Student ID Card (ISIC)*; anybody aged 26 or less qualifies for the **International Youth Travel Card**; and teachers qualify for the **International Teacher Card** – all carrying the same benefits. Check ⓦwww.isiccard.com for details of outlets selling the cards. Reductions and discounts for under-18s and over-65s are also usually available for major attractions and state museums.

# Getting around

The easiest and quickest way to travel between Florence and Siena is by bus; trains nearly always involve a change at Empoli – see p.223 for more information. If you want to travel further afield, use of a car is a major advantage. You can still get to all the major places by public transport but away from main routes services can be slow and sporadic. In general, trains are more convenient for longer journeys, buses for local routes.

## By train

The **train** service offered by Italian State Railways (*Trenitalia*) between major towns and cities is relatively inexpensive, reasonably comprehensive and – despite its reputation – fairly efficient. It's worth bearing in mind that while Florence and Pisa have centrally located stations, Siena does not.

**Eurocity** trains (EC) connect major cities across Europe, perhaps stopping at only two or three places in each country; **Cisalpino** (CIS) operates tilting Pendolino trains on trans-Alpine routes between Switzerland, Germany and Italy; **Eurostar Italia** (ES) runs between major cities and is faster and more efficient than **Intercity** (IC) trains. You need

29

to reserve for all these services, and pay a supplement of about thirty percent of the ordinary fare. There are no supplements for the **Espresso** (EX), medium-fast trains that stop at major towns and cities, **Interregionali** (IR), similar to the Espresso, but usually with more stops, or **Regionali** (Reg), slow trains that generally stop at every station.

At train stations, separate posters are used for departures (*partenze* – usually **yellow**) and arrivals (*arrivi* – usually **white**); be careful not to confuse the two. Florence's main station has a large information centre. If you're planning to travel extensively by train it's worth buying a copy of the twice-yearly *In Treno In Tutt'Italia* timetable (€4.50), which covers the main routes and is normally on sale at train-station newsstands; make sure the booklet is valid during the period in which you want to travel. Pay attention to the **timetable notes**, which may specify the dates between which some services run ("*si effetua dal... al...*"), or whether a service is seasonal (*periodico*). The term *giornaliero* means the service runs daily, *feriale* from Monday to Saturday, *festivi* on Sundays and holidays only.

**Italian State Railways** ☎848.888.088, ⊛www .trenitalia.it. The state-owned national network.

### Tickets and fares

Fares are calculated by the kilometre: a return fare (*andata e ritorno*) is exactly twice that of a single (*andata*). A ticket (*un biglietto*) can be bought from a station ticket office (*la biglietteria*), from some travel agents, and – to avoid long queues – from many station news kiosks or bars (for short trips). In Florence, the queues for tickets can be

### Ticket machines

All stations have small yellow machines at the end of the platforms or in ticket halls in which you must **stamp your ticket** immediately before getting on the train; however, don't stamp the return portion of your ticket until you embark on the return journey. If you don't validate your ticket, you become liable for an on-the-spot fine.

extremely long, so you'd be well advised to either buy a ticket the day before or allow plenty of time before your train departs. All tickets must be **validated** just before travel (see box): once validated, tickets for journeys up to 200km are valid for six hours, over 200km for 24 hours. Make sure you pay any **supplement** when you buy your ticket: it will cost you more if you pay on board.

A **reservation** (*una prenotazione*) is obligatory on EuroStar trains, and worthwhile for InterCity trains in the summer. **Sleepers** (*cuccetta*) are available on most long-distance services; prices vary according to length of journey and whether or not you're sharing.

### By bus

A plethora of regional **bus** companies operate out of Florence and Siena, running services that generally are slightly less expensive and almost as quick as the equivalent trains. For details on buses between Florence and Siena, see p.223. For details on transport within Florence, see p.49; for Siena, see p.225.

### By car

Travelling **by car** in Italy is relatively painless. The roads are good, the motorway (*autostrada*) network comprehensive, and Italian drivers rather less erratic than their reputation suggests. Most motorways are **toll-roads**. Take a ticket as you join and pay as you exit; the amount due is flashed up on a screen in front of you. Rates aren't especially high but they can mount up on a long journey. **Speed limits** are 50kph in built-up areas, 110kph on main roads (dual carriageways) and 130kph on motorways. If you **break down**, dial ☎116 at the nearest phone and tell the operator where you are, the type of car and your number plate; the Automobile Club d'Italia (ACI) will send someone out to fix your car – at a price, so you might consider getting cover with a motoring organization in your home country before you leave. Never leave anything visible in the car when parked, including the radio, and always push your aerial down or you might find it snapped off. Most cities and ports have paid garages where you can park safely.

Bringing your own vehicle, you need a valid full driving licence (with paper counterpart if you have a photocard licence) and an international driving permit if you are a non-EU licence-holder. It's compulsory to carry your car documents and passport while you're driving: you may be required to present them if stopped by the police – not an uncommon occurrence.

**Car rental** is pricey, with costs for a Fiat Panda or Renault Twingo (standard "subcompact" models) more than £200/$360 per week with unlimited mileage. Italian firms might be a bit cheaper than the multinationals; there are plenty of companies with desks at Pisa airport, but it usually works out cheapest to book before leaving, either by arranging a fly-drive package through a travel agent or by going direct to the rental agency. Most firms will only rent to drivers over 21 who have held a licence for a year.

## Car rental agencies

**Avis** UK ☎0870/606 0100, ⓦwww.avis.co.uk, US ☎1-800/331-1084, Canada ☎1-800/272-5871, ⓦwww.avis.com, Republic of Ireland ☎01/605 7500, ⓦwww.avis.ie, Australia ☎13 63 33, ⓦwww.avis.com.au, NZ ☎09/526 2847, ⓦwww.avis.co.nz.

**Budget** UK ☎0800/181 181, ⓦwww.budget.co.uk, Republic of Ireland ☎0903/27711, ⓦwww.budget.ie, US ☎1-800/527-0700, ⓦwww.budget.com, Australia ☎1300/362 848, ⓦwww.budget.com.au, NZ ☎09/976 2222, ⓦwww.budget.co.nz.

**Europcar** UK ☎0870/607 5000, Republic of Ireland ☎01/614 2800, US & Canada ☎1-877/940-6900, Australia ☎1300/13 13 90, ⓦwww.europcar.com.

**Hertz** UK ☎0870/848 4848, ⓦwww.hertz.co.uk, Republic of Ireland ☎01/676 7476, ⓦwww.hertz.ie, US ☎1-800/654-3001, Canada ☎1-800/263-0600, ⓦwww.hertz.com, Australia ☎13 30 39, ⓦwww.hertz.com.au, NZ ☎0800/654 321, ⓦwww.hertz.co.nz.

**Holiday Autos** UK ☎0870/400 0099, Republic of Ireland ☎01/872 9366, US ☎1-800/422-7737, Australia ☎1300/554 432, New Zealand ☎0800/144 040, ⓦwww.holidayautos.com.

**National** UK ☎0870/536 5365, ⓦwww.nationalcar.co.uk, US ☎1-800/227-7368, ⓦwww.nationalcar.com, Australia ☎13 10 45, ⓦwww.nationalcar.com.au, NZ ☎0800/800 115, ⓦwww.nationalcar.co.nz.

**Thrifty** UK ☎01494/751 600, ⓦwww.thrifty.co.uk, Republic of Ireland ☎1800/515 800, ⓦwww.thrifty.ie, US ☎1-800/367-2277, ⓦwww.thrifty.com, Australia ☎1300/367 227, ⓦwww.thrifty.com.au, NZ ☎09/309 0111, ⓦwww.thrifty.co.nz.

## By bike or motorbike

**Cycling** is seen as more of a sport than a way of getting around: on a Sunday you'll see plenty of people out for a spin on their Campagnolo-equipped machines, but you'll not come across many luggage-laden tourers. Only in major towns will you find a shop stocking spares for non-racing bikes, so make sure you take a supply of inner tubes, spokes and any other bits you think might be handy. It's possible to rent bikes in both Florence and Siena; see p.218 and p.309 for rental outlets.

**Mopeds** and **scooters** are easier to rent: although they're not built for long-distance travel, they're ideal for shooting around towns. Expect to pay around €40–50 a day rental. Wearing crash helmets is compulsory.

# Accommodation

Accommodation is a major cost in Florence and Siena. The hotels are more upmarket than in most Italian regions, with a preponderance of two- and three-star places. Prices of hotels in all categories tend to rise annually, as there's effectively an infinite demand. There are few really inexpensive hotels and only a scattering of hostels. Even campsites are fairly pricey.

Accommodation in Italy is strictly regulated. All hotels are **star-rated** from one to five; prices are set by law for each room – rates can vary within a hotel – and must be posted at the hotel reception and in individual rooms (usually on the back of the door). Ask to see a variety of rooms if the first you're shown is too expensive or not up to scratch; there may be cheaper rooms available, perhaps without a private bathroom. Tourist offices carry full **lists of hotels** and other accommodation such as private rooms.

It is essential to **book rooms in advance** for Florence and Siena, especially around Easter, Christmas and summer. Always establish the full price of your room – including or excluding breakfast and other extras (tax and service charges are usually included) – before you accept it. You should also always call a day or so before arrival to **confirm your room booking**. If you're going to be arriving late in the evening, it's even worth another call that morning to reconfirm: it's not uncommon for cheaper places to let your room go if you haven't checked in by lunchtime.

## Hotels

Hotels in Italy are known by a variety of names. Most are simply tagged **hotel** or **albergo**. Others may be called a **locanda**, traditionally the cheapest sort of inn, but now sometimes rather self-consciously applied to smart new hotels. A **pensione** was also traditionally a cheap place to stay, though the name now lacks any official status: anywhere still describing itself as a "*pensione*" is probably a hotel in the one-star class.

The star system is the best way to get an idea of what you can expect from a hotel, though it's essential to realize the system is based on an often eccentric set of criteria relating to facilities (say, the presence of a restaurant or an in-room TV) rather than notions about comfort, character or location. A three-star, for example, must have a phone in every room: if it hasn't, it remains a two-star, no matter how magnificent the rest of the hotel. Equally, a two-star hotel may have phones, but lack some other facility that might have taken it up a rating.

Prices in Florence and Siena are much higher than anywhere else in Tuscany. **One-star** places start at about €75 for a double room without private bath; **two-star** hotels cost around €100–150 for an en-suite double; **three-star** places – with a phone and a TV – tend to cost in the region of €200 in Florence, but can be found more cheaply in Siena; and **four-star** hotels start at around €250–300. For **five-star** hotels expect to pay more than €300 a night.

It's not unusual for hotels to impose a **minimum stay** of three nights in high season. If **breakfast** is not included in the price of your room, you can save money by getting breakfast in a bar or café – where the quality is likely to be better anyway. You can cut costs slightly by cramming three into a double room, but most hotels will charge you an extra 35 percent for this. Note also that people **travelling alone** may be hit for the price of a double room even when taking a single, although kindlier hoteliers – if they have no singles available – may offer you a double room at the single rate.

## Self-catering

High hotel prices in Florence and Siena are making **self-catering** an increasingly attractive proposition: for the price of a week's stay in high summer in a three-star double hotel room in central Florence you should be able to find a two-bedroomed apartment in an equally good location, or an entire villa out in the countryside. Many package company firms offer self-catering as an alternative to hotel accommodation, but better selections of apartments are provided by specialist agents such as the UK companies listed below, all of which have a good reputation. See also p.297 for a couple of Siena-based companies and p.21 for companies that can offer self-catering accommodation packages with flights as well.

**Bridgewater** ☎0161/787 8587, 🌐www .bridgewater-travel.co.uk. A company with over 25 years' experience of apartments in Florence and Siena – and of *agriturismo* in the surrounding countryside.
**Holiday Rentals** 🌐www.holiday-rentals.co.uk. This site puts you directly in touch with the owners of dozens of Tuscan properties.
**Interhome** ☎020/8891 1294, 🌐www.interhome .com. Large international villa- and apartment-rental firm with properties around the two cities.
**IST Italian Breaks** ☎020/8660 0082, 🌐www .italianbreaks.com. A range of apartments in Florence and a couple of rather special ones in Siena overlooking the Campo.
**Owners' Syndicate** ☎020/7801 9807, 🌐www .ownerssyndicate.com. Leading operator, with 85 properties, right outside Siena and around 20km from Florence. Good, informative website.
**Traditional Tuscany** ☎01553/810 003, 🌐www .traditionaltuscany.co.uk. Offers B&B in Florentine palaces and on working farms and vineyards, plus a selection of some 25 villas and converted farms at competitive prices.
**Tuscan Holidays** ☎01539/431 120, 🌐www .tuscanholidays.co.uk. A small company with carefully selected homes around Florence and Siena, most with pools in working vineyards, as well as hotels in town.
**Veronica Tomasso Cotgrove** ☎020/7267 2423, 🌐www.vtcitaly.com. Carefully chosen villas and apartments, including some very exclusive properties.

## Hostels and student accommodation

When the extras are factored in, **hostels** don't always represent a saving for two people travelling together – especially when you take into account that some are inconveniently located and require bus journeys to get into town. However, if you're travelling alone, hostels are certainly sociable and can

work out economically; many have facilities such as self-catering kitchens and bargain-basement restaurants that enable you to cut costs further. In Florence and Siena prices start at around €17 a night for a dormitory bed, and you may have to add on extra for breakfast and a shower.

Most hostels belong to the **Hostelling International (HI)** network (🌐www.iyhf.org), and strictly speaking you need to be an HI member to stay at them. Many, however, allow you to join on the spot, or simply charge you a small supplement. Whether or not you're an HI member, you'll need to **book ahead** in the summer months. The most efficient way to book – at main city hostels only – is using HI's own International Booking Network (🌐www.hostelbooking .com); for more out-of-the-way locations, you should contact the hostel direct, sending a thirty-percent deposit (or more) with your booking.

### HI hostel associations

**Australia** ☎02/9261 1111, 🌐www.yha.org.au.
**Canada** ☎1-800/663-5777, 🌐www.hihostels.ca.
**England & Wales** ☎0870/770 8868, 🌐www .yha.org.uk.
**Italy** ☎06.487.1152, 🌐www.ostellionline.org.
**New Zealand** ☎03/379 9970, 🌐www.yha.org.nz.
**Northern Ireland** ☎028/9032 4733, 🌐www .hini.org.uk.
**Republic of Ireland** ☎01/830 4555, 🌐www .irelandyha.org.
**Scotland** ☎0870/155 3255, 🌐www.syha.org.uk.
**USA** ☎301/495-1240, 🌐www.hiayh.org.

## Religious organizations

**Religious organizations** offer cheap accommodation: often the lodgings are annexed to **convents** or **monasteries**, or pilgrim hostels, and in most cases amount to simple hotels. Most have rooms with and without bathrooms; only a few have dorm rooms with bunks. Some accept women only, others familes only or single travellers of either sex. Most have a curfew, but few, contrary to expectations, pay much heed to your coming and going. Virtually none offers meals.

## Camping

**Camping** doesn't always work out any cheaper than staying in a hotel or hostel:

prices in high season start from €12 per person, plus €10/15 per tent/caravan, and around €3 for each vehicle. If you're camping extensively, it's worth checking Italy's very informative camping website, Ⓦwww.camping.it, for details of each site and booking facilities. Camping gas for small portable stoves is easy enough to buy, either from a hardware store (*ferramenta*) or camping/sports shops.

# Food and drink

## Breakfast and snacks

Most Italians start their day in a bar, **breakfast** (*prima colazione*) consisting of a coffee and the ubiquitous *cornetto* or *brioche* – a jam-, custard- or chocolate-filled croissant, which you usually take yourself from the counter. Unfilled croissants can be hard to find; ask for *un cornetto vuoto* or *normale*. Breakfast in a hotel will often be a limp affair, usually worth avoiding, although some upper-bracket places present good breakfast buffets.

At other times of the day, **sandwiches** (*panini*) can be pretty substantial, a filled breadstick or roll for €1.50–2.50. Specialized sandwich bars (*paninoteche*) can be found in many larger towns; grocers' shops (*alimentari*), who'll make sandwiches to order, are another standard source. Bars may also offer *tramezzini*, ready-made sliced white bread with mixed fillings – tasty and slightly cheaper than the average *panino*. Toasted sandwiches (*toast*) are common too: in a *paninoteca* you can get whatever you want toasted; in ordinary bars it's more likely to be a variation on cheese or ham with tomato.

There are a number of options for **takeaway food**. It's possible to find slices of pizza (*pizza a taglio* or *pizza rustica*) pretty much everywhere – buy it by weight (an *etto* is 100g) – while you can get pasta, chips and even hot meals in a **tavola calda**, a sort of snack bar that's at its best in the morning when everything is fresh. Some are self-service with limited seating, found mostly in the bigger towns and inside larger train stations. They are, however, a dying breed, as is the **rosticceria**, where the speciality is usually spit-roasted chicken alongside fast foods such as pizza slices, chips and hamburgers.

Other sources of quick snacks are **markets**, some of which sell take-away food from stalls, including *focacce*, oven-baked pastries topped with cheese or tomato or filled with spinach, fried offal or meat; and *arancini* or *suppli*, deep-fried balls of rice filled with meat (*rosso*) or butter and cheese (*bianco*). **Supermarkets**, also, are an obvious stop for a picnic lunch: Co-op, Conad and PuntoSma are the most common chains in Tuscany.

## Pizza

All across Italy, **pizza** comes thin and flat, not deep-pan, and the choice of toppings is fairly limited – none of the pineapple and sweetcorn variations common in Britain and America. Most are cooked in the traditional way, in wood-fired ovens (*forno a legna*): they arrive blasted and bubbling on the surface, and with a distinctive charcoal taste. *Pizzerie* range from a stand-up counter selling slices (*a taglio*) to a fully fledged sit-down restaurant, and on the whole they don't sell much else besides pizza and drinks, though in large towns you'll come across some that

See the Food and drink colour section for more information on Tuscan cuisine and wine. There's a detailed menu reader of Italian terms on p.355.

## Vegetarian dishes

You can generally manage fine, travelling in Tuscany as a **vegetarian**. If you eat fish and seafood you'll have no problem at all, but even if you don't, you'll find several pasta sauces and pizza varieties without meat, as well as good, filling salads. Beware vegetable soups, which may be made with meat stock. The only real problem is one of comprehension: many Italians don't really understand someone not eating meat, and stating the obvious doesn't always get the point across. Saying you're a vegetarian (*"Sono vegetariano"* – or *"vegetariana"* if you're female) and asking if a dish has meat in (*"c'è carne dentro?"*) might still turn up a poultry or *prosciutto* dish. Better to ask what a dish is made with before you order (*"com'è fatto?"*), so that you can spot the ingredients.

also do simple pasta dishes. Some straight restaurants often have pizza on the menu too. A basic cheese-and-tomato pizza (*margherita*) costs around €5, a fancier variety anything up to €8 or more; it's quite acceptable to cut it into slices and eat it with your fingers. Check the menu reader on p.356 for a list of varieties.

### Ice cream

Italian **ice cream** (*gelato*) is justifiably famous: a cone (*un cono*) or better-value "cup" (*una coppa*) are indispensable accessories to the evening *passeggiata*. Most bars have a fairly good selection, but for real choice go to a **gelateria**, where the range is a tribute to the Italian imagination and flair for display. You'll sometimes have to go by appearance rather than attempting to decipher their exotic names, many of which don't mean much even to Italians; often the basics – chocolate, strawberry, vanilla – are best. There's no problem locating the finest *gelateria* in town: it's the one that draws the crowds. The procedure is to ask for a *cono* or *coppa*, indicating the size you want: a two-dollop cone costs around €1.20.

## Restaurants

Traditionally, Tuscan **restaurant** meals (lunch is *pranzo*, dinner is *cena*) are long and pretty solid affairs, starting with an *antipasto*, followed by a risotto or a pasta dish, leading on to a fish or meat course, cheese, and finished with fresh fruit and coffee. Even everyday meals are a miniaturized version of this. Modern minimalism has made inroads into the more expensive restaurants, but

the staple fare at the majority of places is exactly what it might have been a century ago. Vegetarianism is a concept that's also been slow to catch on, though vegetarians shouldn't have too many problems finding meat-free dishes at most places (see box, above).

Restaurants are most commonly called either **trattorie** or **ristoranti**. Traditionally, a trattoria is a cheaper and more basic purveyor of home-style cooking (*cucina casalinga*), while a *ristorante* is more upmarket, with aproned waiters and tablecloths. These days, however, there's a fine line between the two, as it's become rather chic for an expensive restaurant to call itself a trattoria. It's in the rural areas that you're most likely to come across an old-style trattoria, the sort of place where there's no written menu (the waiter will simply reel off a list of what's available) and no bottled wine (it comes straight from the vats of the local farm). A true *ristorante* will always have a written menu and a reasonable choice of wines, though even in smart places it's standard to choose the ordinary house wine. In Florence, you may well find restaurants unwilling to serve anything less than a full meal: no lunchtime restraint of a pasta and salad allowed.

Increasingly, too, you'll come across **osterie**. These used to be old-fashioned places specializing in home cooking, though recently they have had quite a vogue and the *osteria* tag more often signifies a youngish ownership and clientele, and adventurous foods. Other types of restaurant include **spaghetterie** and **birrerie**, restaurant-bars which serve basic pasta dishes, or beer and snacks, and are again often youngish hangouts.

## The menu and the bill

The cheapest – though not the most rewarding way – to eat in bigger city restaurants is to opt for a set price **menù turistico**. This will give you a first course (pasta or soup), main course, dessert (usually a piece of fruit), half a litre of water and a quarter litre of wine per person. Beware the increasingly common *prezzo fisso* menu, which excludes cover, service, dessert and beverages.

Working your way through an Italian menu (*la lista*, or sometimes *il menù*) is pretty straightforward. **Antipasto** (literally "before the meal") is a course generally consisting of various cold cuts of meat, seafood and various cold vegetable dishes. *Prosciutto* is a common antipasto dish, ham either cooked (*cotto*) or just cured and hung (*crudo*), served alone or with melon, figs or mozzarella cheese. Also very common are *crostini*, canapés of minced chicken liver and other toppings.

The next course, **il primo**, consists of soup or a risotto, polenta or pasta dish. This is followed by **il secondo** – the meat or fish course, usually served alone, except for perhaps a wedge of lemon or tomato. Watch out when ordering fish or Florence's famous *bistecca alla fiorentina,* which will usually be served by weight: 250g is usually plenty for one person, or ask to have a look at the fish before it's cooked. Anything marked *S.Q.* or *hg* means you are paying by weight: *hg* stands for a hectogram (*etto* in Italian) – 100g, or around 4oz. Vegetables (**il contorno**) and salads (**insalata**) are ordered and served separately, and often there won't be much choice, if any: most common are beans (*fagioli*), potatoes (*patate*), and salads either green (*verde*) or mixed (*mista*).

For afters, you nearly always get a choice of fresh fruit (*frutta*) and a selection of desserts (**dolci**) often focused on ice cream or usually dull home-made flans (*torta della casa*).

At the end of the meal, ask for the bill/check (**il conto**). In many *trattorie* this amounts to no more than an illegible scrap of paper, and if you want to be sure you're not being ripped off, ask to have a receipt (*ricevuta*), something all bars and restaurants are legally bound to provide anyway. Bear in mind that almost everywhere you'll pay a **cover charge** (*pane e coperto* or just *coperto*) on top of your food of €1–1.50 a head. Legally backed efforts to do away with this, on the grounds that it amounts to charging extra for what should be incorporated in a restaurant's margins, have not yet succeeded. As well as the *coperto*, **service** (*servizio*) will often be added, generally about ten percent; if it isn't, you should perhaps **tip** about the same amount, though *trattorie* outside the large cities won't necessarily expect tips.

## Drinking

**Drinking** is essentially an accompaniment to food: there's little emphasis on drinking for its own sake. Locals sitting around in bars or cafés – whatever their age – will spend hours chatting over one drink. And even in bars, most people you see imbibing one of the delicious Italian grappas or brandies will take just one, then be on their way. The snag is that, since Italians drink so little, prices can be high.

**Bars** are often very functional, brightly lit places, with a chrome counter, a Gaggia coffee machine and a picture of the local football team on the wall. There are no set licensing hours and children are always allowed in; bars often have a public phone and sell snacks and ice creams as well as drinks. People come to bars for ordinary drinking – a coffee in the morning, a quick beer, or a cup of tea – but don't generally idle away the day or evening in them. It's nearly always cheapest to drink **standing** at the counter (there's often nowhere to sit anyway), in which case you often pay first at the cash desk (*la cassa*), present your receipt (*scontrino*) to the barperson and give your order; sometimes you simply order your drink and pay as you leave. There's always a list of prices (*listino prezzi*) behind the bar. If there's waiter service, you can **sit** where you like, though bear in mind that to do this means your drink will cost perhaps twice as much, especially if you **sit outside** on the terrace. These different prices for the same drinks are shown on the price list as *bar*, *tavola* and *terrazza*.

## Coffee, tea and soft drinks

One of the most distinctive smells in an Italian street is that of fresh **coffee**, usually wafting out of a bar. The basic choice is either small and black (*espresso*, or just *caffè*), or white and frothy (*cappuccino*). If you want a longer *espresso* ask for a *caffè lungo* or *americano*; a double *espresso* is *una doppia*, while a short, extra-strong *espresso* is a *ristretto*. A coffee topped with unfrothed milk is a *caffè latte*; with a drop of milk it's *caffè macchiato*; with a shot of alcohol it's *caffè corretto*. Although most places let you help yourself to sugar, a few add it routinely; if you don't want it, you can make sure by asking for *caffè senza zucchero*. Many places also now sell decaffeinated coffee (ask for the brand-name Hag, even when it isn't). In summer you might want to have your coffee cold (*caffè freddo*); for a real treat, ask for *caffè granita*, cold coffee with crushed ice, usually topped with cream. Hot **tea** (*tè caldo*) comes with lemon (*con limone*) as standard, unless you ask for milk (*con latte*); in summer you can drink it cold (*tè freddo*). **Milk** itself is drunk hot as often as cold, or you can get it with a dash of coffee (*latte macchiato*) and sometimes as a milkshake (*frappé*).

There are numerous **soft drinks** (*analcoliche*). A *spremuta* is a fruit juice, usually orange (*...d'arancia*), lemon (*...di limone*) or grapefruit (*...di pompelmo*), fresh-squeezed at the bar, with optional added sugar. A *succo di frutta* is a bottled fruit juice, widely drunk at breakfast. There are also crushed-ice **granite** in several flavours, and the usual range of fizzy drinks and concentrated juices: the home-grown Italian cola, Chinotto, is less sweet than Coke – good with a slice of lemon. An excellent thirst-quencher is Lemon Soda (the brand name), a widely available bitter-lemon drink; Orange Soda is not as good.

**Tap water** (*acqua normale* or *acqua dal rubinetto*) is quite drinkable, and free in bars. **Mineral water** (*acqua minerale*) is a more common choice, either still (*senza gas*, *liscia*, *non gassata* or *naturale*) or sparkling (*con gas*, *gassata* or *frizzante*).

## Beer and spirits

**Beer** (*birra*) is nearly always a lager-type brew which comes in bottles or on tap (*alla spina*) – standard measures are a third of a litre (*piccola*) and two-thirds of a litre (*media*). Commonest and cheapest are the Italian brands Peroni, Moretti and Dreher, all of which are very drinkable; to order these, either state the brand name or ask for *birra nazionale* – otherwise you may be given a more expensive imported beer. You may also come across darker beers (*birra scura* or *birra rossa*), which have a sweeter, maltier taste and resemble stout or bitter.

All the usual **spirits** are on sale and known mostly by their generic names. There are also Italian brands of the main varieties: the best local brandies are Stock and Vecchia Romagna. A generous shot of these costs about €2, much more for imported stuff or in smart city bars. The home-grown Italian firewater is **grappa**, originally from Bassano di Grappa in the Veneto but now produced just about everywhere. Grappas are made from the leftovers of the winemaking process (skins, stalks and the like) and drunk as *digestivi* after a meal. The best Tuscan varieties are from Montalcino (Brunello) and Montepulciano.

You'll also find **fortified wines** like Martini, Cinzano and Campari. For the real thing, order *un Campari bitter*; ask for a "Campari-soda" and you'll get a ready-mixed version from a little bottle. Lemon Soda (see above) and Campari bitter makes a delicious and dangerously drinkable combination. The non-alcoholic Crodino, easily recognizable by its lurid orange colour, is also a popular *aperitivo*. You might also try Cynar, an artichoke-based sherry-type liquid often drunk as an aperitif.

There's a daunting selection of **liqueurs**. Amaro is a bitter after-dinner drink, and probably the most popular way among Italians to round off a meal. The top brands, in rising order of bitterness, are Montenegro, Ramazotti, Averna and Fernet-Branca. Amaretto is a much sweeter concoction with a strong taste of marzipan. Sambuca is a sticky-sweet aniseed brew, often served with a coffee bean in it and set on fire. Strega is another drink you'll see in every bar – the yellow stuff in elongated bottles: it's as sweet as it looks but not unpleasant. Also popular, though considered slightly naff in Italy, is *limoncello*, a bitter-sweet lemon spirit that's becoming increasingly trendy abroad.

## Wine

Pursuit of **wine** is as good a reason as any for a visit to Tuscany. The province constitutes the heartland of Italian wine production, with sales of Chianti accounting for much of the country's wine exports, and the towns of Montalcino and Montepulciano producing two of the very finest Italian vintages (Brunello and Vino Nobile respectively).

Until recently, most Tuscan wines – including Chianti – were criticized by wine buffs for methods geared principally to high yields, low prices, and never mind the quality. However, nudged along by the **DOC** laws (see the Food and drink colour section) standards have steadily risen. Besides the finer tuning of established names, there's a good deal of experimentation going on, with French grape varieties such as Chardonnay, Sauvignon and the Pinots being added to the blends of Tuscan wines, and producers using the French technique of *barriques*, 225-litre oak casks, for ageing reds and whites.

The snobbery associated with "serious" wine drinking remains for the most part mercifully absent. Light reds, such as those made from the *dolcetto* grape, are refrigerated in hot weather, while some full-bodied whites are drunk at or near room temperature. Wine is also **very inexpensive**: in some bars you can get a glass of good local produce for €0.60 or so, and table wine in restaurants – often decanted from the barrel – rarely costs more than €6 per litre. Major-name bottles are pricier but still very good value; expect to pay from around €10–15 a bottle in a restaurant, less than half that from a shop or supermarket.

# Communications

## Post

Opening hours of main **post offices** are usually Mon–Sat 8.30am–7.30pm, although smaller offices are open mornings only (Mon–Fri 8.30am–1.00pm, Sat 8.30am–noon). You can also buy **stamps** (*francobolli*) in *tabacchi*, and in some gift shops. The Italian postal system is one of the slowest in Europe so if your letter is urgent make sure you send it *posta prioritaria*, which has varying rates according to weight and destination. Letters can be sent **poste restante** (general delivery) to any Italian post office by addressing them "*Fermo Posta*" followed by the name of the town; your surname should be double-underlined for easier identification, as filing is often diabolical: when picking items up take your passport, and – in case of difficulty – make sure they also check under your middle names and initials.

## Phones

Public **phones**, run by Telecom Italia, come in various forms, usually with clear instructions in English; if you can't find a phone box, bars will often have a phone you can use – look for the yellow or red phone symbol. Coin phones are virtually extinct, so you'll almost certainly have to buy a **phonecard** (*carta* or *scheda telefonica*), available from *tabacchi* and newsstands. **Tariffs** are among the most expensive in Europe. For national calls, the off-peak period runs Mon–Fri 6.30pm–8am, then Sat 1pm until Mon 8am.

**Phone numbers** change with amazing frequency in Italy; if in doubt, consult the local directory – there's a copy in most bars, hotels and phone offices. Area codes are now an integral part of the number and must always be dialled, regardless of where you're calling from. Numbers beginning ☎800 are free, an English-speaking operator is on ☎170, and international directory enquiries is ☎176.

To use your **mobile phone**, check with your provider whether it will work in Italy and what the charges will be. Technology in Italy is GSM (🌐www.gsmworld.com). Unless you have a triband phone, it's unlikely that a mobile bought for use in North America will work elsewhere. Most mobiles in Australia and New Zealand are GSM, but it pays to check before you leave home.

### Phoning home from Italy

You can call abroad from most public phones with an international **phone card** (*carta* or *scheda telefonica internazionale*). These are on sale at many newspaper kiosks and *tabacchi* and start at €5 – though you will need more than that for anything but the briefest of chats.

Alternatively, you might consider a **phone charge card** from your phone company back home; most providers in Europe, North America, Australia and New Zealand have their own versions. Using a PIN number, they let you make calls from most hotel, public and private phones – via a toll-free Italian number – that are charged to your home account. Most are free to obtain, but bear in mind that rates aren't necessarily cheaper than calling from a public phone.

Without these cards, you can make **reverse-charge** or **collect calls** (*chiamata con addebito destinatario*) by dialling ☎170 and following the recorded instructions. Dialling **direct**, the off-peak period for international calls is Mon–Sat 10pm–8am and all day Sun.

**To the UK** ☎0044 + area code without the zero + number.
**To Ireland** ☎00353 + area code without the zero + number.
**To the US or Canada** ☎001 + area code + number.
**To Australia** ☎0061 + area code without the zero + number.
**To New Zealand** ☎0064 + area code without the zero + number.

### Calling Italy from abroad

First dial your **international access code** (00 from the UK, Ireland and New Zealand; 011 from the US and Canada; 0011 from Australia), followed by **39** for Italy, followed by the full Italian number **including the leading zero**.

## Email

An easy way to keep in touch while travelling is to sign up for a free Internet **email** address that can be accessed from anywhere via the World Wide Web; YahooMail (🌐www.yahoo.com) and Hotmail (🌐www.hotmail.com) are the two most popular, but there are thousands of others. Once you've set up an account, you can use the company's website to pick up and send mail from any Internet café, or hotel with Internet access. Internet points are now widespread in Florence and Siena. Listings of **Internet cafés** in Florence are given on p.218 and for Siena on p.309. Reckon on paying around €4 for half an hour online, less if you're a student.

# The media

Local and national newspapers are readily available and form an essential accompaniment to bar culture: in small towns, folk are drawn to a bar for a read, not a drink. However, television plays a central role in Italian life: it's a rare household that doesn't have the TV switched on from morning to night, regardless of the poor quality of Italy's numerous local and heavily censored national channels.

## Newspapers

Tuscany's major **newspaper** is the Florence-based *La Nazione*. This is technically a national paper but its sales are concentrated in the central provinces of Italy. It produces local editions, with supplements, including informative entertainments listings, for virtually every major Tuscan town. Of the other nationals, the centre-left *La Repubblica* and authoritative right-slanted *Corriere della Sera* are the two most widely read and available. *L'Unità*, the Democratic Left (PDS) party organ, has experienced hard times, even in the party's Tuscan strongholds; it now seems to have regained some lost ground under new editorship. The most avidly read papers of all are the pink *Gazzetta dello Sport* and *Corriere dello Sport*; essential reading for the serious Italian sports fan, they devote as much attention to players' ankle problems as most papers would give to the resignation of a government. News magazines are also widely read in Italy, from the similar *L'Espresso* and *Panorama* to the lighter offerings of *Gente*, *Oggi* and *Novella 2000*.

**English** and **US newspapers** can be found for two or three times the normal price in all the larger towns and established resorts, usually on the day of issue in bigger cities like Florence and Siena. Pan-European editions of Britain's *Guardian* and *Financial Times* and the Rome editions of the *International Herald Tribune* and *USA Today* are also usually available on the day of publication.

## TV and radio

Italy's three main national **TV** channels are RAI 1, 2 and 3. Silvio Berlusconi's Fininvest runs three additional nationwide channels: Canale 5, TG4 and Italia 1. Although all six are blatantly pro-Berlusconi, the degree of sycophancy displayed on the TG4 news has reached such ludicrous heights (newscaster Emilio Fede is variously overcome by tears of joy or despair, depending on the fortunes of Berlusconi) that most Italians now tune in solely for a giggle. The other main channel is Telemontecarlo, currently reaching seventy percent of the country. Although the stories of Italian TV's stripping housewives are overplayed, the output is pretty bland across the board, with the accent on quiz shows, soaps and plenty of American imports. The RAI channels carry less advertising and try to mix the dross with above-average documentaries and news coverage. Numerous other channels concentrate on sport; if you want to see the weekend's Italian League football action, settle into a bar from 5pm on a Sunday.

While there are always exceptions, you shouldn't expect too much from a hotel TV: if satellite channels are available at all, English-language options are generally restricted to BBC World, CNN and little else.

The situation in **radio** is even more anarchic, with FM so crowded that you continually pick up new stations whether you want to or not. There are some good small-scale stations if you search hard enough, but on the whole the RAI stations are the most professional – though even with them daytime listening is virtually undiluted dance music. The **BBC World Service** (ⓦwww.bbc.co.uk) is in English on 648kHz medium wave most of the day; they also broadcast continuously online, as do Voice of America (ⓦwww.voa.gov) and Radio Canada (ⓦwww.rcinet.ca).

# Opening hours and holidays

## Opening hours

Most shops and businesses in Florence and Siena are open daily from 8 or 9am until around 1pm, and again from about 4pm until 7 or 8pm. In Siena food shops tend to close on Sunday and many non-food shops are closed on Monday mornings in the two cities.

Opening hours for museums, galleries and churches vary and are prone to change; we've detailed them wherever possible throughout the Guide.

## National holidays

Whenever you visit, you may well find your travel plans disrupted by **national holidays**

and local saints' days. Local religious holidays don't generally close down shops and businesses, but they do mean that accommodation space may be tight. However everything, except some bars and restaurants, closes on Italy's official national holidays, which are:

**Jan 1**
**Jan 6** (Epiphany)
**Easter Monday**
**April 25** (Liberation Day)
**May 1** (Labour Day)
**Aug 15** (Ferragosto; Assumption)
**Nov 1** (Ognissanti; All Saints)
**Dec 8** (Immaculate Conception)
**Dec 25**
**Dec 26**

# Trouble and the police

In Florence and Siena, the only trouble you're likely to come across are gangs of *scippatori* ("snatchers"), often kids, who operate in crowded streets or markets, train stations and packed tourist sights. As well as handbags, *scippatori* grab wallets, tear off any visible jewellery and, if they're really adroit, unstrap watches.

You can **minimize the risk** of this happening by being discreet: wear money in a belt or pouch; don't put anything down on café or restaurant tables; don't flash anything of value; keep a firm hand on your camera; and carry shoulder bags slung across your body, as Italian women do. It's a good idea, too, to entrust money and credit cards to hotel managers. Never leave anything valuable in your **car** and park in car parks or well-lit, well-used streets.

Italy's reputation for **sexual harassment** of women is based largely on experiences in the south of the country. However, even in the "civilized" north, travelling on your own, or

with another woman, you can expect to be tooted and hissed at from time to time and may attract occasional unwelcome attention in bars or restaurants. This pestering is not usually made with any kind of violent intent,

### Emergency phone numbers

**Police** (Carabinieri) ☎112
**Any emergency service** (Soccorso Pubblico di Emergenza) ☎113
**Fire service** (Vigili del Fuoco) ☎115
**Roadside assistance** (Soccorso Stradale) ☎116

but it's still annoying and frustrating. There are few things you can do to ward it off. Indifference is often the most effective policy, as is looking as confident as possible, walking with a purposeful stride and maintaining a directed gaze. Sitting around in **parks** – especially Florence's Cascine – it's best to pick a spot close to other people.

## The police

In Italy there are several different branches of the **police**, ostensibly to prevent any single branch seizing power. You're not likely to have much contact with the Guardia di Finanza, who investigate smuggling, tax evasion and other finance-related felonies. Drivers may well come up against the **Polizia Urbana**, or town police, who are mainly concerned with traffic and parking offences, and also the **Polizia Stradale**, who patrol motorways.

If you're unlucky, you may have dealings with the **Carabinieri**, dressed in military-style uniforms and white shoulder belts (they're part of the army), who deal with general crime, public order and drugs control. These are the ones Italians are most rude about, but a lot of this stems from the usual north–south divide. Eighty percent of the Carabinieri are from southern Italy; joining the police is one way to escape the poverty trap.

The **Polizia Statale**, the other general crime-fighting branch, enjoy a fierce rivalry with the Carabinieri, and are the ones to whom thefts should be reported at their base, the **Questura** (police station) – you'll find Questura addresses throughout the guide, and in the local phonebook. They'll issue you with a *denuncia*, an impressively stamped report form which you'll need for any insurance claims after you get home. The Questura is also where you should to go to obtain a visa extension or a *permesso di soggiorno*.

In any brush with the authorities, your experience will depend on the individuals you're dealing with. It's not unheard of – and is perfectly legal – to be stopped and searched simply for being young and carrying a rucksack. These are usually just routine spot checks, but don't expect easy treatment if you're picked up for any offence, especially if it's **drugs**-related. Any distinction between "hard" and "soft" drugs is blurred: everything is illegal above the possession of a small amount of marijuana "for personal use", though there's no proper definition of what this means.

# Travellers with disabilities

As part of the European *Turismo per Tutti* (Tourism for All) project – administered in Italy by the national disabled support organization CO.IN – museum, transport and accommodation facilities have improved remarkably in Florence. However, access may be through a different door: in Florence, for example, disabled access to the Duomo is through the doors on the south side, and at the Palazzo Vecchio, through the gates on the north side. Generally, while stairs and steps present the most obvious difficulties – restaurants tend to have their bathrooms downstairs, for instance – other problems arise from oblivious traffic,

cars parked on pavements and the sheer distances of car parks from old-town centres. Public transport is becoming more attuned, though you still need to give 24 hours' notice for porter service or special help at any train station. In Florence, one factor to note is that the streets and pavements are often cobbled, making for an extremely bumpy ride.

### Contacts for travellers with disabilities

#### UK and Ireland

**Holiday Care** ☎0845/124-9971, Minicom: ☎0845/124 9976, ⓦwww.holidaycare.org.uk.

Provides free lists of accessible accommodation abroad.

**Irish Wheelchair Association** ☎01/818 6400, ⓦwww.iwa.ie. Useful information about travelling abroad with a wheelchair.

**Tripscope** The Vasall Centre, Gill Ave, Bristol BS16 2QQ ☎0845/758 5641 ⓦwww.tripscope .org.uk. This registered charity provides a national telephone information service offering free advice on UK and international transport for those with mobility problems.

### North America

**Access-Able** ⓦwww.access-able.com. Online resource for travellers with disabilities.

**Directions Unlimited** ☎1-800/533-5343 or 914/241-1700. Tour operator specializing in custom tours for people with disabilities.

**Mobility International USA** Voice and TDD ☎541/343-1284, ⓦwww.miusa.org. Information and referral services, access guides, tours and exchange programmes. Annual membership $35 (includes quarterly newsletter).

**Society for the Advancement of Travelers with Handicaps (SATH)** ☎212/447-7284, ⓦwww.sath.org. Non-profit educational organization actively representing travellers with disabilities.

**Wheels Up!** ☎1-888/389-4335, ⓦwww.wheelsup .com. Discounted airfares and tours for disabled travellers, plus information on financial help for holidays.

### Australia and New Zealand

**ACROD (Australian Council for Rehabilitation of the Disabled)** ☎02/6282 4333 & 02/9554 3666. Provides lists of travel agencies and tour operators for people with disabilities.

**Disabled Persons Assembly** ☎04/801 9100, ⓦwww.dpa.org.nz. Resource centre with lists of travel agencies and tour operators.

### Italy

**CO.IN** ☎06.2326.9231, ⓦwww.coinsociale.it. National disabled support organization.

**Accessible Italy** ☎0549.875.392, ⓦwww .accessibleitaly.com. Group or individual tours to Florence.

# Gay and lesbian travellers

Attitudes to gays and lesbians in Florence and Siena are on the whole tolerant, and Florence has a particularly thriving gay scene. The national gay organization ARCI-Gay (☎051.649.3055, ⓦwww.arcigay.it) has branches in most big towns; *Babilonia* (ⓦwww.babiloniaweb.it), the national gay magazine, is published monthly (€5); and ⓦwww.gay.it (in association with ⓦwww .gay.com) has a wealth of information for gays and lesbians in Italy. The age of consent is 16.

> Contacts for gay and lesbian travellers

### UK

**Gay Travel** ⓦwww.gaytravel.co.uk. Online travel agent, offering good deals on all types of holiday. Also lists gay- and lesbian-friendly hotels around the world.

**Madison Travel** ☎01273/202 532, ⓦwww .madisontravel.co.uk. Established travel agents

specializing in packages to gay- and lesbian-friendly mainstream destinations, and also to gay/lesbian destinations.

### US and Canada

**Damron Company** ☎1-800/462-6654 or 415/255-0404, ⓦwww.damron.com. Publisher of the *Men's Travel Guide*, a pocket-sized yearbook full of listings of hotels, bars, clubs and resources for gay men; the *Women's Traveler*, which provides similar listings for lesbians; and *Damron Accommodations*, which provides detailed listings of over 1000 accommodations for gays and lesbians worldwide.

### Australia and New Zealand

**Parkside Travel** ☎08/8274 1222, Ⓔparkside@herveyworld.com.au. Gay travel agent associated with local branch of Hervey World Travel; all aspects of gay and lesbian travel worldwide.

**Silke's Travel** ☎1800/807 860 or 02/8347 2000, ⓦwww.silkes.com.au. Long-established gay and lesbian specialist, with the emphasis on women's travel.

# Directory

**Children** Kids are adored in Italy and will be made a fuss of in the street, and welcomed and catered for in bars and restaurants. Two recent laws have improved the situation for parents even further: the ban on smoking in restaurants and bars has transformed the air and made them far more family-friendly, while the law on disabled access make it far easier to take a pushchair (*passeggino*) into museums and churches. Hotels normally charge around thirty percent extra to put a bed or cot in your room. The only hazards in summer are the heat and sun; sunblock can be bought in any pharmacy, and bonnets or straw hats in most markets. Take advantage of the less intense periods – mornings and evenings – for travelling, and use the quiet of siesta-time to recover flagging energy. The rhythms of the southern climate soon modify established patterns, and you'll find it quite natural carrying on later into the night, past normal bedtimes. In summer, it's not unusual to see Italian children out at midnight, and not looking much the worse for it.

You can buy **baby** equipment – nappies, creams and foods – in chemists. See the website ⓦ www.travelforkids.com for more information on child-friendly sights and activities in Florence and Siena.

**Electricity** The supply is 220V, though anything requiring 240V will work. Most plugs are two round pins: UK equipment will need an adaptor, US equipment a 220-to-110 transformer as well.

**Language courses** An excellent way of learning Italian is to attend a residential course in Florence or Siena. There are a great many places where you can do this, usually offering courses of varying levels of intensity for between one and three months. Reckon on paying around £490/$870 for a two-week course, including accommodation, which will normally be with an Italian family. For details, contact the long-established British Institute of Florence (ⓦ www.britishinstitute.it) or the Università Italiana per Stranieri in Siena (ⓦ www.unistrasi.it). Euro-Academy (ⓦ www.euroacademy.co.uk) and CESA Languages Abroad (ⓦ www.cesalanguages.com) in the UK, and Languages Abroad (ⓦ www.languagesabroad.com) in the US, run Italian courses in Florence.

**Mosquitoes** A hazard for much of the summer in the centre of Florence: you are advised to take insect repellent with you – though you can also get it, along with repelling devices for your room, in chemists.

**Tax** If you are thinking of splashing out on a designer outfit or some other expensive item, bear in mind that visitors from outside the EU are entitled to an IVA (purchase tax) rebate on single items valued at over €154.94. The procedure is to get a full receipt from the shop, describing the purchase in detail. This receipt must be presented to customs on your return home, and then sent back to the shop within ninety days of the date of the receipt; the shop will then refund the IVA component of the price, a saving of eighteen percent.

**Time** Italy is on Central European Time (CET): 1hr ahead of London, 6hr ahead of New York and 8hr behind Sydney.

# Arriving in Florence: Practicalities

Florence is an easy city to find your way around: most of the main sights lie north of the Arno, the river which bisects the city from west to east, but a handful are scattered in the district to the south, an area known as the Oltrarno. In both cases distances between sights are easily manageable on foot, with very few exceptions.

North of the river the city hinges around two main piazzas, **Piazza del Duomo** and **Piazza della Signoria**, and their connecting street, Via dei Calzaiuoli. Here you'll find some of the big set-piece sights – the Duomo, Baptistery and Uffizi gallery – as well as attractions such as the Palazzo Vecchio and the Museo dell'Opera del Duomo (the cathedral museum).

Immediately to the east of these pivotal squares there's a tangle of streets around the **Bargello** sculpture gallery (an area that has several associations with Dante), and beyond that lies an appealing district which goes by the name of the great church at its heart, **Santa Croce**. To the north of the centre you'll find the **San Lorenzo** quarter, visited primarily for its markets, its church, and the Michelangelo sculptures in the Cappelle Medicee. Further north, the **San Marco** area has two key sights: the Museo di San Marco, a monastery filled with paintings by Fra' Angelico, and the Accademia, home to Michelangelo's *David*. On the western flank of the city centre, the streets around the medieval church of **Orsanmichele** hide some low-key attractions among clusters of designer shops. Further north and west of here, near the train station, lies a less prepossessing area where the principal attraction is the remarkable church of **Santa Maria Novella**.

South of the river, in the **Oltrarno**, the city has a different feel: somewhat quieter on the whole, and a touch more pleasant to explore for its own sake. The central area, just across the Ponte Vecchio, centres on the huge **Palazzo Pitti**, with its major picture gallery and the formal Bóboli gardens behind. To the west are two important churches and their equally well known squares: **Santo Spirito**'s piazza is the focus of a lively and increasingly gentrified neighbourhood, while **Santa Maria del Carmine** is home to the Cappella Brancacci and its famous fresco cycle. The chief sight of eastern Oltrarno is the exquisite hilltop church of **San Miniato al Monte**, one of Florence's principal landmarks.

## Arrival

Unless you're driving into the city, your point of arrival will be **Santa Maria Novella station**, which is located within a few minutes' walk of the heart of the historic centre: rail and bus connections from the three airports that serve the city all terminate at the station, as do international trains and buses from all over Tuscany.

### By air

If you're flying to **Pisa** – the routine approach – it's an effortless hour's journey by train from the airport into Florence. Flying to Florence's own ever-expanding airport at **Perètola**, it's about twenty minutes by shuttle bus or taxi to the city centre. An alternative arrival point is **Bologna** (Marconi airport), though this takes longer and involves both bus and train transfers.

### Pisa airport

Most scheduled and charter flights fly to **Pisa**'s Galileo Galilei airport (①050.849.300, ⓦwww.pisa-airport.com), 95km west of Florence and 3km from the centre of Pisa. If you've arrived on one of the budget airlines, you can use the shuttle **buses** that leave roughly every hour from in front of the terminal and arrive at Florence's Santa Maria Novella station seventy minutes later. You can buy tickets (€7.50 single) at the stand right in front of you as you come out into the airport concourse. Otherwise you'll have to take a train, which is cheaper (€5), if often slower (70–100min in total, depending on connections at Pisa Centrale); there are only seven direct trains daily (6.40am–10.20pm; no service between 12.40pm and 6pm), but every thirty minutes a shuttle train runs from the airport to Pisa Centrale (6min), where you can change to one of the hourly trains to Florence (journey time 1hr). Trains depart from a platform at the end of the airport concourse, to the left as you emerge from arrivals. Tickets can be bought from the office at the opposite end of the concourse from the station. Remember to validate your ticket in the platform machines before boarding the train. If you're arriving late, you'll have to take the five-minute bus (€1; every 20min), train or taxi ride to Pisa Centrale, from where trains to Florence start running from around 4am. Returning from Florence to Pisa Aeroporto, shuttle buses run from 5.50am to 7.30pm. After that, there is a direct train at 8.37pm, but otherwise you'll have to take the train to Pisa Centrale and catch a connecting bus, train or taxi.

### Perètola airport

An increasing number of international air services use Florence's **Perètola** (Amerigo Vespucci) airport (℡055.306.1300, ⓦ www .aeroporto.firenze.it), 5km northwest of the city centre. There's a tiny arrivals hall with exchange machine, half a dozen car rental desks, a lost-baggage counter and a small tourist office (daily 7.30am–11.30pm; ℡055.315.874). The SITA and ATAF bus companies operate a joint service called **Vola in bus** (ⓦwww.ataf.net), which provides half-hourly shuttles into the city from immediately outside the arrivals area. The first bus into the city is at 6am (last 11.30pm), the first out to the airport at 5.30am (last 11pm). Tickets (€4) can be bought on board or from machines at the airport and bus station, and the journey takes thirty minutes. Most buses arrive at and depart from the main SITA bus terminal on Via di Santa Caterina da Siena, off Piazza della Stazione, a few steps west of Santa Maria Novella train station; after 9pm, however, the buses depart from outside *Bar Cristallo* in Largo Alinari, off the eastern side of Piazza della Stazione. A **taxi** from Perètola into central Florence should cost about €15–20, and take around twenty minutes.

### Bologna airport

A few airlines use **Bologna** (ⓦwww.bologna -airport.it) – about the same distance from Florence as Pisa – as a gateway airport for Florence. Aerobus shuttles depart every twenty minutes (7.30am–11.45pm) from outside the

Note that there is a double **address** system in Florence, one for businesses and one for all other properties – that, at least, is the theory behind it, though in fact the distinction is far from rigorous. Business addresses are followed by the letter **r** (for *rosso*) and are marked on the building with a red number on a white plate, sometimes with an r after the numeral, but not always. There's no connection between the two series: no. 20 might be a long way from no. 20r.

airport's Terminal A (*Arrivi*) to Bologna's main train station (about 25min), from where regular trains run to Florence's Santa Maria Novella station in about an hour. Note, however, that Ryanair services to Bologna in fact fly to Forlì airport, which is more than 60km southeast of Bologna, and very inconvenient for Florence.

### By train

Most **trains** arrive at Florence's main station, **Santa Maria Novella** ("Firenze SMN" on timetables), located just north of the church and square of Santa Maria Novella, ten minutes' unhurried walk west of the Duomo. In the station you'll find left-luggage facilities (see p.219), a 24-hour pharmacy and a fee-charging accommodation agency (by platform 5). In the vicinity of the station you should keep a close eye on your bags at all times: it's a prime hunting-ground for thieves. Also avoid the concourse's various taxi and hotel touts, however friendly they may appear.

### By car

Only residents are allowed to park on the streets in the centre, so you have to leave your **car** in one of the city's main car parks. North of the Arno, the car parks nearest the centre are: underneath the train station; Fortezza da Basso (usually the one with most space); Mercato Centrale; and along the Arno at Lungarno Amerigo Vespucci, Lungarno delle Grazie and Lungarno della Zecca Vecchia. South of the river the best options are Piazza del Carmine, Piazza

Cestello or around Porta San Frediano (there's a cluster of car parks here). You can also find parking spaces alongside the city's main ring roads (the *Viali*). The lowest tariff you'll find is around €1 per hour; a more typical rate is €5 for two hours.

If you want to leave your car for a prolonged period, try Piazzale Michelangelo, the nearest substantial **free parking** area to the centre. It's about twenty minutes' walk to the Piazza della Signoria from here, or a short ride into the centre of town on bus #12 or #13. Watch out for a scam in which bogus car-park attendants direct you into a parking space, thus implying there's a charge: there isn't.

## Information

For information about Florence's sights and events, the main **tourist office** is at Via Cavour 1r, five minutes' walk north of the Duomo (Mon–Sat 8.30am–6.30pm, Sun 8.30am–1.30pm; ℡055.290.832 or 055.290.833, ⓦwww.firenzeturismo.it). A quieter office, run by the town council, is just off Piazza Santa Croce at Borgo Santa Croce 29r (Mon–Sat 9am 7pm, Sun 9am–2pm; ℡055.234.0444). There's also a convenient office close to the train station, to the right of the back of Santa Maria Novella church, on the far side of the large Piazza della Stazione (Mon–Sat 8.30am–7pm, Sun 8.30am–2pm; ℡055.212.245).

All three provide an adequate **map** and various leaflets, including a sheet with updated opening hours and entrance charges. The office at Via Cavour also handles information on the whole of Florence province. None of these offices will book accommodation, but can give you the names of private booking agencies. They also hand out the free information booklets *Informacittà* and *Vivifirenze*. One of the best sources of information on events is *Firenze Spettacolo* (€1.60), a monthly, partly bilingual listings magazine available from bookshops and larger newsstands.

## City transport

Finding your way around central Florence is straightforward – it's just ten minutes' **walk** from Santa Maria Novella to the central Piazza del Duomo, along Via de' Panzani and Via de' Cerretani. You can't really miss these roads: stand with your back to the train station and they form the main thoroughfare sweeping away in front of you and to the left. The great majority of the major sights are within a few minutes of the Duomo.

Within the historic centre, walking is generally the most efficient way of getting around, and the imposition of the **zona a traffico limitato** (ZTL) – which limits traffic in the centre to residents' cars, delivery vehicles and public transport – has reduced the once unbearable pollution and noise. On the other hand, the ZTL has increased the average speed of the traffic, so you should be especially careful before stepping off the narrow pavements.

## Buses

If you want to cross town in a hurry, or visit some of the peripheral sights, your best option is to use one of the frequent and speedy orange ATAF **buses**.

## Florence on the Internet

**Tourist information** ⓦwww.firenze.turismo.toscana.it. An official tourist office site (there are many), with an English-language option. Useful for information on forthcoming exhibitions and hotel listings.

**Firenze Online** ⓦwww.fionline.it/turismo. Classy if commercially oriented site from one of Florence's main service providers, with information on art, music, theatre, cinema, shopping – and even finding a job.

**Firenze.net** ⓦwww.firenze.net. Smart, stylish website, packed with city info and links.

**Uffizi Gallery** ⓦwww.uffizi.firenze.it. The official website of the Uffizi, with images of the paintings, historical notes, news, virtual reality tours of some rooms and an index of artists.

**Your Way to Florence** ⓦwww.arca.net/florence.htm. The most comprehensive site, with news plus information on transport, accommodation and opening hours.

Tickets are valid for unlimited travel within one hour (€1), three hours (€1.80), 24 hours (€4.50), two days (€7.60), three days (€9.60) and seven days (€16). A *Biglietto Multiplo* gives four sixty-minute tickets for €3.90. You can buy tickets from the main ATAF **information office** in the bays to the east of Santa Maria Novella train station (daily 7am–8pm; ⓦwww.ataf.net), from any shops and stalls displaying the ATAF sign and from automatic machines all over Florence; tickets cannot be bought on buses. Once you're on board, you must stamp your ticket in the machine to begin its period of validity. There's a hefty on-the-spot **fine** for any passenger without a validated ticket.

Most of the routes that are useful to tourists stop by the station, notably #7 (for Fiesole), and #12/13: #13 goes clockwise through Piazzale Michelangelo, San Miniato and Porta Romana (all on the south side of the river), while #12 goes anticlockwise round the same route). In addition to these, small **electric buses** run along four very convenient central city routes. Bus #A runs from the station right through the historic centre, passing close by the Duomo and

Signoria, then heading east just north of Santa Croce; #B follows the north bank of the Arno; while #C descends from Piazza San Marco, heading south past Santa Croce and across the Ponte delle Grazie on its way to Via Bardi. These three buses follow similar routes on their return journeys. Bus #D leaves the station and crosses the river at Ponte Vespucci; from here it becomes a handy Oltrarno bus, running right along the south bank of the river and, on the return journey, jinking up past Palazzo Pitti, Santo Spirito and the Carmine church on its way back to the Ponte Vespucci.

## Taxis

**Taxis** are white with yellow trim. It's difficult to flag down a cab on the street but there are plenty of central ranks: key locations include the station, Piazza della Repubblica, Piazza del Duomo, Piazza Santa Maria Novella, Piazza San Marco, Piazza Santa Croce and Piazza Santa Trinita. You can also call a "radio taxi" on ☎055.4242, 055.4798 or 055.4390. If you do, you'll be given the car's code name – usually a town, city or

## Florence museum admission

All of Florence's state-run museums belong to an association called **Firenze Musei** (ⓦwww.firenzemusei.it), which sets aside a daily quota of tickets that can be **reserved in advance**. The Uffizi, the Accademia and the Bargello belong to this group, as do the Palazzo Pitti museums, the Bóboli garden, the Medici chapels in San Lorenzo, the archeological museum and the San Marco museum. For the first trio you should certainly consider making use of this facility, because in high season the queues for tickets on the door can be enormous.

For the Uffizi you can reserve tickets at the reception area, or use the **telephone booking line**, which currently is the only outlet for reserved tickets for the other museums in the Firenze Musei scheme. You call ☎055.294.883 (Mon–Fri 8.30am–6.30pm, Sat 8.30am–12.30pm) and an English-speaking operator allocates you a ticket (with a €3 booking fee) for a specific hour; the ticket is collected at the museum, again at a specific time, shortly before entry. That's the theory, but in reality the phone line tends to be engaged for long periods at a stretch, so perseverance is nearly always required. And if you're going to pre-book a visit, you should do it as soon as possible, because the allocation of reservable tickets is often sold out many days ahead. (For more details on the Uffizi, see p.77.)

Note that on-the-door admission to all state-run museums is free for EU citizens under 18 and over 65, on presentation of a passport, and that nearly all of Florence's major museums are routinely **closed on Monday**, though some are open for a couple of Mondays each month. In the majority of cases, museum ticket offices close thirty minutes before the museum itself. At the Palazzo Vecchio and Museo Stibbert however, it's one hour before, while at the Uffizi, Bargello, Museo dell'Opera del Duomo, the dome of the Duomo, the Campanile and Pitti museums it's 45 minutes.

country – and its number, both of which are emblazoned on the cab, together with the phone number of the company. Italians tend not to order cabs far in advance: simply call up a few minutes beforehand.

All rides are metered; expect to pay €5–8 for a short hop within the centre. Supplements on the metered fare are payable between 10pm and 6am (€2.78), all day on Sunday and public holidays (€1.65), for journeys outside the city limits (to Fiesole, for example) and for each piece of luggage placed in the boot (€0.60). If you call a cab it will arrive with a small sum on the meter, which the driver switches on when he begins the journey to pick you up.

# Piazza del Duomo

From the train station, all first-time visitors gravitate towards **Piazza del Duomo**, beckoned by the pinnacle of Brunelleschi's dome, which lords it over the cityscape with an authority unmatched by any architectural creation in any other Italian city. Yet even though the magnitude of the **Duomo** is apparent from a distance, first sight of the church and the adjacent **Baptistery** still comes as a jolt, their colourful patterned exteriors making a startling contrast with the dun-toned buildings around. Each of these great buildings is as remarkable inside as out, and an ascent of the cathedral's **dome** will give you astounding views over the city to the hazy Tuscan hills beyond.

After exploring the cathedral, you can escape the crowds by climbing the **Campanile**, the Duomo's detached bell-tower, or visit the **Museo dell'Opera del Duomo**, a repository for works of art removed over the centuries from the Duomo, Baptistery and Campanile. With pieces by Donatello, Michelangelo and many others, it's the city's second-ranking sculpture collection after the Bargello. On a considerably smaller scale, the **Loggia del Bigallo** contains a

tiny and beguiling museum relating to one of the city's oldest philanthropic institutions, while the **Museo di Firenze com'era** – a short distance east of the piazza – is devoted to the evolution of the Florentine cityscape.

# The Duomo

Some time in the seventh century the seat of the Bishop of Florence was transferred from San Lorenzo to Santa Reparata, a sixth-century church which stood on the site of the present-day **Duomo**, or **Santa Maria del Fiore** (Mon–Fri 10am–5pm, Thurs closes 3.30pm, Sat 10am–4.45pm, Sun 1.30–4.45pm; on 1st Sat of month closes 3.30pm). Later generations modified this older church until 1294, when Florence's ruling priorate was stung into action by the magnificence of newly commissioned cathedrals in Pisa and Siena. Their own cathedral, they lamented, was too "crudely built and too small for such a city".

A suitably immodest plan to remedy this shortcoming was ordered from Arnolfo di Cambio, who drafted a scheme to create the largest church in the Roman Catholic world and "surpass anything of its kind produced by the Greeks and Romans in the times of their greatest power". Progress on the project faltered after Arnolfo's death in 1302, but by 1380 Francesco Talenti and a string of mostly jobbing architects had brought the nave to completion. By 1418 the tribunes (apses) and the dome's supporting drum were also completed. Only the dome itself – no small matter – remained unfinished (see p.58).

△ The Duomo and Campanile, viewed from the south

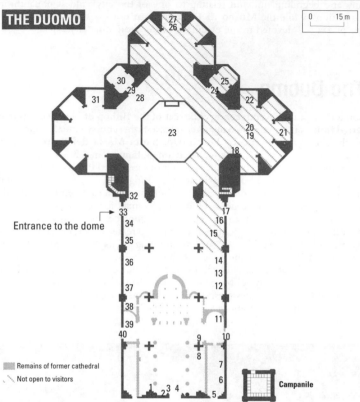

# THE DUOMO

0       15 m

Entrance to the dome

Campanile

■ Remains of former cathedral

⬝⬝ Not open to visitors

1 Stained glass: St Stephen (left), Assumption (centre) and St Lawrence (right), Lorenzo Ghiberti
2 Tomb of Antonio d'Orso, bishop of Florence (1323), Tino da Camaino
3 Mosaic: *Coronation of the Virgin* (1300), attributed to Gaddo Gaddi
4 Clock (1443) – decoration, Paolo Uccello
5 Stained glass: *St Lawrence and Angels*, Lorenzo Ghiberti
6 Tondo: *Bust of Brunelleschi* (1447), Andrea Cavalcanti
7 Bust: *Giotto at Work* (1490), Benedetto da Maiano
8 Gothic water stoup (1380), attributed to Urbano da Cortona
9 Entrance and steps to Santa Reparata
10 Porta del Campanile
11 Painting: *St Bartholomew Enthroned* (1408), Rossello di Jacopo Franchi
12 Painted sepulchral monument: Fra Luigi Marsili (1439), Bicci di Lorenzo
13 Statue: *Isaiah* (1427), Bernardo Ciuffagni
14 Painted sepulchral monument: Archbishop Pietro Corsino of Florence (1422), Bicci di Lorenzo
15 Stained glass: *Six Saints* (1395), Agnolo Gaddi
16 Bust: Marsilio Ficino (1521), philosopher friend of Cosimo I, holding a copy of Plato's works
17 Porta dei Canoncini: sculpture (1395–99), Lorenzo d'Ambrogio
18 Eight statues of the Apostles (1547–72) against the pillars of the octagon
19 Tribune: each tribune has five chapels; each chapel has two levels of stained glass, most by Lorenzo Ghiberti
20 Frescoes below windows of west and east tribunes: *Saints* (1440), attributed to Bicci di Lorenzo
21 Altar, attributed to Michelozzo
22 Fresco fragment: *Madonna del Popolo* (13th century), attributed to Giotto
23 Dome fresco cycle: *The Last Judgement* (1572–79), Giorgio Vasari and Federico Zuccari
24 Enamelled terracotta (above door): *Ascension* (1450), Luca della Robbia
25 Sagrestia Vecchia (Old Sacristy)
26 Bronze reliquary (1432–42) of St Zenobius (below altar), Lorenzo Ghiberti
27 Candle-holders: *Two Angels* (1450), Luca della Robbia
28 Enamelled terracotta: *Resurrection* (1444), Luca della Robbia
29 Bronze doors (1446–67), Luca della Robbia and Michelozzo
30 Sagrestia Nuova (New Sacristy): intarsia (1436–45), Benedetto and Giuliano da Maiano
31 Former site of Michelangelo's *Pietà*, currently in the Museo dell'Opera
32 Entrance and stairs to the dome
33 Porta della Mandorla: sculpture, Nanni di Banco and Donatello
34 Painting: *Dante explaining the Divine Comedy* (1465), Domenico di Michelino
35 Fresco: *SS Cosmas and Damian* (1429), Bicci di Lorenzo; two windows by Agnolo Gaddi
36 Statue (in recess) designed for old cathedral facade: *King David* (1434), Bernardo Ciuffagni
37 Equestrian portrait: *Sir John Hawkwood* (1436), Paolo Uccello
38 Equestrian portrait: *Niccolò da Tolentino* (1456), Andrea del Castagno
39 Bust: *Antonio Squarcialupi* (former cathedral organist, 1490), Benedetto da Maiano
40 *The Prophet Joshua* (1415), Nanni di Bartolo; the head is by Donatello

# The exterior

Parts of the Duomo's **exterior** date back to Arnolfo's era, but most of the overblown and pernickety main **facade** is a nineteenth-century simulacrum of a Gothic front. The original facade, which was never more than quarter-finished, was pulled down in 1587 on the orders of Ferdinand I. A competition to produce a new front proved fruitless, and for three centuries the cathedral remained faceless. After Florence became capital of the newly unified Italy in 1865, however, no fewer than 92 plans were submitted. The winning entry, by the otherwise obscure Emilio de Fabris, was completed in 1887. To its credit, the new frontage at least retained the original colour scheme and materials, with marble quarried from three different sources: white from Carrara, red from the Maremma and green from Prato.

The cathedral's south (right) side is the oldest part of the exterior – both its side portals deserve a glance – but the most attractive adornment is the **Porta della Mandorla** (number 33 on our plan), on the other side. This takes its name from the almond-shaped frame (or *mandorla*) that contains the grime-streaked relief of *The Assumption of the Virgin* (1414–21), sculpted by Nanni di Banco; the lunette features a mosaic of the *Annunciation* (1491) to a design by Ghirlandaio. The two heads in profile either side of the gable may be early works by Donatello.

# The interior

The Duomo's **interior** is the converse of the exterior – a vast, uncluttered enclosure of bare masonry. Its ambience is more that of a great assembly hall than a devotional building, and yet its apparently barren walls hold a far greater accumulation of treasures than at first appears.

The most conspicuous decorations are a pair of memorials to *condottieri* (mercenary commanders). Paolo Uccello's monument to **Sir John Hawkwood** (37), created in 1436, is often cited as the epitome of Florentine mean-spiritedness; according to local folklore – unsupported by any evidence – the mercenary captain of Florence's army was promised a proper equestrian statue as his memorial, then was posthumously fobbed off with this trompe l'oeil version. Perhaps the slight was deserved. Before being employed by Florence, Hawkwood and his White Company had marauded their way through Tuscany, holding entire cities to ransom under threat of ransack. The monument features a strange shift of perspective, with the pedestal depicted from a different angle from what's on it; it's known that Uccello was ordered to repaint the horse and rider, presumably because he'd shown them from the same point of view as the base, which must have displayed the horse's belly and not much else. Look back at the entrance wall and you'll see another Uccello contribution to the interior – a **clock** (4) adorned with four rather abstracted Evangelists. It uses the old *hora italica*, common in Italy until the eighteenth century, when the 24th hour of the day ended at sunset.

Andrea del Castagno's monument to **Niccolò da Tolentino** (38), created twenty years later, is clearly derived from Uccello's fresco, but has an aggressive edge that's typical of this artist. Just beyond the horsemen, Domenico di Michelino's 1465 work *Dante Explaining the Divine Comedy* (34) gives Brunelleschi's dome – then only nearing completion – a place scarcely less prominent than the mountain of Purgatory. Dante stands outside the walls, a symbol of his exile from Florence.

Judged by mere size, the major work of art in the Duomo is the 1572–79 fresco of **The Last Judgement** (23), which fills much of the interior of

## The Pazzi Conspiracy

The **Pazzi Conspiracy**, perhaps the most compelling of all Florence's murkier acts of treachery, had its roots in the election in 1472 of **Sixtus IV**, a pope who distributed money and favours with a largesse remarkable even by papal standards. Six of his nephews were made cardinals, one of them, the uncouth **Girolamo Riario**, coming in for particularly preferential treatment, probably because he was Sixtus's son. Sixtus's plan was that Riario should take over the town of Imola as a base for papal expansion, and accordingly he approached Lorenzo de' Medici for the necessary loan. Aware that Imola was too close to Milan and Bologna to be allowed to fall into papal hands, Lorenzo rebuffed the pope, despite the importance of the Vatican account with the Medici bank, and the family's role as agents for the papacy's alum mines in Tuscany (alum was a vital part of the dyeing industry, and therefore essential to Florence's textile trade). Enraged by the snub, and by Lorenzo's refusal to recognize **Francesco Salviati** as archbishop of Pisa (Sixtus had ignored an agreement by which appointments within the Florentine domain could only be made by mutual agreement), Sixtus turned to the Pazzi, the Medici's leading Florentine rivals as bankers in Rome.

Three co-conspirators met in Rome in the early months of 1477: Riario, now in possession of Imola but eager for greater spoils; Salviati, incandescent at Lorenzo's veto and desperate to become archbishop of Florence; and **Francesco de' Pazzi**, head of the Pazzis' Rome operation and determined to usurp Medici power in Florence. Any plot, however, required military muscle, and the man chosen to provide it, a plain-speaking mercenary called **Montesecco**, proved intensely wary of the whole enterprise: "Beware of what you do," he counselled, "Florence is a big affair." In the end he made his cooperation conditional on papal blessing, a benediction that was readily obtained. "I do not wish the death of anyone on any account," was Sixtus's mealy-mouthed observation, "since it does not accord with our office to consent to such a thing" – yet he knew full well Lorenzo's death was essential if the plot was to succeed. "Go, and do what you wish," he added, "provided there be no killing." **Jacopo de' Pazzi**, the Pazzis' wizened godfather, was also won over by Sixtus's disingenuous support, despite being on good terms with the Medici – indeed, one of his nephews was married to Lorenzo's sister.

the dome. At the time of its execution, however, a substantial body of opinion thought Vasari's and Zuccari's combined effort did nothing but deface Brunelleschi's masterpiece, and quite a few people today are of the same opinion.

To the side of the high altar a barrier prevents you from going any further, but glass doors allow you to look into the **Sagrestia Nuova** (30), where the lavish panelling is inlaid with beautiful intarsia work (1436–45) by Benedetto and Giuliano Maiano, notably a delicate trompe l'oeil *Annunciation* in the centre of the wall facing the door. The relief of the *Resurrection* (1442) above the entrance is by Luca della Robbia, his first important commission in the enamelled terracotta for which he became famous. The stunning **sacristy door** (1445–69), created in conjunction with Michelozzo, was his only work in bronze. It was in this sacristy that Lorenzo de' Medici took refuge in 1478 after his brother Giuliano had been mortally stabbed on the altar steps by the Pazzi conspirators (see above): the bulk of della Robbia's recently installed doors protected him from his would-be assassins. Small portraits on the handles commemorate the brothers.

Across the way, in the section that's closed off to visitors, della Robbia's *Ascension* (1450) can be seen above the door of the **Sagrestia Vecchia** (25); it was once accompanied by Donatello's sublime *cantoria*, or choir-loft, now

After numerous false starts, it was decided to **murder** Lorenzo and Giuliano whilst they attended Mass in the cathedral. The date set was Sunday, April 26, 1478. Montesecco, however, now refused "to add sacrilege to murder", so Lorenzo's murder was delegated to two embittered priests, Maffei and Bagnone, whereas Giuliano was to be dispatched by Francesco de' Pazzi and **Bernardo Baroncelli**, a violent Pazzi sidekick deeply in debt to the family. Salviati, meanwhile, accompanied by an armed troop, was to seize control of the Palazzo della Signoria.

It all went horribly wrong. Giuliano was killed in a crazed frenzy, his skull shattered and his body rent with nineteen stab wounds, but Lorenzo managed to escape, fleeing wounded to the Duomo's new sacristy, where he and his supporters barricaded themselves behind its heavy bronze doors. Across the city, Salviati was separated from his troops, thanks to newly installed secret doors and locks in the Palazzo della Signoria, and arrested by the *Gonfaloniere*, Cesare Petrucci.

Apprised of the plot, a furious mob dispensed summary justice to several of the conspirators: Salviati's troops were massacred to a man, whilst Salviati and Francesco de' Pazzi were hanged from a window of the Palazzo della Signoria. Of the latter execution, Poliziano, the eminent humanist, noted that "as the archbishop rolled and struggled at the end of his rope, his eyes goggling in his head, he fixed his teeth into Francesco de' Pazzi's naked body". Maffei and Bagnone, the bungling priests, were castrated and hanged. Baroncelli escaped to Constantinople but was extradited and executed. Montesecco was tortured, but given a soldier's execution in the Bargello. Jacopo's end was the most sordid. Having escaped Florence, he was recaptured, tortured, stripped naked, and hanged alongside the decomposing Salviati. He was then buried in Santa Croce, but exhumed by the mob, who blamed heavy rains on his evil spirit. His corpse was dragged through the streets, tipped in a ditch, and finally propped up outside the Pazzi palace, where his rotting head was used as door knocker. Eventually the putrefying body was thrown in the Arno, fished out, flogged and hanged again by a gang of children, and finally cast back into the river.

in the Museo dell'Opera (see p.64). Luca della Robbia's equally mesmeric *cantoria*, in the same museum, occupied a matching position above the Sagrestia Nuova.

## Santa Reparata

In the 1960s, remnants of the Duomo's predecessor, **Santa Reparata** (9), were uncovered underneath the west end of the nave, where a flight of steps leads down into the excavation. The remains (admission €3) are extensive, as the nave of the Duomo was built, on the same alignment, several feet above that of the old church, which was thus not fully demolished. Subsequent excavations have revealed a complicated jigsaw of Roman, Paleochristian and Romanesque remains, plus fragments of mosaic and fourteenth-century frescoes. The explanatory diagrams tend to intensify the confusion: to make sense of it all, you'll have to keep referring to the colour-coded model in the farthest recess of the crypt. In 1972, further digging revealed **Brunelleschi's tomb**, an unassuming marble slab so simple that it had lain forgotten under the south aisle. The tombstone's present position is hardly any more glorious (it can be seen, without paying, through a grille to the left at the foot of the steps), but the architect does at least have the honour of being one of the very few Florentines to be buried in the Duomo itself.

## Brunelleschi's dome

Since Arnolfo di Cambio's scale model of the Duomo collapsed under its own weight some time in the fourteenth century, nobody has been sure quite how he intended to crown his achievement. In 1367 Neri di Fioraventi proposed the construction of a magnificent **cupola** (dome) that was to span nearly 43m, broader than the dome of Rome's Pantheon, which had remained the world's largest for 1300 years, and rise from a base some 55m above the floor of the nave – taller than the highest vaulting of any Gothic cathedral. Just as radical was Fioraventi's decision to dispense with flying buttresses, regarded as ugly vestiges of the Gothic barbarism of enemy states such as France and Milan.

There was just one problem: nobody had worked out how to build the thing. Medieval arches were usually built on wooden "centring", a network of timbers that held the stone in place until the mortar set. In the case of the Duomo, the weight of the stone would have been too great for the timber (the entire dome is thought to weigh some 33,000 tonnes), and the space to be spanned was too great for the measuring cords that would be needed to guide the masons – any cord strung across the church would sag and stretch too much for accuracy. A committee of the masons' guild was set up to solve the dilemma. One idea was to build the dome from pumice. Another, according to Vasari, was to support the dome on a vast mound of earth that would be seeded with thousands of coins; when the dome was finished, the mound would be cleared by inviting Florence's citizens to excavate the money.

After years of bickering the project was thrown open to competition. A goldsmith and clockmaker called **Filippo Brunelleschi** presented the winning scheme, defeating Ghiberti in the process – revenge of sorts for Ghiberti's triumph seventeen years earlier in the competition to design the Baptistery doors (see p.61). Doom-mongers, Ghiberti among them, criticized Brunelleschi at every turn, eventually forcing the authorities to employ both rivals. An exasperated Brunelleschi feigned illness and resigned. Ghiberti, left to his own devices, found himself baffled, and in 1423 Brunelleschi was invited to become the dome's sole "inventor and chief director".

The key to Brunelleschi's success lay in the construction of the dome as two masonry shells, each built as a stack of ever-diminishing rings. Secured with hidden stone beams and enormous iron chains, these concentric circles formed a lattice that was filled with lightweight bricks laid in a herringbone pattern that prevented the higher sections from falling inward. Brunelleschi's relentless inventiveness extended to a new hoist with a reverse gear, a new type of crane, and even a boat for transporting marble that was so ungainly it was nicknamed *Il Badalone* (The Monster).

The dome's completion was marked by the **consecration** of the cathedral on March 25, 1436 – Annunciation Day, and the Florentine New Year – in a ceremony conducted by the pope. Even then, the topmost piece, the lantern, remained unfinished, with many people convinced the dome could support no further weight. But once again Brunelleschi won the day, beginning work on the dome's final stage in 1446, just a few months before his death. The whole thing was finally completed in the late 1460s, when the cross and gilded ball, both cast by Verrocchio, were hoisted into place.

Today it is still the largest masonry dome in the world. Only the gallery around the base remains incomplete – abandoned with just one face finished after Michelangelo compared it to "cages for crickets". This criticism aside, Michelangelo was awestruck: gazing on the cupola he is supposed to have said: *Come te non voglio, meglio di te non posso* ("Similar to you I will not, better than you I cannot").

# The dome

Climbing the **dome** (Mon–Fri 8.30am–7pm, Sat 8.30am–5.40pm; 1st Sat of month closes 4pm; €6) is an amazing experience, both for the views from the top and for the insights it offers into Brunelleschi's engineering genius (see box). Be prepared for the queue that usually stretches from the entrance, on the north flank of the nave; it does, however, move fairly briskly. Also be ready for the 463 lung-busting steps. Claustrophobics should note that the climb involves some very confined spaces.

After an initial ascent, you emerge onto a narrow gallery that runs around the interior of the dome, with a dizzying view down onto the maze-patterned pavement of the nave. It's also the best vantage point from which to inspect the seven **stained-glass roundels**, designed by Uccello, Ghiberti, Castagno and Donatello, below Vasari's *Last Judgement* fresco. Beyond the gallery, you enter the more cramped confines of the dome itself. As you clamber up between the inner and outer shells, you can observe many ingenious features of Brunelleschi's construction: the ribs and arches, the herringbone brickwork, the wooden struts that support the outer shell – even the hooks and holes left for future generations of repairers. From the base of the white marble lantern that crowns the dome, the views across the city are breathtaking.

# The Campanile

The **Campanile** (daily 8.30am–7.30pm; €6) – the cathedral's bell-tower – was begun in 1334 by Giotto during his period as official city architect and *capo maestro* (head of works) in charge of the Duomo. By the time of his death three years later, the base, the first of five eventual levels, had been completed. Andrea Pisano, fresh from creating the Baptistery's south doors (see p.60), continued construction of the second storey (1337–42), probably in accordance with Giotto's plans. Work was rounded off by Francesco Talenti, who rectified deficiencies in Giotto's original calculations in the process: the base's original walls teetered on the brink of collapse until he doubled their thickness. When completed, the bell-tower reached 84.7m, well over the limit set by the city in 1324 for civic towers, the building of which had long been a means of expressing aristocratic or mercantile power.

These days a climb to the summit is one of the highlights of any Florentine trip, though it's worth first taking in the tower's decorative **sculptures and reliefs** (most are now copies, but you can get a closer look at the age-blackened originals in the Museo dell'Opera del Duomo). As it moved up the tower, the decoration was intended to mirror humankind's progress from original sin to a state of divine grace, a progress facilitated by manual labour, the arts and the sacraments, and guided by the influence of the planets and the cardinal and theological virtues. Thus the first storey is studded with two rows of bas-reliefs; the lower register, in hexagonal frames – some designed by Giotto, but all executed by Pisano and pupils – illustrates the *Creation, Art and Works of Man*, while in the diamond-shaped panels of the upper register are allegories of the *Seven Planets* (then believed to influence human lives), *Seven Sacraments* (which sanctify human existence) and *Seven Virtues* (which shape human behaviour). A century or so later Luca della Robbia added the *Five Liberal Arts* (*Grammar*, *Philosophy*, *Music*, *Arithmetic* and *Astrology*) – which shape the human spirit – on the north face. Further works in the second-storey niches by Pisano were eventually replaced by Donatello and Nanni di Bartolo's figures of the *Prophets*, *Sibyls*, *Patriarchs* and *Kings* (1415–36).

The parapet at the top of the tower is a less lofty but in many ways more satisfying viewpoint than the cathedral dome, if only because the view takes in the Duomo itself. Be warned, though, that there are 414 steps to the summit – and no lift. George Eliot made the ascent in 1861, finding it "a very sublime getting upstairs indeed", her "muscles much astonished at the unusual exercise".

# The Baptistery

Florence's **Baptistery** (Mon–Sat noon–6.30pm, Sun 8.30am–1.30pm; €3) stands immediately west of the Duomo, whose geometrically patterned marble cladding mirrors that of the smaller, older building. Generally thought to date from the sixth or seventh century, the Baptistery is the oldest building in Florence, first documented in 897, when it was recorded as the city's cathedral before Santa Reparata. Though its origins lie buried in the Dark Ages, no building better illustrates the special relationship between Florence and the Roman world.

The Florentines were always conscious of their **Roman** ancestry, and for centuries believed that the Baptistery was a converted Roman temple to Mars, originally built to celebrate the defeat of Fiesole and the city's foundation. This belief was bolstered by the interior's ancient granite columns, probably taken from the city's old Roman Capitol (other columns from this site found their way to San Miniato). Further proof was apparently provided by traces of an ancient pavement mosaic, remains now thought to belong to an old Roman bakery. But if the building itself is not Roman, its exterior marble cladding – applied in a Romanesque reworking between about 1059 and 1128 – is clearly classical in inspiration, while its most famous embellishments, the gilded **bronze doors**, mark the emergence of a more scholarly, self-conscious interest in the art of the ancient world.

## The south doors

Responsibility for the Baptistery's improvement and upkeep lay with the *Arte di Calimala*, the most powerful of Florence's guilds. It was they who initiated

△ A detail of the Baptistery's mosaics

the building's eleventh-century revamp, and they who in the 1320s turned their attention to the exterior, and in particular to the question of a suitably majestic entrance. In this they were stung into action by arch-rival Pisa, whose cathedral was not only famous for its bronze portals, but whose craftsmen had recently completed some celebrated bronze doors for the great cathedral at Monreale in Sicily.

The arrival of Andrea Pisano in Florence in 1330 offered the chance of similar glories. Within three months the Pisan sculptor had created wax models for what would become the Baptistery's **south doors**. (They were originally placed in the east portal, but were displaced when Ghiberti's "Gates of Paradise" – see below – were finished.) Over the next eight years the models were cast in bronze, probably with the assistance of Venetian bell-makers, then Italy's most accomplished bronzesmiths. Twenty of the doors' 28 panels, installed in 1339, form a narrative on the life of St John the Baptist, patron saint of Florence and the Baptistery's dedicatee; the lowest eight reliefs depict Humility and the Cardinal and Theological Virtues. The bronze frame (1452–62) is the work of Vittorio Ghiberti, son of the more famous Lorenzo. The figures above the portal – the Baptist, Salome and executioner – are copies of late sixteenth-century additions; the originals are in the Museo dell'Opera del Duomo.

## The north doors

Some sixty years of financial and political turmoil, and the ravages of the Black Death, prevented further work on the Baptistery's other entrances until 1401. That year a competition was held to design a new set of doors, each of the six main entrants being asked to create a panel showing the Sacrifice of Isaac. The doors were to be a votive offering, a gift to God to celebrate the passing of another plague epidemic.

The judges found themselves equally impressed by the work of two young goldsmiths, Brunelleschi and **Lorenzo Ghiberti** (both winning entries are displayed in the Bargello). Unable to choose between the pair, it appears that the judges suggested that the two work in tandem. Brunelleschi replied that if he couldn't do the job alone he wasn't interested – whereupon the contract was handed to Ghiberti, leaving his rival to stomp off to study architecture in Rome. Ghiberti, barely 20 years old, was to devote much of the next 25 years to this one project, albeit in the company of distinguished assistants such as Masolino, Donatello and Paolo Uccello. His fame rests almost entirely on the extraordinary result.

His **north doors** (1403–24) show a new naturalism and classicized sense of composition, copying Pisano's 28-panel arrangement while transcending its traditional Gothic approach: the upper twenty panels depict Scenes from the New Testament, while the eight lower panels describe the Four Evangelists and Four Doctors of the Church.

## The east doors

The north doors, while extraordinary, are as nothing to the sublime **east doors** (1425–52), ordered from Ghiberti as soon as the first set was finished. The artist would spend some 27 years on the new project, work which he pursued, in his own words, "with the greatest diligence and greatest love". These doors have long been known as the "Gates of Paradise", supposedly because Michelangelo once remarked that they were so beautiful they deserved to be the portals of heaven. However, it's more likely that the name came about because these doors face

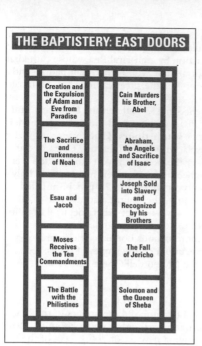

## THE BAPTISTERY: EAST DOORS

| | |
|---|---|
| Creation and the Expulsion of Adam and Eve from Paradise | Cain Murders his Brother, Abel |
| The Sacrifice and Drunkenness of Noah | Abraham, the Angels and Sacrifice of Isaac |
| Esau and Jacob | Joseph Sold into Slavery and Recognized by his Brothers |
| Moses Receives the Ten Commandments | The Fall of Jericho |
| The Battle with the Philistines | Solomon and the Queen of Sheba |

the cathedral – the space between a cathedral and its baptistery was known as the *Paradiso*, because the sacrament of baptism put its recipient on the threshold of paradise.

The doors have just ten panels, a departure from both previous sets of doors, while their enclosing squares abandon the Gothic diamond or quatrefoil frame. Unprecedented in the subtlety of their casting, the **Old Testament scenes** – the Creation, the Ten Commandments, the Sacrifice of Isaac, and so on – are a primer of early Renaissance art, using rigorous perspective, gesture and sophisticated groupings to intensify the drama of each scene. Ghiberti's power of compression and detail is such that several narratives are often woven into a single scene. The sculptor has also included an understandably self-satisfied self-portrait in the frame of the left-hand door: his is the fourth head from the top of the right-hand band – the bald chap with the smirk.

The other 23 medallions portray various of Ghiberti's artistic contemporaries, while the 24 statuettes depict the Prophets and Sibyls. The gorgeous golden doors now in place are reproductions, as the original panels have been restored and exhibited, to great effect, in the Museo dell'Opera del Duomo.

The pair of pitted **marble columns** to the side of the east doors were presented by the city of Pisa in the twelfth century, and would have been slotted into the walls had they not turned out to be too weak to bear any substantial weight. The story goes that when the Pisans set off to attack Mallorca in 1117 they were so fearful of a raid by the city of Lucca in their absence that they begged the Florentines to watch over their city. In gratitude, on their return they made Florence a gift of the two pillars, part of the booty seized during the Mallorcan raid. However, the columns were deemed to have magic powers too valuable to be left to the Florentines – their polished surfaces were meant to foretell acts of treason – and the Pisans are said to have deliberately ruined and weakened the pillars by baking them in embers.

Another marble column, just north of the Baptistery, is decorated with bronze branches and leaves to commemorate a miracle of January 429 AD, brought about by the body of St Zenobius, Florence's first bishop; as the corpse was being carried from San Lorenzo into Santa Reparata it brushed against a barren elm here, which thereupon sprang into leaf.

## The interior

The Baptistery **interior** is stunning, with its black and white marble cladding and miscellany of ancient columns below a blazing **mosaic ceiling**. Mosaics were not a Florentine speciality – in the centuries to come they would give way to fresco, but in the thirteenth century they were the predominant decorative medium. Encouraged by the interest surrounding the restoration of mosaics then taking place in the early Christian basilicas of Rome and Ravenna, the city was keen to match its rivals, principally Venice.

The earliest mosaics (1225) lie above the square apse, and depict the Virgin and John the Baptist. Above them, a wheel of prophets encircles the Lamb of God. The main vault is dominated by a vast figure of Christ in Judgement, flanked by depictions of Paradise and Hell. Just to the left of the monstrous, man-eating Lucifer, the poet Virgil (in a white cloak) can be seen leading Dante (in black) through the Inferno. The figures were a later insertion, added after the poet's death during something of a frenzy of recognition. The other five sections of the octagonal ceiling depict Biblical scenes, beginning above the north doors with the Creation, and proceeding through the stories of Joseph and John the Baptist towards the Crucifixion and Resurrection, seen above the south doors.

The interior's semi-abstract **mosaic pavement** also dates from the thirteenth century. The empty octagon at its centre marks the spot once occupied by the huge font in which every child born in the city during the previous twelve months would be baptized on March 25 (New Year's Day in the old Florentine calendar). When a child was born, a coloured bean was dropped into an urn in the Baptistery: black for a boy, white for a girl – a system which allowed the birth rate to be calculated.

To the right of the altar lies the **tomb of Baldassare Cossa**, the schismatic Pope John XXIII, who was deposed in 1415 and died in Florence in 1419. At the time of his death he was a guest of his financial adviser and close friend, Giovanni di Bicci de' Medici, the man who established the Medici at the political forefront of Florence. It was through Pope John that Giovanni became chief banker to the Papal Curia, a deal that laid the foundations of the Medici fortune: for years over half the Medici's profits would come from just two Rome-based banks. That Pope John achieved a resting place here was certainly not due to his piousness. At his deposition he was accused of heresy, murder and the seduction of more than two hundred women in Bologna during his sojourn in the city as papal representative. His monument, draped by an illusionistic marble canopy, is the work of Donatello and his pupil Michelozzo.

# The Museo dell'Opera del Duomo

In 1296 a body called the Opera del Duomo, literally the "Work of the Duomo", was created to oversee the maintenance of the Duomo. Since the early fifteenth century its home has been the building behind the east end of the cathedral at Piazza del Duomo 9, which now also houses the **Museo dell'Opera del Duomo** (Mon–Sat 9am–7.30pm, Sun 9am–1.40pm; €6), a repository of the most precious and fragile works of art from the Duomo, Baptistery and Campanile. As an overview of the sculpture of Florence the museum is second only to the Bargello. (Incidentally, you can see the stonemasons of the present-day Opera at work in their studio at Via dello Studio 23a, on the south side of the Duomo.)

## The ground floor

Beyond the ticket office, rooms devoted to sculpture from the Baptistery (mostly works by Tino da Camaino) and the Duomo's lateral doors precede the museum's **courtyard**, a site thick with historical associations despite its ultra-modern makeover: it was here that much of Michelangelo's *David* was sculpted. Now glazed over, the courtyard is home to all eight of Ghiberti's panels from the "Doors of Paradise" (see p.61), finally brought together following restoration, and now sharing the space with the graceful *Baptism of Christ* (1502–25), by Andrea Sansovino and assistants.

The largest room on this floor is a large hall devoted to the original sculptures of the cathedral's west front, foremost among which are works by the cathedral's first architect, **Arnolfo di Cambio** (and his workshop), including an eerily glass-eyed *Madonna and Child*; all were rescued from Arnolfo's quarter-finished cathedral facade which was pulled down by Ferdinand I in 1587. Equally striking is the sculptor's vase-carrying figure of *St Reparata*, one of Florence's patron saints, a work long thought to be of Greek or Roman origin. Also noteworthy is the ramrod-straight statue of Boniface VIII, one of the most unpleasant of all medieval popes. Along the entrance wall are four seated figures of the Evangelists, also wrenched from the facade: Nanni di Banco's *St Luke* and **Donatello**'s *St John* are particularly fine.

The room off the far end of the hall features a sequence of **marble reliefs** (1547–72), by Bacio Bandinelli and Giovanni Bandini, part of an unfinished sequence of 300 panels proposed for the choir of the cathedral. Also here is a collection of paintings from a series of altars in the cathedral, all torn from their original home in 1838 as they were considered an affront to the purity of the building. One of the most eye-catching is Giovanni di Biondo's triptych portraying episodes from the *Martyrdom of St Sebastian*: study the smaller predella panels for some of the more hair-raising events in the saint's life, notably a violent cudgelling and the panel in which he is tipped head-first into a well.

The adjoining modern **octagonal chapel** features an assembly of reliquaries which contain, among other saintly remains, the jaw of Saint Jerome and an index finger of John the Baptist. From here a vaulted gallery leads to the museum's main stairs – note the marker on the right-hand wall indicating the water level in the building after the 1966 flood. It's easy to miss the room off to the right of the **Lapidarium** (a collection of modest works in stone), which contains items removed from the cathedral's Porta della Mandorla, including a lovely terracotta *Creation of Eve* (1410) attributed to Donatello.

## The upper floor

Up the stairs on the mezzanine level stands **Michelangelo**'s anguished **Pietà** (1550–53), moved from the cathedral as recently as 1981 while restoration of the dome was in progress, but probably fated to stay here. This is one of the sculptor's last works, carved when he was almost 80, and was intended for his own tomb; Vasari records that the face of Nicodemus is a self-portrait. Dissatisfied with the quality of the marble, Michelangelo mutilated the group by hammering off the left leg and arm of Christ; his pupil Tiberio Calcagni restored the arm, then finished off the figure of Mary Magdalene, turning her into a whey-faced supporting player.

Although he's represented on the lower floor, it's upstairs that **Donatello**, the greatest of Michelangelo's precursors, really comes to the fore. The first room at the top of the stairs features his magnificent **Cantoria**, or choir-loft (1433–39), with its playground of boisterous *putti*. Facing it is another splendid *cantoria* (1431–38), the first-known major commission of the young **Luca della Robbia** (the originals are underneath, with casts replacing them in the *cantoria* itself); the earnest musicians embody the text from Psalm 33 which is inscribed on the frame: "Praise the Lord with harp. Sing unto Him with the psaltery and instrument of ten strings." Both lofts were dismantled and removed from their position above the cathedral's sacristies in 1688 on the occasion of the ill-fated marriage of Violante Beatrice of Bavaria to Ferdinand de' Medici, the hopelessly ineffectual heir of Cosimo III. The ceremony gave the cathedral authorities the excuse to decorate the cathedral in a more fitting "modern" style. The ensuing clear-out left the *cantorie* languishing in dusty storage for some two centuries.

Around the room are arrayed the life-size figures that Donatello carved for the Campanile, perhaps the most powerful of which is the prophet Habbakuk, the intensity of whose gaze is said to have prompted the sculptor to seize it and yell "Speak, speak!" Donatello was apparently also responsible for the statue's nickname *Lo Zuccone* (the Pumpkin) – after its bald head. Keeping company with Donatello's work are four Prophets (1348–50) and two Sybils (1342–8) attributed to Andrea Pisano, and *The Sacrifice of Isaac* (1421), a collaboration between Nanni di Bartolo and Donatello.

Donatello's later style is exemplified by the gaunt wooden figure of Mary Magdalene (1453–5), which confronts you on entering the room off the *cantorie* room. The *Magdalene* came from the Baptistery, as did the silver altar-front at the far end of the room, a dazzling summary of the life of St John the Baptist. Begun in 1366, the piece was completed in 1480, the culmination of a century of labour by, among others, Michelozzo (responsible for the central figure of *John the Baptist*), Verrocchio (the *Decapitation* to the right) and Antonio del Pollaiuolo (the *Birth of Jesus* on the left side), who was the chief creator of the silver cross atop the altar. Ranged around the walls are more reliquaries, fabrics, copes and other religious vestments, including 27 sublimely worked **needlework panels** – former vestments and altar panels from the Baptistery – produced between 1466 and 1487 by French, Flemish and Florentine artists, including members of the Arte di Calimala (one of the key textile guilds) working to designs by Pollaiuolo. Not surprisingly, given their provenance, they portray scenes from the life of the Baptist, one of Florence's patrons and the Baptistery's dedicatee.

In the room on the other side of the *cantorie* room you'll find the **bas-reliefs** that once adorned the Campanile. Though darkened with age, their allegorical panels remain both striking and intelligible, depicting the spiritual refinement of humanity through labour, the arts and, ultimately, the virtues and sacraments. The display reproduces the reliefs' original arrangement, the key panels being the hexagonal reliefs of the lower tier, all of which – save for the last five, by Luca della Robbia (1437–39) – were the work of Andrea Pisano and his son Nino (c.1348–50), probably to designs by Giotto.

A corridor at the end of Room II leads past a mock-up of Brunelleschi's building site, complete with broken bricks, wooden scaffolding and some of the tools that were used to build the dome, many invented specifically for the purpose by the architect himself. More arresting is Brunelleschi's **death mask**, which almost – but not quite – looks out of the window at the dome just across the way.

The sequence of rooms beyond displays various proposals for completing the balcony of the drum below the cupola (see p.58) and the Duomo's west front, including models created by Michelangelo, Giuliano da Maiano, Giambologna, Antonio da Sangallo, Andrea Sansovino and other leading architects. The wooden model of the **cathedral lantern** is presumed to have been made by Brunelleschi as part of his winning proposal for the design of the lantern in 1436. The final room, just off the main staircase, shows plans submitted to the three competitions held in the 1860s, when Florence was briefly capital of

Italy and the question of the facade standing "ignominious in faded stucco", as George Eliot put it, once more became pressing. They mostly provoke relief that none came to fruition, while Emilio de Fabris's winning design of 1876 is mostly remarkable for how little it differs from the other nineteenth-century Gothic pastiches.

# The Museo del Bigallo

On the other side of Piazza del Duomo, at the top of Via de' Calzaiuoli, stands the **Loggia del Bigallo**, which was built in the 1350s for the Compagnia della Misericordia, a charitable organization founded by St Peter Martyr in 1244, to give aid to the sick and to bury the dead. (The Misericordia still exists: their headquarters is just across the way, with their ambulances parked outside.) By the time the loggia was built, the Misericordia was also functioning as an orphanage – the building was commissioned as a place to display abandoned babies, in the hope that they might be recognized before being given to foster parents. For most of the fifteenth century the Misericordia was united with another orphanage, Compagnia del Bigallo (from the village in which it began), hence the loggia's name. Nowadays it houses the three-room **Museo del Bigallo** (daily except Tues 10am–6pm; €2), which contains a tiny collection of religious paintings commissioned by the two companies. As you might expect, the Madonna and Child is a dominant theme, and St Peter Martyr is present as well, but the two highlights are a remnant of a fresco painted on the outside of the loggia in 1386, showing the transfer of infants to their adoptive parents, and the *Madonna of the Misericordia*, painted by a follower of Bernardo Daddi in 1342, which features the oldest known panorama of Florence.

# The Museo di Firenze com'era

The top of Via del Proconsolo, just a few yards from the Museo dell'Opera del Duomo, forms a major junction with Via dell'Oriuolo, home to the **Museo di Firenze com'era** (daily except Thurs 9am–2pm; €2.70). This "Museum of Florence as it used to be" is one of the city's unsung museums, but its contents and setting – in a pleasant garden-fronted palazzo – are delightful. There are plans to move the museum to the Palazzo Vecchio, but the transfer does not appear to be imminent.

The story begins with a collection of models, plans and photographs of the excavation of the Piazza della Signoria that took place in the 1980s. As one would expect, a number of discoveries were made, but for want of any better ideas the piazza was simply paved over once the dig was complete. A large, somewhat speculative model of the **Roman city** stands at the far end of the room, with coloured sections showing the buildings whose locations the archeologists are sure of.

The long, vaulted main gallery stands on the other side of the entrance corridor. Maps, prints, photos and topographical paintings chart the growth of Florence from the fifteenth century to the present, and while none of the exhibits is a masterpiece, most of them are at least informative. Perhaps the most impressive item comes right at the start: a meticulous 1887 reproduction of a colossal 1472 aerial view of Florence called the *Pianta della Catena* (Chain Map), the original of which was destroyed in Berlin during World War II. It's the oldest accurate representation of the city's layout.

Almost as appealing are the twelve lunette pictures (1555) of the **Medici villas**, reproductions of which you'll see on postcards and posters across the city. They're the work of Flemish painter Justus Utens and were painted for the Medicis' Villa dell'Artimino. A poignant wooden model portrays the labyrinthine jumble of the **Mercato Vecchio**, the city's ancient heart, which was demolished to make space for the Piazza della Repubblica at the end of the nineteenth century. Elsewhere, a graphic picture portrays Savonarola's execution (see p.123), and eighteenth-century Florence is celebrated in the elegiac engravings of Giuseppe Zocchi.

# 2

# Piazza della Signoria and the Uffizi

Whereas the Piazza del Duomo provides the focus for the city's religious life, the **Piazza della Signoria** – site of the magnificent **Palazzo Vecchio** and forecourt to the **Uffizi** – has always been the centre of its secular existence. Always busy, it's at its liveliest for political rallies and other civic events, when speakers address the crowds from the terrace in front of the Palazzo Vecchio. (The terrace is called the *arringhiera*, from the same root as the English word "harangue".) Tempers can get frayed at these gatherings, but things used to be a lot wilder: in 1343, for example, one inflammatory meeting ended with a man being eaten by a mob. Most famously, it was here that Savonarola held his "Bonfires of the Vanities" (see p.123) – on the very spot where, on May 23, 1498, he was to be executed for heresy. A plaque near the fountain marks the place.

For so important a square, the history of the Piazza della Signoria is one of oddly haphazard and piecemeal development. Originally the area belonged to the Uberti family, leading members of the city's Ghibelline faction. When the Ghibellines were defeated in 1268, the land and buildings on it were confiscated and allowed to fall into ruin, supposedly as a lasting memorial to Ghibelline treachery. In time, part of the area was paved, a further act of humiliation designed to prevent the Uberti – exiled from the city – from ever raising another building within its precincts. The alleged reluctance of the city authorities to encroach on this "tainted" land partly explains the asymmetrical shape of the square and the Palazzo Vecchio.

The piazza took on a public role in 1307, when a small area was laid out to provide a setting for the Palazzo Vecchio, then known as the Palazzo dei Priori. All efforts to enlarge it over the next hundred years – a job sub-contracted to the Opera del Duomo, the city's largest construction company – were hampered by work on the palace and Loggia della Signoria. Contemporary accounts talk of decades when the area was little more than a rubble-filled building site, but by 1385 it was completely paved, and wheeled traffic was banned from the area (as it still is). Further restructuring occurred during Cosimo I's reordering of the Uffizi around 1560, and more alterations followed in 1871, when the medieval Loggia dei Pisani was demolished, opening up much of the square's present-day westward sweep. By this time, some of the piazza's most salient features – its statues – were already firmly in place.

# The statues

Florence's political volatility is encapsulated by the Piazza della Signoria's peculiar array of **statues**, most of which were arranged in the sixteenth century to accentuate the axis of the Uffizi. From left to right, the line-up starts with Giambologna's equestrian statue of **Cosimo I** (1587–94). An echo

## The Florentine Republic

Dante compared Florence's constant political struggles to a sick man forever shifting his position in bed, and indeed its medieval history often appears a catalogue of incessant civic unrest. Yet between 1293 and 1534 – bar the odd ruction – the city maintained a **republican** constitution that was embodied in well-defined institutions. The nucleus of this structure was formed by the city's merchants and guilds, who covertly controlled Florence as early as the twelfth century and formalized their influence during the so-called **Primo Popolo** (1248–59), a quasi-democratic regime whose ten-year rule, claimed Dante, was the only period of civic peace in Florence's history. During the **Secondo Popolo** (1284), the leading guilds, the *Arti Maggiori*, introduced the **Ordinamenti della Giustizia** (1293), a written constitution that entrenched mercantile power still further and was to be the basis of Florence's government for the next two hundred and fifty years.

The rulers of this much vaunted republic were drawn exclusively from the ranks of guild members over the age of 30, and were chosen in a public ceremony held every two months, the short tenure being designed to prevent individuals or cliques assuming too much power. At this ceremony, the names of selected guild members were placed in eight leather bags (*borse*) kept in the sacristy of Santa Croce; the ones picked from the bags duly became the **Priori** (or *Signori*), forming a government called the **Signoria**, usually comprising nine men, most of them from the *Arti Maggiori*. Once elected, the *Priori* moved into the Palazzo della Signoria, where they were expected to stay, virtually incommunicado, for their period of office – though they were waited on hand and foot, and enjoyed the services of a professional joke-teller, the *Buffone*.

Headed by the **Gonfaloniere** (literally the "Standard-Bearer"), the *Signoria* consulted two elected councils or **Collegi** – the **Dodici Buonomini** (Twelve Citizens) and **Sedici Gonfalonieri** (Sixteen Standard Bearers) – as well as committees introduced to deal with specific crises (the Ten of War, the Eight of Security, the Six of Commerce…). Permanent officials included the Chancellor (a post once held by Machiavelli) and the **Podestà**, a chief magistrate brought in from a neighbouring city as an independent arbitrator, and housed in the Bargello. In times of extreme crisis, such as the Pazzi Conspiracy (see p.56), all male citizens over the age of 14 were summoned to a **Parlamento** in Piazza della Signoria by the tolling of the Palazzo Vecchio's famous bell, known as the *Vacca* (Cow), after its deep, bovine tone. When a two-thirds quorum was reached, the people were asked to approve a **Balìa**, a committee delegated to deal with the situation as it saw fit.

All this looked good on paper but in practice the set-up was far from democratic. The lowliest workers, the **Popolo Minuto**, were totally excluded, as were the **Grandi**, or nobles. And despite the *Signoria*'s apparently random selection process, political cliques had few problems ensuring that only the names of likely supporters found their way into the *borse*. If a rogue candidate slipped through the net, or things went awry, then a *Parlamento* was summoned, a *Balìa* formed, and the offending person replaced by a more pliable candidate. It was by such means that the great mercantile dynasties of Florence – the Peruzzi, the Albizzi, the Strozzi, and of course the Medici – retained their power even when not technically in office.

**PIAZZA DELLA SIGNORIA**

PIAZZA DELLA SIGNORIA

Neptune Fountain

River Arno

| RESTAURANTS | | BARS & CAFÉS | |
|---|---|---|---|
| Antico Fattore | 11 | Caffè Italiano | 5 |
| Da Ganino | 4 | Cantinetta dei | |
| **GELATERIE** | | Verrazzano | 1 |
| Café delle Carizze | 12 | Gustavino | 6 |
| Perchè No! | 2 | Quasigratis | 9 |
| **CLUBS** | | Rivoire | 8 |
| Caruso Jazz Café | 10 | Vini | 3 |
| Tabasco | 7 | | |

of the famous Marcus Aurelius statue in Rome, it was designed to draw parallels between the power of medieval Florence (and thus Cosimo) and the glory of imperial Rome. Three bas-reliefs at the base portray key events in Cosimo's career: becoming duke of Florence (1537), the conquest of Siena (1555), and acquiring the title Grand Duke of Tuscany (1569) from Pius V.

Next comes Ammannati's fatuous **Neptune Fountain** (1565–75), a tribute to Cosimo's prowess as a naval commander. Neptune himself is a lumpen lout of a figure, who provoked Michelangelo to coin the rhyming put-down *Ammannato, Ammannato, che bel marmo hai rovinato* (". . . what a fine piece of marble you've ruined"). Ammannati doesn't seem to have been too embarrassed, though in a late phase of piety he did come to regret the lasciviousness of the figures round the base, created with the assistance of Giambologna and other junior sculptors. Florentine superstition has it that Neptune wanders around the piazza when struck by the light of a full moon.

After a copy of Donatello's **Marzocco** (1418–20), the original of which is in the Bargello, comes a copy of the same sculptor's **Judith and Holofernes** (1456–60), which freezes the action at the moment Judith's arm begins its scything stroke – a dramatic conception that no other sculptor of the period would have attempted. Commissioned by Cosimo de' Medici, this statue doubled as a fountain in the Palazzo Medici but was removed to the Piazza della Signoria after the expulsion of the family in 1495, to be displayed as an emblem of vanquished tyranny; a new inscription on the base reinforced the message for those too obtuse to get it. The original is in the Palazzo Vecchio.

Michelangelo's **David**, at first intended for the Duomo, was also installed here as a declaration of civic solidarity by the Florentine Republic; the original is now cooped up in the Accademia. Conceived as partner piece to the *David* is Bandinelli's **Hercules and Cacus** (1534), designed as a personal emblem of Cosimo I and a symbol of Florentine fortitude. Benvenuto Cellini described the musclebound figure as looking like "a sackful of melons", and it's a sobering thought that the marble might well have ended up as something more inspiring. In the late 1520s, when the Florentines were once again busy tearing the Medici emblem from every building on which it had been stuck, Michelangelo offered to carve a monumental figure of Samson to celebrate the Republic's latest victory over tyranny; other demands on the artist's time put paid to this project, and the stone passed to Bandinelli, who duly vented his mediocrity on it. A year later Bandinelli carved one of the two figures which served as posts for a chain across the palace entrance; the other is the work of an anonymous contemporary.

## The Loggia della Signoria

The square's grace note, the **Loggia della Signoria**, was begun in 1376, prompted by that year's heavy rains, which had washed out Florence's entire

△ Cellini's Perseus

calendar of public ceremonies. It was completed in 1382, serving as a dais for city dignitaries, a forum for meeting foreign emissaries, and a platform for the swearing-in of public officials. Its alternative name, the Loggia dei Lanzi, comes from Cosimo I's bodyguard of Swiss lancers, who were garrisoned nearby; its third name, the Loggia dell'Orcagna, derives from the idea that Orcagna (Andrea del Cione) may have had a hand in its original design.

Although Donatello's *Judith and Holofernes* was placed here as early as 1506, it was only in the late eighteenth century that the loggia became exclusively a showcase for sculpture. In the corner nearest the Palazzo Vecchio stands a figure that has become one of the iconic images of the Renaissance, Benvenuto Cellini's **Perseus** (1545), now back in its rightful place after a painstaking restoration. (The base is a copy, however; the original is on display in the Bargello). Made for Cosimo I, the statue symbolizes the triumph of firm Grand Ducal rule over the monstrous indiscipline of all other forms of government. The traumatic process of the statue's creation is vividly described in Cellini's rip-roaring and self-serving autobiography: seeing the molten bronze beginning to solidify too early, the ever-resourceful hero saved the day by flinging all his pewter plates into the mix. When the bronze cooled the figure emerged from the mould missing only three toes, which were added later.

Equally attention-seeking is Giambologna's last work, to the right, **The Rape of the Sabine** (1583), conjured from the largest piece of sculptural marble ever seen in Florence, and the epitome of the Mannerist obsession with spiralling forms. The sculptor supposedly intended the piece merely as a study of old age, male strength and female beauty: the present name was coined later. The figures along the back wall are Roman works, traditionally believed to portray Roman empresses, while of the three central statues only one – Giambologna's **Hercules Slaying the Centaur** (1599) – deserves its place. The seven figures in the spandrels between the arches above depict the Virtues (1384–89), all carved to designs by Agnolo Gaddi save the head of *Faith*, which was replaced by Donatello when the original crashed to the ground.

# The Palazzo Vecchio

Probably designed by Arnolfo di Cambio, Florence's fortress-like town hall, the **Palazzo Vecchio** (daily 9am–7pm; Thurs closes 2pm; €6 – or joint ticket with the Cappella Brancacci €8), was begun as the Palazzo dei Priori in the last year of the thirteenth century to provide premises for the *Priori* or *Signoria*, the highest tier of the city's republican government. Changes in the Florentine constitution over the years entailed alterations to the layout of the palace, the most radical coming in 1540, when Cosimo I moved his retinue here from the Palazzo Medici and grafted a huge extension onto the rear. The Medici remained in residence for only nine years before moving to the Palazzo Pitti – largely, it seems, at the insistence of Cosimo's wife, Eleonora di Toledo who dipped into her fortune to purchase the more spacious accommodation on the south side of the river. (As well as finding the Palazzo Vecchio too cramped, she objected to the stink and din created by the lions that were kept caged at the back of the palace, in Via dei Leoni, and also didn't much care for the drunken nocturnal carousings of the Swiss guards who were garrisoned in the Loggia dei Lanzi.) The "old" (*vecchio*) palace, which they left to their son, Francesco, then acquired its present name. Between 1865 and 1870, during Florence's brief tenure as capital of a newly united Italy, the palace housed the country's parliament and foreign ministry.

As for the sights, much of the palace's decoration comprises a relentless eulogy to Cosimo and his relations, propaganda that's made tolerable by some of the palace's examples of Mannerist art – among the finest pieces produced by that ultra-sophisticated and self-conscious movement. There are also frescoes by Domenico Ghirlandaio and some outstanding sculptures, not least works by Michelangelo and Donatello. It's also possible to visit hidden parts of the palace on hour-long guided tours known as **Percorsi Segreti**, while for the youngsters there's the innovative **Emozioni da Museo** programme (see box on p.76).

## The courtyard and first floor

Work on the palace's beautiful inner **courtyard** was begun by Michelozzo in 1453. The decoration was largely added by Vasari, court architect from 1555 until his death in 1574, on the occasion of Francesco de' Medici's marriage to Johanna of Austria in 1565. The bride's origin explains the otherwise puzzling presence of cities belonging to the Habsburg Empire amid the wall's painted townscapes. Vasari also designed the central fountain, though the winsome putto and dolphin (1476) at its crown are the work of Verrocchio (the present statues are copies; the originals are on the Terrazzo di Giunone on the palace's second floor). Vasari was also let loose on the **monumental staircase** (marked 1 on our plan), a far more satisfying affair which leads to the palace's first floor (though visitors are sometimes directed to take a different route upstairs).

Vasari was given fuller rein in the huge **Salone dei Cinquecento** at the top of the stairs, where tickets are checked. It was originally built in 1495 as the meeting hall for the Consiglio Maggiore (Great Council), the ruling assembly of the penultimate republic. The chamber might have had one of Italy's most remarkable decorative schemes: Leonardo da Vinci and Michelangelo were employed to paint frescoes on opposite sides of the room, but Leonardo's work, *The Battle of Anghiari*, was abandoned (or destroyed) after his experimental technique went wrong, while Michelangelo's *The Battle of Cascina* had got no further than a fragmentary cartoon when he

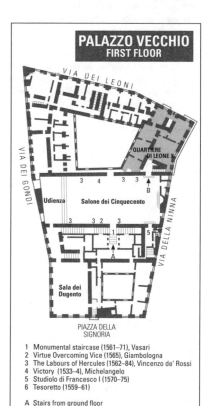

**PALAZZO VECCHIO**
**FIRST FLOOR**

1   Monumental staircase (1561–71), Vasari
2   Virtue Overcoming Vice (1565), Giambologna
3   The Labours of Hercules (1562–84), Vincenzo de' Rossi
4   Victory (1533–4), Michelangelo
5   Studiolo di Francesco I (1570–75)
6   Tesoretto (1559–61)

A   Stairs from ground floor
B   Stairs to second floor

## Percorsi Segreti

The Palazzo Vecchio's various so-called **Percorsi Segreti** ("Secret Passageways") allow access – on guided tours only – to parts of the building that are normally off limits. Most visually impressive is the trip up through the palace and into the **Attic of the Salone del Cinquecento**. From the vantage point of a balcony high above the hall, the guide describes the complex way in which Vasari created such a huge space within the medieval structure, and explains the allegorical meaning of the paintings. You are then led up into the vast attic itself, where two sets of trusses support the roof above and the ceiling below. Some of the beams are over 20m long.

Less magnificent, but still worth it for the guides' commentary, is the route leading from the street outside up through the secret **Stairway of the Duke of Athens**. The doorway was knocked through the exterior wall of the Palazzo in 1342 as an emergency escape route for the duke, who briefly took up the reins of power here. He never in fact used the staircase, but only because his fall from grace came rather sooner than he had imagined.

Another Percorso Segreto allows you inside the **Studiolo di Francesco I**, then through one of the hidden doors and up a secret little staircase to the *studiolino* or **Tesoretto** (6), Cosimo's tiny private study, which was built ten years before the *studiolo*.

All three tours (each costs €7 and includes admission to Palazzo Vecchio) last roughly an hour; further tours cost €2. These are not accessible for visitors in wheelchairs. Tours go every day in Italian, French and/or English, but exactly what language the tours are conducted in depends on demand, so it is worth asking about tours in English either at the desk by the ticket office or by phone (☎055.276.8224). Guides usually take one party on each Percorso Segreto from Monday to Friday at 9.30am and 11am, on Saturday at 3.30pm, 4.30pm and 5.30pm, and on Sunday at 10am, 11am and noon (though times change frequently); as a rule, there's at least one English-language party for each Percorso every day above . Further *percorsi* are planned, depending on the success of the present tours.

was summoned to Rome by Pope Julius II in 1506. Instead the hall received six drearily bombastic murals (1563–65) – painted either by Vasari or under his direction – illustrating Florentine military triumphs over Pisa (1496–1509) and Siena (1554–55). It has generally been assumed that Vasari obliterated whatever remained of Leonardo's fresco before beginning his work, but the discovery of a cavity behind *The Battle of Marciano* has raised the possibility that Vasari instead contructed a false wall for his fresco, to preserve his great predecessor's painting. Investigations are proceeding.

The **ceiling**'s 39 panels, again by Vasari, celebrate the *Apotheosis of Cosimo I* (centre), a scene surrounded by the crests of the city's guilds and further paeans to the prowess of Florence and the Medici. (One of the Percorsi Segreti takes you into the attic above the roof, an extraordinary space where it's possible to see how Vasari pulled off the trick of suspending such a large ceiling without visible supports.) The **sculptural** highlight is Michelangelo's *Victory* (4), almost opposite the entrance door. Carved for the tomb of Pope Julius II, the statue was donated to the Medici by the artist's nephew, then installed here by Vasari in 1565 to celebrate Cosimo's defeat of the Sienese ten years earlier. Directly opposite, on the entrance wall, is the original plaster model of a companion piece for the *Victory*, Giambologna's **Virtue Overcoming Vice (2)**, another artistic metaphor for Florentine military might – this time Florence's victory over Pisa. The remaining statues, the masterpiece of sixteenth-century artist Vincenzo de' Rossi, portray the

**Labours of Hercules (3)** and are yet another example of Florentine heroic propaganda: the innocuously classical Hercules is also one of Florence's many civic symbols.

### The Studiolo di Francesco I

From the Salone del Cinquecento, a roped-off door allows a glimpse of the most bizarre room in the building, the **Studiolo di Francesco I (5)**. Created by Vasari towards the end of his career and decorated by no fewer than thirty Mannerist artists (1570–74), this windowless cell was created as a retreat for the introverted son of Cosimo and Eleonora. Each of the miniature bronzes and nearly all the paintings reflect Francesco's interest in the sciences and alchemy: the entrance wall pictures illustrate the theme of Earth, while the others, reading clockwise, signify Water, Air and Fire. The outstanding paintings are the two that don't fit the scheme: Bronzino's portraits of the occupant's parents, facing each other across the room. The oval paintings on the panels at the base hinted at the presence of Francesco's most treasured knick-knacks, which were once concealed in the compartments behind; the wooden structure is actually a nineteenth-century re-creation, though the paintings are original.

Much of the rest of this floor is still used by council officials, though if the seven rooms of the **Quartiere di Leone X** and **Sala dei Dugento** are open (they rarely are), don't miss the opportunity. The latter, in particular, is outstanding: Benedetto and Giuliano da Maiano, excellent sculptors both, were responsible for the design (1472–77) and for the fine wooden ceiling; the tapestries (1546–53) were created to designs by Bronzino, Pontormo and others.

### The second floor

Steps lead from the Salone to the **second floor**, passing an intriguing fireworks fresco (1558) showing Piazza della Signoria during the celebrations for the feast of St John the Baptist. Turn left at the top of the stairs and you enter the **Quartiere degli Elementi**, one of the floor's three distinct suites of rooms. All five salons here are slavishly devoted to a different member of the Medici clan. Persevere, though, if only to enjoy the city **views** from the Terrazza di Saturno and Verrocchio's original *Putto and Dolphin* statue on the Terrazzo di Giunone.

Return to the stairs and head straight on and you cross a gallery with views down into the Salone. Immediately afterwards come the six rooms of the **Quartiere di Eleonora di Toledo**, the private

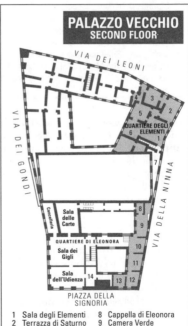

PALAZZO VECCHIO
SECOND FLOOR

VIA DEI LEONI
VIA DEI GONDI
VIA DELLA NINNA

QUARTIERE DEGLI ELEMENTI
Sala delle Carte
Cancelleria
QUARTIERE DI ELEONORA
Sala dei Gigli
Sala dell'Udienza
PIAZZA DELLA SIGNORIA

| 1 | Sala degli Elementi | 8 | Cappella di Eleonora |
|---|---|---|---|
| 2 | Terrazza di Saturno | 9 | Camera Verde |
| 3 | Sala di Ercole | 10 | Camera delle Sabine |
| 4 | Terrazza di Giunone | 11 | Sala di Ester |
| 5 | Sala di Giove | 12 | Camera di Penelope |
| 6 | Sala di Opi | 13 | Camera di Gualdrada |
| 7 | Gallery | 14 | Cappella della Signoria |

75

2

## For the kids: Emozioni da Museo and Encounters

**Emozioni da Museo** (from €6) is anything but a traditional museum experience, though there's a whiff of the classroom about the "interactive workshops" held in rooms dotted around the palace. These are aimed more at local *ragazzi* than visitors' kids, but some classes are held in English, usually at weekends.

Most satisfying is perhaps **"Clothing and the Body"**. Guides lead the group through a secret door in the Sala delle Carte and down to a vaulted space dominated by a four-poster bed in which an actress playing Eleonora di Toledo lies sleeping. Her maid enters and gets her mistress washed, combed, primped and ready for the day: Eleonora ends up dressed exactly as in Bronzino's portrait in the Uffizi. Meanwhile, their gossipy conversation, joined by Duke Cosimo and his servant, leads into a discussion that compares clothing and attitudes to the body now and in the Renaissance. Even when the actresses are speaking Italian, English-speaking guides are on hand to translate.

In **"Architecture of the Palazzo"** the children create, walk upon and, inevitably, destroy a load-bearing arch made from special bricks, and reconstruct a model of the Palazzo Vecchio in order to see how it was built. **"The Magic of Lenses"** allows the kids to play with various lenses, learn about optical effects and then put together a basic telescope. From the basement classroom it's up to the balcony of the palace to test out designs perfected by Galileo, among others. More scientific still is **"Horror Vacui?"** – ("[Nature] abhors a vacuum?") – which reproduces the experiments of the Florentine mathematician Torricelli, who proved the existence of atmospheric pressure.

Organized by the Associazione Museo dei Ragazzi di Firenze, **Encounters** are guided tours led by costumed actors that are aimed at both children and adults, but probably will appeal most to the youngsters. Vasari himself leads a tour of the Palazzo Vecchio, Galileo explains his radical inventions in the Museo di Storia della Scienza, and Suleiman the Magnificent takes a group of captured Christians round his armoury in the Museo Stibbert. During the school holidays, at least one tour a day is normally given in English; call ☎055.276.8224 to book.

apartments of Cosimo I's wife. The first room, the **Camera Verde (9)** has some charming wildlife on its ceiling, but the star turn is the tiny and exquisite **Cappella di Eleonora (8)**, vividly decorated by Bronzino in the 1540s. It seems that the artist used a novel and time-consuming technique to give these wall paintings the same glassy surface as his canvases, executing a first draft in fresco and then glazing it with a layer of tempera. The wall paintings show scenes from the life of Moses, episodes probably intended to draw parallels with the life of Cosimo. In the *Annunciation* that flanks the *Deposition* on the back wall, Bronzino is said to have used Cosimo's and Eleonora's eldest daughter as the model for the Virgin.

Those who find all this Mannerist stuff unhealthily airless can take refuge in the more summery rooms which follow. The **Sala dell'Udienza**, originally the audience chamber of the Republic, boasts a stunning gilt-coffered ceiling by Giuliano da Maiano. The Mannerists reassert themselves with a vast fresco sequence (1545–48) by Cecchino Salviati, a cycle widely considered to be this artist's most accomplished work.

Giuliano was also responsible, with his brother Benedetto, for the intarsia work on the doors and the lovely doorway that leads into the **Sala dei Gigli**, a room that takes its name from the lilies (*gigli*) that adorn most of its surfaces – the lily is the emblem of St Zenobius and of the Virgin, both patron saints of Florence. The room has another splendid ceiling by the Maiano brothers, and a wall frescoed by Domenico Ghirlandaio with *SS Zenobius, Stephen and Lorenzo* (1481–85) and lunettes portraying *Six Heroes of Ancient Rome*. The undoubted highlight here, however, is Donatello's original *Judith and Holofernes* (1455–60), removed from Piazza della Signoria.

Two small rooms are attached to the Sala dei Gigli: the **Cancelleria**, once Machiavelli's office and now containing a bust and portrait of the oft-maligned political thinker, and the lovely **Sala delle Carte**, formerly the Guardaroba (Wardrobe), the repository of Cosimo's state finery. Now it is decorated with 57 maps painted in 1563 by the court astronomer Fra' Ignazio Danti, depicting what was then the entire known world. One of the maps, in the far right-hand corner, conceals a door to a hidden staircase.

A door leads out from the second floor onto the broad balcony of the Palazzo Vecchio's **tower**. The views are superb, if not as good as those enjoyed from the cell in the body of the tower above, which was known ironically as the Alberghinetto (Little Hotel); such troublemakers as Cosimo de' Medici and Savonarola were once imprisoned here. The final section of the museum, just before the exit, is something of an afterthought, and is devoted to second-rate pictures once owned by the American collector Loeser.

# The Uffizi

Florence can prompt an over-eagerness to reach for superlatives; in the case of the **Galleria degli Uffizi**, the superlatives are simply the bare truth: this is the finest picture gallery in Italy. So many masterpieces are collected here that it's not even possible to skate over the surface in a single visit. Though you may not want to emulate Edward Gibbon, who visited the Uffizi fourteen times on a single trip to Florence, it makes sense to limit your initial tour to the first fifteen rooms, where the Florentine Renaissance works are concentrated, and to explore the rest another time.

The gallery is housed in what were once government offices (*uffizi*) built by Vasari for Cosimo I in 1560. After Vasari's death, work on the elongated U-shaped building was continued by Buontalenti, who was asked by Francesco I to glaze the upper storey so that it could house his art collection. Each of the succeeding Medici added to the family's trove of art treasures. The accumulated collection was preserved for public inspection by the last member of the family, Anna Maria Lodovica, whose will specified that it should be left to the people of Florence and never be allowed to leave the city. In the nineteenth century a large proportion of the statuary was transferred to the Bargello, while most of the antiquities went to the Museo Archeologico, leaving the Uffizi as essentially a gallery of paintings supplemented with some classical sculptures.

## Uffizi practicalities

The Uffizi is open Tuesday to Sunday 8.15am to 6.50pm; in high summer and at festive periods it sometimes stays open until 10pm. This is the busiest single building in the country, with over one and a half million visitors a year, so during peak season you've almost no chance of getting in without paying the €3 surcharge for booking a ticket **in advance**. For next-day tickets, there's a reservations desk that opens at 8.15am at Door 2, and has an allocation of just 200. For reservations further in advance, go to Door 3, or call the Firenze Musei

## The Uffizi bombing

At 1am on May 27, 1993, a colossal **explosion** occurred on the west side of the Uffizi, killing five people, demolishing the headquarters of Europe's oldest agricultural academy, blasting holes through the walls of the Uffizi itself, and damaging numerous paintings inside, some of them irreparably. Initially it was supposed that a gas leak might have been responsible, but within hours the country's head prosecutor, after discussions with forensic experts and the anti-terrorist squad, issued a statement: "Gas does not come into it. We have found a crater one and a half metres wide. The evidence is unequivocal." Fragments of the car that had carried the estimated 100kg of TNT had been found some 30m from the rubble.

Instantly it was put about that the **Mafia** lay behind the atrocity, though it was not explained what the Mafia had to gain from the killing of the academy's curator and her family, or from the mutilation of a few Renaissance paintings. While many were willing to believe that the Mafia may have planted the bomb, most Florentines were convinced that the orders had originated within the country's political and military establishment. Frightened by the political realignments taking place all over Italy, with the rise of northern separatists, the reformed communist party and various newly formed groupings, the old guard were evidently employing the tactics of destabilization – a repeat of the 1970s' "Strategy of Tension", when organized criminals and right-wing politicians colluded in a sequence of terrorist attacks to ensure the public's loyalty to the supposedly threatened state. Just days before the Uffizi bombing, the Italian secret service had been implicated in the murders of Giovanni Falcone and Paolo Borsellino, the country's most powerful anti-Mafia investigators, and it seemed plain that the same unholy alliances had been at work in Florence.

Three Mafia bosses and eleven underlings were sentenced in June 1998 to life imprisonment for the Uffizi bombing and for two subsequent car bombings in Rome. The prosecution had argued that the Sicilian mobsters had intended to destabilize the government and damage Italy's image abroad. In the opinion of many Italians, however, the true reasons for the outrage remain unrevealed.

line on ☎055.294.883 (see p.50 for more information). Full admission costs €6.50 but EU citizens aged 18–25 pay half-price and entry is free to under-18s and over-65s; there are, however, frequent special exhibitions, during which the full price is raised to €9.50. You should be aware that it's very rare for the whole Uffizi to be open; a board by the entrance tells you which sections are closed. In 2004 it was announced that over the next few years the Uffizi would be doubling the number of rooms open to the public, in order to show some eight hundred works that have usually been kept in storage. This sixty-million-euro project got off to a rather inauspicious start, when excavations in preparation for the building of a new exit (a controversial high-rise canopy designed by Japanese architect Arata Isozaki) unearthed the remains of the medieval houses that were demolished in the 1560s to make way for the Uffizi. The new exit was promptly scrapped, but work on the exhibition spaces should soon be starting, which will inevitably mean that some pictures will not be on show precisely where they appear in the following account.

## Rooms 1 to 7

On the ground floor, in rooms that once formed part of the eleventh-century church of San Pier Scheraggio, are shown **Andrea del Castagno**'s frescoes of celebrated Florentines; the imaginary portraits include Dante and Boccaccio, both of whom spoke in debates at the church. Close to a Botticelli *Annunciation*,

△ The courtyard of the Uffizi

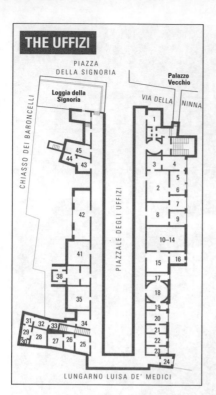

THE UFFIZI

PIAZZA DELLA SIGNORIA

Palazzo Vecchio

Loggia della Signoria

VIA DELLA NINNA

CHIASSO DEI BARONCELLI

PIAZZALE DEGLI UFFIZI

LUNGARNO LUISA DE' MEDICI

a lift goes up to the galleries; if you take the staircase instead, you'll pass the entrance to the prints and drawings collection, the bulk of which is reserved for scholarly scrutiny, though samples are often on public show.

Upstairs, all the rooms lead off the statue-lined monumental corridor that runs round the building. **Room 1**, housing an assembly of antique sculptures, many of which were used as a kind of source book by Renaissance artists, is often shut. The beginnings of the stylistic evolution of that period can be traced in the three altarpieces of the *Maestà* (Madonna Enthroned) that dominate **Room 2**: the *Madonna Rucellai*, *Maestà di Santa Trìnita* and *Madonna d'Ognissanti*, by **Duccio**, **Cimabue** and **Giotto** respectively. These great works, which dwarf everything around them, show the softening of the hieratic Byzantine style into a more tactile form of representation.

Painters from fourteenth-century Siena fill **Room 3**, with several pieces by Ambrogio and Pietro Lorenzetti and **Simone Martini**'s glorious *Annunciation*, the Virgin cowering from the angel amid a field of pure gold.

Other trecento artists follow in **rooms 5 and 6**, among them Florence's first-rank Gothic painters, **Orcagna** and **Lorenzo Monaco**, whose majestic *Coronation of the Virgin* catches the eye first. The *Adoration of the Magi* by **Gentile da Fabriano** is the summit of the precious style known as International Gothic, spangled with gold so thick in places that the crowns of the kings, for instance, are like low-relief jewellery. It's crammed with so much detail that there's no real distinction between what's crucial and what's peripheral, with as much attention lavished on incidentals such as a snarling cheetah as on the supposed protagonists. The right-hand panel of the predella, below, was stolen by Napoleon and replaced with a copy which, unlike the rest of the painting, is not painted directly onto gold – hence the relative matt dullness of its surface. Nearby is the *Thebaid*, a beguiling little narrative that depicts monastic life in the Egyptian desert as a sort of holy fairytale; though sometimes assigned to the young Fra Angelico, it's more generally thought to be by the now-obscure Gherardo di Jacopo Starnina, who in his time (he died around 1410) was one of Florence's major artists, and is thought to have been the master of Masolino.

Gothic golds are left behind in **Room 7**, which reveals the sheer diversity of early Renaissance painting. **Paolo Uccello**'s *The Battle of San Romano* once hung in Lorenzo the Magnificent's bedchamber, in company with its two companion pieces now in the Louvre and London's National Gallery. Warfare is the ostensible subject, but this is really a semi-abstract compendium of perspectival effects – a toppling knight, a horse and rider keeled onto their sides, the foreshortened legs of a kicking horse, a thicket of lances – creating a fight scene with no real sense of violence. *The Madonna and Child with SS Francis, John the Baptist, Zenobius and Lucy* is one of only twelve extant paintings by **Domenico Veneziano**, who spent much of his life in Venice but died destitute in Florence.

Veneziano's greatest pupil, **Piero della Francesca**, is represented in **Room 8** by the paired portraits of *Federico da Montefeltro and Battista Sforza*, the duke and duchess of Urbino. These panels were painted two years after Battista's death; in the background of her portrait is the town of Gubbio, where she died giving birth to her ninth child and only son, Guidobaldo. Most space in Room 8 is given over to **Filippo Lippi**, whose *Madonna and Child with Two Angels* supplies one of the gallery's most popular faces, and one of its least otherworldly devotional images: the model was Lucrezia Buti, a convent novice who became the object of one of his more enduring sexual obsessions. That liaison produced a son, the aptly named **Filippino** "Little Philip" **Lippi**, whose lustrous *Madonna degli Otto* shows the later influence of Leonardo.

# Rooms 9 to 17

Lippi's pupil, Botticelli, steals some of the thunder in **Room 9**, where the artists centre-stage are **Piero** and **Antonio del Pollaiuolo**; their sinewy *SS Vincent, James and Eustace*, one of their best works, is chiefly the work of Antonio. This room also contains the *Portrait of Young Man in a Red Hat*, sometimes referred to as a self-portrait by Filippino, but now widely believed to be an eighteenth-century fraud.

It's in the merged **rooms 10–14** that the greatest of **Botticelli**'s productions are gathered. A century ago most people walked past his pictures without breaking stride; nowadays – despite their elusiveness – the *Primavera* and the *Birth of Venus* stop all visitors in their tracks. The identities of the characters in the **Primavera** are not contentious: on the right Zephyrus, god of the west wind, chases the nymph Cloris, who is then transfigured into Flora, the pregnant goddess of spring; Venus stands in the centre, to the side of the three Graces, who are targeted by Cupid; on the left Mercury wards off the clouds of winter. What this all means, however, has occupied scholars for decades. Some see it as an allegory of the four seasons, but the consensus now seems to be that it shows the triumph of Venus, with the Graces as the physical embodiment of her beauty and Flora the symbol of her fruitfulness – an interpretation supported by the fact that the picture was placed outside the wedding suite of Lorenzo di Pierfrancesco de' Medici.

Botticelli's most winsome painting, the **Birth of Venus**, probably takes as its source the myth that the goddess emerged from the sea after it had been impregnated by the castration of Uranus, an allegory for the creation of beauty through the mingling of the spirit (Uranus) and the physical world. The supporting players are the nymph, Cloris, and Zephyrus, god of the west wind. Zephyrus blows the risen Venus to the shore where the goddess is clothed by Hora, daughter and attendant of Aurora, goddess of dawn. A third allegory hangs close by: *Pallas and the Centaur*, perhaps symbolizing the ambivalent triumph of reason over instinct. (Incidentally, the *Birth of Venus* was one of the first large-scale works to be painted onto canvas.)

Botticelli's devotional paintings are generally less perplexing. *The Adoration of the Magi* is traditionally thought to contain a gallery of Medici portraits: Cosimo il Vecchio as the first king, his sons Giovanni and Piero as the other two kings,

Lorenzo the Magnificent on the far left, and his brother Giuliano as the black-haired young man in profile on the right. Only the identification of Cosimo is reasonably certain, along with that of Botticelli himself, on the right in the yellow robe. In later life, influenced by Savonarola's teaching, Botticelli confined himself to devotional pictures and moral fables, and his style became increasingly severe and didactic. The transformation is clear when comparing the easy grace of the *Madonna of the Magnificat* and the *Madonna of the Pomegranate* with the more rigidly composed *Pala di Sant'Ambrogio* or the angular and agitated *Calumny*. Even the *Annunciation* (1489), painted just as Savonarola's preaching began to grip Florence, reveals a new intensity in the expression of the angel and in the twisting treatment of the body of the Virgin, who appears almost blown back by the force of the message.

Not quite every masterpiece in this room is by Botticelli. Set away from the walls is the *Adoration of the Shepherds* by his Flemish contemporary **Hugo van der Goes**. Brought to Florence in 1483 by Tommaso Portinari, the Medici agent in Bruges, it provided the city's artists with their first large-scale demonstration of the realism of Northern European oil painting, and had a great influence on the way the medium was exploited here.

Works in **Room 15** trace the formative years of **Leonardo da Vinci**, whose distinctive touch appears first in the *Baptism of Christ* (in Room 14) by his master Verrocchio. Vasari claimed that only the wistful angel in profile was by the 18-year-old apprentice, and the misty landscape in the background, but recent X-rays have revealed that Leonardo also worked heavily on the figure of Christ. A similar terrain of soft-focus mountains and water occupies the far distance in Leonardo's slightly later *Annunciation*, in which a diffused light falls on a scene where everything is observed with a scientist's precision: the petals of the flowers on which the angel alights, the fall of the Virgin's drapery, the carving on the lectern at which she reads. In restless contrast to the aristocratic poise of the *Annunciation*, the sketch of *The Adoration of the Magi* – abandoned when Leonardo left Florence for Milan in early 1482 – presents the infant Christ as the eye of a vortex of figures, all drawn into his presence by a force as irresistible as a whirlpool.

Most of the rest of the room is given over to Raphael's teacher, **Perugino**, who is represented by a typically contemplative *Madonna and Child with Saints* (1493), and a glassily meditative *Pietà* (1494–95). It also contains a bizarre *Incarnation* by **Piero di Cosimo**, the wild man of the Florentine Renaissance. Shunning civilized company, Piero did everything he could to bring his life close to a state of uncompromised nature, living in a house that was never cleaned, in the midst of a garden he refused to tend, and eating nothing but hard-boiled eggs. Where his contemporaries might seek inspiration in commentaries on Plato, he would spend hours staring at the sky, at peeling walls, at the pavement – at anything where abstract patterns might conjure fabulous scenes in his imagination. His wildness is most obviously realized in the nightmarish *Perseus Freeing Andromeda*, where even the rocks and the sea seem to twist and boil monstrously.

# Rooms 18 to 23

**Room 18**, the octagonal **Tribuna**, now houses the most important of the Medici's collection of classical sculptures, chief among which is the *Medici Venus*, a first-century BC copy of the Praxitelean *Aphrodite of Cnidos*. She was kept in the Villa Medici in Rome until Cosimo III began to fret that she was having a detrimental effect on the morals of the city's art students, and ordered her removal to Florence. The move clearly didn't affect the statue's sexual charisma, however: it became traditional for eighteenth-century visitors to Florence to caress her buttocks. Around the walls are hung some fascinating portraits by **Bronzino**: Cosimo de' Medici, Eleonora di Toledo, Bartolomeo Panciatichi and his wife Lucrezia Panciatichi, all painted as figures of porcelain, placed in a bloodless, sunless world. More vital is Andrea del Sarto's flirtatious *Ritratto d'Ignota* (*Portrait of a Young Woman*), and there's a deceptive naturalism to Vasari's portrait of Lorenzo the Magnificent and Pontormo's of Cosimo il Vecchio, both painted long after the death of their subjects.

The last section of this wing throws together Renaissance paintings from outside Florence, with some notable Venetian and Flemish works. **Signorelli** and **Perugino** – with some photo-sharp portraits – are the principal artists in **Room 19**, and after them comes a room largely devoted to **Cranach** and **Dürer**. Each has an *Adam and Eve* here, Dürer taking the opportunity to show off his proficiency as a painter of wildlife. Dürer's power as a portraitist is displayed in the *Portrait of the Artist's Father*, his earliest authenticated painting, and Cranach has a couple of acute pictures of Luther on display, one of them a double with his wife.

A taste of the Uffizi's remarkable collection of Venetian painting follows, with an impenetrable *Sacred Allegory* by **Giovanni Bellini**, and three rare works by **Giorgione** (if you accept the attribution of the mesmerizing portrait of a young soldier traditionally known as the *Gattemelata*). A clutch of Northern European paintings is chiefly notable for **Holbein**'s *Portrait of Sir Richard Southwell*, while a crystalline triptych by **Mantegna** in Room 23 is not in fact a real triptych, but rather a trio of small paintings shackled together. To the side are a couple of other pictures by Mantegna – a swarthy portrait of Carlo de' Medici and the tiny *Madonna of the Stonecutters*, set against a mountain that looks like a gigantic fir cone.

# Rooms 24 to 28

Beyond the stockpile of statues in the short corridor overlooking the Arno, the main attraction in **Room 25** is **Michelangelo**'s *Doni Tondo*, the only easel painting he came close to completing. (Regarding sculpture as the noblest of the visual arts, Michelangelo dismissed all non-fresco painting as a demeaning chore.) Nobody has yet explained the precise significance of every aspect of this picture, but plausible explanations for parts of it have been put forward. The five naked figures behind the Holy Family seem to be standing in a half-moon-shaped cistern or font, which would relate to the infant Baptist to the right, who – in the words of St Paul – prefigures the coming of Christ just as the new moon is "a shadow of things to come". In the same epistle, Paul goes on to commend the virtues of mercy, benignity, humility, modesty and patience, which are perhaps what the five youths represent.

**Room 26** contains **Andrea del Sarto**'s sultry *Madonna of the Harpies* and a number of compositions by **Raphael**, including the lovely *Madonna of the Goldfinch* and the late *Pope Leo X with Cardinals Giulio de' Medici and Luigi de' Rossi* – as shifty a group of ecclesiastics as was ever gathered in one frame. The Michelangelo tondo's contorted gestures, hermetic meaning and virulent colours were greatly influential on the Mannerist painters of the sixteenth century, as can be gauged from *Moses Defending the Daughters of Jethro* by **Rosso Fiorentino**, one of the seminal figures of the movement, whose works hang in **Room 27**, along with two major religious works by Bronzino and his adoptive father, Pontormo – one of the very few painters not seen at his best in the Uffizi.

**Room 28** is entirely given over to another of the titanic figures of sixteenth-century art, **Titian**, with nine paintings on show. His *Flora* and *A Knight of Malta* are stunning, but most eyes tend to swivel towards the *Urbino Venus*, the most fleshy and provocative of all Renaissance nudes, described by Mark Twain as "the foulest, the vilest, the obscenest picture the world possesses".

A brief diversion through the painters of the sixteenth-century Emilian school follows, centred on **Parmigianino**, whose *Madonna of the Long Neck* is one of the pivotal Mannerist creations. Parmigianino was a febrile and introverted character who abandoned painting for alchemy towards the end of his short life, and many of his works are marked by a sort of morbid refinement, none more so than this one. The Madonna's tunic clings to every contour, an angel advances a perfectly turned leg, the infant Christ drapes himself languorously on his mother's lap – prefiguring the dead Christ of the Pietà – while in the background an emaciated figure unrolls a scroll of parchment by a colonnade so severely foreshortened that it looks like a single column.

## Rooms 31 to 45

**Rooms 31 to 34** feature artists from Venice and the Veneto, with outstanding paintings such as **Moroni**'s *Portrait of Count Pietro Secco Suardi*, **Paolo Veronese**'s *Annunciation* and *Holy Family with St Barbara*, and **Tintoretto**'s *Leda*. Sebastiano del Piombo's *Death of Adonis* was reduced to little more than postage-stamp tatters by the 1993 bomb the restoration is little short of miraculous.

**Room 41**, entered off the main corridor, is dominated by **Rubens** and **Van Dyck**. The former's *Portrait of Isabella Brandt* makes its point more quietly than most of the stuff around it. Rubens lets rip in *Henry IV at the Battle of Ivry* and *The Triumphal Entry of Henry IV into Paris* – Henry's marriage to Marie de' Medici is the connection with Florence. Rubens's equally histrionic contemporary, **Caravaggio**, has a cluster of pieces in **Room 43**, including a screaming severed head of *Medusa*, a smug little *Bacchus*, and a throat-grabbing *Sacrifice of Isaac*.

Alongside, **Room 44** is in effect a showcase for the portraiture of **Rembrandt**. His sorrow-laden *Self-Portrait as an Old Man*, painted five years or so before his death, makes a poignant contrast with the self-confident self-portrait of thirty years earlier. Although there are some good pieces from **Tiepolo**, portraits again command the attention in the following room of eighteenth-century works, especially the two of Maria Theresa painted by **Goya**, and **Chardin**'s demure children at play.

On the way out, in the hall at the top of the exit stairs squats one of the city's talismans, the *Wild Boar*, a Roman copy of a third-century BC Hellenistic sculpture; it was the model for the *Porcellino* fountain in the Mercato Nuovo.

## The Corridoio Vasariano

A door on the west corridor, between rooms 25 and 34, opens onto the **Corridoio Vasariano**, a passageway built by Vasari in 1565 to link the Palazzo Vecchio to the Palazzo Pitti through the Uffizi. Winding its way down to the river, over the Ponte Vecchio, through the church of Santa Felìcita and into the Giardino di Bóboli, it gives a fascinating series of clandestine views of the city. As if that weren't pleasure enough, the corridor is completely lined with paintings, the larger portion of which comprises a gallery of **self-portraits**. Once you're past the portrait of Vasari, the series proceeds chronologically, littered with illustrious names: Raphael, Andrea del Sarto, Bronzino, Bernini, Rubens, Rembrandt, Velázquez, David, Delacroix and Ingres.

Because of staff shortages and strict limits on numbers allowed into the corridor (there is no fire escape), access is extremely difficult. At the time of going to press, **tours** are being conducted on some mornings, usually on Wednesday and Friday, but there is no definite schedule, so for the latest situation you should ask at the gallery's ticket office, or ring ☎055.294.883.

# West of the centre: from Via dei Calzaiuoli to the Cascine

The main catwalk of the Florentine *passeggiata* is **Via dei Calzaiuoli**, the broad pedestrianized avenue that links Piazza della Signoria with Piazza del Duomo. Shop-lined for most of its length, it boasts one stupendous monument, the church of **Orsanmichele**. Despite the urban improvement schemes of the nineteenth century and the bombings of World War II, several streets south of here retain their medieval character: an amble through streets such as Via Porta Rossa, Via delle Terme and Borgo Santi Apostoli will give you some idea of the feel of Florence in the Middle Ages, when every important house was an urban fortress. Best of these medieval redoubts is the **Palazzo Davanzati**, whose interior looks little different from the way it did six hundred years ago but has been off-limits for a long time now, owing to a lengthy structural rescue job. Nearby, the fine church of **Santa Trìnita** is home to an outstanding fresco cycle by Domenico Ghirlandaio, while beyond the glitzy **Via de' Tornabuoni** – Florence's prime shopping street – you'll find a marvellous chapel designed by Alberti and a museum devoted to the work of Marino Marini. The most significant sight in this quarter of the city, though, is the profusely frescoed church of **Santa Maria Novella**, where you can see masterpieces by Paolo Uccello, Giotto, Filippino Lippi, Masaccio and another superb cycle by Ghirlandaio. A few minutes' walk away, there's yet more Ghirlandaio, and work by Botticelli, in the church of **Ognissanti**. And if all this art is beginning to take its toll, you could take a break in the tree-lined avenues of the **Cascine** park, right on the western edge of the city centre.

# Piazza della Repubblica and Orsanmichele

Halfway along Via dei Calzaiuoli, Via dei Speziali connects with the vacant expanse of **Piazza della Repubblica**. Impressive solely for its size, this square was planned in the late 1860s, when it was decided to demolish the central marketplace (Mercato Vecchio) and the tenements of the Jewish quarter in order to give Florence a public space befitting the capital of the recently formed Italian nation. The most ambitious element in a programme of civic improvements that saw the widening of streets leading to the new train station and the creation of various avenues and squares (such as Via Nazionale and Piazza della Indipendenza), the clearance of the Mercato Vecchio had not even begun when, in 1870, the capital was transferred to Rome. In the same year work began on the new market area, by San Lorenzo, but it wasn't until 1885 that the Mercato Vecchio and its disease-ridden slums were finally swept away. On the west side a vast **arch** bears the triumphant inscription: "The ancient city centre restored to new life from the squalor of centuries." The free-standing **column** is the solitary trace of the piazza's history. Once surrounded by stalls, it used to be topped by Donatello's statue of *Abundance*, and a bell that was rung to signal the start and close of trading. The column was taken down during the construction of the piazza, long after the statue had rotted away, but was replaced in 1956.

Nowadays, Piazza della Repubblica is best known for the three large and expensive **cafés** that stand on the perimeter: the *Gilli*, founded way back in 1733 (albeit on a different site – it moved here in 1910), and the most attractive of the trio; the *Giubbe Rosse*, once the intellectuals' café of choice (the Futurist manifesto was launched here in 1909); and the *Paszkowski*, which began business as a beer hall in the 1840s, is now a listed historic monument, and bears the suffix "Caffè Concerto", betokening the smarmy music with which it pollutes the piazza most evenings.

## Orsanmichele

Standing like a truncated military tower towards the southern end of Via dei Calzaiuoli, **Orsanmichele** (Mon–Fri 9am–noon & 4–6pm, Sat & Sun 9am–1pm & 4–6pm; closed 1st & last Mon of month) is the oddest-looking church in Florence. Not only is the building itself a major monument, but its exterior was once the most impressive outdoor sculpture gallery in the city. Several of the pieces have been or are being restored, however, after which they will be displayed in the Bargello and elsewhere; their places at Orsanmichele are taken by replicas. Copies or not, this church is one of the city's great sights.

The first building here was a small oratory secreted in the orchard or vegetable garden (*orto*) of a now-vanished Benedictine monastery. A larger church stood on the site from the ninth century: San Michele ad Hortum, later San Michele in Orte – hence the compacted form of Orsanmichele. Even after the church was replaced by a **grain market** in the thirteenth century, the place retained its religious associations. In 1300, the chronicler Giovanni Villani claimed "the lame walked and the possessed were liberated" after visiting a miraculous image of the Virgin painted on one of the market pillars.

After a fire in 1304, the building was eventually replaced by a **loggia** designed by Francesco Talenti to serve as a trade hall for the *Arti Maggiori*, the Great Guilds which governed the city. Between 1367 and 1380 the loggia

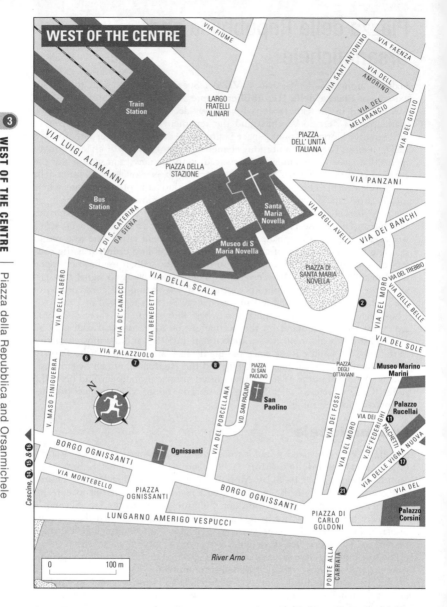

was walled in, after which the site was again dedicated almost exclusively to religious functions, while leaving two upper storeys for use as emergency grain stores.

As far back as 1339, plans had been made to adorn each pillar of the building with a patron statue, each assigned to a different guild. In the event, only one statue was produced in sixty years – a *St Stephen* commissioned by the *Arte della*

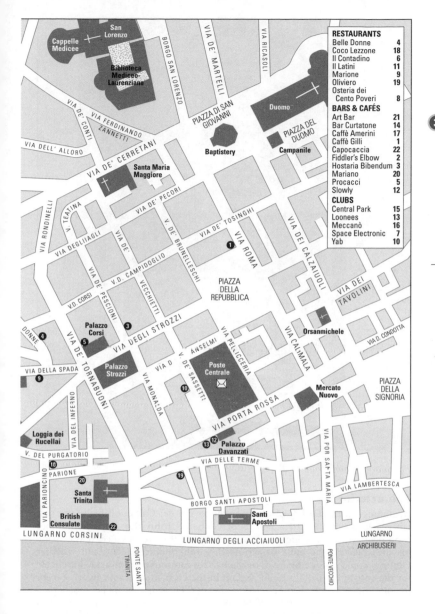

**RESTAURANTS**

| | |
|---|---|
| Belle Donne | 4 |
| Coco Lezzone | 18 |
| Il Contadino | 6 |
| Il Latini | 11 |
| Marione | 9 |
| Oliviero | 19 |
| Osteria dei Cento Poveri | 8 |

**BARS & CAFÉS**

| | |
|---|---|
| Art Bar | 21 |
| Bar Curtatone | 14 |
| Caffè Amerini | 17 |
| Caffè Gilli | 1 |
| Capocaccia | 22 |
| Fiddler's Elbow | 2 |
| Hostaria Bibendum | 3 |
| Mariano | 20 |
| Procacci | 5 |
| Slowly | 12 |

**CLUBS**

| | |
|---|---|
| Central Park | 15 |
| Loonees | 13 |
| Meccanò | 16 |
| Space Electronic | 7 |
| Yab | 10 |

*Lana.* In 1408, weary of the delay, the city elders set a ten-year deadline, warning that the niches would be allocated to rival guilds if commissions remained unfulfilled. The delay was to posterity's benefit, for the statues that were eventually produced spanned the emergent years of the Renaissance: sixty years earlier, lesser talents than Donatello, Ghiberti, Verrocchio and Luca della Robbia would have been put to work on the project.

△ The Madonna della Rosa

## The exterior

Beginning on the far left of Orsanmichele's Via dei Calzaiuoli flank, the first tabernacle is occupied by a replica of Ghiberti's **John the Baptist** (number 1 on plan), the earliest life-size bronze statue of the Renaissance. It was made for the *Calimala*, the guild of wholesale cloth importers. Doubtful whether Ghiberti could cast the figure in one piece, his cautious patrons made him liable for the cost of the metal should he fail. In the event it came out intact, except for one toe, which had to be welded on later. The adjacent niche is occupied by a replica of *The Incredulity of St Thomas* (2) by Verrocchio, which replaced an earlier gilded statue by Donatello, *St Louis of Toulouse*, now in the Museo dell'Opera del Duomo; Giambologna's *St Luke* (3) similarly replaced an earlier statue by Lamberti now in the Bargello.

Round the corner, Brunelleschi's *St Peter* (4) is followed by two works from Nanni di Banco: *St Philip* (5) and the so-called **Quattro Coronati** (6). These four Christian stonemasons executed by Diocletian for refusing to carve a pagan idol were patron saints of the masons' guild, sponsors of this niche. Their name comes from the manner of their execution: they were killed by having an iron crown (*corona*) driven onto their heads. The story goes that Nanni di Banco misjudged the space available for his *Quattro Coronati*; when only three figures would fit in the niche, he consulted his friend Donatello, who simply had his assistants file away at the saints until they had been slimmed down sufficiently. The bas-reliefs of architects and sculptors at work are also by Nanni; the medallion above is by Luca della Robbia. A copy of Donatello's *St George* (7) occupies the next niche – the original is in the Bargello, as is the original accompanying bas-relief of *St George and the Dragon*.

On the church's west side stand *St Matthew* (8) and *St Stephen* (9), both by Ghiberti, and *St Eligius* (10) by Nanni di Banco; the *St Matthew*, posed and clad like a Roman orator, makes a telling comparison with the same artist's *St John*, cast just ten years before but still semi-Gothic in its sharp-edged drapery and arching lines. Earlier than either is Donatello's **St Mark** (11), made in 1411 when the artist was 25; the work is often considered one of the first statues of the Renaissance, a title based on the naturalism of St Mark's stance and the brooding intensity of his gaze. A replica of Pietro Lamberti's *St James* (12) precedes the benign **Madonna della Rosa** (13), probably by Simone Talenti. The latter was damaged in 1493 when one Signor Marrona went berserk and set about axing lumps out of every statue of the Madonna he could find. A lynch mob of Savonarola's monks caught up with him just after he'd gouged out one of the eyes of the infant Christ. The weakest of the sculptures, Baccio da Montelupo's *John the Evangelist* (14), brings up the rear.

**ORSANMICHELE**

VIA DEI CALZAIUOLI

VIA ORSANMICHELE

VIA DE' LAMBERTI

Entrance

1 John the Baptist (1412–16), Lorenzo Ghiberti (copy) for the Arte di Calimala (Textiles Guild); niche, Albizo di Piero to a design by Ghiberti
2 The Incredulity of St Thomas (1473–83), Verrocchio (copy) for the Mercatanzia (Merchants' Tribunal); niche (1423–5), Donatello and Michelozzo
3 St Luke (1610), Giambologna for the Giudici e Notai (judges and notaries); niche, Niccolò di Pietro Lamberti (1404–6)
4 St Peter (1408–13), attrib. Brunollocchi (copy) for the Beccai (butchers)
5 St Philip (1412–15), Nanni di Banco (copy) for the Conciapelli (tanners)
6 Quattro Coronati (1409–17), Nanni di Banco for the Maestri di Pietre e Legname (masons and carpenters)
7 St George (1416–9) and relief of St George and Dragon, Donatello (copies) for the Corazzai (armourers)
8 St Matthew (1419–22), Lorenzo Ghiberti for the Cambio (bankers); tabernacle to a design by Ghiberti
9 St Stephen (1425–8), Lorenzo Ghiberti for the Arte della Lana (wool)
10 St Eligius (1417–21), Nanni di Banco (copy) for the Maniscalchi (smiths)
11 St Mark (1411–13), Donatello (copy) for the Linaiuoli (linen-drapers); niche (1411), Perfetto di Giovanni and Albizo di Piero
12 St James (1420) and bas relief of the Martyrdom of St James, attrib. Niccolò di Pietro Lamberti (copy) for the Pellicciai (furriers)
13 Madonna della Rosa (1400), attrib. Simone Talenti (copy) for the Medici e Speziali (doctors and pharmacists); Madonna Enthroned (above), Luca della Robbia (1465)
14 St John the Evangelist (1515), Baccio da Montelupo for the Setaiuoli (silk)

## The interior

Orsanmichele's interior centrepiece is a pavilion-sized glass and marble **tabernacle** by Orcagna, the only significant sculptural work by the artist. Decorated with lapis lazuli and gold, it cost 86,000 florins in 1355. The iconography is obscure, but concerns salvation through the Virgin. It frames a *Madonna delle Grazie* painted in 1347 by Bernardo Daddi as a replacement for the miraculous image of the Virgin destroyed by the 1304 fire. The brotherhood that administered Orsanmichele paid for the tabernacle from thanksgiving donations in the aftermath of the Black Death; so many people attributed their survival to the Madonna's intervention that the money received in 1348 alone was greater than the annual tax income of the city coffers. Other paintings can be seen on the pillars: devotional images of the guilds' patron saints, they can be regarded as the low-cost ancestors of the Orsanmichele statues.

The original lines of the bricked-up loggia are still clear, while the vaulted halls of the upper granary – one of the city's most imposing medieval interiors – also survive. The halls now house the **Museo di Orsanmichele** (tours daily 9am, 10am & 11am; closed 1st and last Mon of month; free), entered via the footbridge from the Palazzo dell'Arte della Lana, the building opposite the church entrance. In practice, opening times can be affected by the use of the space for temporary exhibitions. If you get the chance, be sure to visit, not only for the fine interior, but also for the chance to see several of the most important original exterior statues. As restoration work is completed, it is planned that all the statues will eventually be exhibited here, though no one expects to wrest the most famous of all, Donatello's *St George*, from the clutches of the Bargello.

# From the Mercato Nuovo to Santi Apostoli

One block west of the southern end of Via dei Calzaiuoli lies the **Mercato Nuovo**, or Mercato del Porcellino (mid-Feb to mid-Nov daily 9am–7pm; mid-Nov to mid-Feb Tues–Sat 9am–5pm), where there's been a market since the eleventh century, though the present loggia dates from the sixteenth. Having forked out their euros at the souvenir stalls, most people join the small group that's invariably gathered round the bronze boar known as *Il Porcellino*: you're supposed to earn yourself some good luck by getting a coin to fall from the animal's mouth through the grille below his head. This superstition has a social function, as the coins go to an organization that runs homes for abandoned children.

## The Palazzo Davanzati

Perhaps the most imposing exterior in this district is to be seen just to the south of the market – the thirteenth-century Palazzo di Parte Guelfa, financed from the confiscated property of the Ghibelline faction and later expanded by Brunelleschi. However, for a more complete re-creation of medieval Florence you should visit the fourteenth-century **Palazzo Davanzati** in Via Porta Rossa. In the nineteenth century the palazzo was divided into flats, but at the beginning of the twentieth it was restored to something very close to the modified appearance of the 1500s, when a loggia replaced the battlements on the roof, and the Davanzati stuck their coat of arms on the front. (The immense amount of metalwork on the exterior was used variously for tying up animals, draping wool and washing out to dry, suspending bird cages or fixing banners, carpets and other hangings on the occasion of festivities and processions.) Apart from those haute-bourgeois emendations, the place now looks much as it did when first inhabited. Virtually every room is furnished and decorated in predominantly medieval style, using genuine artefacts gathered from a variety of sources.

Nowadays the palazzo is maintained as the **Museo della Casa Fiorentina Antica**. The building was closed in 1995 for a major structural restoration, and a token photographic exhibition of the holdings of the museum has since been on display in the entrance hall (Tues–Sun 9am–2pm; also 2nd and 4th Mon and 1st, 3rd and 5th Sun of month same hours). The description that follows gives you an idea of the interior of the museum before closure, but as yet no full opening date has been fixed.

## The lower floors

The owners of this house were obviously well prepared for the adversities of urban living, as can be seen in the siege-resistant doors, the huge storerooms for the hoarding of provisions, and the private water supply. The courtyard's **well** was something of a luxury at a time when much of Florence was still dependent on public fountains: a complex series of ropes and pulleys allowed it to serve the entire house; similarly the palace's **toilets**, state-of-the art affairs by the standards of 1330. Such arrangements were far from common: Boccaccio describes the more basic facilities of most Florentines in the *Decameron* – two planks of wood suspended over a small pit.

An ancient staircase – the only one of its kind to survive in the city – leads to the **first floor** and the Sala Grande or **Sala Madornale**. This room, used for family gatherings, underlines the dual nature of the house: furnished in the best style of the day, it also has four wood-covered hatches in the floor to allow the bombarding of a besieging enemy. Merchants' houses in the fourteenth century would typically have had elaborately painted walls in the main rooms, and the Palazzo Davanzati preserves some fine examples of such decor, especially in the dining room or **Sala dei Pappagalli**, where the imitation wall hangings of the lower walls are patterned with a parrot (*pappagallo*) motif, while the upper walls depict a garden terrace.

Before the development of systems of credit, wealth had to be sunk into tangible assets such as the tapestries, ceramics, sculpture and lacework that alleviate the austerity of many of these rooms; any surplus cash would have been locked away in a strongbox like the extraordinary example in the **Sala Piccola**, whose locking mechanism looks like the innards of a primitive clock. There's also a fine collection of *cassoni*, the painted chests in which the wife's dowry would be stored.

Plushest of the rooms is the first-floor **bedroom**, or Sala dei Pavoni – complete with en-suite bathroom. It takes its name from the beautiful frescoed frieze of trees, peacocks (*pavoni*) and other exotic birds: the coats of arms woven into the decoration are the crests of families related to the Davanzati. The rare Sicilian linen bed-cover is decorated with scenes from the story of Tristan.

## The upper floors

The arrangements of the rooms on the upper two floors, together with their beautiful array of furniture and decoration, mirror that of the first floor. For all the splendour of the lower rooms, the spot where the palace's occupants would have been likeliest to linger is the third-floor **kitchen**. Located on the uppermost floor to minimize damage if a fire broke out, it would have been the warmest room in the house. A fascinating array of utensils is on show here: the *girapolenta*, the polenta-stirrer, is extraordinary. Set into one wall is a service shaft connecting the kitchen to all floors of the building. The leaded glass – like the toilets – was considered a marvel at a time when many windows were covered with turpentine-soaked rags stretched across frames to repel rainwater.

## Santi Apostoli

Between Via Porta Rossa and the Arno, on Piazza del Limbo (the former burial ground of unbaptized children), stands the ancient church of **Santi Apostoli** (Mon–Sat 10am–noon & 4–5.30pm, Sun 4–5.30pm). Legend has it that this was founded by Charlemagne, but it's not quite that ancient – the eleventh century seems the likeliest date of origin. Santi Apostoli possesses some peculiar relics, in the form of stone fragments allegedly brought from the Holy Sepulchre in Jerusalem by a crusading Florentine; on Holy Saturday sparks struck from these stones are used to light the flame that ignites the "dove" that in turn sets off the fireworks in front of the Duomo (see p.209). Orderly and graceful, the interior of grey *pietra serena* against white walls looks like an anticipation of the architecture of Brunelleschi.

# Piazza and Ponte Santa Trìnita

West of the Palazzo Davanzati, Via Porta Rossa runs into **Piazza Santa Trìnita** – not really a square, just a widening of the city's most expensive street, Via de' Tornabuoni. The centrepiece of the piazza is the Colonna della Giustizia (Column of Justice), which Pope Pius IV uprooted from the Baths of Caracalla and sent to Cosimo I, who in 1565 raised it on the spot where, in August 1537, he had heard of the defeat of the anti-Medici faction at Montemurlo. The column stands on the axis of the sleek **Ponte Santa Trìnita**, construction of which was begun in 1567 on Cosimo's orders, ten years after its predecessor was demolished in a flood – and ten years after Siena had finally become part of Florentine territory, a subjugation which the bridge was intended to commemorate. The roads on both sides of the river were raised and widened to accentuate the dramatic potential of the new link between the city centre and the Oltrarno, but what makes this the classiest bridge in Florence is the sensuous curve of its arches, a curve so shallow that engineers have been baffled as to how the bridge bears up under the strain. Ostensibly the design was conjured up by Ammannati, one of the Medici's favourite artists, but the curves so closely resemble the arc of Michelangelo's Medici tombs that it's likely the credit belongs to him.

In 1944 the Nazis blew the bridge to smithereens and a seven-year argument ensued before it was agreed to rebuild it using as much of the original material as could be dredged from the Arno. To ensure maximum authenticity in the reconstruction, all the new stone that was needed was quarried from the Bóboli gardens – where the stone for Ammannati's bridge had been cut – and hand tools were used to trim it, as electric blades would have given the blocks too harsh a finish. Twelve years after the war, the reconstructed bridge was opened, lacking only the head from the statue of *Spring*, which had not been found despite the incentive of a hefty reward. At last, in 1961, the missing head was fished from the riverbed; having lain in state for a few days on a scarlet cushion in the Palazzo Vecchio, it was returned to its home.

# Santa Trìnita church

The antiquity of the church of **Santa Trìnita** (Mon–Sat 8am–noon & 4–6pm, Sun 4–6pm) is manifest in the Latinate pronunciation of its name: modern Italian stresses the last, not the first syllable. The church was founded in 1092 by a Florentine nobleman called **Giovanni Gualberto**, scenes from whose life

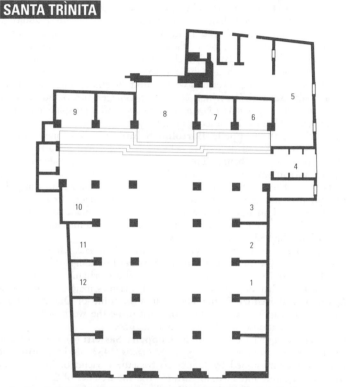

SANTA TRÌNITA

1   Cappella Cialli-Sernigi: Mystic Marriage of St Catherine (1390–95), Spinello Aretino
2   Cappella Bartolini-Salimbeni: Scenes from the Life of the Virgin (1420–25), Lorenzo Monaco
3   Cappella Ardinghelli: Pietà (1424), Giovanni Toscani; altar tabernacle (1505–13), Benedetto da Rovezzano
4   Passage with remnants of avelli (graves) that once lined church's flanks
5   Sacristy: tomb of Onofrio Strozzi (1425), attrib. Michelozzo
6   Cappella Sassetti: Scenes from the Life of St Francis (1483–6); Adoration of the Shepherds altarpiece (1485), Domenico Ghirlandaio
7   Cappella Doni: "Miraculous" crucifix removed from the church of San Miniato al Monte
8   Chancel
9   Cappella Scali: tomb of Benozzo Federighi (1454–7), Luca della Robbia (left wall)
10  Cappella Spini: wooden statue of Mary Magdalen (1455), Desiderio da Settignano and Benedetto da Maiano
11  Cappella Compagni: entrance arch – San Giovanni Gualberto Pardons his Brother's Murderer (1440), Lorenzo di Bicci; right wall – Annunciation; altar wall – San Giovanni Gualberto and Members of the Vallombrosan Order (1455), Neri di Bicci
12  Cappella Davanzati: altarpiece – Coronation of the Virgin and Twelve Saints (1430), Bicci di Lorenzo; left wall – Tomb of Giuliano Davanzati (d.1444), attrib. Bernardo Rossellino (includes third-century Roman sarcophagus)

are illustrated in the frescoes in the fourth chapel of the left aisle. One Good Friday, so the story goes, Gualberto set off intent on avenging the murder of his brother. On finding the murderer he decided to spare his life – it was Good Friday – and proceeded to San Miniato (see p.168), where a crucifix is said to have bowed its head to honour his act of mercy. Giovanni went on to become a Benedictine monk and found the reforming Vallombrosan order and – notwithstanding the mayhem created on Florence's streets by his militant supporters – was eventually canonized.

The church was rebuilt between about 1300 and 1330, work being interrupted by the plague of 1348. Further rebuilding took place between 1365 and 1405, while the facade – by Buontalenti – was added in 1594. Piecemeal additions over the years have lent the church a pleasantly hybrid air: the largely Gothic interior contrasts with the Mannerist facade, itself at odds with the Romanesque interior facade. Santa Trìnita's architecture is softened by a number of works of art, the best of which are Ghirlandaio's frescoes. Resist the temptation to head straight for these, however, and work round the church, beginning at the **Cappella Cialli-Sernigi** (1), which contains a damaged fresco and detached *sinopia* depicting the *Mystical Marriage of St Catherine* (1389) by Spinello Aretino, recently discovered below the frescoes in the adjoining chapel.

The next chapel, the **Cappella Bartolini–Salimbeni** (2), is one of only a handful in the city whose decorative scheme has remained uncorrupted by subsequent additions and changes. The frescoes (1420–25) of episodes from the **Life of the Virgin** (2) are by Lorenzo Monaco, who also painted its *Annunciation* altarpiece. The lunette and right wall of the next chapel, the **Cappella Ardinghelli (3)**, features Giovanni Toscani's contemporaneous frescoes of the *Pietà* (1424–25) and an unfinished altar tabernacle by Benedetto da Rovezzano (1505–13): the latter, intended for the tomb of Giovanni Gualberto, was damaged during the 1530 siege of the city.

A small **passage** (4) lined with graves, or *avelli*, is usually closed, but the adjacent sacristy, or **Cappella di Onofrio Strozzi** (5), designed by Ghiberti between 1418 and 1423, is often open; if not, the sacristan will show you around. The main altar once held Gentile da Fabriano's majestic *Adoration of the Magi*, now in the Uffizi. To the altar's left is the tomb of Onofrio Strozzi, scion of a major banking dynasty: long thought to be the work of Donatello, the tomb is now cautiously attributed to Michelozzo.

Next comes the church's highlight, the **Cappella Sassetti** (6), famous for its cycle of frescoes of scenes from the *Life of St Francis* (1483–86) by **Domenico Ghirlandaio**. Commissioned by Francesco Sassetti, a friend of Lorenzo the Magnificent, they were intended, in part, to rival the frescoes of Sassetti's rival, Giovanni Tornabuoni, in Santa Maria Novella, also by Ghirlandaio (see p.102). Sassetti and his wife, the chapel's donors, are buried in Giuliano da Sangallo's black tombs under the side arches. Ghirlandaio's frescoes are concerned as much with a portrayal of fifteenth-century Florence as with the narrative of their religious themes. St Francis is shown healing a sick child in Piazza Santa Trìnita: the church of Santa Trìnita is in the background, painted as it then appeared, still with its pre-Buontalenti Gothic facade. *St Francis Receiving the Rule* (in the lunette above the altar) sets the action in Piazza della Signoria – note the Loggia della Signoria – and features (right foreground) a portrait of Sassetti between his son, Federigo, and Lorenzo the Magnificent (Sassetti was general manager of the Medici bank). On the steps below them are the humanist Poliziano and three of his pupils, Lorenzo's sons. Ghirlandaio (hand on hip) is present as a self-portrait.

Ghirlandaio also painted the chapel's altarpiece, the *Adoration of the Shepherds* (1485), a persuasive Renaissance fusion of Classical and Christian iconography.

Mary and the shepherds are painted amid Classical columns, a Roman sarcophagus (used as the manger) and a triumphal arch transplanted from the Roman forum. The figures of the donors – Sassetti and his wife, Nera Corsi – kneel to either side.

Displayed in the neighbouring **Cappella Doni** (7) is the miraculous crucifix, formerly in San Miniato, that's said to have bowed its head to Gualberto. The **chancel** (8) features further early fresco fragments – similar tantalizing fragments are dotted around the church. Its high altar once held another major painting now in the Uffizi – Cimabue's pioneering *Maestà*.

The third of the church's major works, a powerful composition by Luca della Robbia – the **tomb of Benozzo Federighi, bishop of Fiesole** (9) – occupies the left wall of the Cappella Scali; moulded and carved for the church of San Pancrazio, it was transported here in 1896. The fine wooden **statue of Mary Magdalene** (10), which owes much to Donatello's *Magdalene* in the Museo dell'Opera del Duomo, was begun by Desiderio da Settignano and completed, according to Vasari, by Benedetto da Maiano. Before you leave, various of the fifteenth-century paintings in the remaining **side chapels** (11–12) are well worth a look.

# Via de' Tornabuoni to the Rucellai chapel

The shops of **Via de' Tornabuoni** are effectively out of bounds to those who don't travel first class. Versace, Ferragamo, Prada, Cavalli, Gucci and Armani have their outlets here: indeed, in recent years they have come to monopolize the street (and nearby Piazza Strozzi), to the dismay of many, who see further evidence of the loss of Florentine identity in the eviction of local institutions such as the Seeber bookshop, the Farmacia Inglese and the *Giacosa* café. The last of this trio – famed as the birthplace of the Negroni cocktail – now exists in name only, as an adjunct to the huge Roberto Cavalli shop, with footage of Cavalli catwalk shows projected onto a big screen for the customers' entertainment. A rather more discreet conversion was carried out at the former Seeber premises: it's now occupied by fashion house MaxMara, whose architects uncovered two sets of frescoes (one sixteenth-century, the other nineteenth-century) when the old paintwork was stripped away. Trumpeting the refined taste of MaxMara boss Achille Maramotti (a major collector of modern art), a MaxMara spokesperson said of the decision to leave the paintings on show: "It may take up floor space in terms of selling, but it is more important to fill people with knowledge and beauty than sell an extra coat."

Conspicuous wealth is nothing new on Via de' Tornabuoni. Looming above everything is the vast **Palazzo Strozzi**, the most intimidating of all Florentine Renaissance palaces, with windows as big as gateways and embossed with lumps of stone the size of boulders. It was begun by the banker Filippo Strozzi, a figure so powerful that he was once described as "the first man of Italy", and whose family provided the ringleaders of the anti-Medici faction in Florence. He bought and demolished a dozen town houses to make space for Giuliano da Sangallo's inhabitable strongbox, and the construction of it lasted from 1489 to 1536. The interior of the palazzo is open only for special exhibitions.

# The Palazzo Rucellai

Some of Florence's other plutocrats made an impression with a touch more subtlety than the Strozzi. In the 1440s Giovanni Rucellai, one of the richest businessmen in the city (and an esteemed scholar too), decided to commission a new house from Leon Battista Alberti, whose accomplishments as architect, mathematician, linguist and theorist of the arts prompted a contemporary to exclaim, "Where shall I put Battista Alberti: in what category of learned men shall I place him?" The resultant **Palazzo Rucellai**, two minutes' walk from the Strozzi house at Via della Vigna Nuova 18, was the first palace in Florence to follow the rules of classical architecture; its tiers of pilasters, incised into smooth blocks of stone, evoke the exterior wall of the Colosseum. Alberti later produced another, equally elegant design for the same patron – the front of the church of Santa Maria Novella. In contrast to the feud between the Medici and the Strozzi, the Rucellai were on the closest terms with the city's *de facto* royal family: the **Loggia dei Rucellai**, across the street (now a clothes shop), was in all likelihood built for the wedding of Giovanni's son to the granddaughter of Cosimo il Vecchio, and the frieze on the Palazzo Rucellai features the heraldic devices of the two families, the Medici emblem alongside the Rucellai sail.

## The Museo Marino Marini and the Cappella di San Sepolcro

Round the corner from the Palazzo Rucellai stands the ex-church of San Pancrazio, deconsecrated by Napoleon, then successively the offices of the state lottery, the magistrates' court, a tobacco factory and an arsenal. It is now the swish **Museo Marino Marini** (June, July & Sept Mon & Wed–Fri 10am–5pm; Oct–May Mon & Wed–Sat 10am–5pm; closed Aug; €4), where the attire and demeanour of the attendants might make you think you'd strayed into a well-appointed fashion house. Holding around two hundred works left to the city in Marini's will, the museum itself is perhaps the most intriguing artefact and it's debatable whether Marini's pieces can stand up to the reverential atmosphere imposed by the display techniques. Variations on the sculptor's trademark horse-and-rider theme – familiar from civic environments all over Europe – make up much of the show.

Once part of the church but now entirely separate from the museum, the **Cappella Rucellai**, which was redesigned by Alberti, houses the **Cappella di San Sepolcro**, the most exquisite of his creations (June–Sept hours vary but usually Mon–Fri 10am–noon; Oct–May Mon–Sat 10am–noon & 5–5.30pm; free). Designed as the funerary monument to Giovanni Rucellai, it takes the form of a diminutive reconstruction of Jerusalem's Church of the Holy Sepulchre.

# Piazza Santa Maria Novella

Scurrying from the train station in search of a room, or fretting in the queues for a rail ticket, most people barely give a glance to **Santa Maria Novella train station**, but this is a building that deserves as much attention as many of the city's conventional monuments. Its principal architect, Giovanni Michelucci – who died in January 1991 just two days short of his hundredth birthday – was one of the leading figures of the Modernist movement, which in Mussolini's Italy was marginalized by the officially approved pomposities of the Neoclassical tendency. Accordingly, there was some astonishment when, in 1933, Michelucci and his colleagues won the open competition to design the main rail terminal for one of the country's showpiece cities. It's a piece of impeccably rational planning, so perfectly designed for its function that no major alterations have been necessary in the half-century since its completion.

Cross the road from the front of the train station, and you're on the edge of a zone free from the hazards of speeding traffic and petrol fumes. On the other side of the church of Santa Maria Novella – whose back directly faces the station – lies **Piazza Santa Maria Novella**, a square with a distinctly squalid undertone, though the development of an upmarket hotel complex on the eastern side (formerly something of a backpackers' den) will doubtless be followed by more stringent policing of the area.

## The church of Santa Maria Novella

From its graceful green, white and pink marble facade, you'd never guess that the church of **Santa Maria Novella** (Mon–Thurs and Sat 9am–5pm, Fri & Sun 1–5pm; €2.50) was the Florentine base of the austere Dominican order, fearsome vigilantes of thirteenth-century Catholicism. A more humble church, Santa Maria delle Vigne, which had existed here since the eleventh century, was handed to the Dominicans in 1221; they then set about altering the place to their taste. By 1360 the interior was finished, but only the Romanesque lower part of the **facade** had been completed. This state of affairs lasted until 1456,

---

### St Peter Martyr and the Paterenes

In the twelfth century Florence became the crucible of one of the reforming religious movements that periodically cropped up in medieval Italy. The **Paterenes**, who were so numerous that they had their own clerical hierarchy in parallel with that of the mainstream Church, were convinced that everything worldly was touched by the Devil. Accordingly they despised the papacy for its claims to temporal power and spurned the adoration of all relics and images. Furthermore, they rejected all forms of prayer and all contracts – including marriage vows – and were staunch pacifists.

Inevitably their campaign against the financial and moral corruption of the Catholic Church brought them into conflict with Rome; the displeasure of the Vatican eventually found its means of expression in the equally zealous but decidedly non-pacific figure of the Dominican known as **St Peter Martyr**. Operating from the monastery of Santa Maria Novella, this papal inquisitor headed a couple of anti-Paterene fraternities, the Crocesegnati and the Compagnia della Fede, which were in effect his private army. In 1244 he led them into battle across the Piazza Santa Maria Novella, where they proceeded to massacre hundreds of the theological enemy. The epicentre of the carnage is marked by the Croce del Trebbio in Via delle Belle Donne, off the eastern side of the piazza.

After this, the Dominicans turned to less militant work, founding the charitable organization called the Misericordia, which is still in existence today (see p.66). In 1252 Peter was knifed to death by a pair of assassins in the pay of a couple of Venetians whose property he'd confiscated, which is why he's usually depicted with a blade embedded in his skull. The official version, however, identifies the assassins as Paterene heretics, and relates that the dying man managed to write out the Credo with his own blood before expiring – an incident depicted in the frescoes in Santa Maria Novella's Cappellone degli Spagnoli. Within the year he'd been made a saint.

when Giovanni Rucellai paid for Alberti to design a classicized upper storey (1456–70) that would blend with the older section while improving the facade's proportions. The sponsor's name is picked out across the facade in Roman capitals (iohanes·oricellarivs…), while the Rucellai family emblem, the billowing sail of Fortune, runs as a motif through the central frieze. One other external feature is worth noting: the route into the church takes you through the cemetery, which – uniquely – is ringed by an arcade of *avelli*, the collective burial vaults of upper-class families.

Santa Maria Novella's **interior** was designed specifically to enable preachers to address their sermons to as large a congregation as possible: acoustic effects may even have been a consideration in the adoption of the French fashion for stone vaults (timbered roofs had hitherto been the norm in Tuscan churches). Its architects were not content with sheer physical size alone, however, and created a further illusion of space with an ingenious trompe l'oeil: the distance between the columns diminishes with proximity to the altar, a perspectival illusion to make the nave seem longer. Treasures aplenty fill the

**SANTA MARIA NOVELLA**

0    25 m

1 Annunciation, anon. 14th-century Florentine painter
2 Nativity (lunette above door), attrib. Botticelli
3 Annunciation (1602), Santi di Tito
4 Tomb of Beata Villana delle Botti (d. 1361), a Dominican nun, by Bernardo Rossellini (1451) and Desiderio da Settignano
5 Pulpit (1443), Brunelleschi
6 Trinity (1427), Masaccio
7 Crucifix, Giotto (c. 1288–90)
8 Tomb of the Patriarch of Constantinople (d.1440)
9 Cappella Rucellai (1303–52): Madonna and Child (1348), Mino da Fiesole; tombplate of Leonardo Dati (1425–6), Ghiberti
10 Cappella Bardi: 14th-century frescoes
11 Cappella di Filippo Strozzi: frescoes (1489–1502), Filippino Lippi; tomb of Filippo Strozzi (1491–5), Benedetto da Maiano
12 Chancel: fresco cycle (1485–90), Domenico Ghirlandaio
13 Cappella Gondi: crucifix (1410–14), attrib. Brunelleschi
14 Cappella Strozzi: frescoes (1350–7), Narno di Cione; altarpiece (1357), Orcagna
15 Chiostro Verde
16 The Flood (1425–30), Paolo Uccello
17 Cappellone degli Spagnoli
18 Chiostrino dei Morti
19 Chiostro Grande

interior, not least a ground-breaking painting by Masaccio, a crucifix by Giotto and no fewer than three major **fresco cycles**. There would be even more had it not been for the antics of Vasari and his minions in the 1560s, who ran amok here in a frenzy of "improvement", ripping out the rood screen and the choir and bleaching over the frescoes; restorers in the nineteenth century managed to reverse much of his handiwork.

## The nave

Entwined around the second nave pillar on the left is a **pulpit**, designed by Brunelleschi and notorious as the spot from which the Dominicans first denounced Galileo for espousing the Copernican theory of the heavens. The actual carving was completed by Buggiano, Brunelleschi's adopted son, who may well have advised Masaccio on the Renaissance architectural details present in the background of his extraordinary 1427 fresco of the **Trinity** (number 6 on our plan), which is painted on the wall nearby. This was one of the earliest works in which the rules of perspective and classical proportion were rigorously employed, and Florentines queued to view the illusion on its unveiling, stunned by a painting which appeared to create three-dimensional space on a solid wall. Amazingly, the picture was concealed behind an altar in 1570 and rediscovered only in 1861. The painting's theme was suggested by the fact that the Dominicans' calendar began with the Feast of the Trinity. Surmounting a stark image of the state to which all flesh is reduced, the main scene is a dramatized diagram of the mechanics of Christian redemption. The lines of the painting lead from the picture's donors, the judge Lorenzo Lenzi and his wife (the figures flanking the pair of painted pillars), through the Virgin and the Baptist (humanity's mystical link with the Holy Trinity), to the crucified Christ and the stern figure of God the Father at the pinnacle. The skeleton beneath the picture bears a motto with the none too cheery couplet: "I was that which you are / You will be that which I am."

**Giotto's Crucifix** (7), a radically naturalistic and probably very early work (c.1288–90), now hangs in what is thought to be its intended position, poised dramatically over the centre of the nave. Hitherto, it had been hidden away in the sacristy, veiled by a layer of dirt so thick that many scholars refused to recognize it as the work of the great master; the attribution is still disputed, a common complaint being that Christ's body is depicted in an unusually heavy way. But as seen from below, suspended in an eerily life-like manner, the weight of flesh seems only to contribute to its painful realism.

Nothing else in the main part of the church has quite the same resonance as these three works, but the wealth of decoration is astounding. In the right transept lies the **tomb** of the Patriarch of Constantinople (8), who died in the adjoining convent in 1440 after unsuccessful negotiations to unite the Roman and Byzantine churches at the 1439 Council of Florence. Raised above the pavement of the transept, the **Cappella Rucellai** (9), often closed, contains a marble *Madonna and Child* on the main altar signed by Nino Pisano, and – in the centre of the floor – Ghiberti's bronze tomb of the Dominican general Francesco Leonardo Dati.

### The Cappella di Filippo Strozzi

In 1486 the chapel to the right of the chancel (11) was bought by Filippo **Strozzi**, a wealthy banker, who then commissioned Filippino Lippi to paint a much-interrupted fresco cycle (1489–1502) on the life of his namesake, St Philip the Apostle, a saint rarely portrayed in Italian art. The paintings, a departure from anything seen in Florence at the time, were completed well after Strozzi's death in 1491. Lippi, it's interesting to note, received a payment of 300 florins for the work – ten times the cost of Strozzi's funeral.

Before starting the project Filippino spent some time in Rome, and the work he carried out on his return displays an archeologist's obsession with ancient Roman culture. The right wall depicts Philip's *Crucifixion* and his *Miracle before the Temple of Mars*. In the latter, the Apostle uses the cross to banish a dragon which had been an object of pagan worship in a Temple of Mars. The enraged temple priests then capture and crucify the saint. The figures swooning from the dragon's stench are almost overwhelmed by an architectural fantasy derived from Rome's recently excavated Golden House of Nero. Look carefully in the top right-hand corner and you'll see a miniscule figure of Christ, about the same size as one of the vases behind the figure of Mars.

The left wall depicts *The Raising of Drusiana* and the *Attempted Martyrdom of St John*: the latter scene alludes to the persecutions of the Emperor Domitian, during which John was dipped in boiling oil in an attempt to kill him – but the Apostle emerged miraculously unscathed and rejuvenated by the experience. The vaults portray Adam, Noah, Jacob and Abraham and, like the chapel's stained glass and impressive trompe l'oeil decoration, were also the work of Lippi. Behind the altar of this chapel is **Strozzi's tomb** (1491–95), beautifully carved by Benedetto da Maiano.

## The chancel (Cappella Tornabuoni)

As a chronicle of fifteenth-century life in Florence, no series of frescoes is more fascinating than **Domenico Ghirlandaio**'s pictures around the **chancel** (12) and high altar. The artist's masterpiece, the pictures ostensibly depict scenes from the life of the Virgin (left wall) and episodes from the life of St John the Baptist, and were designed to replace works on similar themes by Orcagna destroyed a century earlier, reputedly by a bolt of lightning. However, the fact that the paintings were commissioned by **Giovanni Tornabuoni**, a banker and uncle of Lorenzo de' Medici (Lorenzo the Magnificent), means they are liberally sprinkled with contemporary portraits and narrative details – which explains why certain illustrious ladies of the Tornabuoni family are present at the births of both John the Baptist and the Virgin. Such self-glorification made the frescoes the object of special ire after they were completed, drawing the vitriol of Savonarola during his hellfire and brimstone sermons. Stuffier art critics have also labelled them too "superficial" for serious comment: John Ruskin, their most notable detractor, observed that "if you are a nice person, they are not nice enough", and "if you are a vulgar person, not vulgar enough".

In truth, there are few frescoes in the city with such immediate charm, and none which are so self-conscious a celebration of Florence at its zenith – it's no accident that one of the frescoes **(S)** includes a prominent Latin inscription (on an arch to the right) which reads: "The year 1490, when the most beautiful city renowned for abundance, victories, arts and noble buildings profoundly enjoyed salubrity and peace." Having found the inscription, you might then want to identify some of the portraits scattered around the paintings. Ghirlandaio features as a self-portrait in **(A)**, in which Joachim, the Virgin's father, is chased from the temple because he has been unable to have children – the painter is the figure in the right-hand group with hand on hip. In the next fresco **(B)**, the young woman in the white and gold dress leading the group of women is Ludovica, Tornabuoni's only daughter, who died in childbirth aged 15: it's doubtless no accident that the scene painted in the fresco depicts the birth of the Virgin. Across the chancel, on the right wall, the **Visitation** **(Q)** features Giovanna degli Albizi, Tornabuoni's daughter-in-law, who also died in childbirth – she's the first of the trio of women to the

**SANTA MARIA NOVELLA**
**CHANCEL FRESCOES**

A Joachim chased from the Temple
B The Birth of the Virgin
C Presentation in the Temple
D The Marriage of the Virgin
E The Adoration of the Magi
F The Massacre of the Innocents
G The Death of the Virgin and Assumption
H Giovanni Tornabuoni (donor) at prayer
J Francesca Pitti, wife of Giovanni Tornabuoni
K The Annunciation
L St John in the Wilderness

M St Dominic burning heretical books
N St Peter Martyr
P The Coronation of the Virgin
Q The Visitation
R The angel appears to Zachariah
S Zachariah writes down the name of his son
T The birth of St John Baptist
U The baptism of Christ
V St John the Baptist preaching
W The Feast of Herod

right of the Virgin. The **Birth of St John the Baptist (T)** features Torn-abuoni's sister, Lucrezia, better known as the mother of Lorenzo de' Medici (the Magnificent): she's the woman in front of the servant carrying the fruit on her head.

## The Cappella Strozzi

The next chapel beyond the chancel is the **Cappella Gondi** (13), which houses Brunelleschi's crucifix, supposedly carved as a riposte to the uncouthness of Donatello's cross in Santa Croce. It is the artist's only surviving sculpture in wood. Legend claims that Donatello was so struck on seeing his rival's work that he dropped a basket of eggs.

Even more startling, however, is the great fresco cycle in the next chapel but one, the **Cappella Strozzi** (14), which lies above the level of the rest of the church at the end of the north (left) transept. Its frescoes (1350–57) were commissioned as an expiation of the sin of usury by Tommaso Strozzi, an ancestor of Filippo Strozzi, patron of the chapel across the church. The pictures are the masterpiece of Nardo di Cione, brother of the better-known Orcagna (Andrea di Cione), with whom Nardo collaborated to design the chapel's stained glass.

Orcagna alone painted the chapel's magnificent high altarpiece, *Christ Presenting the Keys to St Peter and the Book of Wisdom to Thomas Aquinas* (1357). A propaganda exercise on behalf of the Dominicans, the picture shows Christ bestowing favour on both St Peter and St Thomas Aquinas, the latter a figure second only to St Dominic in the order's hierarchy. The stern and implacable figures are perfect advertisements for the Dominicans' unbending authority. Behind the altar, the central fresco depicts the *Last Judgement*, with Dante featured as one of the saved (in white, third from the left, second row from the top). So, too, are Tommaso Strozzi and his wife, shown being led by St Michael into paradise, with an angel helping the righteous up through a trapdoor; on the right of the altar, a devil forks the damned down into hell. The theme of judgement is continued in the bleached fresco of Dante's *Inferno* on the right wall, faced by a thronged *Paradiso* on the left. The entrance arch features a frieze of saints, while the vaults depict St Thomas Aquinas and the Virtues.

# The Museo di Santa Maria Novella

Further remarkable paintings are to be found in the spacious Romanesque conventual buildings to the left of the church of Santa Maria Novella, home to the **Museo di Santa Maria Novella** (Mon–Thurs & Sat 9am–5pm, Sun 9am–2pm; €2.70). The first set of cloisters beyond the entrance, the **Chiostro Verde** (15), dating from 1332 to 1350, features frescoes of *Stories from Genesis* (1425–30) executed by Paolo Uccello and his workshop. The cloister takes its name from the green base *terra verde* pigment they used, and which now gives the paintings a spectral undertone.

The windswept image of **The Flood** (16), the best-preserved of the cloister's frescoes, is rendered almost unintelligible by the telescoping perspective and the double appearance of the ark (before and after the flood), whose flanks form a receding corridor in the centre of the picture: on the left, the ark is rising on the deluge, on the right it has come to rest as the waters subside. In the foreground, two men fight each other in their desperation to stay alive; the chequered life-belt that one of these men is wearing around his neck is a favourite Uccello device for demonstrating a mastery of perspective – it's a *mazzocchio*, a 72-faceted wicker ring round which a turbanned headdress was wrapped. Another

## Paolo Uccello

Some of the most curious and haunting images to come out of the Florentine Renaissance are the products of **Paolo Uccello**'s obsession with the problems of perspective and foreshortening. Born in 1396, he trained in Ghiberti's workshop before moving to Venice, where he was employed on mosaics for the Basilica di San Marco. He worked periodically in Florence, returning for an extended period in 1431. Five years later he was contracted to paint the commemorative portrait of Sir John Hawkwood in the Duomo, the trompe l'oeil painting which gives the first evidence of his interest in foreshortening.

After an interlude in Padua, Uccello completed the frescoes for the cloister of Santa Maria Novella, in which his systematic but non-naturalistic use of perspective is seen at its most extreme. In the following decade he painted the three-scene sequence of the **Battle of San Romano** (Louvre, London National Gallery and Uffizi) for the Medici – his most ambitious non-fresco paintings, and similarly notable for their unsettling multiple perspectives and strange use of foreshortening.

Uccello was driven halfway round the bend by the study of **perspective**, locking himself away for weeks at a time when he'd got his teeth into a particularly thorny problem. Chronically incapable of looking after his more mundane concerns, he was destitute by the time of his death in 1475: "I am old and without means of livelihood. My wife is sick and I am unable to work any more." Yet he left behind some of the most arresting paintings of the Renaissance, in which his preoccupation with mathematical precision coexists with a fundamentally Gothic sense of pageantry.

man grabs the ankles of the visionary figure in the foreground – presumably Noah, though he is a much younger Noah than the hirsute patriarch leaning out of the ark on the right to receive the dove's olive branch. In the right foreground there's a preview of the universal devastation, with tiny corpses laid out on the deck, and a crow gobbling an eyeball from one of the drowned.

### The Cappellone degli Spagnoli

Off the cloister opens what was once the chapterhouse of the immensely rich convent of Santa Maria, the **Cappellone degli Spagnoli** (17), or Spanish Chapel. For a time it was also the headquarters of the Inquisition. It received its present name after Eleonora di Toledo, wife of Cosimo I, reserved it for the use of her Spanish entourage. Presumably she derived much inspiration from its majestic fresco cycle (1367–69) by Andrea di Firenze, an extended depiction of the triumph of the Catholic Church that was described by Ruskin as "the most noble piece of pictorial philosophy in Italy".

Virtually every patch of the walls is covered with frescoes, whose theme is the role of the Dominicans in the battle against heresy and in the salvation of Christian souls. The **left wall** as you enter depicts *The Triumph of Divine Wisdom*, a triumph exemplified by Thomas Aquinas, who is portrayed enthroned below the Virgin and Apostles amidst the winged Virtues and the "wise men" of the Old and New Testaments (the so-called Doctors of the Church). Below these are fourteen figures who symbolize the Arts and Sciences, branches of learning brought to fruition by the Holy Spirit (symbolized by the dove above the Virgin) working through the Catholic faith.

The more spectacular **right wall** depicts *The Triumph of the Church*, or more specifically, the "Mission, Work and Triumph of the Dominican Order". Everything here conforms to a strict and logical hierarchy, beginning at the crown of the painting (on the ceiling) with the boat of St Peter, a symbol of the Church.

At the bottom is a building supposed to be Florence's cathedral, a pinky-purple creation imagined one hundred years before the structure was completed. Before it stand the pope and Holy Roman Emperor, society's ultimate spiritual and temporal rulers. Before them stand ranks of figures representing religious orders, among which the Dominicans are naturally pre-eminent. In particular, note St Dominic, the order's founder, unleashing the "hounds of the lord", or *Domini Canes*, a pun on the Dominicans' name: heretics, the dogs' victims, are shown as wolves.

Among the group of pilgrims (in the centre, just below the Duomo) are several portraits, real or imagined: Cimabue (standing in a large brown cloak); Giotto (beside him in profile, wearing a green cloak); Boccaccio (further right, in purple, holding a closed book); Petrarch (above, with a cloak and white ermine hood); and Dante (alongside Petrarch in profile, with a white cap). Above and to the right, are scenes of young people dancing, hawking, playing music and engaging in other pleasures of the sort that the Dominicans so heartily condemned.

Those able to resist such abominations – the saved – are shown being marshalled by a nearby friar who hears their confession before dispatching them towards St Peter and the Gate of Paradise. Once through the gate, the blessed are shown in adoration of God and the angels with the Virgin at their midst. Foremost among those confessing is the chapel's donor, one Buonamico Guidalotti (shown kneeling), who paid for the chapel in honour of his wife, who died during the 1348 plague. The far wall shows scenes connected with the Crucifixion, with some very unhappy devils in the bottom right-hand corner, while the near (entrance) wall, which is excluded from the frescoes'

△ St Dominic and the "hounds of the Lord"

unified theme, contains scenes from the life of St Peter Martyr, one of the Dominicans' leading lights.

The contemporaneous decoration of the **Chiostrino dei Morti** (18), the oldest part of the complex, has not aged so robustly; it was closed for restoration at the time of writing. The **Chiostro Grande** (19), to the west, is also out of bounds, but for the more unusual reason that it is a practice parade ground for aspiring carabinieri (Italy's semi-military police force). The small museum adjoining the Chiostro Grande is notable chiefly for some peculiarly glamorous fourteenth- and fifteenth-century reliquary busts, containing remnants of St Ursula and Mary Magdalene, among others.

# Ognissanti to the Cascine

In medieval times one of the main areas of cloth production – the mainstay of the Florentine economy – was in the western part of the city. **Ognissanti** (daily 7.30am–12.30pm & 3.30–7.30pm), or All Saints, the main church of this quarter, stands on a piazza that might be taken as a symbol of the state of the present-day Florentine economy, dominated as it is by the five-star *Grand* and *Excelsior* hotels.

The church was founded in 1256 by the Umiliati, a Benedictine order from Lombardy whose speciality was the weaving of woollen cloth – they it was who commissioned the great Giotto altarpiece of the *Maestà* in the Uffizi. In 1561 the Franciscans took over the church, the new tenure being marked by a Baroque overhaul which spared only the medieval campanile. The facade (1637) of the church is of historical interest as one of the earliest eruptions of the Baroque in Florence – it was abhorred by many Florentines at the time as an affront to the city's Renaissance traditions. The building within, however, is made appealing by earlier features – **frescoes** by Domenico Ghirlandaio and Sandro Botticelli.

The young face squeezed between the Madonna and the dark-cloaked man in Ghirlandaio's *Madonna della Misericordia* (1473), the higher of the two works over the second altar on the right, is said to be that of Amerigo Vespucci (1451–1512), an agent for the Medici in Seville, whose two voyages in 1499 and 1501 would lend his name to a continent. The altar was paid for by the Vespucci, a family of silk merchants from the surrounding district, which is why other members of the clan appear beneath the Madonna's protective cloak. Among them is Simonetta Vespucci (at the Virgin's left hand), the mistress of Giuliano de' Medici and reputedly the most beautiful woman of her age – she is said to have been the model for Botticelli's *Venus*, now in the Uffizi.

The idea may not be so far-fetched, for Botticelli also lived locally, and the Vespucci and Filipepi families were on good terms. Botticelli is buried in the church, beneath a round tomb slab in the south transept, and his painting of *St Augustine's Vision of St Jerome* (1480) lies on the same wall as the Madonna, between the third and fourth altars. Facing it is Ghirlandaio's more earthbound *St Jerome*, also painted in 1480.

In the same year Ghirlandaio painted the well-preserved *Last Supper* that covers one wall of the **refectory**, reached through the cloister entered to the left of the church (Mon, Tues & Sat 9am–noon; free). It's a characteristically placid scene, the most animated characters being the birds in flight over the fruit-laden lemon trees above the heads of the disciples.

# The Cascine

Florence's public park, the **Cascine**, begins close to the Ponte della Vittoria (bus #17e from the Duomo, station or youth hostel) and dwindles away 3km downstream, at the confluence of the Arno and the Mugnone, where there's a statue of the Maharajah of Kohlapur – he died in Florence in 1870 and the prescribed funeral rites demanded that his body be cremated at a spot where two rivers met.

Once the Medici dairy farm (*cascina*), then a hunting reserve, this narrow strip of green mutated into a high-society venue in the eighteenth century: if there was nothing happening at the opera, all of Florence's *beau monde* turned out to promenade under the trees of the Cascine. A fountain in the park bears a dedication to Shelley, who was inspired to write his *Ode to the West Wind* while strolling here on a blustery day in 1819.

Thousands of people come out here on Tuesday mornings for the colossal market beyond the former train station (which now houses a new arts centre, the Stazione Leopolda), and on any day of the week the Cascine swarms with joggers, cyclists and roller-bladers. Parents bring their kids out here too, to play on the grass (a rare commodity in Florence) or visit the small zoo. However, the Cascine also has a reputation as haunt for the city's junkies, and it's emphatically not a place for a nocturnal stroll, as it has long been a hunting ground for the city's pimps.

# North of the centre: the San Lorenzo, San Marco and Annunziata districts

A few blocks from the train station and the Duomo lies the San Lorenzo district, the city's main market area, with scores of stalls encircling a vast and wonderful food hall. The racks of T-shirts, leather jackets and belts almost engulf the church of **San Lorenzo**, a building of major importance that's often overlooked in the rush to the Duomo and the Uffizi. Attached to the church is another of the city's major draws, the **Cappelle Medicee** (Medici Chapels). While various of the Medici's most important members are buried in the main part of San Lorenzo, dozens of lesser lights are interred in these chapels, with two of the most venal being celebrated by some of **Michelangelo**'s finest funerary sculpture. The Medici also account for the area's other major sight, the **Palazzo Medici-Riccardi**, with its exquisite fresco-covered chapel, while the most celebrated of all Michelangelo's works in stone – the *David* – can be admired in the nearby galleries of the **Accademia**. The devotional art of Fra' Angelico fills the nearby **Museo di San Marco**, which in turn is but a stroll away from **Piazza Santissima Annunziata**, one of Florence's most photogenic locales, thanks to Brunelleschi's **Spedale degli Innocenti** and the church of **Santissima Annunziata**.

## San Lorenzo

Founded in 393, **San Lorenzo** (Mon–Sat 10am–5pm; €2.50) has a claim to be the oldest church in Florence. For some three hundred years it was the city's

## Michelangelo

One of the titanic figures of the Italian Renaissance, **Michelangelo Buonarroti** (1475–1564) was born in Caprese in eastern Tuscany. His family soon moved to Florence, where he became a pupil of Ghirlandaio, making his first stone reliefs for Lorenzo de' Medici. After the Medici were expelled from the city the young Michelangelo went to Rome in 1496. There, he secured a reputation as the most skilled sculptor of his day with the *Bacchus* (now in the Bargello) and the *Pietà* for St Peter's.

After his return to Florence in 1501, Michelangelo carved the **David** and the *St Matthew* (both in the Accademia). He was also employed to paint a fresco of the *Battle of Cascina* in the Palazzo Vecchio. Only the cartoon was finished, but this became the single most influential work of art in the city, its twisting nudes a recurrent motif in later Mannerist art. Work was suspended in 1505 when Michelangelo was called to Rome by Pope Julius II to create his tomb; the *Slaves* in the Accademia were intended for this grandiose project which, like many of Michelangelo's schemes, was never finished.

In 1508 Michelangelo began his other superhuman project, the decoration of the **Sistine Chapel** ceiling in Rome. Back in Florence, he started work on the San Lorenzo complex in 1516, staying on in the city to supervise its defences when it was besieged by the Medici and Charles V in 1530. Four years later he left for ever, and spent his last thirty years in Rome, the period that produced the *Last Judgement* in the Sistine Chapel. Florence has one work from this final phase of Michelangelo's long career, the **Pietà** he intended for his own tomb (now in the Museo dell'Opera del Duomo).

cathedral, before renouncing its title to Santa Reparata, the precursor of the Duomo. By 1060 a sizeable Romanesque church had been constructed on the site, a building which in time became the Medici's parish church, benefiting greatly over the years from the family's munificence.

The family was in a particularly generous mood in 1419, when a committee of eight parishioners headed by Giovanni di Bicci de' Medici, founder of the Medici fortune, offered to finance a new church. **Brunelleschi** was commissioned to begin the project, starting work on the Sagrestia Vecchia (Old Sacristy) before being given the go-ahead two years later to build the entire church. Construction lapsed over the next twenty years, hampered by financial problems, political upheavals and Brunelleschi's simultaneous work on the cathedral dome. Giovanni's son, Cosimo de' Medici, eventually gave the work fresh impetus with a grant of 40,000 *fiorini* (florins) – at a time when 150 florins would support a Florentine family for a year. Cosimo's largesse saved the day, but was still not sufficient to provide the church with a facade. No less a figure than Michelangelo laboured to remedy the omission, one of many to devote time to a scheme to provide a suitable frontage. None of the efforts was to any avail: to this day the exterior's bare brick has never been clad.

## The interior

When you step inside the church, what strikes you first is the cool rationality of Brunelleschi's design, an instantly calming contrast to the hubbub outside. San Lorenzo was the earlier of Brunelleschi's great Florentine churches (the other is Santo Spirito) but already displays his mastery of Classical decorative motifs and mathematically planned proportions.

The first work of art to catch your attention, in the second chapel on the right, is Rosso Fiorentino's **Marriage of the Virgin** (marked 1 on our plan),

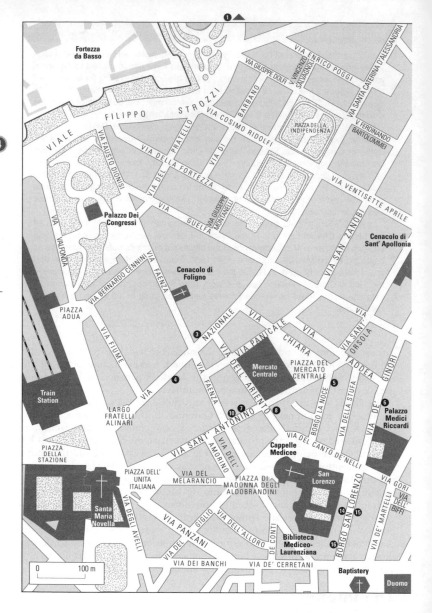

with its uniquely golden-haired and youthful Joseph. There's another arresting painting at the top of the left aisle – Bronzino's enormous fresco of *The Martyrdom of St Lawrence* (10) – but it seems a shallow piece of work alongside the nearby bronze pulpits (2) by **Donatello**. Clad with reliefs depicting scenes preceding and following the Crucifixion, these are the artist's last works (begun c.1460), and were completed by his pupils as increasing paralysis limited their

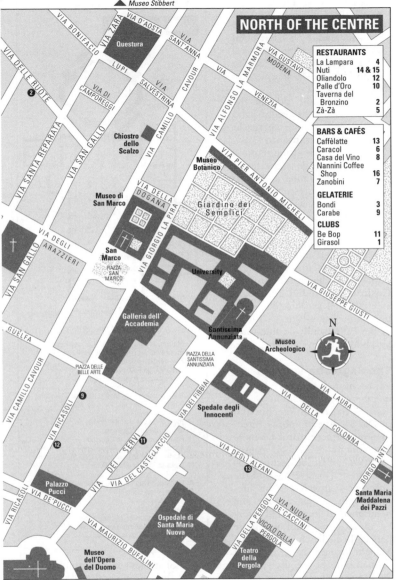

Museo Stibbert

**RESTAURANTS**

| | |
|---|---|
| La Lampara | 4 |
| Nuti | 14 & 15 |
| Oliandolo | 12 |
| Palle d'Oro | 10 |
| Taverna del Bronzino | 2 |
| Zà-Zà | 5 |

**BARS & CAFÉS**

| | |
|---|---|
| Caffèlatte | 13 |
| Caracol | 6 |
| Casa del Vino | 8 |
| Nannini Coffee Shop | 16 |
| Zanobini | 7 |

**GELATERIE**

| | |
|---|---|
| Bondi | 3 |
| Carabe | 9 |

**CLUBS**

| | |
|---|---|
| Be Bop | 11 |
| Girasol | 1 |

master's ability to model in wax. Jagged and discomforting, charged with more energy than the space can contain, these panels are more like brutal sketches in bronze than conventional reliefs. The overpopulated *Deposition*, for example, has demented mourners sobbing beneath crosses which disappear into the void beyond the frame, while in the background a group of horsemen gather on a hill whose contours are left unmarked. Donatello is buried in the nave of the church, next to his patron, Cosimo de' Medici, and commemorated by a **memorial** (8) on the right wall of the chapel in the north transept, close to Filippo Lippi's 1440 altarpiece of the *Annunciation* (9).

On the opposite side of the church, near the right-hand pulpit, there's a fine tabernacle, the **Pala del Sacramento** (3), by Desiderio da Settignano. Round the corner to the right lies a chapel (4) containing a Roman sarcophagus, a fresco fragment of the Virgin, a wooden crucifix by Antonio del Pollaiuolo and two modern works in *pietra dura*, a peculiarly Florentine kind of technicolour marquetry using semi-precious stones. In· the centre of the church, the **tomb of Cosimo de' Medici** (5), known as Cosimo il Vecchio, bears the inscription "Pater Patriae" (Father of the Fatherland) – a title once borne by Roman emperors.

## The Sagrestia Vecchia

Four more leading Medici members lie buried in the neighbouring **Sagrestia Vecchia** (D) or Old Sacristy, a minor architectural masterpiece that is far more than simply a Medici mausoleum. One of Brunelleschi's earliest projects (1421–26) – and the only one completed in his lifetime – the design, a cube and hemispherical dome, could hardly be more simple and yet more perfect. Brunelleschi's biographer, Manetti, wrote that "it astounded

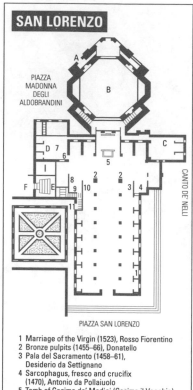

**SAN LORENZO**

PIAZZA MADONNA DEGLI ALDOBRANDINI

CANTO DE' NELLI

PIAZZA SAN LORENZO

1  Marriage of the Virgin (1523), Rosso Fiorentino
2  Bronze pulpits (1455–66), Donatello
3  Pala del Sacramento (1458–61),
   Desiderio da Settignano
4  Sarcophagus, fresco and crucifix
   (1470), Antonio da Pollaiuolo
5  Tomb of Cosimo de' Medici (Cosimo il Vecchio)
6  Tomb of Giovanni and Piero de' Medici
   (Cosimo's sons)
7  Tomb of Giovanni and Piccarda de'
   Medici (Cosimo's parents)
8  Funerary memorial to Donatello
9  Annunciation (1440), Filippo Lippi
10 Martyrdom of St Lawrence (1565–9), Bronzino
11 Stairs to Ricetto and Biblioteca

A  Entrance to the Cappelle Medicee
B  Cappella dei Principi
C  Sagrestia Nuova
D  Sagrestia Vecchia
E  Ricetto (vestibule), Michelangelo
F  Biblioteca Medicea-Laurenziana

all men both of the city and foreigners . . . for its new and beautiful manner. And so many people came continuously that they greatly bothered those who worked there."

The space was commissioned by Giovanni Bicci de' Medici, the principal founder of the Medici fortune, as a private chapel. The dedication is to St John the Evangelist, patron saint of Giovanni (John), but note that it is the Medici *palle* motif (see p.117) that dominates. On his death, Giovanni, along with his wife Piccarda, was buried beneath the massive marble slab at the centre of the **chapel** (7). Another **tomb** (6), easily missed, lies immediately on the left as you enter: the last resting place of Giovanni's grandsons, Giovanni and Piero de'

Medici, it was commissioned from Verrocchio in 1472 by Lorenzo de' Medici. To the modern eye the tomb looks relatively plain, but a Florentine of the day would have been abundantly aware that it was made from the three most precious materials of antiquity – marble, porphyry and bronze.

More arresting than either of the tombs, however, is the chapel's ornamentation. Here Brunelleschi's genius was complemented by the decorative acumen of Donatello, who worked in the sacristy between 1434 and 1443, some twenty years before sculpting the pulpits in the main body of the church. He was responsible for both the cherub-filled frieze and the eight extraordinary tondos above it, four of the latter a striking orangey-pink, the rest crafted in a more muted white against grey. The tondos' subjects are the four Evangelists and a quartet of scenes from the life of St John the Evangelist. The terracotta bust of St Lawrence (Lorenzo) is attributed to either Donatello or Desiderio da Settignano.

Two large **reliefs**, also probably by Donatello, adorn the space above the two doors on the end wall: one shows SS Lawrence and Stephen, twin protectors of Florence, the other SS Cosmas and Damian. These last two, twins and early Christian martyrs, were the patron saints of doctors (*medici*) and thus of the Medici, who were probably descended from doctors or apothecaries. By happy coincidence, Cosimo de' Medici, the church's chief patron, was born on the saints' feast day (27 September), so the two are often seen in paintings or buildings commissioned or connected with him.

Donatello was also responsible for the two bronze doors below with their combative martyrs to the left, and the Apostles and Fathers of the Church to the right. The chapel beyond the left door has a sublime little marble *lavabo*, probably by Verrocchio: many of its fantastic creatures have Medici connections – the falcon and lamb, for example, are the heraldic symbols of Piero de' Medici, who commissioned the work.

Lastly, the **stellar fresco** on the dome above the recessed altar inevitably draws your eye: opinion differs as to whether the position of the painted stars is synonymous with the state of the heavens on July 16, 1416, the birthday of Piero de' Medici, or on July 6, 1439, the date on which the union of the Eastern and Western churches was celebrated at the Council of Florence.

## The Biblioteca Medicea-Laurenziana

A gateway to the left of the church facade leads through a pleasant cloister and through a doorway (11) up to the **Biblioteca Medicea-Laurenziana** (F) (Mon–Sat 8.30am–1.30pm; free, except during special exhibitions). Wishing to create a suitably grandiose home for the precious manuscripts assembled by Cosimo and Lorenzo de' Medici, Pope Clement VII – Lorenzo's nephew – asked Michelangelo to design a new Medici library in 1524. The **Ricetto** (E), or vestibule (1559–71), of the building he eventually came up with is a revolutionary showpiece of Mannerist architecture, delighting in paradoxical display: brackets that support nothing, columns that sink into the walls rather than stand out from them, and a flight of steps so large that it almost fills the room, spilling down like a solidified lava flow.

From this eccentric space, you're sometimes allowed into the tranquil **reading room**; here, too, almost everything is the work of Michelangelo, even the inlaid desks. Exhibitions in the connecting rooms draw on the 15,000-piece Medici collection, which includes manuscripts as diverse as a fifth-century copy of Virgil – the collection's oldest item – and a treatise on architecture by Leonardo. Note how the coffered ceiling and terracotta floor mirror each other's designs.

# The Cappelle Medicee

Michelangelo's most celebrated contribution to the San Lorenzo complex forms part of the **Cappelle Medicee** (Tues–Sat 8.15am–4.50pm; 1st, 3rd & 5th Sun of month and 2nd & 4th Mon of month same hours; €6), entered from Piazza Madonna degli Aldobrandini, at the back of the church. These chapels divide into three sections: the crypt, burial place of many minor Medici; the **Cappella dei Principi**, housing the tombs of six of the more major Medici; and the **Sagrestia Nuova**, home to three major groups of Michelangelo sculpture.

## The crypt

Hardly any of the Medici, however humble, suffered the indignity of a modest grave. Some might have expected more, though, than the low-vaulted **crypt** of the Cappelle Medicee, home to the brass-railed tombs of many of the family's lesser lights. Most were placed here in 1791 by Ferdinand III with what appears to have been scant regard for his ancestors: one contemporary recorded how the duke had the corpses thrown "together pell-mell . . . caring scarcely to distinguish one from the other".

This haphazard arrangement prevailed until 1857, when it was decided – after much controversy – to exhume 49 of the bodies and provide them with a more dignified interment. William Wetmore Story, an American sculptor present at the exhumation, described the event with obvious relish: "Dark and parchment-dried faces were seen, with thin golden hair, rich as ever, and twisted with gems and pearls and golden nets. . . Anna Luisa, almost a skeleton, lay robed in rich violet velvet, with the electoral crown surmounting a black, ghastly face. . . Francesco, her uncle, lay beside her, a mass of putrid robes and rags." Since 2004 researchers have been conducting exhumations in another Medici crypt below the church, where they have discovered that the dead Medici are not quite as well-ordered as one would expect: the skeleton of a one-year-old was found in the tomb of Filippino de' Medici (son of Grand Duke Francesco I), who was almost five when he died, and the crypt also contains the remains of eight children who feature on no Medici family tree.

## Cappella dei Principi

After filing through the crypt, you climb steps at its rear into the larger of the chapels, the **Cappella dei Principi** (Chapel of the Princes), a morbid and dowdy marble-plated hall built as a mausoleum for Cosimo I and the grand dukes who succeeded him. The octagonal chapel took as its inspiration the floorplan of no less a building than the Baptistery, and the extent of Medici conceit was underlined by the chapel's intended centrepiece – the Holy Sepulchre of Christ, a prize that had to be forfeited when the pasha refused to sell it and an expedition sent to Jerusalem to steal it returned empty-handed.

Dismissed by Byron as a "fine frippery in great slabs of various expensive stones, to commemorate rotten and forgotten carcasses", this was the most expensive building project ever financed by the Medici, and the family were still paying for it in 1743 when the last of the line, Anna Maria Ludovica, joined her forebears in the basement. It could have looked even worse – the massive statues in the niches were intended to be made from semiprecious stones, like those used in the heraldic devices set into the walls (the crests are those of Tuscan and other towns within the Medici domain). Captured Turkish slaves formed the bulk of the workforce set to haul and hack the stone into manageable pieces. Only two of the massive statues were ever completed.

Scaffolding, suitably rich in gold and black, has adorned the walls since a section of cornice fell off in January 2000, revealing major structural faults.

## The Sagrestia Nuova

Begun in 1520, the **Sagrestia Nuova** (C) was designed by Michelangelo as a tribute to, and reinvention of, Brunelleschi's Sagrestia Vecchia in the main body of San Lorenzo. Architectural experts go into raptures over the sophistication of the architecture, notably the empty niches above the doors, which play complex games with the vocabulary of classical architecture, but the lay person will be drawn to the three fabulous **Medici tombs** (1520–34), two wholly and one partly by Michelangelo. The sculptor was awarded the commissions by Pope

△ Tomb of Lorenzo, duke of Urbino

Leo X – a Medici – and the pope's cousin, Cardinal Giulio de' Medici, later to become Pope Clement VII.

With your back to the entrance door, the tomb on the left belongs to **Lorenzo, duke of Urbino**, the grandson of Lorenzo the Magnificent. Michelangelo depicts him as a man of thought, and his sarcophagus bears figures of *Dawn* and *Dusk*, the times of day whose ambiguities appeal to the contemplative mind. Opposite stands the tomb of Lorenzo de' Medici's youngest son, **Giuliano, duke of Nemours**; as a man of action, his character is symbolized by the clear antithesis of *Day* and *Night*. A contemporary writer recorded that the sculptor gave his subjects "a greatness, a proportion, a dignity . . . which seemed to him would have brought them more praise, saying that a thousand years hence no one would be able to know that they were otherwise." The protagonists were very much otherwise: Giuliano was in fact an easygoing but feckless individual, while Lorenzo combined ineffectuality with unbearable arrogance. Both died young and unlamented of tuberculosis, combined in Lorenzo's case with syphilis. Michelangelo was not unaware of the ironies; some critics have suggested that Lorenzo's absurd hat may well have been a sly hint as to the subject's feeble-mindedness.

The two principal effigies were intended to face the equally grand tombs of Lorenzo de' Medici and his brother Giuliano, two Medici who had genuine claims to fame. The only part of the project completed by Michelangelo is the **Madonna and Child**, the last image of the Madonna he ever sculpted. The figures to either side are Cosmas and Damian, patron saints of doctors (*medici*) and the Medici family. Although completed by others, they follow Michelangelo's original design. Wax and clay models exist in the Casa Buonarroti (see p.149) and British Museum of other figures Michelangelo planned for the tomb. Among these were allegorical figures of Heaven and Earth and statues of river gods representing the Tiber and Arno, the last two intended to symbolize the provinces of Tuscany and Lazio, both briefly ruled by Giuliano. Sketches relating to this scheme are visible behind the altar (visitors are allowed to see them, under supervision, every thirty minutes), but the chapel was never completed as Michelangelo intended: in 1534, four years after the Medici had returned to Florence in the wretched form of Alessandro, Michelangelo decamped to Rome, where he stayed for the rest of his life.

# The Palazzo Medici-Riccardi

On the edge of the square in front of San Lorenzo stands the **Palazzo Medici-Riccardi** (daily except Wed 9am–7pm; €4), built for Cosimo de' Medici by Michelozzo between 1444 and 1462, possibly to a plan by Brunelleschi. Another story has it that Cosimo did indeed ask Brunelleschi to design the new palace, but the result was so grandiose that Cosimo rejected it on political grounds, saying "envy is a plant one should never water". Brunelleschi, who was renowned for his temper, is said to have smashed the splendid model in rage. With its heavily rusticated exterior, the monolithic palace was the prototype for several major Florentine buildings, most notably the Palazzo Pitti and Palazzo Strozzi. According to Michelozzo, rustication – the practice of facing buildings with vast, rough-hewn blocks of stone – was desirable as it united "an appearance of solidity and strength with the light and shade so essential to beauty under the glare of an Italian sun".

The palace remained the family home and Medici business headquarters until Cosimo I moved to the Palazzo Vecchio in 1540. In Cosimo de' Medici's

## The Medici balls

You come across the **Medici emblem** – a cluster of red balls (palle) un ª nnld background – all over Florence, yet its origins are shrouded in mystery. Legend claims the family was descended from a Carolingian knight named Averardo, who fought and killed a giant in the Mugello, north of Florence. During the encounter his shield received six massive blows from the giant's mace, so Charlemagne, as a reward for his bravery, allowed Averardo to represent the dents as red balls on his coat of arms.

Rival families claimed that the balls had less exalted origins, that they were medicinal pills or cupping glasses, recalling the family's origins as apothecaries or doctors (medici). Others claim they are bezants, Byzantine coins, inspired by the arms of the Arte del Cambio, the money-changers' guild to which the Medici belonged. In a similar vein, some say the balls are coins, the traditional symbols of pawnbrokers.

Whatever the origin, the number of palle was never constant. In the thirteenth century, for example, there were twelve. By Cosimo de' Medici's time the number had dropped to seven, though San Lorenzo's Old Sacristy, a Cosimo commission, strangely has eight, while Verrocchio's roundel in the same church's chancel has six and Grand Duke Cosimo I's tomb, in the Cappella dei Principi, has five. Cosimo il Vecchio was said to be so fond of displaying the palle on the buildings he had funded that a rival alleged that even the monks' privies in San Marco were adorned with Medici balls.

prime, around fifty members of the Medici clan lived in the palace, though after the deaths of his son Giovanni and grandson Cosimino, the embittered, gouty old man was said to repeatedly complain that the palace had become "too large a house for so small a family". In its day, Donatello's statue of *Judith and Holofernes* (now in the Palazzo Vecchio) adorned the walled garden, a rarity in Florence; the same artist's *David*, now in the Bargello, stood in the entrance courtyard.

After 1659 the palace was greatly altered by its new owners, the Riccardi, and it now houses the offices of the provincial government. The chief attraction for tourists is the cycle of Gozzoli **frescoes** in the chapel, which a maximum of seven people may view at any one time. To avoid the queues, book tickets in advance at the ticket office, at Via Cavour 3, or call ☎055.276.0340.

### The Gozzoli frescoes

Today all that survives of the interior of the original palace is Michelozzo's deep, colonnaded courtyard, which closely follows the new style established by Brunelleschi in the foundling hospital (see p.129), and a tiny **chapel**, reached by stairs leading directly from the court. The walls of the chapel are covered by some of the city's most charming frescoes: **Benozzo Gozzoli**'s sequence depicting *The Journey of the Magi*, painted around 1460 and recently restored to magnificent effect. The landscape scenes to either side of the altar are by the same artist.

Despite the frescoes' ostensible subject, the cycle probably portrays the pageant of the Compagnia dei Magi, the most patrician of the city's religious confraternities, whose annual procession took place at Epiphany. Several of the Medici, inevitably, were prominent members, including Piero de' Medici (Piero il Gottoso – the Gouty), who may have commissioned the pictures. It's known that several of the Medici household are featured in the procession, but putting names to these prettified faces is a problem. The man leading the cavalcade on a white horse is almost certainly Piero, while the figure behind him, in the black cloak, is probably his father, Cosimo il Vecchio. Piero's older son, the future Lorenzo il Magnifico, eleven years old at the time the fresco was painted, is probably the gold-clad young king in the foreground, riding the grey horse detached from the rest of the procession, while his brother, Giuliano, is probably the one preceded by the black bowman, to the left of Cosimo il Vecchio. The artist himself is in the crowd at the rear of the procession, his red beret signed with the words "Opus Benotii" in gold. Finally, the bearded characters among the throng might be portraits of the retinue of the Byzantine emperor John Paleologus III, who had attended the Council of Florence twenty years before the fresco was painted.

### The first floor

Another set of stairs leads from the passageway beside the courtyard up to the **first floor**, where a display case in the lobby of the main gallery contains a *Madonna and Child* by **Filippo Lippi**, one of Cosimo de' Medici's more troublesome protégés. Even as a novice in the convent of Santa Maria del Carmine, Filippo managed to earn himself a reputation as a drunken womanizer: in the words of Vasari, he was "so lustful that he would give anything to enjoy a woman he wanted . . . and if he couldn't buy what he wanted, then he would cool his passion by painting her portrait". Cosimo set up a workshop for him in the Medici palace, from which he often absented himself to go chasing women. On one occasion Cosimo actually locked the artist in the studio, but Filippo escaped down a rope of bed sheets; having cajoled him into returning, Cosimo declared that he would in future manage the painter with "affection and kindness", a policy that seems to have worked more successfully.

The ceiling of the grandiloquent **gallery** glows with Luca Giordano's enthusiastic fresco of *The Apotheosis of the Medici*, from which one can only deduce that Giordano had no sense of shame. Perhaps he had no time to consider the commission – he was known as Luca Fa-presto (Luca Does-It-Quickly). Accompanying Cosimo III on his flight into the ether is his son, the last male Medici, Gian Gastone (d. 1737), who grew to be a man so dissolute and inert that he could rarely summon the energy to get out of bed in the morning.

Even more sumptuous interior decoration can be seen in the **Biblioteca Riccardiana-Moreniana**, on the opposite side of the palace (entered from Via Ginori; Mon–Sat 9am–1pm; free), one of the Riccardi's more successful remodellings. It is still a working library, but brief, silent visits can be made to see the array of gilded eighteenth-century shelves, overlooked by Luca Giordano's allegory of *Intellect Liberated from the Bonds of Ignorance* (1685).

# From the Mercato Centrale to the Fortezza da Basso

The **Mercato Centrale** is Europe's largest covered food hall, built in stone, iron and glass by Giuseppe Mengoni, architect of Milan's famous Galleria. Opened in 1874, it received a major overhaul a century later, reopening in 1980 with a new first floor. Butchers, *alimentari*, tripe-sellers, greengrocers, pasta stalls – they're all gathered under the one roof, and all charging prices lower than you'll readily find elsewhere in the city. Get there close to the end of the working day at 2pm and you'll get some good reductions.

Each day from 8am to 7pm the streets around the Mercato Centrale are thronged with **stalls** selling bags, belts, shoes, trousers – some of it of doubtful quality. This is the busiest of Florence's daily street markets, and a half-hour's immersion in the haggling mass of customers provides as good a break as any from a pursuit of the city's art.

## The Cenacolo di Foligno

One of Florence's more obscure *cenacoli* (Last Suppers), the **Cenacolo di Foligno**, is to be found a short distance from the market at Via Faenza 42, in the ex-convent of the Franciscans of Foligno (Mon, Tues & Sat 9am–noon; free). It was once thought to be by Raphael but is now reckoned to have been painted in the 1490s by Perugino. Certainly it shows many of Perugino's stylistic idiosyncrasies – the figures arranged in flat ranks, their gestures compiled from a repertoire of poses that can be seen in many of his other works.

## The Fortezza da Basso

Beyond Via Faenza, the **Fortezza da Basso** was built to intimidate the people of Florence by the vile Alessandro de' Medici, who ordained himself duke of Florence after a ten-month siege by the army of Charles V and Pope Clement VII (possibly Alessandro's father) had forcibly restored the Medici. Michelangelo, the most talented Florentine architect of the day, had played a major role in the defence of the city during the siege; the job of designing the fortress fell to the more pliant Antonio da Sangallo.

Within a few years the cruelties of Alessandro had become intolerable; a petition to Charles V spoke of the Fortezza da Basso as "a prison and a slaughterhouse for the unhappy citizens". Charles's response to the catalogue of Alessandro's atrocities was to marry his daughter to the tyrant. In the end, another Medici came to the rescue: in 1537 the distantly related **Lorenzaccio de' Medici** stabbed the duke to death as he waited for an amorous assignation in Lorenzaccio's house. The reasons for the murder have never been clear but it seems that Lorenzaccio's mental health was little better than Alessandro's: in his earlier years he and Alessandro had regularly launched lecherous sorties on the city's convents, and he had been expelled from Rome after lopping the heads off statues on the Arch of Constantine. The assassination, however, had favourable consequences for the city: as Alessandro died heirless, the council proposed that the leadership of the Florentine republic should be offered to **Cosimo de' Medici**, the great-grandson of Lorenzo il Magnifico. Subsequent Medici dukes had no need of a citizen-proof fort, and the Fortezza da Basso fell into dereliction after use as a gaol and barracks.

Since 1978 there's been a vast modern shed in the centre of the complex, used for trade fairs and shows such as the *Pitti Moda* fashion jamborees in January and July. The public gardens by the walls are fairly pleasant, if you want an open-air spot to relax before catching a train.

# The San Marco district

Much of central Florence's traffic is funnelled along Via Cavour, the thoroughfare connecting the Duomo area to Piazza della Libertà, a junction of the city's *viali* (ring roads). Except as a place to catch buses out to Fiesole and other points north, the street itself has little to recommend it, but halfway along it lies **Piazza San Marco**, home of the **Museo di San Marco**, a museum devoted chiefly to the paintings of Fra' Angelico. In the same district lies the **Accademia**, a museum that comes second only to the Uffizi in the popularity stakes, because it possesses half a dozen sculptures by **Michelangelo**, among them the *David* – symbol of the city's republican pride and of the illimitable ambition of the Renaissance artist. So great is the public appetite for this one work in particular that you'd be well advised to book tickets in advance (see p.50).

# The Accademia

Florence's first academy of drawing, the Accademia del Disegno, was founded in 1563 by Bronzino, Ammannati and Vasari. Initially based in Santissima Annunziata, it moved in 1764 to Via Ricasoli, and soon afterwards was transformed into a general arts academy, the Accademia di Belle Arti. Twenty years later the Grand Duke Pietro Leopoldo I founded the nearby **Galleria dell'Accademia** (Tues–Sun 8.15am–6.50pm; €6.50, or €9.50 during special exhibitions), filling its rooms with paintings for the edification of the students. Later augmented with pieces from suppressed religious foundations and other sources, the Accademia has an extensive collection of paintings, especially of Florentine work of the fourteenth and fifteenth centuries.

The **picture galleries** which flank the main sculpture hall are quite small and generally unexciting, with copious examples of the work of "Unknown Florentine" and "Follower of . . . ". The pieces likeliest to make an impact are Pontormo's *Venus and Cupid* (1532), painted to a cartoon by Michelangelo; a *Madonna of the Sea* (1470) attributed to Botticelli; and the painted fifteenth-century *Adimari Chest*, showing a Florentine wedding ceremony in the Piazza del Duomo. A cluster of rooms near the exit house gilded religious works from the thirteenth and fourteenth centuries, including an altarpiece of the *Pentecost* by Andrea Orcagna (c.1365).

## Michelangelo's David

Commissioned by the Opera del Duomo in 1501, the **David** was conceived to invoke parallels with Florence's freedom from outside domination (despite the superior force of its enemies), and its recent liberation from Savonarola and the Medici. It's an incomparable show of technical bravura, all the more impressive given the difficulties posed by the marble from which it was carved. The four-metre block of stone – thin, shallow and riddled with cracks – had been quarried from Carrara forty years earlier. Several artists had already attempted to work with it, notably Agostino di Duccio, Andrea Sansovino and Leonardo da Vinci. Michelangelo succeeded where others had failed, completing the work in 1504 when he was still just 29.

Four days and a team of forty men were then required to move the statue from the Opera del Duomo to the site that was eventually chosen for it, in the Piazza della Signoria; another three weeks were needed to raise it onto its plinth. During the move the statue required protection day and night to prevent it being stoned by Medici supporters all too aware of its symbolism. Damage was done a few years later, in 1527, when the Medici were again expelled from the city: a bench, flung from a window of the Palazzo Vecchio by anti-Medici rioters, struck and smashed the left arm, but the pieces were gathered up and reassembled. The statue remained in its outdoor setting, exposed to the elements, until it was sent to the Accademia in 1873, by which time it had lost its gilded hair and the gilded band across its chest. Also missing these days is a skirt of copper leaves added to spare the blushes of Florence's more sensitive citizens.

Thoroughly cleaned in 2002, *David* now occupies a specially built alcove, protected by a glass barrier that was built in 1991, after one of its toes was cracked by a hammer-wielding artist. With its massive head and gangling arms, the *David* looks to some people like a monstrous adolescent, but its proportions would not have appeared so graceless in the setting for which it was conceived: the *David* was commisioned as a piece of monumental sculpture for the Duomo, where it would have been placed at rather higher altitude, and at a greater distance from the public, than the position it occupies in the Accademia's chapel-like space.

## The Slaves

Michelangelo once described the process of carving as being the liberation of the form from within the stone, a notion that seems to be embodied by the remarkable unfinished **Slaves** (or Prisoners). His procedure, clearly demonstrated here, was to cut the figure as if it were a deep relief, and then to free the three-dimensional figure; often his assistants would perform the initial operation, working from the master's pencil marks, so it's possible that Michelangelo's own chisel never actually touched these stones.

Probably carved in the late 1520s, the statues were originally destined for the tomb of Julius II, intended perhaps to symbolize the liberal arts left "enslaved" by Julius's demise. The tomb underwent innumerable permutations before its eventual abandonment, however, and in 1564 the artist's nephew gave the carvings to the Medici, who installed them in the grotto of the Bóboli garden. Four of the original six statues came to the Accademia in 1909. Two others found their way to the Louvre in Paris.

Close by is another unfinished work, *St Matthew* (1505–06), started soon after completion of the *David* as a commission from the Opera del Duomo; they actually requested a full series of the Apostles from Michelangelo, but this is the only one he ever began. It languished half-forgotten in the cathedral vaults until 1831.

# The Museo di San Marco

A whole side of Piazza San Marco is taken up by the Dominican convent and church of San Marco, the former building now the home of the **Museo di San Marco** (Tues–Fri 8.15am–1.50pm, Sat 8.15am–6.50pm; also 1st, 3rd & 5th Mon of month 8.15am–1.50pm, and 2nd & 4th Sun of month 8.15am–6.50pm; €4). The Dominicans acquired the site in 1436, after being forced to move from their former home in Fiesole, and the complex promptly became the recipient of Cosimo's most lavish patronage. In the 1430s he financed Michelozzo's enlargement of the conventual buildings (1437–52), and went on to establish a vast library here. Abashed by the wealth he was transferring to them, the friars of San Marco suggested to Cosimo that he need not continue to support them on such a scale, to which he replied, "Never shall I be able to give God enough to set him down as my debtor." Ironically, the convent became the centre of resistance to the Medici later in the century: Girolamo **Savonarola**, leader of the government of Florence after the expulsion of the Medici in 1494, was the prior of San Marco. In 1537 Duke Cosimo expelled the Dominicans once more, reminding them that it was another Cosimo who had established the building's magnificence in the first place.

Girolamo **Savonarola** was born in 1452, the son of the physician to the Ferrara court. He grew up to be an abstemious and melancholic youth, sleeping on a bare straw mattress and spending much of his time reading the Bible and writing dirges. At the age of 23 he absconded to a Dominican monastery in Bologna, informing his father by letter that he was "unable to endure the evil conduct of the heedless people of Italy".

Within a few years, the Dominicans had dispatched him to preach all over northern Italy, an enterprise which got off to an unpromising start. Not the most attractive of men – he was frail, with a beak of a nose and a blubbery mouth – Savonarola was further hampered by an uningratiating voice and a particularly inelegant way of gesturing. Nonetheless, the intensity of his manner and his message attracted a committed following when he settled permanently in the monastery of **San Marco** in 1489.

By 1491, Savonarola's sermons had become so popular that he was asked to deliver his Lent address in the Duomo. Proclaiming that God was speaking through him, he berated the city for its decadence, for its paintings that made the Virgin "look like a whore", and for the tyranny of its Medici-led government. Following the death of Lorenzo il Magnifico, the rhetoric became even more apocalyptic. "Wait no longer, for there may be no more time for repentance," he told the Duomo congregation, summoning images of plagues, invasions and destruction.

When Charles VIII of France marched into Italy in September 1494 to press his claim to the throne of Naples, Savonarola presented him as the instrument of God's vengeance. Violating Piero de' Medici's declaration of Tuscan neutrality, the French army massacred the garrison at Fivizzano, and Florence prepared for the onslaught, as Savonarola declaimed, "The Sword has descended; the scourge has fallen." With support for resistance ebbing, Piero capitulated to Charles; within days the Medici had fled and their palace had been plundered. Hailed by Savonarola as "the Minister of God, the Minister of Justice", Charles and his vast army passed peacefully through Florence on their way to Rome.

The political vacuum in Florence was filled by the declaration of a **republican constitution**, but Savonarola was now in effect the ruler of the city. Continual decrees were issued from San Marco: profane carnivals were to be outlawed, fasting

As Michelozzo was altering and expanding San Marco, the convent's walls were being decorated by one of its friars and a future prior, **Fra' Angelico**, a Tuscan painter in whom a medieval simplicity of faith was uniquely allied to a Renaissance sophistication of manner. He was born in Vicchio di Mugello (a village in the hills to the northeast of Florence), son of a wealthy landowner, some time between the late 1380s and 1400. He entered the Dominican monastery of nearby Fiesole aged around 20, where he was known as Fra' Giovanni da Fiesole. Already recognized as an accomplished artist, he flourished when he came to San Marco.

Here he was encouraged by the theologian Antonino Pierozzi – the future St Antonine – the convent's first prior and later archbishop of Florence. By the time Fra' Giovanni succeeded Pierozzi as prior, the pictures he had created for the monastery over the course of a decade and others for numerous churches in Florence and elsewhere – principally Orvieto cathedral and the Vatican – had earned him the title "the angelic painter", the name by which he's been known ever since. In 1982 he was beatified (a halfway house to sainthood), thus formalizing the name by which he had long been known, Beato Angelico, or the Blessed Angelico.

was to be observed more frequently, children were to act as the agents of the righteous, informing the authorities whenever their parents transgressed the Eternal Law. Irreligious books and paintings, expensive clothes, cosmetics, mirrors, board games, trivialities and luxuries of all types were destroyed, a ritual purging that reached a crescendo with a colossal **"Bonfire of the Vanities"** on the Piazza della Signoria.

Meanwhile, Charles VIII was installed in Naples and a formidable alliance was being assembled to overthrow him: the papacy, Milan, Venice, Ferdinand of Aragon and the Emperor Maximilian. In July 1495 the army of this Holy League confronted the French and was badly defeated. Charles's army continued northwards back to France, and Savonarola was summoned to the Vatican to explain why he had been unable to join the campaign against the intruder. He declined to attend, claiming that it was not God's will that he should make the journey, and thus set off a chain of exchanges that ended with his **excommunication** in June 1497. Defying Pope Alexander's order, Savonarola celebrated Mass in the Duomo on Christmas Day, which prompted a final threat from Rome: send Savonarola to the Vatican or imprison him in Florence, otherwise the whole city would join him in excommunication.

Despite Savonarola's insistence that the Borgia pope was already consigned to hell, the people of Florence began to desert him. The region's crops had failed, plague had broken out again, and the city was at war with Pisa, which Charles had handed over to its citizens rather than return to Florence's control, as he had promised. The Franciscans of Florence, sceptical of the Dominican monk's claim to divine approval, now issued a terrible challenge. One of their community and one of Savonarola's would walk through an avenue of fire in the Piazza della Signoria: if the Dominican died, then Savonarola would be banished; if the Franciscan died, then Savonarola's main critic, Fra' Francesco da Puglia, would be expelled.

A thunderstorm prevented the trial from taking place, but the mood in the city had anyway turned irrevocably. The following day, Palm Sunday 1498, a siege of the monastery of San Marco ended with Savonarola's **arrest**. Accused of heresy, he was tortured to the point of death, then **burned at the stake** in front of the Palazzo Vecchio, with two of his supporters. When the flames had finally been extinguished, the ashes were thrown into the river, to prevent anyone from gathering them as relics.

## The ground floor

Immediately beyond the **entrance** (marked 1 on the plan) lies the **Chiostro di Sant'Antonino** (2), designed by Michelozzo and now dominated by a vast cedar of Lebanon. Most of the cloister's faded frescoes are sixteenth-century depictions of episodes from the life of Antonino Pierozzi, Angelico's mentor and the convent's first prior. Angelico himself painted the frescoes in its four corners, of which the most striking is the lunette of *St Dominic at the Foot of the Cross* (3).

This weather-bleached work pales alongside the twenty or so paintings by the artist gathered in the **Ospizio dei Pellegrini** (5), or Pilgrims' Hospice, which lies between the cloister and the piazza. Many of the works – including several of Angelico's most famous – were brought here from churches and galleries around Florence; all display the artist's brilliant colouring and spatial clarity, and an air of imperturbable piety. On the right wall as you enter is a *Deposition* (4), 1432–35, originally hung in the church of Santa Trìnita. Commissioned by the Strozzi family, the painting was begun by Lorenzo Monaco, who died after completing the upper trio of triangular pinnacles, and continued by Fra' Angelico. At the opposite end of the room hangs the *Madonna dei Linaiuoli* (6),

Angelico's first major public painting (1433), commissioned by the *linaiuoli* or flax-workers' guild, for their headquarters. The grandiose marble frame is the work of Ghiberti. Halfway down the room, on the inner wall, the so-called *Pala di San Marco* (1440), though badly damaged by the passage of time and a disastrous restoration, demonstrates Fra' Angelico's familiarity with the latest developments in artistic theory. Its figures are arranged in lines that taper towards a central vanishing point, in accordance with the principles laid out in Alberti's *Della Pittura* (*On Painting*), published in Italian just two years before the picture was executed. The work was commissioned by the Medici as an altarpiece for the church of San Marco, hence the presence of the family's patron saints Cosmas and Damian, who can be seen at work as doctors (*medici*), in the small panel immediately to the right.

Back in the cloister, a doorway in its top right-hand corner opens into the **Sala del Lavabo** (7), where the monks washed before eating. Its entrance wall has a *Crucifixion with Saints* by Angelico, and its right wall two panels with a pair of saints, also by Angelico. The left wall contains a damaged lunette fresco of the *Madonna and Child* by Paolo Uccello, plus part of a predella by the same artist. The impressive room to the right, the **Refettorio Grande** (8), or Large Refectory, is dominated by a large fresco of the *Crucifixion* by

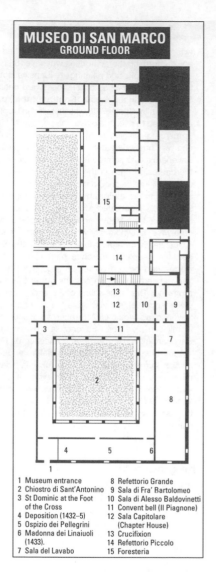

**MUSEO DI SAN MARCO**
GROUND FLOOR

1 Museum entrance
2 Chiostro di Sant'Antonino
3 St Dominic at the Foot of the Cross
4 Deposition (1432–5)
5 Ospizio dei Pellegrini
6 Madonna dei Linaiuoli (1433).
7 Sala del Lavabo
8 Refettorio Grande
9 Sala di Fra' Bartolomeo
10 Sala di Alesso Baldovinetti
11 Convent bell (Il Piagnone)
12 Sala Capitolare (Chapter House)
13 Crucifixion
14 Refettorio Piccolo
15 Foresteria

the sixteenth-century painter Giovanni Sogliani. Of more artistic interest are the rooms devoted to paintings by **Fra' Bartolomeo** (9) and **Alesso Baldovinetti** (10). Note in particular Fra' Bartolomeo's suitably intense portrait of Savonarola, and his unfinished *Pala della Signoria* (1512), originally destined for the Salone dei Cinquecento in the Palazzo Vecchio.

Further round the cloister lies the **Sala Capitolare** (12), or Chapter House, which now houses a large conventual bell, the Piagnone (11), which was rung to summon help on Savonarola's arrest on the eve of April 8, 1498: it became a symbol of anti-Medici sentiment ever after. Here, too, is a powerful fresco of the *Crucifixion* (13), painted by Angelico and assistants in 1441. At the rear of this room, entered via a passageway alongside the Chapter House, lies the **Refettorio Piccolo** (14), or Small Refectory, with a lustrous *Last Supper* (1480) by Ghirlandaio. This forms an anteroom to the **Foresteria** (15), home to the convent's former guest rooms, which is cluttered with architectural bits and pieces salvaged during nineteenth-century urban improvement schemes. The corridor provides good views into the (closed) Chiostro di San Domenico.

## The first floor

Stairs off the cloister by the entrance to the Foresteria lead up to the first floor, where almost immediately you're confronted with one of the most sublime paintings in Italy. For the drama of its setting and the lucidity of its composition, nothing in San Marco matches Angelico's **Annunciation** (A). The pallid, submissive Virgin is one of the most touching images in Renaissance art, and the courteous angel, with his scintillating unfurled wings, is as convincing a heavenly messenger as any ever painted. An inscription on this fresco reminds the passing monks to say a Hail Mary as they venerate the image.

Angelico and his assistants also painted the simple and piously restrained pictures in each of the 44 **dormitory cells** on this floor, into which the brothers would withdraw for solitary contemplation and sleep. Such privacy was a novelty, allowed only after a papal concession of 1419 that freed the Dominicans from sleeping in dormitories. Given the speed with which the monks began their construction, the cells must have been a welcome change, but

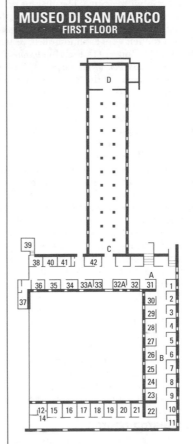

**MUSEO DI SAN MARCO**
FIRST FLOOR

A Annunciation
B Madonna delle Ombre
C Library
D Sala Greca

1 Noli Me Tangere
2 The Body of Christ
3 Annunciation
4 Crucifixion
5 Nativity
6 Transfiguration
7 Mockery of Christ
8 The Marys at the Sepulchre
9 Coronation of the Virgin
10 Presentation in the Temple
11 Madonna and Child with Saints
12-14 Savonarola's cells
22 Crucifixion with the Virgin
23 Crucifixion with the Virgin and St Dominic
24 Baptism of Christ
25 Crucifixion with the Virgin, Magdalen and St Dominic

26 Pietà with St Dominic or St Thomas
27 Christ at the Column with the Virgin and St Dominic
28 Christ Carrying the Cross
29 Crucifixion with the Virgin and St Dominic
30 Crucifixion with the Virgin and St Dominic
31 Christ in Limbo
32 Sermon on the Mount
33 Arrest of Christ
34 Agony in the Garden
35 Institution of the Eucharist
36 Crucifixion
37 Crucifixion
38 Adoration of the Magi
39 Crucifixion with SS. Cosmas and Damian
40 Crucifixion
41 Crucifixion
42 Crucifixion with SS. Mark, Dominic, Mary and Martha

they came with a price. The realism of the frescoes, in particular the copious amounts of blood present in some of the Crucifixion scenes, is said to have caused some of the more timorous monks to faint. The outer cells of the corridor on the left (1–11) almost all have works by Angelico himself – don't miss the *Noli Me Tangere* (1), the *Annunciation* (3), the outstanding *Transfiguration* (6) and the *Coronation of the Virgin* (9). The marvellous **Madonna delle Ombre** (B), or Madonna of the Shadows, on the wall facing these cells, is probably also by Angelico. Several of the scenes include one or both of a pair of monastic onlookers, serving as intermediaries between the occupant of the cell and the personages in the pictures: the one with the star above his head is St Dominic; the one with the split skull is St Peter Martyr (see p.99).

At the end of the far corridor is a knot of rooms (12–14) once occupied by Savonarola. These now contain various relics – a belt, a cape, a torn vest – questionably authenticated as worn by the man himself; most dubious of all is the piece of wood from his funeral pyre, which is depicted in a couple of paintings here. If you turn right at the main *Annunciation* and continue to the end of the corridor you'll come to cells 38 and 39: these more luxuriously appointed retreats were the personal domain of Cosimo de' Medici. The fresco of the *Adoration of the Magi* (38) may well be the work of Angelico's star pupil Benozzo Gozzoli. Its subject may have been suggested by Cosimo himself, who liked to think of himself as a latter-day wise man, or at least as a gift-giving king.

On the way to these VIP cells you'll pass the entrance to **Michelozzo's Library** (C), built in 1441–44 to a design that exudes an atmosphere of calm study, though – as the plaque by the doorway tells you – it was here that Savonarola was finally cornered and arrested in 1498. Cosimo's agents roamed as far as the Near East garnering precious manuscripts and books; in turn, Cosimo handed all the religious items over to the monastery, stipulating that they should be accessible to all, making it Europe's first public library. On the left-hand wall, halfway down, the original green wall paint, a colour held to be conducive to meditation, has been exposed. At the far end, a door leads through to the **Sala Greca** (D; usually open for guided visits on the hour), which was added to house a growing collection of Greek codices.

### San Marco church

Greatly altered since Michelozzo's intervention, the church of **San Marco** (Mon–Sat 9.30am–noon & 4–5.30pm) is worth a quick call for two works on the second and third altars on the right: a *Madonna and Saints* painted in 1509 by Fra' Bartolomeo, and an eighth-century mosaic of *The Madonna in Prayer* (surrounded by later additions), brought here from the Constantine basilica in Rome. This had to be cut in half in transit, and you can still see the break across the Virgin's midriff.

# West and north of Piazza San Marco

Within a couple of minutes' stroll west and north of **Piazza San Marco** are two little-visited art attractions, one of the city's obscurer parks, and a cluster of specialist museums. None would feature in a rushed itinerary, but the first pair in particular are worth the diversion on any high-culture point-to-point.

### The Cenacolo di Sant'Apollonia

Running off the west side of Piazza San Marco, Via degli Arazzieri soon becomes Via XXVII Aprile, where the former Benedictine convent of **Sant'Apollonia** stands at no. 1 (Tues–Sat 8.15am–1.50pm; 2nd & 4th Sun of month and 1st, 3rd & 5th Mon of month same hours; free). Most of the complex has now been turned into apartments, but one entire wall of the former refectory houses Andrea del Castagno's *Last Supper*, one of the most disturbing versions of the event painted in the Renaissance. Blood-red is the dominant tone, and the most commanding figure is the diabolic, black-bearded Judas, who sits on the near side of the table. The seething patterns in the marbled panels behind the Apostles seem to mimic the turmoil in the mind of each, as he hears Christ's announcement of the betrayal. Painted around 1450, the fresco was plastered over by the nuns before being uncovered in the middle of the nineteenth century. Above the illusionistic recess in which the supper takes place are the faded remains of a *Resurrection, Crucifixion and Deposition* by Castagno, revealed when the frescoes were taken off the wall for restoration. The *sinopie* (preparatory drawings) of these and of a *Pietà* are displayed opposite.

## The Chiostro dello Scalzo

To the north of San Marco, at Via Cavour 69, is **Lo Scalzo**, the home of the Brotherhood of St John, whose vows of poverty entailed walking around barefoot (*scalzo*). The order was suppressed in 1785 and their monastery sold off, except for the **cloister** (Mon, Thurs & Sat 8.15am–1.50pm; free). This was the training ground for Andrea del Sarto, an artist venerated in the nineteenth century as a painter with no imperfections, but now regarded with slightly less enthusiasm on account of this very smoothness. His monochrome paintings of the *Cardinal Virtues* and *Scenes from the Life of the Baptist* occupied him off and on for a decade from 1511, beginning with the *Baptism*, finishing with the *Birth of St John*. A couple of the sixteen scenes – *John in the Wilderness* and *John Meeting Christ* – were executed by his pupil Franciabigio in 1518, when del Sarto was away in Paris.

## The Giardino dei Semplici and natural history museums

The **Giardino dei Semplici** or **Orto Botanico** (April–Oct Tues 9am–1pm & 3–6pm, Wed–Fri 9am–1pm; Nov–March Mon–Fri 9am–1pm; €4), northeast of San Marco, was set up in 1545 for Cosimo I as a medicinal garden, following the examples of Padua and Pisa. Entered from Via La Pira, it now covers five acres, most of the area being taken up by the original flowerbeds and avenues. It's the nearest equivalent to the Bóboli garden on the north side of the city, but unfortunately it closes at exactly the time you could use it for a midday break.

The garden entrance at Via Micheli 3 also gives access to a number of **museums** administered by the university. The **Museo Botanico** (currently open only to scholars; ☎055.275.7462), set up for Leopoldo II of Lorraine, contains over four million botanical specimens, supplemented by plaster mushrooms and wax models of plants. Masses of rocks are on show in the **Museo di Minerologia e Litologia** (June–Sept Wed & Fri 9am–1pm; Oct–May Tues 9am–1pm & 2–5pm, Wed–Sat 9am–1pm; €6 joint ticket with the next museum), including a 150-kilo topaz from Brazil and a load of worked stones from the Medici collection – snuff boxes, little vases, a quartz boat. The **Museo di Geologia e Paleontologia** (same hours and ticket as above) is one of Italy's biggest fossil shows, featuring such delights as prehistoric elephant skeletons from the upper Valdarno and a skeleton from Grosseto once touted as the missing link between monkeys and *Homo sapiens*. There's a plan to move all these natural history museums into a new home on Via Circondaria, making what will be the largest museum of its kind in Italy, but the project has spent years stuck on the drawing board.

# Piazza Santissima Annunziata

Nineteenth-century urban renewal schemes left many of Florence's squares rather grim places, which makes the pedestrianized **Piazza Santissima Annunziata**, with its distinctive arcades, all the more attractive a public space. It has a special importance for the city, too. Until the end of the eighteenth century the Florentine year used to begin on March 25, the Festival of the Annunciation – hence the Florentine predilection for paintings of the Annunciation, and the fashionableness of the Annunziata church, which has long been the place for society weddings. The festival is still marked by a huge fair in the piazza and the streets leading off it; later in the year, on the first weekend in September, the square is used for Tuscany's largest crafts fair.

△ Pietro Tacca's fountain

Brunelleschi began the piazza in the 1420s, with additions made later by Ammannati and Antonio da Sangallo. The equestrian **statue** of Grand Duke Ferdinand I (1608) at its centre was Giambologna's final work, and was cast by his pupil Pietro Tacca from cannons captured at the Battle of Lepanto. Tacca was also the creator of the bizarre **fountains** (1629), on each of which a pair of aquatic monkeys spit water at two whiskered sea slugs.

## The Spedale degli Innocenti

Piazza Santissima Annunziata's tone is set by the **Spedale degli Innocenti**, or Ospedale (Mon, Tues & Thurs–Sun 8.30am–2pm; €4). Commissioned in 1419 by the *Arte della Seta*, the silk-weavers' guild, it opened in 1445 as the first foundlings' hospital in Europe, and is still an orphanage today. It was largely designed by Brunelleschi (whose activity as a goldsmith, strangely, allowed him membership of the guild), and his nine-arched loggia was one of Europe's earliest examples of the new classically influenced style.

Andrea della Robbia's blue-backed ceramic tondi (1487) of well-swaddled babies advertise the building's function, but their gaiety belies the misery associated with it. Slavery was part of the Florentine economy as late as the fifteenth century (it's probable that Leonardo da Vinci's mother was a slave), and many of the infants given over to the care of the Innocenti were born to domestic slaves. A far-from-untypical entry in the Innocenti archives records the abandonment of twins "from the house of Agostino Capponi, born of Polonia his slave . . . They arrived half dead: if they had been two dogs they would have been better cared for." From 1660 children could be abandoned anonymously in the *rota*, a small revolving door whose bricked-up remains are still visible at the extreme left of the facade; it remained in use until 1875.

The building within centres on two beautiful cloisters, Brunelleschi's central **Chiostro degli Uomini** (Men's Cloister) and the narrow, graceful **Chiostro delle Donne** (Women's Cloister) to the right. Stairs from the left-hand corner of the former lead up to the **museum**, a miscellany of Florentine Renaissance art that includes some of Luca della Robbia's most beguiling Madonnas and an *Adoration of the Magi* (1488) by Domenico Ghirlandaio. The latter, commissioned as the altarpiece of the building's church, features a background depicting the *Massacre of the Innocents*. The parallel of the slaughter of Bethlehem's first-born with the orphanage's foundlings, or *innocenti*, was deliberately made.

## Santissima Annunziata

**Santissima Annunziata** (daily 7am–12.30pm & 4–6.30pm) is the mother church of the Servites, or Servi di Maria (Servants of Mary), a religious order founded by Filippo Benizzi and six Florentine aristocrats in 1234. From humble beginnings, the order blossomed after 1252, when a painting of the Virgin begun by one of the monks – abandoned in despair because of his inability to create a truly beautiful image – was completed by an angel while he slept. So many people came to venerate the image that by 1444 a new church, financed by the Medici, was commissioned from Michelozzo (who happened to be the brother of the Servites' head prior). The project, completed by Leon Battista Alberti in 1481, involved laying out the present-day Via dei Servi, designed to link Santissima Annunziata and the cathedral, thus uniting the city's two most important churches dedicated to the Madonna.

## The Chiostrino dei Voti

As the number of pilgrims to the church increased, so it became a custom to leave wax votive offerings (*voti*) in honour of its miraculous Madonna. In the early days these were placed around the walls. Later they were hung from the nave ceiling. Eventually they became so numerous that in 1447 a special atrium, the **Chiostrino dei Voti**, was built onto the church. In time this came to house some six hundred statues, some of them life-sized depictions of the donor, with full-sized wax horse in close attendance. The collection was one of the city's great tourist attractions until 1786, when the whole lot was melted down to make candles.

More lasting alterations to the cloister's appearance, in the shape of a major **fresco cycle**, were made in 1516 on the occasion of the canonization of Filippo Benizzi, the Servites' founding father. Three leading artists of the day, Andrea del Sarto, Jacopo Pontormo and Rosso Fiorentino, were involved, together with several lesser painters. Some of the panels are in a poor state – all were removed from the walls and restored after the 1966 flood (see p.143) – but their overall effect is superb.

The entrance wall, together with the right (south) and far (east) walls, depict scenes from the *Life of the Virgin* – an obvious theme given the church's Marian dedication – while the remaining two walls portray scenes from the *Life of St*

**SANTISSIMA ANNUNZIATA: CHIOSTRINO DEI VOTI**

PIAZZA SANTISSIMA ANNUNZIATA

1 Assumption (1513–4), Rosso Fiorentino
2 Visitation (1514–6), Pontormo
3 Marriage of the Virgin (1513), Franciabigio
4 The Birth of the Virgin (1511), Andrea del Sarto
5 Journey of the Magi (1511), Andrea del Sarto
6 Nativity (1460–2), Alesso Baldovinetti
7 Vocation and Investiture of San Filippo Benizzi (1476), Cosimo Rosselli
8 The Saint Covers a Leper with His Shirt (1509–10), Andrea del Sarto

9 The Saint Punishes Blasphemers (1509–10), Andrea del Sarto
10 The Saint Cures a Possessed Woman (1509–10), Andrea del Sarto
11 The Saint Raises a Child (1509–10), Andrea del Sarto
12 The Saint Cures a Sick Child (1509–10), Andrea del Sarto

A  Main entrance
B  Entrance to Chiostro dei Morti
C  Entrance to church

*Filippo Benizzi.* Moving right around the cloister, the sequence works backwards from the Virgin's death, beginning with an **Assumption** (1) by Rosso Fiorentino, one of his first works, painted when he was aged around 19. The authorities immediately found fault with it (for one thing, the *putti* bearing Mary to heaven seem to be having an unseemly amount of fun), asking Andrea del Sarto to paint a new version over it, but in the event it was never altered.

Alongside lies Pontormo's **Visitation** (2), which was said to have taken some eighteen months to paint; del Sarto's **Journey of the Magi** (5), by contrast, across the atrium, took a little over three months. In the next alcove note Franciabigio's **Marriage of the Virgin** (3), in which the painter is said to have taken a hammer to the Virgin's face: apparently he was angry at the monks for having secretly looked at the work before its completion; after the artist's tantrum no one had the courage to repair the damage.

Before the next lunette comes a fine marble bas-relief of the *Madonna and Child* attributed to Michelozzo, followed by the cloister's masterpiece, Andrea del Sarto's **Birth of the Virgin** (4). To the right of the large church door is the same artist's **Journey of the Magi** (5), which includes a self-portrait in the right-hand corner. Left of the door lies Alesso Baldovinetti's **Nativity** (6), its faded appearance the result of poor initial preparation on the part of the artist. The sequence devoted to Filippo Benizzi begins on the next wall with Cosimo Rosselli's **Vocation and Investiture of the Saint** (7); the five remaining damaged panels (8–12) are all the work of Andrea del Sarto.

## The interior

Few Florentine interiors are as striking at first sight as Santissima Annunziata, but in order to be sure of seeing it you should visit in the afternoon: this church commands the devotion of a large congregation, and there are Masses every hour all morning. Beyond the startling first impression made by the gilt and stucco gloss that was applied in the seventeenth and eighteenth centuries, the church contains few genuine treasures. One notable exception is the ornate **tabernacle** (1448–61) immediately on your left as you enter, designed by Michelozzo to house the miraculous image of the Madonna. Michelozzo's patron, Piero di Cosimo de' Medici, made sure that nobody remained unaware of the money he sank into the shrine: an inscription reads *Costò fior. 4 mila el marmo solo* ("The marble alone cost 4000 florins"). The painting encased in the marble has been repainted into illegibility, and is usually kept covered anyway. It is further obscured by a vast array of lamps, candles and votive offerings: Florentine brides still traditionally visit the shrine to leave their bridal bouquets with the Madonna.

To the tabernacle's right lies a chapel (1453–63) originally created as an oratory for the Medici, adorned with five panels of inlaid stone depicting the Virgin's principal symbols (sun, moon, star, lily and rose) and a small picture of the *Redeemer* (1515) by Andrea del Sarto. Piero de' Medici loaned out the space to visiting dignitaries to allow them a privileged view of the Madonna.

The **Cappella Feroni**, next door, features a restrained fresco by Andrea del Castagno of *Christ and St Julian* (1455–56). The adjacent chapel contains a more striking fresco by the same artist, the *Holy Trinity and St Jerome* (1454). Now restored, both frescoes were obliterated after Vasari spread the rumour that Castagno had poisoned his erstwhile friend, Domenico Veneziano, motivated by envy of the other's skill with oil paint. Castagno was saddled with this crime until the nineteenth century, when an archivist discovered that the alleged murderer in fact predeceased his victim by four years.

Separated from the nave by a triumphal arch is the unusual **tribune**, begun by Michelozzo but completed to designs by Alberti; you get into it along a corridor from the north transept. The chapel at the farthest point was altered by Giambologna into a monument to himself, complete with bronze reliefs and a crucifix by the sculptor. The chapel to its left contains a sizeable *Resurrection* (1550) by Bronzino. Look out, too, for the magnificent **organ** at the head of the aisle; built in 1628, it's the city's oldest and the second oldest in Italy.

The spacious **Chiostro dei Morti** is worth visiting for Andrea del Sarto's intimate *Madonna del Sacco* (1525), over the door that opens from the north transept (if you can't find the sacristan to open it, you may be able to enter the cloister from the street – the entrance is to the left of the main entrance); depicting the *Rest during the Flight into Egypt*, the picture takes its curious name from the sack on which St Joseph is leaning.

## The Museo Archeologico

On the other side of Via della Colonna from the side wall of Santissima Annunziata, the **Museo Archeologico** (Mon 2–7pm, Tues & Thurs 8.30am–7pm, Wed & Fri–Sun 8.30am–2pm; €4) houses the most important collection of its kind in northern Italy. It suffered terrible damage in the flood of 1966 and the task of restoring the exhibits is still not quite finished, so the arrangement of the rooms is subject to sudden changes.

Its special strength is its **Etruscan** finds, many of them part of the Medici bequest. On the ground floor there's a comprehensive display of Etruscan funerary figures, but even more arresting than these is the *François Vase*, an Attic krater (bowl) from the sixth century BC, discovered in an Etruscan tomb at Chiusi. Pride of place in the first-floor **Egyptian collection**, where the rooms are handsomely decorated in mock-Egyptian funerary style, goes to a Hittite chariot made of bone and wood and dating from the fourteenth century BC. The grisly exposed mummies may be popular with children.

The rest of this floor and much of the floor above are given over to the **Etruscan, Greek and Roman collections**, arranged with variable clarity. Of the Roman pieces the outstanding item is the *Idolino*, probably a copy of a fifth-century BC Greek original. Nearby is a massive Hellenistic horse's head, which once adorned the garden of the Palazzo Medici, where it was studied by

---

### The Museo Stibbert

About 1500m north of San Marco, at Via Stibbert 26 (bus #4 from the station), is the loopiest of Florence's museums, the **Museo Stibbert** (Mon–Wed 10am–2pm, Fri–Sun 10am–6pm; guided tour €5). This rambling, murky mansion was the home of the half-Scottish half-Italian Frederick Stibbert, who in his twenties made a name for himself in Garibaldi's army. Later he inherited a fourteenth-century house from his mother, then bought the neighbouring mansion and joined the two together, thus creating a place big enough to accommodate the fruits of his compulsive collecting. The 64 rooms contain over fifty thousand items, ranging from snuff boxes to paintings by Carlo Crivelli and a possible Botticelli.

Militaria were Frederick's chief enthusiasm, and the Stibbert **armour** collection is reckoned one of the world's best. It includes Roman, Etruscan and Japanese examples (the highlight of the whole museum), as well as a fifteenth-century *condottiere*'s outfit and the armour worn by the great Medici commander Giovanni delle Bande Nere, retrieved from his grave in San Lorenzo in 1857. The big production number comes in the great hall, between the two houses, where a platoon of mannequins is clad in full sixteenth-century gear. Also on show is the regalia in which Napoleon was crowned king of Italy.

Donatello and Verrocchio. In the long gallery you'll find the best of the Etrus-can pieces: the *Arringatore* (Orator), the only known Etruscan large bronze from the Hellenistic period, and the *Chimera*, a triple-headed monster of the fifth century BC. A symbol of the three-season pre-Christian Mediterranean year, the *Chimera* was much admired by Cosimo I's retinue of Mannerist artists and all subsequent connoisseurs of the offbeat.

# 5

# East of the centre: from the Bargello to Campo di Marte

The dense network of streets northeast of the Piazza della Signoria is dominated by the campanile of the **Badìa Fiorentina**, the most important of several buildings in the area that have the strongest associations with Florence's – indeed Italy's – foremost poet, Dante Alighieri. Immediately opposite the church stands the forbidding bulk of the **Bargello**, once the city's prison, now home to a superb assemblage of sculpture, plus excellent collections of enamels, ivories, glassware, silverware and other *objets d'art*. To get a full idea of the achievement of the Florentine Renaissance, a visit to the Bargello is as important as a day in the Uffizi, and as a corrective to the notion that Florence's contribution to European civilization has been limited to the arts, you should call in at the fascinating **Museo di Storia della Scienza** at the back of the Uffizi. Further east rises the vast Franciscan church of **Santa Croce**, whose architecture and frescoes make it one of the most compelling sights in Florence. The church is the centrepiece of a district that was one of Florence's more densely populated areas before November 4, 1966, when the Arno burst its banks and the low-lying Santa Croce area, packed with tenements and small workshops, was very badly damaged. Many residents moved out permanently in the following years, but now the more traditional shops, bars and restaurants that survived the flood have been joined by a growing number of new and often extremely good bars and restaurants, a transformation that's particularly noticeable around the **Sant'Ambrogio** market. In addition to the great church and its museum, the other main cultural attractions in this part of the city are the **Museo Horne**, a modest but pleasing collection of art treasures, and the **Casa Buonarroti**, a less than entirely satisfying homage to Michelangelo.

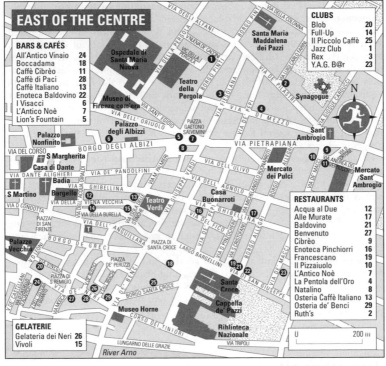

# The Museo di Storia della Scienza

Down the Uffizi's east flank runs Via dei Leoni, named after the lions that were once housed in this street. When the ancestors of these ferocious mascots were brought to the city, in the thirteenth century, they were caged close to the Baptistery, on the site now occupied by the Loggia del Bigallo. In 1319 the lions were moved into an enclosure on Piazza della Signoria, whence they were in turn evicted half a century later, to make way for the Loggia dei Lanzi. They remained in their new quarters on Via dei Leoni until the time of Cosimo I, whose wife – Eleanor of Toledo – insisted that the malodorous and raucous beasts had to go.

At the river end, the street opens into Piazza dei Giudici, so called from the tribunal that used to meet in the building now housing the city's science museum, the **Museo di Storia della Scienza** (Mon & Wed–Fri 9.30am–5pm, Tues & Sat 9.30am–1pm; Oct–May open Sat till 5pm and 2nd Sun of month 10am–1pm; €7.50). Long after Florence had declined from its artistic apogee, the intellectual reputation of the city was maintained by its scientists, many of them directly encouraged by the ruling Medici-Lorraine dynasty. Two of the latter, Grand Duke Ferdinando II and his brother Leopoldo, both of whom studied with Galileo, founded a scientific academy at the Pitti in 1657. Called the Accademia del Cimento (Academy of Experiment), its motto was "Try and try again". The instruments made and acquired by this academy are the core of the museum.

The first eleven exhibition rooms feature **measuring instruments**, notably a selection of beautiful Arab astrolabes. There's also a massive armillary sphere made for Ferdinando I to provide a visual demonstration of the supposed veracity of the earth-centred Ptolemaic system and the fallacy of Copernicus's heliocentric universe. Galileo's original instruments are on show here, such as the lens with which he discovered the four moons of Jupiter (which he tactfully named the Medicean planets). On this floor you'll also find the museum's equivalent of a religious relic – a bone from one of Galileo's fingers. Other cases display items belonging to Michelangelo, and objects such as ancient quadrants and calculating machines that have the beauty of works of art. The most impressive of several fascinating rooms is Room 7, filled with dozens of gorgeous globes and old maps.

On the floor above there are all kinds of **scientific and mechanical equipment**, some – such as a perpetual motion machine – from the quasi-magical realms of scientific endeavour. Room 12 sets the tone, with dozens of old clocks and timepieces. There are also a couple of remarkable outsized exhibits: the huge lens made for Cosimo III, with which Faraday and Davy managed to ignite a diamond by focusing the rays of the sun, and the enormous lodestone given by Galileo to Ferdinando II. Other rooms feature pharmaceutical and chemical apparatus.

The best is saved for last: a **medical section** full of alarming surgical instruments and anatomical wax models for teaching obstetrics. Room 19 concludes with the contents of a medieval pharmacy, displaying such unlikely cure-alls as Sangue del Drago (Dragon's Blood) and Confetti di Seme Santo (Confections of Blessed Seed).

# The Bargello

In Renaissance Florence, sculpture assumed an importance unmatched in any other part of Italy, perhaps because this most public of arts was especially appropriate to a city with such a highly developed sense of itself as a special and cohesive community. On a less abstract level, Florence is surrounded by quarries, and the art of stonecutting had always been nurtured here. Whatever the reason for this pre-eminence, the Renaissance sculpture collection of the **Museo Nazionale del Bargello** (Tues–Sat 8.15am–1.50pm; 2nd & 4th Sun of month and 1st, 3rd & 5th Mon of month same hours; €4), at Via del Proconsolo 4, is the richest in Italy. Sculpture apart, the museum also devotes a vast amount of space to the decorative arts: superb carpets, enamels, ivories, glassware, tapestries, silverware and other *objets d'art*. Although they receive scant attention from most visitors, it would be as easy to spend as much time on the dozen or more rooms filled with these treasures as the four rooms devoted to sculpture.

The Bargello's home, the daunting Palazzo del Bargello, was built in 1255 immediately after the overthrow of the aristocratic regime. The first of the city's public palaces, it soon became the seat of the *Podestà*, the city's chief magistrate, and the site of the main law court. Numerous malefactors were tortured, tried, sentenced and executed here, the elegant courtyard having been the site of the city's gallows and block. The building acquired its present name after 1574, when the Medici abolished the post of *Podestà*, the building becoming home to the chief of police – the *Bargello*. Torture and capital punishment were banned in 1786 (the first such abolition in Europe), though the building remained a prison until 1859.

△ The Bargello

## The ground floor

You've no time to catch your breath in the Bargello: the first room to the right of the ticket office is crammed with treasures, chief of which are the work of **Michelangelo**, in whose shadow every Florentine sculptor laboured from the sixteenth century onwards. The tipsy, soft-bellied figure of *Bacchus* (1496–97) was his first major sculpture, carved at the age of 22, a year or so before his great *Pietà* in Rome. Michelangelo's style later evolved into something less immediately striking, as is shown by the delicate *Tondo Pitti* of the Madonna and Child (1503–05). The square-jawed *Bust of Brutus* (1539–40) is the artist's sole work of this kind; a powerful portrait sketch in stone, it's a coded celebration of anti-Medicean republicanism, carved soon after the murder of the nightmarish Duke Alessandro de' Medici (see p.119).

Works by Michelangelo's followers and contemporaries are ranged in the immediate vicinity; some of them would command prolonged attention in less exalted company. **Benvenuto Cellini**'s huge *Bust of Cosimo I* (1545–47), his first work in bronze, was a sort of technical trial for the casting of the *Perseus*, his most famous work. Alongside the two preparatory models for the *Perseus* in wax and bronze are displayed the original marble base and four statuettes that comprise the statue's pedestal; *Perseus* himself still stands in his intended spot, in the Loggia della Signoria.

Close by, **Giambologna**'s voluptuous *Florence Defeating Pisa* (1575) – a disingenuous pretext for a glamour display if ever there were one – takes up a lot of space, but is eclipsed by his best-known creation, the wonderful *Mercury* (1564), a nimble figure with no bad angles. Comic relief is provided by the reliably inept Bandinelli, whose coiffured *Adam and Eve* look like a grandee and his wife taking an *au naturel* stroll through their country estate. The powerfully erotic *Leda and the Swan* by **Ammannati** (1540–50) was inspired by a painting of the subject by Michelangelo that was later destroyed.

Part two of the ground floor's collection lies across the Gothic **courtyard**, which is plastered with the coats of arms of the *Podestà*. Against the far wall stand six allegorical figures by Ammannati from the fountain of the Palazzo Pitti courtyard. Of the two rooms across the yard, the one to the left features largely fourteenth-century works, notably pieces by Arnolfo di Cambio and Tino da Camaino; temporary exhibitions are often held in the room to the right.

## The first floor

At the top of Giuliano da Sangallo's courtyard **staircase** (1502), the first-floor loggia has been turned into a menagerie for Giambologna's quaint bronze animals and birds, imported from the Medici villa at Castello, just outside Florence. The nearer doorway to the right opens into the tall, Gothic **Salone del Consiglio Generale**, the museum's second key room. Here again the number of masterpieces is breathtaking, though this time the presiding genius is **Donatello**, the fountainhead of Renaissance sculpture.

Vestiges of the sinuous Gothic manner are evident in the drapery of his marble *David* (1408), but there's nothing antiquated in the **St George** (1416), carved for the tabernacle of the armourers' guild at Orsanmichele and installed in a replica of its original niche at the far end of the room. If any one sculpture could be said to embody the shift of sensibility that occurred in quattrocento Florence, this is it: whereas St George had previously been little more than a symbol of valour, this alert, tensed figure represents not the act of heroism but the volition behind it. The slaying of the dragon is depicted in the small, badly eroded marble panel underneath, a piece as revolutionary as the figure of the saint, with its seamless interweaving of foreground and background.

Also here is the sexually ambivalent bronze **David**, the first freestanding nude figure created since classical times (1430–40). A decade later the sculptor produced the strange prancing figure known as *Amor-Atys*, afterwards mistaken for a genuine statue from classical antiquity. This was the highest compliment the artist could have wished for – as is attested by the story of Michelangelo's heaping soil over one of his first works, a sleeping cupid, in order to give it the appearance of an unearthed ancient piece. Donatello was just as comfortable with portraiture as with Christian or pagan imagery, as his breathtakingly vivid terracotta *Bust of Niccolò da Uzzano* demonstrates; it may be the earliest Renaissance portrait bust. When the occasion demanded, Donatello could also produce a straightforwardly monumental piece like the nearby *Marzocco* (1418–20), Florence's heraldic lion.

Donatello's master, **Ghiberti**, is represented by his relief of *Abraham's Sacrifice*, his entry in the competition to design the Baptistery doors in 1401, easily missed on the right-hand wall; the treatment of the theme submitted by

Brunelleschi, effectively the runner-up, is hung alongside. Set around the walls of the room, **Luca della Robbia**'s simple sweet-natured humanism is embodied in a sequence of glazed terracotta Madonnas.

The rest of this floor is occupied by a superb collection of European and Islamic applied art, with dazzling specimens of work in enamel, glass, silver, majolica and ivory: among the ivory pieces from Byzantium and medieval France you'll find combs, boxes, chess pieces, and devotional panels featuring scores of figures crammed into a space the size of a paperback. Room 9, the **Cappella di Santa Maria Maddalena**, is decorated with frescoes discovered in 1841 when the room was converted from a prison cell; long attributed to Giotto, they're now thought to be by followers. The scenes from *Paradiso* on the altar (end) wall feature a portrait of Dante holding *The Divine Comedy* – he's the figure in maroon in the right-hand group, fifth from the left. The chapel's beautiful pulpit, lectern and stalls (1483–88) all came from San Miniato al Monte (see p.168), while the impressive altar triptych is a mid-fifteenth-century work by Giovanni di Francesco.

## The second floor

Sculpture resumes upstairs, with rooms devoted to the della Robbia family, a prelude to the **Sala dei Bronzetti**, Italy's best assembly of small Renaissance bronzes. Giambologna's spiralling designs predominate, a testament to his popularity in late sixteenth-century Florence: look out for the *Hercules* series (Ercole, in Italian), showing the hero variously wrestling and clubbing his opponents into submission. An interesting contrast is provided by **Antonio del Pollaiuolo**'s earlier and much more violent *Hercules and Antaeus* (c.1478), which stands on a pillar nearby. Like Leonardo, Pollaiuolo unravelled the complexities of human musculature by dissecting corpses.

Also on this floor there's a splendid display of bronze medals, featuring specimens from the great pioneer of this form of portable art, Pisanello, among whose coin-sized portraits you'll see Leonello d'Este (the lord of Ferrara), Sigismondo Malatesta (the lord of Rimini) and John Paleologus III (the penultimate emperor of Byzantium). Lastly, there's a room devoted mainly to **Renaissance portrait busts**, including Mino da Fiesole's busts of Giovanni de' Medici and Piero il Gottoso (the sons of Cosimo de' Medici). Antonio del Pollaiuolo's *Young Cavalier* is probably another thinly disguised Medici portrait, while the bust labelled *Ritratto d'Ignoto* (Portrait of an Unknown Man), beside Verrocchio's *Madonna and Child*, may in fact depict the face of Macchiavelli. Also outstanding are Francesco Laurana's *Battista Sforza*, an interesting comparison with the Piero della Francesca portrait in the Uffizi, and the *Woman Holding Flowers* by Verrocchio. The centre of the room is shared by Verrocchio's *David*, clearly influenced by the Donatello figure downstairs, and a wooden crucifix (c.1471) attributed to the same artist.

# The Badìa Fiorentina

Directly opposite the Bargello lies the **Badìa Fiorentina**, now approaching the end of many years of restoration. Tourist visits are allowed on Monday afternoons (3–6pm); at other times the church is open for prayer only, following the monastic rules of the Fraternity of Jerusalem, whose church this is.

The dark interior and fresco-covered cloister are well worth a few minutes. The *Badìa* (Abbey) is also a place of reverence for admirers of **Dante**, for this was the parish church of Beatrice Portinari, for whom he conceived a lifelong love as he watched her at Mass here. Furthermore, it was here that Boccaccio delivered his celebrated lectures on Dante's theological epic.

Founded in 978 by Willa, widow of the Margrave of Tuscany, in honour of her husband, the Badìa was one of the focal buildings in medieval Florence: the city's sick were treated in a hospital founded here in 1031, while the main bell marked the divisions of the working day. The hospital also owed much to Willa's son, Ugo, who further endowed his mother's foundation after a vision of the hellish torments which awaited him by "reason of his worldly life, unless he should repent". The 1280s saw the church overhauled along Cistercian Gothic lines, probably under the direction of Arnolfo di Cambio, architect of the Duomo and Palazzo Vecchio. Only a few years later, in 1307, part of the new structure was demolished as punishment of the resident monks for refusal to pay a tax. Later Baroque additions smothered much of the old church in 1627, though the narrow **campanile** – Romanesque at its base, Gothic towards its apex – escaped unharmed. Completed between 1310 and 1330, it remains a prominent feature of the Florentine skyline.

On the left, as you enter from Via Dante Alighieri, hangs **Filippino Lippi**'s superb *Apparition of the Virgin to St Bernard*, painted in 1485 for the Benedictine monastery at Campora and commissioned by Piero del Pugliese: Lippi has included a portrait of the donor at the bottom of the painting, which is still enclosed by its original frame. Bernard is shown in the act of writing a homily aimed at those caught between the "rocks" of tribulation and the "chains" of sin; the presence of the four monks reinforces the message that redemption lies in the contemplative life.

Set back to the right is the church's second highlight, the **tomb monument** to Ugo, sculpted by Mino da Fiesole between 1469 and 1481. Mino was also responsible for the nearby tomb of Bernardo Giugni and an altar frontal of the *Madonna and Child with SS Leonard and Lawrence*. Giugni was a lawyer and diplomat, hence the figures of Justice and Faith accompanying his effigy.

A staircase leads from the choir – take the door immediately right of the high altar – to the upper storey of the **Chiostro degli Aranci** (Cloister of the Oranges), named after the fruit trees that used to be grown here. Two of its flanks are graced with an anonymous but highly distinctive fresco cycle (1436–39) on the life of St Benedict. A later panel – showing the saint throwing himself into bushes to resist temptation – is by the young Bronzino (1526–28). The cloister itself (1432–38) is the work of Bernardo Rossellino, one of the leading lights of early Renaissance architecture.

# Dante's district

After visiting the Badìa Fiorentina, you might want to explore the city's knot of buildings with **Dante** associations – some of them admittedly spurious – that cluster together in the grid of minor streets behind the Badìa, between Piazza del Duomo and Piazza della Signoria. Start your peregrinations at the Baptistery, Dante's "bel San Giovanni", and one of only three Florentine churches mentioned by the poet. Nearby, south of the Duomo, search out the so-called **Sasso di Dante** (Dante's Stone), set between Via dello Studio and Via del

Proconsolo. Dante is supposed to have sat here and watched the construction of the cathedral. Walk down Via dello Studio, and at its junction with Via del Corso lies the **Palazzo Salviati**, site of Beatrice's former home. The courtyard still contains the so-called *Nicchia di Dante* (Dante's Niche), from which the young Dante is said to have watched his *inamorata*.

Cross Via del Corso from the Palazzo Salviati then head down Via Santa Margherita and you come to a small piazza fronting the **Casa di Dante** (summer: Mon & Wed–Sat 10am–6pm, Sun 10am–2pm; winter Mon & Wed–Sat 10am–4pm, Sun 10am–2pm; €2.60). Somewhat fraudulently marketed as Dante's house, the building is actually a medieval pastiche dating from 1910. The modest museum upstairs (frequently closed for restoration) is a homage to the poet rather than a shrine: it contains nothing directly related to his life,

---

## Dante Alighieri

**Dante** signed himself "Dante Alighieri, a Florentine by birth but not by character", a bitter allusion to the city he served as a politician but which later cast him into exile and was to inspire some of the most vitriolic passages in his great epic poem, *La Divina Commedia* (The Divine Comedy).

The poet was born in 1265 into a minor and impoverished noble family. He was educated at Bologna and later at Padua, where he studied philosophy and astronomy. The defining moment in his life came in 1274 when he met the 8-year-old **Beatrice Portinari**, a young girl whom Boccaccio described as possessed of "habits and language more serious and modest than her age warranted". Her features were "so delicate and so beautifully formed," he went on, "and full, besides mere beauty, of so much candid loveliness that many thought her almost an angel."

Dante – just 9 at the time of the meeting – later described his own feeling following the encounter: "Love ruled my soul," he wrote, "and began to hold such sway over me... that it was necessary for me to do completely all his pleasure. He commanded me often that I should endeavour to see this so youthful angel, and I saw in her such noble and praiseworthy deportment that truly of her might be said these words of the poet Homer – *She appeared to be born not of mortal man but of God*."

Unhappily, Beatrice's family had decided their daughter was to marry someone else – Simone de' Bardi. The ceremony took place when she was 17; seven years later she was dead. Dante, for his part, had been promised – aged 12 – to Gemma Donati. The wedding took place in 1295, when the poet was 30.

His romantic hopes dashed, Dante settled down to a military and political career. In 1289 he fought for Florence against Arezzo and helped in a campaign against Pisa. Later he joined the Apothecaries' Guild, serving on a variety of minor civic committees. In 1300 he was dispatched to San Gimignano, where he was entrusted with the job of coaxing the town into an alliance against Pope Boniface VIII, who had designs on Tuscany. In June of the same year he sought to settle the widening breach between the **Black** (anti-imperial) and **White** (more conciliatory) factions of Florence's ruling Guelph party. The dispute had its roots in money: the Whites contained leading bankers to the imperial powers (the Cerchi, Mozzi, Davanzati and Frescobaldi), while the Blacks counted the Pazzi, Bardi and Donati amongst their number, all prominent papal bankers. Boniface, not surprisingly, sided with the Blacks, who eventually emerged triumphant.

Dante's White sympathies sealed his fate. In 1302, following trumped-up charges of corruption, he was sentenced with other Whites to two years' exile. While many of the deportees subsequently returned, Dante rejected his city of "self-made men and fast-got gain". He wandered instead between Forlì, Verona, Padua, Luni and Venice, writing much of *The Divine Comedy* as he went, before finally settling in Ravenna, where he died in 1321.

and in all likelihood Dante was born not on the house's site but somewhere in the street that bears his name. Numerous editions of the *Divina Commedia* are on show – including a poster printed with the whole text in minuscule type – along with copies of Botticelli's illustrations to the poem.

As contentious as the Casa di Dante's claims is the story that Dante married Gemma Donati in **Santa Margherita de' Cerchi** (Mon–Sat 10am–noon & 3–6pm, Sun 10am–noon), the ancient little church up the street from the Casa di Dante on the right. Documented as early as 1032, the building does, however, contain several tombs belonging to the Portinari, Beatrice's family name; the porch also features the Donati family crest, as this was also their local parish church. These are probably the limits of the Dantesque associations, though the church is worth a look anyway, chiefly for a nice altarpiece of the *Madonna and Four Saints* by Neri di Bicci.

Over Via Dante Alighieri from the poet's house, on Piazza San Martino, lies the tiny **San Martino del Vescovo** (Mon–Thurs & Sat 10am–noon & 3–5pm, Fri 10am–noon), built on the site of a small oratory founded in 986 that served as the Alighieri's parish church. Rebuilt in 1479, it later became the headquarters of the Compagnia di Buonomini, a charitable body dedicated to aiding impoverished better-class citizens for whom begging was too demeaning a prospect. The Buonomini commissioned from Ghirlandaio's workshop a sequence of frescoes showing various altruistic acts and scenes from the life of St Martin, and the result is as absorbing a record of daily life in Renaissance Florence as the Ghirlandaio frescoes in Santa Maria Novella. The chapel also contains a couple of fine Madonnas, one Byzantine, the other probably by Niccolò Soggia, a pupil of Perugino.

Opposite San Martino soars the thirteenth-century **Torre della Castagna**, meeting place of the city's *priori* before they decamped to the Palazzo Vecchio. This is one of the most striking remnants of Florence's medieval townscape, when over 150 such towers rose between the river and the Duomo, many of them over two hundred feet high. Allied clans would link their towers with wooden catwalks, creating a sort of upper-class promenade above the heads of the lowlier citizens. In 1250 the government of the *Primo Popolo* ordered that the towers be reduced by two-thirds of their height; the resulting rubble was voluminous enough to extend the city walls beyond the Arno.

# Santa Croce

The focal point of the eastern quarter of the city centre is **Piazza Santa Croce**, one of Florence's largest squares and traditionally one of the city's main arenas for ceremonials and festivities. Thus when Lorenzo the Magnificent was married to the Roman heiress Clarice Orsini, the wedding was celebrated on this square, with a tournament that was more a fashion event than a contest of skill: Lorenzo's knightly outfit, for instance, was adorned with pearls, diamonds and rubies. It's still used as the pitch for the Gioco di Calcio Storico, a football tournament between the city's four *quartieri*; the game, held three times in St John's week (see p.209), is characterized by incomprehensible rules and a level of violence which the sixteenth-century costumes do little to inhibit.

The church of **Santa Croce** (Mon–Sat 9.30am–5.30pm, Sun 1–5.30pm; €4) is the Franciscans' principal church in Florence – a rival to the Dominicans' Santa Maria Novella – and is often said to have been founded by St Francis himself. In truth it was probably begun seventy or so years after Francis's death, in 1294, possibly by the architect of the Duomo, Arnolfo di Cambio. It replaced a smaller church on the site, a building that had become too small for the vast congregations gathering to hear the Franciscans' homilies on poverty, chastity and obedience in what was then one of the city's poorest areas. Francis – who never became a priest – had intended his monks to live as itinerants, begging for alms when necessary, and preaching without the use of churches, never mind churches the size of Santa Croce. After his death, this radical stance was quickly abandoned by many of his followers, with the backing of a papacy anxious to institutionalize a potentially dangerous mass movement.

Ironically, it was Florence's richest families who funded the construction of Santa Croce, to atone for the sin of usury on which their fortunes were based.

## Florence's floods

The calamity of the November 1966 flood had plenty of precedents. Great areas of the city were destroyed by a flood in **1178**, a disaster exacerbated by plague and famine. In **1269** the Carraia and Trinita bridges were carried away on a torrent so heavy that "a great part of the city of Florence became a lake". The flood of **1333** was preceded by a four-day storm, with thunder and rain so violent that all the city's bells were tolled to drive away the evil spirits thought to be behind the tempest: bridges were demolished and the original *Marzocco* – a figure of Mars rather than the leonine figure that inherited its name – was carried away by the raging Arno. Cosimo I instituted an urban beautification scheme after a deluge put nearly twenty feet of muddy water over parts of the city in **1557**; on that occasion the Trinita bridge was hit so suddenly that everyone on it was drowned, except for two children who were left stranded on a pillar in midstream, where for two days they were fed by means of a rope slung over from the bank.

It rained continuously for forty days prior to **November 4, 1966**, with nearly half a metre of rain falling in the preceding two days. When the water pressure in an upstream reservoir threatened to break the dam, it was decided to open the sluices. The only people to be warned about the rapidly rising level of the river were the jewellers of the Ponte Vecchio, whose private nightwatchman phoned them in the small hours of the morning with news that the bridge was starting to shake. Police watching the shopkeepers clearing their displays were asked why they weren't spreading the alarm. They replied, "We have received no orders." When the banks of the Arno finally broke down, a flash flood dumped around 500,000 tonnes of water and mud on the streets, moving with such speed that people were drowned in the underpass of Santa Maria Novella train station. In all, 35 Florentines were killed, 6000 shops put out of business, more than 10,000 homes made uninhabitable, some 15,000 cars wrecked, and thousands of works of art damaged, many of them ruined by heating oil flushed out of basements.

Within hours an impromptu army of rescue workers had been formed – many of them students – to haul pictures out of slime-filled churches and gather fragments of paint in plastic bags. Donations came in from all over the world, but the task was so immense that the restoration of many pieces is still unaccomplished. Some rooms in the archeological museum, for example, have remained closed since the flood, and many possessions of the National Library are still in the laboratories. In total around two-thirds of the 3000 paintings damaged in the flood are now on view again, and two massive laboratories – one for paintings and one for stonework – are operating full time in Florence, developing restoration techniques that are often taken up by galleries all over the world. Today, throughout the city, you can see small marble plaques with a red line showing the level the floodwaters reached on that dreadful day in 1966.

Plutocrats such as the Bardi, Peruzzi and Baroncelli sponsored the extraordinary **fresco cycles** that were lavished on the chapels over the years, particularly during the fourteenth century, when artists of the stature of Giotto and the Gaddi family worked here. In further contradiction of the Franciscan ideal of humility, Santa Croce has long served as the national pantheon: the walls and nave floor are lined with the **monuments** to more than 270 illustrious Italians, many of them Tuscan, including Michelangelo, Galileo, Machiavelli, Alberti, Dante, and the great physicist Enrico Fermi (though the last two are not buried here).

Of all the events that have happened at Santa Croce, none was more momentous than the **Council of Florence**, held in 1439 in an attempt to reconcile the differences between the Roman and Eastern churches. Attended by the pope, the Byzantine emperor and the Patriarch of Constantinople, the council arrived at a compromise that lasted only until the Byzantine delegation returned home. Its more enduring effect was that it brought scores of classical scholars to the city, some of whom stayed on to give an important impetus to the Florentine Renaissance.

# The interior

The church's **facade** is a neo-Gothic sham which dates from as recently as 1863. The church had languished for centuries without a suitable frontage, a situation remedied when someone claimed to have discovered long-lost plans for the "original" facade; in truth the scheme was no more than a giant-sized pastiche of Orcagna's tabernacle in Orsanmichele (see p.91). The vast interior is infinitely more satisfying, and feels rather more airy than it would originally have done: a large partition, built to separate the monks' choir from the area reserved for the congregation, used to interrupt the nave (a similar partition existed at Santa Maria Novella). Both the partition and choir were torn down in 1566 on the orders of Cosimo I, acting on Counter-Reformation dictates which proscribed such arrangements. Unfortunately the changes gave Vasari a chance to interfere, opening up the side altars and damaging frescoes by Orcagna, tantalizing traces of which still adorn parts of the walls.

## The south aisle

Hurry towards the high altar and the Giotto-painted chapels to its right if all you want to see are the church's most famous works of art. Otherwise, take a more measured walk down the **south aisle**. Against the first pillar stands the tomb of Francesco Nori, one of the victims of the Pazzi Conspiracy (see p.56), surmounted by Antonio Rossellino's lovely relief of the *Madonna del Latte* (marked 1 on our plan). Nearby is Vasari's **tomb of Michelangelo** (2); the sculptor's body was brought back from Rome to Florence in July 1574, ten years after his death, and his tomb is said to have been positioned close to the church's entrance at his own request, so that when the graves fly open on the Day of Judgement, the first thing to catch his eye will be Brunelleschi's cathedral dome.

The Neoclassical **monument to Dante** (3) is a cenotaph rather than a tomb, as the exiled poet is buried in Ravenna, where he died in 1321. Three centuries before Dante finally received this bland nineteenth-century tribute, Michelangelo had offered to carve the poet's tomb – a tantalizing thought. Against the third pillar there's a marvellous **pulpit** (4) by Benedetto da Maiano, adorned with niche statuettes of the virtues and scenes from the life of St Francis.

# Tuscan
# food & drink

**The traditional dishes of Tuscany are Italy's most influential cuisine: the ingredients and culinary techniques of the region have made their mark not just on the menus of the rest of Italy but also abroad. Wine too has always been central to the area's economy and way of life, familiar names such as Chianti and Vino Nobile di Montepulciano representing just a portion of the enormous output from Tuscan vineyards.**

Bistecca alla Fiorentina

## Food in Florence and Siena

Each major Tuscan town has its culinary specialities, but the biggest influences on the region's cuisine are the simple rustic dishes of Florence, the most famous of which is *bistecca alla fiorentina*, a thick T-bone steak grilled over charcoal, usually served rare. The meat for true Florentine *bistecca* comes from the Valdichiana area south of Arezzo, from an animal no more than two and a half years old. The Florentines are also fond of the unpretentious *arista*, roast pork loin stuffed with rosemary and garlic, and of *pollo alla diavola*, a flattened chicken marinated in pepper, olive oil and lemon juice or white wine, then dressed with herbs before grilling. Wild hare features on many menus, as *lepre in dolce e forte* (cooked in wine and tomatoes with raisins, pine nuts, candied orange peel and herbs), or as *pappardelle con lepre* (noodles topped with hare, fried bacon and tomatoes). These are basically peasant meals that have become staples of the regional cuisine, as have dishes like *trippa e zampa* – tripe with calf's feet, onions, tomatoes, white wine, garlic and nutmeg.

## Olive oil

The most important ingredient of Tuscan cooking is **olive oil**, which comes into almost every dish – as a dressing for salads, a medium for frying, or simply drizzled over vegetables and into soups and stews just before serving. Olive-picking begins around November, before the olives are fully ripe; the oil produced from the first pressing is termed *extra virgine*, the purest and most alkaline, with less than one-percent acidity. The quality of the oil declines with subsequent pressings.

Many of the specialities of Siena are similarly carnivorous, being based on the meat of various local breeds of pig. *Salsicce secche* (dried sausages) is one ubiquitous example that's been eaten in the city for centuries, and on many Sienese menus you'll encounter *buristo*, a salami made from a mixture of bacon, blood and the meat from a pig's head, seasoned with lemon peel, garlic, pine nuts and sultanas. Siena has its own local type of pasta as well: called *pici*, it's a sort of thick and irregular handmade spaghetti, and is often served with a sauce of tomatoes, *pancetta* (bacon cured in salt and spices), sausage and chicken.

Soups are central to the cuisine of both cities, the most famous being *ribollita*, a thick vegetable concoction traditionally including left-over beans (hence "reboiled"). *Pappa al pomodoro* is a popular broth with bread, tomatoes and basil cooked to a sustaining stodge. As secondi, you'll find a lot of "hunters' dishes" (*cacciatore*), most commonly *cinghiale* (wild boar) or *pollo* (chicken). White *cannellini* beans are the favourite vegetables, boiled with rosemary and doused with olive oil, or cooked with tomatoes (*all'uccelletto*).

Broad beans, peas, artichokes and asparagus are other much-used vegetables, but none is as typically Tuscan as spinach, which is served as a side vegetable, in combination with omelettes, poached eggs or fish, mixed with ricotta to make *gnocchi*, or as a filling for crespoline (pancakes). Spinach and green beans are often eaten cold, usually with a squeeze of lemon.

Chef at work

Despite some crop reductions caused by outbreaks of tree disease, wild chestnuts remain another staple of Tuscan cooking: there's a long tradition of specialities based on dried chestnuts and chestnut flour, such as the delicious *castagnaccio* (chestnut cake), made with pine nuts, raisins and rosemary. Sheep's milk *pecorino* is the best-known Tuscan cheese abroad (the ewes that produce it are reared on the hills of the Crete, to the south of Siena), but just as widespread locally is the oval *marzolino* from the Chianti region, which is eaten either fresh or ripened, and is often grated over meat dishes.

Dessert menus will often include *cantuccini*, hard biscuits which are dipped in a glass of Vinsanto, or *zuccotto*, a brandy-soaked sponge cake filled with cream mixed with chocolate powder, almonds and hazelnuts – like *tiramisù* elsewhere in Italy.

Asparagus on sale in a local market

# Denominazione d'Origine

The designation **Denominazione d'Origine Controllata (DOC)** guarantees the origin of the wine and that it has been made to the specification of the rules for the zone in which it's produced. Denomination zones are set by government decree and specify where a certain named wine may be made, what grape varieties may be used, the maximum yield of grapes per hectare and for how long the wine should be aged. *Vino da tavola* (table wine) is simply wine that does not conform to the DOC laws, although that doesn't necessarily mean it's bad. Though the DOC system has undoubtedly raised standards, the rigidity of the rules can throw up misleading anomalies: depending on the vintage, Chianti, for instance, can denote a wine of pedigree to be treated with reverence, a quaffable lunchtime drink, or a simply appalling plonk – yet all qualify for a DOC label regardless. Increasingly, producers in Tuscany (and elsewhere) who are eager to experiment are disregarding the rules; the sometimes expensive new wines they produce qualify as among Italy's best, and have been nicknamed "Super-Tuscans", despite still officially being labelled *vino da tavola*.

**Denominazione d'Origine Controllata e Garantita (DOCG)** is perhaps the only designation that has any real meaning. The 21 wines sold under this label not only have to conform to DOC laws, but are also quality tested by government-appointed inspectors.

# Tuscan wine

The wines of Tuscany are predominantly based on the local Sangiovese grape, the foundation of heavyweights such as Chianti, Brunello di Montalcino and Vino Nobile di Montepulciano. Traditionally, the best Tuscan wines are reds, but new techniques have boosted the quality of many whites.

Chianti, the archetypal Italian wine, is the most difficult to characterize, as the vintages vary from the lightest swillable stuff to deep-toned masterpieces aged in the cellars of ancient castles. The core of Chianti country is the Chianti Classico region between Florence and Siena, and even within this well-defined zone there are so many variables of climate and terrain that the character of the wine bottled in one estate might be entirely distinct from the neighbouring product. This makes it as difficult to get a full grasp of the subject of Chianti wine as it is to master the intricacies of Bordeaux, but it does make a tasting tour a highly rewarding experience.

Rosso di Montalcino

The greatest Tuscan red, Brunello di Montalcino, is produced just outside the Chianti region, around the hill-town of Montalcino south of Siena. First created a little over a century ago, it's a powerful, complex and long-lasting wine, whose finest vintages sell at stratospheric prices. More accessible is the youthful Rosso di Montalcino, offering a cut-price glimpse of Brunello's majesty. The mighty, if inconsistent, Vino Nobile di Montepulciano completes the upper tier of the Tuscan wine hierarchy, and, similarly, Montepulciano has a good regular red produced by less complex methods.

Non-DOC wines include some of the most fashionable and innovative Tuscan products, such as Sassicaia, described by Hugh Johnson as "perhaps Italy's best red wine", and the top-rated Tignanello made from a combination of Sangiovese and Cabernet Sauvignon grapes by the Chianti-based Antinori estate, a pillar of the Tuscan wine establishment.

## A Tuscan wine checklist

**Bianco di Pitigliano** Delicate dry white from southern Tuscany.

**Bianco Vergine della Valdichiana** Soft dry white from the area south of Arezzo.

**Brunello di Montalcino** Full-bodied red from south of Siena; one of Italy's finest wines.

**Carmignano** A highly regarded dry red produced in the region west of Florence; this area also produces Vin Ruspo, a fresh rosé.

**Chianti** Produced in seven distinct central Tuscan districts. Ranges from the roughest table wine to some of Italy's most elegant reds.

**Colline Lucchesi** A soft and lively DOC red from the hills east of Lucca.

**Galestro** Light, dry summer white produced in Chianti.

**Grattamacco** Produced southeast of Livorno, this non-DOC wine comes as a fruity white and a full, dry red.

**Montecarlo** A full and dry white – one of Tuscany's finest – from east of Lucca.

**Montecucco** New DOC red from Cinigiano and Civitella Paganico near Grosseto.

**Monteregio di Massa Marittima** Another newish DOC red from the Alta Maremma region.

**Morellino di Scansano** A fairly dry, robust, up-and-coming DOC red, made southeast of Grosseto.

**Pomino** New DOC from near Rúfina; red, white and Vinsanto.

**Rosso di Montalcino** A full-bodied DOC from the Montalcino area, aged less than the great Brunello di Montalcino.

**Rosso di Montepulciano** Excellent-value red table wine.

**Sammarco** Big Cabernet wine from the Chianti region.

**Sassicaia** Full ruby wine, best left a few years; from near Livorno.

**Solaia** Another Cabernet Sauvignon from the Antinori estate.

**Spumante** Sparkling wine made using the *champenoise* or *charmat* method.

**Tavernelle** California-style red from western Chianti.

**Tignanello** Traditional Sangiovese Chianti, again from Antinori.

**Vernaccia di San Gimignano** Subtle dry white DOC of variable quality from the hills of San Gimignano.

**Vino Nobile di Montepulciano** A full, classy red DOCG from around Montepulciano, south of Siena.

**Vinsanto Toscano** Aromatic wine, ranging from dry to sweet, and often served at dessert.

Canova's **monument to Alfieri** (5) commemorates an eighteenth-century Italian poet and dramatist as famous for his amatory liaisons as his literary endeavours. The tomb was paid for by his mistress, the so-called Countess of Albany, erstwhile wife of Charles Edward Stuart (aka Bonnie Prince Charlie). Albany herself modelled for the tomb's main figure, an allegory of Italy bereaved by Alfieri's death. The nearby **tomb of Machiavelli** (6), carved 260

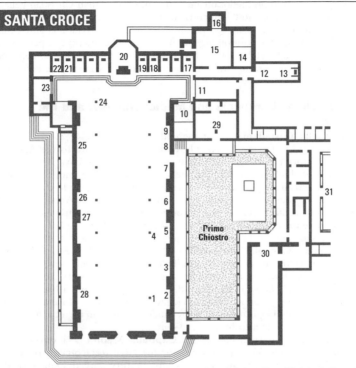

1  Madonna del Latte (1478), Antonio Rossellino
2  Tomb of Michelangelo (1570), Giorgio Vasari
3  Cenotaph to Dante (1829), Stefano Ricci
4  Pulpit (1472–6), Benedetto da Maiano
5  Monument to Vittorio Alfieri (1810), Antonio Canova
6  Tomb of Niccolò Machiavelli (1787), Innocenzo Spinazzi
7  Annunciation (1435), Donatello
8  Tomb of Leonardo Bruni (1446–7), Bernardo Rossellino
9  Tomb of Giacchino Rossini (1900), Giuseppe Cassioli
10  Cappella Castellani: frescoes (1385), Agnolo Gaddi
11  Cappella Baroncelli: frescoes (1332–8), Taddeo Gaddi
12  Cappella Medici (1434), designed by Michelozzo
13  Madonna and Child altarpiece (1480), Andrea della Robbia
14  Church shop
15  Sacristy
16  Cappella Rinuccini: frescoes (1365), Giovanni da Milano
17  Cappella Velluti: altarpiece, Giovanni di Biondo

18  Cappella Peruzzi: Lives of St John the Evangelist and St John the Baptist (1326–30), Giotto
19  Cappella Bardi: Life of St Francis (1315–20), Giotto
20  Chancel: Frescoes and stained glass (1380), Agnolo Gaddi
21  Cappella Pulci-Beradi: Martyrdom of SS Lorenzo and Stefano (1330) frescoes, Bernardo Daddi
22  Cappella Bardi di Vernio: Scenes from the Life of San Silvestro (1340) frescoes, Maso di Banco
23  Cappella Bardi: wooden crucifix (1412), Donatello
24  Monument to Leon Battista Alberti (d. 1472), Lorenzo Bartolini (early 19th-century)
25  Tomb of Carlo Marsuppini (1453), Desiderio da Settignano
26  Pietà (1560), Agnolo Bronzino
27  Tomb of Lorenzo Ghiberti and his son Vittorio (pavement slab)
28  Tomb of Galileo (1737), Giulio Foggini
29  Cappella dei Pazzi
30  Refectory and museum
31  Inner Cloister

years after his death, is unexceptional save for its famous inscription: *Tanto nomini nullum par elogium* ("No praise can be high enough for so great a name"). The side door at the end of the aisle is flanked by Donatello's gilded stone relief of the *Annunciation* (7).

Beyond the door is Bernardo Rossellino's much-imitated **tomb of Leonardo Bruni** (8), chancellor of the Republic, humanist scholar and author of the first history of the city – his effigy is holding a copy. Bruni, who died in 1444, was the first man of any great eminence to be buried in the church, which is a little surprising given his predominantly humanist rather than Christian beliefs. The tomb, one of the most influential of the Renaissance, makes the point: for the first time the human figure dominates, with the Madonna and Child banished to a peripheral position high in the lunette. The inscription, penned by Carlo Marsuppini, his successor as chancellor, reads: "After Leonardo departed life, history is in mourning and eloquence is dumb." Marsuppini himself is buried in the opposite aisle.

## The Castellani, Baroncelli and Medici chapels, and the sacristy

The **Cappella Castellani** (10), at the end of the south aisle, is strikingly, if patchily, covered in frescoes by Agnolo Gaddi and his pupils. To the right are depicted the stories of St John the Baptist and St Nicholas of Bari: the latter, the patron saint of children – he's the St Nicholas of Santa Claus fame – is shown saving three girls from prostitution and reviving three murdered boys. The left wall features episodes from the lives of St John and St Antony Abbot; the latter gave away his wealth, making him a favourite of the poverty-inspired Franciscans. Also note the chapel's fine tabernacle, the work of Mino da Fiesole, and its funerary monuments, including that of the Countess of Albany.

The adjoining **Cappella Baroncelli** (11) was decorated by Agnolo's father, Taddeo, a long-time assistant to Giotto. Taddeo's cycle, largely devoted to the life of the Virgin, features one of the first night scenes in Western painting, *The Annunciation to the Shepherds*, in which the angel appears amid a blaze of light that's believed to be a representation of Halley's Comet. The main altar painting, the *Coronation of the Virgin*, may also be by Taddeo, though an increasing number of critics now attribute it to his master, Giotto.

The corridor to the right ends at the **Cappella Medici** (12), usually open only for those taking Mass. It's notable for the large terracotta altarpiece by Andrea della Robbia (13) and a nineteenth-century forged Donatello; the chapel, like the corridor, was designed by Michelozzo, the Medici's pet architect. Finely carved wooden doors lead off the corridor into the beautifully panelled **Sacristy** (15), where the highlight is a marvellous *Crucifixion* by Taddeo on the left. The tiny **Cappella Rinuccini** (16), separated from the sacristy by a grille, is impressively covered with frescoes on the life of the Virgin (on the left) and St Mary Magdalene (on the right); the Lombard artist responsible, Giovanni da Milano, was one of Giotto's most accomplished followers.

## The east chapels: Giotto's frescoes

Both the **Cappella Peruzzi** (18) and the **Cappella Bardi** (19) – the two chapels on the right of the chancel – are entirely covered with frescoes by Giotto, with some assistance in the latter. Their deterioration was partly caused by Giotto's having painted some of the pictures onto dry plaster, rather than the wet plaster employed in true fresco technique, but the vandalism of later generations was far more destructive. In the eighteenth century they were covered in whitewash, then they were heavily retouched in the nineteenth; restoration in the 1950s returned them to as close to their original state as was possible.

Scenes from the lives of St John the Evangelist and St John the Baptist cover the Peruzzi chapel, while a better-preserved cycle of the life of St Francis fills the Bardi. Despite the areas of paint destroyed when a tomb was attached to the wall, the *Funeral of St Francis* is still a composition of extraordinary impact, the grief-stricken mourners suggesting an affinity with the lamentation over the body of Christ – one of them even probes the wound in Francis's side, echoing the gesture of Doubting Thomas. The *Ordeal by Fire*, showing Francis about to demonstrate his faith to the sultan by walking through fire, shows Giotto's mastery of understated drama, with the sultan's entourage skulking off to the left in anticipation of the monk's triumph. On the wall above the chapel's entrance arch is the most powerful scene of all, *St Francis Receiving the Stigmata*, in which the power of Christ's apparition seems to force the chosen one to his knees.

Agnolo Gaddi was responsible for the design of the **stained glass** in the lancet windows round the high altar, and for all the chancel **frescoes** (20), which depict the legend of the True Cross – a complicated tale tracing the wood of the Cross from its origins as the Tree of Paradise. The vast polyptych on the high altar is a composite of panels by several artists.

The **Cappella Bardi di Vernio** (22) was painted by Maso di Banco, perhaps the most inventive of Giotto's followers. Following tradition, the frescoes, showing scenes from the life of St Sylvester, portray the saint baptizing Emperor Constantine, notwithstanding the fact that Sylvester died some time before the emperor's actual baptism. The second **Cappella Bardi** (23) houses a wooden crucifix by Donatello, supposedly criticized by Brunelleschi as resembling a "peasant on the Cross". According to Vasari, Brunelleschi went off and created his own crucifix for Santa Maria Novella to show Donatello how it should be done (see p.103).

### The north aisle

As you walk back towards the entrance along the north aisle, the first pillar you pass features a ghastly nineteenth-century **monument to Leon Battista Alberti** (24), the Renaissance architect and artistic theorist whose writings did much to influence Rossellino in his carving of the Bruni tomb across the nave. The Bruni tomb in turn influenced the outstanding **tomb of Carlo Marsuppini** (25) by Desiderio da Settignano. Marsuppini's lack of Christian qualifications for so prominent a church burial is even more striking than Bruni's: he's said to have died without taking confession or communion. The tomb inscription opens with the words, "Stay and see the marbles which enshrine a great sage, one for whose mind there was not world enough."

A *Pietà* (26) by the young Bronzino, a future Mannerist star, briefly disturbs the parade of tombs that follows. A surprisingly modest pavement slab marks the **tomb of Lorenzo Ghiberti** (27) – the artist responsible for the Baptistery's marvellous doors – and his son Vittorio. The **tomb of Galileo** (28) is more ostentatious, though it was some ninety years after his death in 1642 that the "heretic" scientist was deemed worthy of a Christian burial in Florence's pantheon.

# The Cappella dei Pazzi

The door in the south (right) aisle leads through into the church's Primo Chiostro (First Cloister), site of Brunelleschi's **Cappella dei Pazzi** (29), the epitome of the learned, harmonious spirit of early Renaissance architecture. Begun in 1429 as a chapterhouse for Santa Croce, it was commissioned by Andrea de' Pazzi, a member of a banking dynasty that played a prominent role in the Pazzi Conspiracy. Its exterior remained unfinished at the time of the plot, however, and it seems none of the family was ever buried here.

Brunelleschi worked on the chapel between 1442 and his death in 1446, though financial problems meant that work was only completed in the 1470s. Geometrically perfect without seeming pedantic, the chapel is exemplary in its proportion and in the way its decorative detail harmonizes with the design. The polychrome lining of the portico's shallow cupola is by Luca della Robbia, as is the garland of fruit which surrounds the Pazzi family crest. The frieze of angels' heads is by Desiderio da Settignano, though Luca was responsible for the tondo of *St Andrew* (1461) over the door. The portico itself may be the work of Giuliano da Maiano, while the majestic wooden doors (1472) are the product of a collaboration between the brothers Maiano, Giuliano and Benedetto. Inside, the twelve blue and white tondi of the *Apostles* are by Luca della Robbia, while the four vividly coloured tondi of the *Evangelists* in the upper roundels were produced in the della Robbia workshop, possibly to designs by Donatello and Brunelleschi.

## The Museo dell'Opera di Santa Croce and the inner cloister

The **Museo dell'Opera di Santa Croce** (30), which flanks the first cloister, houses a miscellany of works of art, the best of which are gathered in the Refettorio (refectory). Foremost of these is Cimabue's famous *Crucifixion*, very badly damaged in 1966 and now the emblem of the havoc caused by the flood. Other highlights include a detached fresco of the *Last Supper* (1333), considered the finest work by Taddeo Gaddi (end wall), and the earliest surviving example of the many Last Suppers (*Cenacoli*) dotted around the city. This theme was of obvious relevance given its position, which – as here – was invariably the refectory where monks gathered to eat. Equally compelling is Donatello's enormous gilded *St Louis of Toulouse* (1424), made for Orsanmichele. Other fine works saved from Vasari's meddling in the main church include six fresco fragments by Orcagna (on the side walls) and Domenico Veneziano's *SS John and Francis*.

A series of rooms sparsely filled with various damaged fragments leads you towards the spacious **Inner Cloister** (31), another late project by Brunelleschi. Completed in 1453, after the architect's death, it is the most peaceful spot in the centre of Florence, achieving its atmosphere by the slow rhythm of the narrow, widely spaced columns.

# The Museo Horne

On the south side of Santa Croce, down by the river at Via dei Benci 6, stands one of Florence's more recondite museums, the **Museo della Fondazione Horne** (Mon–Sat 9am–1pm; €5). Its collection was left to the state by the English art historian Herbert Percy Horne (1864–1916), who was instrumental in rescuing Botticelli from neglect with a pioneering biography. The half a dozen or so rooms of paintings, sculptures, pottery, furniture and other domestic objects contain no real masterpieces, but are diverting enough if you've already done the major collections. With winning eccentricity, the exhibits are labelled with numbers only and you have to carry round a key in the form of a long list, available from the ticket office. The museum building, the Palazzo Corsi-Alberti (1489), is worth more than a glance even if you're not going into the museum. Commissioned by the Corsi family, it's a typical merchant's house of the period, with huge cellars in which wool would have been dyed, and an open gallery above the courtyard for drying the finished cloth.

The pride of Horne's collection was its drawings, which are now salted away in the Uffizi, though a small, usually captivating display is maintained in the room on the right of the **ground floor**. Of what's left, the pick in the left-hand downstairs room is a bas-relief of the *Madonna and Child* attributed to Jacopo Sansovino. On the **first floor**, the highlights of Room 1 are a worn crucifix by Filippino Lippi; part of a predella with a tiny age-bowed panel of *St Julian* by Masaccio; a dark *Deposition* by Gozzoli, his last documented work; and a group of saints by Pietro Lorenzetti. The next room contains the collection's big draw, Giotto's *St Stephen* (a fragment from a polyptych), followed in Room 3 by Beccafumi's *Holy Family*, shown in its original frame. The wooden figure of *St Jerome* nearby is by Verrocchio. One of the main exhibits on the **second floor** is a piece of little artistic merit but great historical interest: a copy of part of Leonardo's *Battle of Anghiari*, once frescoed on a wall of the Palazzo Vecchio. Here, too, are further works by such big names as Filippo and Filippino Lippi, Simone Martini and Beccafumi, as well as some lovely pieces of furniture.

# Casa Buonarroti and the Sant'Ambrogio district

The enticing name of the **Casa Buonarroti**, located north of Santa Croce at Via Ghibellina 70 (daily except Tues 9.30am–2pm; €6.50), is somewhat misleading. Michelangelo Buonarroti certainly owned three houses here in 1508, and probably lived on the site intermittently between 1516 and 1525, but thereafter the properties' associations with the artist become increasingly tenuous. On Michelangelo's death, for example, they passed to his nephew, Leonardo, whose son converted them into a single palazzo, leaving little trace of the earlier houses (though he built a gallery dedicated to his great-uncle). Michelangelo's last descendant, Cosimo, left the building to the city on his death in 1858. Today the house contains a smart but low-key museum. Many of the rooms are pleasing enough, all nicely decorated in period style and adorned with beautiful furniture, *objets d'art*, frescoed ceilings and the like, but among the jumble of works collected here, only a handful are by Michelangelo: most were created simply in homage to the great man.

Etruscan and Roman fragments have been wrested back from the archeological museum to languish on the ground floor once more, but the two main treasures are to be found in the room on the left at the top of the stairs. The **Madonna della Scala** (c.1490–92) is Michelangelo's earliest known work, a delicate relief carved when he was no older than 16. The similarly unfinished *Battle of the Centaurs* was created shortly afterwards, when the boy was living in the Medici household. In the adjacent room you'll find the artist's wooden model (1517) for the facade of San Lorenzo. Close by is the largest of all the sculptural models on display, the torso of a **River God** (1524), a work in wood and wax probably intended for the Medici chapel in San Lorenzo. Other rooms contain small and fragmentary pieces, possibly by the master, possibly copies of works by him.

## The Sant'Ambrogio markets

Two of Florence's markets lie within a few minutes' stroll of the Casa Buonarroti. To the north, the Piazza dei Ciompi is the venue for the **Mercato delle Pulci** or Flea Market (summer Mon–Sat 10am–1pm & 4–7pm; winter Mon–Sat 9am–1pm & 3–7pm; also open same hours on last Sun of month). Much of the junk maintains the city's reputation for inflated prices, though you can find a few interesting items at modest cost – old postcards, posters and so on. Vasari's Loggia del Pesce (1567) gives the square a touch of style; built for the fishmongers of the Mercato Vecchio in what is now Piazza della Repubblica, it was dismantled when that square was laid out, and rebuilt here in 1951.

A short distance to the east, out of the orbit of nearly all tourists, is the **Mercato di Sant'Ambrogio** (Mon–Sat 7am–2pm), a smaller, tattier but even more enjoyable version of the San Lorenzo food hall. The *tavola calda* (snacks and meals stall) here is one of Florence's lunchtime bargains, and – as at San Lorenzo – the stalls bring their prices down in the last hour of trading.

## The church of Sant'Ambrogio

Nearby **Sant'Ambrogio** (daily 8am–12.30pm & 4–7pm) is one of Florence's older churches, having been documented in 988, though rebuilding over the centuries means that it is now somewhat bland in appearance. Inside you'll find a *Madonna Enthroned with SS John the Baptist and Bartholomew* (second altar on

△ Sant'Ambrogio market

the right), attributed to Orcagna (or the school of Orcagna), and a recently restored triptych in the chapel to the right of the main altar, attributed to Lorenzo di Bicci or Bicci di Lorenzo. More compelling than either painting, though, is the Cappella del Miracolo, the chapel to the left of the high altar, and its tabernacle (1481–83) by Mino da Fiesole, an accomplished sculptor whose name crops up time and again across Tuscany. This was one of Mino's last works – he died in 1484 – making it fitting that he should be buried close by, in a tomb marked by a pavement slab at the chapel entrance. Another great artist, the multi-talented Verrocchio (d.1488), is buried in the fourth chapel. The narrative **fresco** (1486) alongside Mino's tabernacle alludes to the miracle which gave the Cappella del Miracolo its name. The work of Cosimo Rosselli, best known for his frescoes in Santissima Annunziata, it describes the discovery and display of a chalice full of blood in 1230. The Florentines believed the chalice saved them from, among other things, the effects of a virulent plague outbreak of 1340. The painting is full of portraits of Rosselli's contemporaries, making it another of Florence's vivid pieces of Renaissance social reportage: Rosselli himself is the figure in the black beret at the extreme left of the picture.

# From the synagogue to the English cemetery

The enormous domed building rising to the north of Sant'Ambrogio church is the **Synagogue**; the ghetto established in this district by Cosimo I was not demolished until the mid-nineteenth century, which is when the present Moorish-style synagogue was built. It contains a small **museum** that charts the history of Florence's Jewish population (April–Oct Sun–Thurs 10am–5/6pm, Fri 10am–2pm; Nov–March Sun–Thurs 10am–3pm, Fri 10am–2pm; €4).

West of the synagogue, on Borgo Pinti, stands the church of **Santa Maria Maddalena dei Pazzi** (Mon–Sat 9–11.50am & 5–5.20pm & 6.10–6.50pm, Sun 9–10.45am & 5–6.50pm), named after a Florentine nun who was famed for her religious ecstasies: when possessed by the holy spirit she would spew words at such a rate that a team of eight novices was needed to transcribe her inspired dictation. She was also prone to pouring boiling wax over her arms, and was fond of reclining naked on a bed of thorns. This unflinching piety was much honoured in Counter-Reformation Florence: when Maria de' Medici went off to marry Henry IV of France, Maria Maddalena transmitted the news that the Virgin expected her to re-admit the Jesuits to France and exterminate the Huguenots, which she duly did.

Founded in the thirteenth century but kitted out in Baroque style, the church is not itself much of an attraction, but its chapterhouse – reached by a tortuous subterranean passageway that's accessed from the top of the right aisle – is decorated with a radiant **Perugino** fresco of the *Crucifixion* (€1). Based on the terrain around Lago Trasimeno, the scene is painted as a continuous panorama on a wall divided into three arches, giving the effect of looking out through a loggia onto a springtime landscape. As always with Perugino, there is nothing troubling here, the Crucifixion being depicted not as an agonizing death but rather as the necessary prelude to the Resurrection.

North of the Pazzi church, at the end of Borgo Pinti, is the **English Cemetery** at Piazza Donatello (daily 9am–noon & 3–6pm). Now a funerary traffic island, this patch of garden is the resting place of Elizabeth Barrett Browning and a number of contemporaneous artistic Brits, among them Walter Savage Landor and Arthur Hugh Clough.

# San Salvi and Campo di Marte

Twenty minutes' walk beyond Piazza Beccaria, east of Sant'Ambrogio (or bus #10 from the station, or #6 from Piazza San Marco), is the ex-convent of **San Salvi**, which was reopened in 1982 after the restoration of its most precious possession, the *Last Supper* by Andrea del Sarto (Tues–Sun 8.15am–1.50pm). As a prelude to this picture, there's a gallery of big but otherwise unremarkable Renaissance altarpieces, a gathering of pictures by various del Sarto acolytes, and the beautiful reliefs from the tomb of Giovanni Gualberto, founder of the

## Crisis and revival at Campo di Marte

In recent years there have been some tough times for the team known as the *Viola*, after the distinctive violet colour of their shirts. Some would argue that things started to go downhill back in 1990, when the great **Roberto Baggio** was transferred – for what was then a world record fee – to Juventus, amid scenes of fervent protest. In 1996, with Argentinian striker Gabriel Batistuta (aka "**Batigol**") attracting the sort of morbid affection that Baggio once commanded, Fiorentina won the Italian cup, and they came close to a league championship in 1999, finishing third. But then Batigol was lured to Roma, sparking demonstrations of such violence that the club's owner, TV and film magnate Vittorio Cecchi-Gori, required police protection. Roma promptly rubbed salt into the wound by becoming champions of Serie A (Italy's top division), but far worse was to come in 2002, when Fiorentina became the most spectacular casualty of the financial crisis that engulfed what used to be the world's wealthiest league. For many years the clubs in Serie A had been paying insupportable salaries on the basis of projected TV revenue, while consistently failing in the lucrative Champions' League. By 2002 the aggregate debts of the Serie A teams had passed $750 million, and for Fiorentina the situation was almost terminal: declared **bankrupt**, they were kicked out of Serie A and demoted to Serie C2B – in effect, the bottom of the heap.

The once-great club was reformed as **Fiorentina 1926 Florentia**, or **Florentia Viola** for short (ⓦ www.fiorentina2000.net), under the new ownership of footwear millionaire Diego della Valle. The star players – Nuno Gomes, Adani, Enrico Chiesa – all exercised their right to a free transfer when the bankruptcy was confirmed, leaving former Juventus and Italy midfielder Angelo di Livio as the linchpin of a team composed mainly of teenagers. Yet the club quickly fought its way back up the leagues, returning to Serie A for the 2004/2005 season (when they just about avoided relegation to Serie B), and the support at the Stadio Franchi – stoked by the fans' longstanding sense of themselves as the unloved outsiders of Italian football – remains as intense as ever, so **tickets** can be hard to obtain. (They cost from around €20 and can be bought at the ground itself, or three or four days in advance from the *Toto* booth on the west side of Piazza della Repubblica. For information on availability, call ☏ 055.292.363).

Though the club is now solvent and successful once more, the whiff of scandal is still in the air: a public prosecutor is currently investigating the premature deaths of three ex-Fiorentina players between 1987 and 2004, and other cases of severe ill-health (including heart and kidney disease, and cancer) among men who appeared for the club in the 1970s. The suspicion is that players might have been doped with strength-building drugs, administered in the form of a coffee-like drink. Nello Saltutti, who played for the *Viola* from 1972 to 1975 and died of a heart attack in 2003, spoke to an investigator in 1997, after his first cardiac arrest, and told him: "That 'coffee' was very good for us. We all played very well and played twice as fast as usual. The day after, however, we were all destroyed."

Vallombrosan order to whom this monastery belonged. The tomb was smashed up by Charles V's troops in 1530 but they refused to damage the *Last Supper*, which is still in the refectory for which it was painted, accompanied by three del Sarto frescoes brought here from other churches in Florence. Painted around 1520 and evidently much influenced by Leonardo's work, this is the epitome of del Sarto's soft, suave technique – emotionally undernourished for some tastes, but faultlessly carried out.

## The Stadio Comunale

As befits this monument-stuffed city, Florence's football team play in a stadium that's listed as a building of cultural significance, the **Stadio Comunale** (or **Stadio Artemio Franchi**) at **Campo di Marte** (bus #17 from the train station). It was designed by Pier Luigi Nervi in 1930, as a consequence of two decisions: to create a new football club for Florence and to stage the 1934 World Cup in Italy.

The stadium was the first major sports venue to exploit the shape-making potential of reinforced concrete, and its spiral ramps, cantilevered roof and slim central tower still make most other arenas look dreary. From the spectator's point of view, however, it's far from perfect: for instance, the peculiar D-shape of the stands – necessitated by the straight 200-metre sprint track – means that visibility from some parts of the ground is awful. But the architectural importance of Nervi's work meant that when Florence was chosen as one of the hosts for the 1990 World Cup there could be no question of simply building a replacement (as was done brilliantly at Bari), nor of radically altering the existing one (as happened at most grounds). Much of the seventy billion lire spent on the refurbishment of the Stadio Comunale was thus spent ensuring that the improvements did not ruin the clean modernistic lines, and most of the extra space in the all-seater stadium was created by lowering the pitch a couple of metres below its previous level, in order to insert another layer of seats where the track had been.

# 6

# Oltrarno

Visitors to Florence might perceive the River Arno as a simple inter-
ruption in the urban fabric, but some Florentines still talk as though a
ravine runs through their city. North of the river is known as *Arno di quà*
("over here"), while the other side, hemmed in by a ridge of hills that
rises a short distance from the river, is *Arno di là* ("over there"). More formally,
it's known as the **Oltrarno** – literally "beyond the Arno" – a terminology that
has its roots in medieval times, when the district was not as accessible as the
numerous bridges now make it.

Traditionally an artisans' quarter, the Oltrarno has nonetheless always
contained more prosperous enclaves: many of Florence's ruling families chose
to settle in this area, and nowadays some of the city's plushest shops line the
streets parallel to the river's southern bank. Further in, the area around **Santo
Spirito** and **Piazza del Carmine** is a good place to come in the evening, as
it's here you'll find some of Florence's best bars and restaurants. Window-shop-
ping, eating and drinking are not the area's sole pleasures, however, as the district
also contains several of the city's key sights, most notably the **Palazzo Pitti** and
the frescoes of **Santa Maria del Carmine**.

# Central Oltrarno

The most famous bridge in the city, the **Ponte Vecchio**, links the northern
bank to the Oltrarno's central area, home to the **Palazzo Pitti**, a rambling
palace complex whose cluster of museums includes the city's second-ranking picture gallery. Close by lies the **Giardino di Bóboli**, Italy's most visited
garden, a leafy retreat from the sightseeing. Lesser attractions include the ancient
church of **Santa Felìcita**, known for one of the city's stranger paintings, and
the extraordinary medical waxworks of **La Specola**.

## The Ponte Vecchio

The direct route from the city centre to the heart of the Oltrarno crosses the
Arno via the **Ponte Vecchio**, the last in a line of bridges at the river's narrowest
point that stretches back to Etruscan and Roman times. Some believe that this
was the bridging point for the Via Cassia, the principal road between Rome
and the north; others maintain that the Roman crossing was a touch further
upstream. Until 1218 the crossing here was the city's only bridge, though the
version you see today dates from 1345, built to replace a wooden bridge swept

away by floods twelve years earlier. The name, which means the Old Bridge, was coined to distinguish it from the Ponte alla Carraia, the bridge raised in 1218. Over its arcades runs Vasari's concealed passageway (see p.84), commissioned by the Medici in 1565 to allow them to pass unobserved from the Palazzo Vecchio to the Palazzo Pitti. Much later in its history the Ponte Vecchio was the only bridge not mined by the Nazis in 1944 as they retreated before the advancing American Fifth Army; Field Marshal Kesselring is said to have spared it on Hitler's express orders. Much of the rest of the city, including medieval quarters at either end of the bridge, was not so lucky: the Nazis reneged on a promise to spare the city (as had happened in Rome), blowing up swathes of old buildings to hamper the Allied advance.

The bridge's present-day **shops** and **hawkers** can come as a shock, but the Ponte Vecchio has always been loaded with stores like those now propped over the water. Their earliest inhabitants were butchers and fishmongers, attracted to the site by the proximity of the river, which provided a convenient dumping ground for their waste. Next came the tanners, who used the river to soak their hides before tanning them with horses' urine. The current plethora of jewellers dates from 1593, when Ferdinando I evicted the butchers' stalls and other practitioners of what he called "vile arts". In their place he installed eight jewellers and 41 **goldsmiths**, also taking the opportunity to double the rents. Florence had long revered the art of the goldsmith, and several of its major artists were skilled in the craft: Ghiberti, Donatello and Cellini, for example. The third of this trio is celebrated by a bust in the centre of the bridge, the night-time meeting point for Florence's unreconstructed hippies and local lads on the pull.

# Santa Felìcita

**Santa Felìcita** (Mon–Sat 9.30am–12.30pm & 3–6.30pm) might be the oldest church in Florence, having possibly been founded in the second century by Greek or Syrian merchants, pioneers of Christianity in the city. It was built close to the Via Cassia over an early Christian cemetery, commemorated by a column

## Jacopo Pontormo

Born near Empoli, Jacopo Carrucci (1494–1556), better known as **Pontormo** after his native village, studied under Andrea del Sarto in Florence in the early 1510s. His early independent works include the frescoes in the atrium of Santissima Annunziata in Florence, which have an edgy quality quite unlike that of his master. In the 1520s he was hired by the Medici to decorate part of their villa at Poggio a Caiano, after which he executed a *Passion* cycle for the Certosa, to the south of the city. His masterpiece in Florence is the *Deposition* in Santa Felìcita; the major project of his later years, a fresco cycle in San Lorenzo, has been totally destroyed, though some of his other paintings can be seen in the Uffizi.

A crucial figure in the evolution of the hyper-refined Mannerist style, Pontormo was every bit as strange as his bizarre *Deposition* suggests. A chronic hypochondriac – his diary is a tally of the state of his kidneys, bowel disorders and other assorted ailments – he seems to have found the company of others almost intolerable, spending much of his time in a top-floor room that could be reached only by a ladder, which he drew up behind him. So eccentric was his behaviour that he was virtually mythologized by his contemporaries. One writer attributed to him an all-consuming terror of death and called his room a "beast's lair", while another insisted that he kept corpses in a tub as models for a *Deluge* that he was painting – an antisocial research project that allegedly brought protests from the neighbours.

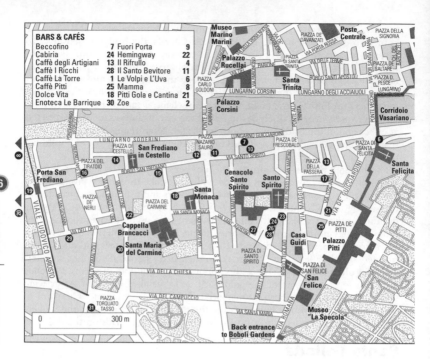

| BARS & CAFÉS | | |
|---|---|---|
| Beccofino | 7 | Fuori Porta | 9 |
| Cabiria | 24 | Hemingway | 22 |
| Caffè degli Artigiani | 13 | Il Rifrullo | 4 |
| Caffè I Ricchi | 28 | Il Santo Bevitore | 11 |
| Caffè La Torre | 1 | Le Volpi e L'Uva | 6 |
| Caffè Pitti | 25 | Mamma | 8 |
| Dolce Vita | 18 | Pitti Gola e Cantina | 21 |
| Enoteca Le Barrique | 30 | Zoe | 2 |

(1381) in Piazza della Felìcita. It's known for certain that a church existed on the site by the fifth century – a tombstone dated 405 has been found nearby – by which time it had been dedicated to St Felicity, an early Roman martyr who is often shown in Renaissance paintings with her seven sons, each of whom was executed in front of her for refusing to renounce his faith (the saint herself was either beheaded or thrown into boiling oil). New churches were built on the site in the eleventh and fourteenth centuries, while in 1565 Vasari added an elaborate portico to accommodate the *corridoio* linking the Uffizi and Palazzo Pitti; a window from the corridor looks directly into the church. All but the facade was extensively remodelled between 1736 and 1739.

The interior demands a visit for the amazing Pontormo paintings in the **Cappella Capponi**, which lies to the right of the main door, surrounded by irritating railings. The chapel was designed in the 1420s by Brunelleschi, but subsequently much altered – notably by Vasari, who destroyed the Pontormo fresco in the cupola when building his corridor. Under the cupola are four tondi of the *Evangelists* (painted with help from his adoptive son, Bronzino), while on opposite sides of the window on the right wall are the Virgin and the angel of Pontormo's delightfully simple *Annunciation*, the arrangement alluding to the Incarnation as the means by which the Light came into the world. The low level of light admitted by this window was a determining factor in the startling colour scheme of Pontormo's weirdly erotic **Deposition** (1525–28), one of the masterworks of Florentine Mannerism. Nothing in this picture is conventional: the figure of Mary is on a different scale from her attendants; the figures bearing Christ's body are androgynous figures clad in billows of acidic sky-blue, puce green and candy-floss pink drapery; and there's no sign of the cross, the thieves, soldiers or any of the other scene-setting devices usual in

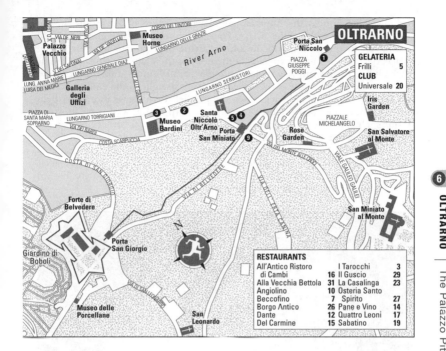

**OLTRARNO**

| GELATERIA | |
|---|---|
| Frilli | 5 |
| **CLUB** | |
| Universale | 20 |

| RESTAURANTS | | | |
|---|---|---|---|
| All'Antico Ristoro | | I Tarocchi | 3 |
| di Cambi | 16 | Il Guscio | 29 |
| Alla Vecchia Bettola | 31 | La Casalinga | 23 |
| Angiolino | 10 | Osteria Santo | |
| Beccofino | 7 | Spirito | 27 |
| Borgo Antico | 26 | Pane e Vino | 14 |
| Dante | 12 | Quattro Leoni | 17 |
| Del Carmine | 15 | Sabatino | 19 |

paintings of this subject; the sole background detail is a solitary ghostly cloud. The bearded brown-cloaked figure on the extreme right is believed to be a self-portrait of the artist.

## The Palazzo Pitti

Beyond Santa Felìcita, the street opens out at Piazza Pitti, forecourt of the largest palace in Florence, the **Palazzo Pitti**. Banker and merchant Luca Pitti commissioned the palace to outdo his rivals, the Medici. Work started around 1457, possibly using a design by Brunelleschi which had been rejected by Cosimo de' Medici for being too grand. No sooner was the palace completed, however, than the Pitti's fortunes began to decline, and by 1549 they were forced to sell out to the Medici. The Pitti subsequently became the Medici's base in Florence, growing in bulk until the seventeenth century, when it achieved its present gargantuan dimensions. Later, during Florence's brief tenure as the Italian capital between 1865 and 1870, it housed the Italian kings.

Today the Palazzo Pitti and the pavilions of the Giardino di Bóboli contain eight museums, of which the foremost is the **Galleria Palatina**, a painting collection second in importance only to the Uffizi. Separate tickets are required for the Galleria and **Museo degli Argenti**, the most compelling of the palace's other collections, and for the **Galleria d'Arte Moderna** – these tickets, however, cover entry into other museums in the complex.

### The Galleria Palatina and Appartamenti Reali

Many of the paintings gathered by the Medici in the seventeenth century are now arranged in the **Galleria Palatina** (Tues–Sun 8.15am–6.50pm; €8.50, includes admission to the Appartamenti Reali), a suite of 29 rooms on the first floor of one wing of the palace. The ticket office and the grand staircase leading up to the gallery both lie off the main courtyard to the rear of the palace. Beyond the huge chandelier at the head of the stairs, the first two rooms – which have wonderful views – lead into two parallel suites of six rooms. If you want to head for the meat of the collection, walk straight to the end of the first section, then turn left and back down the parallel row of state rooms. It's here that you'll find the gallery's eleven paintings by **Raphael**, as well as the fourteen **Titians**. The pictures are not arranged in the sort of didactic order observed by most galleries, but are instead hung as they would have been in the days of their acquisition, three deep in places, with the aim of making each room pleasurably varied. The best thing to do is wander at random until a picture takes your fancy. The big names just keep on coming, and the highlights are many, so you'll need several hours to see the collection properly.

△ *La Velata*, by Raphaell

The current itinerary takes you straight through into the suite containing mostly less famous works, though some individual paintings are well worth seeking out, notably: **Fra' Bartolomeo**'s *Deposition*; a tondo of the *Madonna and Child with Scenes from the Life of St Anne* (1452) by **Filippo Lippi**; his son Filippino's *Death of Lucrezia*; a *Sleeping Cupid* (1608) by **Caravaggio**; and Cristofano Allori's sexy **Judith and Holofernes**, for which Allori himself, his mother and his mistress provided the models for the principal characters. Also in this section are the Corridoio del Volterrano, which houses mainly Florentine works of the seventeenth century, and the Corridoio della Colonna, which has a Flemish theme.

In the second, more captivating part of the gallery, **Andrea del Sarto** is represented in strength, his seventeen works including a beautifully grave *Annunciation*. Even more remarkable is the Pitti's collection of paintings by his great contemporary, **Raphael**. When Raphael settled in Florence in 1505, he was besieged with commissions from patrons delighted to find an artist for whom the creative process involved so little agonizing. In the next three years he painted scores of pictures for such people as Angelo Doni, the man who commissioned Michelangelo's *Doni Tondo*, now in the Uffizi. Raphael's portraits of Doni and his wife, Maddalena (1506–7), display an unhesitating facility and perfect poise; if the Maddalena's pose looks familiar, incidentally, it's because it's copied directly from Leonardo's *Mona Lisa*. Similar poise illuminates Raphael's splendidly framed 1515 *Madonna della Seggiola*, or Madonna of the Chair, in which the figures are curved into the rounded shape of the panel (which is said to have come from the bottom of a wine barrel), with no sense of artificiality. For centuries this was Italy's most popular image of the Virgin; nineteenth-century copyists had to join a five-year waiting list to study the picture. *La Gravida* (1504–8), in the Sala dell'Iliade, shows Raphael in earthier vein; it's a rare work which tentatively portrays the pregnant bulge of an expectant mother. According to Vasari, the model for the famous *Donna Velata* (Veiled Woman), in the Sala di Giove, was the painter's mistress, a Roman baker's daughter known to posterity as La Fornarina; recent research seems to have established that Raphael and his model had married before the picture was completed.

The assembly of paintings by the Venetian artist **Titian** includes a number of his most trenchant portraits. The lecherous and scurrilous Pietro Aretino – journalist, critic, poet and one of Titian's closest friends – was so thrilled by his 1545 portrait that he gave it to Cosimo I; Titian painted him on several other occasions, sometimes using him as the model for Pontius Pilate. Also here are likenesses of Philip II of Spain and the young Cardinal Ippolito de' Medici (1532) – who fought in the defence of Vienna against the Ottomans only to be poisoned at the age of 24 – and the so-called *Portrait of an Englishman* (1540), who scrutinizes the viewer with unflinching sea-grey eyes. To his left, by way of contrast, is the same artist's sensuous and much-copied *Mary Magdalene* (1531), the first of a series on this theme produced for the duke of Urbino. In the same room, look out for Rosso Fiorentino's recently restored *Madonna Enthroned with Saints* (1522), and the gallery's outstanding sculpture, Canova's *Venus Italica*, commissioned by Napoleon as a replacement for the *Venus de' Medici*, which he had whisked off to Paris.

Much of the rest of the Pitti's first floor comprises the **Appartamenti Reali**, the Pitti's state rooms. They were renovated by the dukes of Lorraine in the eighteenth century, and then by Vittorio Emanuele when Florence became the country's capital, so the rooms display three distinct decorative phases. The gallery leads straight through into the apartments, and after Raphael and Titian it can be difficult to sustain a great deal of enthusiasm for such ducal elegance, notwithstanding the sumptuousness of the furnishings.

# The other Pitti museums

On the floor above the Palatina is the **Galleria d'Arte Moderna** (Tues–Sat 8.15am–1.50pm; also 1st, 3rd & 5th Sun of month and 2nd & 4th Mon of month same hours; joint ticket with Galleria del Costume €5), a chronological survey of primarily Tuscan art from the mid-eighteenth century to 1945. Most rewarding are the products of the *Macchiaioli*, the Italian division of the Impressionist movement; most startling, however, are the sculptures, featuring sublime kitsch such as Antonio Ciseri's *Pregnant Nun*.

The **Museo degli Argenti** (daily 8.15am–2pm; closed 1st & last Mon of month; joint ticket with Museo delle Porcellane and Giardino di Bóboli €6), entered from the main palace courtyard, is a museum not just of silverware but of luxury artefacts in general. The lavishly frescoed reception rooms themselves fall into this category: the first hall, the Sala di Giovanni da San Giovanni, shows Lorenzo de' Medici giving refuge to the Muses; the other three ceremonial rooms have trompe l'oeil paintings by seventeenth-century Bolognese artists. As for the exhibits, the least ambivalent response is likely to be aroused by Lorenzo the Magnificent's trove of antique vases, all of them marked with their owner's name. The later the date of the pieces, though, the greater the discrepancy between the skill of the craftsman and the taste by which it was governed; by the time you reach the end of the jewellery show on the first floor, you'll have lost all capacity to be surprised or revolted by seashell figurines, cups made from ostrich eggs, portraits in stone inlay, and the like. Exhibitions are sometimes held here, which can affect the ticket price and opening hours.

Visitors without a specialist interest are unlikely to be riveted by the other Pitti museums that are currently open. In the Palazzina della Meridiana, the eighteenth-century southern wing of the Pitti, the **Galleria del Costume** (same hours & ticket as Galleria d'Arte Moderna) provides the opportunity to see the dress that Eleonora di Toledo was buried in, though you can admire it easily enough in Bronzino's portrait of her in the Palazzo Vecchio. Also housed in the Meridiana is the **Collezione Contini Bonacossi** (free tours usually Thurs & Sat 9.45am; booking essential a week ahead at the Uffizi ☏055.23.885), on long-term loan to the Pitti. Its prize pieces are its Spanish paintings, in particular Velázquez's *Water Carrier of Seville*. The well-presented but esoteric collection of porcelain, the **Museo delle Porcellane**, is located on the other side of the Bóboli garden (same days – see below – and ticket as garden, but closes 2.30pm), while the **Museo delle Carrozze** (Carriage Museum) has been closed for years and, despite what the Pitti handouts tell you, will almost certainly remain so for the foreseeable future to the chagrin of very few.

# The Giardino di Bóboli

The delightful formal gardens of the Palazzo Pitti, the **Giardino di Bóboli** (daily: Jan, Feb, Nov & Dec 8.15am–4.30pm; March 8.15am–5.30pm; April, May, Sept & Oct 8.15am–6.30pm; June–Aug 8.15am–7.30pm; closed 1st & last Mon of month; joint ticket with Museo delle Porcellane and Museo degli Argenti €6), takes its name from the Bóboli family, erstwhile owners of much of this area, which was once a quarry; the bedrock here is one of the sources of the yellow sandstone known as *pietra forte* (strong stone) that gives much of Florence its dominant hue. Carefully shaped into a rough, boulder-like texture, this stone was also used to "rusticate" the Palazzo Pitti's great facade. When the Medici acquired the house in 1549 they set to work transforming their

## The birth of opera

The Medici pageants in the gardens of the Pitti were the last word in extravagance, and the palace has a claim to be the birthplace of the most extravagant modern performing art, **opera**. The roots of the genre are convoluted, but its ancestry certainly owes much to the singing and dancing tableaux called *intermedii*, with which high-society Florentine weddings were padded out. Influenced by these shows, the academy known as the Camerata Fiorentina began, at the end of the sixteenth century, to blend the principles of Greek drama with a semi-musical style of declamation. The first composition recognizable as an opera is *Dafne*, written by two members of the Camerata, Jacopo Peri and Ottavio Rinucci, and performed in 1597; the earliest opera whose music has survived in its entirety is the same duo's *Euridice*, premiered in the Pitti palace on the occasion of the proxy marriage of Maria de' Medici to Henry IV.

back yard into an enormous 111-acre garden, its every statue, view and grotto designed to elevate nature by the judicious application of art.

Work continued into the early seventeenth century, by which stage this steep hillside had been turned into a maze of statue-strewn avenues and well-trimmed vegetation. Opened to the public in 1766, it is the only really extensive area of accessible greenery in the centre of the city, and can be one of the most pleasant spots for a midday picnic or coffee. (There's a café, the *Kaffeehaus*, with a panoramic view in the garden.) It's no place to seek solitude, however: some five million visitors annually, more than at any other Italian garden, take time out here. (If the queues at the main entrance are too daunting, walk about three hundred metres further along the main road, the Via Romana, where you'll find another, invariaby quieter, entrance.)

Aligned with the central block of the palazzo, the garden's **amphitheatre** was designed in the early seventeenth century as an arena for Medici entertainments. The site had previously been laid out by Ammannati in 1599 over an earlier stone quarry as a garden in the shape of a Roman circus. For the wedding of Cosimo III and Princess Marguerite-Louise, cousin of Louis XIV, twenty thousand guests were packed onto the stone benches to watch a production that began with the appearance of a gigantic effigy of Atlas with the globe on his back; the show got under way when the planet split apart, releasing a cascade of earth that transformed the giant into the Atlas mountain. Such frivolities did little to reconcile Marguerite-Louise to either Florence or her husband, and after several acrimonious years this miserable dynastic marriage came to an effective end with her return to Paris, where she professed to care about little "as long as I never have to set eyes on the grand duke again".

Of all the garden's Mannerist embellishments, the most celebrated is the **Grotta del Buontalenti** (1583–88), to the left of the entrance, beyond Giambologna's much-reproduced statue of Cosimo I's favourite dwarf astride a giant tortoise. Embedded in the grotto's faked stalactites and encrustations are replicas of Michelangelo's *Slaves* – the originals were lodged here until 1908. Lurking in the deepest recesses of the cave, and normally viewable only from afar, is Giambologna's *Venus Emerging from Her Bath*, leered at by attendant imps.

Another spectacular set piece is the fountain island called the **Isolotto**, which is the focal point of the far end of the garden; from within the Bóboli the most dramatic approach is along the central cypress avenue known as the **Viottolone**, many of whose statues are Roman originals. These lower parts of the garden are its most pleasant – and least visited – sections. You come upon them quickly if you enter the Bóboli by the Porta Romana entrance. Birdwatchers might sample the special nature trail, laid out in 1994. Until 1772 the garden's wooded thickets were used for netting small birds for the Medici dinner table.

## The Casa Guidi and La Specola

Within a stone's throw of the Pitti, on the opposite side of the road, on the junction of Via Maggio and Via Romana, you'll find the home of Robert Browning and Elizabeth Barrett Browning, the **Casa Guidi** (April–Nov Mon, Wed & Fri 3–6pm; free, but donations welcome). It's something of a shrine to Elizabeth, who wrote much of her most popular verse here (including, naturally enough, *Casa Guidi Windows*) and died here. Virtually all the Casa Guidi's furniture went under the hammer at Sotheby's in 1913, and there's just one oil painting left, but two of the three rooms still manage to conjure up something of the spirit. It makes a spectacular place to stay – you can rent it through the Landmark Trust but it is booked months ahead and is far from cheap (ⓦwww.landmarktrust.org.uk)

There's more to enjoy on the third floor of the university buildings at Via Romana 17, in what can reasonably claim to be the strangest museum in the city. Taking its name from the telescope (*specola*) on its roof, **La Specola** (Mon, Tues, Thurs, Fri & Sun 9am–1pm, Sat 9am–5pm; €5; ⓦwww.specola.unifi .it/cere) is a twin-sectioned museum of zoology. The first part is conventional enough, with ranks of shells, insects and crustaceans, followed by a mortician's ark of animals stuffed, pickled and desiccated, including a hippo, given to Grand Duke Pietro Leopardo, which used to reside in the Bóboli garden. Beyond some rather frayed-looking sharks lie the exhibits everyone comes to see, the **Cere Anatomiche** (Anatomical Waxworks). Wax arms, legs and organs cover the walls, arrayed around satin beds on which wax cadavers recline in progressive stages of deconstruction, each muscle fibre and nerve cluster moulded and dyed with absolute precision. Most of the six hundred models – and nearly all of the amazing full-body mannequins – were made between 1775 and 1791 by one Clemente Susini, under the supervision of the physiologist Tommaso Bonicoli, and were intended as teaching aids, in an age when medical ethics and refrigeration techniques were not what they are today.

In a separate room towards the end, after the obstetrics display and a few zoological waxworks, you'll find the grisliest section of La Specola, a trio of tableaux created by **Gaetano Zumbo**, a cleric from Sicily, to satisfy the hypochondriacal obsessions of Cosimo III, a Jesuit-indoctrinated bigot who regarded all genuine scientific enquiry with suspicion. Enclosed in tasteful display cabinets, they depict Florence during the plague: rats teasing the intestines from green-fleshed corpses, mushrooms growing from the mulch of fleshly debris, and the pink bodies of the freshly dead heaped on the suppurating semi-decomposed. A fourth tableau, illustrating the horrors of syphilis, was damaged in the 1966 flood, and now consists of a loose gathering of the dead and diseased. In the centre of the room lies a dissected waxwork head, built on the foundation of a real skull; it's as fastidious as any of Susini's creations, but Zumbo couldn't resist giving the skin a tint of putrefaction, before applying a dribble of blood to the mouth and nose.

# Western Oltrarno

**Western Oltrarno** is one of the city's earthier districts, though in recent years it's been steadily colonized by bars, restaurants and shops that are turning it into a south-of-the-river equivalent of the lively area around Sant'Ambrogio. Some indication of the importance of the parish of **Santo Spirito**, the Oltrarno's social and geographical heart, is given by the fact that when Florence was divided into four administrative *quartieri* in the fourteenth century, the entire area south of the Arno was given its name. The busy piazza in front of Santo Spirito church, with its market stalls, cafés and restaurants, encapsulates the self-sufficient character of this part of the Oltrarno, an area not hopelessly compromised by the encroachments of tourism, even though there's a steady stream of day-trippers heading for the great fresco cycle in the church of **Santa Maria del Carmine**.

# Santo Spirito

Designed in 1434 as a replacement for a thirteenth-century church, **Santo Spirito** (Mon, Tues & Thurs–Sat 8.30am–noon & 4–6pm, Sun 4–6pm) was one of Brunelleschi's last projects, a swansong later described by Bernini as "the most beautiful church in the world". Many have concurred since, though the interior's measured monochrome of grey *pietra serena* and off-white *intacco* (plaster) can seem severe to modern eyes.

Work on the church began in 1444, but only a single column had been raised by the time the architect died two years later. Brunelleschi had wanted the church to enjoy an uninterrupted view of the Arno, but was thwarted by the aristocratic families whose homes would have had to have been demolished. Many of the same families helped pay for the church, however, whose chief source of income was sponsorship of its many side chapels. One Frescobaldi aristocrat donated a thousand florins, a huge sum at the time, as long as "no coat of arms other than that of the Frescobaldi were placed in the sepulchre" of his chapel. Funds were supplemented in more modest fashion by Augustinian monks from the neighbouring monastery, who sacrificed a meal a day as a money-raising example to others.

## The interior

The church is so perfectly proportioned that nothing could seem more artless, yet the plan is extremely sophisticated: a Latin cross with a continuous chain of 38 chapels round the outside and a line of 35 columns running without a break round the nave, transepts and chancel. The exterior wall was originally designed to follow the curves of the chapels' walls, creating a flowing, corrugated effect. As built, however, the exterior is a plain, straight wall, and even the main facade remained incomplete, disguised today by a simple plastering job. Inside the church, only the Baroque baldachin, about as nicely integrated as a jukebox in a Greek temple, disrupts the harmony.

A fire in 1471 destroyed most of Santo Spirito's medieval works, including famed frescoes by Cimabue and the Gaddi family, but as a result, the altar paintings in the many chapels comprise an unusually unified collection of religious works, most having been commissioned in the aftermath of the fire. For the first time, single painted panels replaced the previously preferred genre of the polyptych, and there was a new emphasis on the so-called *Sacra Conversazione*, representing the Madonna and Child surrounded by saints, each apparently lost in private meditation. Most prolific among the artists is the so-called **Maestro di Santo Spirito**, but some of the best paintings are found in the transepts.

In the south transept is Filippino Lippi's so-called **Nerli Altarpiece**, an age-darkened Madonna and Child with saints (second chapel from the left of the four chapels on the transept's south wall). The Nerli were the family who commissioned the chapel and the painting, the donors Tanai and Nanna dei Nerli being portrayed amidst the latter's saints; their Florentine home, the Palazzo dei Nerli near Porta San Frediano, is depicted in the background.

Across the church, in the north transept, is an unusual **St Monica and Augustinian Nuns** (1460–70), probably by Verrocchio or Francesco Botticini, that's virtually a study in monochrome, with black-clad nuns flocking round their black-clad paragon; it's in the second chapel on the right wall as you stand with your back to the high altar. Two chapels to the left, on the facing wall, the Cappella Corbinelli features a fine sculpted altarpiece (1492) by the young Andrea Sansovino.

A door in the north aisle leads through to Giuliano da Sangallo's stunning vestibule and **sacristy** (1489–93), the latter designed in conscious imitation of Brunelleschi's Pazzi chapel. The meticulously planned proportions and soft grey and white tones create an atmosphere of extraordinary calm that is only disrupted by the exuberantly botanical carvings of the capitals, some of which were designed by Sansovino. Hanging above the altar is a wooden crucifix, attributed to **Michelangelo**. With its distinctive, tenderly feminized body, its existence had long been documented, but it was feared lost until discovered in Santo Spirito in 1963. For years it festered in the Casa Buonarotti until it was restored and returned to Santo Spirito in December 2000.

### The Chiostro dei Morti and the Cenacolo di Santo Spirito

A glass door at the far end of the vestibule, usually locked, gives out onto the **Chiostro dei Morti**, the only cloister in the complex that is still part of the Augustinian monastery. The 1471 fire destroyed much of the rest of the monastery, with the exception of its refectory (entered to the left of the main church, at Piazza Santo Spirito 29), which is now the home of the **Cenacolo di Santo Spirito** (Tues–Sun: April–Nov 9am–2pm; Dec–March 10.30am–1.30pm; €2.20), a one-room collection comprising an assortment of carvings, many of them Roman-esque, and a huge fresco of *The Crucifixion* (1365) by Orcagna and his workshop.

# Santa Maria del Carmine

Nowhere in Florence is there a more startling contrast between exterior and interior than in **Santa Maria del Carmine**, a couple of blocks west of Santo Spirito in Piazza del Carmine. Outside it's a drab box of shabby brick; inside – in the frescoes of the **Cappella Brancacci** (Mon & Wed–Sat 10am–5pm, Sun 1–5pm; €4 or €8 joint ticket with Palazzo Vecchio) – it provides one of Italy's supreme artistic experiences. The chapel is barricaded off from the rest of the Carmine, and visits are restricted to a maximum of thirty people at a time, for just fifteen minutes. The time limit is strictly enforced in high season, but tends to become more flexible as the crowds ebb away. (You can either book a slot on ☎055.276.8224 or pay at the ticket office; if you choose the latter option, bear in mind that tickets are timed, so you may have to come back some time after buying them.)

### The Cappella Brancacci

The **Cappella Brancacci** frescoes were commissioned in 1424 by Felice Brancacci, a silk merchant and leading patrician figure, shortly after his return from a stint in Egypt as the Florentine ambassador. The decoration of the chapel was begun in the same year by **Masolino** (1383–1447), fresh from working as an assistant to Lorenzo Ghiberti on the Baptistery doors. Alongside Masolino was Tommaso di Ser Giovanni di Mone Cassai – known ever since as **Masaccio** (1401–28), a nickname meaning "Mad Tom". The former was aged 41, the latter just 22.

Two years into the project Masolino was recalled to Budapest, where he was official painter to the Hungarian court. Left to his own devices Masaccio began to blossom. When Masolino returned in 1427 the teacher was soon taking lessons from the supposed pupil, whose grasp of the texture of the real world, of the principles of perspective and of the dramatic potential of the biblical texts they were illustrating far exceeded that of his precursors. In 1428 Masolino was called away to Rome, where he was followed by Masaccio a few months later. Neither would return to the chapel. Masaccio died the same year, aged just 27, but, in the words of Vasari, "all the most celebrated sculptors and painters since Masaccio's day have become excellent and illustrious by studying their art in this chapel". (Michelangelo used to come here to make drawings of Masaccio's scenes, and had his nose broken on the chapel steps by a young sculptor whom he enraged with his condescension.) Any thought of further work on the frescoes ceased in 1436, when Brancacci (married to the daughter of Palla Strozzi, leader of the city's anti-Medici faction) was exiled by Cosimo de' Medici. The Carmelite monks in charge of the chapel and its frescoes promptly removed all portraits and other references to the disgraced donor.

Work resumed between 1480 and 1485, some fifty years later, when the paintings were completed by **Filippino Lippi**. So accomplished were Lippi's copying skills that his work was only recognized as distinct from that of his predecessors in 1838. By then public taste had performed an about-face; back in the late seventeenth century, it had been seriously proposed that the frescoes be removed. That suggestion was overruled, but approval was given for building alterations that destroyed frescoes in the lunettes above the main scenes. The surviving scenes were blurred by smoke from a fire that destroyed much of the church and adjoining convent in 1771, and subsequent varnishings smothered them in layers of grime that continued to darken over the decades. When critic Bernard Berenson saw the frescoes in 1930 he described them as "dust-bitten and ruined". Then, in 1932, an art historian removed part of the altar that had been installed in the eighteenth century, and discovered areas of almost pristine paint; half a century later, work finally got under way to restore the

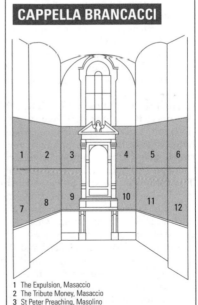

**CAPPELLA BRANCACCI**

1  The Expulsion, Masaccio
2  The Tribute Money, Masaccio
3  St Peter Preaching, Masolino
4  The Baptism of the Neophytes, Masaccio
5  The Healing of the Cripple and the Raising of Tabitha, Masolino–Masaccio
6  The Temptation, Masolino
7  St Paul Visits St Peter in Prison, Filippino Lippi
8  The Raising of the Son of Theophilus and St Peter Enthroned, Masaccio–Lippi
9  St Peter Healing the Sick with his Shadow, Masaccio
10 The Distribution of Alms and the Death of Ananias, Masaccio
11 The Disputation, Filippino Lippi
12 St Peter Freed from Prison, Filippino Lippi

chapel to the condition of the uncovered patch, revealing figures that exemplify what Berenson singled out as the "tactile quality" of Florentine art.

The small scene on the left of the entrance arch is the quintessence of Masaccio's art. Plenty of artists had depicted **The Expulsion of Adam and Eve** (1) before, but none had captured the desolation of the sinners so graphically: Adam presses his hands to his face in bottomless despair, Eve raises her head and screams. The monumentalism of these stark naked figures – whose modesty was preserved by strategically placed sprigs of foliage prior to the restoration – reveals the influence of Donatello, who may have been involved in the planning of the chapel. In contrast to the emotional charge and sculptural presence of Masaccio's couple, Masolino's almost dainty **Adam and Eve** (6) on the opposite arch, pose as if to have their portraits painted.

St Peter is chief protagonist of all the remaining scenes. It's possible that the cycle was intended as propaganda on behalf of the embattled papacy, which had only recently resolved the long and bitter Great Schism, during which one pope held court in Rome and another in Avignon. By celebrating the primacy of St Peter, the rock upon whom the Church is built, the frescoes by implication extol the apostolic succession from which the pope derives his authority.

Three scenes by Masaccio are especially compelling. First off is the **Tribute Money** (2), most widely praised of the paintings and the Renaissance's first monumental fresco. The narrative is complex, with no fewer than three separate events portrayed within a single frame. The central episode shows Christ outside the gates of Capernaum being asked to pay a tribute owing to the city. To the left, St Peter fetches coins from the mouth of a fish in order to pay the tribute, Christ in the central panel having pointed to where the money will be found. The third scene, to the right, depicts Peter handing over the money to the tax official.

Masaccio's second great panel is **St Peter Healing the Sick** (9), in which the shadow of the stern and self-possessed saint (followed by St John) cures the infirm as it passes over them, a miracle invested with the aura of a solemn ceremonial. The third panel is **The Distribution of Alms and Death of Ananias** (10), in which St Peter instructs the people to give up their possessions to the poor. One individual, Ananias, retains some of his wealth with the knowledge of his wife, Sapphira. Rebuked by Peter, Ananias dies on the spot, closely followed by a similarly castigated Sapphira.

Filippino Lippi's work included the finishing of Masaccio's **Raising of Theophilus's Son and St Peter Enthroned** (8), which depicts St Peter raising the son of Theophilus, the Prefect of Antioch (apparently after he'd been dead for fourteen years). The people of Antioch, suitably impressed by the miracle, build a throne from which St Peter can preach, shown as a separate episode to the right. The three figures to the right of the throne are thought to be portraits of Masaccio, Alberti and Brunelleschi, who made a trip to Rome together. Masaccio originally painted himself touching Peter's robe, a reference to the enthroned statue of Peter in Rome, which pilgrims touch for good luck. Lippi considered the contact of the artist and saint to be improper and painted out the arm; at the moment, his fastidious over-painting has been allowed to remain, but you can clearly see where the arm used to be.

Lippi left another portrait in the combined scene of **St Peter in Disputation with Agrippa** (or Nero) and his crucifixion (11): the central figure looking out from the painting in the trio right of the crucifixion is Botticelli, the painter's teacher, while Filippino himself can be seen at the far right.

(Like the Palazzo Vecchio, the Carmine is part of the **Emozioni da Museo** programme (see p.76), offering guided tours of the Brancacci chapel, as well as parts of the convent otherwise closed to the public.)

# Eastern Oltrarno

On the tourist map of Florence, **eastern Oltrarno** is something of a dead zone: as on the opposite bank of the river, blocks of historic buildings were destroyed by mines left behind by the Nazis in 1944. Some characterful parts remain, however, notably the medieval Via de' Bardi and its continuation, Via San Niccolò. These narrow, palazzo-lined streets will take you past the eclectic **Museo Bardini** and the medieval church of **San Niccolò**, both of which can be visited as part of the walk up to **San Miniato al Monte**, widely regarded as one of the most beautiful Romanesque churches in Tuscany. Another target for an Oltrarno hike might be the **Forte di Belvedere**, a Medici fortress now used mainly for temporary exhibitions.

## The Museo Bardini

The best way to reach the Bardini museum from the Ponte Vecchio and elsewhere in the Oltrarno is to take Via de' Bardi, known in the Middle Ages as the Borgo Pitiglioso – the "miserable" or "flea-bitten" street. Part way down the street on the left, beyond the small Piazza di Santa Maria Soprarno, you'll pass the tiny church of **Santa Lucia dei Magnoli**, founded in 1078. Pop inside if you're lucky enough to find it open: the first altar on the left has a panel of *St Lucy* by the Sienese master Pietro Lorenzetti.

The **Museo Bardini** (closed for restoration at the time of writing), which stands at the end of the street at Piazza de' Mozzi 1, is like the Museo Horne just across the Arno, in that it was built around the bequest of a private collector. Whereas Horne was a moderately well-off connoisseur, however, his contemporary Sergio Bardini (1836–1922) was once the largest art dealer in Italy. His tireless activity, at a time when Renaissance art was relatively cheap and unfashionable, laid the cornerstone of many important modern-day European and North American collections. Determined that no visitor to his native city should remain unaware of his success, he ripped down a church that stood on the site and built a vast home, studding it with fragments of old buildings. Doorways, ceiling panels and other orphaned pieces are strewn all over the place: the first floor windows, for instance, are actually altars from a church in Pistoia. The more portable items are equally wide-ranging: musical instruments, carvings, ceramics, armour, furniture, carpets, pictures – if it was vaguely arty and had a price tag, Bardini snapped it up. His artistic potpourri was bequeathed to the city on his death. The museum may lack genuine masterpieces, but it's larger and more satisfying than the Museo Horne, as well as being crammed with a sufficiently wide variety of beautiful objects to appeal to most tastes. Displays are spread over a couple of floors and some twenty rooms, though only the more precious exhibits are fully labelled.

On the **ground floor**, beyond the open-plan spread of rooms in the vestibule, Tino da Camaino's *Charity* (Room 7) stands out. In Room 10, upstairs, there's a room of funerary monuments arranged as if in a crypt, with an enamelled terracotta altarpiece attributed to Andrea della Robbia. On the **first floor**, beyond several rooms of weapons, three pieces in Room 14 also grab the attention: a polychrome terracotta of the *Madonna and Child* by Donatello; an extraordinarily modern-looking stucco, mosaic and glass relief of the *Madonna dei Cordai* (1443), also probably by Donatello; and a terracotta *Madonna and Child with San Giovannino* by Benedetto da Maiano. Room 16 has some lovely *cassoni*, or medieval chests, and several of the museum's many depictions of the Madonna and Child, a subject with which Bardini appears to have been obsessed. Other highlights of the final rooms include some gorgeous carpets and Domenico Beccafumi's *Hercules at the Crossroads between Vice and Virtue* (Room 15); Michele Giambono's *St John the Baptist* (Room 16); a painted relief in terracotta from the workshop of Jacopo della Quercia (Room 17); a *St Michael* by Antonio del Pollaiuolo and a beautiful terracotta *Virgin Annunciate*, an anonymous piece from fifteenth-century Siena (Room 18).

## From San Niccolò to Piazzale Michelangelo

Beyond the Museo Bardini, Via San Niccolò swings past **San Niccolò sopr'Arno** (daily 10am–noon), another of this quarter's interesting little churches. Restoration work after the 1966 flood uncovered several frescoes underneath the altars, but none is as appealing as the fifteenth-century fresco in the sacristy; known as *The Madonna of the Girdle*, it was probably painted by Baldovinetti. In medieval times the church was close to the edge of the city, and two of Florence's fourteenth-century gates still stand in the vicinity: the diminutive **Porta San Miniato**, set in a portion of the walls, and the huge **Porta San Niccolò**, overlooking the Arno. From either of these gates you can begin the climb up to San Miniato: the path from Porta San Niccolò weaves up through **Piazzale Michelangelo**, with its replica *David* and bumper-to-bumper tour coaches; the more direct path from Porta San Miniato offers a choice between the steep Via del Monte alle Croci or the stepped Via di San Salvatore al Monte, both of which emerge a short distance uphill from Piazzale Michelangelo.

In spring you can break the walk by visiting one of the gardens on the slopes just below the Piazzale: to the west on Via di San Salvatore al Monte is the pleasant Rose Garden (May to mid-June daily 8am–8pm; free), but more striking is the **Iris Garden** (3 weeks in May daily 10am–12.30am & 3–7pm; free), whose entrance lies at the southeast corner of the square. The iris is one of the city's many symbols, and in May the garden hosts the Italian Iris Society's Florence Prize, an international competition that turns this olive grove into a mass of colour.

## San Miniato al Monte

Arguably the finest Romanesque structure in Tuscany, **San Miniato al Monte** (daily: summer 8am–7.30pm; winter 8am–5.30pm) is also the oldest surviving church building in Florence after the Baptistery. Its brilliant multicoloured facade lures troops of visitors up the hill from Oltrarno, and the church and its magnificent interior and works of art more than fulfil the promise of its distant appearance. The **walk** up to San Miniato has some steep sections; if you don't fancy the climb, take **bus** #12 or #13 as far as Piazzale Michelangelo and then continue on foot.

The church's dedicatee, **St Minias**, was Florence's first home-grown martyr. Possibly a Greek merchant or the son of an Armenian king, he originally left home to make a pilgrimage to Rome. Around 250 he moved to Florence, where he became caught up in the anti-Christian persecutions of the Emperor Decius. Legend has it that after martyrdom by decapitation – close to the site of Piazza della Signoria – the saintly corpse was seen to carry his severed head over the river and up the hill to this spot, an area where he'd previously lived as a hermit: a shrine was subsequently erected on the slope. The hill, known as **Mons Fiorentinus**, was already the site of several pagan temples and a secret oratory dedicated to Peter the Apostle. A chapel to Miniato is documented on the site in the eighth century, though construction of the present building began in 1013. It was raised by Alibrando, bishop of Florence, and endowed by Emperor Henry II "for the good of his soul". Initially run as a Benedictine foundation, the building passed to the Cluniacs until 1373, and then to the **Olivetans**, a Benedictine offshoot, who reside here to this day. The monks sell their famous liquors, honeys and tisanes from the shop next to the church, as well as souvenirs and divers unguents, proof against complaints ranging from anxiety and depression to varicose veins and "lowering of the voice".

## The exterior

San Miniato's gorgeous marble **facade** alludes to the Baptistery in its geometrical patterning, and, like its model, the church was often mistaken for a structure of classical provenance during the later Middle Ages. The lower part of the facade is possibly eleventh-century, while the angular upper levels date from the twelfth century onwards, and were financed in part by the *Arte di Calimala* (cloth merchants' guild), the body responsible for the church's upkeep from 1288: their trademark, a gilded copper eagle clutching a bale of cloth, perches on the roof. The mosaic of *Christ between the Virgin and St Minias* dates from 1260. The original **bell-tower** collapsed in 1499 and was replaced in the 1520s by the present campanile, still unfinished. During the 1530 siege of Florence it was used as an artillery post, thus attracting the attention of enemy gunners. Michelangelo, then advising on the city's defences, had it wrapped in woollen mattresses to protect it from cannon balls.

## The interior

With its choir raised on a platform above the large crypt, the sublime **interior** of San Miniato is like no other in the city, and its general appearance has changed little since the mid-eleventh century. The main additions and decorations in no way spoil its serenity, though the nineteenth-century recoating of the marble columns is a little lurid: the columns' capitals, however, are Roman

△ San Miniato al Monte

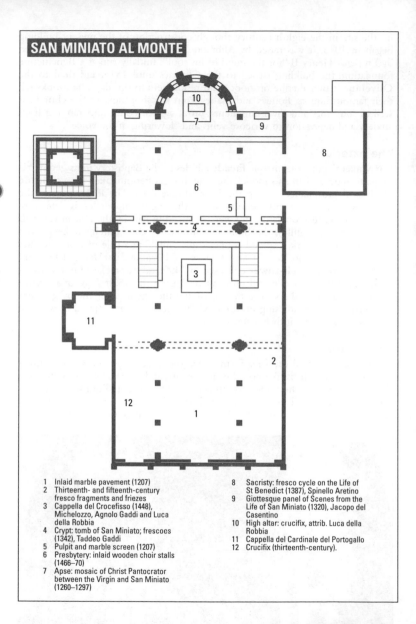

**SAN MINIATO AL MONTE**

1 Inlaid marble pavement (1207)
2 Thirteenth- and fifteenth-century fresco fragments and friezes
3 Cappella del Crocefisso (1448), Michelozzo, Agnolo Gaddi and Luca della Robbia
4 Crypt: tomb of San Miniato; frescoes (1342), Taddeo Gaddi
5 Pulpit and marble screen (1207)
6 Presbytery: inlaid wooden choir stalls (1466–70)
7 Apse: mosaic of Christ Pantocrator between the Virgin and San Miniato (1260–1297)

8 Sacristy: fresco cycle on the Life of St Benedict (1387), Spinello Aretino
9 Giottesque panel of Scenes from the Life of San Miniato (1320), Jacopo del Casentino
10 High altar: crucifix, attrib. Luca della Robbia
11 Cappella del Cardinale del Portogallo
12 Crucifix (thirteenth-century).

and Byzantine originals removed from older buildings. The intricately patterned panels of the **pavement** (1) are dated 1207; some claim the zodiac and strange beast motifs were inspired by Sicilian fabrics, others that they are of Byzantine origin, introduced into Italy through trade and the Crusades.

The lovely tabernacle, or **Cappella del Crocefisso** (3), which dominates the middle of the nave, was designed in 1448 by Michelozzo. The date is significant, for the piece is one of the few works commissioned by Piero de' Medici, or Piero il Gottoso (the Gouty), during his brief tenure as head of the Medici dynasty. The marble medallion to the rear and other parts of the work are adorned with Piero's motto (*Semper*) and several Medici symbols – the eagle holding three feathers and a diamond ring, the latter a symbol of durability and toughness. The chapel originally housed the miraculous crucifix associated with St Giovanni Gualberto (see p.95), which was moved to Santa Trinita in 1671. Today it contains painted **panels** by Agnolo Gaddi depicting the *Annunciation, Stories of the Passion* and *SS Giovanni Gualberto and Miniato* (1394–96). These were originally arranged in the form of a cross to act as a frame for the now vanished crucifix. Maso di Bartolomeo crafted the twin eagles (1449), symbols of the *Calimala*, to stress that while Piero was the work's sponsor, the guild was responsible for overseeing all stages of its construction. The terracotta in the barrel vault is by Luca della Robbia.

Steps either side of the cappella lead down to the **crypt** (4), the oldest part of the church, where the original high altar still contains the bones that Bishop Alibrando confirmed as those of St Minias in the eleventh century (ignoring a well-founded belief that the real bones had been removed to Metz by a relic-obsessed German). The vaults, supported by 36 wonderfully mismatched pillars, contain gilt-backed frescoes (1341) of the saints, martyrs, prophets, virgins and Evangelists by Taddeo Gaddi.

Back in the main body of the church, steps beside the Cappella del Crocefisso lead to the raised **choir** and **presbytery** (6), where there's a magnificent Romanesque **pulpit** (5) and screen dating from 1207. The odd totem-like figures supporting the lectern may represent three of the four Evangelists or, possibly, humanity placed in a middle state between the animal world (the lion) and the divine (the eagle). The great **mosaic** (7) in the apse was created in 1297, probably by the same artist who created the facade mosaic, as their subjects are identical – *Christ Pantocrator* enthroned between the Virgin and San Miniato. The **crucifix** (10) above the high altar is attributed to Luca della Robbia. Off the presbytery lies the **sacristy** (8), whose walls are almost completely covered in a superlative fresco cycle by Spinello Aretino (1387), the first such complete cycle in Tuscany devoted to the *Life of St Benedict*.

Back in the lower body of the church, the **Cappella del Cardinale del Portogallo** (11), dating from a few years after the Cappella del Crocefisso, is one of the masterpieces of Renaissance chapel design and a marvellous example of artistic collaboration. Completed in 1473, it was built as a memorial to Cardinal James of Lusitania, who died in Florence in 1459, aged 25. The cultured nephew of King Alfonso V of Portugal, James was sent to study law in Perugia, later becoming archbishop of Lisbon, a cardinal, and subsequently the ambassador to Florence. Close to death in the city, he asked to be buried in San Miniato. The cardinal's aunt and his humanist friends and admirers jointly sponsored his tomb. Aside from that of Minias himself, this is – remarkably – the church's only tomb.

The chapel's basic design was the work of Antonio di Manetto (or Manetti), a pupil and biographer of Brunelleschi, who borrowed heavily from his master's work in San Lorenzo's Sagrestia Vecchia. The **tomb** itself was carved by Antonio and Bernardo Rossellino; their elder brother Giovanni oversaw the chapel's construction after Manetto's death. Antonio Rossellino's tondo of the *Madonna and Child* keeps watch over the deceased.

The chapel's architectural and sculptural work was followed in 1466 by carefully integrated frescoes and **paintings**: an *Annunciation* (to the left) and the *Evangelists* and *Doctors of the Church* by Alesso Baldovinetti (lunettes and beside the arches). Antonio and Piero del Pollaiuolo produced the **altarpiece** depicting the cardinal's patron saint, St James, with SS Vincent and Eustace: the present picture is a copy, the original being in the Uffizi. The ceiling's tiled decoration and four glazed terracotta medallions, perhaps the finest such work in the city, were provided by Luca della Robbia.

All the decorative details were carefully designed to complement one another and create a unified artistic whole. Thus Rossellino's tondo of the *Madonna and Child*, for example, echoes the round windows of the walls; the colours in Baldovinetti's *Annunciation* deliberately echo the tones of the surrounding porphyry and serpentine inlays; and the curtain held aside by angels on the cardinal's tomb is repeated in a similar curtain half-shielding the altar.

## ⑥ From the Forte di Belvedere to San Leonardo in Arcetri

The **Forte di Belvedere**, standing on the crest of the hill above the Bóboli garden, was built by Buontalenti on the orders of Ferdinando I between 1590 and 1595, ostensibly to protect the city, but in fact to intimidate the grand duke's subjects. The urban panorama from here is superb, and ambitious exhibitions are often held in and around the shed-like palace in the centre of the fortress, as are occasional summer-evening film screenings. The city's new Museo delle Arme (Arms and Armour Museum) is also due to open here soon.

In the past it has sometimes been possible to get up to the fort from the Bóboli gardens, but if you want to be certain of getting in, approach the fort from the **Costa di San Giorgio**, a lane which you can reach by backtracking slightly from the Museo Bardini, or pick up directly from the rear of Santa Felìcita. Look out for the villa at no. 19, home to Galileo between 1610 and 1631.

East from the Belvedere stretches the best-preserved section of Florence's fortified **walls**, paralleled by Via di Belvedere. South of the Belvedere, Via San Leonardo leads past olive groves to the church of **San Leonardo in Arcetri** (daily 10am–noon), site of a beautiful thirteenth-century pulpit brought here from a church now incorporated into the Uffizi. Dante and Boccaccio are both said to have preached from the spot.

# Fiesole

T he hill-town of **FIESOLE**, which spreads over a cluster of hills above the Mugnone and Arno valleys some 8km northeast of Florence, is conventionally described as a pleasant retreat from the crowds and heat of summertime Florence. Unfortunately, its tranquillity has been so well advertised that in high season it's now hardly less busy than Florence itself; you'd probably also need paranormal sensitivity to detect much climatic difference between the two on an airless August afternoon.

That said, Fiesole offers a grandstand view of the city, has something of the feel of a country village, and bears many traces of its history – which is actually lengthier than that of Florence. First settled in the Bronze Age, then later by the Etruscans, and then absorbed by the Romans, it rivalled its neighbour until the early twelfth century, when the Florentines overran the town. From that time it became a satellite, favoured as a semi-rural second home for wealthier citizens such as the ubiquitous Medici.

Fiesole is one of the easiest short trips from Florence: ATAF city **bus** #7 runs from Santa Maria Novella train station to Fiesole's central Piazza Mino da Fiesole (every 15–20min; takes 20min; €0.80). Fiesole's **tourist office** (March–Oct Mon–Sat 9am–6pm, Sun 10am–1pm, 2–6pm; Nov–Feb Mon–Sat 9am–5pm, Sun 10am–4pm; ☎055.598.720, ⊛www.comune.fiesole.fi.it) is nearby at Via Portigiani 3/5, next to the entrance to the archeological site.

## The Town

When the Florentines wrecked Fiesole in 1125, the only major building they spared was the **Duomo** (daily 7.30am–noon & 3–6pm; till 5pm in winter), on the edge of Piazza Mino. Subsequently, nineteenth-century restorers managed to ruin the exterior, which is now notable only for its lofty campanile. The most interesting part of the bare interior is the raised choir: the altarpiece is a polyptych, painted in the 1440s by Bicci di Lorenzo, and the Cappella Salutati, to the right, contains two fine pieces carved around the same time by Mino da Fiesole: an altar frontal of the Madonna and Saints and the tomb of Bishop Salutati. Fiesole's patron saint, St Romulus, is buried underneath the choir in the ancient crypt. Behind the Duomo at Via Dupré 1, the **Museo Bandini** (summer daily 10am–7pm; winter open 10am–5pm, closed Tues; joint ticket valid all day covering admission to all Fiesole's museums €6.50; ⊛www.fiesolemusei.it) possesses a collection of glazed terracotta in the style of the della Robbias, the odd piece of Byzantine ivory work and a few thirteenth- and fourteenth-century Tuscan pictures, none of them inspiring.

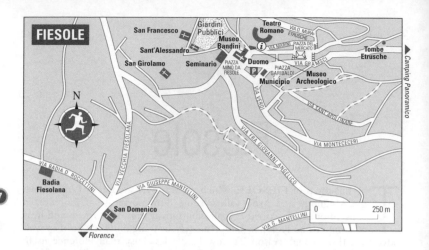

Across the road from the museum are the town's other museums: the **Teatro Romano** and the **Museo Archeologico** (same times and ticket as Museo Bandini). Built in the first century BC, the 3000-seat theatre was excavated towards the end of the nineteenth century and is in such good repair that it's used for performances during the Estate Fiesolana festival (see p.210). Parts of the site may be closed as excavation work continues. Most of the exhibits in the site's small **museum** were excavated in this area and encompass pieces from the Bronze Age to Roman occupation.

Fiesole's other major churches, Sant'Alessandro and San Francesco, are at the top of the steep Via San Francesco, which runs past the **Oratorio di San Jacopo** (Sat & Sun 10am–7pm; same ticket as the museums), a little chapel containing a fifteenth-century fresco and some ecclesiastical treasures. A little further up, a terrace offers a knockout view of Florence. **Sant'Alessandro** (open for occasional exhibitions only) was founded in the sixth century on the site of Etruscan and Roman temples; repairs have rendered the outside a white-washed nonentity, but the beautiful *marmorino cipollino* (onion marble) columns of the basilical interior make it the most atmospheric building in Fiesole. Again, restoration has not improved the Gothic **San Francesco** (daily 9am–noon & 3–7pm; till 6pm Oct–March), which occupies the site of the acropolis: the interior is a twentieth-century renovation, but the tiny cloisters are genuine. The church itself contains an *Immaculate Conception* by Piero di Cosimo (second altar on the right), and below the church is a small museum featuring material gathered mainly by missions to the Far East, much of it from China, as well as a piece of Etruscan wall. From the front of San Francesco a gate opens into a wooded public park, the most pleasant descent back to Piazza Mino.

If you want to wring every last drop of historical significance from Fiesole, you could follow the signposts from here up the hill to the east of the Teatro, to the ruins of a couple of **Etruscan tombs** from the third century BC.

## To San Domenico

The most enjoyable excursion from Fiesole is a wander down the narrow Via Vecchia Fiesolana, which passes the **Villa Medici** – built for Cosimo il Vecchio by Michelozzo – on its way to the hamlet of **SAN DOMENICO**. Fra'

Angelico was once prior of the Dominican **monastery** at this village and the church retains a *Madonna and Angels* by him, in the first chapel on the left; the chapterhouse also has a Fra' Angelico fresco of *The Crucifixion* (ring at no. 4).

Five minutes' walk northwest from San Domenico stands the **Badìa Fiesolana** (Mon–Fri 8.30am–6.30pm), Fiesole's cathedral from the ninth century to the eleventh. Cosimo il Vecchio had the church altered in the 1460s, a project which kept the magnificent Romanesque facade intact while transforming the interior into a superb Renaissance building.

# Listings

# Listings

# 8

# Accommodation

A ccommodation in Florence can be a problem: hotels are plentiful, but prices are high and standards often less than alluring. Worse still, the tourist invasion has very few slack spots: "low season" is defined by most hotels as meaning mid-July to the end of August (the weeks during which nearly all Italians head for the beaches or the mountains), and from mid-November to mid-March, except for the Christmas and New Year period. Between March and October you'll need to book your room well in advance or reconcile yourself to staying some way from the centre. If you're considering a package deal, check the location of your hotel carefully. There's a handful of **hostels** and a couple of **campsites**, but few are within the city boundaries.

If you haven't reserved ahead, the main tourist office (p.49) can give you the numbers of various private booking agencies, but there is no longer an official accommodation booking service in Florence. Be wary of resorting to touts, who hang around the queues for this office and around the station in general: some of their hotels are genuine but are likely to be expensive or far from the centre, while others are unlicensed private houses whose safety standards may be dubious.

For more general information on accommodation see p.32. Central Florence accommodation is marked on the map on pp.180–181, while more outlying places are shown on the map on pp.186–187.

## Hotels

**Hotels** in Italy are graded on a scale running from one-star to five-star (see p.32), but bear in mind that prices in Florence are higher than anywhere else in the country except Venice: one-star establishments in this city cost as much as two-star – even three-star – places elsewhere in Tuscany.

The main concentration of lowish-cost hotels is to the east of the station, centred on Via Faenza and Via Nazionale, with a smaller cluster along Via della Scala, which extends westwards from Piazza della Stazione. Neither of these zones is very pleasant: the Faenza/Nazionale area has a sizeable night-time population of assorted lowlife, with pimps and prostitutes on every corner, while Via della Scala is a major traffic artery and feels more remote from the heart of the city. Note that some of the places in these areas are unlicensed; if you're at all doubtful about a hotel, give it a miss. Our reviews are grouped by district, with subdivisions by price: "Budget" hotels are those which have doubles for under €100; "Inexpensive" hotels should have rooms for €100–150; "Moderate" means €150–200; "Expensive" means €200–300; and in our "Very Expensive" hotels you'll be paying upwards of €300.

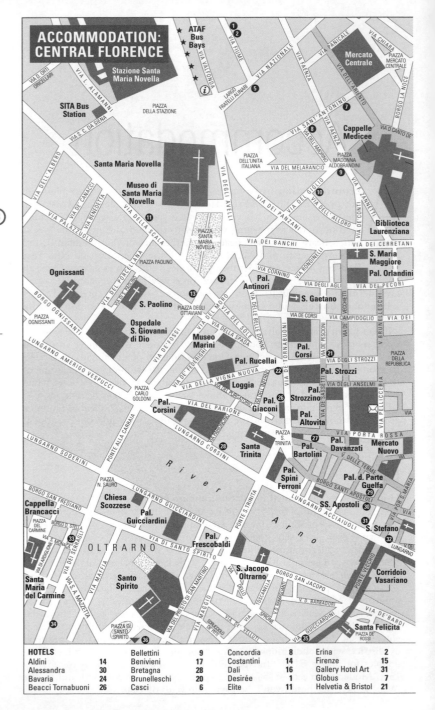

# ACCOMMODATION: CENTRAL FLORENCE

ATAF Bus Bays

Stazione Santa Maria Novella

SITA Bus Station

PIAZZA DELLA STAZIONE

Mercato Centrale

PIAZZA MERCATO CENTRALE

BORGO LA NOCE

VIA D'ORTI ORICELLARI

VIA L. ALAMANNI

VIA FIUME

VIA VALFONDA

LARGO FRATELLI ALINARI

VIA NAZIONALE

VIA FAENZA

VIA PANICALE

VIA CHIARA

PIAZZA

VIA DELL'ARIENTO

VIA S. C. DA SIENA

Santa Maria Novella

Museo di Santa Maria Novella

VIA DELL'ALBERO

VIA DE' CANACCI

VIA DELLA SCALA

VIA PALAZZUOLO

VIA DELLA SCALA

PIAZZA PAOLINO

PIAZZA SANTA MARIA NOVELLA

VIA DEGLI AVELLI

PIAZZA DELL'UNITA ITALIANA

VIA DEL MELARANCIO

VIA DEI PANZANI

VIA DEI BANCHI

PIAZZA MADONNA ALDOBRANDINI

Cappelle Medicee

VIA D CANTO DE

VIA SANT'ANTONINO

VIA DEL GIGLIO

VIA DELL'ALLORO

VIA DEI CERRETANI

Biblioteca Laurenziana

VIA DE' CONTI

VIA F. ZANNETTI

S. Maria Maggiore

Pal. Orlandini

Ognissanti

PIAZZA OGNISSANTI

BORGO OGNISSANTI

S. Paolino

Ospedale S. Giovanni di Dio

LUNGARNO AMERIGO VESPUCCI

VIA DEL PORCELLANA

VIA DEL MORO

VIA DE'FOSSI

PIAZZA DEGLI OTTAVIANI

VIA DELLA SPADA

Museo Marini

Pal. Rucellai

Loggia

VIA CORNINO

Pal. Antinori

VIA DELLE BELLE DONNE

VIA DEGLI AGLI

S. Gaetano

VIA DE CORSI

VIA DE PESCIONI

Pal. Corsi

Pal. Strozzi

VIA DE' TORNABUONI

VIA DELLA VIGNA NUOVA

VIA DEL PARIONE

Pal. Corsini

PIAZZA CARLO GOLDONI

VIA DELLE TERME

Pal. Giaconi

Pal. Strozzino

Pal. Altovita

VIA DEGLI STROZZI

VIA DEGLI ANSELMI

VIA DE' SASSETTI

VIA DE' BRUNELLESCHI

PIAZZA DELLA REPUBBLICA

VIA DEI

VIA DE CAMPIDOGLIO

VIA DEL PECORI

VECCHIETTI

VIA PORTA ROSSA

VIA FELLICCERIA

Mercato Nuovo

Pal. Davanzati

Pal. Bartolini

Santa Trinita

PIAZZA S. TRINITA

LUNGARNO CORSINI

PONTE ALLA CARRAIA

LUNGARNO SODERINI

River

Arno

PIAZZA N. SAURO

Chiesa Scozzese

Pal. Guicciardini

Cappella Brancacci

PIAZZA DEL CARMINE

BORGO D. STELLA

BORGO SAN FREDIANO

LUNGARNO GUICCIARDINI

Pal. Spini Ferroni

Pal. d. Parte Guelfa

BORGO SANTI APOSTOLI

SS. Apostoli

LUNGARNO ACCIAIUOLI

S. Stefano

PONTE VECCHIO

Corridoio Vasariano

Santa Maria del Carmine

OLTRARNO

Santo Spirito

Pal. Frescobaldi

S. Jacopo Oltrarno

BORGO SAN JACOPO

VIA DI SANTO SPIRITO

VIA MAFFIA

VIA DE' SERRAGLI

VIA S. MONACA

VIA SANT'AGOSTINO

VIA S.A. MAZZETTA

PIAZZA DI SANTO SPIRITO

VIA MAGGIO

VIA DEL PRESTO DI SAN MARTINO

VIA DE' VELLUTI

VIA TOSCANELLA

VIA DE' BARDI

Santa Felicita

PIAZZA DE' ROSSI

① ②

⑤

⑦

⑧

⑨

⑩

⑪

⑫

⑬

㉑

㉒

㉖

㉗

㉘

㉙

㉚

㉛

㉜

㉝

㉞

㉟

㊱

| HOTELS | | | | | | | |
|---|---|---|---|---|---|---|---|
| Aldini | 14 | Bellettini | 9 | Concordia | 8 | Erina | 2 |
| Alessandra | 30 | Benivieni | 17 | Costantini | 14 | Firenze | 15 |
| Bavaria | 24 | Bretagna | 28 | Dali | 16 | Gallery Hotel Art | 31 |
| Beacci Tornabuoni | 26 | Brunelleschi | 20 | Desirée | 1 | Globus | 7 |
| | | Casci | 6 | Elite | 11 | Helvetia & Bristol | 21 |

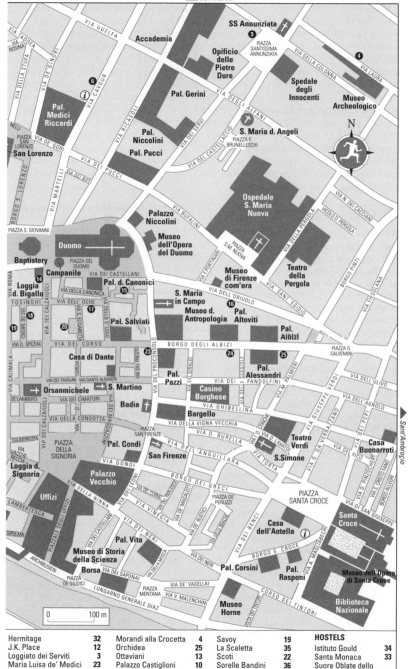

| Hermitage | **32** | Morandi alla Crocetta | **4** | Savoy | **19** | **HOSTELS** | |
|---|---|---|---|---|---|---|---|
| J.K. Place | **12** | Orchidea | **25** | La Scaletta | **35** | Istituto Gould | **34** |
| Loggiato dei Serviti | **3** | Ottaviani | **13** | Scoti | **22** | Santa Monaca | **33** |
| Maria Luisa de' Medici | **23** | Palazzo Castiglioni | **10** | Sorelle Bandini | **36** | Suore Oblate dello | |
| Maxim | **18** | Porta Rossa | **27** | Torre Guelfa | **29** | Spirito Santo | **5** |

The **prices** in the reviews relate to the high season; you will often find lower rates between mid–November and mid–March as well in July and August. Smaller hotels may regard the whole year as peak period, but it is always worth asking, since most hotels will drop their prices to fill rooms. Watch out for the hidden extra cost of breakfast: some hotels include it in the room price, but many don't (it's always cheaper and usually nicer to eat in a bar or café if you have the option). Prices for rooms may also vary within the same hotel, so if the first price you're quoted seems high, ask if there's anything cheaper – rooms without a private bathroom always cost less. As ever in big cities, **single rooms** are at a premium: you'll do well to get away with less than two-thirds the cost of a double. The maximum cost of a room, plus any charge for breakfast, should be posted on the back of the door; if it isn't, or if you have any other complaints, contact the tourist office. Note that many hotels require a **deposit** to secure booking, which will involve sending credit card details; if a hotel demands a cash deposit, go elsewhere.

## City centre

### Budget

**Bavaria** Borgo degli Albizi 26 ☎ & ℗055.234.0313, ⓦwww.eidinet.com /hotelbavaria. A simple and decent one-star near the city centre (second floor, no lift) with just nine rooms, including some palatial chambers on the upper floor, and a couple of inexpensive rooms with shared bathroom. The hotel occupies part of a sixteenth-century *palazzo* built for a follower of Eleonora di Toledo. Be sure to book, especially in summer, when it's popular with student tour groups. It has a range of prices: doubles with shower for €90, with bathroom just over €100, and there are cheaper rooms with shared bathrooms as well as single rooms.
**Dali** Via dell' Oriuolo 17 ☎ & ℗055.234.0706, ⓦwww.hoteldali.com. One of the least expensive one-star options close to the centre. The nine rooms, three with bath (€80 – those without are €15 cheaper), are plain and rather basic, but the location – on the top floor of a *palazzo* built in 1492 – helps, as does the view from the back rooms of the giant magnolia in the garden below. The friendly young owners speak good English.
**Maria Luisa de' Medici** Via del Corso 1 ☎055.280.048. Slightly run-down, quirky one-star, on the first floor (no lift), with painting-by-numbers portraits of the Medici in the rooms. But it is comfortable, central, small (nine rooms, two with private bathroom) and quiet. No credit cards. Booking by phone only. Curfew 11.30pm. €95 with en-suite bathroom, or €15 cheaper without.
**Maxim** entrances at Via dei Calzaiuoli 11 (lift) and Via de' Medici 4 (stairs) ☎055.217.474,

℗055.283.729, ⓦwww.hotelmaximfirenze.it. Few one-star hotels offer a better location than this friendly 26-room place just a minute from the Duomo. The clean air-conditioned double rooms are good value at around €95; the quietest look onto a central courtyard.
**Orchidea** Borgo degli Albizi 11 ☎055.248.0346, ⓦwww.hotelorchidea florence.it. On the first floor of a lovely twelfth-century building, with seven big rooms, including three doubles, one with a shower in the room. Doubles are a bargain at €80.

### Inexpensive

**Aldini** Via dei Calzaiuoli 13 ☎055.214.752, ℗055.291.621, ⓦwww.hotelaldini.it. A two-star at a very convenient address on the corner of Piazza Duomo. Of its fourteen rooms, all the doubles (from around €135) come with private bathrooms; the singles (€90) come with and without.
**Bretagna** Lungarno Corsini 6 ☎055.289.618, ℗055.289.619, ⓦwww .hotelbretagna.net. This one-star riverfront hotel has a superb location and Rococo-style breakfast and living rooms. The new management is increasing to six the number of rooms overlooking the Arno, and by the start of 2006 all 24 rooms should have en-suite bathrooms and air-conditioning. At present, doubles are from around €100.
**Firenze** Piazza dei Donati 4 ☎055.214.203, ℗055.212.370, ⓦwww.albergofirenze.net. Clean and central no-frills one-star hotel. It has 57 rooms, so there's a better chance of finding space here than in some of the smaller places. Most rooms are doubles

costing around €100; all have private bathrooms. Rooms on top floors enjoy a touch more daylight. No credit cards.

**Scoti Via de' Tornabuoni 7** ℡ & ℻ 055.292.128, 🅦 www.hotelscoti.com. The best budget option on this notoriously expensive street, with doubles available for around €100 without breakfast. Just eleven rooms, most with bathrooms, but all more than decent. Until they put a sign up in the street it will be easy to miss.

## Moderate

🏃 **Alessandra Borgo Santi Apostoli 17** ℡ 055.283.438, 🅦 www.hotelalessandra .com. One of the best and friendliest of the central two-stars, with 27 rooms (20 with bathroom) occupying a sixteenth-century *palazzo* and furnished in a mixture of antique and modern styles. Used by the fashion-show crowd, so booking is essential in September. Discreetly signed on the street, so easy to miss. Doubles from around €170; you pay €10 more for a river view, and €40 less for those with shared bathrooms.

**Costantini Via dei Calzaiuoli 13** ℡ 055.213.995, ℻ 055.215.128, 🅦 www.hotelcostantini.it. This fourteen-room two-star shares a great location with the *Aldini*, on the city's main pedestrian street, close to the Duomo and Piazza della Signoria. Offers en-suite doubles for around €150.

**Porta Rossa Via Porta Rossa 19** ℡ 055.287.551, ℻ 055.282.179, 🅦 www.hotelportarossa.it. Florence has smarter three-star hotels, but none as venerable as the 78-room *Porta Rossa*, which has been a hotel since the fourteenth century and hosted, among others, Byron and Stendhal. You come here for character and nineteenth-century ambience, rather than luxurious modern touches. Doubles (five have baths, the rest have showers) cost €150–180, or for €100 more you can splash out on one of the two fabulous tower rooms.

🏃 **Torre Guelfa Borgo SS Apostoli 8** ℡ 055.239.6338, 🅦 ww.hoteltorreguelfa .com. Twenty tastefully furnished rooms are crammed on to the third floor of this ancient tower, the tallest private building in the city. Guests can enjoy the marvellous views all over the city from the tower's small roof garden. There are also six cheaper doubles on the first floor (no TV and more noise from the road). Very charismatic, and very

popular, with good-value rooms – €190 up top, €150 on the first floor.

## Expensive

**Beacci Tornabuoni Via de' Tornabuoni 3** ℡ 055.212.645, ℻ 055.283.594, 🅦 www .tornabuonihotels.com. With 28 rooms occupying the top two floors of a fifteenth-century *palazzo*, this is a beguilingly antiques-stuffed three-star hotel, perfectly placed on Florence's poshest shopping street. The roof garden is superb, especially in spring, when the jasmine is blossoming. Doubles usually cost from €260, but special offers are available on the website.

**Benivieni Via delle Oche 5** ℡ 055.238.2133, ℻ 055.239.8248, 🅦 www.hotelbenivieni.it. This small, friendly and family-run three-star is situated between the Duomo and Piazza della Signoria, tucked away on a quiet backstreet. Fifteen smallish rooms are ranged around two floors of a former synagogue; the rooms on the upper floor are brighter but all are simple, modern and in perfect condition. As they should be: the place only opened in 2001. Doubles at around €225 – but they sometimes have rooms going at almost half that price, so it's always worth asking.

🏃 **Hermitage Vicolo Marzio 1/Piazza del Pesce** ℡ 055.287.216, ℻ 055.212.208, 🅦 www.hermitagehotel.com. Pre-booking is essential to secure one of the 28 rooms in this superbly located three-star hotel right next to the Ponte Vecchio, with unbeatable views from some rooms as well as from the flower-filled roof garden. The service is friendly, and rooms are cosy, decorated with the odd antique flourish; bathrooms are small but nicely done. Double-glazing has eliminated the noise problems once suffered by the front rooms, and you'll need to book many months in advance to secure one of these. Doubles from €240, and for €15 more you get one of the sixteen rooms with a Jacuzzi.

## Very expensive

**Brunelleschi Piazza Santa Elisabetta 3** ℡ 055.27.370, ℻ 055.219.653, 🅦 www.hotel brunelleschi.it. Designed by leading architect Italo Gamberini, this four-star hotel is built around a Byzantine chapel and fifth-century tower. A small in-house museum displays Roman and other fragments found during building work. Decor is simple and stylish, with the original brick and stone offset by lots of wood; the 95 rooms are spacious – the best, on the fourth floor, have views of the Duomo and Campanile. The rack rate for a double is upwards of €370, but there are often special deals to be had.

**Gallery Hotel Art** Vicolo dell'Oro 5 ⊕055.27.263, ⓦ www.lungarnohotels.com/gallery. This immensely stylish four-star is unlike any other hotel in central Florence. A member of the Design Hotels group, it has a sleek, minimalist and hyper-modern look – lots of dark wood and neutral colours – and taste-ful contemporary art displayed in the recep-tion and all 74 rooms. There is a small but smart bar, a sushi restaurant, and an attrac-tive lounge with art-filled bookshelves and comfortable sofas. The location is perfect, in a small, quiet square ten seconds' walk from the Ponte Vecchio. Doubles from €385 and (way) up.

▽ *Helvetia & Bristol* main entrance

🏃 **Helvetia & Bristol** Via dei Pescioni 2 ⊕055.266.51, ⓦ www.royaldemeure .com. In business since 1894 and favoured by such luminaries as Pirandello, Stravinsky and Gary Cooper. Following a refit in the 1990s, this is now undoubt-edly Florence's finest small-scale five-star hotel. The public spaces and 67 bedrooms and suites (each unique) are faultlessly designed and fitted, mixing antique furnishings and modern facilities – such as Jacuzzis in many bathrooms – to create a style that evokes the Belle Epoque without being suffocatingly nostalgic or twee. If you're going to treat yourself, this is a leading contender. Rooms start at around €440 without breakfast.

**Savoy** Piazza della Repubblica 7 ⊕055.27.351, ⓦ www.roccofortehotels .com. The *Savoy* had become something of a doddery old dowager before being taken in hand by the Rocco Forte group. Now it's once again one of the city's very best hotels, having been refurbished in discreetly luxurious modern style, with plenty of bare wood, stone-coloured fabrics and peat-coloured marble. And the location could not be more central. Costs vary according to the time of year and whether there are special offers, but you can expect to pay from €485 upwards for a double, and more than €2000 for the Repubblica suite. Prices do not include breakfast.

## Santa Maria Novella district

### Budget

🏃 **Elite** Via della Scala 12 ⊕055.215.395, ⓕ055.213.832. A tiny two-star run by one of the most pleasant managers in town. Five double rooms have private bathrooms and are available for less than €100 – one cheaper room has a shower but shares a toilet with two single rooms. Quieter rooms are at the back.

**Ottaviani** Piazza degli Ottaviani 1 ⊕055.239.6223, ⓕ055.293.355, ⓔ pensioneottaviani@hotmail.com. The best of this one-star's nineteen rooms (only two with private bathrooms) overlook Piazza Santa Maria Novella; others aren't so good, but still remain inexpensive (from €60 with a shower, €70 with bathroom) and conven-ient. No credit cards.

### Very expensive

**J.K. Place** Piazza Santa Maria Novella 7 ⊕055.264.5181, ⓦ www.jkplace.com. One of the newest and most appealing of Florence's designer hotels occupies a fine eighteenth-century building on Piazza Santa Maria Novella. *J.K. Place*'s big idea is to create a homely rather than hotel-like atmosphere, with a hostess rather than a receptionist, a bar from which you help yourself, and a communal breakfast table where you can chat with fellow guests. The twenty rooms bear designer Michele Bönan's exotic-elegant stamp, and have DVD players and flat-screen TVs. Doubles from €325.

## Station and San Lorenzo district

### Budget

🏃 **Giovanna Via Faenza 69** ⊕ &
ⓕ 055.238.1353, ⓦ www.albergogiovanna
.it. Third-floor hotel (no lift) that's small, tidy
and as cheap as any on Via Faenza. It has
just seven rooms from around €70, a handful with private bathrooms. The *Nella* on the
second floor (⊕ 055.265.4346, ⓦ www
.hotelnella.net) has rooms from €90, for
which you also get air-conditioning and en-
suite bathrooms.

**Marcella Via Faenza 58** ⊕ & ⓕ 055.213.232.
Seven good-sized rooms in this third-floor
one-star, one with private bathroom. From
around €70. No credit cards.

**Nazionale Via Nazionale 22** ⊕ 055.238.2203,
ⓦ www.nazionalehotel.it. An average but
serviceable family-run one-star place with
nine rooms, five with private bathroom
(planned renovations will give all rooms
en-suite bathrooms), equidistant from the
train station and the San Lorenzo market.
Doubles with bathrooms are €100, those
without are €20 less, and singles without
are a mere €50.

**Via Faenza 56** Several budget hotels are
crammed into this address near the station
– note there is no lift. Best of the one-stars
is the *Paola* (⊕ 055.213.682, ⓦ www
.albergopaola.com), up on the top floor,
with seven rooms (from €70) all painted in
bright colours and all with shower cubicles
in the corner of the rooms. Toilets are on
the corridor. On the same floor is the *Merlini*
(⊕ 055.212.848, ⓦ www.hotelmerlini.it),
which has ten rooms, six with private bathrooms. You'll pay from €95 for a double
here (€15 less for one without a bathroom),
but you have to be in by the 1am curfew.
On the second floor there's the twelve-room
*Marini* (⊕ 055.284.824; €75), which is
comfortable but bland, as is the seven-room
*Armonia* (⊕ 055.211.146), one floor down
again, where rooms go for around €65. On
the ground and first floor you'll also find the
slightly pricier, two-star *Azzi* (⊕ 055.213.806,
ⓦ www.hotelazzi.it), which has friendly staff
and garden views from some of its sixteen
rooms. Doubles here go from €115 with
bathroom, and €20 less without.

### Inexpensive

🏃 **Ausonia e Rimini and Kursaal Via
Nazionale 24** ⊕ 055.496.547 &

ⓕ 055.496.324, ⓦ www.kursonia.com. Two co-
managed and nicely refurbished hotels near
the station: the two-star *Kursaal* is on the
second floor and the one-star *Ausonia* on
the third. Altogether they have thirty rooms:
twenty superior doubles with air-conditioning and en-suite bathrooms (around €130)
and ten standard rooms without bathrooms
(next winter's renovations will turn some of
these into superior rooms) costing around
€30 less. They also offer Internet access
and a laundry service.

**Concordia Via dell'Amorino 14** ⊕ 055.213.233,
ⓦ www.albergoconcordia.it. An extremely
convenient first-floor hotel (no lift), located at
the back of San Lorenzo church. There are
sixteen rooms, all with private bathrooms,
for around €110 a night. The rooms have
been given a warm, tastefully coloured look,
as part of an upgrade to two-star status.

**Desirée Via Fiume 20** ⊕ 055.238.2382, ⓦ www
.desireehotel.com. Completely overhauled
two-star featuring stained-glass windows,
simulated antique furniture and a bath in each
of the eighteen rooms. Located one block
east of the station, so there are better-situ-
ated hotels at this price, but it's nonetheless a
reasonable choice. Doubles from €135.

**Erina Via Fiume 17** ⊕ 055.288.294,
ⓕ 055.284.343. A two-star hotel located on
the third floor of an old *palazzo*, very close
to the station. Has fourteen double rooms
at €135 (one without en-suite bathroom is
€30 cheaper).

**Globus Via Sant'Antonino 24** ⊕ 055.211.062,
ⓦ www.hotelglobus.com. Recently renovated
three-star close to San Lorenzo. The 23 air-
conditioned rooms are furnished in modern
style, and very good value. Doubles around
€100.

### Moderate

🏃 **Bellettini Via dei Conti 7** ⊕ 055.213.561,
ⓦ www.hotelbellettini.com. The warm
welcome of owner Signora Gina counts for
much in this 27-room two-star, close to San
Lorenzo; so, too, do her copious breakfasts.
Most of the simple rooms have private bathrooms, all have TVs and air-conditioning; the
price is around €150 for an en-suite double.

🏃 **Casci Via Cavour 13** ⊕ 055.211.686,
ⓦ www.hotelcasci.it. It would be
hard to find a better two-star in central
Florence than this 26-room hotel. Only two
(sound-proofed) rooms face the busy street:
the rest are quiet, clean and well fitted-out,

# FLORENCE ACCOMMODATION: AROUND THE CENTRE

▲ Stadio Comunale

▲ Fiesole

▲ Museo Stibbert

▲ Prato & Pistoia

**HOTELS**
| | |
|---|---|
| Annalena | S |
| Ausonia e Rimini | K |
| Benvenuti | C |
| Cimabue | E |
| Genzianella | C |
| Giovanna | M |
| J & J | P |
| Kursaal | K |
| Marcella | J |
| Nazionale | N |
| Orto de' Medici | H |
| Panorama | G |
| Residenza JohannaDue | B |
| Residenza JohannaUno | D |
| Residenza JohleaDue | F |
| Residenza JohleaUno | F |
| Silla | R |
| Via Faenza 56 | L |

**HOSTELS**
| | |
|---|---|
| Ostello Archi Rossi | I |
| Ostello Villa Camerata | A |
| Pio X–Artigianelli | Q |
| Suore Oblate dell' Assunzione | O |

Stazione Campo di Marte

Cimitero degli Inglesi

Giardino della Gherardesca

Museo Botanico

Giardino dei Semplici

Museo Archeologico

Scalzo

Museo di San Marco

SS. Annunziata

Spedale degli Innocenti

Accademia

Sant'Apollonia

Cenacolo di Foligno

Palazzo delle Mostre

Fortezza da Basso

Stazione Santa Maria Novella

See 'Central Florence' map for detail

Bus Station

River Mugnone

N

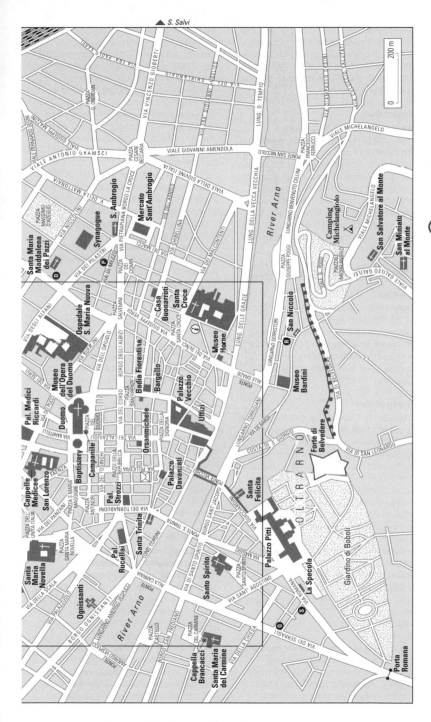

plus they're well priced at around €155 for a double. The welcome is warm and the owners are unfailingly helpful and courteous. The big buffet breakfast in the vaulted and frescoed reception area is a major plus, as is free Internet access.

### Expensive

**Residenza Castiglioni** Via del Giglio 8 ☎055.239.6013, ⓕ055.264.7251, ⓦwww.residenzacastiglioni.com. Run by the same team as runs the *Torre Guelfa*, this is a discreet and hugely stylish hideaway that does not feel like a hotel at all. Just half a dozen spacious en-suite double rooms (three of them frescoed) on the second floor of a *palazzo* very close to San Lorenzo church. All credit cards except for Amex accepted. Doubles from around €200.

## San Marco and Annunziata districts

### Budget

**Benvenuti** and **Genzianella** Via Cavour 112 ☎055.572.141, ⓔbensecc@iol.it. Two dependable if unthrilling *pensioni* sharing the same reception, with 27 rooms in all, virtually on the Piazza della Libertà, which means a bus or long walk to the sights. Doubles from €90.

### Inexpensive

**Cimabue** Via Bonifacio Lupi 7 ☎055.471.989, ⓕ055.463.0906, ⓦwww.hotelcimabue.it. This sixteen-room hotel offers more than the usual two-star establishment, though its location is a touch remote. Some of the double and triple rooms have frescoed ceilings, and all are kitted out with antiques and pleasant fabrics. All rooms have (mostly small) private bathrooms; the family atmosphere is welcoming and the breakfasts more than generous. Doubles around €115. Cheaper singles also available.
**Panorama** Via Cavour 60 ☎055.238.2043, ⓕ055.264.404. A 31-room two-star that's a favourite with school groups, in the university area just north of San Marco on the city's main north-running road. Doubles from €100.
🏃 **Residenza JohannaUno** Via Bonifacio Lupi 14 ☎055.481.896, ⓦwww.johanna.it. Genteel place that feels very much a "residence" rather than a hotel, hidden away in the same apartment

building as the Swedish Consulate in a very quiet, leafy corner of the city, five minutes' walk north of San Marco; ring the bell on the brass plaque by the wrought-iron gates and go in the door on the right-hand side. Rooms are cosy and well kept, there are books and magazines, and the two *signore* who run the place are as friendly and helpful as you could hope for. The very similar *Residenza JohannaDue* (☎055.473.377) is located a bit further from the main sights, at Via Cinque Giornate 12, to the north of the Fortezza da Basso, and has parking spaces. Both cost in the region of €100 a night, with one cheaper single room. You need to check in before 7pm on the first day to pick up your key. No credit cards.
🏃 **Residenza JohleaUno** Via San Gallo 80 ☎055.463.3292, ⓦwww.johanna.it. Another venture from the people who created the nearby *Residenza Johanna* (see above), offering the same low-cost, high-comfort package, with the same level of hospitality, but slightly plusher, more spacious and more expensive – though it's still outstanding value by Florentine standards. At neighbouring Via San Gallo 76 you'll find *JohleaDue* (☎055.461.185), which in design, atmosphere and cost is indistinguishable from *Uno*. Rooms €100–110 (the superiors are larger and have marble bathrooms). Some rooms have showers, some baths. As with *Johanna*, you must check in by 7pm. Further down at no.72 is yet another, rather smarter, establishment run by the same team, the *Antica Dimora* (☎055.462.7296, ⓦwww.anticadimorafirenze.it), with doubles from around €125. No credit cards.

### Expensive

🏃 **Loggiato dei Serviti** Piazza Santissima Annunziata 3 ☎055.289.592, ⓕ055.289.595, ⓦwww.loggiatodeiservitihotel.it. This elegant, extremely tasteful and well-priced three-star hotel is situated on one of Florence's most celebrated squares. Its 39 rooms (five in the new annexe nearby) have been stylishly incorporated into a structure designed in the sixteenth century in imitation of the Brunelleschi hospital across the square, to accommodate the Servite priests who worked there and provide lodgings for itinerant Servites.

Their relative plainness reflects something of the building's history, but all are decorated with fine fabrics and antiques, and look out either onto the piazza or peaceful gardens to the rear: top-floor rooms have glimpses of the Duomo. Doubles cost upwards of €200.

**Morandi alla Crocetta Via Laura 50** ☎055.234.4747, Ⓦwww.hotelmorandi .it. An intimate three-star gem, whose small size and friendly welcome ensure a home-from-home atmosphere. Rooms are tastefully decorated with antiques and old prints, and vivid carpets laid on parquet floors. Two rooms have balconies opening onto a modest garden: the best room – with fresco fragments and medieval nooks and crannies – was converted from the site's former convent chapel. Doubles cost around €200.

**Orto de' Medici Via San Gallo 30** ☎055.483.427, Ⓦwww.ortodeimedici.it. A 31-room frescoed and antique-furnished three-star, occupying a quiet *palazzo* in the university area. Via San Gallo is not the most attractive street in Florence, but the hotel has been very recently and impressively refurbished, and there is a breakfast terrace. Rooms – with baths or showers – cost from around €190, and for €265 a superior room also gives you a balcony. See its website for excellent offers.

## Sant'Ambrogio district

**J & J Via di Mezzo 20** ☎055.263.121, Ⓦwww .cavalierehotels.com. The bland exterior of this former fifteenth-century convent, located very close to Piazza Sant'Ambrogio, conceals a romantic nineteen-room four-star hotel. Some rooms are vast split-level affairs – but all have charm and are furnished with modern fittings, attractive fabrics and a few antiques. Common areas are decked with flowers, and retain frescoes and vaulted ceilings from the original building. In summer breakfast is served in the convent's lovely old cloister. Doubles from around the €300 mark.

## Oltrarno

### Inexpensive
**La Scaletta Via Guicciardini 13** ☎055.283.028, Ⓦwww.lascaletta.com. An eleven-room two-star hotel under new management; a/c rooms with tiled floors, three of them with

views across to the Bóboli gardens. Drinks served on the rooftop terrace, where you look across the Bóboli in one direction and the city in the other. Around €145 for a double room (€10 discount when paid in cash).

**Sorelle Bandini Piazza Santo Spirito 9** ☎055.215.308, Ⓕ055.282.761. Some of the twelve rooms in this one-star *pensione* are vast and have marble fireplaces, but other rooms are grim – so make sure you inspect before paying. Location is a plus: the hotel is on Piazza Santa Spirito, one of the city's more happening squares, and the hotel's loggia, which runs round two sides of the building, gives you a grandstand view. Prices are roughly €115 without bath, or €140 en-suite.

### Moderate
**Annalena Via Romana 34** ☎055.222.402, Ⓦwww.hotelannalena.it. Situated a short way beyond Palazzo Pitti (and right by an entrance to the Bóboli gardens), this twenty-room three-star, once owned by the Medici, passed to a young Florentine noblewoman (Annalena) who retired from the world after a disastrous love affair and bequeathed the building to the Dominicans. The best rooms open onto a gallery with garden views, and a sprinkling of antiques lend a hint of old-world charm. Rooms cost around €175.

**Silla Via de' Renai 5** ☎055.234.2888, Ⓔhotel .silla@tin.it. Three-star place occupying a fifteenth-century *palazzo* building that has been somewhat masked by a 1980s refit, but the 35 rooms are in good shape and reasonably sized – and nine have a view over a small park and road to the river. Breakfast is served on the terrace in summer. Doubles are usually around €180, but it's worth asking about special offers.

## Fiesole

**Villa San Michele Via Doccia 4** ☎055.567.8200, Ⓦwww.villasanmichele.orient-express.com. The astronomically expensive *Villa San Michele* is one of Italy's most sybaritic hotels. Occupying a former monastery that was designed in part by Michelangelo, it's surrounded by gorgeous parkland, offers terrific views of Florence, and boasts a great restaurant. A once-in-a-lifetime kind of place. Doubles from over €800.

# Hostels

Florence has only a handful of **hostels** and the best of these is some distance from the centre. To help matters a little, there are a number of places run by religious bodies, plus student institutions which provide beds for non-natives at the city universities. Out of term time (June–Oct) some of these places are open to young tourists, and a few even have accommodation throughout the year. In addition to the houses listed below, there are also a number of *Case dello Studente*, which are run by the university authorities and occasionally made available to visitors; for latest information on these, ask at the tourist office.

**Istituto Gould Via dei Serragli 49**
☎055.212.576, ⊛www.istitutogould.it.
Occupies part of a former seventeenth-century *palazzo* (the doorbell is easily missed). Its 97 beds are extremely popular, so it's wise to book in advance, especially during the academic year. Street-front rooms can be noisy (rear rooms are better), but the old courtyard, terracotta floors and stone staircases provide atmosphere throughout. Open for check-in Mon–Fri 8.45am–1pm & 3–7.30pm, Sat 9am–1.30pm & 2–6pm but closed Sun. Singles (with/without private bathroom) €41/36; doubles (per person) €29/25; triples €24/21; quads €23/21. No curfew.

**Ostello Archi Rossi Via Faenza 94r**
☎055.290.804, ⊛www.hostelarchirossi.com. A five-minute walk from the train station, this privately owned hostel is spotlessly clean and decorated with guests' wall-paintings and graffiti. It's popular – the 96 places fill up quickly – and has a pleasant garden and terrace. Evening meals are available at extra cost; spacious dining room with satellite TV and films shown on request. Single rooms around €30. Dorm beds €20–25, depending on size of dorm (4–9 beds) and whether or not there's an internal bathroom; all prices include breakfast and thirty minutes' Internet time. Disabled access rooms available. Curfew at 2am for dorms.

**Ostello Villa Camerata Viale Augusto Righi 2–4** ☎055.601.451, ℻055.610.300, ⊛www.ostellionline.org. An HI hostel tucked away in a beautiful park to the northeast of the city. This is one of Europe's most attractive hostels, a sixteenth-century house with frescoed ceilings, fronted by lemon trees in terracotta pots. Doors open at 2pm; if you'll arrive later, call ahead to make sure there's space – bookings by email or fax only. Midnight curfew. There are 322 dorm places, and a few family rooms. Breakfast and sheets are included, but there are no

kitchen facilities; optional supper costs about €9. Films in English are shown every night. Dorm beds €17; two-/three-bed rooms €23/19 per person. Take bus #17b from the train station (takes about 30min).

**Pio X – Artigianelli Via dei Serragli 106** ☎ & ℻055.225.044. One of the cheapest options in town, often booked up by school groups. Don't be put off by the huge picture of Pope Pius X at the top of the steps; the management is friendly and the atmosphere relaxed. Get there by 9am, as the 64 beds are quickly taken. Showers are free. Beds in doubles, triples, quads and quins cost around €17, or €19 with en-suite bathrooms; minimum stay two nights, maximum five. Open all day throughout the year; midnight curfew; no reservations by phone.

**Santa Monaca Via Santa Monaca 6**
☎055.268.338, ⊛www.ostello.it. Privately owned hostel in Oltrarno, close to Santa Maria del Carmine. Has 114 beds, arranged in a dozen dorms with between four and twenty beds. Kitchen facilities (no utensils), washing machines, free hot showers, and a useful noticeboard with information on lifts and onward travel. It's a fifteen-minute walk from the station, or take bus #11, #36 or #37 to the second stop after the bridge. Credit cards accepted. Open for check-in 9.30am–1pm and 2pm–12.30am. Dorm beds €17. Curfew 1am.

**Suore Oblate dell'Assunzione Via Borgo Pinti 15**
☎055.248.0583, ℻055.234.6291. Not far from the Duomo, this convent-run hostel is open to both men and women, as long as rooms are not required by the nuns or their visitors. There's no breakfast. Singles €38, doubles €37 per person, both with private bathrooms. Triples and quads also available.

**Suore Oblate dello Spirito Santo Via Nazionale 8** ☎055.239.8202, ℻055.239.8129. Also run by nuns, this clean and pleasant hostel, a few steps from the station, is open to women, families and married couples only, and is closed to the public during school terms. Doubles, triples and quads all have private bathroom. Breakfast included, and there's a minimum stay of two nights. Doubles and triples cost €27 per person.

# Campsites

The situation for **camping** isn't very good: in summer, you're almost certain to find that the only available spaces are at the *Area di Sosta*, an emergency accommodation area sometimes set aside by the city authorities which usually amounts to a patch of ground sheltered by a rudimentary roof, with a shower block attached. Contact the tourist offices for details, if any, of the current location.

**Camping Michelangiolo Viale Michelangelo 80** ☎055.681.1977, ⓦ www.ecvacanze.it. A 240-pitch site that's always crowded, owing to its superb hillside location in an olive grove. Kitchen facilities and well-stocked, if expensive, shop nearby. Take #13 bus from the station. April–Oct.
**Camping Panoramico Via Peramondo 1, Fiesole** ☎055.559.069, ⓦ www.florencecamping.com.

Located in Fiesole, a fifteen-minute ride on bus #7 from Florence train station, this 120-pitch site has a bar, restaurant, pool and small supermarket.
**Villa Camerata Viale Augusto Righi 2–4** ☎055.601.451, ⓦ www.ostellionline.org. Basic 55-pitch site in the grounds of the *Villa Camerata* HI hostel.

# Eating and drinking

F or a small city, Florence has plenty of big-city attractions: scores of **cafés and restaurants**, a full calendar of cultural events and a lot of very chic shops to give focus to the evening *passeggiata*. The main problem is one of identity, in a city whose inhabitants are heavily outnumbered by outsiders from March to October. Restaurant standards are often patchy and prices pitched at whatever level the tourists can bear, while many of the locals swear there's scarcely a single genuine Tuscan place left in the Tuscan capital – an exaggeration, of course, but a reflection of a general feeling that too much has been lost to tourism. Yet the situation is nowhere near as bad as some reports would have it, and if anything, it's been improving in recent years, with the appearance of several stylish and good-value restaurants, alongside some superb wine bars.

## Restaurants

In gastronomic circles, **Florentine cuisine** is accorded as much reverence as Florentine art, a reverence encapsulated in the myth that French eating habits acquired their sophistication in the wake of Catherine de' Medici's marriage to the future Henry II of France. In fact, Florentine food has always been characterized by modest raw materials and simple technique: beefsteak (*bistecca*), tripe (*trippa*) and liver (*fegato*) are typical ingredients, while grilling (*alla Fiorentina*) is a favoured method of preparation. In addition, white beans (*fagioli*) will feature on most menus, either on their own, garnished with liberal quantities of local olive oil, or as the basis of such dishes as *ribollita*.

There aren't many **restaurants** where you can get away with spending less than €30 per person for three courses plus wine, although Florence has some decent low-budget places serving food that at least give some idea of the region's characteristic dishes, and even the simplest trattoria should offer *bistecca alla Fiorentina* – though you should bear in mind that this dish is priced per hundred grams, so your bill will be considerably higher than the figure written on the menu. And, of course, if the budget is tight, there's always the option of a pizzeria: Florence has several very good ones, usually charging in the region of €7–8.

The restaurants below are organized by area. Very roughly, the cheapest places tend to be near the station and San Lorenzo market, while the main concentrations of mid-range and top-class restaurants are around Santa Croce and Sant'Ambrogio and over in the Oltrarno. You can of course keep costs down even in more expensive places by having just two courses (pasta and main), and retiring to a bar for ice cream or coffee and *digestif*. Remember, too, that

If you want to put together a picnic, an obvious place to shop is the Mercato Centrale by San Lorenzo church (Mon–Sat 7am–2pm, plus Sat 4–8pm in winter), where everything you could possibly need can be bought under one roof: bread, ham, cheese, fruit, wine, ready-made sandwiches. Also comprehensive is the Mercato Sant'Ambrogio over by Santa Croce (Mon–Fri 7am–2pm). Every district has its *alimentari*, which in addition to selling the choicest Tuscan produce often provide sandwiches. *Vera*, at the southern end of Ponte Santa Trìnita, Piazza Frescobaldi 3r, is a fine example of a Florentine deli; other excellent central *alimentari* include *Tassini*, Borgo Santi Apostoli 24r; *Pegna*, near the Duomo at Via dello Studio 26r (closed Wed afternoons); and *Alessi Paride*, Via delle Oche 27–29r. Chocoholics should check out *Andrea Bianchini*, near the Sant'Ambrogio market at Via de' Macci 50 (Tues–Sat 10am–noon & 4–7.30pm), which sells delectable chilli-flavoured chocolates and a riot of other flavours. *Vestri*, Borgo degli Albizi 11r (Ⓦ www.cioccolateriavestri.com), offers deliciously thick chocolate to drink (hot or cold depending on the season) and a mouth-watering array of chocolate products, including ice cream.

For a hearty sit-down lunchtime snack, each of the two markets has an excellent *tavola calda*, serving meatballs, pasta, stews, soups and sandwiches: *Nerbone* (Mon–Sat 7am–2pm) in the Mercato Centrale, and *Tavola Calda da Rocco* (Mon–Sat noon–2.30pm), in the Mercato di Sant'Ambrogio.

If you really want to go native, you could join the throng of office workers around the mobile tripe stall in Piazza dei Cimatori (Mon–Fri 8.30am–8.30pm). Its speciality is the local delicacy called *lampredotto*: hot tripe served in a bun with a spicy sauce. (Or rather, two cuts of tripe – *gala*, famed for its delicate, pink-crested ridges and exquisite taste, and the fattier, heavier *spannocchia*.) The stall also sells wine, so you can wash the taste away should you realize you've made a horrible mistake. There's a similar operation – *Da Sergio e Pierpaolo* – near the Sant'Ambrogio market, in Via de' Macci (Mon–Sat 7.15am–3pm).

you often needn't buy a whole bottle of wine: ask for a half-bottle or quarter-bottle or jug of house wine (*mezza bottiglia* or *un quartino*). Another useful tip is that any place displaying the Slow Food sign is likely to be good; founded in 1986, the Slow Food movement promotes the use of fresh local food and well-executed cooking.

Many restaurants are **closed on Sunday**, so if you want to be sure of a table it's a good idea to make a reservation for that night. And bear in mind that simple meals – not just snacks – are served in many Florentine bars, so if you're exploring a particular area of the city and fancy a quick bite to eat rather than a full-blown restaurant meal, take a look at the relevant section in the "Cafés and bars" and "Wine bars" listings below.

All listings below are located on the corresponding chapter maps.

### Piazza della Signoria

The listings in this section are marked on the map on p.70.

**Antico Fattore** Via Lambertesca 1–3r ℡ 055.288.975. Simple Tuscan dishes dominate the menu, and the soups are particularly good; close to the Piazza della Signoria, but not as expensive as its prime location might suggest. Service can be grim, though. Mains cost around €10–14.

Closed Sun, plus Sat in summer, Mon in winter, & Aug.

**Da Ganino** Piazza dei Cimatori 4r, off Via Dante Alighieri ℡ 055.214.125. One of only a handful of recommendable places close to the Signoria. Produces good home-made pasta and desserts, though the prices reflect the locale as much as the quality of the kitchen – mains from €10. In summer, when tables are moved out onto the tiny square, it's essential to book. Mon–Sat 7pm–1am.

The listings in this section are marked on the map on pp.88–89.

**Belle Donne Via delle Belle Donne 16r.** A tiny, convivial, faux-rustic trattoria, where you sit elbow-to-elbow on bare benches and stools, under swags of foliage, drinking your wine from a tumbler. Not a place to linger over your meal, but it's honest food, cheerfully presented at honest prices – main courses €7–12 – and serves up seasonal specialities such as *baccelli* (raw broad beans in their pods) with pecorino. Open every day, except for August, when it's closed for the annual holiday.

**Coco Lezzone Via del Parioncino 26r, corner of Via del Purgatorio** ☎055.287.178. Stumble on this back-street place and you'd swear you'd found one of the great old-world Florentine trattorias. The prices are moderate (mains from €10), the food is sometimes good and sometimes not, and the service is frequently offhand – this place has been very fashionable for so long that the proprietors often seem to think they don't need to make an effort any more. No credit cards are accepted and no coffee served. Closed Sun & mid-July to mid-Aug.

**Il Contadino Via Palazzuolo 71r.** Small, popular place with simple black and white interior and fascinating large photos of old Florence on the walls. Fast, friendly service, shared tables (no booking), very cheap but good fare. Fixed price for three-course lunch and dinner (around €10, plus a small extra charge for a *quartino* of wine). No written menu: the four or so choices for each course are recited rapidly. Daily noon–2.30pm & 6–9.30pm.

**Il Latini Via dei Palchetti 6r** ☎055.210.916. Once a trattoria of the old school, the quasi-legendary *Latini* is now something of a caricature of itself. It still looks the part – hams hanging from the ceiling, family photos on the wall, simple tables and old rush chairs. Food quality, though, is average (the *bistecca* is an honourable exception), and prices well above those of most trattorias (mains from €10). Old regulars still eat here, but you'll find the queues in the evenings (booking is difficult) are full of foreigners. 11am–midnight; closed Mon & lunch Tues.

**Marione Via della Spada 27r** ☎055.214.756. Simple, good-value Tuscan cooking, at prices that are a pleasant surprise for this location, a stone's throw from Via Tornabuoni. Mains from €6. Daily noon–3pm & 7–11.30pm. Closed first two weeks of Aug.

**Oliviero Via delle Terme 51r** ☎055.240.618. Currently enjoys a reputation for some of Florence's best food, but at a price. It has a welcoming and old-fashioned feel – something like an Italian restaurant of the 1960s. The innovative food is predominantly Tuscan, but includes other Italian dishes; desserts, for once, are excellent. The menu includes fresh fish when available, something of a rarity in Florence. Expect to pay upwards of €50, without wine. Mon–Sat 11am–3pm & 7pm–1am. Closed Aug.

**Osteria dei Cento Poveri Via Palazzuolo 31r** ☎055.218.846. A small and busy restaurant (you won't be the only tourist here) with a strong Pugliese accent and offering more fish than is customary in this city. The lobster gnocchi (€17) is an interesting novelty – the pasta is made across the road – and there's always a fish of the day. Fairly expensive, with main courses at around €18. May–Sept Tues–Sun 7pm–midnight, Sun 12.30am–2.30pm; Oct–April also open for lunch Tues–Sat.

## North of the centre

The listings in this section are marked on the map on pp.110–111.

**La Lampara Via Nazionale 36r** ☎055.215.164. The narrow entrance is deceptive: this is a huge place that goes back and back and has a terrace, too, at the rear. Don't be put off by the multilingual menus: the food is very good, the prices moderate (mains €9–13) and the waiters attentive. Packed with locals at lunchtime and evening, so try to book a table. Daily noon–midnight.

**Nuti Borgo San Lorenzo 39r** ☎055.210.410. This massive place, with a restaurant on one side of the street and a pizzeria on the other, claims to be the oldest pizzeria in town; the menu isn't limited to pizzas, and prices are reasonable (pizzas from €6.50, two-course menus from €12) – though the service sometimes isn't. Open 11.30pm–1am. Closed Sun in winter.

**Oliandolo Via Ricasoli 38–40r** ☎055.211.296. A small, fast and very cheap spot (dishes from €4) that's very popular with locals at lunchtime – you'll probably have to queue if you come after 12.30pm. Good roast pork and beans, and excellent baked cheesecake. Mon–Sat 8am–7pm.

**Palle d'Oro Via Sant'Antonino 43r**
℡055.288.383. Close to San Lorenzo
market, this is the plainest possible type
of trattoria, serving very good fare – such
as chicken in a green peppercorn sauce
for €7. Packed at lunchtime. Besides full
meals, they do sandwiches to take away.
Mon–Sat noon–2.30pm & 6.30–9.45pm.

**Taverna del Bronzino Via delle Ruote 27r**
℡055.495.220. Located a short walk northwest of San Marco, with the sort of look
– vaulted ceiling and terracotta floors – that
guarantees a steady flow of upper-bracket
tourists. The menu is conservatively stylish
and it never disappoints. Closed Sun.

**Zà-Zà Piazza del Mercato Centrale 26r**
℡055.210.756, ⍟www.trattoriazaza.it.
In business for more than twenty years, and
perhaps the best of several trattorias close to
the Mercato Centrale. In recent years it has
raised its profile to the extent that booking is
virtually obligatory in summer. The interior is
dark, stone-walled and brick-arched, with a
handful of tables – though in summer there
are more tables on the outside terraces.
There's usually a set-price menu for less than
€15 which offers a choice of three or four
pastas and main courses; otherwise you'll
pay around €25–30 per head. The omelette
with a creamy truffle sauce is exquisite
(€8.50) and the mixed antipasti are generous
and tasty. Daily 11am–11pm; closed Aug.

### East of the centre

The listings in this section are marked
on the map on p.135.

**Acqua al Due Via dell'Acqua 2r/Via della Vigna
Vecchia 40r** ℡055.284.170. Always packed
(often with foreigners but with Italians too),
chiefly on account of its offbeat decor,
lively atmosphere and *assaggio di primi*
– a succession of pasta dishes shared by
everyone at the table. Evenings only; main
courses from around €12.

**Alle Murate Via Ghibellina 52r** ℡055.240.618.
A highly regarded and highly professional
operation, offering a couple of tempting
set menus (the "Toscano" and "Creativo",
for €52 and €60), but only if all the people
at the table order them. The wine vault is
particularly well stocked, and a few tables
have been set up down there for the benefit
of visiting oenophiles. You pay for the quality: starters cost €18 and main courses are
€22–24. Tues–Sun 7.30pm–1am.

**Baldovino Via San Giuseppe 22r**
℡055.241.773, ⍟www.baldovino.com.
This superb place, run by an imaginative
Scottish couple, is renowned above all for its
pizzas (made in a wood-fired oven according
to Neapolitan principles), but the main menu
(which changes monthly) is full of excellent
Tuscan and Italian dishes, with mains around
€12–17 – although you pay the usual
premium for the succulent *bistecca alla
Fiorentina*. Portions are very generous. Open
Tues–Sun 11am–3pm & 7pm–1am.

**Benvenuto Via della Mosca 15r, corner Via de'
Neri.** Just a couple of minutes' walk from
Piazza della Signoria, this place has been
around for years and maintains its reputation for low prices. What it lacks in atmosphere it makes up for with reliable cooking.
Mains from €9. Closed Wed & Sun.

▽ *Cibrèo*

**Cibrèo Via de' Macci 118r**
℡055.234.1100. The *Cibrèo* restaurant – which has now spawned a café,
trattoria and shop – is the first Florentine
port-of-call for many foodies, having
achieved fame well beyond the city. The
recipe for success is simple: superb food
with a creative take on Tuscan classics,
in a tasteful dining room with friendly
and professional service. You'll need to
book days in advance for a table in the
main part of the restaurant, but next door
there's a small, somewhat spartan and
sometimes overly busy trattoria section
where the food is virtually the same,
no bookings are taken and the prices
are much lower: around €15 for the
main course, as opposed to €30 in the
restaurant. 12.30–2.30pm & 7–11.15pm.
Closed Sun, Mon & all Aug.

**Enoteca Pinchiorri Via Ghibellina 87**
☎055.242.777, ⓦ www.enotecapinchiorri.com.
No one seriously disputes the *Pinchiorri*'s
claim to be Florence's best restaurant,
certainly not Michelin, who've given it three
of their coveted rosettes. The food is as
magnificent as you'd expect, given the
plaudits, but the ceremony that surrounds
its presentation strikes many as excessive.
Choose from 200 different wines, including some of the rarest and most expensive
vintages on the planet. None of this comes
cheap – you could easily spend in excess
of €150 per person, excluding wine – but
there's nowhere better for the never-to-be
repeated Florentine treat. Closed Mon &
Wed lunch, all day Sun & Aug.

**Francescano Largo Bargellini 16** ☎055.241.605.
*Francescano* began life as a sibling of
*Baldovino*, and though it is now independently owned, still offers similarly good food
in a friendly, clean-cut setting. The menu is
simpler, smaller and a little less expensive
than at *Baldovino* (mains €10 and up), but
it's reliably good. Noon–2.30pm & 7–11pm.
Oct–May closed Tues.

🏃 **Il Pizzaiuolo Via de' Macci 113r**
☎055.241.171. Many Florentines
reckon the pizzas here are the best in the
city. Wines and other menu items have a
Neapolitan touch, as does the atmosphere,
which is friendly and high-spirited. Booking's a good idea, at least in the evening.
The kitchen stays open until a little after
midnight. 12.30–3pm & 7pm–1am. Closed
Sun & Aug.

**L'Antico Noè Volta di San Piero 6r**
☎055.234.0838. Situated next door to the
*vinaio* of the same name, this tiny trattoria
has a very insalubrious setting (you'll doubtless pass a drunk or two on your way to
the door), but the food is fine and the prices
low – mains from €9. Mon–Sat noon–3pm
& 7–11pm.

🏃 **La Pentola dell'Oro Via di Mezzo 24r**
☎055.241.821. Run by Giuseppe
Alessi, the owner of a fine upmarket
restaurant in Fiesole, *La Pentola* has one
of the more imaginative menus in Florence,
mingling the innovative with the profoundly
traditional (some recipes date back to the
sixteenth century). The main basement
restaurant has the cosiest of dining rooms,
but the quality is difficult to match for the
price. Expect to pay upwards of €35, or a
little less in the more informal ground-floor

section, which focuses on traditional rather
than aristocratic cuisine. Mon–Sat noon–
3.30pm & 9pm–midnight.

**Natalino Borgo degli Albizi 17r**
☎055.289.404. Slighly pricier than your
average trattoria, but excellent food,
untouristy for the location and has
outside tables. The truffled courgettes
with pecorino are astounding. Tues–Sun
noon–3pm & 7–11pm.

🏃 **Osteria Caffè Italiano Via Isola delle
Stinche 11–13r** ☎055.289.368. The
high vaulted ceilings lend a medieval touch
to this café, wine bar and restaurant,
but the clientele are *à la mode* Florentine
– smart but relaxed. The cuisine is typically
Tuscan – lots of beef, veal and wild boar
– and first-rate, even the cakes; expect to
pay upwards of €35 per head. Tues–Sun
10am–1am.

🏃 **Osteria de' Benci Via de' Benci 13r**
☎055.234.4923. A modern, busy
and reasonably priced *osteria*, with bar
attached. The interior is pretty and pleasant, and is augmented by outside tables
when it's warm enough – in summer it
attracts big crowds. The tables have paper
tablecloths and you eat off chunky ceramic
plates. The moderately priced menu offers
well-prepared standards plus innovative
Tuscan cuisine. The strawberry risotto is
an unexpected and delicious starter (€9)
and the *goloso* and *piccante* steaks are
very good. Staff are young, and the atmosphere friendly. Restaurant open Mon–Sat
1–2.45pm & 7.30–10.45pm; bar open
8am–midnight.

**Ruth's Via Luigi Carlo Farini 2a** ☎055.248.0888.
Next to the synagogue, this is one of the
few kosher places in Florence, and is
gaining a reputation as a good vegetarian
restaurant. Mains €9–16. Open 12.30–
3.30pm & 8–10.30pm; closed Fri eve & Sat
lunchtime.

### Oltrarno

The listings in this section are marked
on the map on pp.156–157.

**All'Antico Ristoro di Cambi Via Sant'Onofrio 1r**
☎055.217.134, ⓦ www.anticoristorodicambi
.it. Run by the same family since the 1940s,
this rough and ready trattoria is particularly
good for meaty Florentine standards such
as wild boar and steak, and has a very
good wine list. It's vast, but nonetheless

gets packed on a Saturday night, when even the large terrace fills up. Main dishes from €10. Mon–Sat 12.30am–2.30pm & 7.30–11pm.

**Alla Vecchia Bettola Viale Lodovico Ariosto 32–34r ☎055.224.158.** Located on a major traffic intersection a couple of minutes' walk from the Carmine, this place – with its long tables – has something of the atmosphere of a drinking den, which is what it once was; the menu boasts a good repertoire of Tuscan meat dishes, with main courses reasonably priced from €10. Noon–2.30pm & 7.30–10.30pm. Closed Sun & Mon.

**Angiolino Via Santo Spirito 36r ☎055.239.8976.** Long a no-nonsense Oltrarno favourite, with a menu that's short and to the point, featuring Tuscan classics such as *bistecca*, *ribollita* and *pappa al pomodoro*. Some nights it's as good as any restaurant in its (moderate) price range – mains are €12–15 – but quality can be very erratic and service problematic. Oct–March closed Mon.

**Beccofino Piazza degli Scarlatti 1r ☎055.290.076, ⓦwww.beccofino.com.** The most upmarket venture from David Gardner, the Scottish boss of *Baldovino* (see p.195) – indeed, some might find its cooking and expensively austere decor a bit too self-consciously cutting edge. Prices are above average – €18–22 for *secondi* – but so is the quality. If you'd like to test the waters first, have a drink at the attached wine bar. Tues–Sun 7–11pm, plus Sun lunch.

**🏃 Borgo Antico Piazza di Santo Spirito 6r ☎055.210.437.** The spartan chic of *Borgo Antico*'s white tile and pink plaster decor reflects the increasingly trendy character of this once notoriously sleazy Oltrarno piazza, and there's no Oltrarno restaurant trendier than this place. It's usually very crowded and very noisy, though in summer the tables outside offer relative quiet. Choose from a menu of pizzas or a range of Tuscan standards at reasonable prices (€13–18). Salads here are particularly good, and there's often a selection of fresh fish and seafood pastas. Servings – on the restaurant's famous huge plates – are generous to a fault. Open daily noon–midnight.

**Dante Piazza Nazario Sauro 10r ☎055.219.219.** *Dante* is another Oltrarno institution, popular mainly for its pizzas (€7), though it also offers a menu of pasta, fish and meat dishes (from €10 for mains). Closed Wed & last 2 weeks of Aug.

**Del Carmine Piazza del Carmine 18r ☎055.218.601.** Years ago this was an unsung local trattoria; now the tourists have taken over, but it hasn't altogether lost its soul. Uncomplicated Florentine cooking, with a frequently changing menu. Mon–Sat noon–3pm & 6.30–10.30pm.

**Il Guscio Via dell'Orto 49 ☎055.224.421.** A long-established upper-range Oltrano favourite: high-quality Tuscan meat dishes, home-made pasta and superb desserts, plus a wide-ranging wine list. Evenings only; closed Sat & Aug.

**I Tarocchi Via dei Renai 12r ☎055.234.3912.** There are a few simple dishes on the menu, but this is essentially an inexpensive pizzeria – and one of the best in the city. Tues–Fri 12.30–2.30pm & 7–10pm, Sat & Sun 7–10pm only. Closed Mon.

**🏃 La Casalinga Via del Michelozzo 9r ☎055.218.624.** Located in a side-street off Piazza di Santa Spirito, this long-established family-run trattoria serves up some of the best low-cost Tuscan dishes in town (€10 for a *secondo*). No frills – paper tablecloths, so-so house wine by the flask and brisk service – but most nights it's filled with regulars and a good few outsiders. Closed Sun & last 3 weeks of Aug.

**🏃 Osteria Santo Spirito Piazza di Santo Spirito 16r/Via Sant'Agostino ☎055.238.2383.** Run by the owners of the *Borgo Antico* (see above), this *osteria* is part of the new wave of Florentine restaurants. Informal and modern, its walls are painted deep red and blue, and the lighting is bright over hearty Tuscan dishes presented with contemporary flair. Tables are on two floors, and in summer you can eat outdoors on the piazza. Pasta dishes €6–12, mains €12–20. Open daily until midnight.

**Pane e Vino Piazza di Cestello 3r ☎055.247.6956.** *Pane e Vino* began life as a bar (over by San Niccolò), so it's no surprise that the wine list is excellent and well priced, with bottles from €13. In its new home, the ambience is stylish yet relaxed and the menu small (*primi* around €10, *secondi* €15), featuring a very enticing *menu degustazione* (€30). Small TV screens in the dining area show the chefs beavering away in the kitchen, producing some of the best food in town – the ravioli with asparagus in a lemon cream melts in your mouth. Mon–Sat 8pm–1am.

**Quattro Leoni** Via dei Vellutini 1r/ Piazza della Passera ⓣ055.218.562, Ⓦwww.4leoni.com. Occupying a three-roomed medieval interior, this is a young, relaxed place with wooden beams and splashy modern paintings strung across the rough stone walls. In summer you can also eat al fresco under vast canvas umbrellas in the tiny Piazza della Passera – one of the most appealing outdoor eating venues in the city. It's popular with visiting stars – Dustin Hoffman and Sting feature on the walls, and Anthony Hopkins ate here while filming *Hannibal*. For everyone else booking is essential. You can eat very well for around €30 a head. Noon–2.30pm & 7–11pm; closed Wed lunch.

**Sabatino** Via Pisani 2r ⓣ055.225.955. Situated right by Porta San Frediano, this old-fashioned, no-frills, long-running family trattoria is not a gourmet venue, but it's excellent value and the atmosphere is always terrific. Closed Sat, Sun & Aug.

# Cafés and bars

Virtually every street in central Florence has a **café** or **bar** of some sort; what follows is a guide to the best and the most popular. Predictably enough, there's a heavy concentration on and around the big tourist streets and squares: Piazza della Repubblica, Piazza del Duomo, Via dei Calzaiuoli and so on. Many of these are expensive and characterless, but some – as listed below – are expensive and very good, especially when it comes to cakes and other sweet delicacies. To find places where prices are lower and non-Florentine faces fewer, only a little effort is needed: a short walk east from the Signoria gets you into the burgeoning Santa Croce area, and it's just as easy to get over into the Oltrarno, the most authentic quarter of the historic centre.

As elsewhere in Italy, the distinction between bars and cafés is tricky to the point of impossibility, as almost every café serves alcohol and almost every bar serves coffee. It's really just a question of degrees of emphasis: in some cafés, most of the custom comes first thing in the morning, as people on their way to work stop off for a dash of caffeine and a brioche or cornetto (croissant); in others, the tables are busiest late at night, when people drop by after an evening out, to relax over a Campari or a glass of wine.

There's one category of bar that's quite distinct from cafés, and that's the **enoteca**, where the enjoyment of wine is the chief point of the exercise – though in this case the complicating factor is that almost all *enoteche* serve food, which in some instances makes them almost indistinguishable from restaurants. You'll find *enoteche* and more humble wine dens reviewed in the "Wine bars" section (see p.201). Bars where **music** – live or recorded – is the main attraction are reviewed in "Nightlife" (see p.207).

## Piazza del Duomo

The listings in this section are marked on the map on p.52.

**Astor Caffè** Piazza del Duomo 20r. From its modest street-front opposite the northeast corner of the Duomo you wouldn't guess that this was the hottest spot on the piazza, but inside you'll find a glitzy and spacious three-storey set-up. Food is served in the upstairs restaurant, in the basement you get DJs playing anything from hip-hop to Brazilian music most nights, and in the ground-floor bar you sip cocktails with the city's gilded youth. Mon–Sat 10am–3am.

**Chiaroscuro** Via del Corso 36r. Nice cakes, but caffeine's the main draw, as you might guess from the coffee-related paraphernalia in the window. Also a good place for a quick, cheap lunch – choose food at the bar and take it to tables at the back. Mon–Sat 8am–9.30pm, Sun 3–8.30pm.

## Piazza della Signoria

The listings in this section are marked on the map on p.170.

**Caffè Italiano** Via della Condotta 56r. Located one block north of the piazza, this is a combination of old-fashioned stand-up bar and smart café, with lots of dark wood, silver teapots and superb cakes, coffees and teas. Lunch is inexpensive and excellent, as you'd expect from a place owned by Umberto Montano, boss of the outstanding *Osteria Caffè Italiano* (see p.196). 8am–8.30pm; June–Sept closed Sun.

**Rivoire Piazza della Signoria 5r.** If you want to people-watch on Florence's main square, this is the place to do so, and the outside tables are invariably packed. Founded in 1872, the café started life specializing in hot chocolate, still its main claim to fame. Ice creams are also fairly good, but the sandwiches and snacks are overpriced and poor: this is a place for one pricey beer or cappuccino, just to say you've done it. Closed Mon.

## West of the centre

The listings in this section are marked on the map on pp.88–89.

**Art Bar Via del Moro 4r.** A fine little bar near Piazza di Carlo Goldoni. The interior looks like an antique shop, while the club-like atmosphere attracts a rather smart crowd. Especially busy at happy hour (7–9pm), when the low-priced cocktails are in heavy demand. The after-hours ambience is also ideal for a laid-back nightcap. Mon–Sat 7pm–1am.

**Bar Curtatone Borgo Ognissanti 167r.** Despite the name, this big and slick establishment is more a café than a bar; a good place to recharge over an espresso and a slab of cake. Sept–June Mon & Wed–Sun 7am–1am; July Mon & Wed–Fri 7am–1am, Sat & Sun 7am–3pm; closed Aug.

**Caffè Amerini Via della Vigna Nuova 63r.** The intimate interior's medieval brick arching contrasts with modern furniture and a couple of Art Deco mirrors. Sandwiches, salads and snacks are particularly good – point at what you want from the bar and then sit down to be served: there's only a small premium for sitting down. Mon–Sat 8am–8pm.

**Caffè Gilli Piazza della Repubblica 36–39r.** Founded in 1733, this most appealing of the square's expensive cafés moved to its present site in 1910. The staggering Belle Epoque interior is a sight in itself, but most people choose to sit on the big outdoor terrace. On a cold afternoon try the famous

hot chocolate – it comes in five blended flavours: almond, orange, coffee, gianduia and cocoa. 8am–1am; closed Tues.

▽ *Capocaccia*

🏃 **Capocaccia Lungarno Corsini 12–14r,** ⓦ www.capocaccia.com. The well-designed interior is roomy and has plenty of tables and stools; there's a DJ every night; and you'll be mixing almost entirely with fashionable locals, especially later on – it's been voted the Florentines' favourite night-time rendezvous several times. If you have neither youth nor beauty on your side, however, you'd best stay away. Sushi aperitifs on Tuesdays – you pay €1–2 on top of the drink price to get access to the substantial snacks. Sunday brunch 12.30–3.30pm. Open daily noon–4pm & 6pm–1am.

**Hostaria Bibendum Via dei Pescioni 2.** New, Belle Epoque–styled bar that achieves the same low-key relaxed feel and quality of service as the *Helvetia & Bristol* hotel to which it is attached. Good wine list, excellent "H&B" cocktails, and small, expensive main courses (€18–24), but interesting menu that's strong on fish and has an excellent dish of cheeses and truffled honey. Kitchen open 11am–2.30pm & 7.30–10.30pm; bar open until 1am.

**Mariano Via Parione 19r.** It just says *Alimentari* above the door, but this is a smartish local café-bar behind the Santa Trìnita church that does brisk lunchtime business with its freshly prepared sandwiches and snacks, including *panini tartufati*. 8am–3pm & 5–7.30pm; closed Sat afternoon.

**Procacci Via de' Tornabuoni 64r.** Famous café that doesn't serve coffee, just wine and cold drinks. Its reputation comes from the extraordinary *tartufati*, or truffle-butter rolls (€1.60), which are delicious, if not exactly filling. Mon–Sat 10.30am–8pm; closed Aug.

**Slowly Via Porta Rossa 63.** This extremely trendy bar attracts a showy, beautifully dressed young crowd, chatting over pricey cocktails and high-end bar snacks. Time will tell whether its appearance in all the designer magazines will lead to style tourists edging out the Florentines. Mon–Sat 7pm–2.30am. Closed July & Aug.

## North of the centre

The listings in this section are marked on the map on pp.110–111.

**Caffèlatte Via degli Alfani 39r** ☏055.247.8878. *Caffèlatte* began life in the 1920s, when a milk and coffee supplier opened here. Nowadays, it's expanded its operation to include an organic bakery, which produces delicious breads and cakes, served in the one-room café. The speciality drink, as you'd expect, is *caffè latte*, served in huge bowls. Laid-back music and temporary exhibitions of paintings and photographs enhance the vaguely "alternative" mood. Mon–Sat 8am–8pm, Sun 10am–4pm.

**Caracol Via Ginori 10r.** Florence has a few pseudo–Latin American dives, of which this is by far the best. A big wooden bar and ranks of tequila bottles create the right look and feel, while a multiethnic crowd provides the noise and energy levels. Happy hour (6–8.30pm) is the best and busiest time to show up: cocktails are cheap, and there are snacks and tortillas to help them down. Tues–Sun 6pm–2am. Closed June–Sept.

**Nannini Coffee Shop Via Borgo San Lorenzo 7r.** The Florentine outpost of Siena's *Nannini* operation, famed for its superb coffee and tooth-wrecking *panforte*, an extremely dense and delicious cake. Daily 7.30am–8pm.

## East of the centre

The listings in this section are marked on the map on p.135.

🏃 **Caffè Cibrèo Via Andrea del Verrocchio 5r.** Possibly the prettiest café in Florence, with a chi-chi clientele to match. Opened in 1989, but the wood-panelled interior looks at least two hundred years older. Cakes and desserts are great, and the light meals bear the culinary stamp of the *Cibrèo* restaurant kitchens opposite. Tues–Sat 8am–1am.

**Caffè di Paci Via dei Neri 37r.** Friendly, small bar with tables at the back, serving a range of delicious truffle-flavoured dishes plus home-made pasta and a few other Florentine staples. Mon–Sat 7am–midnight.

**I Visacci Borgo degli Albizi 82r.** A bright, stylish and popular small bar, serving *crostini* and a few more substantial dishes. Tues–Sat 10am–2.30am (May–Aug closes earlier), Sun & Mon 10am–10pm.

## Oltrarno

The listings in this section are marked on the map on pp.156–157.

**Cabiria Piazza di Santo Spirito 4r.** Trendy in look, feel and clientele, but still rather cosy. The main seating area is in the room to the rear, but plenty of punters (some locals and lots of foreigners) sit out on the piazza, or crowd into the bar area at the front. There's a DJ-run soundtrack most nights from around 9pm – drinks are cheaper until then. Open 8am–1.30am; closed Tues & 10 days in mid-Aug.

**Caffè degli Artigiani Via dello Sprone 16r.** Slightly ramshackle and very welcoming café on a delightful small square near the Ponte Vecchio, much used by local students. Serves salads and sandwiches. Mon 7am–7pm, Tues–Sat 7am–1am.

🏃 **Caffè Pitti Piazza Pitti 9r.** Sit outside or in the old-style interior, which is nicely done out with wooden floors and subdued gold-yellow walls. Panini and other snacks are available at lunch, with a full dinner menu later – a *menu degustazione* for €30, and mains €15–19. Daily 10am–2am; June & July closed Mon.

**Caffè I Ricchi Piazza di Santo Spirito 9r.** The most relaxed of the cafés on this square. Menus change daily, and there's a good selection of cakes, ice cream and sandwiches. Summer Mon–Sat 7am–1am; winter closes 8pm.

🏃 **Caffè La Torre Lungarno Cellini 65r.** This bar changes its decor every year, which is one reason it has managed to remain one of the most fashionable bars in Florence. The other is its superb location, in the shadow of the tower of the Porta

San Niccolò, close to the Arno, with lots of outdoor seating. Excellent, imaginative cocktails complete the picture. Daily 10.30am–3am.

**Dolce Vita Piazza del Carmine.** A smart, modern-looking and extremely popular bar that's been going for more than a decade and has stayed ahead of the game through constant updating; aluminium bar stools, sleek black-and-white photos on the walls and the chance to preen with Florence's beautiful things, who like to drop in here for a cocktail on their way to a club. Daily 5pm–2am.

**Hemingway Piazza Piattellina 9r, off Piazza del Carmine.** Self-consciously trendy, but don't let that put you off – there's nothing else like it in Florence. Choose from one of countless speciality teas, sample over twenty coffees, or knock back one of the "tea cocktails". Owners Paul de Bondt and Andrea Slitti are members of the Compagnia del Cioccolato, a chocolate appreciation society – and it shows: the handmade chocolates are sublime. Tues–Sun 4.30pm–1am.

**Mamma Lungarno Santa Rosa, ⓦwww .mammasanfrediano.it.** Delightful venue for summer nights, occupying a small park in the shadow of the high city walls behind the Porta San Frediano. Romantic at dusk,

when candles are set out, it becomes hugely busy later on – more than a thousand people have been known to come out here on fine nights. DJs two or three nights a week keep the fashionable, cocktail-drinking and almost entirely Italian crowd happy. Occasional live gigs; antipasti available from the bistro. April–Oct Mon–Thurs & Sun 11am–2am, Fri & Sat till 3am.

**Il Rifrullo Via San Niccolò 53–57r.** New owners have smartened and expanded this bar, which is still a nice place to unwind after the hike up to San Miniato, or for a nightcap. Lying to the east of the Ponte Vecchio–Pitti Palace route, it attracts fewer tourists than many Oltrarno cafés. Has pleasant garden terrace, too. Serves tapas in the early evening, larger dishes after that, and offers brunch (€18) on Sat & Sun. Mon–Sat 7am–1am, Sun 7am–7pm.

**Zoe Via dei Renai 13.** Just set back from the Arno, on the south side of the grassy Piazza Demidoff, *Zoe* and neighbouring bar *Negroni* are perennially popular for summer evening drinks. *Zoe* is a little louder, a little trendier and a little younger in spirit. Both bars specialize in the *aperitivo*, with a free buffet laid out between 7.30 and 10.30pm, and attract lots of young Florentines right through into the small hours. Mon–Sat 8am–2.30am, Sun 4pm–2am.

# Wine bars

As you'd expect in a city that lies close to some of the best vineyards in the country, Florence has plenty of bars dedicated to the wines of Chianti and other Tuscan producers. At one end of the scale there's the endangered species known as the *vinaio* (see box, overleaf), which consists of little more than a niche with a few shelves of generally workaday wines, plus a counter of snacks. At the opposite pole there's the *enoteca*, which is in effect a restaurant devoted to wine: all of them have kitchens (cooking excellent food in many cases), but the wine menu will be far more extensive, often running to hundreds of different vintages. Increasingly popular among younger Florentines, the city's *enoteche* are becoming more numerous with every passing year, and their quality is consistently high.

## Piazza del Duomo

**Fiaschetteria Nuvoli Piazza dell'Olio 15 (see map on p.52).** It's something of a surprise to find such a traditional place so close to the Duomo. The tiny, dark, bottled-lined shop is dominated by a counter laden with cold meats, *crostini* and other snacks, plus a few opened wine bottles. There's room inside to

eat sitting down, but most of the customers are content with a quick glass at the bar. Mon–Sat 8am–8pm.

## Piazza della Signoria

The listings in this section are marked on the map on p.70.

**Cantinetta dei Verrazzano Via dei Tavolini 18–20r.** Owned by Castello dei

**9**

## Vinaii

The *vinaio* was once a real Florentine institution. These tiny places with no seating would typically see customers lingering for no more than a couple of minutes – long enough to down a tumbler of basic red wine and exchange a few words with the proprietor. The number of *vinaii* has declined markedly in recent years; the following are the notable survivors.

**All'Antico Vinaio** Via dei Neri 65r (see map on p.135). Though recently revamped, this place – located between the Uffizi and Santa Croce – preserves much of the rough-and-ready atmosphere that's made it one of Florence's most popular wine bars for the last hundred years. Also serves coffee, rolls and plates of pasta. Mon–Sat 8am–10pm; closed 3 weeks in late July & early Aug.

**L'Antico Noè** Volta di San Piero 6r. A long-established stand-up wine bar, tucked into an uninviting little alley to the north of Santa Croce, at the eastern end of Borgo degli Albizi. Mon–Sat noon–3pm & 7pm–midnight.

**Quasigratis** Piazza del Grano 10 (formerly known as Via dei Castellani; see map on p.70). Little more than a window in a wall at the back of the Uffizi, and it doesn't say *Quasigratis* ("Almost free") anywhere – just "Vini". Rolls, nibbles and wine – in tiny glasses called *rasini* – are consumed standing up. Daily 10am–11pm; closed Jan–Feb.

**Vini** Via dei Cimatori 38r (see map on p.52). Formally named *I Fratellini*, though there's no sign outside except *Vini*, this minuscule dirt-cheap wine bar is somehow clinging on in the immediate vicinity of the high-rent Via dei Calzaiuoli. Serves decent panini and local wines. Mid-June to Aug Mon–Fri 8am–5pm; Sept to mid-June daily 8am–8pm.

Verrazzano, a major Chianti vineyard, this wood-panelled place near Orsanmichele is part-bar, part-café and part-bakery, making its own excellent pizza, *focaccia* and cakes. A perfect spot for a light lunch or an early evening drink. July & Aug Mon–Sat 8am–4pm; Sept–June Mon–Sat 8am–9pm.

**Gustavino** Via della Condotta 37r, @www .gustavino.it. A minute's walk from Piazza della Signoria, this *enoteca con cucina* is the antithesis of the faux-rustic Tuscan wine bar, with its steel chairs and glass-topped tables. Some might find it a bit too businesslike, but it has a more than adequate selection of wines, and the kitchen turns out some interesting dishes – such as black *tagliolini* with sea urchin and zucchini-flower pesto (€12). The *cucina* itself is on full view, both from the tables and from the street. Its wine shop next door has a cosier feel (noon–midnight daily), serving snacks. Tues–Sun noon–3pm & 7.30pm–midnight.

### North of the centre

The listings in this section are marked on the map on pp.110–111.

**Casa del Vino** Via dell'Ariento 16r. Located just west of the Mercato Centrale, and passed by hordes of tourists daily – yet probably visited by only a handful. Patrons are mostly Florentines, who pitch up for a drink, a chat with owner Gianni Migliorini and an assault on various panini, *crostini*, and saltless Tuscan bread and salami. Mon–Fri 9.30am–7pm.

**Zanobini** Via Sant'Antonino 47r. Like the *Casa del Vino*, its rival just around the corner, this is an authentic Florentine place, whose feel owes much to the presence of locals and traders from the nearby Mercato Centrale. Offers acceptable snacks, but most people are simply here for a chat over a glass of wine. Mon–Sat 8am–2pm & 3.30–8pm.

### East of the centre

The listings in this section are marked on the map on p.135.

**Boccadama** Piazza Santa Croce 25–26r. A smart and well-stocked wine bar, offering vintages from all over the country and a good selection of snacks. The restaurant next door is OK, but not one of the area's best. Tues–Sun 3.30–11pm; also March–Oct Mon 3.30–11pm.

**Caffè Italiano Via Isola delle Stinche 11–13r.** As well as serving a superb range of mainly Tuscan wines, the wine-bar section of *Caffè Italiano* has an excellent kitchen – but only three tables and little standing room, so the queues outside can be long. No credit cards. Tues–Sun 7.30–1am.

**Enoteca Baldovino Via San Giuseppe 18r.** An offshoot of the excellent *Baldovino* restaurant across the road, this is a stylish place to sample gastronomic snacks or drink top-quality wine, either at the bar or one of the tables to the rear. Small menu of sandwiches, soups, pizza and home-made cakes. Summer daily noon–midnight; winter Tues–Sun noon–4pm & 6pm–midnight.

## Oltrarno

The listings in this section are marked on the map on pp.156–157.

**Beccofino Piazza degli Scarlatti 1r.** Like the restaurant to which it's attached, this wine bar is a sophisticatedly stylish establishment tho selection of wines is terrific, and there's a menu of innovative dishes from the restaurant's kitchen, at somewhat lower prices. Tues–Sun 7pm–midnight.

**Enoteca Le Barrique Via del Leone 40r.** A fine small wine bar, a short distance west of Santa Maria del Carmine, with a wide-ranging list of vintages and a modest menu of full meals. Tues–Fri & Sun 4.30pm–1am.

**Fuori Porta Via del Monte alle Croci 10r ☎055.234.2483, ⊛www.fuoriporta.it.** If you're climbing up to San Miniato you could take a breather at this superb and justly famous wine bar–*osteria*. There are over four hundred wines to choose from by the bottle, and an ever-changing selection of wines by the glass, as well as a wide selection of grappas and malt whiskies. Bread, cheese, ham and salami are available, together with a choice of pasta dishes and tasty salads, all very elegantly presented. Has a summertime terrace and large dining area, but it's still wise to book if you're coming here to eat. Mon–Sat 12.30–3.30pm & 7pm–12.30am; closed 2 weeks in mid-Aug.

**Il Santo Bevitore Via Santo Spirito 64–66r ☎055.211.264.** The Holy Drinker is an airy and stylish "gastronomic *enoteca*" with a small but classy food menu (around €20 for a meal without drinks) to complement its enticing menu of wines. Good range of salads at lunchtime, with a more extensive evening menu. Mon–Sat 12.30–2.30pm & 7.30–11.30pm.

## Pubs

Every Italian town of any size now has at least one pub, generally with an Irish theme, in which the clientele tends to be a mix of local lads and students sipping slowly at their half-pints, and English-speaking tourists showing them how it's really done. Florence has an increasing number of such places, of which the following trio are more convincing than most of the rest.

**Fiddler's Elbow** Piazza di Santa Maria Novella 7r (see map on pp.88–89). Part of an Italy-wide chain, with just one smoky, dark and wood-panelled room, invariably heaving with homesick foreigners – fortunately there's also seating out on the piazza. Women travellers are likely to find themselves the object of concerted attention from packs of Guinness-sozzled Italians. Daily noon–2am.

**Lion's Fountain** Borgo degli Albizi 34r (see map on p.52). Background music isn't traditional, but it's inoffensive; the decor is pseudo-Irish, and the bar staff and atmosphere are generally friendly. Food is simple and good – lots of salads and sandwiches – and you can catch big sporting events on the TVs. Drinks are reasonably priced, and include a good range of cocktails as well as the ubiquitous Guinness. Daily 6pm–2am.

**Robin Hood's Tavern** Via dell'Oriuolo 58r (see map on p.52). One of the biggest and most successful of several places that try to affect the look of an English pub – probably because it was started by a former biker from Birmingham. Happy hour 5–9pm. Open daily 2pm–3am.

**Le Volpi e L'Uva Piazza dei Rossi 1r, off Piazza di Santa Felìcita, ⓦ www.levolpie-luva.com.** This discreet, friendly little place, just over the Ponte Vecchio, does good business by concentrating on the wines of small producers and providing tasty cold meats and snacks to help them down (the selection of cheeses in particular is tremendous). At any one time you can choose from at least two dozen different wines by the glass. Mon–Sat 10am–8pm.

**Pitti Gola e Cantina Piazza Pitti 16.** A small and friendly wine bar, very handily placed for a glass of Chianti after a slog around the Pitti museums. Tues–Sun 10am–11.30pm. Closed 2 weeks in mid-Aug.

# Gelaterie

Devotees of Italian **ice cream** will find that Florence offers plenty of opportunities to indulge: the city has some superb *gelaterie*, and some would claim that *Vivoli* (see below) is the best purveyor in the country.

The procedure is the same wherever you buy. First decide whether you want a cone (*un cono*) or a cup (*una coppa*). Then decide how much you want to pay: cone and cup sizes tend to start around €2, going up in €1 increments. Unless you plump for the smallest size you'll usually be able to choose a combination of two or three flavours. Finally, you may be asked if you want a squirt of cream (*panna*) on top – it's usually free.

**Bondi (also known as Il Triangolo delle Bermude) Via Nazionale 61r (see map on pp.110–111).** The Bondi family make some of the most unusual concoctions in town, such as cinnamon, Oreo (made from the American biscuit) and Mars bar. Closed Mon.

**Café delle Carizze Piazza Pesce 3r (see map on p.70).** Good outlet right by the Ponte Vecchio. Daily except Wed 11am–8pm.

**Caffè I Ricchi Piazza di Santo Spirito 9r (see map on pp.156–157).** Excellent ice cream at a popular location – flavours include English trifle.

**Carabe Via Ricasoli 60r (see map on pp.110–111).** Wonderful Sicilian ice cream made with Sicilian ingredients as only they know how. Also serves a variety of cakes. May–Oct daily 10am–midnight; Nov, March & April daily noon–7.30pm; first half of Dec & last half of Jan Tues–Sun noon–7.30pm; closed mid-Dec to mid-Jan.

**Festival del Gelato Via del Corso 75r (see map on p.52).** Around seventy varieties of ice cream, with some very exotic combinations. Tues–Sun 10am–midnight.

**Frilli Via San Miniato 5r (see map on pp.156–157).** Tiny family operation just inside the San Miniato gate in the San Niccolò district: recommended are the orange and lemon mousse. Open Tues–Sun 10am–8pm, but open till midnight on summer weekends.

**Gelateria dei Neri Via dei Neri 20–22r (see map on p.135).** Small place in contention for the best ice cream in town. Close to the Uffizi but away from the crowds. The range of flavours is fantastic – fig and walnut, Mexican chocolate (very spicy), rice – and they also have some non-dairy ice cream. Daily 11am–midnight.

**Perchè No! Via de' Tavolini 19r (see map on p.70).** Superb *gelateria*, in business since the 1930s; go for the rum-laced *tiramisù*, the chocolate or the gorgeous pistachio. Daily 11am–midnight, except Tues 11am–7.30pm; closed Nov.

**Vivoli Via Isola delle Stinche 7r (see map on p.135).** Operating from deceptively unprepossessing premises in a side-street close to Santa Croce, this has long been rated the best ice-cream-maker in Florence – and some say in Italy. Tues–Sun 7.30am–1am. Closed Aug.

# 10

# Nightlife and cultural events

lorence has a reputation for catering primarily to the middle-aged and affluent, but like every university town it has its pockets of **nightlife** activity, not to mention the added nocturnal buzz generated by thousands of summer visitors.

Full details of the city's dependable club and live music venues are given below, but for up-to-the-minute **information** about what's on, call in at the tourist office in Via Cavour or at Box Office, which has outlets at Via Almanni 39 (☎055.210.804; Mon 3.30–7.30pm, Tues–Sat 10am–7.30pm) and Via Porta Rossa 82r, near the corner with Via de' Tornabuoni (☎055.219.402; Mon 1–8pm, Tues–Sat 9am–8pm). Tickets for most events are available at Box Office; otherwise, keep your eyes peeled for advertising posters, or pick up monthly magazines such as *Firenze Spettacolo* (€1.60), which has an English section ("Florenscope") as well as a map of places open after midnight.

## Clubs

Put together balmy summer evenings, a big student population and Florence's huge summer surge of young travellers, and you have a recipe for a massive **club** scene. Unfortunately, those same ingredients don't necessarily add up to produce the most sophisticated of venues, and in any case, clubs in Italy don't resemble their equivalents in London or other big cities. For one thing, most Florentines aren't in clubs to dance or drink; they're there to see and be seen, and dress up to the nines. Foreigners are a different matter, and one or two – mostly central – clubs have a slightly more sweaty and familiar atmosphere as a result.

The streets of central Florence are generally safe at night, but women should be wary of strolling through the red-light districts alone: the area around the **station** and **Piazza Ognissanti** have a particularly dodgy reputation, and kerb-crawling is not unknown. Unaccompanied tourists of either sex should stay well clear of the **Cascine park** at night: if you're going to one of the clubs located there, get a taxi there and back.

NIGHTLIFE AND CULTURAL EVENTS | Clubs

205

Florence's history is scattered with the names of some of history's greatest gay and bisexual artists, including Michelangelo, Leonardo and Botticelli: *Florenzer* was, during the seventeenth century at least, German slang for gay. The city remains, for the most part, tolerant towards gay and lesbian visitors. The leading gay bar is **Crisco**, a short distance east of the Duomo at Via Sant'Egidio 43r (see map on p.52; ☎055.248.0580, ⓦwww.crisco.it; Mon & Wed–Sun 10/11pm till late), but the ambience can be a bit heavy for some tastes. **Il Piccolo Caffè**, Borgo Santa Croce 23r (see map on p.135; ☎055.241.704; daily 5pm till late), has a more chilled-out atmosphere, while **Y.A.G. B@r**, also near Santa Croce at Via de' Macci 8r (see map on p.135; ☎055.246.9022, ⓦwww.yagbar.com), is stylish and draws a trendy, mixed crowd. The key bar-club is the pioneering **Tabasco**, which has been going for more than thirty years at Piazza Santa Cecilia 3r (see map on p.70; ☎055.213.000, ⓦwww.tabascogay.it; daily 10pm–6am, with music Thurs–Sun). For more information and contacts, check out ⓦwww.gay.it/pinklily. For lesbian contacts, check the noticeboard at the women's bookshop Libreria delle Donne, Via Fiesolana 2b (Mon 3.30–7.30pm, Tues–Sat 9am–1pm & 3.30–7.30pm).

Faced with a low income from the bar, most clubs charge a fairly stiff **admission**: reckon on €15 and up for the bigger and better-known places. This is not quite as bad as it sounds, for the admission often includes a drink. Prices at the bar after that are usually pretty steep. Other more insidious admission procedures include a card system, where you're given a card on (usually free) entry that gets stamped every time you spend money at the bar. By the end of the night you have to have spent a minimum sum; if not, you have to pay the difference before the bouncers will let you out. And of course everyone loses their card. Alternatively, the card may be used just to keep tabs on your drinks, with the bill settled at the end of the evening. Payment always has to be in cash: credit cards are not accepted.

Opening and closing times for clubs are rarely set, though the weekly closing day, if there is one, doesn't usually vary. Clubs are also prone to closure, or to closing and then opening up under a different name.

### West of the centre

The listings in this section are marked on the map on pp.88–89.

**Central Park Via Fosso Macinante 2, Parco delle Cascine.** One of the city's biggest and most commercial clubs, with adventurous, wide-ranging and up-to-the-minute music on several dance floors from DJs who know what they're doing and have access to a superb sound system. A card system operates for drinks, and the first drink is included in the admission – around €20 after midnight, usually free before. It's unsafe to wander around the park outside, especially for women. Summer Tues–Sat 11pm–4am; winter Fri & Sat same hours.

**Loonees Via Porta Rossa 15r.** Run by a former biker from Birmingham, this is a relaxed bar in the centre of town, with live music Wed–Sat. Daily 9pm–2am.

**Meccanò Viale degli Olmi 1/Piazzale delle Cascine** ☎055.331.371. People flock here for a night out from across half of Tuscany. The place is labyrinthine, with a trio of lounge and bar areas, and a huge and invariably packed dance floor playing mostly house. In summer, when the action spills out of doors, you can cool off in the gardens bordering the Cascine. The €15 admission (usually less during the week) includes your first drink. Summer Wed–Sat 8.30pm–4am; winter Thurs–Sat same hours; closed Nov & two weeks in Aug.

**Space Electronic Via Palazzuolo 37** ☎055.293.082, ⓦwww.spaceelectronic.net. You'll find all the disco clichés of a big Continental club here – glass dance floors and mirrored walls – and one or two less

10 | NIGHTLIFE AND CULTURAL EVENTS | Clubs

familiar features, such as the piranha tank in the downstairs bar, near the karaoke area. Cooler-than-thou clubbers might be sniffy about its popularity with youthful tourist coach parties and local lads on the pull, but it's fine if all you want to do is dance, and the music can be surprisingly good. Admission €14 with one free drink; drinks are reasonably priced. Mon–Fri & Sun 10pm–2.30am, Sat 10pm–3am; winter closed Mon.

**Yab Via Sassetti 5r** ☎055.215.160, ⓦwww.yab .it. Long-established place crammed into a basement and currently enjoying something of a vogue, especially on a Thursday night. On other nights it doesn't have the most up-to-the-minute playlist in the world, but still offers probably the most relaxed and reliable night's clubbing in central Florence. You're given a card and pay on leaving if you've spent less than €15 at the bar. Aug–April Mon & Wed–Sun 9pm–4am; May–July Mon 11pm–4am.

### East of the centre

The listings in this section are marked on the map on p.135.

**Blob Club Via Vinegia 21r** ☎055.211.209. A favourite with Florentine students, possibly on account of its free admission and the 6–10pm happy hour. Seating upstairs, bar and tiny dance floor downstairs, but don't expect to do much dancing – later on, especially on weekend nights, *Blob* gets packed full with a very happy and very drunken crowd. Quieter in the summer months. Daily 6pm–3am.

**Full-Up Via della Vigna Vecchia 25r** ☎055.293.006. Situated close to the Bargello, this club has been going so long it's become something of an institution,

but new management is trying to move it upmarket. Admission €13. Reckon on around €7 for most drinks. Tues–Sat 11pm–4am. Closed June–Sept.

🏃 **Rex Via Fiesolana 25r** ⓦwww.rexcafe.it. One of the city's big night-time fixtures, a friendly bar-club with a varied and loyal clientele. Vast curving lights droop over the central bar, which is studded with turquoise stone and broken mirror mosaics. Big arched spaces to either side mean there's plenty of room, the cocktails are good and the snacks excellent. DJs provide the sounds at weekends. Daily 5pm–3am. Closed June–Aug.

### Oltrarno

🏃 **Universale Via Pisana 77r** ☎055.221.122, ⓦwww.universale-firenze.it (see map on pp.156–157). Located beyond the city gates, this is perhaps the most stylish night venue in Florence, with a restaurant and various club zones installed in a beautiful converted 1950s cinema. Snobby and nouveau, maybe, but definitely glamorous. The music is predominantly house. Tues–Sun 8.30pm–3am. Closed Mon & May–Sept.

### Perètola

**Tenax Via Pratese 46** ☎055.632.958, ⓦwww .tenax.org. Florence's big-hitting club, pulling in the odd big-name DJ. Given its location in the northwest of town, near the airport (take a taxi), you'll escape the hordes of *internazionalisti* in the more central clubs. With two large floors, it's a major venue for concerts, as well. Admission varies from around €10 to around €20. Thurs–Sat 10.30pm–4am. Closed mid-May to mid-Sept.

# Live music

Florence's **live music** scene isn't the hottest in Italy, but there's a smattering of venues for small-time local outfits, and a couple of big stages for visiting stars. In addition to the recommendations below, a few of the places reviewed under "Bars and cafés" and "Clubs" lay on live bands from time to time: check listings magazines for one-off events.

### Piazza della Signoria

**Caruso Jazz Café Via Lambertesca 14/16r** ☎055.281.940, ⓦwww.carusojazzcafe.com

(see map on p.70). Regular live jazz at this small venue. €8 for admission and first drink. Closed Sun.

The listings in this section are marked on the map on pp.110–111.

**Be Bop Via dei Servi 28r.** A nice and rather classy rock, jazz and blues bar with bow-tied bar staff and faux Art Nouveau decor. Located close to the university district, and often full of students as a result. No dance floor as such; this is more a place to sit and chill out to the music. Daily 6pm–1am.

**Girasol Via del Romito 1** ⊤055.474.948. Florence's liveliest Latin bar, located on a minor road due north of the Fortezza da Basso, is hugely popular. Rather than relying solely on salsa classes, cocktails and the usual vinyl suspects – although it does all these – the place draws in some surprisingly good live acts, with different countries' sounds each day of the week, from Brazilian bossa nova to Cuban son; Friday is party night. Daily 7pm–2.30am.

## East of the centre

**Jazz Club Via Nuova de' Caccini 3** ⊤055.247.9700 (see map on p.135). Florence's foremost jazz venue has been a fixture for years. The €6 "membership" fee gets you down into the medieval brick-vaulted basement, where the atmosphere's informal and there's live music most nights (and an open jam session on Tuesdays). Cocktails are good, and you can also snack on bar nibbles and *focaccia*. Tues–Fri 9.30pm–1.30am, Sat 9.30pm–2.30am. Closed June–Aug.

**Nelson Mandela Forum Viale Pasquale Paoli** ⊤055.210.804. Along with *Tenax* (see below), this place – located a long way east of the centre, at Campo di Marte – is the city's main venue for big-draw mainstream acts, such as Mark Knopfler and Lenny Kravitz.

## Il Poggetto

**Auditorium Flog Via Michele Mercati 24b** ⊤055.490.437, ⓦ www.flog.it. One of the city's best-known mid-sized venues, and a perennial student favourite – with a suitably downbeat studenty look and feel – for all forms of live music (and DJs), but particularly local indie-type bands. It's usually packed, despite a position way out in the northern suburbs at Il Poggetto; to get there take buses #8, #14, #20 or #28.

## Perètola

**Tenax Via Pratese 46** ⊤055.308.160, ⓦ www .dada.it/tenax. The city's longest-running venue for new and established bands, as well as big-name international acts. Keep an eye open for posters around town or call at the tourist office for upcoming gigs. The place is enormous but easy-going, and doubles as a club after hours. There are ranks of bars, pool tables, computer games and plenty of seating.

# Classical music

The **Maggio Musicale**, Italy's oldest and most prestigious music festival, is the most conspicuous sign of the health of the city's classical music scene, though it should be said that the fare tends towards the conservative. In addition to the major festivals listed below, the city has numerous organizations that put on concerts at various times of the year. The **Amici della Musica** hosts a season of chamber concerts with top-name international performers from October to April, mostly in the Teatro della Pergola, occasionally in the Teatro Goldoni. Events are held throughout the year by the **Associazione Giovanile Musicale**: two of their best are the *Concerti di Pasqua*, a series of Easter concerts usually held in the church of Orsanmichele, and the *Festival Estate*, a festival held in July in the courtyard of the Palazzo Pitti.

The **Orchestra da Camera Fiorentina** (Florence Chamber Orchestra; ⓦ www.orcafi.it) plays from March to October, often in Orsanmichele or the Badìa Fiorentina, while from April to September concerts and dances in period dress are staged in the Oratorio di San Bernardino by the **Orchestra Historica di Firenze**. The main concert season of the Filarmonica di Firenze G. Rossini

Florence's main cultural festivals are covered in the "Classical music" section; what follows is a rundown on its more folkloric events.

### Scoppio del Carro

The first major folk festival of the year is Easter Sunday's **Scoppio del Carro** (Explosion of the Cart), when a cartload of fireworks is hauled by six white oxen from the Porta a Prato to the Duomo; there, during the Gloria of the midday Mass, the whole lot is set off by a "dove" that whizzes down a wire from the high altar. The origins of this incendiary descent of the Holy Spirit lie with one Pazzino de' Pazzi, leader of the Florentine contingent on the First Crusade. On getting back to Florence he was entrusted with the care of the flame of Holy Saturday, an honorary office which he turned into something more festive by rigging up a ceremonial wagon to transport the flame round the city. His descendants continued to manage the festival until the Pazzi conspiracy of 1478, which of course lost them the office. Since then, the city authorities have taken care of business.

### Festa del Grillo

On the first Sunday after Ascension Day (forty days after Easter), the **Festa del Grillo** (Festival of the Cricket) is held in the Cascine park. In amongst the stalls and the picnickers you'll find people selling tiny wooden cages containing crickets, which are then released onto the grass – a ritual that may hark back to the days when farmers had to scour their land for locusts, or to the tradition of men placing a cricket on the door of their lovers to serenade them.

### St John's Day and the Calcio Storico

The saint's day of **John the Baptist**, Florence's patron, is June 24 – the occasion for a massive fireworks display up on Piazzale Michelangelo, and for the first game of the **Calcio Storico**. Played in sixteenth-century costume to perpetuate the memory of a game played during the siege of 1530, this uniquely Florentine mayhem is a three-match series staged in this last week of June, with fixtures usually held in Piazza Santa Croce (scene of that first match) and Piazza della Signoria. Each of the four historic quarters fields a team, Santa Croce playing in green, San Giovanni in red, Santa Maria Novella in blue and Santo Spirito in grossly impractical white. The prize for the winning side is a calf, which gets roasted in a street party after the tournament and shared among the four teams and the inhabitants of the winning quarter.

### Festa delle Rificolone

The **Festa delle Rificolone** (Festival of the Lanterns) takes place on the Virgin's birthday, September 7, with a procession of children to Piazza Santissima Annunziata. Each child carries a coloured paper lantern with a candle inside it – a throwback to the days when people from the surrounding countryside would troop by lantern light into the city for the Feast of the Virgin. The procession is followed by a parade of floats and street parties.

### Festa dell'Unità

October's **Festa dell'Unità** is part of a nationwide celebration run by the Italian communists. Florence's is the biggest event after Bologna's, with loads of political stalls and restaurant-marquees. Box Office will have details of venues, while news about the *Feste* and other political events in Florence can be found in *Anteprima*, a local supplement published with Friday's edition of the communist daily *L'Unità*.

is in January and February, but in June it also performs a series of concerts in Piazza della Signoria, and Tuscany's major orchestra, the **Orchestra Regionale Toscana** (ⓦ www.orchestradellatoscana.it), plays one or two concerts a month in the city between November and May in the Teatro Verdi as well as a couple of concerts in the Bóboli gardens. The Lutheran church on Lungarno Torrigiani regularly holds free chamber music and organ recitals.

**Teatro Comunale** Corso Italia 16 ☎055.213.535. Florence's main municipal theatre, out to the west of Santa Maria Novella, which hosts many of the city's major classical music, dance and theatre events. It has its own orchestra, chorus and dance company, attracting top-name international guest performers. The main season (concerts, opera and ballet) runs Jan–April and Sept–Dec, with concerts usually held on Friday, Saturday and Sunday evenings.

**Teatro Goldoni** Via Santa Maria 15 ☎055.210.804. This exquisite little eighteenth-century theatre, located a little way past the Palazzo Pitti, is occasionally used for chamber music and opera performances, but lately it has hosted more dance productions than anything else.

**Teatro della Pergola** Via della Pergola 18 ☎055.226.4316, ⓦwww.pergola.firenze.it. The beautiful little Pergola was built in 1656 and is Italy's oldest surviving theatre – Verdi's *Macbeth* was first performed here. It plays host to chamber concerts, small-scale operas, and some of the best-known Italian theatre companies.

**Teatro Verdi** Via Ghibellina 99–101 ☎055.212.320, ⓦwww.teatroverdifirenze.it. Another of the city's premier music venues.

## Music festivals

**Estate Fiesolana** ⓦwww.estatefiesolana.it. Slightly less exclusive than the Maggio Musicale, concentrating more on chamber and symphonic music. It's held in Fiesole every summer, usually from June to late August. Films and theatre are also featured, and most events are held in the open-air Teatro Romano.

**Maggio Musicale Fiorentino** ⓦwww .maggiofiorentino.com. The highlight of Florence's cultural calendar and one of Europe's leading festivals of opera and classical music; confusingly, it isn't restricted to May (*Maggio*), but lasts for a couple of months from late April or early May. The festival has its own orchestra, chorus and ballet company, plus guest appearances from foreign ensembles. Events are staged at the Teatro Comunale (or its Teatro Piccolo), the Teatro della Pergola, the Palazzo dei Congressi, the Teatro Verdi and occasionally in the Bóboli gardens. Information and tickets can be obtained from the Teatro Comunale.

# Theatre

Should your Italian be up to a performance of the plays of Machiavelli or Pirandello in the original, Florence's **theatres** offer year-round entertainment. In addition to the places listed below, various halls and disused churches are enlisted for one-off performances.

**Teatro Comunale** Corso Italia 16 ☎055.213.535. Florence's principal performance space hosts theatre productions, as well as dance and classical music concerts; offerings here are usually mainstream.

**Teatro Le Laudi** Via Leonardo da Vinci 2r ☎055.572.831. Located northeast of the centre, a few minutes' walk from San Marco; stages a fair amount of modern work.

**Teatro della Pergola** Via della Pergola 18 ☎055.226.4350, ⓦwww.pergola.firenze.it. Fine old theatre, staging productions that are usually Italian, or foreign classics in translation. The season runs from October to April.

**Teatro Verdi** Via Ghibellina 99–101 ☎055.212.320, ⓦwww.teatroverdifirenze.it. Productions at the Teatro Verdi are more or less similar to the mainstream fare of the Teatro Comunale, though you may also catch the odd musical.

**Stazione Leopolda** Viale Fratelli Rosselli 5 ☎055.212.622, ⓦwww.stazione-leopolda.com. New contemporary arts centre in Florence's first railway station, 1km west of Santa Maria Novella. Built in 1848 and closed down in 1861, the old station is a fine Neoclassical space for dance, arts events and occasional concerts.

# Cinema

Florence has a large number of **cinemas**, but very few show subtitled films. The vast majority of English-language films are dubbed, though a couple of cinemas do regularly have undubbed screenings (*versione originale*). See *Firenze Spettacolo* or the listings pages of *La Nazione* for locations and latest screenings.

Florence has two major **film festivals**: Under Florence (first two weeks of Dec), which shows Italian independent films and videos, and the more earnest Festival dei Popoli (2 weeks in Nov or Dec), run by an academic institution concerned with documentary film. For information on both events contact the Cinema Alfieri Atelier, Via dell'Ulivo 6 (☏055.240.720).

**Cinema Goldoni Via dei Serragli 109**
☏055.222.437. Florence's best cinema. Most weeks it has an English-language night, usually Wed. The shows are popular, however, so turn up early to be sure of a seat. Closed June & July.

**Odeon Original Sound Via de' Sassetti 1**
☏055.214.068. Films are screened in their original language at this air-conditioned cinema once a week, generally on Mon, for most of the year, plus Tues and Thurs in summer.

# Shopping

f you're after high-quality **clothes** and accessories, paintings, prints and marbled paper, or any number of other beautiful or luxury objects, then you'll find them in Florence – though this is not a city for the bargain-hunter. Its best-known area of manufacturing expertise is leather goods, with top-quality shoes, bags and gloves sold across the city. The main concentration of outlets is around **Via de' Tornabuoni** – the city's premier

## Markets

**Cascine** Parco del Cascine. The biggest of all Florence's markets happens Tuesday morning at the Cascine park near the banks of the Arno (bus #1, 9, 12 or 17c), where hundreds of stallholders set up an alfresco budget-class department store. Fewer tourists make it out here than to San Lorenzo, so prices are keener. Clothes (some secondhand) and shoes are the best bargains, though for cheaper still, you should check out the weekday-morning stalls at Piazza delle Cure, just beyond Piazza della Libertà (bus #1 or #7; Tues 8am–1pm).

**San Lorenzo** Piazza di San Lorenzo. Another open-air warehouse of cheap clothing. San Lorenzo is as well organized as a shopping mall: huge waterproof awnings ensure that the weather can't stop the trading, and some of the stallholders even accept credit cards. You'll find plenty of leather jackets, T-shirts and other cheap clothes: it may be what you're looking for, but it may not be that much of a bargain. For anything pricey, try to haggle. Daily 8am–7pm.

**Mercato Centrale** Piazza del Mercato Centrale. Europe's largest indoor food hall is situated at the heart of the stall-filled streets around San Lorenzo, and is well worth a sightseeing and people-watching visit whether you intend to buy anything or not. Its popularity as a tourist sight has pushed prices up, but it's still unbeatable for picnic supplies. Mon–Sat 7am–2pm, plus Sat 4–8pm in winter.

**Mercato Nuovo** Loggia del Mercato Nuovo. Just to the west of Piazza della Signoria (and also known as the Mercato del Porcellino), this is the main emporium for straw hats, plastic *David*s and the like. Mid-Feb to mid-Nov daily 9am–7pm; mid-Nov to mid-Feb Tues–Sat 9am–5pm.

**Mercato delle Pulci** Piazza dei Ciompi. A flea market stacked with antiques and bric-a-brac, pitched every day near the Sant'Ambrogio food market. Summer Mon–Sat 10am–1pm & 4–7pm; winter Mon–Sat 9am–1pm & 3–7pm; also open same hours on last Sun of month. More serious antique dealers swell the ranks on the last Sunday of each month (same hours).

**Mercato Sant'Ambrogio** Piazza Ghiberti. Big, cheap market just beyond Santa Croce, with food stalls in the central hall, as well as cheap clothes and leather. Mon–Sat 7am–2pm.

shopping thoroughfare – and the tributaries of Via degli Strozzi and Via della Vigna Nuova, also home to the shops of Italy's top fashion designers. If their prices are too steep, passable imitations (and outright fakes) can be unearthed at the various **street markets**, of which San Lorenzo is the most central. It's also worth having a look in the area of Via Matteo Palmieri and Borgo degli Albizi (a couple of minutes' walk east and north of the Bargello, respectively) for cheaper trendy clothes and jewellery.

If you want everything under one roof, there's also a handful of **department stores**. Marbled paper is another Florentine speciality, and, as you'd expect in this arty city, Florence is also one of the best places in the country to pick up **books** on Italian art, architecture and culture. The whole Ponte Vecchio is crammed with **jewellers'** shops, most of them catering strictly to the financial stratosphere. Those of more limited means could either take a chance on the counterfeits and low-cost originals peddled by the street vendors on and around the bridge, or check out our recommendations below. For delicatessens and **food** stores see the box on p.193.

# Books and maps

**BM Borgo Ognissanti 4r** ☎055.294.575. English-language bookshop selling a wide selection of guidebooks and general titles, with particular emphasis on Italian literature in translation, as well as books on Italian art, cookery and travel in Italy. Mon–Sat 9.30am–7.30pm; April–Dec also Sun 10.30am–1pm & 3.30–7pm.

**Edison Piazza della Repubblica 27r,** ☎055.213.110. This US-style operation is arranged on four floors (with English-language books on the top), the stock is impressive and the opening hours unique. Mon–Sat 9am–midnight, Sun 10am–midnight.

**Feltrinelli Via de' Cerretani 30r** ☎055.238.2652, ⓦwww.feltrinelli.it. This branch of the Feltrinelli chain, a short distance west of the Duomo, is best for Italian titles, maps and guides. Mon–Fri 9am–7.30pm, Sat 10am–8pm, Sun 10.30am–1.30pm & 3.30–7.30pm.

**Feltrinelli International Via Cavour 12–20r** ☎055.219.524. Bright and well staffed, this is the first port of call for English or other foreign-language books, newspapers and videos, as well as posters, cards and magazines. Mon–Sat 9am–7.30pm.

**Libreria EPT Via Condotta 42r** ☎055.240.489.

City maps and walking maps (1:25,000) of surrounding area. Mon 3.30–7.30pm, Tues–Sat 9.30am–1pm & 7.30pm.

**McRae Via de' Neri 32r** ☎055.238.2456, ⓦwww.mcraebooks.com/shop. Run by a former staff member of Seeber (see below), this bookshop, not far from the Uffizi, has one of the finest collections of English-language books in town: guides, cookery books, literature and art all covered. Daily 9am–7.30pm.

**Paperback Exchange Via Fiesolana 31r** ☎055.247.8154, ⓦwww.papex.it. A bit remote – north of Santa Croce – but always has a good stock of English and American books, with the emphasis on Italian-related titles and secondhand stuff; also exchanges secondhand books and has informative and friendly staff. Mon–Fri 9am–7.30pm, Sat 10am–1pm & 3.30–7.30pm.

**Seeber Via de' Cerretani 54r** ☎055.215.697, ⓦwww.melbookstore.it. Displaced from its famous old HQ on Via de' Tornabuoni, the venerable Seeber now occupies a former cinema, and has been thoroughly "modernized" by its new owners. It's lost its soul in the process, but the stock is still impressive. Mon–Sat 9.30am–7.30pm.

# Clothing

**Armani Via de' Tornabuoni 44–50r** ☎055.219.041, ⓦwww.armani.com. Gorgeous clothes from the most

famous designer in Italy, at prices that make you think you must have misread the tag. Mon 10am–2pm & 3–7pm,

Tues–Fri 10am–7pm, Sat 10.30am–7.30pm.

**Compai** Via Matteo Palmieri 6r ℡055.234.0606, Ⓦwww.compai.com. Whacky recycled vintage clothes by young designers. Mon 3.30–8pm, Tues–Sat noon–8pm.

**Dolce e Gabbana** Via della Vigna Nuova 27 ℡055.281.003. The Venetian-Sicilian double act are now in the same big league as Armani and Versace, but their extravagant – often camp – aesthetic hasn't been tamed by success. Mon 3–7pm, Tues–Sat 10am–7pm.

**Emporio Armani** Piazza Strozzi 14–17r ℡055.284.315, Ⓦwww.emporioarmani.com. The lowest-priced wing of the Armani empire, this is the place to go if you're desperate to get the Armani label on your back. Mon 3.30–7.30pm, Tues–Sat 10am–1pm & 3.30–7.30pm.

**Ferragamo** Via de' Tornabuoni 14r ℡055.292.123. Salvatore Ferragamo emigrated to the US at the age of 14 and became the most famous shoemaker in the world, producing everything from pearl-studded numbers for Gloria Swanson to gladiators' sandals for Cecil B. de Mille. Managed by his widow and children, Ferragamo now produces ready-to-wear outfits, but the company's reputation still rests on its beautiful shoes. The shop, occupying virtually the entire ground floor of a colossal palazzo on Piazza Santa Trìnita, is unbelievably grandiose. Mon–Sat 10am–7.30pm.

**Gucci** Via de' Tornabuoni 73r and 81r ℡055.264.011. The Gucci empire was founded at no. 73, which remains the flagship showroom, though the creative head of the company is no longer a member of the Gucci clan – Texan designer Tom Ford masterminded the reinvention of the label as one of the coolest around, before moving on in 2004. Mon 3–7pm, Tues–Sat 10am–7pm.

**Luisa at Via Roma** Via Roma 19–21r ℡055.217.826. A long-standing fixture at this address, gathering together a host of different labels every season, but with a tendency to play it safe. Mon–Sat 10am–7.30pm, Sun 11am–7pm.

**Poncif** Borgo Albizi 35r. Elegant contemporary women's fashion outlet, stocking a range of labels. Mon 3.30–7.30pm, Tues–Thurs 10am–1.30pm & 3.30–7.30pm, Fri & Sat 10am–7.30pm.

**Prada** Via de' Tornabuoni 51–55r & 67r ℡055.283.439, Ⓦwww.prada.it. During the 1990s the severe style of Milanese designer Miuccia Prada became supremely trendy, and she's still riding high. Mon–Sat 10am–7.30pm, last Sun of the month 10am–7pm.

**Pucci** Via de' Tornabuoni 20–22r ℡055.294.028. The Pucci family was one of the city's mercantile dynasties, until Marchese Emilio Pucci gatecrashed the fashion world of the 1950s with his vivid, swirling-patterned silks, which remain the Pucci signature, even though French designer Christian Lacroix has been at the helm since 2002. Mon–Sat 10am–7pm, Sun 2–7pm.

🏃 **Raspini** Via Por Santa Maria 70r & Via Roma 25r ℡055.213.077, Ⓦwww.raspini.com. Florence's biggest multi-label clothes shop, with a good stock of diffusion lines. These are the two main branches, and there's a third one at Via de' Martelli 5–7r. Mon 3.30–7.30pm, Tues–Sat 10.30am–7.30pm.

# Department stores

**Coin** Via dei Calzaiuoli 56r but with entrances on all four sides of the block ℡055.280.531, Ⓦwww.coin.it. Clothes-dominated chain store in an excellent central position. Quality is generally high, though styles are fairly conservative except for one or two youth-oriented franchises on the ground floor. Also a good place for linen and other household goods. Mon–Sat 10am–8pm, Sun 11am–8pm.

**Rinascente** Piazza della Repubblica 1 ℡055.239.8544, Ⓦwww.rinascente.it. Like Coin, Rinascente is part of a countrywide chain, though this store, opened in 1996, is a touch more upmarket than its nearby rival. Sells clothing, linen, cosmetics, household goods and other staples. Mon–Sat 9am–9pm, Sun 10.30am–8pm.

# Jewellery

**Alessandro Dari** Via San Nicolò 115r ℡055.244.747, Ⓦwww.alessandrodari.com.

This goldsmith's workshop, in eastern Oltrarno, produces intricate rings with musical and architectural motifs. You can walk around the display of Alessandro's work to loud classical music as the master works away. Mon–Sat 9.30am–1.30pm & 4–7.30pm.

**Bijoux Cascio Via de' Tornabuoni 32r & Via Por Santa Maria 1r ☎055.238.2851.** The outfit has made a name for itself over the last thirty years as a maker of imitation jewellery. It takes a trained eye to distinguish much of the stuff from that displayed in the windows on the Ponte Vecchio. Mon 3.30–7.30pm, Tues–Sat 9.30am–1pm & 3.30–7.30pm.

**Dettagli per donzelle, comari e sognatori Borgo degli Albizi 40r ☎055.234.0333.** Funky, brightly coloured hand-made jewellery and accessories at reasonable prices. Mon 3.30–7.30pm, Tues–Sat 10am–7.30pm.

**Gatto Bianco Borgo SS Apostoli 12r ☎055.282.989.** Strange combinations of precious and everyday materials are the signature of this outlet, one of the city's more adventurous jewellery workshops. Mon 3.30–7.30pm, Tues–Sat 9.30am–1pm & 3.30–7.30pm.

**Moltissimo Via Matteo Palmieri 27r ☎055.242.038.** Remodelled vintage jewellery – strong on 50s style – and accessories, as well as pleasingly simple designs of retro hand-painted china. Mon–Sat 10.30am–7.30pm.

**Torrini Piazza del Duomo 10r ☎055.230.2401.** Torrini registered its trademark – a distinctive half-clover leaf with spur – as early as 1369. Seven centuries later this store remains one of the premier places to buy Florentine jewellery: gold predominates, but all manner of classic and modern pieces are available, at a price. Mon 3–7pm, Tues–Sat 10am–1.30pm & 2.30–7pm.

# Kitchen shops

**Bartolini Via dei Servi 30r ☎055.211.895, ⓦwww.dinobartolini.it.** Well-stocked shop with all the coffee pots and cappuccino makers you could want. 10am 1pm & 3.30–7.30pm; closed all day Sun & Mon mornings.

**La Ménagère Via de' Ginori 8r ☎055.213.875.** Excellent range of kitchen implements, in a rather beautiful, old-fashioned interior. 9am–1pm & 3.30–7.30pm; closed Mon morning.

# Music

**Alberti Via de' Pucci 16r & Borgo San Lorenzo 45–49r ☎055.284.346.** Founded in 1873, this is the city's leading supplier of domestic hi-fi, videos, records and CDs. The Borgo San Lorenzo store is good for opera, classical and jazz, while the Via de' Pucci shop (a couple of blocks to the east) concentrates on contemporary music (dance, rock etc). June–Sept Mon 3.30–7.30pm, Tues–Sat 9am–7.30pm; Oct–May Mon–Fri 9am–7.30pm, Sat 9am–1pm.

**Data Records 93 Via de' Neri 15r ☎055.287.592.** Huge collection of new and secondhand albums covering rock, pop, reggae, jazz, punk, heavy metal etc, not far from the Uffizi.

**Fenice Via Santa Reparata 8b ☎055.238.1880.** Small record shop in the back streets beyond San Lorenzo, with a fantastic stock of classical music and helpful staff. They also have a smaller selection of jazz and other music. Mon–Sat 9am–1pm & 3.30–7.30pm.

**Ricordi Media Store Via Brunelleschi 8–10r ☎055.214.104.** The city's biggest general CD store, just off Piazza della Repubblica. Mon–Sat 9am–7.30pm, plus Sept–June last Sun of month 3.30–7.30pm.

# Paper, stationery and artists' materials

**Giulio Giannini e Figlio Piazza Pitti 36r ☎055.212.621, ⓦwww.giuliogiannini.it.** Established in 1856, this paper-making and book-binding firm has been honoured with exhibitions dedicated to its work.

Once the only place in Florence to make its own marbled papers, it now offers a wide variety of diaries, address books and so forth as well. Mon–Sat 10am–7.30pm, Sun 10.30am–6.30pm.

Il Papiro Via Cavour 55r ☎055.215.262, Ⓦwww.ilpapirofirenze.it. Huge range of marbled paper and gifts in seven outlets around the city, including Via de' Tavolini 13r and Piazza del Duomo 24r. Mon–Sat 10am–1pm, 2–7.30pm.

Pineider Piazza della Signoria 13r & Via de' Tornabuoni 76r ☎055.284.655. Pineider sell briefcases, picture frames and other accessories for home and office, but their reputation rests on their colour coordinated calling cards, hand-made papers and envelopes – as used by Napoleon, Stendhal, Byron and Shelley, to name just a few past customers. Mon 3–7pm, Tues–Fri 10am–1.30pm & 2.30–7pm,

plus Sat 2.30–7pm in July & Aug; closed 2nd week of Aug.

Il Torchio Via de' Bardi 17 ☎055.234.2862. A marbled-paper workshop using manufacturing techniques known only to the owner. Desk accessories, diaries, albums and other items in paper and leather are also available. Mon–Fri 9am–7.30pm, Sat 9.30am–1pm.

Vernici Colori Belle Arti Via delle Belle Donne 15b ☎055.294.700. Small shop with a good stock of artists' materials not far from Santa Maria Novella. 9am–1pm & 3.30–7pm; closed Sat.

Zecchi Via della Studio 19r. A very good stock of paints, brushes and all artistic equipment, close to the Duomo. Mon–Fri 8.30am–7.30pm, Sat 8.30–12.30am.

## Perfume and toiletries

🏃 Farmacia Santa Maria Novella Via della Scala 16 ☎055.216.276, Ⓦwww.smnovella.it. Occupying the pharmacy of the Santa Maria Novella monastery, this sixteenth-century shop was founded by Dominican monks as an outlet for their potions, ointments and herbal remedies. Many of these are still available, including distillations of flowers and herbs, together with face-creams, shampoos and other, more esoteric, products. The shop's as

famous for its wonderful interior as for its products, which are sold worldwide. Mon–Sat 9.30am–7.30pm, Sun 10.30am–6.30pm.

Spezieria Erborista Palazzo Vecchio Via Vaccherccia 9r ☎055.239.6055. A celebrated old shop, selling its own natural remedies and a range of unique perfumes, such as Acqua di Caterina de' Medici. July & Aug Mon–Fri 9am–7.30pm, Sat 9am–5pm; Sept–June Mon–Sat 9.30am–7.30pm, 1st and last Sun of month 1.30–7pm.

## Prints and photos

🏃 Alinari Largo Alinari 15 ☎055.239.51, Ⓦwww.alinari.com. Founded in 1852, this is the world's oldest photographic business. Owners of the best archive of old photographs in Italy – 400,000 glass plates and 700,000 negatives – they will print any image you choose from their huge catalogue. They also publish books, calendars, posters and cards. Tues–Fri 9am–1pm & 2.30–6.30pm, Sat 9am–1pm & 3–7pm; closed two weeks in mid-Aug.

Giovanni Baccani Via della Vigna Nuova 75r ☎055.214.467. You'll see prints and engravings in shops across Florence, but nowhere is the selection as mouthwatering as in Baccani, a beautiful old shop (established in 1903) that's crammed with all manner of prints, frames and paintings. Prices range from a few euros into the realms of credit-card madness. Mon 3.30–7.30pm, Tues–Sat 9am–1pm & 3.30–7.30pm; July closed Sat afternoons; closed first three weeks of Aug.

## Shoes, bags, gloves and hats

Borsalino Via Porta Rossa 40r ☎055.218.275. Fine trad hat shop for men, with some genuine fold-away Panamas. Another branch at Via della Vigna Nuova 60r sells women's hats and younger styles.

Cellerini Via del Sole 37r ☎055.282.533. Bags, bags and more bags. Everything here is made on the premises under the supervision of the firm's founders, the city's premier exponents of the craft; bags don't

⑪

come more elegant, durable – or costly.
Summer Mon–Fri 9am–1pm & 3–7pm, Sat
9am–1pm; winter Mon 3–7pm, Tues–Sat
9am–1pm & 3–7pm.

**Cristina e i suoi Colori Piazza N. Sauro 8r**
☎055.268.605. Located at the southern
end of Ponte alla Carraia, "Cristina and
her Colours" is as the name suggests
– it's overflowing with dramatic, colourful
handmade hats, bags, jewellery and lovely
flower-shaped lamps. Mon 4–8pm, Tues–
Sat 10.30am–1.30pm & 4–8pm.

**Francesco da Firenze Via Santo Spirito 62r**
☎055.212.428. Handmade shoes for men
and women at very reasonable prices.
Classical footwear combined with striking
designs. Mon–Sat 9am–1pm & 3.30–
7.30pm; Aug closed Sat afternoon.

**Madova Via Guicciardini 1r**
☎055.239.6526. The last word in
gloves – every colour, every size, every style.
Prices range from around €35 to €90.
Mon–Sat 9.30am–7.30pm.

**Mannina Via Guicciardini 16r**
☎055.282.895. This famed Oltrarno
shoemaker has been going for donkey's
years, producing beautifully made and
sensible footwear at prices that are far from
extravagant. Mon–Sat 9.30am–7.30pm, Sun
10.30am–1pm & 2–6pm.

**Stefano Bemer Borgo San Frediano 143r**
☎055.211.356, ⓦwww.bemers.it. If you're
in the market for made-to-measure Italian
shoes, there's no better place than this.
Mon–Sat 9am–1pm & 3.30–7.30pm.

# Directory

**Banks and exchange** Florence's main bank branches are on or around Piazza della Repubblica, but exchange booths (*cambio*) and ATM cash card machines (*bancomat*) for Visa and MasterCard advances can be found across the city. Banks generally open Mon–Fri 8.20am–1.20pm and 2.35–3.35pm, though some are open longer hours. A useful Travelex branch is at Lungarno Acciaiuoli 6r (Mon–Sat 9am–6pm, Sun 9.30am–5pm; ☏055.289.781); American Express is at Via Dante Alighieri 22r (Mon–Fri 9am–5.30pm, Sat 9am–12.30pm; ☏055.50.981).

**Bike, scooter & moped rental** Alinari, Via Guelfa 85r ☏055.280.500, ⓦwww .alinarirental.com; Florence by Bike, Via San Zanobi 120–122r ☏055.488.992, ⓦwww .florencebybike.it (they also do repairs); or Geordie Chopin at Via Fiesolana 10r ☏055.245.013 (Mon–Sat 9am–1pm & 3–7.30pm; for rental or repair of bicycles only). There are more scooter rental places on Borgo Ognissanti.

**Bus information** City buses are run by ATAF ☏800.424.500, ⓦwww.ataf.net. For details of buses to Siena, see p.223.

**Car rental** Avis, Borgo Ognissanti 128r ☏055.239.8826; Europcar, Borgo Ognissanti 53r ☏055.290.437/8; Excelsior, Via Lulli 76 ☏055.321.5397; Hertz, Via Maso Finiguerra 33r ☏055.282.260; Italy by Car/Thrifty, Borgo Ognissanti 134r ☏055.287.161; Maggiore, Via Maso Finiguerra 31r ☏055.210.238; Program, Borgo Ognissanti 135r ☏055.282.916.

**Consulates** UK, Lungarno Corsini 2 ☏055.284.133, ©consular.florence@fco .gov.uk; US, Lungarno Amerigo Vespucci 38 ☏055.266.951.

**Doctors** The Tourist Medical Service is a private service used to dealing with foreigners; they have doctors on call 24 hours a day on ☏055.475.411 (ⓦwww .medicalservice.firenze.it), or you can visit their clinic at Via Lorenzo il Magnifico 59 (Mon–Fri 11am–noon & 5–6pm, Sat 11am–noon). Note that you'll need insurance cover to recoup the cost of a consultation, which will be at least €50. Florence's central hospital is on Piazza Santa Maria Nuova.

**Emergencies** Police ☏112 or ☏113; Fire ☏115; car breakdown ☏116; first aid ☏118. If your passport is lost or stolen, report it to the police and contact your consulate.

**Flight information** Aeroporto Galileo Galilei, Pisa ☏050.849.300, ⓦwww.pisa-airport .com; information also from the check-in desk at Santa Maria Novella train station, platform 5 (daily 7am–8pm). Aeroporto Florence-Perètola (Amerigo Vespucci), Via del Termine 11 ☏055.306.1300, ⓦwww.safnet .it – for recorded information on international flights call ☏055.306.1702, on domestic flights ☏055.306.1700. Aeroporto G. Marconi, Bologna ☏051.647.9615, ⓦwww .bologna-airport.it.

**Internet cafés** *D@dov@go*, Via dei Seragli 80r; *Internet Train* (ⓦwww.internettrain.it) – more than a dozen outlets, including Via de Benci 36r (open till 1am), Via Guelfa 54/56r and Piazza Stazione 1; *La Ch@t*, Via Ghibellina 98r (open till midnight); *meridiaNet*, Borgo San Frediano 5r (Mon–Fri 11am–10.30pm, Sat & Sun 2–9pm); *Net Village*, Via San Egidio 10r (daily 9am–midnight); *Webpuccino*, Via dei Conti 22r (Mon–Sat 10am–10pm, Sun noon–9pm); *WWW village*, Via degli Alfini 11/13. Most charge around €4.50 an hour; the tourist office has a full list.

**Laundry** Florence has plenty of self-service *lavanderie* costing around €3–4 for a complete wash, with the main concentration being near the one-star hotels of the station and San Lorenzo districts. Ask at your hotel for the nearest, or head for one of the following: Guelfa, Via Guelfa 106r; Onda Blu, Via degli Alfani 24r; Self Service, Via Faenza 26r; Wash & Dry, which has eleven sites in the city open till 10pm, including Via dei Servi 105r, Via della Scala 52r, Via del Sole 29r, Via Ghibellina 143r, Via dei Serragli 87r and Via Nazionale 129r.

**Left luggage** Santa Maria Novella station by platform 16 (daily 6am–midnight); €3.80 per piece for 5hr, then €0.60 per hour. You'll need to produce some form of identification.

**Lost property** Lost property handed into the city or railway police ends up at Via Circondaria 17b (Sept–July Mon, Wed, Fri & Sat 9am–noon, Tues & Thurs 9am–noon & 2.30–4.30pm; Aug Mon–Fri 9am–noon; ⊕055.367.943; take bus #23 to Viale Corsica). There's also a lost property office at Santa Maria Novella station, on platform 16 next to left luggage (daily 7am–noon; ⊕055.235.2190).

**Pharmacies** The Farmacia Comunale, on the train station concourse, is open 24hr, as is All' Insegna del Moro, Piazza San Giovanni 20r, on the north side of the Baptistery, and Farmacia Molteni, Via dei Calzaiuoli 7r. Normal opening hours for pharmacies are Mon–Sat 8.30am–1pm & 4–8pm. All pharmacies display a late-night roster in their window; otherwise ring ⊕182 for information.

**Police** Emergency ⊕112 or 113. The Questura, where you should report a lost passport or a theft, is at Via Zara 2 (daily 8am–8pm; translator on hand 8am–2pm; ⊕055.49.771). If you do report a theft or other crime, you will have to fill out a form (*una denuncia*): this may be time-consuming, but it's essential if you want to make a claim on your travel insurance on returning home.

**Post office** The main central post office is near Piazza della Repubblica at Via Pelliceria 8 (Mon–Sat 8.15am–7pm); the poste restante section is through the door immediately on the left as you enter. If you're having mail sent to you poste restante, make sure it's marked for Via Pelliceria, otherwise it will go to Florence's biggest post office, at Via Pietrapiana 53–55 (Mon–Fri 8.15am–7pm, Sat 8.15am–12.30pm). If all you want are stamps (*francobolli*), then it's easier to buy them at a tobacconist's (*tabaccaio*), which are marked by a sign outside with a white "T" on a blue background.

**Toilets** Public toilets are usually open 10am–6pm daily and cost €0.60. They are marked on a map given out by the tourist office. Locations include the top of Via Filippina behind the Bargello; at the tourist office on Borgo Santa Croce; in the subway at Santa Maria Novella station; and Via della Stuffa 25, near the Mercato Centrale.

# Siena

# The City

# Arriving in Siena: Practicalities

The centre of Siena is its great square, the Campo, built at the intersection of a Y-shaped configuration of hills and the convergence of the city's principal roads, the Banchi di Sopra, Banchi di Sotto and Via di Città. Each of these roads leads out across a ridge, straddled by one of the city's three medieval districts, or *terzi* (literally "thirds"): the Terzo di Città to the southwest, the Terzo di San Martino to the southeast and the Terzo di Camollia to the north.

This central core – almost entirely medieval in plan and appearance – is initially a little disorienting, though with the Campo as a point of reference you won't go far wrong. Movement around is also made easier by the fact that the city centre has been effectively pedestrianized since the 1960s. Everywhere of use or interest in the city is within easy walking distance, with the exception of St Bernardino's monastic retreat, L'Osservanza, the *Guidoriccio* hostel and the campsite.

## Arrival

It's an easy journey from Florence to Siena by either bus or train, with buses pulling into centrally located Piazza Gramsci-La Lizza and trains arriving at the station at Piazza Fratelli Rosselli, less conveniently sited, outside the town.

### By bus

Intercity **buses** from Florence to Siena are run by TRA-IN (℡0577.204.246, Ⓦwww.trainspa.it), which confusingly has nothing to do with trains. They depart from the bus station near Santa Maria Novella at Via Santa Caterina da Siena 17r. There are two services: the Corse Rapide, or Rapida, is the quicker of the two (1hr 15min), with at least hourly (and often more frequent) services, except on Sunday, when they are considerably curtailed (around 5 daily). Tickets cost €6.50 if bought beforehand, €8 if bought on board. The hourly Corse Dirette, or Diretta, sounds as if it should be quicker and direct, but it runs via Colle di Val d'Elsa and Poggibonsi and takes 1hr 35min; it costs €4.50 (€6 on board). Both services arrive in the city at Piazza Gramsci-La Lizza, a short walk north of the centre. Ticket offices beneath Piazza Gramsci have information on all routes in and out of the city. **Left luggage** is

also available here: half a day (7am–1pm or 1–7.45pm) costs €2, one day (7am–7.45pm) €3.50. Bags can only be left for one day, and there's a fine of €15.50 if you don't pick up your bag by 7.45pm.

### By train

If you are coming to Siena by **train** from Florence Santa Maria Novella, the chances are you will have to change trains at Empoli: the connections are usually good, and Empoli station, with its two or three platforms, is straightforward. Reckon on 95 minutes to two hours for the complete journey. There is also a handful of direct Florence-Siena trains which take 1hr 27min. Siena's **train station** is inconveniently sited at Piazza Fratelli Rosselli, down in the valley, 2km northeast of the historic centre. Its foyer has a small train information office, exchange facilities, basic tourist information and a separate counter selling city bus tickets (also available from automatic machines). Considerable work and road-building is in progress around the station, and arrangements for picking up buses to the centre are currently in flux, but in general just about any city bus leaving from the more distant bus stop (not the one immediately outside the station) will take you to the centre. The ticket counter will help out if you have problems.

It shouldn't cost more than a few euros to take a **city taxi** to the centre. There are ranks by the train station (℡0577.44.504) and on Piazza Matteotti (℡0577.289.350), or cabs can be called elsewhere between 7am and 9pm by phone (℡0577.49.222). Note, however, that in Siena it's virtually impossible to book taxis in advance and you should allow plenty of time for cabs to reach you through the city's labyrinthine one-way system.

## By car

Coming to Siena by **car** is not particularly recommended. The approach is easy enough: it's linked to Florence by a fast four-lane highway which starts from the Firenze Certosa junction on the A1 autostrada, 6km south of Florence; from central Florence, head through the Oltrarno to the Porta Romana and follow "Certosa" signs.

**Parking**, however, in Siena's old centre is almost completely prohibited, and at busy times the many **garages** (see Ⓦwww.siena parcheggi.com for information on these) on the approach roads, while clearly signposted, secure and affordable, are often full. If you find one with space, cut your losses and use it. The two biggest are also misleadingly named: "Parcheggio Il Campo" is a long way from the Campo, just inside the Porta Tufi, and "Parcheggio Il Duomo" is just within Porta San Marco and nowhere near the Duomo. **Street-**parking outside the city walls is free, but extremely difficult to find. Beware that many spaces are actually resident-only: your car will be towed away if you park here. Follow signs to the *centro* and try to find a parking space at one of the following: around Piazza Gramsci or the large triangle of La Lizza; opposite San Domenico in the car park alongside the stadium; off the Viale Manzoni, which loops around the northeast wall of the city; or around the Porta Romana. Viale Manzoni is free parking; at the others a machine or an attendant issues tickets, usually by the hour: rates are reasonable. If you know you'll be driving in, you'd do well to arrange parking with your hotel in advance. You can drive through the old town alleys only in order to load or unload luggage at your hotel – but you must have it arranged in advance. Note that you cannot park around La Lizza on Wednesday mornings (8am–2pm), when the market takes place; offending cars are towed away.

## Siena museum admission

Rather than paying admission at each attraction, it's worth picking up a **pass** or **joint ticket** (*biglietto cumulativo*) covering entry to several sites. Siena has an array of these, though they have a tendency to change from year to year. Usually they are buyable at any of the participating museums. All, though, permit only a single entry to each attraction.

The **cathedral authorities** have an "Opera" pass, which gives entry to the Museo dell'Opera, the Baptistery and San Bernardino for €10 and is valid for three days.

The **civic museum authorities** have their own two-day pass, which gives entry to the Museo Civico (but *not* the Torre del Mangia), Santa Maria della Scala and the Palazzo delle Papesse, for €10. A joint ticket covering only the Museo Civico and Torre del Mangia is also €10.

Finally, there are seasonal versions of an all-encompassing seven-day "Art Itinerary" pass – the **SIA Inverno**, or **Itinerario d'Arte Inverno** (Winter Art Itinerary; available Nov to mid-March), covering entry to the Museo dell'Opera, the Baptistery, Libreria Piccolomini, Museo Civico, Santa Maria della Scala and Palazzo delle Papesse for €13; or the **SIA Estate**, or **Itinerario d'Arte Estate** (Summer Art Itinerary; available mid-March to Oct), valid for all these plus the Oratorio San Bernardino, Museo Diocesano and the church of Sant'Agostino, for €16.

Note that the Pinacoteca Nazionale is administered by a separate body from all the above, and so is not included on any of the passes.

Although queues in Siena are never as bad as in Florence, it is possible to reserve a date and admission time to any of Siena's civic museums (with the exception of the Pinacoteca) by contacting the city council by phone, fax or email (℡0577.41.169, ℻0577.226.265). You will be issued with a pass that enables you to go directly to the museum ticket office to pay for your visit at the appointed time. Booking in advance also entitles you to a small (usually €1) discount per person. Bookings for the Duomo, Museo dell'Opera, Baptistery and San Bernardino can be made by calling ℡0577.283.048.

## Information

Siena's main **tourist office** is at Piazza del Campo 56 (Mon–Sat 9am–7pm; ☏0577.280.551, ⓦwww.terresiena .it). They provide hotel lists, a town map and a range of information booklets. "Ecco Siena" **guided walks** (in English) start from the Campo (April–Oct Mon–Fri 3pm; €15 per person); book with the tourist office, Siena Hotels Promotion (☏0577.288.084, ⓦwww.hotelsiena.com) or visit ⓦwww .guidesiena.it.

## City transport

Most sights in Siena are within easy walking distance, but if you want to cross town in a hurry your best option is to use one of the frequent TRA-IN **buses** (main office in Piazza Gramsci ☏0577.204.246, ⓦwww.trainspa .it). Siena is divided into four zones (A–D), and most journeys you make are likely to be in zone A, or Fascia A (up to 4km from the city centre). Tickets cost €0.90 in this zone and are valid for any number of journeys within an hour. Tickets for journeys taking in Fascia B (5–8km from the city centre), or crossing from A to B, cost €1.

**ARRIVING IN SIENA: PRACTICALITIES**

# The Campo

Piazza del Campo, more often known simply as **the Campo**, is Europe's finest medieval square and the centre of Siena in every sense: the main streets lead into it, the Palio takes place around its perimeter, its position determines the rest of the city's urban structure, and in the evening and during much of the day it is the natural point to which visitors and residents gravitate. Even after several visits, the effect of walking from the cramped streets and narrow alleys nearby into its sudden and dramatic open space never pales. Four hundred years ago, Montaigne described it as the most beautiful square in the world – an assessment it still seems hard to dispute.

With its amphitheatre curve, the Campo appears an almost organic piece of city planning. In fact, much of the square's early development was arbitrary. In its earliest days it was an impractically steep and badly drained patch of open pasture – the word *campo* in Italian means "field". Probably the first major intervention was the building of ditches and channels in an attempt to improve drainage on the Campo's slopes, and especially the precipitous drop that is still apparent around and beyond Piazza del Mercato behind the Palazzo Pubblico, the city's main civic palace and the square's principal building. The street on the Campo's perimeter at its highest point, near the intersection of Via di Città and Banchi di Sopra, marks the position of one of the earliest major bastions, built in conjunction with the drainage schemes to prevent landslips and erosion.

For many years after these first developments, Siena's citizens overlooked the Campo's potential, only gradually beginning to build temporarily or half-heartedly on its various levels and terraces during the twelfth century. The first documented attempt to consolidate the area's piecemeal growth came on March 11, 1169, when the city acquired a patch of land known as Campo San Paolo (Vicolo San Paolo, an alley into the square, still exists on the western side of the Loggia della Mercanzia). This was the first of many acquisitions, revealing an increasingly coordinated and determined attempt on the part of the city elders to create a formal communal space.

THE CAMPO

| RESTAURANTS | | | BARS & CAFÉS | |
|---|---|---|---|---|
| Le Campane | 5 | Osteria Le | Brividio | 4 |
| Osteria Il | | Logge | 3 | La Costarelli | 2 |
| Carroccio | 7 | Ristorante | | Key Largo | 1 |
| | | Garibaldi | 6 | | |

△ The Campo seen from the Torre del Mangia

Though myth attributes its origins to Senius and Acius, sons of Remus (hence the she-wolf emblem of the city), **Siena** was in fact founded by the Etruscans and refounded as a Roman colony – Saena Julia – by Augustus. Over the course of the next millennium it grew to be an independent republic, and in the thirteenth and fourteenth centuries was one of the major cities of Europe. It was almost the size of Paris, controlled most of southern Tuscany and its flourishing wool industry, dominated the trade routes from France to Rome, and maintained Italy's richest banks. The city also developed a highly sophisticated civic life, with its own written constitution and a quasi-democratic council – the *comune*. It was in this great period that the city was shaped, and in which most of its art and monuments are rooted.

This golden era, when the Republic of Siena controlled a great area of central and southern Tuscany, reached an apotheosis with the defeat of a much superior Florentine army at the **Battle of Montaperti** in 1260. Although the result was reversed nine years later, shifting the fulcrum of political power towards Florence, Siena's merchants and middle classes – the so-called *Popolo Grasso* – embarked on an unrivalled urban development; from 1287 to 1355, under the rule of the **Council of Nine**, the city underwrote first the completion of the **Duomo** and then the extraordinary **Campo**, with its exuberant **Palazzo Pubblico**. Sienese bankers, meanwhile, had spread their operations throughout Europe, and with Duccio, Martini and the Lorenzetti, the city was at the forefront of Italian art.

Prosperity and innovation came to an abrupt halt with the **Black Death**, which reached Siena in May 1348. By October, when the disease had run its course, the population had dropped from 100,000 to 30,000. The city was never fully to recover (the population today is around 60,000) and its politics, always factional, moved into a period of intrigue and chaos. Its art, too, became highly conservative, as patrons looked back to the old hierarchical religious images. The chief figures in these war-ridden and anarchic years were the city's two nationally renowned saints, **Caterina** (1347–80) and **Bernardino** (1380–1444), who both exercised enormous influence, amid two further outbreaks of the plague.

As the sixteenth century opened, a period of autocratic rule under the tyrannical Pandolfo Petrucci (the self-styled Il Magnifico) brought a further military victory over

---

The definitive division between what would become the Campo and Piazza del Mercato to the southwest came in 1194, when a large bastion separating the areas was built so as to improve drainage further and control erosion. It was at this point that the square assumed its conch-like shape and saw the nucleus of what would become the Palazzo Pubblico, built atop the new bastion. Slope and drainage problems aside, the site was ideal, as it lay at the convergence of the city quarters, but was a part of none (old market places and the old Roman forum were probably also situated here or nearby). By 1297, the status of the square was such that the *comune* was prescribing what could and could not be built, specifying, for example, that only two- or three-columned windows were allowed (a glance around the square today suggests that the rule was not always obeyed). The piazza itself was completed around 1347, when the city's Council of Nine, the then ruling body, laid its nine segments of paving to commemorate their highly civic rule and pay homage to the Virgin, the folds of whose cloak it was intended to symbolize.

From the start, the stage-like Campo was a focus of city life. As well as its continuing role as the city's marketplace – for livestock as well as produce – it was the scene of executions, bullfights, communal boxing matches, and, of course, the Palio. St Bernardino preached here, too, holding before him the monogram of Christ's name in Greek ("IHS"), which he urged the nobles

Florence, but ended with the city embroiled in ever-expanding intrigues involving the Borgias, the Florentines, the papacy, the French and the empire of **Charles V**. The last proved too big to handle for the Sienese; imperial troops imposed a fortress and garrison, and then, after the Sienese had turned to the French for help to expel them, the imperials laid siege to the city and the surrounding countryside. The effects of the siege (1554–55) proved more terrible even than the Black Death, with the population plummeting from 40,000 to as few as 8000. The republic was over, although a band of loyalists – comprising around 700 families – took refuge at Montalcino and prolonged it there for a while, at least in name.

Two years after the siege, Philip II, Charles's successor, gave up Siena to **Cosimo I**, Florence's Medici overlord, in payment for war services, the city subsequently becoming part of Cosimo's Grand Duchy of Tuscany. This was the death knell. For sixty years the Sienese were forbidden even to operate banks, while control of what was by now an increasingly minor provincial town reverted, under Medici patronage, to the nobles.

Siena's swift decline from republican capital to little more than a market centre explains the city's astonishing state of medieval preservation. Little was built and still less demolished, while allotments and vineyards occupied the spaces between the ancient quarters, as they do today. And while nearby towns like Poggibonsi were badly damaged in World War II, Siena was taken, unopposed, by the French Expeditionary Force on July 3, 1944, and escaped unscathed.

Since the war, Siena has recovered some of its prosperity, partly thanks to **tourism** and partly the resurgence of the **Monte dei Paschi di Siena**. This bank, founded in Siena in 1472, is one of the major players in Italian finance and in its home base is one of the city's largest employers.

The Monte dei Paschi coexists, apparently easily enough, with one of Italy's strongest **left-wing councils**. Though this quiet, rather bourgeois provincial capital may not look like a red city, some 35,000 of the 250,000 population of Siena province are card-carrying PDS or Communist Party members – a loyalty partly won by the communists' role in the resistance during the last war.

to adopt in place of their own vainglorious coats of arms. A few did so (the monogram is to be seen on various palazzi), and it was adopted by the council on the facade of the Palazzo Pubblico, alongside the city's she-wolf symbol, which is itself a reference to Siena's legendary foundation by the sons of Remus.

It's easy enough to soak up the atmosphere of the Campo simply by strolling through or sitting out in it. The many bars, cafés and restaurants around its perimeter tend to be expensive of course, but you might consider paying over the odds just this once for the privilege of enjoying the sublime space and spectacle of Europe's greatest medieval public arena; see p.299 for recommendations of the better places to eat and drink in or just outside the square. On the northwest flank of the piazza itself stands the **Fonte Gaia**, a copy of a Renaissance fountain by the Sienese sculptor Jacopo della Quercia, while occupying much of the square's southern side is the **Palazzo Pubblico**, containing the **Museo Civico**, which safeguards two of Tuscany's greatest paintings, Simone Martini's *Maestà* and Ambrogio's *Allegories of Good and Bad Government*, as well as one of its most controversial, the *Equestrian Portrait of Guidoriccio da Fogliano*. Finally, if you have the legs and the head for heights required, climb the **Torre del Mangia**, the colossal tower flanking the Palazzo Pubblico, for some extraordinary views of Siena and the Tuscan countryside.

# The Fonte Gaia

At the highest point of the Campo is the **Fonte Gaia**, a copy (1856–66) by Tito Sarrocchi of the Renaissance fountain designed and carved for the piazza by Jacopo della Quercia (1374–1438), Siena's greatest medieval sculptor: the original languished for many years in the Palazzo Pubblico, but now has a permanent home in the Fienile section of Santa Maria della Scala (see p.249).

Jacopo signed the contract for the fountain on January 22, 1409, and was given twenty months to complete the work and a fee of 2000 florins. In the event, the contract was only confirmed on June 12, 1412, by which time the sculptor had been paid just 120 florins. Quibbles over money continued, as did problems with securing materials, and for the next six years Jacopo found himself both short-changed and distracted by commissions in Lucca, scene of his first great success and first documented work, the tomb sculpture of Ilaria Carretto in the town's cathedral. In 1401, Jacopo had also taken part – unsuccessfully – in the competition to design the Baptistery doors in Florence. Unlike his fellow competitors, and eventual victors, Brunelleschi and Ghiberti, Jacopo had the audacity to submit not a model, but a completed bronze, a work now lost.

Such ambition and precocity would serve him well in Siena, where the Fonte Gaia, finally completed in 1419, was hailed a masterpiece on its unveiling, and earned Jacopo the name Jacopo della Fontana, or Jacopo of the Fountain. Jacopo worked elsewhere in Siena, notably in the Baptistery, where he created one of the panels for the font, *The Annunciation of the Birth of the Baptist to Zaccaria* (1417–30), but none of his subsequent work matched the Fonte Gaia.

The fountain's conception – the Virgin at the centre, flanked by the Virtues – was a conscious emulation of Lorenzetti's frescoes on *Good and Bad Government* in the Palazzo Pubblico (see p.237). The scheme also included statues of Acca Larentia and Rea Silvia, carved a little later than the fountain, probably with the help of Francesco di Valdambrino (1380–1435), a friend of Jacopo who sculpted part of the Carretto tomb and was a fellow protagonist in the competition to design Florence's Baptistery doors. Rea Silvia's presence is explained by the fact that she was the mother of Romulus and Remus, who according to legend played a part in Siena's foundation (see p.228); Acca Larentia was a lover of Hercules and foster mother of Romulus and Remus. The fountain's name comes from festivities celebrating its inauguration in 1419, the climax of a long process that began in the 1340s, when masons managed to channel water into the square.

# The Palazzo Pubblico

Making no bones about its expression of civic pride, the **Palazzo Pubblico**, bristling with crenellations and glorious medieval detail, occupies virtually the entire south side of the Campo, shadowed by its giant bell-tower, the **Torre del Mangia**. For centuries the *palazzo* was the headquarters of Siena's rulers and ruling councils, in all their various guises, but today, most of the space on the upper floor is given over to the **Museo Civico**, Siena's main civic museum, consisting of medieval salons, chambers, vestibules and corridors decorated with frescoes and other works commissioned by the city elders over the years, among them some of the finest masterpieces in Siena, if not in the country.

△ The Palazzo Pubblico

Construction of a palace on the site probably began around 1194, the year a colossal bulwark was built to bolster and separate the area now occupied by the Campo from the precipitous slope to the southwest. In 1280 Siena experienced one of the more radical of the many changes to its quasi-democratic system, when the magistrature of the Trentasei ("The Thirty-Six") was reduced to fifteen governors. Four years later, a chronicle records that the then *Podestà*, one of the leading lights of the administration, one Count Ghinolfo da Romena, transferred the office of the Dogana (customs and excise) to the Campo. He then became the first documented administrator to reside in the square, also installing the offices of the Gabella, one of two bodies, along with the Biccherna (see p.262), responsible for the city's finances. The first reference to a fresco being commissioned for the Palazzo Pubblico appears in 1289. By 1305, work was completed on the central part of the palace, and five years later the two flanks were finished, giving the palace more or less the appearance it has today. The Torre del Mangia was built between 1338 and 1348 (see p.238), and the Cappella di Piazza, or Cappella del Voto (see below) between 1352 and 1376.

The palace's lower level of arcading is characteristic of Sienese Gothic, as are the columns separating the windows. The council was so pleased with this aspect of the design that they ordered its emulation on all other buildings on the square. It was gracefully adapted on the twelfth-century Palazzo Sansedoni on the north side – but ignored elsewhere.

The other main exterior feature of the Palazzo Pubblico is the **Cappella di Piazza**, a stone loggia set at the base of the tower, which the council vowed to build at the end of the Black Death in 1348 as a votive offering (hence its alternative name of the Cappella del Voto). Work began in 1352, but funds were slow to materialize, and by 1376, when the chief mason at the cathedral, Giovanni di Cecco, turned his hand to its design, new Florentine ideas were already making their influence felt. The final stage of construction, almost a century later between 1468 and 1470, when the chapel was heightened and a canopy added, was wholly Renaissance in concept. The architect responsible was Antonio Federighi (1420–90), a leading artistic light of the time, who also worked in, among other places, the Baptistery, the Loggia del Papa, the Loggia di Mercanzia and on the pavement of the Duomo. For all its undoubted élan, however, it's hard not to feel that this Renaissance masterpiece is something of an anomaly here and an architectural affront to the palace's Gothic integrity.

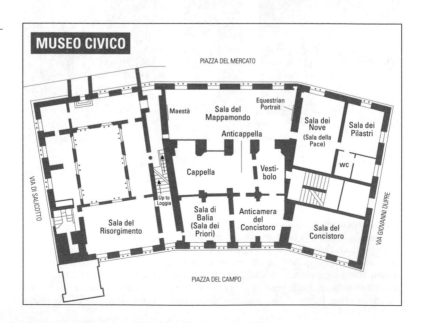

# The Museo Civico

In the days of the *comune*, the Palazzo Pubblico housed the city accounts and council offices. Parts of the building still have an administrative function, but its principal upper rooms have been converted into the **Museo Civico** (daily: Jan 7–Feb 15 & Nov 26–Dec 22 10am–5.30pm; Feb 16–March 15, Nov 1–25 & Dec 23–Jan 6 10am–6.30pm; March 16–Oct 31 10am–7pm; €7, or €10 with the Torre del Mangia; for other joint tickets see p.224), entered through the courtyard to the right of the Cappella di Piazza. Note that tickets are sold separately for the museum and the tower. The museum starts on the first floor of the *palazzo*, opening with a disappointing, miscellaneous five-room picture collection dominated by nineteenth-century hunting scenes. Fear not, however, for this is a poor start to what is a fine museum. Most of the works described below, being frescoes, are always in situ, but some rooms may be closed, and some freestanding sculptures or panel paintings are occasionally moved or absent on loan.

## Sala del Risorgimento

The first major room is the **Sala del Risorgimento** (1878–90), painted with scenes commemorating the life of Vittorio Emanuele, first king of Italy, from 1849 to his death in 1878. These depict various battle campaigns, the king's coronation and his earlier meeting with Garibaldi and his army on the road to Capua, where he refused Garibaldi's governorship of the Neapolitan provinces, instead inflicting a decade of martial rule. The ceiling is decorated with allegorical figures representing the regions and provinces of Italy, and the walls are adorned with miscellaneous sculptures of famous and less-than-famous Italians, notably Camillo Cavour, one of the prime political movers in the campaign for Italian unification. Other works here are by Tito Sarrocchi, the sculptor responsible for the copy of the Fonte Gaia.

## Sala di Balia

The first of the rooms of any real interest is the **Sala di Balia** (or Sala dei Priori), frescoed by **Spinello Aretino** and his son, Parri, in 1407 with episodes from the life of Siena-born Rolando Bandinelli, better known as Pope Alexander III, whose pontificate ran from 1159 to 1181. The artist's last major work, the frescoes are particularly concerned with Alexander's conflict with Frederick Barbarossa, the German Holy Roman Emperor. Barbarossa opposed Alexander's papacy, and instigated a schism (1160–77), during which he backed three rival anti-popes, Victor IV, Pasquale III and Callisto III. Alexander was also the pope who imposed a penance on England's Henry II following the assassination of Thomas à Becket, and who convened the Lateran Council of 1179 which laid down the requirement for papal elections – still in place today – that required a two-thirds majority among the voting cardinals.

The pope and emperor came into even greater conflict following Barbarossa's destruction of Milan in 1162, an event that caused the formation of a Lombard League of Italian states, supported by the Vatican and the Venetians. Sixteen major **frescoes** depict this and other events, though they're not in any particular order. On the wall immediately on your left as you enter, for example, the key fresco depicts the reconciliation of Alexander, the Doge of Venice and Barbarossa in Rome after Barbarossa's defeat in 1176. On the wall to its right are panels showing the foundation of the Egyptian city of Alexandria, named in Pope Alexander's honour, and a supine Barbarossa pledging his fidelity to the

**THE CAMPO** | The Palazzo Pubblico

pope. On the same wall to the right the story backtracks to Alexander receiving the papal crown and a meeting between the pope and the Doge. Elsewhere, on the far right of the room (right of the exit), the story is picked up halfway through, and Alexander is shown fleeing Rome (entered by Barbarossa in 1166) disguised as a monk, but recognized by a French pilgrim. The finest of the frescoes, around the exit, shows the **Battle of Punta Salvatore**, in which the Venetian fleet defeated that of Barbarossa. The superbly realized naval conflict includes the Venetians capturing the emperor's son and the Germans desperately trying to rescue him.

The ceiling frescoes of the **Sixteen Virtues** (1407–48) are by another Sienese painter, the fiery **Martino di Bartolomeo**, an artist who seemed preoccupied by the theme, for he was probably also responsible for the panel of the *Cardinal Virtues* on the pavement of the Duomo. Martino was a friend of Jacopo della Quercia, but enjoyed less than cordial relations with other local artists, notably Taddeo di Bartolo, whom, court records recall, he slandered in 1412.

## Anticamera del Concistoro

Beyond is the **Anticamera del Concistoro**, also known as the Sala dei Cardinali or Sala di Passeggio. By the entrance door is a detached fresco, the *Three Saints and Donor*, attributed to Ambrogio Lorenzetti and transferred here in the nineteenth century. It was probably once part of a much larger work depicting the Madonna and Child: in such pictures the donor – the individual responsible for commissioning the picture – would have been shown kneeling at the feet of the Madonna. To its right as you face the entrance door is *Christ on the Tree of Life* by an anonymous sixteenth-century sculptor. Near the centre of the adjoining wall to the right is a beautiful *Madonna and Child with Four Angels*, attributed to Matteo di Giovanni, whose Madonna has the unquiet look typical of this painter: his propensity for the unsettling found expression in several grisly depictions of the *Massacre of the Innocents*, one of which you'll see later on in the museum. The figure of San Nicola nearby is by Antonio Federighi, architect of the Loggia del Papa (see p.263) and sculptor of accomplished works in the Duomo (a water stoup and font) and on the facade of the Loggia della Mercanzia. On the far right of the same wall is a fine fresco of Sant'Onofrio by an anonymous fifteenth-century Sienese painter, while on the adjoining wall, left of the exit door, is *St Paul* (1425) by Martino di Bartolomeo, artist of the ceiling frescoes in the previous room.

## Sala del Concistoro

The next room is the **Sala del Concistoro**, entered via an ornate marble doorway (1448) by Bernardo Rossellino, the sculptor and architect who redesigned much of the southern Tuscan town of Pienza for Pope Pius II. Notice the two angels holding the coat of arms of Siena. The room's vault was superbly frescoed by the Mannerist star, **Domenico Beccafumi**, between 1529 and 1535, a period during which he was also working on the pavement of the Duomo and the majestic *St Michael* in the church of San Niccolò al Carmine (see p.273). The frescoes were commissioned after the Sienese secured their freedom from the autocratic regime of Pandolfo Petrucci and had defeated the Medici pope of the time, Clement VII. Proud of their reacquired republican status, the city elders decided on a scheme that, in part at least, celebrated the ideals of the ancient Roman republic. As a result, the panels are either allegories or describe rather obscure events from Greek and Roman history, but only in so much

– like virtually every painting in the palazzo – as they evoke parallels with the civic virtues or historical achievements of Siena itself. The three panels in the centre of the ceiling are straight allegories and the most intelligible of the frescoes: the circular central panel depicts Justice, with images of Concord and *Love of Country* (Patriae Amor) to either side.

## Vestibolo and Anticappella

Doors from the Anticamera behind you lead into the **Vestibolo**, which contains a damaged fresco of the *Madonna and Child* (1340) by Ambrogio Lorenzetti and a gilded bronze of the *She-Wolf Suckling Romulus and Remus* (1429) by the Torinese artists, Giovanni and Lorenzo di Torino, an allusion to the city's mythical foundation by Senius, son of Remus. On the left is the more interesting **Anticappella**, frescoed between 1407 and 1414 by Taddeo di Bartolo, the last major exponent of Siena's conservative Gothic style. Immediately striking is the vast *St Christopher*, though it's painted in a rather cumbersome manner, in marked contrast to the sort of grace of which Taddeo was capable, not least in his glorious triptych in the Oratorio di Santa Caterina della Notte in Santa Maria della Scala (see p.255).

His other **frescoes** here are also more accomplished than the *St Christopher*, and, like those in the Sala del Concistoro, have Greek and Roman themes that reflect Siena's civic concerns. This was the first such cycle painted for a civic palace, such laudatory schemes having previously been created for popes and temporal princes and rulers. The lunettes under the vaults carry representations of five political virtues: Strength, Justice and Prudence (also Cardinal Virtues), plus Religion and Magnanimity, all shown with their relative attributes. Between them are portraits of eminent political figures from the Roman era and below them six figures holding epigraphs in Latin. The entire fresco cycle is "presented" to the onlooker by Aristotle, who is portrayed at the entrance to the Vestibolo. In front of him are the figures of Julius Caesar and Pompey, intended not as exemplars of the political art, but as warning on the perils of over-ambition and discord. The epigraph below underlines the fact, describing how the majesty of Rome (*maiestas romana*), which once held the world in thrall, crumbled in the face of an ambition that brought about the loss of liberty. There is a circular map of Rome itself in the under-arch, flanked by pairs of pagan gods representing war and peace (Jove and Mars and Apollo and Pallas) and their traditional symbolic animals and attributes.

## Cappella

Taddeo also frescoed the adjoining **Cappella** with episodes from the *Life of the Virgin* (1407–08), interesting for their narrative realism, one of Taddeo's main strengths. The cycle is rather overshadowed, though, by Sodoma's altarpiece, a vast wrought-iron screen (1435–45) – attributed to Jacopo della Quercia – and an exceptional set of twenty-two inlaid choir stalls (1415–28). The last are the work of **Domenico di Niccolò**, ever after known as Domenic dei Cori (Dominic of the Choir Stalls), an artist, sculptor and architect who was also a director of works at Orvieto's great cathedral. The panels portray the Articles of the Creed, meticulously precise definitions of the orthodox faith drawn up to combat heresy. It was a subject only very rarely depicted in medieval or Renaissance art – one of the handful of other examples is here in Siena, in Santa Maria della Scala (see p.253). The images are beautifully executed but also graphic and simple, in keeping with the blunt, simple language of the Creed itself, the articles of which are inscribed at the bottom of each panel.

## Sala del Mappamondo

Fascinating as the preceding works are, they amount to little more than a warm-up for the **Sala del Mappamondo**, one of the great set-pieces of Italian art. Taking its name from the now scarcely visible ceiling fresco of a map of the cosmos – executed by Ambrogio Lorenzetti – the room was used for several centuries as the city's law court and contains one of the greatest of all Italian frescoes, **Simone Martini**'s fabulous and recently restored **Maestà**, a painting of almost translucent colour and the *comune*'s first major commission for the palace. Its political dimension is apparent in the depiction of the Christ Child holding a parchment inscribed with the city's motto of justice and the inscription of two stanzas from Dante on the steps below the throne, warning that the Virgin will not intercede for those who betray her or oppress the poor. It is one of Martini's earliest known works, painted in 1315 at the age of 30, and, remarkably, just four years after the completion of Duccio's *Maestà*, the only comparable Sienese masterpiece; before this extraordinary debut not a thing is known of the painter. He touched up parts of the picture, following damage from damp, six years later, by which time his style had markedly changed, as can be seen by comparing the head of the Madonna, painted in 1315, and the later, restored head of the Maddalena to the left, compositionally the same (inclined down and facing left), but very different in manner and tone.

The Maestà, or Madonna in Majesty (or Enthroned), surrounded by her celestial court, was a distinctly Sienese conceit, and had no precedents in Romanesque or Byzantine art. Its origins and inspiration were probably literary, references to the Virgin as a crowned Queen of Heaven appearing in Italian religious poetry – via French courtly poetry – at the end of the thirteenth century. Martini's richly decorative style is archetypal Sienese Gothic and its arrangement makes a fascinating comparison with Duccio's *Maestà* (with whom Martini perhaps trained), now in the Museo dell'Opera del Duomo. Martini's great innovation was the use of a canopy and a frieze of medallions which frame and organize the figures – a sense of space and hint of perspective that suggest a knowledge of Giotto's work. Martini also substitutes a distinctly Gothic throne for the Romanesque one painted by Duccio, and uses a "realistic" sky blue for the background in contrast to the stylized Byzantine gold background of his predecessor. He links the individual figures, as well as uniting the Madonna and her court, whereas in Duccio's painting the figures are clearly intended to inhabit distinct worlds. Martini's work also has a far more obvious fluidity and ease, as seen in the billowing, sinuous curves of the canopy.

The fresco on the opposite wall, the marvellous **Equestrian Portrait of Guidoriccio da Fogliano**, is a motif for medieval chivalric Siena, and was, until recently, also credited to Martini. Depicting the knight setting forth from his battle camp to besiege a walled hill town (thought to be Montemassi, a village southwest of Siena near Roccastrada), it would, if it were by Martini, be accounted one of the earliest Italian portrait paintings. Art historians, however, have long puzzled over the apparently anachronistic castles: according to some, they are of a much later architectural style than the painting's supposed date of 1328. The work would also seem to be part-painted over a fresco to the right by Lippo Vanni, which is dated 1364. In the mid-1980s the waters were further muddied when, during restoration, another apparently anachronistic fresco was found – the painting now beneath the equestrian portrait showing two men in front of a castle, believed to be the one at Arcidosso in southern Tuscany; it has been variously attributed to Martini, Duccio, Pietro Lorenzetti or Memmi di Filippuccio. The current state of the debate is confused, with a number of historians – led by the American Gordon Moran (whom the council for a while banned from the Palazzo Pubblico and accused of belonging to the CIA) – interpreting the *Guidoriccio* as a sixteenth-century fake, and others – including an Italian commission of experts – maintaining that it is a genuine Martini overpainted by subsequent restorers. Things reached such a pitch that a neutral referee – an Englishman, Professor Andrew Martindale – was called in to arbitrate; his findings, however, proved inconclusive. Tempers recently boiled over when the Americans accused the Sienese of deliberately destroying evidence that would support their case during a "routine" restoration. Much rests on a scrupulous analysis of Siena's vast archives in the Palazzo Piccolomini: details contained in the records of payments for various paintings of the period may well help solve the mystery. The only other option – often suggested but not yet countenanced – is to strip away all the frescoes concerned to study exactly what overlays what.

At least there's no problem with the coffered figures to the right and left of the uncovered fresco beneath the equestrian portrait; these are a pair of saints by Sodoma dating from 1529. The other large frescoes in the room also depict Sienese military victories, namely the *Victory at the Val di Chiana* (1364) by Lippo Vanni (on the long wall) and the *Victory at Poggio Imperiale* (1480) by Cristoforo Ghini and Francesco d'Andrea. Don't miss the fine figures on the pilasters below the latter: from left to right they are Sodoma's *Blessed Tolomei* (1533), founder of the abbey at Monte Oliveto Maggiore; *St Bernardino* (1450) by Sano di Pietro; and *St Catherine of Siena* (1461) by Vecchietta.

## Sala dei Nove (Sala della Pace)

Almost equally important and interesting frescoes adorn the **Sala dei Nove** (or **Sala della Pace**) next door: Ambrogio Lorenzetti's *Allegories of Good and Bad Government*, commissioned in 1338 to remind the councillors of the effects of their duties, and widely considered one of Europe's most important surviving cycles of secular paintings. The walled city the frescoes depict is clearly Siena, along with its countryside and domains, and the paintings are full of details of medieval life: agriculture, craftwork, trade and building, even hawking and dancing. They form the first-known panorama in Western art and show an innovative approach to the human figure – the beautiful, reclining Peace (Pax) in the *Good Government* hierarchy is based on a Roman sarcophagus still on display in the Palazzo Pubblico. An odd detail is that the "dancing maidens" in *Good Government* are probably young men: women dancing in public, according to the historian Jane Bridgeman, would have been too shocking in medieval Siena, and the figures' short hair and slit skirts were characteristic of professional male entertainers.

The moral theme of the frescoes is expressed in a complex iconography of allegorical virtues and figures. *Good Government*, painted on the more brightly lit walls and better preserved, is dominated by a throned figure representing the *comune* (he is dressed in Siena's colours of black and white), flanked by the Virtues (Peace – from which the room takes its name – is the nonchalantly reclining figure in white) and with Faith, Hope and Charity buzzing about his head. To the left, on a throne, Justice (with Wisdom in the air above) dispenses rewards and punishments, while below her throne Concordia advises the republic's councillors on their duties. All hold ropes, symbol of agreement. *Bad Government* is ruled by the figure of Tyranny or Fear (or the Devil), who bears a cup of poison and whose scroll reads: "Because he looks for his own good in the world, he places justice beneath tyranny. So nobody walks this road without Fear: robbery thrives inside and outside the city gates." Fear is surrounded by figures symbolizing the Vices and three Deadly Sins. To its left are figures that include Discord, dressed in black and white and with the words "Sì" and "No" on its skin. As in *Good Government*, the allegorical figures are surrounded by wonderfully graphic concrete images of the consequences of *Bad Government*.

Ironically, within a decade of the frescoes' completion, Siena was engulfed by the Black Death – in which Lorenzetti and his family were among the victims – and the city was under tyrannical government. However, the paintings retained an impact on the citizenry: St Bernardino preached sermons on their themes.

### Sala dei Pilastri and loggia

The room adjoining the Sala della Pace, the **Sala dei Pilastri** (or **delle Colonne**), displays panel paintings from the thirteenth to the fifteenth century, whose conservatism and strict formulaic composition points up the scale of Lorenzetti's achievement. Notable among them is one of the earliest Sienese masterpieces, Guido da Siena's gripping *Maestà* (1221 or 1262–65), for which Duccio may have repainted the Virgin's face; the throne and six angels at the top of the painting are small, and the iconographic emphasis is still on the Mother and Child, but it is clear that this is a prototype *Maestà*, the ancestor of the later great *Maestà* of Martini and Duccio. Also here is a fascinating picture of *St Bernardino Preaching in the Campo* by Neroccio di Bartolomeo (note how the men and women in the crowd are separated by a white cloth); and a graphically violent *Massacre of the Innocents* removed from Sant'Agostino, painted by Matteo di Giovanni – one of four he completed in the city. The stained-glass figure of St Michael in one of the windows is attributed to Ambrogio Lorenzetti.

Backtracking through the museum, it is worth climbing the stairs between the Sala del Risorgimento and Sala di Balia to the rear **loggia**, where you can enjoy a view over the Piazza del Mercato, now mainly a car park with a belvedere-like platform and a couple of pleasant café-pizzerias and restaurants (see p.300 for a review of the *Antica Trattoria Papei*, the better of these). It is on the loggia that you realize how abruptly the town ends: buildings rise to the right and left for a few hundred metres along the ridges of the Terzo di San Martino and Terzo di Città, but in the centre the land drops away to a rural valley.

# The Torre del Mangia

Within the Palazzo Pubblico's courtyard, opposite the entrance to the Museo Civico, is separate access to the **Torre del Mangia** (daily 10am–6.15/7pm; Nov to mid-March closes 4pm; €6 or €10 with the Museo Civico), 87m high, or 102m if you include the lightning conductor. Climb the 388 steps and you have fabulous, vertigo-inducing views across town and countryside. Note that there is no lift, and that the tower is closed for safety reasons during heavy rain.

Built between 1325 and 1348 – the cresting was designed by Lippo Memmi – the tower takes its name from its first watchman, Giovanni di Duccio, a spendthrift (*mangiaguadagni*) who is commemorated by an eighteenth-century statue in the courtyard. It was the last great project of the *comune* before the Black Death and exercised a highly civic function: its bell was rung to order the opening of the city gates at dawn, the break for lunch, the end of work at sunset and the closing of the city gates three hours later. The first clock was added in 1360, but substituted in 1400 for works designed by Don Gasparo di Simone degli Ubaldini, a master clock-maker who had already created timepieces for the Rialto in Venice and the towns of Orvieto and Città di Castello in Umbria. The present main bell dates from 1666 and weighs 6.76 tonnes.

# 14

# Piazza del Duomo

S tanding atop a hill and visible from many parts of the city, Siena's glorious **Duomo** is the focus of an ensemble of buildings arrayed around the **Piazza del Duomo**. The Duomo is one of Tuscany's great sights, its facade a multicoloured medley of sculpture, decorative marbles, mosaics and stained glass. Inside is a bewildering variety of art, including one of Italy's finest pulpits, a sublime fresco cycle by Pinturicchio and sculptures by Michelangelo, Donatello and others.

On its southwest side the piazza is hedged in by another artistic treasure-house, the medieval **Santa Maria della Scala**, Siena's main hospital for over eight hundred years and now a museum and arts complex containing some staggering medieval frescoes, a fascinating miscellany of subterranean chapels and museums, and an entire church. A number of other historic buildings line the square, including the Palazzo dei Vescovi (Archbishop's Palace); the Palazzo del Magnifico, built for Petrucci in 1508; and the Palazzo Granducale, built later the same century for the Medici.

In the form of an "L", the square itself is an unusual shape and is barely large enough to do justice to the Duomo. This stems from the site's limited scope in a cramped medieval city and from the strange history of the Duomo (see below), which at one time involved a part-finished extension (the shell of which still survives) into what is now Piazza San Jacopo della Quercia. Part of this side square contains the **Museo dell'Opera del Duomo**, home to Siena's single greatest work of art – **Duccio's Maestà** – and a range of other significant sculptures and paintings.

## The Duomo

Few buildings reveal so much of a city's history and aspirations as Siena's **Duomo** (€3: March to late Aug Mon–Sat 10.30am–7.30pm, Sun 1.30–7.30pm; late Oct–Feb Mon–Sat 10.30am–6.30pm, Sun 1.30–6.30pm; €6: late Aug to late Oct daily 9.30am–7.30pm,

**PIAZZA DEL DUOMO** N

**RESTAURANTS**
| | |
|---|---|
| Al Marsili | 2 |
| Antica Osteria da Divo | 1 |
| La Taverna del Capitano | 3 |

VIA FRANCIOSA
PIAZZA SAN GIOVANNI
VIA DI FUSARI
VIA FRANCIOSA
VIA DI SAN GIROLAMO
PIAZZETTA DELLA SELVA
Santissima Annunziata
VICOLO DI SAN GIROLAMO
Baptistery
Duomo
PIAZZA JACOPO DELLA QUERCIA
PIAZZA DEL DUOMO
VIA DEL CASTORO
Prefettura
Santa Maria della Scala
VIA DEL CAPITANO
VIA DEL POGGIO
Palazzo del Capitano
PIAZZA DI POSTIERLA

0     200 m

the period when the pavement is on display – see below). And few buildings so dominate a city's skyline: the dome and tower are visible not just from Siena's various hills and ridges, but from many of the far-flung hinterland towns and villages that once formed part of the Sienese Republic. Where Florence's dome casts the city in its shadow, Siena's striped campanile, together with the Torre del Mangia, its civic twin, reaches much farther into Tuscany's rural heartland, both literally and metaphorically – a tangible reminder of the still strong ties binding the outlying towns of the old Republic.

Both the elaborate exterior and rich interior are unmissable, though the latter is compromised by the vast summer crowds streaming through its turnstiles (the entrance fee required to enter the interior is a recent – and controversial – innovation). The **exterior** is an amazing conglomeration of Romanesque and Gothic, delineated by bands of black and white marble, an idea adapted from Pisa and Lucca. Inside are more treasures, notably the **Altare Piccolimini**, with sculptures by Michelangelo; the **Libreria Piccolomini**, home to a superb fresco cycle by Pintoricchio; the art-filled **Cappella di San Giovanni Battista**; and Nicola Pisano's remarkable **pulpit**, one of the greatest of all Tuscan sculptures. Smaller, but no less sublime, artworks include the Pecci tomb by Donatello and Tino da Camaino's *Tomb of Cardinal Riccardo Petroni* (both in the Cappella di Sant'Ansano); Beccafumi's bronze angels in the apse; and the Cappella Chigi, the last major artistic masterpiece commissioned for the building. Easily missed, if only because it is often partially or completely covered for safekeeping, is the entire **pavement**, or floor, of the interior, adorned with a sequence of 56 decorated stone panels created or designed over the course of two hundred years by some of the greatest artists of their day.

## Some history

The site of the Duomo, one of Siena's highest points, has long made it a place of special significance. The city's most important Roman temple, a shrine to Minerva, was probably built here, and it seems likely that there was a church on the site from at least the ninth century, possibly earlier. The first documented record of a move to erect a cathedral comes in 1136, when a group of citizens, the Opera del Duomo, was charged with creating a church at the *comune*'s expense. The Siena-born pope, Alexander III, is traditionally held to have consecrated the work in 1179, though by this date it's unlikely that much had been built. In 1258, the "Opera di Santa Maria", as it was now called, was entrusted to the monks of San Galgano, an abbey southwest of Siena, who had a reputation for efficiency and expertise. They were also responsible for the city's accounts, as you'll see if you visit the Palazzo Piccolomini (see p.261), and remained in charge of the Duomo's construction until 1314.

In 1265, when the building's basic structure was complete, one of the Galgano monks, Fra Melano, went to Pisa to commission a pulpit from Nicola Pisano, while in 1280 Nicola's son, Giovanni, was employed to work on the facade. By 1297, however, Giovanni left the project, angered by arguments with the *comune*, who, the rumour goes, had been staggered to find the business side of the facade in chaos and Giovanni and his team working with no care for, or control of finance, accounting or materials. Worse was to come. In 1317 a group of prominent citizens decided the cathedral was too small, and said so, leading the Republic to order, on August 23, 1339, a building that, had it been realized, would have been Europe's largest church outside Rome.

The idea was to create a baptistery on the slope to the east and use this as a foundation for a rebuilt nave, but the work ground to a halt as the walls gaped under the pressure. For a while, the authorities pondered knocking down the whole building and starting from scratch in accordance with the new architectural principles of the day. Eventually they hit on a new scheme to reorientate the cathedral instead, using the existing nave as a transept and building a **new nave** out towards the Campo. Again cracks appeared, and then in 1348 came the Black Death. With the population halved and funds suddenly cut off, the plan was abandoned once and for all in 1355. The part-built extension still stands at the north end of the square. Finishing touches were made to the facade in 1377, though it would be some time before it was definitively completed – the mosaics were added in 1877 and the bronze door in 1958.

## The exterior

The Duomo's **facade** is one of the most striking of any in Italy, only the very similar frontage of Orvieto's cathedral in nearby Umbria matching its almost excessive weight and variety of decoration. Although baffling on first viewing, the inspired mixture of sculptures, stained glass, mosaics and intricate stonework has a unifying theme, and one where the Madonna, always important to the Sienese, plays an important role. In essence it's based on a traditional view of the Virgin's life and the manner in which Christ's coming was foretold in antiquity. Thus the pagan sibyls and the prophets, heralds of the Incarnation, feature prominently, as do the stories of the Virgin's parents, St Anne and St Joachim. The same theme is followed in the pavement panels inside the cathedral (see p.248).

△ Siena's Duomo: detail of the facade

In the time he worked on the facade and flanking walls, Giovanni Pisano and his workshop carved much of the **statuary** on the second tier, including fourteen statues of the prophets, philosophers and sibyls, now transferred to the Museo dell'Opera and replaced by copies. The **bas reliefs** (1297–1300) above the central door are the work of Tino di Camaino, a Sienese sculptor who about fifteen years later would carve the Petroni tomb inside the cathedral, creating one of Tuscany's most important funerary monuments (see p.247). The subjects portrayed include St Joachim chased from the Temple (partly because of his failure to have children in twenty years of marriage); the annunciation of the birth of the Virgin to Joachim; the birth of the Virgin; and the presentation of the Virgin in the temple. The central **door** below from 1958 also contains reliefs of scenes from the *Life of the Virgin*, as do the poorly executed **mosaics**, while the thirty-six busts of the prophets and patriarchs around the **rose window** are copies by Tito Sarocchi (who also copied the Fonte Gaia in the Campo) of fourteenth-century originals. Immediately above the central door, note St Bernardino's bronze monogram of Christ's name.

Before entering the cathedral, walk to the right (south) side of the exterior. Once the entire elevated area off this right exterior flanking wall was occupied by a Bishop's Palace and only removed in the nineteenth century, after which (in 1898) the four large upper windows were added. Above the door at the foot of the **campanile**, built in 1313, is a lovely relief of the *Madonna and Child* (1458), by **Donatello**, who had returned to Siena in 1457 hoping to be commissioned to create the cathedral's main bronze door. In the event he was rebuffed, and this is one of only a handful of works from the period, executed thirty years after he had created the Pecci tomb inside the cathedral. The relief was only unveiled after his death in 1466.

# The interior

The cathedral **interior** is immediately arresting, a blaze of colour and detail, with its zebra-stripe bands of marble, and the line of popes' heads – including several Sienese – set above the pillars. These stucco busts were added in the fifteenth and sixteenth centuries and many seem sculpted with an apparent eye to their perversity: the same hollow-cheeked scowls crop up repeatedly. The hubbub and crowds can be off-putting at busy times, but it's worth persevering and resisting the temptation to wander at random. Our account begins on the left (north) side of the cathedral, just past the ticket office, and proceeds clockwise. Numbers in square brackets refer to the plan on p.244/overleaf. It concludes with the pavement, where the key panels are also highlighted on the same plan, but note that only in late August and September (precise dates vary from year to year) is the full pavement exposed.

## The Altare Piccolomini

Ignore the forgettable first three altars in the left aisle and make straight for the fourth, the **Altare Piccolomini [1]**, commissioned in 1491 from the Lombard sculptor, Andrea Bregno, by Cardinal Francesco Piccolomini, later Pope Pius III. It's a striking and richly carved work, made all the more remarkable by the fact that four of its principal statues are almost certainly by Michelangelo: these are saints Gregory and Paul in the two main niches on the right, and saints Pius and Peter in the two niches on the left. The figure of St Francis in the upper left niche was also begun by Michelangelo, but completed by a Florentine, Pietro Torrigiani. Michelangelo was commissioned to carve a whole series of statues here, but after completing this set, probably sculpted between 1501 and 1503,

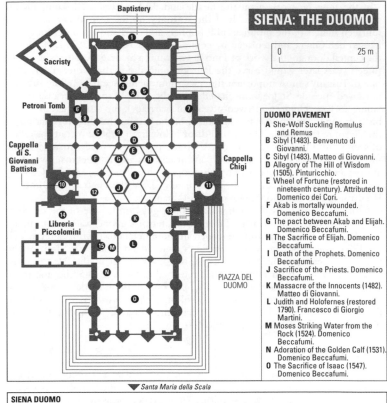

**Baptistery**

# SIENA: THE DUOMO

**Sacristy**

0             25 m

**Petroni Tomb**

**Cappella di S. Giovanni Battista**

**Cappella Chigi**

**Libreria Piccolomini**

PIAZZA DEL DUOMO

▼ *Santa Maria della Scala*

### DUOMO PAVEMENT

**A** She-Wolf Suckling Romulus and Remus
**B** Sibyl (1483). Benvenuto di Giovanni.
**C** Sibyl (1483). Matteo di Giovanni.
**D** Allegory of The Hill of Wisdom (1505). Pinturicchio.
**E** Wheel of Fortune (restored in nineteenth century). Attributed to Domenico dei Cori.
**F** Akab is mortally wounded. Domenico Beccafumi.
**G** The pact between Akab and Elijah. Domenico Beccafumi.
**H** The Sacrifice of Elijah. Domenico Beccafumi.
**I** Death of the Prophets. Domenico Beccafumi.
**J** Sacrifice of the Priests. Domenico Beccafumi.
**K** Massacre of the Innocents (1482). Matteo di Giovanni.
**L** Judith and Holofernes (restored 1790). Francesco di Giorgio Martini.
**M** Moses Striking Water from the Rock (1524). Domenico Beccafumi.
**N** Adoration of the Golden Calf (1531). Domenico Beccafumi.
**O** The Sacrifice of Isaac (1547). Domenico Beccafumi.

### SIENA DUOMO

**15** Altare Piccolomini (1491). Andrea Bregno. Sculptures by Michelangelo.
**14** Libreria Piccolomini. Frescoes on the life of Pope Pius II (1505–07) by Pinturicchio.
**12** Flagpole from the Battle of Montaperti.
**10** Cappella di San Giovanni Battista. Frescoes (1501–04) by Pinturicchio; bronze by Donatello of St John the Baptist (1457).
**9** Pulpit. Nicola Pisano and assistants (1268).
**8** Tomb of Bishop Pecci of Grosseto (1426–7). Donatello.
**6** Tomb of Cardinal Riccardo Petroni (1314–18). Tino da Camaino.
**4** Bronze candleholders (1548–50). Domenico Beccafumi.
**5** Bronze candleholders (1497–99). Francesco di Giorgio Martini.
**2** High altar (1532). Baldassare Peruzzi.
**3** Ciborio (1467–72). Vecchietta.
**1** Stained glass (1288). To a design by Duccio.
**7** Cappella del Sacramento. Bas-reliefs (1425) by Domenico dei Cori.
**11** Cappella Chigi (1659–62). To a design by Gian Lorenzo Bernini.
**13** Tomb of Tommaso Piccolomini (1484–5). Neroccio di Bartolomeo Landi. Below: bas-reliefs of Episodes from the Life of the Virgin (1451) by Urbano da Cortona.

he left for a more tempting contract in Florence – the *David*. The sculptures of a young Michelangelo are joined by that of another precocious sculptor, Jacopo della Quercia, whose Madonna in the main, central upper niche was probably one of his earliest works.

## Libreria Piccolomini

Midway along the nave, on the left, Pinturicchio's brilliantly coloured fresco of the *Coronation of Pius II* marks the entrance to the **Libreria Piccolomini [2]**, well worth a visit for the beautiful fresco cycle within. The frescoes (1505–7) and library were commissioned by Francesco Piccolomini (who for ten days was Pope Pius III) to house the books of his uncle, Aeneas Sylvius Piccolomini (Pius II). The frescoes do justice to the man whom Jacob Burckhardt adopted almost as a hero in his classic *The Civilization of the Renaissance in Italy*. Pius II, born at nearby Pienza in 1405, was the archetypal Renaissance man, writing poetry, a geography and the *Commentaries*, a deeply humanist work in which he enthuses over landscape, antiquity and architecture and describes the languages, customs and industries encountered on his travels.

Pinturicchio's **frescoes**, painted with an equal love of nature and classical decor, as well as a keen sense of drama, commemorate the gamut of Pius II's career. Rather confusingly, the cycle begins at the rear to the right of the window with Aeneas's secular career as a diplomat: he is seen attending the Council of Basle as secretary to an Italian bishop (panel 1); presenting himself as an envoy to James II of Scotland (panel 2); being crowned poet laureate by the Holy Roman Emperor, Frederick III (panel 3); and then representing Frederick on a visit to Pope Eugenius IV (panel 4). Aeneas subsequently returned to Italy and took holy orders, becoming first Bishop of Trieste and then of Siena, in which role he is depicted presiding over the meeting of Frederick III and his bride-to-be, Eleonora of Portugal, outside the city's Porta Camollia (panel 5).

In 1456 Aeneas was made a cardinal (panel 6) and just two years later was elected pope (panel 7), taking the title Pius II. In political terms, his eight-year rule was not a great papacy, despite his undoubted humanism and diplomatic skill, with much of the time wasted in crushing the barons of Romagna and the Marche. The crusade he called in 1456 at Mantua (panel 8) to regain Constantinople from the Turks – who took the city in 1453 – came to nothing, and the last picture of the series (panel 10) shows his death at Ancona, where he had gone to encourage the troops. It was said that his death was brought on by grief for the failure to get the crusade off the ground, or possibly by poisoning by the troops, eager to terminate their pledge. Between these two panels is the event for which Siena most remembers him – the canonization of St Catherine.

In art history terms, Pinturicchio stands as a relatively minor figure. Born in Perugia, he worked with Perugino on the Sistine Chapel before beginning his, his acknowledged masterpiece, in 1502. His skills lie in the brilliant colouring, the naturalistic detail – the storm scene in Aeneas's departure for Basle is one of the first in Western art – and in an easy disposition of crowds, ideal for the pageants here, and enhanced by their illusionistic placing within a series of loggias.

The library is now used to display the cathedral's **choirbooks**, illuminated by Sano di Pietro and other Sienese Gothic artists. At the centre of the room stands a Roman statue of the **Three Graces**, supposedly copied from a lost Greek work by Praxiteles. It was bought by the Piccolomini nephew and was used as a model by Pinturicchio and Raphael.

## Cappella di San Giovanni Battista

Tucked away round the corner from the entrance to the Libreria, past a vast **flagpole [3]** carried by the Sienese at the Battle of Montaperti in 1260, the **Cappella di San Giovanni Battista [4]** is easily overlooked. However, it is well worth close scrutiny, for its decorative scheme features first-rate sculptures, paintings and other details. The *cappella* is dedicated to St John the Baptist, mainly because it contains a reliquary housing what is allegedly the Baptist's right arm (the reliquary is displayed only on the saint's feast day). The chapel is the work of Giovanni di Stefano, son of the painter Sassetta, and was completed in 1482. The decorated columns at the entrance were long thought to have come from a Roman altar, but that on the right (1486) is now attributed to **Antonio Federighi**, also responsible for part of the cathedral pavement and the beautiful water stoups near the cathedral entrance (see p.248). In addition, Federighi is credited with the chapel's **font** (1484), adorned with reliefs depicting the story of Adam and Eve and other details. The chapel's central niche has a superb bronze statue of the Baptist by **Donatello**, created in 1457 in Florence (and damaged during its transit to Siena), shortly after his extraordinary Florentine *Mary Magdalene* (see p.65) and very similar to his Bargello statue of the Baptist. The painting (1487) in the niche on the left portrays Sant'Ansano, one of Siena's patron saints (see p.275), and is the work of Giovanni di Stefano. From an artistic point of view it is overshadowed by five more accomplished and eye-catching **frescoes** by **Pinturicchio**, painted (before those in the Libreria) between 1501 and 1504. The four other frescoes here by the same artist are inferior, the result of poor restoration in 1608 and 1868. One of the best of the frescoes, on the lower part of the chapel wall on the right, shows a kneeling and praying Alberto Aringhieri, a committee member of the Opera del Duomo responsible for commissioning the chapel and much of the cathedral pavement; he's portrayed here as a knight.

## The pulpit

Perhaps the cathedral's greatest individual art treasure is the **pulpit [5]**, completed by Nicola Pisano in 1268, soon after his pulpit for the Baptistery at Pisa, with help from his son Giovanni and Arnolfo di Cambio. The design of the panels duplicates those in Pisa, though they are executed with much greater detail and high relief. The carving's distance from the art of the Byzantine world is perhaps best illustrated by the statuette of the *Madonna*, whose breast is visible beneath her cloak – the first such instance in Italian art.

The work is loaded with imagery and symbolism: the **lions and lionesses** supporting the pillars represent strength, majesty and justice, as well as the triumph of Christ over the Antichrist (symbolized by the lions devouring a horse) and the Church nourishing its adherents (illustrated by the lionesses suckling their young). At the top of the pillars, on the angle of each corner, are figures representing the **Virtues**, the basis on which a Christian life on earth should be lived, each with children whispering in their ears. Above these are figures symbolizing the **Liberal Arts** (Grammar, Rhetoric, Dialectic, Geometry, Arithmetic, Music, Philosophy and Astronomy), the practice of such arts being an intellectual means by which humanity can elevate itself towards God.

Between the figures of the Liberal Arts, the incredibly detailed **main panels** of the pulpit itself illustrate key events from the Life of Christ. From left to right these are: the *Annunciation, Nativity, Isaiah Announces the Coming of Christ*, the *Voyage and Adoration of the Magi, The Virgin Presenting her Son, The Presentation at the Temple and Flight into Egypt, The Massacre of the Innocents, Christ of the Apocalypse* (with the Tree of Life springing from Christ's side), and the *Crucifixion*. This last is sublime, Christ's persecutors huddled on the right, heads facing up, his supporters, and the lamenting Madonna and other women, in dramatic compositional and emotional counterpoint, shown to the left, their heads downcast.

## Cappella di Sant'Ansano

Much as the Libreria Piccolomini can overshadow the Baptist's chapel, so Pisano's pulpit can detract from two very different but important pieces of funerary sculpture close by in the **Cappella di Sant'Ansano**. The first of these is the (easily missed) bronze pavement **Tomb of Bishop Pecci of Grosseto [6]** (1426–7) by Donatello, created thirty years before his other work inside and outside the cathedral (see above), but at more or less the same time as his panel for Siena's baptistery (see p.249). Behind it on the wall is arguably the cathedral's finest sculpture after the pulpit, the **Tomb of Cardinal Riccardo Petroni [7]** carved by Tino da Camaino fifty years after Pisano's masterpiece between 1314 and 1318. A prototype for Italian tomb architecture over the next century, it introduced, among other things, the use of supporting caryatids to Tuscan sculpture, an idea Tino would develop in his masterpiece, the tomb of the Angevin kings in Naples. It is interesting to note the date of the sculpture, just a year or so after Duccio completed his *Maestà*, Siena's supreme painting (see p.255), for the tomb's main narrative elements owe much to the iconography of Duccio's work. This is most apparent in the scenes either side of the central figure of the risen Christ below the reclining figure of Petroni. To the left is *Christ Appearing to the Magdalen* and to the right the *Incredulity of St Thomas*, the latter – keep it in your mind for later – a virtual facsimile of the same episode as portrayed by Duccio in the *Maestà* in the Museo dell'Opera.

## The presbytery, apse and high altar

Beyond the arch that heralds the start of the presbytery, on small columns on either side of the presbytery itself, are two rows of four superb bronze candleholders **[8]** (1548–50), created by Domenico Beccafumi, almost exclusively known as a painter, in the last years of his life. It is worth comparing these with two more pairs of candlesticks, also disguised as angels, which sit on the upper tiers of the altar. Those **[9]** on either side of the lower tier (1497–99) are by Francesco di Giorgio Martini, an artist, sculptor, writer and, above all, military engineer, whose name crops up time and again in different roles across the city. The candleholders on the upper tier, weak in comparison with those of Martini and Beccafumi, are by Giovanni di Stefano, architect of the earlier Baptist chapel.

The **high altar [10]** (1532) itself is the work of another artist, architect and painter whose name reappears across Siena, Baldassare Peruzzi, best known as the architect and collaborator of Raphael in the Palazzo Farnesina in Rome, built for the Sienese banker Agostino Chigi (the family responsible for the Cappella Chigi: see below). The large bronze **ciborio [11]**, or urn (1467–72), on top of the altar is by Vecchietta, and is full of touching and often exquisite details – though you'll need binoculars or good eyes to see them.

The choir stalls (1362–97 and 1567–70 for the central stalls) are a supreme example of the genre, with some exquisite carving and inlay, while the **stained glass [12]** in the large round window was created to a design by Duccio in 1288, making it some of the oldest in Italy. Among the subjects portrayed is one of the earliest depictions of the Assumption of the Virgin, an event with no biblical or other sound theological foundation, and an obvious counterpoint to Duccio's later *Maestà*, or *Madonna Enthroned* (see p.255), the painting that would adorn the high altar below from 1311 to 1505.

## The Cappella Chigi and south aisle

The Duomo's south side contains relatively thin pickings after the riches of the north side. Exceptions include the **Cappella del Sacramento [13]** (nine chapels down), whose right wall has five excellent bas-reliefs (1425), probably removed from a pulpit sculpted by Domenico dei Cori and later dismantled.

Moving towards the main door, you come to the **Cappella Chigi [14]**, or Cappella del Voto, the last major addition to the Duomo. It was created between 1659 and 1662 at the behest of Alexander VII, another Sienese pope, scion of the fabulously wealthy Chigi banking dynasty (see p.267 for more on the Chigi). Built to a design by **Gian Lorenzo Bernini** (1598–1680), the great genius of the Roman Baroque, it was intended as a new setting for the *Madonna del Voto*, an anonymous thirteenth-century painting that commemorated the Sienese dedication of their city to the Virgin on the eve of the Battle of Montaperti. It may be that this painting occupied the Duomo's high altar for several years, superseding the *Madonna dagli Occhi Grossi* (now in the Museo dell'Opera) and preceding the elevation of Duccio's *Maestà*. The chapel's style, not surprisingly given its designer, is pure Roman Baroque, most notably seen in the four **niche statues**, two of which are by Bernini himself – wild, semi-clad figures of Mary Magdalene and St Jerome (1662–3), the latter holding a cross in ecstasy like some 1970s rock guitarist. Outside the chapel, the walls are covered in a mass of devotional objects – silver limbs and hearts, *contrada* scarves, even the odd Palio costume and crash helmet.

Moving to the **fifth altar** down from the door in the south aisle, opposite the Piccolomini altar, you find another fine funerary sculpture above the door to the campanile, the *Tomb of Tommaso Piccolomini* (1484–5), bishop of Pienza, by Neroccio di Bartolomeo Landi. Below it are **bas-reliefs** (1451) with episodes from the life of the Virgin by Urbano da Cortona, a collaborator of Donatello and best known in Siena for his *Tomb of Cristoforo Felici* in San Francesco (see p.284). Various fragments from the same work are found on the left main pillar of the central main door. By this pillar and the door's right-hand pillar are the last of the cathedral's treasures, two beautiful **water stoups** (1466) by Antonio Federighi.

### The pavement

The facade's use of black and white decoration is echoed by the Duomo's great marble **pavement**, which begins with geometric patterns and a few scenes outside the church and takes off into a startling sequence of 56 figurative panels within. These were completed between 1349 and 1547, with virtually every artist who worked in the city trying his hand on a design. The earliest employed a simple *sgraffito* technique, which involved chiselling holes and lines in the marble and then filling them in with pitch; later tableaux are considerably more ambitious, worked in multicoloured marble. Unfortunately, the whole effect can only be seen for about a couple of months in late summer (usually September and October, but dates vary); the rest of the year, most of the panels are rather unimaginatively protected by underfoot boarding.

The subjects chosen for the panels are a strange mix, incorporating biblical themes, secular commemorations and allegories that echo the iconography of the facade. The most ordered part of the scheme are the ten Sibyls – mythic prophetesses who foretold the coming of Christ – on either side of the beginning of the main aisle (the finest of which are marked as [B] and [C] on our plan). Fashioned towards the end of the fifteenth century, when Sienese painters were still imprinting gold around their conventional Madonnas, they are totally Renaissance in spirit. Between them, in the central nave, are the much earlier *She-Wolf Suckling Romulus and Remus* and the twelve cities allied with the Sienese Republic and their animal symbols [A] and the *Wheel of Fortune* [E], along with Pinturicchio's *Allegory of Virtue*, or *Allegory of the Hill of Wisdom* [D]). Further down the nave, the twelve panels of the central hexagon contain Domenico Beccafumi's *Stories from the Life of Elijah* [H–J]. Beccafumi worked intermittently on the pavement from 1518 to 1547, also designing the vast friezes of *Moses Striking Water from the Rock* [M], just beyond, and *The Sacrifice of Isaac* [O], in front of the high altar. To the left of the hexagon is a *Massacre of the Innocents* [K], almost inevitably the chosen subject of Matteo di Giovanni, who tackled the same theme at least twice more in Siena – the paintings are in Santa Maria dei Servi (see p.266) and the Palazzo Pubblico (see p.238).

## The Baptistery

The cathedral **Baptistery** (daily: March–May, Sept & Oct 9.30am–7.30pm; June–Aug hours vary, but usually 9am–7.30pm; Nov–Feb 10am–1pm & 2–5pm; €3; or €10 joint ticket – see p.224) contains one of the city's great Renaissance works – a hexagonal font with scenes illustrating the Baptist's life. It's unusual in being placed beneath the main body of the church: to reach it, turn left out of the Duomo, follow the walls left and then take the flight of steps leading down behind the cathedral.

The cathedral chapter responsible for the **font** (1417–30) must have had a good sense of what was happening in Florence at the time, for they managed to commission panels by **Lorenzo Ghiberti** (*Baptism of Christ* and *John in Prison*) and **Donatello** (*Herod's Feast*), as well as by the local sculptor **Jacopo della Quercia** (*The Angel Announcing the Baptist's Birth*). Jacopo also executed the marble tabernacle above, and the summit statue of *John the Baptist* and five niche statues of the Prophets. Of the main panels, Donatello's scene, in particular, is a superb piece of drama, with Herod and his cronies recoiling at the appearance of the Baptist's head. Donatello was also responsible for two of the corner angels (*Faith* and *Hope*) and (with Giovanni di Turino) for the miniature angels on the tabernacle above.

The lavishly frescoed **walls** almost overshadow the font, their nineteenth-century overpainting having been removed after a vigorous assault by the restorers. With your back to the entrance the best include (on the left arched vault lunette) a fresco of scenes from the life of St Anthony (1460) by Benvenuto di Giovanni, a pupil of Vecchietta; scenes from the life of Christ by Vecchietta himself (inside left wall of the central stepped chapel); and the same artist's *Prophets*, *Sibyls* and *Articles of the Creed* (the main vaults), the last a repeat of a theme he would use in the Santa Maria della Scala.

# Santa Maria della Scala

The complex of **Santa Maria della Scala** (daily: mid-March to Oct 10.30am–6.30pm; rest of year 10.30am–4.30pm; €6 or €5.50 if booked or bought the previous day; joint tickets see p.224; ⓦwww.santamaria.comune.siena.it), opposite the Duomo, saw use as the city's hospital for over eight hundred years, listing among its charitable workers St Catherine and St Bernardino. Its closure in 1995 aroused mixed feelings, for the functioning building gave a sense of purpose to the cathedral square, which won't be matched by its intended use as Siena's principal cultural and museum space. At the same time, the *comune*'s grandiose plans for the enormous building – which include a new home for the Pinacoteca Nazionale – mean that some extraordinary works, long hidden from all but the most determined visitors, are now on public view for the first time in centuries.

## A history of Santa Maria della Scala

According to legend, the hospital of Santa Maria della Scala was founded by **Beato Sorore**, a ninth-century cobbler-turned-monk who worked among orphans, a story given credence by the reputed discovery of his "tomb" in 1492. Sorore, however, was almost certainly mythical, his name a corruption of *suore*, or nuns, who for centuries tended the sick as a part of their vocation. The hospital was probably founded by the cathedral's canons, the first written record of its existence appearing in 1090. Its development was prompted by the proximity of the **Via Francigena**, a vital trade and pilgrimage route between Rome and northern Europe, which in the early Middle Ages replaced the deteriorating Roman consular roads used previously. Its route passed below Siena's walls, giving rise to the growth of numerous rest-places (*ospedali*) where travellers and pilgrims could seek shelter and succour. Some forty of these grew up in Sienese territory alone, the most important of which was Santa Maria della Scala. Initially pilgrims were the main concern; hospital work, in the modern sense, came later: "hospitality rather than hospitalization" was the credo.

The foundation was one of the first European examples of the Xenodochium, literally an "abode", a hospital that not only looked after the sick but could also be used as a refuge and food kitchen for an entire town in times of famine and plague. This role made it a vital part of the city's social fabric, its importance leading to a long-running and ill-mannered tussle between lay and secular authorities. In time it passed from the cathedral canons into the hands of hospital friars, and in 1404, after an intense dispute, into the care of the *comune*, who appointed its rectors and governing body. Alms and bequests of money over the centuries kept it richly endowed, the Sienese taking to heart St Paul's stricture that charity was the most important of the three Cardinal Virtues.

Some of the donated funds were diverted away from humanitarian concerns, and into artistic and architectural commissions: as early as 1252, Siena's bishop gave permission for Santa Maria's abbot to build a **church**, the precursor of the present Santissima Annunziata. In 1335 the hospital commissioned Simone Martini and Pietro and Ambrogio Lorenzetti, the city's three leading painters, to fresco the building's exterior facade (works that have since been lost to the elements). In 1359 it paid an exorbitant sum to acquire from Constantinople a nail used during the Passion, a piece of the True Cross, and a part of the Virgin's girdle, along with a miscellany of **saints' relics**. In 1378 it financed the setting of a stone bench along the length of the hospital's exterior, its original purpose being to provide the hospital's dignitaries with somewhere to sit during the city's interminable religious and civic ceremonies – and still much used today as a shady spot from which to view the facade of the Duomo.

While some of the complex still remains off-limits, the last few years have seen the restoration and opening of the church of **Santissima Annunziata**; the **Cappella del Sacro Chiodo** with its highly acclaimed fresco cycle by Vecchietta; a beautiful Beccafumi fresco in the **Cappella del Manto**; the **Oratorio di Santa Caterina della Notte**, a finely decorated subterranean chapel used by, among others, St Catherine; and, adjacent to this, Jacopo della Quercia's original marble panels from the secular Fonte Gaia in the **Fienile**. Best of all, in the **Sala del Pellegrinaio**, is a vast secular fresco cycle by Domenico di Bartolo, a work now talked of as third only to the frescoes in the Duomo and Palazzo Pubblico in Siena's artistic pantheon. Siena's **Museo Archeologico** now occupies most of the converted basement of the building.

# Santissima Annunziata and the Cappella del Manto

To the left of the ticket desk, and also with its own door onto Piazza del Duomo, is the church of **Santissima Annunziata**, wholly within the complex of Santa Maria della Scala. Remodelled in the fifteenth century, the church is disappointingly bland, but worth a look for the high altar's marvellous bronze statue of the *Risen Christ* by Vecchietta, its features so gaunt the veins show through the skin. Vecchietta clearly understood and absorbed the new approach of Donatello, and several art historians consider this the finest Renaissance sculpture in the city. Before the church's remodelling, frescoes by Vecchietta had entirely covered its walls, a loss as tantalizing as the missing Martini and Lorenzetti frescoes on the hospital's exterior.

Heading right from the ticket office takes you into a small vestibule known as the **Cappella del Manto**, which contains an arresting and beautifully restored fresco of *St Anne and St Joachim* (1512), the earliest major work in Siena by the Mannerist Domenico Beccafumi. The protagonists depicted are the parents of the Virgin, whose story – popular in Tuscan painting – is told in the apocryphal gospels, biblical adjuncts reintroduced to the medieval world in the *Golden Legend* by Jacopo da Voragine. Having failed to conceive during twenty years of marriage, each is told by an angel to meet at Jerusalem's Golden Gate. Here they kiss (the scene depicted in the fresco), a moment which symbolizes the Immaculate Conception of their daughter.

# Sala del Pellegrinaio

Uplifted by contemplation of this event, you turn left from the Cappella del Manto into a vast hall, a majestic whitewashed space typical of the "longitudinal" architectural elements introduced into Italy by French Cistercians travelling the Via Francigena, and now partly used as a bookshop. Turning immediately left (rooms off to the right are used for temporary exhibitions) brings you into another similarly elongated space, the **Sala del Pellegrinaio**, its walls completely covered in a fresco cycle of episodes from the history of Santa Maria della Scala by Domenico di Bartolo and Vecchietta. Incredibly, this astounding space was used as a hospital ward until relatively recently.

The ward was built around 1380 and the frescoes begun in 1440, their aim being not only to record scenes from the hospital's history, but also to promote the notion of charity towards the sick and – in particular – the orphaned, whose care had been a large part of the hospital's early function. Their almost entirely **secular** content was extraordinary at the time they were painted, still some years short of the period when Renaissance ideas would allow for other than religious narratives. It's well worth taking the trouble to study the eight major panels in detail – each is full of insights into Sienese daily life of the time – along with two paintings on the end wall by the window. The cycle starts on the left wall and moves clockwise.

### The left wall

The **first panel**, *The Dream of the Mother of Beato Sorore*, is by Vecchietta, his only contribution to the cycle. It depicts in part a dream in which the mother of Sorore, the hospital's mythical founder, foresees her son's destiny. Her vision focuses on the abandoned children of the hospital, the *gettatelli* (from *gettare*, to throw away), who are shown ascending to Paradise and the waiting arms of the

Madonna. Sorore is shown twice: on the right of the painting with upraised hand receiving the first *gettatello*, and kneeling at the foot of the child-filled ladder. This ladder (*scala*) is the key to the Santa Maria della Scala, which may take its name from this part of the legend. Another version of the story suggests that a three-runged ladder, a symbol of the Trinity, was found during the hospital's construction – although the more likely explanation is that the hospital was simply built opposite the steps, or *scala*, of the Duomo. Whatever the origins, a three-runged ladder surmounted by a cross is the symbol you now see plastered all over the museum's literature and displays.

The **second panel**, *The Building of the Hospital*, depicts a mounted bishop of Siena at the head of a procession passing the hospital, which is in the process of being built, and almost running down a stonemason in the process. Note the buildings, a strange mixture of Gothic and Renaissance that bear little relation to anything in Siena, and the rector of the hospital, portrayed behind the ladder on the right doffing his hat to the visiting dignitaries. The **third panel**, the weakest of the cycle, is by Priamo della Quercia, brother of the more famous Jacopo, and shows the *Investiture of the Hospital Rector by the Blessed Agostino Novello*, the latter traditionally, but erroneously, credited as being the author of the hospital's first statute. The decorous figure on the left is thought to be a portrait of Emperor Sigismondo (who passed through Siena in 1432), or, more probably, a representation of the Byzantine emperor Paleologus III, who took part in the Council of Florence in 1439. The **fourth panel** shows one of Santa Maria's defining moments, when in 1193 Pope Celestine III gave the hospital the right to elect its own rector, thus transferring power from the religious to lay authorities. For the rest, the fresco is an excuse to portray day-to-day life in Siena – interestingly, there's a preponderance of oriental merchants.

## The end wall

The paintings on either side of the **end wall** are late sixteenth-century works, but illustrate two fascinating aspects of the hospital's work. The vast number of orphans taken in meant that an equally large number of wet nurses, or *baliatici*, were needed to feed the infants. At one time their numbers were such that feeding took place in the vast hall now occupied by the bookshop. The pictures here show the nurses in action, and the payment for their services: in grain (on the left wall) and hard cash (on the right).

## The right wall

On the right wall, the **fifth panel**, the most famous in the cycle, shows *The Tending of the Sick*, a picture crammed with incident, notably the close scrutiny being given to a urine sample by two doctors on the left, the youth with a leg wound being washed, and the rather ominous scene on the right of a monk confessing a patient prior to surgery.

The **sixth panel** shows *The Distribution of Charity*, one of the hospital's main tasks, an event that takes place in the old hospital church (now replaced by Santissima Annunziata) with the central door of the Duomo just visible in the background. Bread is distributed to beggars, pilgrims and children (one of whom passes it on to his mother); at the centre an orphan puts on clothes that it has been given. In one strange vignette a child is shown trying to express milk from its mother's breast. On the left, meanwhile, the hospital's rector is shown doffing his hat, possibly to Sigismondo.

The **seventh panel** illustrates further work of the hospital, underlining the vital part it played in maintaining the social fabric of the city. It shows the reception, education and marriage of one of the female orphans, who were provided with a small grant designed to enable them to marry, stay on in the hospital or join a convent. Also included are details indicating that the hospital not only took in children, but also committed itself to caring for them over a long period. Thus the wet nurses are shown in action on the table to the left, along with scenes suggesting weaning, education and play. Bartolo also shows off his Renaissance credentials by including a wealth of extraneous detail, as well as his arcane knowledge of exotic lands, notably in the carpet under the feet of the married couple, whose dragon and phoenix symbols belong to the period of the Ming dynasty.

The final, **eighth panel**, which depicts the feeding of the poor and the elderly, is less engaging than the rest, partly because of the awkwardly sited window, reputedly built by a nineteenth-century superintendent so that he could survey the sick from his upper-floor office without the bother of having to go down into the ward.

# The Cappella del Sacro Chiodo

Some idea of what was lost in the remodelling of Santissima Annunziata can be grasped in Vecchietta's fresco cycle (1446–49) in the **Cappella del Sacro Chiodo**, so named because it once housed the nail (*chiodo*) from the Passion and other holy relics; it's also known as the **Sagrestia Vecchia**, reached through the small Cappella della Madonna beside the Sala del Pellegrinaio. Some art critics pay these frescoes more attention than the Bartolo cycle in the Sala del Pellegrinaio, but for the casual viewer they are less easy to interpret, because the subject matter – an illustration of the *Articles of the Creed* – requires some theological knowledge. If you can manage the Italian, however, the various panels and vaults are well described. Each lunette illustrates one or more articles, the figure of one of the Apostles to the right holding the text of the article in question, the scenes below or to the left depicting an episode from the Old Testament which embodies the article's meaning.

The frescoes are extremely unusual, partly in that they illustrate a written text – something that remained rare until much later in the Renaissance – and partly in that they revolve around the figure of Christ (depicted twice in the main vaults). The latter is an odd choice in a city dedicated to the Madonna, where virtually every work of note either eulogizes Siena itself or includes Christ only as an adjunct to the Virgin. It's thought that the subject was suggested by the "nail from the Cross" contained in the chapel, a relic with obvious relevance to the story of Christ.

Domenico di Bartolo's **high altarpiece**, the *Madonna della Misericordia* (1444), is more intelligible than much of the cycle, and shows the Madonna casting a protective cloak over various of Siena's inhabitants. This theme, a common one in Sienese and other central Italian works, derives from a vision of the Madonna experienced by a ninth-century Cistercian monk. At first, painters depicted only members of the religious orders beneath the protective cloak, monks to one side, nuns to the other. At the beginning of the twelfth century members of religious confraternities were allowed protection, and a few decades later the privilege was extended to all inhabitants of a town or city. Men and women usually remained segregated, however, which makes this version – in which they're mixed – unusual. The fresco once graced the Cappella del Manto (see above), the Virgin's cloak (*manto*) having given the chapel its name. It was detached and fixed here in 1610, its side parts torn away to fit the dimensions of the new altar; in 1969, however, the discarded fragments were found and reattached.

# The rest of Santa Maria della Scala

Stairs lead down to the **Fienile**, the hospital's old hayloft, now housing Jacopo della Quercia's original marble panels from the **Fonte Gaia** (1409–19), transferred here from the Palazzo Pubblico. Though the panels' serious state of erosion makes it hard to appreciate, Jacopo della Quercia was rated by Vasari on a par with Donatello and Ghiberti, with whom he competed for the commission of Florence's Baptistery doors. Michelangelo, too, was an admirer, struck perhaps by the physicality of the figures in the *Expulsion of Adam and Eve*. See p.230 for more on the fountain and its reliefs.

△ Statue from the Fonte Gaia in Santa Maria della Scala

Adjacent is the **Oratorio di Santa Caterina della Notte**, which belonged to one of a number of the medieval confraternities who maintained oratories in the basement vaults of the hospital. It's a dark and strangely spooky place, despite the wealth of decoration; you can easily imagine St Catherine passing nocturnal vigils here. Even if you prove immune to the atmosphere, it's worth coming down here for Taddeo di Bartolo's sumptuous triptych of the *Madonna and Child with SS Andrew and John the Baptist* (1400).

Stairs lead down again to the lavishly decorated **Compagnia della Madonna sotto le Volte**, the oratory and meeting-room of the Società di Esecutori di Pie Diposizioni, the oldest of the lay confraternities, where you'll find a wooden crucifix said to be the one which inspired St Bernardino to become a monk.

From the small columned courtyard (**Corticella**) back on the Fienile level you enter the medieval store rooms – now used for temporary exhibitions – from where stairs descend into the spacious labyrinth of the **Museo Archeologico**, which houses private collections from the late nineteenth century and plenty of local finds from excavation work in and around Siena, Chianti, the upper Val d'Elsa and Etruscan Murlo.

# The Museo dell'Opera del Duomo

Tucked into a corner of the proposed – and abandoned – new nave of the Duomo is a building containing the impressive **Museo dell'Opera del Duomo** (daily: mid-March to Sept 9am–7.30pm; Oct 9am–6pm; rest of year 9am–1.30pm; €6; for joint tickets see p.224; @www.operaduomo.it), which offers the bonus of some fine views over Siena.

On the ground floor, in the **Galleria delle Statue**, the statuary by Giovanni Pisano (1250–1314), removed from the Duomo's facade, looks a little bizarre displayed at eye level: the huge, elongated, twisting figures were meant to be viewed from below and deliberately distorted to take account of this. They are totally Gothic in conception, and for all their subject matter – philosophers from antiquity are represented alongside Old Testament prophets and other characters – show little of his father Nicola's experiment with classical forms seen in the cathedral pulpit. In marked contrast is Donatello's ochre-coloured *Madonna and Child*, a much smaller and more delicate piece in the centre of the room (removed from the door of the Duomo's south transept), alongside a bas-relief by Jacopo della Quercia of *St Anthony Abbot and Cardinal Antonio Casini*.

Upstairs, a curator admits you to the **Sala di Duccio**, curtained and carefully lit to display the artist's vast and justly celebrated **Maestà**. Once painted on both sides, it depicts the *Madonna and Child Enthroned* (or *Maestà*) and the *Story of the Passion*. The four saints in the front rank of the main painting, the *Maestà*, are Siena's patron saints at the time, Ansano, Savino, Crescenzio and Vittore, while the ten smaller figures at the rear of the massed ranks represent ten of the Apostles. (Peter and Paul are in the second rank, accompanied by John the Baptist and other saints.) On its completion in 1311 the work was, as far as scholars can ascertain, the most expensive painting ever commissioned, and had occupied Duccio for almost four years. It was taken in a ceremonial procession from Duccio's studio around the Campo and then to a special Mass in the Duomo; everything in the city was closed and virtually the entire population attended. It then remained on the Duomo's high altar until 1505. This is one of the superlative works of Sienese art – its iconic, Byzantine spirituality accentuated by Duccio's flowing composition and a new attention to narrative detail in the panels of the predella and the reverse of the altarpiece, both now displayed to its side.

The *Maestà* – the Virgin as Queen of Heaven surrounded by her "court" of saints – was a Sienese invention, designed as a "sacrifice" to the Virgin, the city's patron (the consecration took place in 1260), a status emphasized by the lavish use of gold. Duccio's rendering of the theme was essentially the prototype for the next three centuries of Sienese painters; his achievement, as Bernard Berenson put it, was to add "the drama of light to that of movement and expression" and a realization of the space in which action takes place.

This quality is best observed in the narrative panels, most of which have been gathered here; the altarpiece was dismembered in 1771 and removed to the museum in 1887. Only a handful of panels are missing and – to quite understandable local disgust – will not be released by their owners to the city: two are in Washington, three in London's National Gallery and three in the Frick and Rockefeller collections in New York. One of the most effective of the surviving panels is the *Betrayal of Judas*, where trees relieve the main group of figures – Christ is "pointed" by the central tree – and rows of lances break the golden sky. The *Descent from the Cross*, too, is a marvellously composed image.

Also in the room is a *Madonna di Crevole*, an early work by Duccio, and Pietro Lorenzetti's triptych of the *Nativity of the Virgin*, the latter remarkable for breaking with the tradition of triptych painting by running a single scene across two of the painting's three panels. The gilded statues in the room off to the right of the *Madonna and Child with Four Saints* are attributed to Jacopo della Quercia, as is the separate statue of *St John the Baptist*. In the room behind the Sala is a fascinating nineteenth-century drawing of the cathedral pavement, providing a unified view impossible on the spot.

For the art that followed Duccio, and some that preceded him, you need to make your way upstairs again. Here you enter the **Sala di Tesoro**, featuring amid its reliquaries the head of St Galgano and a startling *Christ on the Cross* (1280), an important early work in wood by Giovanni Pisano in which Christ is shown on a Y-shaped tree growing out of the skull of Adam. The latter symbolizes the Tree of Life, or Tree of Knowledge, which grew from a sprig planted in the dead Adam's mouth and would – in the apocryphal story – eventually yield the wood used to crucify Christ.

Beyond the Sala di Tesoro you reach the **Sala della Madonna dagli Occhi Grossi**. The work that gives its name to this room is the cathedral's original, pre-Duccio altarpiece – a stark, haunting Byzantine icon (literally the "Madonna of the Big Eyes") in the centre of the room. It occupies a special place in Sienese history, for it was before this painting that Siena's entire population came to pray before their famous victory over the Florentines at Montaperti in 1260. It was also a promise made in front of the painting prior to the battle that saw Siena dedicated to the Madonna in the aftermath of victory. Around it are grouped a fine array of panels, including works by Simone Martini, Pietro Lorenzetti and Sano di Pietro. Note the panels flanking Sano's *Madonna and Child*: one shows St Bernardino preaching in the Campo and Piazza San Francesco (the latter now home to the saint's oratory; see p.284); the other shows St Apollonia, patron saint of dentists, martyred in Alexandria in the fourth century for refusing to make sacrifices to pagan gods.

Don't miss the tiny entrance to the so-called **Panorama dal Facciatone**: this leads to steep spiral stairs that climb out of the building, up within the walls of the abandoned nave. The sensational view from the top over the city and surrounding hills is definitely worth the two-stage climb, but beware that the topmost walkway – teetering along the very summit of the abandoned nave walls – is narrow and scarily exposed.

# San Martino and Città

S
iena's southern sections embrace two of the city's *terzi* (literally "thirds", designating the three districts into which the city is divided), the Terzo di Città and Terzo di San Martino, both of which have a very different feel to the great civic and religious set-pieces that make up Piazza del Campo and Piazza del Duomo. The **Terzo di San Martino** extends over the long, narrow spur reaching to the southeast, a quiet neighbourhood anchored by Via di Pantaneto and a number of parallel streets that culminate in **Santa Maria dei Servi**, a superb, art-filled church that also offers magnificent views back over the city. On its way from the Campo, Via di Pantaneto passes the imposing Renaissance buildings of **Palazzo Piccolomini** and the **Loggia del Papa**, and is lined with workaday shops, fine medieval townhouses and a variety of inexpensive restaurants and pizzerias. Students tend to outnumber visitors in this residential and university-dominated area, especially towards the south gate of the city, the **Porta Romana**. There is plenty of scope for aimless wandering through the quiet backstreets off Via di Pantaneto. You can either loop back to the centre or drop down into the valley behind the Palazzo Pubblico to visit the Terzo di Città.

The **Terzo di Città**, the area around and south of the Duomo, is even quieter than the Terzo di San Martino, especially when you get past its main draw, the **Pinacoteca Nazionale**. This superb gallery is the most important in Tuscany after Florence's Uffizi, and is filled with Sienese paintings from different eras: you'll need the best part of a morning or afternoon to do it justice. In this district, too, there is a major art-rich church, **Sant'Agostino**, but unlike Santa Maria dei Servi, it is only intermittently open, leaving the district's main appeal the many faultlessly preserved medieval streets, especially those in the two small grids behind the Pinacoteca (on and around Via delle Lombarde) and west of Sant'Agostino (between Via San Pietro and Via di San Quirico). The overwhelming sense of the district as peaceful and distinct from the bustle around the Campo is underlined in a pleasant stroll behind the cathedral on Via del Fosso di Sant'Ansano, a pretty walk that underscores the proximity of the Tuscan countryside to the city walls.

## Terzo di San Martino

The **Terzo di San Martino** embraces the southeast of the city and is a welcome contrast to the busy areas immediately around the Campo and Piazza del Duomo. The quiet medieval streets that range along the Terzo's defining

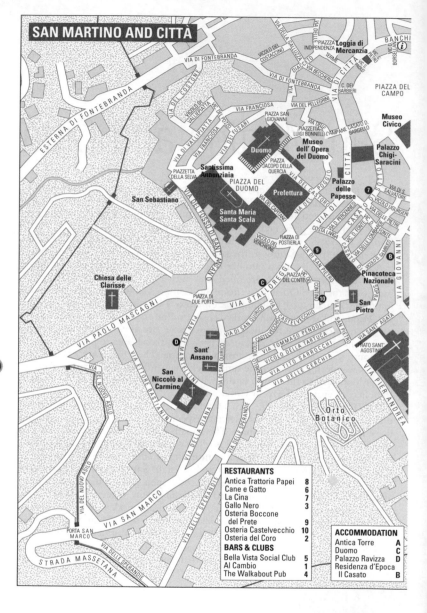

**RESTAURANTS**

| | |
|---|---|
| Antica Trattoria Papei | 8 |
| Cane e Gatto | 6 |
| La Cina | 7 |
| Gallo Nero | 3 |
| Osteria Boccone del Prete | 9 |
| Osteria Castelvecchio | 10 |
| Osteria del Coro | 2 |

**BARS & CLUBS**

| | |
|---|---|
| Bella Vista Social Club | 5 |
| Al Cambio | 1 |
| The Walkabout Pub | 4 |

**ACCOMMODATION**

| | |
|---|---|
| Antica Torre | A |
| Duomo | C |
| Palazzo Ravizza | D |
| Residenza d'Epoca Il Casato | B |

hilly spur see far more locals than visitors and are dotted with numerous little-visited churches, not least **San Martino**, which gives the area its name. The church was also a key seat of power during the Middle Ages for the Piccolomini dynasty, whose colossal former home, the **Palazzo Piccolimini**, and a nearby loggia built by the family, the **Loggia del Papa**, mark the beginning of the district. The Palazzo is well worth a visit, thanks to a collection of unusual

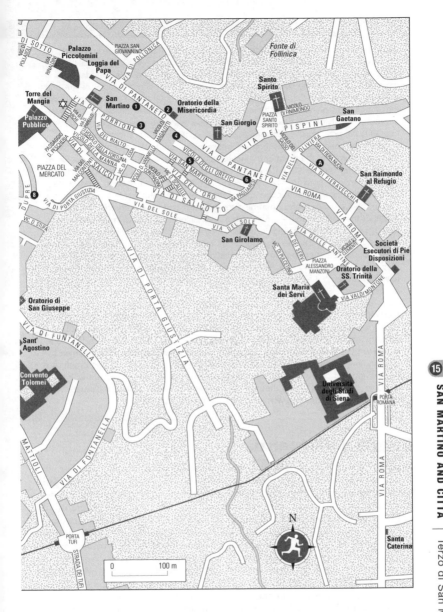

medieval and Renaissance paintings, and so, too, is the area's major church, **Santa Maria dei Servi**, whose medley of frescoes and paintings more than justifies the longish walk to get there. Perhaps the district's biggest draw, though, is the sweeping views, especially from Santa Maria dei Servi, of the city rooftops and the rural valleys beyond.

Within the fabric of the medieval city, Siena preserves its ancient division into wards, or **contrade**. These are integral to the competition of the Palio (see Palio colour section) and sustain a unique neighbourhood identity, clearly visible as you wander around the streets. Each of the seventeen *contrade* has its own church, social centre and museum, as well as a flag and heraldic **animal motif**, after which most of them take their names. The animals – giraffe, snail, goose, porcupine, and others – can be seen all around the city on wall plaques and are represented in a series of modern fountains near the *contrada* churches or headquarters, in each of the city's three *terzi*.

There were once social distinctions between the *contrade*, and although today these are blurred to the point of extinction, allegiance to one's *contrada* – conferred by birth – remains a strong element of social life. After a conventional church baptism, anyone born in a ward division is baptized for a second time in their *contrada* fountain. Subsequently, the *contrada* plays a central role in activities: for kids in the flag-twirling and drumming for the Palio and local *contrada* festivals, for adults in the social clubs – a mix of bar and dining club – and in the attendance of a herald at marriages and funerals. *Contrade* also dispense social assistance to needy members. The respect accorded to the institution of *contrade* is said to have a significant effect on the city's social cohesion. Certainly, for a city of its size, Siena has remarkably low levels of crime and drug usage. Indeed, the only violence tolerated is during the Palio, when *contrada* members may get into fights with their ancient rivals.

For an insight into the workings of the *contrade*, it is worth paying a visit to one of their **museums**, each of which gives pride of place to its displays of Palio trophies. All the museums are open to visitors during the build-up to the Palio and at other times by appointment with at least a week's notice; ask the tourist office to phone if necessary. Each *contrada* also has its own **annual celebration**, accompanied by parades and feasts. And at almost any time of year, you'll see groups practising flag-waving and drum-rolling in the streets. Below is a list of the *contrade* with their symbols, the *terzo* in which they are found, the addresses of their museums, and contact telephone numbers and websites, where appropriate.

# Loggia di Mercanzia

Marking the start of Banchi di Sotto and its extension Via di Pantaneto, the main thoroughfare through Terzo di San Martino, is the three-arched **Loggia di Mercanzia**, or Loggia dei Mercanti, designed as a tribune house where merchants could do their deals. The loggia's hesitant style – a mixture of late Gothic and early Renaissance elements – was the result of extraordinary architectural indecision by the city authorities, the chronicles recording that "on one day they build in a certain way and on the following destroy and rebuild in a different manner". Sano di Matteo did a great deal of the early preparation between 1417 and 1428, Pietro del Minella much of the later work between 1428 and 1444. The latter had worked on the Duomo at Orvieto, the only rival to Siena's (very similar) cathedral in central Italy for sheer scale and decorative splendour. He also created some of the more accomplished panels in the pavement of Siena's cathedral.

The Gothic niches on the loggia's main facade contain statues of saints Paul and Peter (1458–60), rather weak works by Vecchietta, who came to sculpture late in his career; and the figures of San Vittore and Sant'Ansano (1456–63) by Antonio Federighi, also responsible for two celebrated water stoups and panels in the Duomo and the Loggia del Papa (see below).

**Aquila** – Eagle (Città). Casato di Sotto ☎0577.288.086, Ⓦwww.contradadellaquila.it

**Bruco** – Caterpillar (Camollia). Via del Comune 44 ☎0577.44.842

**Chiocciola** – Snail (Città). Via San Marco 37 ☎0577.45.455, Ⓦwww.chiocciola.org

**Civetta** – Owl (San Martino). Piazzetta del Castellare ☎0577.285.505

**Drago** – Dragon (Camollia). Piazza Matteotti 19 ☎0577.40.575, Ⓦwww.contradadeldrago.it

**Giraffa** – Giraffe (Camollia).Via delle Vergini 18 ☎0577.287.091, Ⓦwww.comune.siena.it/giraffa

**Istrice** – Porcupine (Camollia). Via Camollia 87 ☎0577.48.495, Ⓦwww.istrice.org

**Leocorno** – Unicorn (San Martino). Via di Follonico 15 ☎0577.288.549

**Lupa** – She-Wolf (Camollia). Via di Vallerozzi 71/73 ☎0577.270.777

**Nicchio** – Shell (San Martino). Via dei Pispini 68 ☎0577.49.600, Ⓦwww.nobilecontradadelnicchio.it

**Oca** – Goose (Camollia). Vicolo del Tiratoio 11 ☎0577. 285.413, Ⓦwww.contradadelloca.it

**Onda** – Wave (Città). Via Giovanni Dupré 111 ☎0577. 48.384, Ⓦwww.contradacapitanadellonda.it

**Pantera** – Panther (Città). Via San Quirico ☎0577.48.468

**Selva** – Forest (Città). Piazzetta della Selva ☎0577.45.093, Ⓦwww.contradadellaselva.it

**Tartuca** – Turtle (Città). Via Tommaso Pendola 21 ☎0577.49.448, Ⓦwww.tartuca.it

**Torre** – Tower (San Martino). Via Salicotto 76 ☎0577.222.181, Ⓦwww.contradadellatorre.it

**Valdimontone** – Ram (San Martino). Via di Valdimonte 6 ☎0577.222.590, Ⓦwww.valdimonte.it

Inside, the loggia's vaults (1549–51 and 1563–64) are decorated in stucco and frescoes, the work of Pastorino dei Pastorini. The right arm of the interior contains a headless statue of Hercules (1461) by Federighi, the robust muscularity of which is considered by some scholars to have influenced Michelangelo – who worked in Siena between 1501 and 1503 – in his work in Florence's Cappelle Medicee.

# Palazzo Piccolomini

Following Banchi di Sotto from the loggia, you pass the **Palazzo Piccolomini** (at Banchi di Sotto 52), built in more committed Renaissance style and commissioned in 1462 by Pope Pius II, the Pienza-born Aeneas Sylvius Piccolomini. Pius was the city's great Renaissance patron and an indefatigable builder. The palace – one of three the pope built for his family in the city – was designed by Bernardo Rossellino, architect of Piccolomini's famous "new town" of Pienza; note the half-moon symbols, Pius's coat of arms, insinuated across much of the facade. One of Siena's greatest Renaissance buildings, it took its inspiration from Alberti's Palazzo Ruccellai in Florence, completed just eleven years earlier. Both buildings largely eschewed the fortress-like appearance of earlier Florentine and Sienese buildings, exemplified by Michelozzo's Palazzo Medici in Florence. Where Michelozzo built with vast, protruding stones (an effect known as rustication) on the ground floor, leaving onlookers in no doubt as to his fortress-palace's defensive capabilities, Rossellino's facade still emphasizes each individual stone, but in a smooth, elegant and entirely decorative way. The Piccolomini, clearly, felt they had less to fear than the Medici.

## The Archivio di Stato and Museo delle Tavolette di Biccherna

The Palazzo Piccolomini now houses the **Archivio di Stato**, or the city's archive (visits Mon–Fri at 9.30am, 10.30am & 11.30am; free), an unmissable detour, but one made perhaps by one visitor in five hundred to the city. Most people are put off by the fact that you have to be conducted by an employee (no commentary) through the building. En route, you're taken through corridors of archives – great bundles of vellum and leather-bound documents relating to each of the towns and villages in Siena's domain, each one labelled in ancient medieval script with the year in question: 1351, 1352, 1353, etc – a quite overwhelming amount of information for any potential historian, and most of it still unread. If you're lucky you'll also be able to pop out onto the palace's terrace, which offers a rarely seen view of the Campo.

Eventually you reach the **Museo delle Tavolette di Biccherna**, a collection of painted wooden tablets (*tavolette*) and other artefacts, and the main reason for visiting (you're generally left by your guide at this point to look around the displays at your leisure). First documented in 1167, the Biccherna was one of the city's two main financial institutions. It looked after the Republic's direct receipts and public accounts, and controlled and accounted for funds given to civic and public works; the second institution, the Gabella, was responsible for direct and indirect taxes. Both organizations continued, in some shape or form, until the early nineteenth century.

What makes these otherwise dry institutions fascinating is that their records and accounts were contained in books with painted wooden panels as covers, known as *Tavolette*; more interesting still is the fact that the Biccherna commissioned some of the leading painters of the day to execute the beautifully detailed vignettes (the last appeared in 1682). Among those employed were Sano di Pietro, Giovanni di Paolo, Taddeo di Bartolo, Francesco di Giorgio, Domenico Beccafumi and Ambrogio Lorenzetti, the last having painted the 1344 *Gabella* with a version of his *Good Government* fresco in the Palazzo Pubblico.

The earliest *tavolette* are painted with religious subjects; among these is an anonymous portrait of Ugo da San Galgano (1258), who was a Cistercian monk from San Galgano, an abbey south of Siena, and may have come up with the idea of painting the *tavolette*. The city entrusted numerous tasks to such monks, including accounting and other financial work, and in the early years the *camerlingo*, or accountant, would always be a Cistercian monk from San Galgano. Note how only the top half of the panel is decorated, allowing the accounts to be carried without the constant rubbing of hands on the lower portion wearing away the painting.

The panels' paintings soon moved towards secular images of city life, providing a record of six centuries of Sienese history. Later panels were also designed to be displayed as pictures in the council offices, rather than mounted on the books. The city is depicted frequently in the background, protected by the Virgin and mushrooming with towers. Look out, in particular, for Francesco di Giorgio Martini's 1467 panel, which shows the Madonna hovering over an image of the city protecting it from an earthquake in 1466; or Neroccio di Martolomeo's panel from 1480 in which the Virgin recommends the city to Jesus, with the cathedral prominently depicted centre left. Other panels move into specific events – victories over the Florentines; Pius's coronation as pope (1458); the siege of Colle di Val d'Elsa (1479); entrusting the city keys to the Virgin in the Duomo (1483); the demolition of the Spanish fortress (1552); the fall of Montalcino; the Sienese Republic's last stand (1559); the entry into Siena of Cosimo I (1560); war with the Turks (1570); and subsequent Medicean events.

## Loggia del Papa

Like the Palazzo Piccolomini, the rather plain, Renaissance **Loggia del Papa**, or Loggia of the Pope, was commissioned by Pius II, and built in 1462 to a design by Antonio Federighi, whose work you may have just seen in the nearby Loggia di Mercanzia (see above). Across the facade above the arches is the inscription "Pius II Pontifex maximus gentilibus Piccolomineis", words to the effect that the loggia was erected in honour of Pius's Piccolomini family and relatives. In doing so, it underlines the important civic, social and family role played by loggias (even those built by and for popes) in this and other Italian cities at the end of the fourteenth and beginning of the fifteenth century. Today, in a modern urban context, loggias appear to be afterthoughts, decorative and functionless. Formerly, however, every great noble and many mercantile families would ensure that some corner of their palaces, or some point close by, accommodated a loggia, preferably near an area of flat ground that could stage jousts, dances or other ceremonies and celebrations. Above all, loggias were used for dynastic events – to celebrate births or weddings – and, in Siena, for street parties in honour of victories in the Palio. At this last event, nobles and the wealthy would intermingle with ordinary citizens, the loggia thus helping to provide the civic unity and harmony by which the city set such great store.

## San Martino

Before setting off down one of the streets heading southeast into the Terzo di San Martino, Mannerist fans should make a brief visit to the church of **San Martino** (hours vary), founded in the eighth century or earlier, but reconstructed in 1537 and concealed behind a late Renaissance facade from 1613. The key work here is on the third altar on the left (north), an outstanding *Nativity* (1522–24) by Domenico Beccafumi, painted at the same time as the artist was working on the Duomo's pavement. The Virgin's strange gesture, in which she covers the Infant Jesus with a veil, prefigures the Crucifixion, at which she also covers Christ's naked body. The painting also exemplifies Beccafumi's passion for unusual light effects, shapes and compositions, seen notably in the brightly lit sky and the circle created by the hand-holding angels that forms a "crown" for the dove of the Holy Spirit at the top of the picture (Vasari in his *Lives of the Artists* was particularly taken by this last detail). Beccafumi had just returned from Rome at the time of the painting, and for all his Mannerist ambition, was still taken with the classical world, as the work's prominent (but ruined) Roman triumphal arch, clearly out of context in the Bethlehem of the Nativity, makes clear. Its state of ruin is symbolic, suggesting that the birth of Christ marked the start of a new era and an end to the pagan and classical world.

Three other paintings in the church are worth noting, starting with the *Circumcision* (1636) on the second altar on the right (south) wall, the work of the Bolognese artist Guido Reni (1575–1642). It was commissioned by Siena's Gori family and painted close to the artist's death, and, so the story goes, following a flight from Rome (where he had found fame) caused by gambling debts. Reni was heavily influenced by the Caracci, northern Italy's most prominent artists of the time, as was Guercino, a master of seventeenth-century Baroque painting and responsible for the *Martydom of St Bartholemew* in the altar to the left. Also look out for the painting by Giovanni di Lorenzo Cini to the right of the main door as you face the west wall. It shows the Madonna protecting Siena, and was painted to celebrate Siena's victory over the Medici pope, Clement VII, at the Battle of Camollia in 1528.

# Via di Salicotto and Via di Pantaneto

To the south of San Martino, in **Via di Salicotto**, running directly behind the Torre del Mangia, you find yourself in the territory of the Torre (tower) *contrada*. It maintains a museum at no. 76 and a fountain-square a few houses beyond. A famous sign on this street, posted in 1641, informs the citizens that the Florentine governor forbids prostitutes to work in the neighbourhood.

Towards the eastern end of the parallel Via di Pantaneto on the left looms the church of **San Giorgio**, consecrated in 1731 and with an imposing travertine facade (completed 1738), the finest piece of eighteenth-century architecture in Siena, though this is not saying much in a predominantly medieval city. In the unlikely event that the church is open, it's worth popping in to see its best painting, a *Crucifixion* (1601–02) by Francesco Vanni (1563–1609) on the second altar of the left (north) aisle. Vanni was Siena's finest Counter-Reformation artist, and his works can be seen in, among other places, nearby Santo Spirito (see below) and the Cappella di Santa Caterina in San Domenico (see p.287). He is buried here in San Giorgio in a tomb (1656) created by his sons, Raffaello and Michelangelo, to the left of the main entrance door as you face the west wall. Outside the church, try for a glimpse of its Romanesque campanile, difficult to see from the street, built in 1260, the year of the Battle of Montaperti when Siena famously defeated Florence. It has 38 windows, the same number, according to tradition, as the number of companies of knights that took part in the battle.

Almost immediately after San Giorgio, a left turn takes you to the small square containing **Santo Spirito**, sadly also only intermittently open. Doubtless this is because there are insufficient funds to provide security for its outstanding paintings, notably an entire chapel (the first on the right, or south side) entirely decorated by Sodoma in 1520. Among the paintings are *St Nicola of Tolentino* and *St Sebastian*, both invoked against plague – something to which Siena was no stranger – the *Archangel Michael* and *St Antonio Abbot*. The lunette shows the Virgin presenting St Alfonso with the robes of the Augustinians in the presence of saints Rosalia and Lucy. Farther down the right aisle, in the chapel before the high altar, Francesco Vanni painted the vault with *San Giacinto in Glory*, with the same saint's life depicted by Ventura Salimbeni on the walls below.

A final treat on the streets east towards Santa Maria dei Servi is the tiny, intimate church of **San Girolamo**, just off Via di Pantaneto to the south. Knock or ring the bell on the door of the adjoining convent to the left of the church and the cheerful nuns will doubtless be happy to admit you. The convent was the first in Siena belonging to the Gesuati, a religious order founded by the **Beato Giovanni Colombini** in 1354 (see below), passing to the Vergini Abbandonate (the Abandoned Virgins) when the Gesuati were suppressed, and then to the present incumbents, the Figlie della Carità di San Vincenzo de' Paoli. It's a charming church, immaculately kept and boldly striped in black and white. The key painting is to the rear, on the back wall of an antechamber left of the high altar: a *Coronation of the Virgin* by Sano di Pietro, in which the Virgin is flanked by San Girolamo and Beato Colombini. Sano would include the latter figure in two Sienese masterpieces painted for the Gesuati (he became the order's official artist), now in the Pinacoteca Nazionale: the great *Polyptych of the Gesuati* (removed from this convent) and the *Polyptych of St Bonda*.

Colombini was born in 1304 to a wealthy Sienese family, but at the age of 40 renounced wordly pleasures in favour of an extreme life of poverty and hardship in the service of Christ. He and a group of like-minded friends formed "Il Popolo di Gesù", or People of Jesus, later simply the Gesuati, an order that would be promulgated across Italy (Venice, to name but one city, has a large church devoted to the order). Pope Urban V eventually sanctioned the movement, whose members wore white and went barefoot, though its extreme views on the importance of poverty, among other things, would later lead to its downfall and suppression.

## Santa Maria dei Servi

Via di Salicotto or Via San Martino – or Via dei Servi from San Girolamo – bring you to the massive fourteenth-century brick church and campanile of **Santa Maria dei Servi**, the Servites' monastic base. The church (closed 12.30–3pm), which is well worth the walk, is set in a quiet piazza, approached via a row of cypresses and shaded by a couple of spreading trees – good for a midday picnic or siesta. It also offers tremendous **views** across Siena; from here the various ridges of the city and the cathedral's dominant position among them are made clear. The best time to visit is in the morning, when the great sweep of the city skyline is caught in the light of the sun.

The Renaissance-remodelled **interior** is remarkable for a variety of top-notch paintings. The tone is set by a diverting fourteenth-century fresco fragment on the first pillar on the right (south side), an anonymous work showing the *Last Judgement*, with the Virgin liberating souls from Purgatory. The next major painting, above the first main altar on the right (south) wall, is the so-called *Madonna di Bordone* (1261) by **Coppo di Marcovaldo**, a Florentine artist captured by the Sienese at the Battle of Montaperti in 1260 and forced to paint

△ View of Siena's Duomo

this picture as part of his ransom for release. It is his first known major work, one of only a handful that survives from an artist now seen as an important early precursor to Cimabue. The next altar to the left features the *Nativity of the Virgin* (1625) by Rutilio Manetti, Siena's leading follower of Caravaggio.

Two altars down, in the last altar of the right aisle, is Matteo di Giovanni's *Massacre of the Innocents* (1491), one of two versions of this episode in the church, and one of four in the city, including a panel on the pavement of the Duomo, by the infanticide-obsessed Matteo. The popularity of this subject in the late fifteenth century may have been due to the much-publicized massacre of Christian children by the Saracens at Otranto in 1480. Matteo's rendition is a touch less blood-crazed than his Sant'Agostino version, painted two years after the massacre (and moved to the Palazzo Pubblico since its restoration), but only just – certain features are common to both, including the powerful sense of claustrophobia and several unnecessarily perverse details, of which the most disturbing are the woman scratching the face of the soldier about to dispatch her child and the two smiling children watching the massacre from the balcony on the right.

Cheek-by-jowl violence (watched over by Herod from a balcony on the left) also characterizes Pietro Lorenzetti's much earlier version of the *Massacre*, which is found on the right wall of the second chapel to the right of the high altar. In the transept to the right is a large painted Crucifixion attributed to Sassetta. The small, serene *Madonna and Child* above the door is by Segna di Bonaventura (active 1298–1326), nephew of the great Duccio. Lorenzetti is further represented by damaged frescoes of the *Banquet of Herod* and the *Death of John the Evangelist*, located on the right wall of the second chapel to the left of the high altar. The Baptist is shown ascending to heaven with a praying St Drusiana, whom he had brought back to life after her death in Ephesus, Turkey. Also in this chapel is a fine *Adoration of the Shepherds* (1404) by one of Lorenzetti's followers, Taddeo di Bartolo.

Moving to the **left transept** you come to a *Madonna del Manto* (1436) by one of Taddeo's pupils, Giovanni di Paolo, among the finest Sienese exponents of the detailed, courtly style known as International Gothic. The painting was probably part of a much larger polyptych and shows the Virgin sheltering a group of nuns on one side and a group of monks on the other, the latter led by Filippo Benizzi (1235–85), a Florentine general of the Servite order. His story is illustrated by Andrea del Sarto in the Chiostrino dei Voti in Santissima Annunziata in Florence (see p.130). In a strange but pleasing touch, the Virgin's cloak is decorated with images of kneeling prophets framed by Gothic niches. In the church's north aisle, towards the entrance, the last altar before the west wall contains the small but eye-catching *Madonna del Belvedere* (1363), rather lost in its large surround, one of only a handful of works attributed to Jacopo di Mino del Pellicciaio, a pupil of Lippo Memmi.

## Porta Romana

From Santa Maria dei Servi, you're just 100m from the **Porta Romana**, the massively bastioned south gate of the city. Its outer arch bears a fragmentary fresco of the *Coronation of the Virgin*, begun by Taddeo di Bartolo and completed by Sano di Pietro. If you leave the city here, and turn left along Via Girolamo Gigli, you could follow the walls north to the **Porta Pispini**, another impressive example of defensive architecture and again flanked by a fresco of the Virgin, this time a Renaissance effort by Sodoma.

Just within the Porta Romana, opposite the huge ex-convent of San Niccolò (which now houses a psychiatric hospital), is the little church of the **Santuccio**, worth looking into for its seventeenth-century frescoes depicting the life of St Galgano. In the adjacent sacristy, at Via Roma 71, are the premises of the **Società Esecutori di Pie Disposizioni** (the Society of Benevolent Works, formerly the Society of Flagellants). This medieval order, suppressed in the eighteenth century, and later refounded along more secular lines, maintains a small collection of artworks (Mon, Wed & Fri 9am–noon, Tues & Thurs 3–5pm; open on request; free), including a triptych of the *Crucifixion, Flagellation and Burial of Christ* attributed to Duccio.

# Terzo di Città

Via di Città, one of Siena's key streets, cuts across the top of the Campo through the city's oldest quarter, the **Terzo di Città**, the area around the cathedral. The street and its continuation, Via di San Pietro, are fronted by some of Siena's finest private palaces, including the Buonsignori, home to the **Pinacoteca Nazionale**, Siena's main picture gallery. The district is also worth exploring for its own sake and holds a number of churches, such as the art-rich **Sant'Agostino**, as well as some attractive little-known corners.

The district is easily explored, with the Campo as your starting point (the approach assumed in the account below), but you could incorporate it into an itinerary that follows Santa Maria dei Servi by walking west on Via di Salicotto to Piazza del Mercato. Here take the tiny Via del Mercato in the square's northwest corner to Via Giovanni Duprè, an appealing street that climbs past the *contrada* church of the Oratorio di San Giuseppe to Sant'Agostino.

## Palazzo Chigi-Saracini

Walking up Via di Città from the Campo area, you pass the **Palazzo Chigi-Saracini** at Via di Città 82, a Gothic beauty, with its curved facade and back courtyard. Begun in the twelfth century, it was altered many times in the succeeding centuries, not least in 1787, when it was given a neo-Gothic makeover. The tower at its northern end, the first thing you see climbing the street, dates from the building's earliest incarnation, and it was from here in 1260 that Ciretto Ceccolini, watching events as they unfolded in the distance, reported the Sienese victory over Florence at the Battle of Montaperti to his fellow citizens below. Today the building houses the **Accademia Chigiana** (see p.304), founded in 1932 by Guido Chigi-Saracini, which sponsors music programmes throughout the year. It also houses a small but exquisite art collection, including exceptional works by Sassetta, Botticelli and Donatello, formerly almost impossible to see, but recently open to more regular public viewings. Contact the tourist office for the latest details.

Guido Chigi-Saracini was the last in the line of the Chigi-Saracini, one of the great Sienese dynasties. Sapia Saracini, for example, commands several stanzas in Canto XIII of Dante's *Purgatorio*, where she is described as a terrible, but influential rumour-monger. Far more famous was Mariano di Agostino Chigi, a Sienese who founded a bank that under his celebrated son, Agostino, would rival that of the Medici. He employed 20,000 people in various branches as far afield as London, Constantinople and Cairo. More to the point, he became principal banker to Julius II at the end of the fifteenth century, and a direct and indirect patron of Raphael, Michelangelo and many other leading artists then working in Rome. Better was to follow, for Pope Julius III (remembered by a bust in the vestibule) was the son of a Chigi, and though he reigned just five years (1550–55), it was he who confirmed the Jesuit Order and opened the Council of Trent in 1551, designed to roll back the tide of Protestantism. Yet another Chigi – Fabio – became Pope Alexander VII in 1655.

## Palazzo delle Papesse

Almost opposite the Palazzo Chigi-Saracini, at Via di Città 126, is a second Palazzo Piccolomini, the **Palazzo delle Papesse**, this one built to a design by Bernardo Rossellino between 1460 and 1495 as a residence for Pius II's sister, Caterina. Unlike the main Palazzo Pubblico, also designed by Rossellino, the lower level shows the obvious debt to Michelozzo and the Palazzo Medici-Riccardi in Florence. Here, the ground floor is heavily rusticated (that is, formed with large, rough-cut stones that stand proud of the exterior), a throwback to the fortress-like detailing employed by Michelozzo in the 1450s, but abandoned in the main Palazzo Pubblico in favour of a uniformly smooth wall.

Today, the palace houses Siena's **Centro Arte Contemporanea**, a museum of contemporary art (Tues–Sun noon–7pm; €5; joint tickets see p.224; ⓦwww .papesse.org). Its four airy floors house excellent temporary exhibits covering anything from architecture to video art, displayed in rooms, some with nine-teenth-century frescoes, that still conserve many of their original Renaissance structural and decorative features.

## Pinacoteca Nazionale

Via di Città continues to a small piazza, from where Via San Pietro leads left (south) to the fourteenth-century Palazzo Buonsignori at Via San Pietro 29, now the home of the excellent **Pinacoteca Nazionale** (Mon 8.30am–1.30pm, Tues–Sat 8.15am–7.15pm, Sun 8.30am–1.15pm; €4). Its collection is a roll call of Sienese Gothic painting, and if your interest has been spurred by the works by Martini in the Palazzo Pubblico or Duccio in the cathedral museum, a visit is the obvious next step. The collection offers an unrivalled chance to assess the development of art in the city from the twelfth century through to late-Renaissance Mannerism. Note that there have been long-mooted plans to transfer the gallery to Santa Maria della Scala, though no date has been set: indeed, many of the Pinacoteca's rooms are being modernized and reordered, suggesting its continued use for a good while yet. The reordering means certain paintings may not be hung exactly as described below, though identification should always be possible by using the catalogue number given in the text in square brackets.

### Sienese art in the thirteenth and fourteenth centuries

The main rooms are arranged in chronological order, starting on the second floor, where **room 1** begins with the earliest known Sienese work, an altar frontal by the "Maestro di Tressa", dated 1215, of *Christ Flanked by Angels* [1], featuring an almost sculptural Christ carved in relief and side panels depicting the discovery of the True Cross. The figures are clearly Romanesque; the gold background – intricately patterned – was, as you'll see in the coming rooms, to be a standard motif of Sienese art over the next two centuries.

The first identified Sienese painter, Guido da Siena, makes an appearance in the same room: his *Transfiguration, Entry into Jerusalem and Resurrection of Lazarus* [8] from the third quarter of the thirteenth century is one of the first known works painted on canvas. The influences on his work – dated around 1280

– are distinctively Byzantine rather than Romanesque, incorporating studded jewels amid the gold. In some of his narrative panels in this painting his hand seems rather freer, though the colouring is limited to a few delicate shades. It is believed he worked with, or was influenced by, the Florentine Coppo di Marcovaldo, who lived in the city in 1260 after his capture at the Battle of Montaperti (see p.228).

He also almost certainly worked with painters whose reputations are only now, after recent research, being acknowledged and reappraised. These include some of the artists represented in **room 2**, including Dietisalvi di Speme, documented between 1259 and 1291, and the author of numerous Biccherna panels in the Palazzo Piccolomini (see p.261). His diptych [4] showing, among other things, graphic scenes of St Bartholemew's grisly martyrdom (being skinned alive), is especially diverting. More important still is Guido di Graziano, increasingly seen as one of the most accomplished and influential Sienese artists before Duccio. This emerging reputation is borne out by the lovely painting here, *St Peter Enthroned and Scenes from the Life of Christ and St Peter* [15], probably painted around 1270 or 1280, and showing an appreciation of the innovations of Cimabue in Florence and Assisi. Note Peter's inverted crucifixion lower right.

Duccio di Buoninsegna (1260–1319), the dominant figure in early Sienese art, is represented along with his school in **rooms 3 and 4**. Bernard Berenson considered Duccio the last great painter of antiquity, in contrast to Giotto, the first of the moderns. The painter's advances in composition are best assessed in his *Maestà*, in the Museo dell'Opera del Duomo. Here Duccio simply shows that he "fulfilled all that the medieval mind demanded of a painter", in the words of Berenson: his dual purpose being to demonstrate Christianity to an illiterate audience and make an offering (the painting) to God. A rather more Gothic and expressive character is suggested by Ugolino di Nerio's *Crucifixion with St Francis* [34] in room 4, one of the era's most arresting pictures, and graphic confirmation of Ugolino's standing as one of Duccio's most original disciples.

Sienese art over the next century has its departures from Duccio – Lorenzetti's mastery of landscape and life in the *Good and Bad Government* in the Palazzo Pubblico, for example – but the patrons responsible for commissioning works generally wanted more of the same: decorative paintings, whose gold backgrounds made their subjects stand out in the gloom of medieval chapels. As well as specifying the required materials and composition, the Sienese patrons – bankers, guilds, religious orders – would often nominate a particular painting as the model for the style they wanted.

Even within the conventions required by patrons, however, there were painters whose invention and finesse set them apart. One such was **Simone Martini**. Though his innovations – the attention to framing and the introduction of a political dimension – are perhaps best seen in the Palazzo Pubblico, there are several great works on show at the Pinacoteca, mostly in **room 5**, including one of his masterpieces, the large and unmissable *Blessed Agostino Novello and Four of His Miracles*, for a time part of the tomb of Novello in the church of Sant'Agostino. Note the wonderful image (bottom left) of Novello diving to save a falling child. Martini's dulcet and refined style, and his taste for elegance and delicacy – exemplified by the *Madonna and Child* here [9] – would influence most Sienese (and many other) artists in the second half of the fourteenth century, including his brother-in-law and close follower, Lippo Memmi, who also has several fine paintings in this room.

The highlight of **room 6** is an *Adoration of the Magi* [104] by Bartolo di Fredi (1353–1410), the masterpiece of this artist, known for his illustrative and narrative skill. It's a lovely, courtly picture, and a welcome contrast to the many surrounding Madonnas. The works by the Lorenzetti brothers, Pietro and Ambrogio, in **rooms 7 and 8**, are just as rewarding. Pietro's include a Giottoesque *Crucifixion* [147] and the *Carmine Altarpiece*, whose gorgeous but incomplete predella (the missing panels are in American museums, which won't return them) has five skilful narrative scenes of the founding of the Carmelite order. Ambrogio is represented, among others, by a small, exquisite *Madonna and Child Enthroned* [65], and an *Annunciation* [88], signed and dated 1344, making it the last known work by the artist before he died (with Pietro) in the Black Death of 1348. Don't overlook *Saint Galgano* and *Saint Ansano* [43 and 42] by Bartolomeo Bulgarini, probably the earliest works by another mysterious Sienese painter whose importance is only now being recognized by scholars.

**Room 9** is the palace's loggia, with varying temporary exhibits, but it is more than worth a detour for some wonderful **views** of the city.

## The Sienese Renaissance

Sienese art languished behind that of Florence at the start of the fifteenth century, slow – or reluctant – to surrender its placid Madonnas and Childs, stylized Byzantine roots and gold backgrounds to the dynamic new ideas promulgated by the artists working in its rival city. This is not to say that its artists were completely without innovation: Martini and the Lorenzettis, among others, moved Sienese art on in the fourteenth century, and as the Renaissance evolved, Sienese painters such as Taddeo di Bartolo (1362–1422), who is well represented in **room 11**, also began to forge new ideas. Taddeo, the painter of the chapel in the Palazzo Pubblico, still has archaic elements – notably the huge areas of gold around a sketch of landscape – but makes strides in portraiture and renders one of the first pieces of dynamic action in the museum's collection in his *Annunciation and SS Cosmas and Damian* [131].

When Sienese art did start to adopt the new Florentine ideas in earnest, it looked largely to mediators, or artists who set the innovations in a context that continued to pay homage to the comforting Gothic and earlier conventions. The earliest and most important of these painters were Stefano di Giovanni da Cortona, more commonly known as Sassetta (1392–1451); an anonymous artist known as the Maestro dell'Osservanza; and Lorenzo di Pietro, better known as Vecchietta (1412–1480). **Room 12** is the point where Siena seems at last to be entering the mainstream of European Gothic art, starting with two tiny panels, *City by the Sea* and *Castle by a Lake*, which the art historian Enzo Carli claims are the first ever "pure landscapes", without any religious purpose. Formerly attributed to Ambrogio Lorenzetti, they are now given to Sassetta, and are thought to have been painted on a wardrobe, or on a door, one above the other.

Also here is one of the early high points of the Sienese Renaissance, a *Madonna and Child with Musical Angels* [164], dated 1433, by Domenico di Bartolo, the artist responsible for much of Santa Maria della Scala's superb main fresco cycle. The painting's vibrancy shows the influence of Donatello, while the cupids recall Luca della Robbia and the touching, realistic face of the Christ Child the frescoes of Masaccio in the Cappella Brancacci in Florence, works largely executed in the previous decade.

Yet the influence of the past continues to linger, notably in the use of gold and the conservative choice of subject matter. It is also still prevalent in the mass of stereotyped images in the many paintings in this room and **room 13** by Giovanni di Paolo (1403–82), an artist who clearly reveals the conflicting impulses at work in Siena at the time. On the one hand there is the inclination to look back, as in the beautiful *Madonna of Humility* [206] in room 12, the painter's most famous work (of uncertain date), celebrated for its strange and poetic background landscape and lovely trees, constructed on a circular horizon (a common feature of fourteenth-century Sienese paintings). On the other, there is his very different *Presentation at the Temple* [211] from 1447 in room 13, where the Roman temple architecture and almost self-conscious use of perspective reflect an obvious concern with the forward-looking ideas and classical preoccupations of the Renaissance.

In the following **rooms (14–18)** the same tension is found in many other works, mostly by artists from the second half of the fifteenth century influenced by, or trained in, the workshop of Vecchietta (most of whose paintings, rather confusingly, do not appear until room 19). These include Matteo di Giovanni, Neroccio di Bartolomeo Landi, Girolamo di Benvenuto and (probably) Francesco di Giorgio Martini. The last was perhaps the most accomplished, and one of the few Sienese artists of the period to achieve wider fame and obtain commissions outside Siena and Tuscany. His *Madonna and Child with Angel* [288] in room 13 is especially lovely.

Another prominent artist of the period is Sano di Pietro (1406–1481), of whom little is known before his first reliably documented painting in 1444, **room 16**'s *Madonna and Child Enthroned, Angels and Saints* [246], whose predella, sadly, languishes in the Louvre. This late appearance on the scene has led critics to conclude that Sano and the "Maestro dell'Osservanza" are one and the same, and that the latter's works (mostly in room 15b) are actually the early works of Sano. **Room 17** is entirely dedicated to Sano, but confirm the oft-repeated assertion that his paintings, with some exceptions, became increasingly repetitive and monotonous. Indeed, the 1444 *Madonna*, his first known work, is widely considered his masterpiece. Yet in its gold and stylized Madonna it still harks back almost 150 years. It is astonishing to think that the artist's Florentine contemporaries included Uccello and Leonardo.

Vecchietta and his star disciple, Francesco di Giorgio, are seen to best effect in **room 19**. The latter's *Coronation of the Virgin* [440] is the polar opposite of Sano di Pietro's *Madonna*, showing a thoroughly Florentine sensibility (the faces could have been painted by Verrocchio, da Vinci or Botticelli), yet one that still has a lyricism tracing a direct line back to Simone Martini. The two imposing doors [204] at the centre of the room were painted by Vecchietta around 1445 for a cupboard designed to hold some of the many relics accumulated by Santa Maria della Scala.

## Mannerism, Beccafumi and the Collezione Spannocchi

**Rooms 20 to 26** contain a miscellany of paintings by local and visiting artists, of which one stands out: the *Holy Family with the Infant St John* [495], among the gallery's finest works, executed by the Umbrian artist **Pinturicchio**, who also painted the Duomo's Libreria Piccolomini (see p.244).

The last few rooms of the gallery pay homage to the two great names of sixteenth-century Sienese art: Domenico Beccafumi and Antonio Bazzi, better known as Sodoma. **Beccafumi** was a native, and one of Italy's leading exponents of Mannerism, on a par with Pontormo and Rosso Fiorentino. His are dramatic works, distinguished by often extraordinary effects of light and colour, with patches of almost black canvas scattered with flashes of light or bizarrely arranged figures. **Sodoma**, by contrast, came from Vercelli by way of Rome, bringing to Siena the influence of Leonardo da Vinci and the art of Lombardy, as well as that of Raphael (from Rome) and Renaissance masters such as Perugino and Signorelli, both of whom worked in Siena.

Room 27 contains one of Beccafumi's earliest works, the *Triptych of the Trinity* [384], painted around 1512 for the chapel of the Madonna del Manto in Santa Maria della Scala (see p.250). Compare this with the exquisite *Birth of the Madonna* [405] in room 29, a late masterpiece, sporting some extraordinary pinks and greens and the daring use of two sources of light – one in the delivery room, and one in the kitchen to the rear left, where Joachim waits for news of the birth. Don't miss the unfinished *Fall of the Rebel Angels* [423] in room 37, destined for the church of the San Niccolò al Carmine, but rejected because of the nudity of its angels in favour of a more modest version (see p.273). Sodoma is less well represented, but in the *Birth of Jesus with Angel and Infant St John* [512] in **room 32**, painted in around 1510 for the monastery of Lecceto just west of Siena, the gallery has one of the artist's finest works.

Subsequent rooms are dominated by Rutilio Manetti (1571–1639), formely Siena's most celebrated seventeenth-century artist, but now beginning to be eclipsed in the light of new research and changing tastes by Bernardino Mei (1615–76), whose paintings fill **room 33**.

The **third floor** of the museum – not always open – presents the self-contained **Collezione Spannocchi**, a miscellany of Italian, German and Flemish works, including a Dürer, a fine Lorenzo Lotto *Nativity*, Paris Bordone's perfect Renaissance *Annunciation*, and Sofonisba Anguissola's *Bernardo Campi Painting Sofonisba's Portrait* – the only painting in the museum by a woman. Anguissola, who is mentioned by Vasari as a child prodigy, painted at the height of Mannerism; this work is a neat little joke, the artist excelling in her portrait of Campi, but depicting his portrait of her as a flat, stereotyped image.

Immediately outside the gallery to the south, spare a moment to take in the pretty little church of **San Pietro alle Scale**, a thirteenth-century foundation whose eighteenth-century makeover obliterated virtually every trace of the original building. As with too many of Siena's smaller churches, it is rarely open: the interior has fresco fragments portraying St Catherine of Siena and a *Rest on the Flight from Egypt* (1621), one of the masterpieces of Rutilio Manetti, among Siena's leading seventeenth-century painters, whose superb handling of light shows the obvious recent influence of Caravaggio.

## Sant'Agostino and around

Just south of San Pietro and the Pinacoteca is the church of **Sant'Agostino**, which, frustratingly, you can never be sure will be open or not. It was opened after the Millennium and included on some of the city's combined sightseeing tickets with other major sights, a status fully merited by its outstanding collection of paintings. However, at the time of going to press it was once again firmly shut – inquire at the tourist office for the current situation and for news of the church's paintings, some of which disappear for restoration and have a habit of reappearing elsewhere, usually either in the Palazzo Pubblico or Pinacoteca.

The church, built in 1258, ranks alongside Santa Maria dei Servi as one of the city's richest. Augustinian churches in Italy were inevitably built, as here, close to or just outside the walls, mainly because the order was founded relatively late (in the thirteenth century), and space for churches in medieval town centres was by then at a premium. Furthermore, being a preaching order, the Augustinians required vast churches to house the large congregations their sermons attracted.

The key paintings begin with a *Crucifixion* (1506) by Perugino, the finest of Umbria's Renaissance painters, on the second altar of the right, or south aisle. Beyond this, a large chapel opens on the right, the **Cappella Piccolomini**; its

# The
# Siena
# Palio

"The Palio helps Siena to survive in its own mind. It is a metaphor for the continuity of the life of the people."

**Roberto Barzanti, former Siena MEP and mayor**

The **Siena Palio** is the most exciting and spectacular festival event in Italy, a twice-yearly bareback horse race around the Campo, supported by days of preparation, pageantry and intrigue. It has been held since at least the thirteenth century, in honour – like almost everything in Siena – of the Virgin, and it remains a living tradition, felt and performed with an intensity that comes as a shock in these days of cosily preserved folklore. For days around the festivals the air of rivalry is palpable, quite often breaking into violence amid the bragging celebration of victory by one or other of the *contrade*.

Except in times of war, the Palio has virtually always taken place. In 1798, for example, when the city was in chaos after an earthquake, the July Palio was cancelled but the August race took place. The following year, however, the Palio was again cancelled, owing to political unrest: Sienese counter-revolutionaries took the opportunity to rise against the French-held fortress and sacked the ghetto area of the city. In 1919, when half of Italy was in the throes of strikes and rioting, Siena's factions of the left and right agreed to defer such politics until after the Palio.

# The drawing of lots

Even before the race, fortune plays the pre-eminent part: since there's only room for ten riders, each year the seventeen *contrade* have to draw lots to take part. The participants also draw lots both for the horses and for starting positions in the race itself. The jockeys are professional outsiders, traditionally the *butteri*, or cowboys, of the Maremma, employed according to an unreliable and shifting combination of loyalties reinforced by large cash payments and bonuses – and sometimes the threat of violence if they are treacherous. During the run-up to the races they live under the suspicions of their own *contrada* and in fear of the threats of rival *contrade*. They may

## The build-up

Originally the Palio followed a circuit through the town, but since the sixteenth century it has consisted of **three laps** of the Campo, around a track covered with sand and padded with mattresses in an attempt to minimize injury to horses and riders. Despite all probabilities, no jockey has ever been killed.

There are two annual Palios, held on July 2 (formerly the Feast of the Visitation) and August 16 (the day after the Feast of the Assumption), each of which is preceded by a fascinating sequence of events.

**June 29/August 13** The year's horses are presented in the morning at the town hall and drawn by lot. At 7.15pm the first trial race is held in the Campo.

**June 30/August 14** Further trial races are held at 9am and 7.45pm. The evening race is usually followed by a concert in the Campo.

**July 1/August 15** Two more trial races at 9am and 7.45pm, followed by a street banquet and late-night revelry in each of the *contrade*. Restaurants also move their tables outside for these Palio nights.

**July 2/August 16** The day of the Palio begins with a final trial race at 9am. In the early afternoon, each of the ten chosen *contrade* takes its horse to be blessed in its church: "Go, little horse, and return a winner" are the priest's words. It's worth trying to see one of these horse blessings, which are often preceded by an extraordinary struggle to get the animal up or down the entrance steps. It's taken as a good omen if the horse defecates in church. At around 5pm the town hall bell begins to ring and the **corteo storico**, a pageant of horses, riders and medieval-costumed officials, processes through the city to the Campo. The *corteo*

includes *comparse* – symbolic groups of equerries, ensigns, pages and drummers – from each of the *contrade*, who perform various *sbandierata* (flag-twirling) and athletic feats in the square. They are preceded by officials of the *comune* of Siena and representatives from all the ancient towns and villages of the Sienese Republic, led by the standard-bearer of Montalcino, which offered refuge to the last republicans.

be bribed to throw the race, or to whip a rival or his horse; *contrade* have been known to drug horses, and even to mount an ambush on a jockey making his way to the race.

The result of all this is that in any one year perhaps three or four *contrade* go to the start-line with any chance of victory; for those *contrade* disadvantaged by poor horses or jockeys, and the seven *contrade* who aren't even

Contrada flag-throwers

taking part, the race becomes a vehicle for schemes, plots and general mayhem. Each *contrada* has its traditional rival, and ensuring that one's rival loses is as important as winning for oneself. The only rule of the race is that the jockeys cannot interfere with the others' reins; everything else is accepted and practised. And it's the horse that wins – it doesn't matter if the jockey has been thrown en route to victory.

# The race

The race itself begins on July 2 at 7.45pm, on August 16 at 7pm, and lasts for little more than ninety seconds. There's no PA system to tell you what's going on. At the start (in the northwest corner of the Campo) all the horses except one are penned between two ropes; the free one charges the group from behind, when his rivals least expect it, and the race is on. It's a hectic, violent and bizarre spectacle, and the jockeys don't even stop at the finish line but gallop at top speed out of the Campo, followed by a frenzied mass of supporters. Losers can be in danger of assault, especially if there are rumours about of the race being fixed.

The palio – a silk banner – is subsequently presented to the winning *contrada*, who then make their way to the church of Provenanzo (in July) or the Duomo (in August) to give thanks. The younger *contrada* members spend the rest of the night and much of the subsequent week swaggering around the town celebrating their victory, even handing out celebratory sonnets. In the evening all members of the *contrada* hold a jubilant street banquet.

The race

The Chiocciola (snail) contrada

Inevitably, hotel rooms are extremely difficult to find at Palio time, and if you haven't booked, either reckon on staying up all night, or travelling in from a neighbouring town. The races are generally shown live on national television and repeated endlessly all evening.

## Palio practicalities

It's not hard to get a view of any of the practice races or ceremonies, but for the Palio proper you need to plan ahead a little. Tickets for grandstand or balcony seats, ranged around the Campo, cost from €150 to €300 or more, and are sold out months before the race. To secure a seat for next year's event, contact La Palio Viaggi, Piazza La Lizza 12 (☎0577.280.828, ℻0577.289.114 or 0577.533 023; no website). In the UK, contact Liaisons Abroad (☎020.7376.4020, ✆www.liaisonsabroad.com).

Most ordinary spectators crowd for free into the centre of the Campo. For the best view you need to have found a position by 2pm on the inner rail (ideally at the start/ finish line), and to keep it for the next six hours. If you're not installed here, there's really no rush, as you'll be able to see a certain amount from anywhere within the throng. Be prepared to stand your ground: people keep pouring in right up until a few minutes before the race, and the swell of the crowd can be overwhelming. Be aware that you won't be able to leave the Campo for at least two hours after the race. Toilets, shade and refreshment facilities are minimal (which is perhaps why so little drinking goes on). If you arrive late in the day, you might try making your way to Via Giovanni Dupré, behind the Palazzo Pubblico, from where the police usually allow people into the centre of the square an hour or so before the race.

Celebrating after the race

altarpiece is a crowded *Adoration of the Magi* (1518) by Sodoma, who painted a self-portrait in the form of the youth in profile behind the Madonna to the left as you look at the picture. The lunette fresco of the *Madonna and Child with Saints* was discovered during restoration in 1943 and is by Ambrogio Lorenzetti. Note the bizarre-looking Christ Child, arms up in horror, terrified by the bird (symbol of the Passion) held by the Madonna. Two other great paintings that once graced the chapel, Matteo di Giovanni's *Massacre of the Innocents* (1482) and Simone Martini's *Beato Agostino Novello and Four of His Miracles* (circa 1330), have been removed to the Palazzo Pubblico and Pinacoteca respectively. Next artistic stop is the Cappella Bicci, the second chapel to the right of the high altar, which has two lunette medallions by Luca Signorelli and monochrome frescoes of the *Nativity* and *Adoration of the Shepherds* attributed to Francesco di Giorgio Martini (1439–1502). In the chapel alongside to the left is usually a wooden statue of the *Madonna and Child*, long attributed to Jacopo della Quercia, but now considered a work from 1420 by Giovanni di Torino, primarily a goldsmith who also worked on the font in the city's Baptistery, notably the panel depicting the *Nativity of the Baptist* (see p.248).

Outside, the church **piazza** (Prato Sant'Agostino) is a pleasant space, where children play and parents chat. Along with the Campo, this square was the site of violent medieval football matches – or *ballone* – that were eventually displaced in the festival calendar by the Palio.

At no. 5 in the piazza is the **Accademia dei Fisiocritici** (Mon–Wed & Fri 9am–1pm & 3–6pm, Thurs 9am–1pm; ⊛www.accademiafisiocritici.it; free), housing museums of zoology, geology and mineralogy – all a bit pedestrian, though with a few oddities – like terracotta models of *funghi* – to entertain botanists. Continuing the theme, you could make your way across the piazza to the **Orto Botanico** (Mon–Fri 9am–12.30 & 2.30–5.30pm, Sat 8am–noon; free), Via Pier Andrea Mattioli 4, a rare area of green space in the city whose herbarium is stocked with every Tuscan species.

# San Niccolò al Carmine

For a pretty walk from Sant'Agostino, follow **Via della Cerchia** to the Carmelite convent and church of **San Niccolò al Carmine** (or Santa Maria del Carmine) in a predominantly student-populated section of the town. The imposing church was built in the fourteenth century, but was partially remodelled along Renaissance lines by Baldassarre Peruzzi (1481–1536), a Sienese architect who achieved considerable fame in Rome, where he worked, among other things, on the Palazzo della Farnesina, built for a banker of Sienese origin, Agostino Chigi (see p.267).

The single-nave interior contains a sensational *St Michael* by Domenico Beccafumi (midway down the right, or south wall), painted following the monks' rejection of his more intense Mannerist version of the subject in the Pinacoteca (deemed to contain too many nudes for comfort). A hermaphrodite St Michael is shown at the centre of the crowded painting, looked down on by God, who has ordered the saint to earth to dispatch the Devil, whose extraordinary face with gaping mouth and macabre tongue can be seen at the middle of the base of the picture. The lights effects in the painting, as so often in Beccafumi's work, are extraordinary, especially the rays around the head of God and the two vaulted spaces in the work's lower third.

To the painting's left is a fragment of an *Annunciation* confidently attributed to Ambrogio Lorenzetti, while off the right (south) transept is the Cappella del Sacramento, where a rather lacklustre painting by Sodoma, *God the Father and*

△ Medieval street, Siena

*the Birth of the Virgin*, is overshadowed by a fine carved altar by an otherwise little-known Sienese artist, Marrina, or Lorenzo di Mariano (1476–1534), who was also responsible for the facade of the Libreria Piccolomini in the Duomo and the high altar in San Martino.

## Sant'Ansano and San Quirico

The grid of streets on a slight gradient just east of San Niccolò, bookended by Via San Pietro to the east and Via di San Quirico to the west, is one of the most appealing in the city, if only for the area's peace and quiet and thoroughgoing medievalism. There are also a couple of rarely visited churches, easily seen (but with unfortunately erratic opening hours) before walking back to the city centre.

On Via di San Quirico, the church of **Sant'Ansano**, more properly known as the Cappella delle Carceri di Sant'Ansano, is dedicated to one of Siena's patron saints. **Sant'Ansano** was born in Rome in AD 203. At the age of 12 he was baptized by his governess, Massima, and at 19 proclaimed his (illegal) faith openly, upon which his father denounced him to the authorities. He and Massima were then thrown in boiling oil. Massima died, but Ansano survived and was exiled to Siena, where he preached and converted many Sienese. At 20 he was imprisoned and beheaded on the orders of Emperor Diocletian. Among his attributes are the monogram I.H.S., later adopted by St Bernardino, with which he is often depicted in paintings, along with images of him in military dress, in prison or standing in a vat of boiling oil. The saint appears repeatedly in Sienese paintings, including one of the greatest, Duccio's *Maestà* (see p.255), where his appearance in the first file of saints underlines his status.

A clearly anachronistic legend has the saint imprisoned in the tower on the right of the church's facade, which was built, along with the present structure, in the sixteenth century on the site of a far older place of worship. Inside, the oculus above the door contains a rare piece of stained glass depicting St Ansano, who is also portrayed on the high altar (a picture from 1617 by Rustichino) and in fresco fragments on the left wall (with scenes from the *Adoration of the Magi*) attributed to Priamo della Quercia, brother of sculptor Jacopo, best known for his fresco in Santa Maria della Scala (see p.252).

The second church, just to the north, tiny **San Quirico** (or SS Quirico e Giulietta), is less interesting, but is thought to be among the oldest of Siena's religious foundations, having almost certainly been built on the site of a pagan temple. Much of the present building dates from the seventeenth century, but parts of a thirteenth-century church survive, not least the present church's fine Romanesque portal.

# To San Sebastiano

If you return the short distance to San Niccolò al Carmine, it's well worth heading north on Pian dei Mantellini and **Via del Fosso di Sant'Ansano**, a pretty walk on an unexpected country lane above terraced vineyards and allotments. It eventually emerges at the Selva (Wood) *contrada*'s square, **museum** and church of **San Sebastiano**, a surprisingly quiet backwater of the city given its proximity to the Duomo – climb the stepped and atmospheric Vicolo di San Girolamo from here and you come out right in front of the cathedral.

Alternatively, from Sant'Agostino, you could cut back to the Campo along **Via Giovanni Duprè**, where the *Onda* (wave or dolphin) *contrada* has its base at no. 111; to visit the **museum** you need to make an appointment at least a week in advance (see box on p.261 for contact details). The *Onda* church is the **Oratorio di San Giuseppe**, at the Sant'Agostino end of the street, another pleasant and peaceful corner of the city with some fine **views**. The oratorio has a bust (1653) of its eponymous saint above the door, and a pleasing octagonal cupola attributed to Baldassarre Peruzzi (see above).

# Terzo di Camollia

The **Terzo di Camollia** district sits astride Siena's great northern spur and is centred on the ancient **Banchi di Sopra**, a major shopping street and one of the principal arteries linking the Campo to the city's periphery. Two major piazzas interrupt the street's lively march north: Piazza Tolomei and Piazza Salimbeni, both lined with interesting palaces and close to several of the many small churches (most, sadly, only irregularly open) that characterize this part of the city.

At the Terzo's eastern and western margins, like sentinels on the city's outer slopes, are two great churches, **San Francesco** and **San Domenico**, the mother churches of the most important medieval religious orders, the Dominicans and the Franciscans. Each of the vast brick piles has an important association with Siena's major saints, the latter with **Catherine**, the former with **Bernardino**. Catherine is the city's great saint, much loved and venerated. Her major shrine in the city, a chapel in San Domenico, was decorated by Sodoma, one of the leading artists of his day.

Sodoma's work is just one of San Domenico's artistic treasures, all of which are somewhat lost within the church's vast and rather austere interior. Much the same goes for San Francesco, where frescoes by the Lorenzettis, among others, are the main lure. Alongside San Francesco is the **Oratorio di San Bernardino**, relatively unknown but well worth visiting for a fresco cycle by Sodoma and Domenico Beccafumi. Also here are paintings on the life of St Bernardino, whose pilgrim trail in Siena leads out of the city to the north, to the **Osservanza** monastery, his principal retreat.

The obvious way to see the area is to explore Banchi di Sopra, then the streets to the east, including San Francesco, and then, if time is tight, to backtrack to Banchi di Sopra and see San Domenico, perhaps visiting the birthplace of St Catherine en route to the centre. For a flavour of the city's more workaday life, head to the **north** of the Terzo di Camollia, a quieter residential quarter, home to more modern squares and streets such as Piazza Antonio Gramsci and La Lizza, the main bus terminal and site of the city's large Wednesday **market** respectively. To the west, oenophiles shouldn't overlook the **Fortezza di Santa Barbara**, best known for the Enoteca Italiana, a dynamic wine institution that contains examples of virtually every Italian wine.

# Banchi di Sopra

**Banchi di Sopra** is one of Siena's key streets, running through the heart of the north of the medieval quarter. It boasts some of the city's best shops, is the major thoroughfare for the evening *passeggiata* and has a couple of palace-edged squares – **Piazza Tolomei** and **Piazza Salimbeni** – that stand comparison with those of any Tuscan town. Like most Italian streets, it also has its share of easily missed diversions and sights, not least *Nannini* near its southern junction with Via di Città and Banchi di Sotto. Owned by one of Siena's leading modern business dynasties, this institution has long been the city's pre-eminent bar, café and social meeting place (outside the Campo). Although it's perhaps not quite what it was, it still makes an excellent refuelling stop before you start your exploration of the northern city.

## Piazza Tolomei

**Piazza Tolomei** opens off Banchi di Sopra to the right as you walk up the street and is heralded by an easily missed column topped by a statue (1620) of the She-wolf suckling the twins Romulus and Remus, an allusion to the city's legendary foundation (see p.228). On your right rises the three-storey **Palazzo Tolomei**, Siena's oldest and most beautiful palace. It was begun in 1205, and the upper two storeys, with their simple but beautifully elegant windows, were refashioned in 1277. The Tolomei were one of Siena's richest medieval families, a banking dynasty that for centuries was locked in rivalry with the Salimbeni, whose palace lies a short distance up the street (see below). When the palace was built, times were less amenable than they would be a hundred years or so later, and the building has the unmistakable aspect of a fortress; the family would have lived on the upper two floors and the ground floor would have been given over to an armoury and a sizeable corps of guards. Banking riches would make the family virtual overlords of this district for three hundred years. Notice the three half moons over the main door, which signify that the family took part in, or helped finance, three Crusades.

On the opposite, eastern, side of the square is **San Cristoforo**, a church with Romanesque origins that was almost completely rebuilt in 1720 and has a Neoclassical facade added in 1800. The two statues on the facade represent beatifics Bernardo and Nera Tolomei, the former the founder of the Olivetan religious order and the great abbey of Monte Oliveto Maggiore south of Siena. In the days before the building of the Palazzo Pubblico, the church was used as a meeting place for the *comune*. Its opening hours are fluid and its paintings not always on display, but if you're lucky you'll be able to get in and see *St George and the Dragon* (first altar on the south, or right wall), a delightful work attributed to Sano di Pietro. The high altar contains an accomplished sculptural ensemble (1693) by the Baroque sculptor Giovanni Antonio Mazzuoli; at its heart is another depiction of Beato Bernardo Tolomei. The *Madonna and Child with Saints Luca and Romualdo* (1508/1518–20) on the second altar on the right is by Girolamo del Pacchia (1477–1535), whose work alongside Sodoma and Beccafumi you may well see later in the Oratorio di San Bernardino (see p.284).

Outside the church, and down the atmospheric Via del Moro to its left (behind the apse of San Cristoforo), are the remains of a small cloister, still with hints of its ancient Romanesque origins. Note the small stone tomb at the centre of the apse, dedicated to *Deo di Ciecho di Misere Angioliere*, the son of Cecco Angiolieri, a highly celebrated poet and contemporary of Dante.

**16**

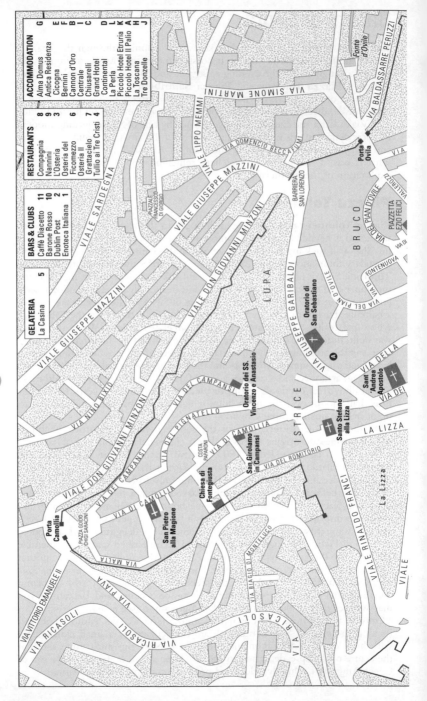

**ACCOMMODATION**

| | |
|---|---|
| Alma Domus | G |
| Antica Residenza | E |
| Cicogna | F |
| Bernini | B |
| Cannon d'Oro | I |
| Centrale | C |
| Chiusarelli | D |
| Grand Hotel | L |
| Continental | K |
| La Perla | A |
| Piccolo Hotel Etruria | H |
| Piccolo Hotel Il Palio | J |
| La Toscana | |
| Tre Donzelle | |

**RESTAURANTS**

| | |
|---|---|
| Compagnia | 8 |
| Nannini | 9 |
| L'Osteria | 3 |
| Osteria del Ficomezzo | 6 |
| Osteria Il Grattacielo | 7 |
| Tullio ai Tre Cristi | 4 |

**BARS & CLUBS**

| | |
|---|---|
| Caffè Diacetto | 11 |
| Barone Rosso | 10 |
| Dublin Post | 2 |
| Enoteca Italiana | 1 |

**GELATERIA**

| | |
|---|---|
| La Casina | 5 |

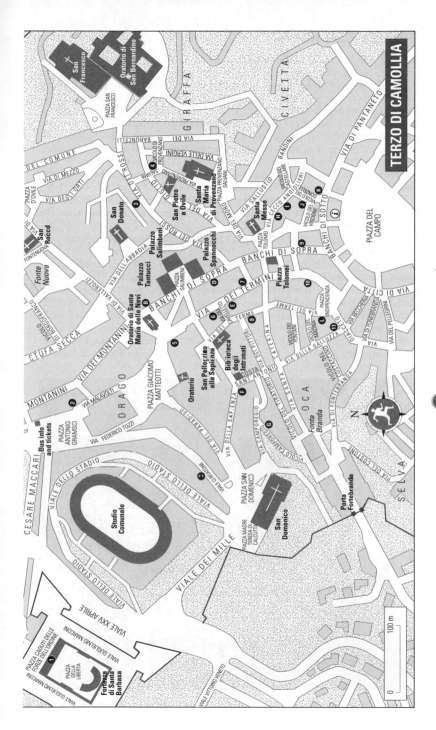

TERZO DI CAMOLLIA

16

279

## Piazza Salimbeni

At first glance, **Piazza Salimbeni** appears to be the superior of Piazza Tolomei, a majestic ensemble of palaces around an ordered medieval square. In fact, the medieval effect is largely contrived, for most of the piazza's fabric, including many of the palaces, was rebuilt or restored in neo-Gothic style in the nineteenth century. On the east side of the piazza, the Palazzo Salimbeni, the palace of the Salimbeni banking family, dates from the fourteenth century, but was almost entirely rebuilt after falling into virtual ruin in 1879. Much the same goes for the Renaissance-style **Palazzo Spannochi** on the south side, restored in 1880 but built in 1473 to a design by Giuliano da Maiano, brother of Benedetto, architect of the similar Palazzo Strozzi in Florence, for which this palace was the prototype. The **Palazzo Tantucci** on the north side dates from 1548, and the statue (1882) at the centre portrays Sallustio Bandini, an eminent Sienese economist, the work of Tito Sarrocchi, the sculptor responsible for the copy of the Fonte Gaia in the Campo.

Since the fifteenth century, the square has been the major power base of the **Monte dei Paschi di Siena**, not only one of Siena's, but one of Italy's foremost financial institutions. Banking was at the heart of medieval Sienese wealth, the town capitalizing on its position on the Via Francigena, the "French road" between Rome and northwest Europe, and the main road between Rome and Florence and Bologna. Sienese banking families go back to the twelfth century and by the end of the thirteenth they were trading widely in France, Germany, Flanders, England and along the Danube, where they maintained networks of corresponding dealers. Activity declined after the Black Death, but in the fifteenth century the Republic set up the Monte dei Paschi di Siena as

△ Piazza Salimbeni, Siena

a lending and charitable institution, to combat the abuses of usury. It consolidated its role under Medici rule and slowly moved into activities more strictly connected with banking. In the twentieth century it merged with other Tuscan and Umbrian banks and further extended its influence.

To appreciate the role of the Monte in Siena you need to tour the building. In 1972, the bank undertook a **radical restructuring**, encasing the building's interior medieval and Renaissance features within an ultra-modern, high-tech framework. This is a sight in itself, the amazing staircase in particular, but it also provides a wonderful showcase for the bank's **art collection** – the bulk of which is housed in the deconsecrated church of San Donato, linked by an underground passage with other parts of the palace complex. The paintings here include some of the finest Gothic works in Siena, among them an exquisitely coloured *Madonna* by Giovanni di Paolo, a *Pietà* by the Maestro dell'Osservanza, Sassetta's *Sant'Antonio Abate*, a *Deposition* by Sano di Pietro and a *Crucifixion* by Pietro Lorenzetti. Also displayed are later works by Beccafumi (including an eerie *St Lucy*), Rutilio Manetti and Bernardino Mei, plus a series of paintings depicting the Palio and its sixteenth-century bullfighting precursor in the Campo.

The bank publicly exhibits its art collections during banking hours by **appointment** only (details from the tourist office). With any luck, you will be shown the archives and major halls of the bank, as well as the paintings, and the visit ends with a trip up to the tower for a view over the Campo.

# Oratorio di Santa Maria delle Nevi

Away from the bustle of Banchi di Sopra, the quiet, mainly medieval streets leading east to San Francesco are more tangled than the relatively ordered grids south and southeast of the Campo. First stop should be the small **Oratorio di Santa Maria delle Nevi**, dedicated to Our Lady of the Snows. It has been "temporarily closed" for restoration on and off for over fifteen years, plans to turn it into a small museum apparently on indefinite hold.

The oratorio dates from 1470, when it was commissioned by the then bishop of Pienza and Montalcino, towns in the Sienese republic, and designed by the Sienese-born **Francesco di Giorgio Martini** (1439–1502). A consummate Renaissance man, Martini was a painter (he worked on the pavement of the Duomo and has several paintings in the Pinacoteca Nazionale), a sculptor (see his *St John the Baptist* in the Museo dell'Opera), architect, miner, writer and – above all – a civil and military engineer who transformed the science of fortification. The great Duke of Urbino, Federico da Montefeltro, would commission 136 defensive and other architectural works from him, including parts of Urbino's Palazzo Ducale, one of Italy's foremost Renaissance palaces. He is also credited with exploding the world's first mine (to help breach the walls of a Tuscan castle in 1495), and designed Santa Maria del Calcinaio in 1485, his architectural masterpiece, at Cortona, central Italy's finest Renaissance church.

His work in the oratory, while more modest, has a pleasing simplicity, best seen on the facade and in the understated interior, where the subtle curves of the vaulting deliberately echo and frame the superb altarpiece (though at the time of writing it had been transferred to the Pinacoteca). The work of Matteo di Giovanni, it depicts the *Madonna della Neve* (1477), a subject that recalls the snow miraculously created by the Madonna in the middle of a Roman summer. The falling snow allegedly marked the outlines of the church that would become

16

Santa Maria Maggiore, one of Rome's quartet of major basilical churches. In time, the snow in such paintings came to symbolize the purity of the Virgin (the fairy-tale of Snow White adopts this association), though the predella of this particular work still contains three scenes illustrating the legend of the origins of Santa Maria Maggiore, including depictions of Rome itself. The main painting has some delightful, if incongruous, details, notably angels presenting the Madonna with bowls of snow and, in the background, cherubs rolling snowballs.

# San Donato to San Francesco

Turn right (east) beyond the oratory down Via di Vallerozzi, then first right on Via dell'Abbadia, and you come to **San Donato**, or, more properly, San Michele al Monte di San Donato, which dates from 1119, when it was built as the Abbazia, or Abbadia di San Michele – hence the name of the street. It soon passed to the Vallombrosan order (whose coat of arms is one of the two at the entrance to the church), and (in 1565) to the Cavalieri di Santo Stefano, whose arms (two red crosses on a white background) can also be seen on the facade. By 1682 it was in the hands of the Carmelites, who transformed much of the church. Immediately on the right, or south, wall in the interior are some early fragments of fresco, possibly from the church's twelfth-century incarnation. The main artistic highlight, however, is a Pietà, sculpted from a single piece of walnut by Vecchietta. A vivid, almost expressionistic work, it shows the obvi-ous influence of Donatello (notably his Mary Magdalene in Florence's Museo dell'Opera), who worked in Siena in the 1420s and between 1457 and 1459.

A short walk east onto Via dei Rossi (turn left) and then Via San Pietro Ovile (first right) brings you to another church that is all too often closed, **San Pietro a Ovile**, begun in the thirteenth century and probably the first base of the Franciscans in the city before their own church was built a short distance to the east (see opposite). Inside, the right wall of the apse contains fresco fragments, probably by Bartolo di Fredi, while above the altar is a fifteenth-century painted Cross by Giovanni di Paolo. Two sublime wooden sculptures that graced the top of the north aisle are "temporarily" in the Museo dell'Opera, and depict the Madonna and St John the Evangelist (probably sculpted around 1415). The work of Domenico dei Cori, who went on to carve the celebrated choir in the chapel of the Palazzo Pubblico (see p.235), they were probably intended for the Duomo, but, after various vicissitudes, found their way to San Pietro. Moving down the north aisle towards the door you pass more early fresco fragments of an *Annunciation* and a copy of a *Maestà* painted for the church in 1350 by the anonymous Maestro di San Pietro a Ovile.

A couple of twists and turns through one of Siena's quietest corners brings you to **Santa Maria di Provenzano**, a church from 1564 whose consider-able size in an otherwise cramped area comes as a surprise, as does its ornate Renaissance and Baroque facade, a rare thing in a predominantly medieval city. Much loved by the Sienese, it owes its fame to a terracotta statue of the Virgin on the high altar, the Madonna del Provenzano, said to have miraculous powers. Numerous ex-votos nearby are testimony to its supposed efficacy, which is said in part to derive from the fact that it once adorned the home of one of Siena's greatest heroes, Provenzano Salviani, the victorous leader at the Battle of Montaperti in 1260, when Siena defeated the Florentines. Unfortunately for devotees, the statue has been dated to around two hundred years after the battle, a fact that has never seemed to worry the Sienese. So powerful is the cult of this Madonna that the second **Palio**, the one held on July 2, has been run in her honour since 1656 (the August Palio has far earlier origins).

Given the victory at Montaperti over Florence, it is ironic that the **pavement** (1685) at the centre of the nave, another major attraction of the church, should bear, at its heart, the arms of Florence's Medici, Siena's and Tuscany's eventual rulers. Elsewhere, look out for the *Messa di San Cerbone* (1630) midway down the right (south) wall, one of the masterpieces of Rutilio Manetti, Siena's leading seventeenth-century artist.

A short distance north – but only worth the detour if you have plenty of time – is one of the city's fountains, the **Fonte Nuova**. A further, highly picturesque fountain, the **Fonte d'Ovile**, can be seen outside the Porta Ovile, a hundred metres or so beyond. Both were built at the end of the twelfth century. Near the Fonte Nuova, in Via di Vallerozzi, is the church of **San Rocco**, home of the Lupa (She-wolf) *contrada*; its museum is at nos. 71–73 (visits by appointment; see p.260 for contact details).

# San Francesco

St Bernardino, born in the year of Catherine's death, began his preaching life at the chill monastic church of **San Francesco**, founded in 1326 on the site of an earlier church from 1228. It was completed around 1475 under the direction of Francesco di Giorgio Martini, whose work you may have seen earlier at the Oratorio di Santa Maria delle Nevi. A huge, hall-like structure, similar to that of the Dominicans' San Domenico, it was heavily restored after damage by fire in 1655 and subsequent use as a barracks. Work between 1894 and 1913 to restore the church to its "original" state further compromised its appearance and atmosphere.

It's therefore hard now to imagine how the church would once have looked, its pavement adorned with tombs, its walls probably almost completely covered in frescoes, banners and coats of arms. Only hints of the decoration remain, beginning on the **west wall** to the right and left of the main door. As you face the wall, high on the left is a detached fresco under a vast canopy, its choir of angels part of an almost vanished *Coronation of the Virgin* (begun 1447) by Sassetta that once decorated the city's original Porta Romana. It was completed in 1450 by Sano di Pietro, a pupil of Sassetta, after the master contracted a fatal chill while working outdoors on the fresco.

Lower down, to the right and left of the door, are the **tombs of the Salimbeni**, the great banking and dynastic rivals of the Tolomei, whose tombs are elsewhere in the church (see below). As in Florence's Santa Croce, another Franciscan church, San Francesco contains many graves of the rich and famous, especially the rich, who sought to be buried among the "humble" Franciscans as a form of penance and heavenly insurance policy: for one thing, usury, the basis of their banking business, was then still considered a sin by the Church. Also to the right of the door, high up, is a fresco of the *Nativity* (1531) by Sodoma, detached from Siena's Porta Pisini. In the corner to the right is an incongruously modern and hyper-realistic painting of Padre Pio (1998), recently sanctified and the most celebrated of latter-day Franciscans.

As you walk down the right (south) aisle, you pass a series of frescoes and fresco fragments, beginning in the first and second niches with anonymous images of the Visitation and various saints. At the end of the aisle you'll find

16

the fourteenth-century **Tomba dei Tolomei**, the best of the church's many funerary monuments. It houses various scions of the Tolomei, one of Siena's grandest medieval families, whose palace lies just off Banchi di Sopra (see p.277). The clan provided numerous of the city's bankers, as well as some of its leading churchmen, among them Bernardo Tolomei, founder of the abbey at Monte Oliveto Maggiore south of the city. Also buried here is Pia de' Tolomei, first wife of Baldo Tolomei, who came to live in Siena after his marriage to his second wife. Pia died, consumed with jealousy, in a castle in the Maremma, prompting Dante's famous reference to her in the *Purgatorio: Siena me fé, disfecemi Maremma* ("Siena made me, the Maremma unmade me").

Two more interesting **tombs** are found on the end wall of the right transept – those of the Garchi family and Angelo Salvetti, the latter a leading sixteenth-century Franciscan. The incised graffiti of the pavement (1541) and the two putti were created to a sketch by Beccafumi, the original of which survives in the Pinacoteca.

The second altar to the right of the high altar has (on the right wall) the *Tomb of Cristoforo Felici* (1462), the masterpiece of Urbano da Cortona, an accomplished disciple of Donatello. The two angels above the figure of Felici, head oddly tilted as if his tomb were too small, clearly echo Donatello's tomb of Giovanni de' Medici in the sacristy of San Lorenzo in Florence (see p.112). The chapel to the left contains a *Madonna and Child* (1398) by Andrea Vanni, best known for his contemporary portrait of St Catherine of Siena in San Domenico (see p.284). This is also an arresting image, made more striking by the obvious damage suffered in the fire of 1655.

The church's remaining major works of art are its most prestigious, starting with a *Crucifixion* (1331) by **Pietro Lorenzetti**, a fresco removed from the chapterhouse of the adjoining convent and now in the first chapel to the left of the high altar. Lorenzo Ghiberti, creator of Florence's celebrated baptistery doors, praised this painting above all others by Lorenzetti for its compositional and emotional impact. The chapel to the left, that is, the third chapel to the left of the high altar, has frescoes worked on jointly by Pietro and Ambrogio Lorenzetti, one depicting *St Louis of Toulouse Becoming a Franciscan* and the other a graphic *Martyrdom of Six Franciscans at Ceuta in Morocco*. They, too, were brought to the chapel from the chapterhouse, all that remains of an entire fresco cycle devoted to St Louis, who renounced the French throne to become a Franciscan. The final chapel on the right contains an accomplished *Madonna and Child* (1400), the Madonna occupying a particularly ornate throne, a painting attributed to Jacopo di Mino.

# Oratorio di San Bernardino

In the piazza to the right of San Francesco as you face the church, adjoining the cloisters, is the **Oratorio di San Bernardino** (mid-March to Oct Mon–Sat 10.30am–1.30pm & 3–5.30pm; €3; joint tickets see p.224). The best artworks here – definitely worth the admission – are in the beautifully wood-panelled upper chapel: fourteen large frescoes by Sodoma, Beccafumi and Girolamo del Pacchia illustrating the *Life of the Virgin*, painted between 1496 and 1518 when Sodoma and Beccafumi were Siena's leading painters. In the lower chapel are seventeenth-century scenes by minor artists of San Bernadino's life, which was taken up by incessant travel throughout Italy, preaching against usury, denouncing

16

## L'Osservanza

If your interest in Bernardino extends to a short pilgrimage, take bus #12 from Piazza Antonio Gramsci to Madonnina Rossa (10–15min), from where it's a short walk uphill to the monastery of **L'Osservanza** (daily 9am–1pm & 4–7pm). Bernardino founded the monastery in 1423 in an attempt to restore the original Franciscan rule, by then corrupted in the cities. Much rebuilt since, the monastery has a small museum devoted to the saint and a largely Renaissance church, whose features include an Andrea della Robbia *Annunciation* and a triptych by Sano di Pietro.

the political strife between the Italian city-states and urging his audience to look for inspiration to the monogram of Christ (the "IPS" that you see all over the city, most notably on the Palazzo Pubblico). Sermons in the Campo, it is said, frequently went on for the best part of a day. His actual political influence was fairly marginal, but he was canonized within six years of his death in 1444, and remains one of the most famous of all Italian preachers. His dictum on rhetoric – "make it clear, short and to the point" – was rewarded in the 1980s with his adoption as the patron saint of advertising.

Attached to the Oratorio is the **Museo Diocesano** (same hours and tickets), containing an array of devotional art from the thirteenth to the seventeenth centuries; the pieces are beautifully displayed, but as a collection it ranks well below the Museo dell'Opera del Duomo.

# North to Porta Camollia

North of Piazza Salimbeni, Banchi di Sopra changes name to **Via dei Montanini** and then **Via di Camollia**, and runs through the less visited parts of the Terzo di Camollia, uninspiring by Sienese standards, but good for regular shopping and largely local-filled bars and restaurants. Via dei Montanini makes for a more pleasant walk than the parallel Via Federico Tozzi and La Lizza to the west, both devoted more or less entirely to the **bus terminal** on and around Piazza Antonio Gramsci.

First stop on Via dei Montanini is **Sant'Andrea Apostolo**, only intermittently open (like all the churches in this district), a building of Romanesque origins that was reordered to dull effect in the eighteenth century. Only a few fragments of fresco survive, notably in the second altar space on the right, with a *Madonna and Child and St Anna* attributed to Martino di Bartolomeo (active 1389–1434), discovered during restoration work in 1959. The key work is the church's high altarpiece, a rather good triptych of the *Coronation of the Virgin with St Peter and St Andrew* (1445) by Giovanni di Paolo. As you leave the church, note the delightful anonymous fifteenth-century bas-relief of the *Madonna and Child* to the right of the door.

A few steps beyond Sant'Andrea Apostolo, the short detour east on Via Giuseppe Garibaldi to the **Oratorio di San Sebastiano**, built in 1492 and altered in the 1650s, is only recommended if you have a passion for seventeenth-century Sienese art, represented here by a number of paintings (most depicting the life of St Sebastian) by Rutilio Manetti and less-accomplished contemporaries such as Pietro Sorri. An even shorter detour west on Via dei Galluzzini brings you to the small church of **Santo Stefano alla**

**Lizza**, founded in the twelfth century and rebuilt in 1675; sadly, at the time of writing, it was firmly bolted and looked almost derelict, and yet it is the rightful home of one of the great Sienese altarpieces, a *Maestà* (1400) by Andrea Vanni.

## Via di Camollia

Back on Via di Camollia, you can detour briefly again northeast on Via Campansi to the **Oratorio dei SS Vincenzo e Anastasio**, property of the Istrice (Porcupine) *contrada* and part of a much larger thirteenth-century architectural ensemble. The ancient facade is plain to the point of being bare, while the interior (see the *contrada* feature on p.261 for contact details for an appointment) contains several precious works of art, including a *Madonna and Child with Saints* by Sano di Pietro and, more notably, an anonymous detached fresco (removed from the facade) of *Christ Pantocrator*, or Christ in the act of blessing. It dates from the early thirteenth century and is believed to be among the oldest, if not *the* oldest, painting in Siena.

Returning to Via di Camollia and continuing north, you come to **San Girolamo in Campansi** on the left, a deconsecrated Francisan monastery from 1420. It is sometimes possible to see the courtyard, at the rear of which is a fresco fragment of an *Annunciation* (1460) by Sano di Pietro, and to visit the first floor of the ex-monastery, where there is a fresco of the *Madonna and Child with Saints* attributed to Beccafumi.

A little way beyond, a short street leads left and down to the **Chiesa di Fontegiusta** (1482–84), built in honour of the Sienese victory at Poggio Imperiale in 1479. The doorway (1489) on the simple Renaissance facade is by Urbano da Cortona, whose much-earlier *Tomb of Cristoforo Felici* you may have seen in San Francesco (see p.284). Above it is a pleasing bas-relief of the *Madonna and Child* attributed to Giovanni di Stefano (1444–1511), best known for his work in the Baptist's chapel in the Duomo. The most beautiful fresco here is on the first altar on the left, *The Sybil Announces the Birth of Christ to the Emperor Augustus* (1528), the work of Sienese Baldassare Peruzzi, better known as an architect (he worked in Rome with Raphael). Peruzzi lived nearby at Via di Camollia 176, almost opposite the simple Lombard-Romanesque church of **San Pietro alla Magione**, built for the Templars, perhaps as early as the tenth century. It later passed to the Knights of Malta, hence Via Malta immediately to its right. The pleasing main facade is clearly ancient in origin, but has an overlarge Gothic door added later, and a still-more incongruous Renaissance chapel tacked on to the right.

**Porta Camollia**, guardian of the road to Florence, bears the famous inscription on its outer arch *Cor magis tibi Sena pandit* – "Siena opens her heart to you wider than this gate." It was here that a vastly superior Florentine force was put to flight in 1526, following the traditional Sienese appeal to the Virgin.

# La Lizza and the Fortezza

Away to the west of Via di Camollia and Via dei Montanini are the gardens of **La Lizza**, laid out in 1779 and taken over on Wednesdays by the town's large market (see p.308). The gardens run almost to the walls of the **Fortezza**

**Medicea**, or **Fortezza di Santa Barbara** (free access). The fortress was built initially by Charles V after the siege of 1554–55, but was subsequently torn down by the people, and rebuilt by Cosimo I, who then moved his troops into the garrison. Its Medicean walls resemble the walls of Lucca, designed by the same architect. Occasional summer concerts are held within the fort, which is also a permanent home to the wine collections and bar of the Enoteca Italiana (see p.303).

# San Domenico

The Dominicans founded their monastery in the city in 1125. Its church, **San Domenico** (daily: April–Oct 7am–1pm & 3–6.30pm; Nov–March 9am–1pm & 3–6pm), was begun in 1226, completed in 1254 and greatly enlarged in 1300. In 1467, when Siena perfected the art of the colossal supporting arch, the vast wall that had previously separated the old nave from the newer transepts was removed, creating, more or less, today's huge and largely Gothic building, typical of the size and austerity of this preaching and militaristic order. Arches that might have blocked a congregation's view of the all-important preacher were avoided where possible.

The church's association with Saint Catherine is immediately asserted. On the right as you enter, at the rear of the church, is a raised area, the **Cappella delle Volte**. The leftmost of three paintings here is a contemporary portrait of the saint by Andrea Vanni, who, according to tradition, captured her likeness from life during one of her ecstasies in 1414. Vanni was both a painter (apprenticed to Lippo Memmi) and diplomat and leading member of the *comune*, but left his civic job on meeting Catherine, becoming her friend and disciple. Below are steps and a niche, where she supposedly received the stigmata, took on the Dominican habit, and performed several of her miracles. Moving down the right (south wall) you come to a glass case (right of a small door) holding various relics, including the thumb of Catherine's right hand and one of the flails she used for self-mortification. The saint's own chapel, the **Cappella di Santa Caterina** (erected in 1488), is beyond the door, located midway down the right (south) side of the church. Its entrance arch bears images of saints Luke and Jerome by Sodoma, while the marble tabernacle on the high altar (1466), the work of Sassetta's son, Giovanni di Stefano, encloses a reliquary containing Catherine's head (most of the rest of her is in Rome). The church's highlights – frescoes by Sodoma (1526) – occupy the walls to the left and right of the chapel's altar and, respectively, depict her swooning and in ecstasy. Sadly, though, their distance from the viewer and the arrangement of the chapel make them difficult to see.

Left of the chapel, above the stairs that lead to the crypt, the large, eye-catching painting is a fine *Adoration of the Shepherds* (1479) by **Francesco di Giorgio Martini**, the leading military architect of his day. His skills as an architect, among many others, are reflected in the ruined triumphal arch in the painting's background. The same skills are also evident in the variety of small buildings ranged across the picture's rural scenes, notably a church on a Greek-cross plan, not dissimilar to his architectural masterpiece, the Renaissance church of the Calcinaio in Cortona, eastern Tuscany.

The church's next notable painting is on the right wall of the first chapel to the right of the high altar: a Matteo di Giovanni **triptych** of the *Madonna* *and Child with SS Jerome and John the Baptist*. The three-part painting was once part of a polyptych, wantonly dismembered at some point – ornate columns would originally have separated the panels. The original lunette is in the Pinacoteca, and three predella panels languish in American collections. As ever in the paintings of Matteo, there is something vaguely unsettling at work, though not to the extent evident in his *Massacre of the Innocents* in Santa Maria dei Servi.

The **high altar** boasts a fine marble tabernacle and two sculpted angels (1465) by the sculptor and architect Benedetto da Maiano, best known for the Palazzo Strozzi in Florence. The **first chapel** to the left of the high altar has a detached fresco of the *Madonna and Child, John the Baptist and Knight* by Pietro Lorenzetti. Also here is a predella by Sodoma depicting the *Fifteen Mysteries of the Rosary*, though note that both the freestanding paintings (the Lorenzetti and Sodoma works) are sometimes moved to other points in the church.

Matteo di Giovanni reappears in the **second chapel** to the left of the main altar, which houses *St Barbara, Angels and SS Catherine of Alexandria and Mary Magdalene* surmounted by an *Epiphany*, considered the artist's masterpiece. Note the tower, invariably included in paintings of Barbara – her father imprisoned her in a tower, angry at her faith; also note the wheel beneath St Catherine (not, in this instance, the Sienese Catherine), the instrument of her martyrdom (hence the "Catherine Wheel" firework). Not in the same league, but diverting all the same, is Rutilio Manetti's *St Anthony Abbot Liberates a Possessed* (fourth altar on the left, or north, wall), the expelled demons streaming into the sky from the exorcised protagonist.

## St Catherine of Siena

**St Catherine** was born Caterina Benincasa, the youngest (it is alleged) of twenty-four children of a dyer, Jacopo, and his wife, Lapa, on March 25, 1347 (1333 in some sources) – Annunciation Day. She had her first visions aged 5 or 6 and took the veil at 8 (16 in some versions), against strong family opposition, not least when they attempted to marry her off at the age of 12. She spent three years in silent contemplation, before experiencing a mystical "Night Obscure". In 1362 she entered a Dominican convent, imposing on herself the strictest of regimes, leaving her cell, it is said, only to go to Mass. Thereafter she went out into the turbulent, post–Black Death city, devoting herself to the poor and sick, and finally turning her hand to politics. She prevented Siena and Pisa joining Florence in rising against Pope Urban V (then absent in Avignon), and proceeded to bring him back to Rome. It was a fulfilment of the ultimate Dominican ideal – a union of the practical and intensely mystical and devotional life, though the saint's political influence and dealings have often been exaggerated. Her attempts to reconcile Florence to the papacy, for example, were repudiated by the Florentines. Catherine returned to Siena to a life of contemplation, visions and stigmata, retaining a political role in her attempts to reconcile the later schism between the popes and anti-popes. All her ideas, and her *Dialogue* and letters, were imparted through dictation or preaching – she never learned to write. She died in Rome in 1380 and was buried in the city in Santa Maria sopra Minerva, but her head found its way back to Siena. She was canonized in 1460 by Pius II, the fact that Pius was a Sienese pope being not entirely coincidental (the scene is portrayed in the Libreria Piccolomini). She joined St Francis as a patron saint of Italy in 1939. John Paul II declared her co-patron of Europe, no less, in 1999. Her symbols are the lily, a crown of thorns, a crucifix and, sometimes, a heart and the flail with which she mortified her flesh. Her feast day – April 30 until 1969 – is now April 29.

# Casa di Santa Caterina and around

St Catherine's family home is just south of San Domenico, down the hill off Costa Sant'Antonio, the **Casa** and **Santuario di Santa Caterina** (daily 9am–12.30pm & 3–6pm; free), though the building has been much adapted, with a Renaissance loggia and a series of oratories – one on the site of her cell. The paintings here are mostly unexceptional Baroque canvases, but it is the life that is important: an extraordinary career that made her Italy's patron saint and among the earliest women to be canonized (see box, p.288).

Near the Santuario is the church of **Santa Caterina**, home of the Oca (goose) *contrada* (☎0577.285.413, ✇www.contradadelloca.it) – known as *gli infami* ("the infamous ones") after its record number of Palio victories. The Casa, Santuario and church are best reached from San Domenico by a panoramic little walk down Via Camporegio and then the stepped alley of Vicolo Camporegio. This route allows you to see the best-preserved of Siena's several fountains, the **Fonte Branda**, which is recorded as early as 1081, though much of the present structure dates from 1246 and after, some of it the work of Giovanni di Stefano, also responsible for one of the Duomo's pavement panels. It's a peaceful and moderately picturesque spot, with views to the south of the ridges and bastions supporting Piazza del Duomo, reached from here by the steeply climbing and rather daunting Via del Costone. Aided by the fountain's reliable water supply, this part of the city was an area for tanneries into the twentieth century. The fountain also features in Sienese folklore as the haunt of werewolves, who would throw themselves into the water at dawn to return to human form. Drinking the water, according to another legend, also causes madness in time.

# To San Pellegrino alla Sapienza

From the Casa e Santuario, walk east up Via della Sapienza or Via dei Pittori, pausing to look up and perhaps explore **Via della Galluzza**, one of Siena's most atmospheric streets, which climbs to the south. Via della Sapienza takes you past the **Biblioteca degli Intronati** (admission by appointment; contact the tourist office for details), founded in 1759 by Sallustio Bandini, one of the founding fathers of economic science, and the man whose statue stands in Piazza Salimbeni, a minute's walk or so up the street (see p.280). The Accademia degli Intronati, whose library this is, dates from 1425, when it was established as a literary (later musical and theatrical) academy. Its 300,000 books and 6000 manuscripts contain many rare works, including a copy of Dante's *Divina Commedia* with illustrations by Botticelli (1481) and (its main treasure) a tenth-century Byzantine copy of the Gospels from the imperial palace in Constantinople.

Continue east and you come to **San Pellegrino alla Sapienza**, on the corner of Via della Sapienza and Via delle Terme, which, like virtually all Sienese churches, has something to make a visit worthwhile – assuming, of course, that it's open and the paintings that should be in situ are actually present. The church dates from at least 1240, when it was first documented, and was enlarged in 1321 by Beato Andrea Gallerani, founder of the Opera della Misericordia, a charitable foundation that looked after orphans and cared for the elderly. The second niche on the right features his portrait: a fine work, possibly by Lippo Memmi, Andrea Vanni or Taddeo di Bartolo. Critics tend towards Memmi, a close collaborator of Simone Martini, evidence coming from the incised gold rays around the figure's head, strikingly similar to the effect used by Martini in his great *Annunciation* in the Uffizi (see p.80). Note the left arm of Gallerani's cloak, which bears the confraternity's symbol, an "M" (for "Misericordia") surmounted by a cross. Memmi or, more probably, his school, was also responsible for the picture of *St Paul* in the fifth niche on the right, and for the matching *St Peter* in the same niche on the opposite wall.

# Listings

# Listings

# Accommodation

A ccommodation in Siena tends to get booked up quickly. The city's history and geography limit its size and the numbers of buildings that can realistically be turned into hotels, so that there are insufficient beds in the historic centre to satisfy an ever-increasing demand. In addition, the large term-time population of students means that less expensive lodgings, particularly the city's 120 or so private rooms (*affittacamere*), are often block-booked for long periods. To make matters worse, there are only four one-star (the cheapest category) hotels, one campsite and one hostel. The busiest times are at Easter, around the Palio (July 2 and August 16), and in late August to October, when the pavement of the Duomo is usually uncovered. It's wise to book well in advance (around six months) if you're planning to visit any time between Easter and October.

Siena is very compact and no hotel in the historic centre is more than a few minutes' walk from the Campo. Note, however, that rooms in old medieval buildings are often small. Larger, more modern, hotels can be found on the outskirts of the city, often just inside or outside the walls. Another option is to base yourself just outside the city, in the Sienese countryside, where you'll find some of Tuscany's most sumptuous hotels – so sumptuous that you'll probably not want to leave them. Or you could plump for an inexpensive farm stay, or *agriturismo*, where you'll often have the option of self-catering. Any accommodation outside the city, however, presents the problem of access, since approaches by car, bus or train are necessarily slow (see p.223).

If you arrive without a booking, and find that all the establishments listed below are full, make your way to the **Siena Hotels Promotion** booth (Mon–Sat 9am–8pm; winter closes 7pm; ☎0577.288.084, ⓦwww.hotelsiena.com), opposite the church of San Domenico on Piazza Madre Teresa di Calcutta. The staff here are generally very helpful and can book rooms in any of the city's hotels. The city's second specialist agency, **Vacanze Senesi**, is situated in the tourist office in the Campo at no. 56 (Mon–Fri 9am–7pm; ☎0577.45.900, ⓦwww.vacanzesenesi.it). **Il Casato Booking Service** is another option, just off the Campo at Via del Casato di Sotto 12 (Mon–Sat 10.30am–6.30pm; ☎0577.46.091, ⓦwww.sienaholiday.com), where you can also buy bus tickets and rent bikes and cars.

For more general information on accommodation, see p.32. All accommodation reviewed in this section is located on a map: the map page-number is indicated at each listing.

# Hotels in Siena

**Antica Residenza Cicogna** Via dei Termini ☎0577.285.613, ⊛www.antica residenzacicogna.it (see map on pp.278–279). A new and little-known bed-and-breakfast option in a perfect location near the *Osteria del Ficomezzo*. The owner, Elisa Trefoloni, is charming, and there are five rooms, all frescoed, delightfully appointed and recently restored – the "Liberty" and "Leoni" rooms are especially nice. All have private bathroom. Breakfast is taken in an extraordinary, high-ceilinged room with colossal beams. Rooms, with breakfast for two, are a bargain at €78.

**Antica Torre** Via Fieravecchia 7 ☎ & ⨍0577.222.255, ⊛www.anticatorresiena .it (see map on pp.258–259). By far the most intimate of the three-star places, with eight smallish and simply, but comfortably, appointed rooms, each with private bathroom and beamed ceilings, squeezed into a tall and very narrow medieval tower dating from the sixteenth century. Rooms have satellite TV, but no air-conditioning. Top rooms are the only ones with any appreciable city views, but the backstreet location in the south of the city means that all rooms are quiet. Breakfast (€7) is served in a claustrophobic little area (a former pottery) in the depths of the building. Doubles with bathroom cost from €120.

**Bernini** Via della Sapienza 15 ☎ & ⨍0577.289.047, ⊛www.albergobernini.com (see map on pp.278–279). A far from prepossessing entrance conceals nine inexpensive and smallish, but well-maintained, rooms at €85, some (nos. 10 and 11 in particular) with views of the city. The one-star rooms are dated, and there's not much in the way of facilities (only two rooms have air-conditioning), but the location is central and quiet, most bathrooms newly renovated, and the owners, the Saracini family, run a relaxed and characterful establishment. Breakfast is extra, at €7, and credit cards are not accepted.

**Cannon d'Oro** Via Montanini 28 ☎0577.44.321, ⨍0577.280.868, ⊛www.cannondoro.com (see map on pp.278–279). A friendly, thirty-room two-star hotel hidden down an alleyway just beyond where Banchi di Sopra becomes Via Montanini. This is one of the better choices among the central mid-price hotels. Rooms cost from €90, and are a reasonable size, with plain walls and an eclectic mixture of fittings and furnishings (some have nice wrought-iron beds and stone walls): although simple, all are clean and well-maintained. Parking is available nearby for around €15.

**Centrale** Via Cecco Angiolieri 26 ☎0577.280.379, ⨍0577.42.152, ⊛hotelcentrale.siena@libero. it (see map on pp.278–279). Just seven large two-star rooms on an upper floor in a quiet street as central as the name suggests, a block north of the Campo. Doubles cost €75 (breakfast is an extra €6), and come with satellite TVs in the rooms and Internet access, but no air-conditioning.

**Chiusarelli** Viale Curtatone 15 ☎0577.280.562, ⊛www.chiusarelli.com (see map on pp.278–279). A nice old three-star Neoclassical villa, with 49 stolid, air-conditioned rooms from €117 (with breakfast) and a terrace and garden at the rear, which overlooks Siena's soccer stadium; but it's midway down a busy street near San Domenico and the bus station, so definitely ask for one of the back rooms, several of which are very large and comfortable. Recent restoration has spruced up the bathrooms a touch, restored the frescoes in some rooms and seen the arrival of rustic "arte povera" furniture. They're still a little functional, though. There's also a big adjoining restaurant under separate management open to non-patrons, and some private parking.

**Duomo** Via Stalloreggi 38 ☎0577.289.088, ⊛www.hotelduomo.it (see map on pp.258–259). A good, solid choice, with reliable, if unexceptional, rooms in a former twelfth-century palace from €130, including satellite TV and air-conditoning. The best of the fifteen rooms in the main hotel (there are another eight in the annexe at Via Stalloreggi 34) have small terraces and great views of the Duomo (ask for no. 54 or one of the "panoramic" rooms). Decor in some rooms has more than a hint of the 1970s, but the upper-floor rooms tend to be brighter and fresher. Rooms aside, this is the best-located of the city's three-star hotels. There's free parking in a nearby garage.

**Garibaldi** Via Giovanni Dupré 18 ☎0577.284.204 (see map on p.226). A good, no-nonsense two-star, with just seven bright, large rooms at €75, very well located above one of the city's better low-cost restaurants, just south of the Campo. Rooms have few facilities, and no TVs. Note that the hotel entrance is separate and to the left of the restaurant.

▽ Ballroom, *Grand Hotel Continental*

pp.278–279). This three-star hotel has forty rooms over five floors of a thirteenth-century townhouse, so may have space when other places are full. The location is atmospheric and central, on an alley behind Piazza Tolomei, and many of the public spaces have a grand medieval air, with vaulted ceilings and redoubtable iron chandeliers. The rooms, though, which start at €85, are more functional and uninspiring. Breakfast costs €8 and parking is available in the hotel's own garage.

🏃 **Palazzo Ravizza** Pian dei Mantellini 34 ☏0577.280.462, ⊛www.palazzoravizza.it (see map on pp.258–259). This elegant 35-room three-star, located in a pleasant area near San Niccolò al Carmine, has been run by the same family (the Grottanelli de' Santi) since opening for business in the 1920s, and has recently been renovated and freshened up without losing its considerable period charm. The rooms are sparingly and tastefully furnished with antiques, and paved with terracotta or parquet tiles, with ceiling frescoes, painted wood beams or small sitting areas in several of them. Some have delightful views of the countryside. In high season, reservations are usually accepted on a half-board basis only; at other times of the year they have doubles and beautiful suites (with Jacuzzis) from around €270 – a touch more than the place is worth. The little garden at the back is a charming place for afternoon tea. Some free parking is available – a not inconsiderable perk.

🏃 **Piccolo Hotel Etruria** Via Donzelle 3 ☏0577.288.088, ⊛www.hoteletruria. com (see map on pp.278–279). A very neat and central family-run two-star, and deservedly popular: advance booking for high season is a must if you want to secure one of its simple, functional and spotless nineteen rooms, recently renovated, with tasteful new, wooden built-in furnishings; all are equipped with satellite TV (but no air-conditioning) and cost €75, plus €5 for a simple breakfast. The little communal sitting area is a pleasant bonus. There are a further nine rooms in the annexe at Via delle Donzelle 10.

**Piccolo Hotel Il Palio** Piazza del Sale 19 ☏0577.281.131, ⊛www.piccolohotelilpalio.it (see map on pp.278–279). Perfectly located for bus and car arrivals, north of the centre, this fifteenth-century two-star hotel was a palace and monastery, and some of the common areas preserve their attractive

🏃 **Grand Hotel Continental** Via Banchi di Sopra 85 ☏0577.56.011, ⊛www .royaldemeure.com (see map on pp.278–279). For years Siena had no luxury five-star hotel – until the vastly expensive restoration of this former palace in a perfect location. The public spaces, especially the grand salon to the rear and left of the reception, are astounding, with superb frescoes and a large covered courtyard. The best rooms and suites are also exceptional – vast, entirely frescoed, and with stunning views of the Duomo. Other rooms are still excellent and superbly appointed, but mostly lack the fabulous period details you'll see in the brochures or on the website. The evening piano bar is a dubious afterthought, horribly out of keeping with the hotel's sense of taste and style. Otherwise this is first choice for a treat: be prepared to say goodbye to around €900 nightly, less for rooms under the eaves, or if you go through a tour operator.

**La Perla** Via delle Terme 25 ☏0577.47.144, ⓔinfo@albergolaperla.191.it (see map on pp.278–279). Just thirteen simple, clean rooms at €65, all with (very compact) bathrooms, in a quiet and appealing little central square, two blocks north of the Campo. This is one of the city's four one-star hotels, so don't expect much of the rooms – there are phones and heating, and that's about it.

**La Toscana** Via Cecco Angiolieri 12 ☏0577.46.097, Ⓕ0577.270.634 (see map on medieval vaulting. Its 26 rooms, costing around €110, are a touch on the small side, though all are clean and come with TV and phone (but not air-conditioning). The staff are friendly and helpful.

**Residenza d'Epoca Il Casato** Via Giovanni Dupré 126; also access via Via Casato di Sopra 33 ☎0577.236.001, ✺www.hotelrooms .it/casato (see map on pp.258–259). A "Residenza d'Epoca" is a specially listed historic building, in this case a frescoed and vaulted fifteenth-century palace and one of Siena's newest accommodation options. The rooms cost between €85 and €100, including breakfast, and are beautifully and simply appointed in period style, vaults and/or frescoes offsetting rich golden fabrics and dark-wood floors. All have private bathrooms, telephones and satellite TV. There is a glorious roof terrace and garden with fine city views.

**Tre Donzelle** Via Donzelle 5 ☎0577.280.358, ⓕ0577.223.933 (see map on pp.278–279). This one-star option right in the heart of town, just off Banchi di Sotto, north of the Campo, is one of Siena's oldest hotels, and it shows. The plain rooms are clean, but are badly in need of updating, and none has TV or air-conditioning. Some also have shared bathrooms, but with prices from €60 and the fine location, this remains an excellent budget option. As a result, it's often booked solid.

## Hotels outside Siena

**Certosa di Maggiano** Via Certosa 82 ☎0577.288.180, ✺www .certosadimaggiano.com. A former fourteenth-century monastery in secluded countryside 1km southeast of Siena, offering extremely stylish and luxurious comfort in just eighteen glorious rooms and suites (€594 plus per night). It's a favourite for honeymoons and romantic weekends, offering an alluring retreat from worldly affairs in its library cloister and tranquil terrace. There's a pool, tennis court, lovely gardens, olive groves, and – should you need it – a heli-pad.

**Santa Caterina** Via E S Piccolomini 7 ☎0577.221.105, ✺www.hscsiena.it. A nineteen-room three-star just outside the walls, fifteen minutes' walk from the Campo, on the street that leads out of town from Porta Romana. Rooms in what began life as an eighteenth-century villa cost €155 and have the advantages of air-conditioning, satellite TV and access to a wonderful garden (with a veranda for breakfast in summer) and parking. Some rooms have views of the unspoiled valley trailing away to the south. The service here is particularly gracious and friendly, and the owners are upgrading the hotel year on year.

**Villa Scacciapensieri** Via di Scacciapensieri 10 ☎0577.41.441, ✺www.villascacciapensieri.it. This family-run four-star country hotel 3km north of Siena is not quite in the *Certosa di Maggiano* league, but it's still classy, luxurious and impressive. Housed in a nineteenth-century villa, it is full of fine old antiques, paintings and beautiful carved ceilings. Its hilltop position means good views of Siena and the Chianti hills to the north, and the formal gardens and parkland provide a bucolic escape. Facilities include tennis courts and a pool. Expect to pay around €235 for one of the 31 rooms.

## Hostels

**Alma Domus** Via Camporegio 31 ☎0577.44.177 (see pp.278–279). This is a quiet, old one-star pilgrim hotel run by the nuns of Santa Caterina, with 27 rooms in a peaceful and rather panoramic position behind San Domenico (follow the signs), but it has the institutional feel of a hostel, not least because of the long, echoing corridors. A handful of rooms have been equipped with air-conditioning. Doubles start at €60, and triples and quads are available, all with private bathrooms. Curfew 11.30pm.

**Ostello della Gioventù "Guidoriccio"** Via Fiorentina 89, Lo Stellino ☎0577.52.212, ✺www.ostellionline.org. Rather sterile and uninspiring HI hostel with 111 beds, located 4km northwest of the centre. Take bus #15 from Piazza Gramsci, or, if you're coming

from Florence, ask to be let off at "Lo Stellino", just after the Siena city sign. It has
several double rooms, a restaurant (meals
from about €10) and bar. Curfew 11.30pm.
Beds cost €13.75, including a simple
breakfast. Doubles are €27.50.

## Campsite

**Campeggio Siena Colleverde Strada di Scaccia-
pensieri 47** ☎ 0577.280.044, ℗ 0577.333.298.
Secure, well-maintained campsite, 2km
north; take bus #8 from Piazza del Sale or
#3 from Piazza Gramsci. Places cost €7.75
per person. Shop, bar and pool. Mid-March
to mid-Nov.

## Long-stay accommodation

For long-stay budget accommodation, call in at the tourist office, which has lists
of **rooms** (*affittacamere*) available in private houses. These are offered mainly to
students, either at the university or on the numerous language and art courses
held in the city, but some are willing to offer shorter lets. They're certainly
worth a try if you're staying for a week or more; rates are around €25 per
person per night, usually for a shared room (less for long-term lets).

Another option is to arrange a let through one of the local *agriturismo* agencies; most rent out **villas** and **farmhouses**, as well as rooms or flats on farms
in the nearby countryside. Prices are usually very reasonable – from as little
as €20 per person per night. The majority offer self-catering, or half- and
full-board options, and many will have swimming pools and activities such as
riding. Siena-based companies include Agriturist Provinciale, Strada Massetana
Romana 50 (☎ 0577.47.669, ⓦ www.agrituristsiena.com), and Casa Club, Via
Veneto 41 (☎ 0577.44.041, ⓦ www.casa-club.com). The accommodation booklet issued by the tourist office has full lists of the *agriturismo* options in the area
and also contains a handful of self-catering apartments in the city.

(17)

# Eating and drinking

Siena feels a little provincial after Florence. The main action of an evening is the *passeggiata* from Piazza Matteotti along Banchi di Sopra to the Campo – and there's not much in the way of nightlife to follow. For most visitors, though, an evening in one of the city's **restaurants** provides diversion enough. While Siena may not possess restaurants to rival the finest in Florence – nothing close to the rarified atmosphere of the *Enoteca Pinchiorri*, for example – eating out has improved considerably in the last decade or so and there's a good choice of simple *osterie* and *trattorie*, as well as plenty of first-rate mid-range places that haven't completely surrendered to the demands of visitors.

**Café life**, however, is much poorer than in Florence, though in the mostly identical and over-priced bars of the Campo, Siena can at least boast one of Europe's great people-watching spots. Bite the bullet and pay over the odds at least once to enjoy the experience.

## Restaurants

Siena used to have a poor reputation for **restaurants**, but over the last few years things have looked up, with a range of imaginative *osterie* opening up and a general hike in standards. The only place where you need surrender gastronomic ideals is in the Campo: the posh restaurant here, *Il Campo*, isn't worth the money – though it's the one to go for if you want to eat in style in the square – which leaves a choice of routine but reasonably priced pizzerias. For cheaper, better-value meals, you'll generally do best walking out a little from the centre, west towards San Niccolò al Carmine, or north towards the Porta Camollia. Via di Pantaneto, in the southeast, also has several inexpensive pizzerias.

**Local specialities** include *pici* (noodle-like pasta with toasted breadcrumbs), *salsicce secche* (dried sausages), *finocchiona* (minced pork flavoured with fennel), *capolocci* (spiced loin of pork), *pappa col pomodoro* (bread and tomato soup), *tortino di carciofi* (artichoke omelette) and *fagioli all'uccelletto* (bean and sausage stew). The city is also famous for a whole range of **cakes and biscuits**, including the ubiquitous *panforte*, a dense and delicious wedge of nuts, fruit and honey that originated with pilgrimage journeys, *cavallucci* (aniseed, nut and spice biscuits), *copate* (nougat wafers) and rich, almond *ricciarelli* biscuits.

All the restaurants below are located on their relevant chapter maps. If you want a romantic meal out of town, then *Il Canto*, the small, exclusive restaurant of the *Certosa di Maggiano* hotel (see p.296) is the place, especially in summer, when you can dine outside. The experience will cost, however – reckon on between €60–85 per person for a meal.

## The Campo

All the restaurants below are located on the map on p.226.

**Le Campane Via delle Campane 6**
☎0577.284.035. High-quality Sienese cuisine at a small, relaxed restaurant with beamed ceiling and rugs on the floor, just west of the Campo. Meat dishes are available, but the menu is predominantly based around fish and seafood. The odd dish can be fussy: *spuma di carote con fonduta di percorino*, for example, is a carrot mousse with pecorino cream cheese. Starters and first courses come in at around €9 each, mains at €12–14. A plus here in summer is the chance to eat out on the small terrace. Closed Mon.

**Osteria Il Carroccio Via del Casato di Sotto 32** ☎0577.41.165. Just 50m from the Campo. A single, L-shaped,

▽ *Osteria Le Logge*

**Osteria Le Logge Via del Porrione 33** ☎0577.48.013. The best-looking restaurant in central Siena occupies a spacious old cabinet-lined *farmacia* off the Campo by the Loggia del Papa. Lunch here is particularly pleasant and relaxed, with charming service, lovely napery, and fresh flowers on the tables, though expect the clientele to be predominantly (but not entirely) foreign. The upstairs dining room is far less pretty. Good pasta and some unusual *secondi*, but the quality of food – once exceptional – is these days merely above average. First courses cost around €8–11, mains €14–18. Closed Sun.

yellow-painted dining room with seating for 35 inside and twenty outside. Opened in 1991, since when it's emerged as a city favourite, thanks to the warm welcome of owner Renata Toppi, and the classic informal *osteria* atmosphere, fair prices (starters and firsts €7–8, mains €15–18, and tasting menu €30) and no-nonsense and generously portioned food. Menus change weekly, and Renata's son, Moreno, has established a wine list of around 120 labels, though inexpensive house wine by the carafe is also available. Closed Wed.

**Ristorante Garibaldi Via Giovanni Dupré 18.** A cheap and basic trattoria, situated in a single-vaulted dining room below the co-owned *Garibaldi* hotel (see p.294) just south of the Campo. It looks rather unappealing (the claustrophobic mezzanine especially), but the reliable and inexpensive food attracts plenty of locals at lunch. Closed Sat.

## Piazza del Duomo

All the restaurants below are located on the map on p.240.

**Al Marsili Via del Castoro 3** ☎0577.47.154, ⓦ www.ristorantealmarsili.it. The lower floor of the old Palazzo Marsili is the home of this elegant and upmarket restaurant (the sort where the waiters wear bow-ties). The cross-vaulted dining room with soothing pale-yellow plaster walls isn't terribly intimate, though there are one or two more private alcoves. The inventive and generally very good Sienese cooking offers many local dishes (including some choice for vegetarians) and the service is attentive if occasionally slightly gruff. The *risotto al limone* is worth dallying over, and they have plenty of more exotic dishes such as the excellent *faraona al Medici* (guinea fowl with prunes, pine nuts and almonds). Be sure to book, especially for the popular Sunday lunch slot. €40 buys a memorable meal. Closed Mon.

**Antica Osteria da Divo Via Franciosa 29** ☎0577.286.054. A close second behind *Osteria Le Logge* (see above) for ambience, thanks to its ancient and extraordinary subterranean dining rooms – the main dining room is a mix of stone (part of the city's second set of walls), medieval brick, bare rock and wooden supports, while the two rear and basement rooms are old

▽ *Antica Osteria da Divo*

Etruscan tombs carved from the living rock. Upstairs is pretty, too, and the creative food is well above average – dishes might include classics such as *pici al ragù di lepre* (thick pasta strands with hare sauce) or the exotic, like duck with *vin santo* and saffron mashed potato. Prices are on the high side, with *primi* at €9 and mains from €16–20 (though this usually includes a side dish), and the classy but canned jazz may not be to all tastes. Closed Tues.

**La Taverna del Capitano Via del Capitano 8** ☎0577.288.094. Has retained its simple, *osteria* feel, look and prices (€25–30 should do the trick here), and the seal of approval from the Slow Food movement, despite being just a stone's throw from the Duomo and its innumerable visitors. A serene dining room divided into four with just forty covers (plus twelve not terribly nice seats outside) under a medieval vaulted ceiling. Cooking is straight-down-the-line Tuscan: *panzanella* (bread salad), *pici*, *pappardelle*, *bistecche* and the like. There's a choice of around sixty decent wines, but also inexpensive stuff by the carafe. Closed Tues.

### San Martino and Città

All the restaurants below are located on the map on pp.258–259.

**Antica Trattoria Papei Piazza del Mercato 6** ☎0577.280.894. Old-style, family-run trattorias such as this are a dying breed, and while this one attracts plenty of locals, it also relies on the patronage of visitors in the know. The setting isn't great: Piazza del Mercato just behind the Palazzo Pubblico is more car park than piazza, but that's not the point – you come here for good, basic food in good, basic surroundings. And, of course, low prices – around €7–10 each for first and main courses. Ignore the brisk show to your table: the service warms up. Aim to sit in the dining room to the left as you enter, as the more modern one on the right is a touch spartan. Closed Mon.

**Cane e Gatto Via Pagliaresi 6** ☎0577.220.751. The "Dog and Cat" (witness the cat in the stained glass near the entrance) has been in business since 1986, and has a curiously dated and less-than-cosy art nouveau feel. There are paintings on white walls and Persian rugs on the floor, but none of the vaulting or brickwork that creates the simple medieval ambience of so many Sienese restaurants. What the place does right is the food and warm welcome, with superb Tuscan *cucina nuova*, featuring seven courses on its *menù degustazione* (tasting menu). This will cost you around €50, with a selection of wines included. Closed Thurs and lunch daily.

**Gallo Nero Via del Porrione** ☎0577.284.356, ⊛www.gallonero.it. Few places, even in Siena, are quite as overwhelmingly medieval in appearance as this large, brick-vaulted restaurant, which takes advantage of its appealing setting to offer themed medieval evenings (usually Friday) with "historic" dishes, wines and musicians. The rest of the time you can choose between à la carte, two set Tuscan menus (€16 and €23) or a set "Medievale" menu at €23. Food might include centuries-old dishes such as bittersweet duck with cheese ravioli and chicken in sweet wine with fruit.

**La Cina Casato di Sotto 56** ☎0577.283.061. Quiet, inexpensive Chinese restaurant 150m from the Campo. The food is adequate, but only worth considering as a change from Siena's otherwise relentless diet of local and regional cuisine.

**Osteria Boccone del Prete Via di San Pietro 17** ☎0577.280.388. One of Siena's newer restaurants, near the Pinacoteca Nazionale, serving a limited menu of delicious crostini, salads and pasta dishes (at just €5) in a stylish setting. Don't be put off by the brightly coloured, high-vaulted dining room when you enter: there's a room with more restrained decor downstairs. Closed Sun.

🏃 **Osteria Castelvecchio Via di Castelvecchio 65** ℡ 0577.49.586, 🌐 www.osteriacastelvecchio.com. Adventurous, first-rate and nicely informal *osteria* with a young, modern edge. There are just two smallish rooms (seating about forty), with fresh, orange-pastel-painted walls under brick vaults. It's a good bet for vegetarians, and there are plenty of meat dishes, home-made pasta and a good wine list. Menus change daily, and you should come away having spent little more than €30 per person on a full meal. Sited off in a quiet corner off Via di San Pietro, near the Pinacoteca Nazionale. Closed Sun.

**Osteria del Coro Via di Pantaneto 85–87** ℡ 0577.222.482, 🌐 www.osteriadelcoro.it. The cosiest and most welcoming of several inexpensive restaurant-pizzerias on this street. A simple, unpretentious interior, with the classic half-wood-panelled walls of this sort of timeless institution. The food is good, with a meal costing around €35, excluding wine (their 130-label list is excellent), and a pizza about €10.

### Terzo di Camollia

All the restaurants below are located on the map on pp.278–279.

**Compagnia Via delle Terme 79–Via dei Pittori 1** ℡ 0577.236.568. Walk down Via delle Terme and the uninviting door and staircase leading to *Compagnia* – if you see them at all – promise little: enter round the corner, however, and you are straight into a relaxed and very pleasant place for a glass of wine, snack or fuller meal. There's the usual Sienese medieval vernacular of beams and brick ceiling, but the soft lighting, leather banquettes and other details add a modern, stylish edge. The food is good and simple and the menu is deliberately limited: just four or five *antipasti* and *primi* (at about €7 and €8–10 respectively), and mains, including a vegetable dish, at €15.

🏃 **L'Osteria Via dei Rossi 79–81** ℡ 0577.287.592. The name says it all: this is a small, simple one-room *osteria*, off the visitor trail with the classic trattoria decor of half-wood-lined walls and old photographs of Siena. There is good basic food (*antipasti* from €2.50, *primi* and *secondi* from €7–10), pleasant service, drinkable wine by the carafe, and a mixture of local residents, students and singletons who just want a quick, cheap meal. Closed Sun.

**Osteria del Ficomezzo Via dei Termini 71** ℡ 0577.222.384. A small, simple *osteria* a little off the tourist track with a cool, pastel interior: good-value lunch, with innovative Tuscan food (menus change weekly), and pricier à la carte that has *antipasti* at €6–9, *primi* from €7 and *secondi* from €9–15. Closed Sun.

**Osteria Il Grattacielo Via Pontani 8** ℡ 0577.289.326. Traditionally a local *vinaio* serving wine and snacks, this tiny *osteria* – with just three tables and ironically named "The Skyscraper" – makes a popular lunch stop for its marinated anchovies, Tuscan beans and salami. Much of the time, though, it seems to operate as a local community centre, busy with chattering old boys, none of whom seem to be eating or drinking. It shuts up shop at 8pm. Closed Sun.

**Tullio ai Tre Cristi Vicolo Provenzano 1** ℡ 0577.280.608. A Sienese institution since 1830, this is the neighbourhood restaurant of the Giraffa *contrada*. It's in a quiet corner of town (though it is signed from hundreds of metres away), which means it sees mainly local traffic. The low-beamed ceilings and vaulted alcoves, nice linen and candles make this a romantic and rather smart spot. The menu is devoted almost entirely to fish and seafood, and changes monthly, with ambitious dishes such as diced monkfish on a bed of potato with leek dressing and truffles. Starters at €9–11, first courses around €13, and mains from €15–18. The *menù degustazione* costs €58. Terrace tables in summer. Closed Wed.

# Cafés, snacks and ice cream

It's a strange Italian town that doesn't have a good number of classic **cafés**, but Siena is one of them, for while there are plenty of workaday bars and cafés for the usual excellent coffee and lunchtime panini, there's only one that has achieved any fame, and that's *Nannini*, Via Banchi di Sopra 24, a Sienese institution owned by a wealthy local family that numbers a rock-star daughter and former Formula-One racing driver son among their offspring. There are seats at the rear, but most people stand at the large, rather functional bar at the front. It's in a good position, though it's hard to see quite what the fuss is about.

Far better, and superior to the many bars on the Campo, are two cafés with secret, little-known terraces that enable you to sip your beer or slurp your *gelato* looking down on the Campo from the first floor of one of the palaces that ring the piazza: one, *La Costarelli*, is in the northwest corner, entered at Via di Città 33; the other, *Key Largo*, is on the east side at Via Rinaldini 17.

*La Costarelli* is also a decent **gelateria**, and *Key Largo* is close to another, *Caribia*, Via Rinaldini 13. *Brividio*, at the corner where Via di Città meets Via dei Pellegrini, is also handy for picking up an ice cream before you wander into the Campo. At the top end of Banchi di Sopra, at no. 97, well placed to catch trade from the *passeggiata*, is *La Casina*, another first-rate *gelateria*.

It's an easy matter to put together your own **picnic**. You can buy **pizza** by weight from many small hole-in-the wall places around the city, or phone an order ahead for fresh-baked pizza (whole or by the slice) from *Mister Pizza*, Via delle Terme 94 (☎0577.221.746; closed Sun). Gourmet supplies are available at the city's sensational and extravagantly stocked **food stores** (see p.307), while on Wednesday a full-scale open-air **market** – with food and clothing stalls – takes place on La Lizza. **Panforte** is best bought fresh by the *etto* (hectogram; 100g) in any of the bakeries or *pasticcerie* along Banchi di Sopra; the gift-packaged slabs aren't so good.

# Nightlife, festivals and the arts

Nightlife is limited in Siena, to say the least, though there are pleasant neighbourhood **bars** in most *contrade*, plus plenty of neon-lit modern establishments and the inevitable Aussie and Irish theme pub. Club life is restricted to just one or two places offering live music and dancing, and a handful of dark and unexceptional late-night bars. Most people, of course, treat the Campo as their evening salon, while locals who want proper clubs and dancing head to the large discos way beyond Siena's margins.

**Festivals and events** are another matter. The Palio takes obvious pride of place, but the city offers several other musical and cultural events, as well as a handful of cinema and theatre options. Look out for posters around Piazza Matteotti and in the Campo backstreets; classical music tastes are the most likely to be rewarded, as the Monte dei Paschi and Accademia Chigiana sponsor impressive concerts throughout the year. The Siena supplement of *La Nazione* newspaper has a "what's on" section, and the tourist office carries numerous flyers and pamphlets of forthcoming events. The website Ⓦ www.terresiena.it is also a good source of information.

## Bars, clubs and live music

**Al Cambio Via di Pantaneto 48** ☎ 0577.220.581 **(see map on pp.258–259).** A dim, moody sort of place, but then there aren't many dance clubs in Siena. Music is conventional and there's usually an admission.

**Bella Vista Social Club Via San Martino** ☎ 0577.221.243 **(see map on pp.258–259).** A dark, wood-filled backstreet space, with twin bars on either side of a single room and a vaulted ceiling covered in posters. Cuban music, drinks and memorabilia.

**Caffè Diacetto Via Diacetto, corner of Via della Galluzza** ☎ 0577.280.426 **(see map on pp.278–279).** An unexceptional bar that has become unaccountably popular with a smart twenty-something crowd, who pack the handful of tables outside on the street, especially early and late evening. Has far more buzz than many a Siena bar. Closed Sun.

**Dublin Post Piazza Gramsci 20–21** ☎ 0577.289.089 **(see map on pp.278–279).** All the dark wood, Guinness, music and ersatz bonhomie you'd expect of an "Irish" pub, though the location on the edge of the modern and nasty Piazza Gramsci alongside the bus bays is anything but appealing. This said, it's popular with visitors and Italians alike.

**Enoteca Italiana Fortezza Medicea, Via Camollia 72** ☎ 0577.288.811,

Ⓦ www.enoteca-italiana.it (see map on pp.278–279). A Sienese institution, this superb and atmospheric *enoteca* within the old Fortezza features virtually every Italian wine (well over a thousand labels), plus many rare and old vintages. Drinks and snacks are served daily noon to midnight, except Mon, when the *enoteca* closes at 8pm.

**Il Barone Rosso Via dei Termini 9**
Ⓣ 0577.286.686, Ⓦ www.barone-rosso.com (see map on pp.278–279). In business since 1993, this is the closest central Siena comes to a proper club, with dancing, drinks, snacks and live music nightly, except Sun, from 9am to 3am.

**Liberamente Piazza del Campo, corner of Casato dei Barbieri.** There's no shortage of places to eat and drink on the Campo, but many die a death after the trippers go home. *Liberamente* is an exception: small, friendly, not too many tables on its narrow piazza frontage, and buzzing into the late evening. Best of all, by Campo standards it's not over-priced.

**The Walkabout Pub Via di Pantaneto 90**
Ⓣ 0577.270.258 (see map on pp.258–259). A boisterous, predictable and friendly "Aussie" pub, with Sky TV for big sports events, Australian and British beers, and a happy hour (5.30–7pm) when all drinks are €3.50.

# Festivals and events

**Accademia Musicale Chigiana Via di Città 89**
Ⓣ 0577.22.091, Ⓦ www.chigiana.it. Siena's foremost cultural association organizes a summer season of classical concerts, the Settimane Musicali di Siena (generally in July), plus other (mostly musical) events such as the Micat in Vertice (motto of the Chigi-Saracini family, which founded the Accademia in 1932) cycle of concerts from November to March.

**Fiera di San Giuseppe** March 19 sees a festival with market stalls and street events in honour of San Giuseppe, patron saint of the Onda (Wave) *contrada*. Similar events take place in other *contrade* at different times of the year. Visit *contrada* websites for details (see box on p.260).

**Fiera di Santa Lucia** Another festival linked to a *contrada* (in this case the Chiocciola, or Snail), but because its day falls close to Christmas – December 13 – it is appropriated by much of the rest of the city. Streets in the *contrada* are filled with stalls selling food and traditional crafts.

**Siena Film Festival** Ⓣ 0577.222.999, Ⓦ www.sienafilmfestival.it. Siena still has some way to go before it challenges the film festivals of Venice or Turin, but its September festival is becoming increasingly popular.

**Siena International Short Film Festival** Ⓦ www.cortoitaliacinema.com. This week-long festival in November has been going from strength to strength since its inception in 1995. A different theme is chosen each year as the inspiration for short films, documentaries and animation. There's also a section devoted to films for children.

**Siena Jazz Fortezza Medicea 10**
Ⓣ 0577.271.401, Ⓦ www.sienajazz.it. A festival of jazz held in venues around the city (and in surrounding towns and villages) in late July and early August. Many events are free. Visit the website for details of other concerts, courses and events throughout the year.

**The Palio Piazza del Campo.** The twice-yearly horse races, and the events on the days before and after the main race, are among Europe's most colourful and exciting. Note that there are trail races on the three days before the July 2 race. See the Palio colour section for full details.

# Cinema

Siena, like most Italian towns and cities, makes few concessions to movie fans who want to see films in the original language. Virtually every film shown is dubbed, and only movies billed as "lingua originale" are screened in English or other "original languages". Contact the tourist office or drop by cinemas such as Cineforum, Piazza dell'Abbadia 6; Fiamma, Via di Pantaneto 141; Metropolitan, Piazza Giacomo Matteotti; or the Odeon, Via Banchi di Sopra 31, on the off-chance that they are screening an undubbbed film.

(19)

# Classical music, dance and theatre

As with cinema, opportunities to enjoy theatre and comedy in Siena are obviously severely restricted unless you have a good command of Italian. Dance and classical music, on the other hand, offer more rewards, especially the latter, with concert cycles throughout much of the year, many organized by the Accademia Musicale Chigiana (see above).

## Classical music

**Classical music** recitals are regularly held in the city's churches, especially the Chiesa Anglicana at Via Garibaldi 32. Visit the tourist office for current details and locations.

## Dance

Performances of classical and contemporary **dance** are usually held in the Teatro dei Rozzi, Piazza Indipendenza 15 ℡0577.46.960, ⓦwww.commune .siena.it. Further information on

dance events and classes in the city can be found by visiting ⓦwww .sienadanza.it.

## Theatre

Siena's main **theatres** are the Teatro dei Rozzi (see "Dance" above); the Teatro dei Rinnovati, Piazza del Campo 1 ℡0577.292.266; and the Teatro Piccolo, Via dei Montanini 118 ℡0577.281.190. Contact the tourist office for latest shows and details of occasional classical music concerts.

19

# Shopping

Shopping in Siena cannot match the big-city scope of Florence, but outside summer the smaller crowds and pleasing streets make for a more intimate and less harried retail experience. This is especially true of shopping for **food and wine**, both good Sienese buys; on the food front, Siena is blessed with several very beautiful and well-stocked delicatessens, and the city is very close to some of Tuscany's key wine regions, notably Montalcino and Montepulciano (as well as Chianti just to the north). One or two of the city's *enoteche* are excellent, with good buys for the casual or serious wine enthusiast.

**Designer clothes** shops cannot match the range available on Florence's Via de'Tornabuoni, but there are a couple of good one-stop stores with well-chosen lines, while shoe shops, as ever in Italy, are first-rate.

## Art, crafts and antiques

**Alvalenti Via di Beccaria 7** ✆0577.286.888. Best known for popular posters and cartoons relating to the *contrade*, but will also take on personal commissions.

**Antichità Monna Agnese Via di Città 45 & 99** ✆0577.282.288. Two branches just 100m or so apart selling a good range of antiques and, in the case of the outlet at no. 45, jewellery as well.

**Bianchi Via di Città 112** ✆0577.282.152, ⓦwww.siena-art.com. This little print and frame shop has been around for years, producing distinctive and reasonably priced brown-ink prints and etchings that you'll see all over the city.

**Bottega delle Cere Via di Pantaneto 103** ✆0577.40.703. One of several shops around the city selling plain, scented and decorated candles.

**Ceramiche Artistiche di Santa Caterina Via di Città 74–76** ✆0577.283.098. Siena has no shortage of ceramic shops: this family-run concern, in business since 1961, is one of the most successful, thanks largely to the fact it sells the distinctive cups used in the movie *Mrs Doubtfire*.

**Cerruti Via di Città 111** ✆0577.223.793. The city's leading gallery of Tuscan and other Italian contemporary art.

**Il Papiro Via di Città 37** ✆0577.284.241. Offers a wealth of stationery and items made from, or decorated with, marbled paper.

**Il Pellicano Via Diacetto 17** ✆0577.247.914. Cheerful and pretty handmade ceramics – the workshop is at Vicolo di Vallepiatta.

**La Parpagliola Via di Città 79** ✆0577.280.849. A vast selection of prints and original art, most of it views and topographical scenes of Siena and Tuscany.

**La Stamperia Via delle Terme 80** ✆0577.280.443. Slightly off the beaten track, but worth searching out for its selection of marbled and other papers, cards, notebooks and general stationery.

**Taddeucci Via di Città 136** ✆0577.289.160. A serious and seriously expensive shop, but the antiques, paintings, chandeliers and other precious items are ravishing.

# Books and newspapers

**Feltrinelli** Banchi di Sopra 52 & 64–66. Italy's leading chain of bookstores has two outlets a few doors away from each other. The shop at no. 52 has a good selection of guides in English, plus British, US and other foreign newspapers and magazines.

**Libreria Senese** Via di Città 64 ☎0577.280.845. Siena's other main source of foreign newspapers and periodicals, and a wide selection of guides, novels and other books in English.

# Clothes, shoes and accessories

**Cortecci** Via Banchi di Sopra 27 ☎0577.280.096 & Piazza del Campo 30–31 ☎0577.280.984. Both branches, but especially the big white store on Via Banchi di Sopra, are among the best places in Siena for a well-chosen selection of clothes and accessories from top Italian and other designer names.

**Dolci Trame** Via del Moro ☎0577.46.168. Although it doesn't have the range of Cortecci (see above), this place stocks a well-chosen selection of more unusual designer clothes for women.

**Furla** Via di Città 6–8 ☎0577.281.287. Outlet of a nationwide chain selling bright, modern and classic women's bags.

**Futuro** Via dei Montanini 65 ☎0577.281.080. Sleek, smart boutique with top-notch women's designer clothes.

**Gazza Ladra** Via Banchi di Sopra ☎0577.283.798. Scarves, scarves and more scarves in every colour, style and fabric imaginable.

**Palumbo** Via San Pietro 5 ☎0577.40.406. Plenty of interesting and slightly out-of-the-ordinary jackets, tops and other clothes for women.

**Romas Mori** Via Banchi di Sopra 30–32 ☎0577.40.598 & Via Banchi di Sopra 68–70 ☎0577.280.528. Vast selection of contemporary and classic shoes for men and women at reasonable prices: if it's not here, it's unlikely to be anywhere else in the city.

**Tessuti a Mano** Via San Pietro 7 ☎0577.282.200. The name means "Handmade Fabrics" (witness the large looms in the shop), but this only tells half the story, for the store sells a wide selection of handmade hats, bags, jumpers, tops and other clothes in wool, silk, mohair and other fabrics.

**TT** Via Banchi di Sopra 12 ☎0577.43.926. Plenty of shoes for women, but also top-notch handbags, belts and other leather accessories.

# Food and wine

**Antico Forno** Piazzetta delle Campane ☎0577.222.299. Delightful bakery just off Via di Città at Via delle Campane; most products are organic and there's a choice of old-fashioned rustic bread and rolls for sandwiches.

**Cantina in Piazza** Via Casato di Sotto 24 ☎0577.222.758. Several large rooms devoted to a vast selection of Tuscan and other wines. Plenty of inexpensive bottles, but the browsing experience is not as pleasant as at the *enoteche* of Palazzo Piccolomini and San Domenico (see overleaf).

**Consorzio Agrario Siena** Via Pianigiani 9 ☎0577.47.449. What started as a humble outlet for the products of local producers has turned into a rather smart emporium selling a vast selection of Tuscan food and wine and a particularly good choice of wine, salami and cheese. The central position (just off Piazza Salimbeni at the top of Banchi di Sopra) and airy layout make this a fine place for one-stop shopping both for picnic supplies and products to take home.

**Drogheria Manganelli** Via di Città ☎0577.280.002. The old glass-fronted cabinets and a delightful interior from 1879 make this one of the city's prettiest food shops, but prices are hardly the cheapest, and close inspection reveals that this is not the wide-ranging delicatessen it first appears: food here is largely restricted to dried goods, oils and wines.

**Enoteca Palazzo Piccolomini Via Rinaldini 1–Chiasso Largo** ☎0577.40.563. Superb wine store just off the Campo, with fair prices, some rare and desirable wines, with an obvious emphasis on Brunello, Chianti and other Tuscan names. Knowledgeable staff, and useful reviews of more interesting vintages from the *Wine Spectator* and other dependable publications.

**Enoteca San Domenico Via del Paradiso 56** ☎0577.271.181. Under the same management as the Enoteca Palazzo Piccolomini, and just as good. The choice of wines here is broader, and there's also a selection of gastronomic treats.

**Panifico Moderno Via dei Montanini 84** ☎0577.280.104. Plenty of basic breads, but the main attraction here is freshly made *panforte*, Siena's rich, classic cake.

**Pizzicheria di Miccoli Via di Città 95.** The nearby Drogheria Manganelli runs it close, but this is Siena's most enticing food shop, worth a visit even if you don't intend to buy. It's especially good for cheese, salami, and the hams that hang from the ceiling.

**Punt Via dei Rossi 88.** One of only a handful of supermarkets in central Siena, Punt is a reasonably convenient spot for basics and foodstuffs at the bottom of this street leading towards San Francesco.

## Homeware

**Chianti Shine Via dei Termini 49** ☎0577.49.781. A shop selling a miscellany of ceramics, homeware, bed linens and other general goods.

**Ditta Zanelli Rino Via dei Fusari 20** ☎0577.280.424. A small neighbourhood shop filled with kitchenware and electrical goods, but also countless classic Barletti and other coffee-makers in all shapes and sizes.

**Muzzi Via dei Termini 97** ☎0577.40.439. Ceramics, glassware, designer and other kitchenware and homeware.

**Siena Ricama Via di Città 61** ☎0577.288.339. Exquisitely embroidered homeware and furnishing inspired by historic pieces. One woman, the dynamic Signora Bruno Brizi Fontani, does all the work.

## Markets

**Antiques market Piazza del Mercato.** Held on the third Sunday of every month, except over Easter and in August, in the large square southwest of the Campo and below the Palazzo Pubblico.

**La Lizza** Siena's vast weekly market takes place on Wednesdays from around 7.30am to 2pm in the area beyond Piazza Gramsci and around the Fortezza.

# Directory

**Banks and exchange** Banks are concentrated along Banchi di Sopra, north of the Campo; most have ATM cash card machines. The train station ticket office will also change cash and travellers' cheques, but the most central option is Exact at Via di Città 80–82 ☎0577.288.115; hours vary from month to month, but it's usually open daily 8.30am–10/11pm.

**Bike and scooter rental** You can rent bikes at DF Bike, Via Massetana Romana 54 ☎0577.271.905; scooters and bikes at DF Moto, Via dei Gazzani 16–18 ☎0577.288.387, or Automotocicli Perozzi, Via del Romitorio 5 ☎0577.223.157.

**Bus information** Ticket offices beneath Piazza Gramsci have information on all routes. The bus company serving Siena and its hinterland, plus buses to and from Florence is called TRA-IN (☎0577.204.246 or 0577.204.225, ⓦwww.trainspa.it). TRA-IN tickets and information are also available at the train station (☎0577.204.228 or 0577.204.245) and some tobacconists (see p.223 for more details). Sena also has its office beneath Piazza Gramsci (☎800.930.960, 0577.247.934 or 0577.283.203, ⓦwww.sena.it) and run services to Assisi, Bologna, Florence, Perugia, Pisa, Milan and southern Italy.

**Car rental** Avis, Via Simone Martini 36 ☎0577.270.305, ⓦwww.avisautonoleggio.it; Hertz, Viale Sardegna 37 ☎0577.45.085, ⓦwww.hertz.it; Maggiore, Via Mentana 18 ☎0577 .345.395, ⓦwww.maggiore.it; Perozzi, Via del Romitorio 5 ☎0577.223.157; De Romanis, Via Duccio di Buoninsegna 10 ☎0577.226.974; Soldatini, Via

Caffarini 33 ☎0577.593.016 (available with driver).

**Hospital** The city's main hospital is Le Scotte, beyond the railway station at Viale Mario Bracci (☎0577.585.111) and has a casualty and first-aid department (Pronto Soccorso ☎0577.585.807 or 0577.585.808). For an ambulance, call ☎118.

**Internet access** Alfieri Internet Train, Via di Pantaneto 54 ☎0577.247.460 (Mon–Fri 10am–8pm, Sat noon–8pm); there is another outlet at Via di Città 121 ☎0577.247.460 (Mon–Fri 8am–8pm, Sun 9am–8pm, closed Sat), with laptop access and arrangements to send packages home with UPS or FedEx.

**Language courses** Scuola Leonardo da Vinci, Via del Paradiso 16 ☎0577.249.097, ⓦwww.scuolaleonardo.com; Società Dante Alighieri, Via Tommaso Pendola 37 ☎0577.49.533, ⓦwww.dantealighieri.com.

**Laundry** Ondablu, Via del Casato di Sotto 17 (daily 8am–10pm); Wash and Dry, Via di Pantaneto 38 (daily 8am–10pm).

**Left luggage** 24hr locker service at the train station; staffed facility at bus station in Piazza Gramsci (daily 7am–7.45pm; €3.50 per bag per day).

**Lost property** *Comune di Siena*, Casato di Sotto 23 (Mon–Sat 9am–12.30pm, Tues also 3–5pm).

**Parking** Siena Parcheggi ☎0577.228.711, ⓦwww.sienaparcheggi.com. Details of car parks, locations and rates.

**Pharmacy** Antica Farmacia Parenti, Via Banchi di Sopra 43 ☎0577.283.269; generally has English-speaking staff.

**Police** The Questura is on Via del Castoro ☎0577.201.111.

**Post office** Piazza Matteotti 1 ⓦwww.poste .it (Mon–Fri 8.15am–7pm, Sat 8.15am–noon).

**Railway station** Piazza Rosselli; call centre ☏892.021, ⓦwww.trenitalia.it.

**Taxis** It is difficult to hail taxis on the street, but there are ranks at the railway station and on the west side of Piazza Matteotti; otherwise, call ☏0577.49.222 or 0577.44.504 or visit ⓦwww.commune .siena.it/taxi.

# Contexts

# Contexts

# The historical background

The story of Florence and Siena is inseparable from the story of Tuscany, the province that Florence grew to dominate. Accordingly, the section that follows gives a broad introduction to Tuscan history, placing the main emphasis on the role played by Florence. Crucial episodes within the narrative of Florence and its culture – for instance, the ascendancy of Savonarola – are covered in greater detail in the chapters on that city; similarly, you'll find an overview of the evolution of Siena on p.228.

## Etruscans and Romans

The name of the province of Tuscany derives from the **Etruscans**, the most powerful civilization of pre-Roman Italy. There's no scholarly consensus on the origins of this people, with some experts insisting that they migrated into Italy from Anatolia at the start of the ninth century BC, and others maintaining that they were an indigenous tribe. All that's known for certain is that the Etruscans were spread thoughout central Italy from the eighth century BC, and that the centre of gravity of their domain was in the southern part of the modern province, roughly along a line drawn from Orbetello to Lago Trasimeno. Their principal settlements in Tuscany were Roselle, Vetulonia, Populonia, Volterra, Chiusi, Cortona, Arezzo and – most northerly of all – Fiesole.

It seems that the Etruscans absorbed elements of those cultures with which they came into contact, thus their trade with Greek settlements produced some classically influenced art that can be seen at its best in Florence's archeological museum and in Cortona. The Etruscan language has still not been fully deciphered (a massive translation programme is under way in Perugia), so at the moment their wall paintings and terracotta funerary sculptures are the main source of information about them, and this information is open to widely differing interpretations. Some people have inferred an almost neurotic fear of death from the evidence of their burial sites and monuments, while others – most notably D.H. Lawrence – have on the contrary intuited an irrepressible and uncomplicated vitality.

There may have been an Etruscan settlement where Florence now stands, but it would have been subservient to their base in the hill-town of Fiesole. The substantial development of Tuscany's chief city began with the **Roman colony of Florentia**, established by Julius Caesar in 59 BC as a settlement for army veterans – by which time Romans had either subsumed or exterminated most Etruscan towns. Expansion of Florentia itself was rapid, with a steady traffic of trading vessels along the Arno providing the basis of accelerated growth in the second and third centuries AD.

This rise under the empire was paralleled by the growth of **Siena**, **Pisa** and **Lucca**, establishing an economic primacy in the north of Tuscany that has endured to the present. According to legend Siena was founded by the sons of Remus, supposedly fleeing their uncle Romulus, while the port at Pisa was developed by the Romans in the second century BC. Lucca was even more important, and it was here that Julius Caesar, Crassus and Pompey established their triumvirate in 56 BC.

# Barbarians and margraves

Under the comparative tranquillity of the Roman colonial regime, **Christianity** began to spread through the region. Lucca claims to have been the first Christian city in Tuscany – evangelized by a disciple of St Peter – though Pisa's church of San Pietro a Grado is said to have been founded by Peter himself. In Florence, the church of San Lorenzo and the martyr's shrine at San Miniato were both established in the fourth century.

This period of calm was shattered in the fifth century by the invasions of the **Goths** from the north, though the scale of the destruction in this first barbarian wave was nothing compared to the havoc of the following century. After the fall of Rome, the empire had split in two, with the western half ruled from Ravenna and the eastern from Constantinople (Byzantium). By the 490s Ravenna was occupied by the Ostrogoths, and forty years later the Byzantine emperor Justinian launched a campaign to repossess the Italian peninsula.

The ensuing mayhem between the Byzantine armies of Belisarius and Narsus and the fast-moving Goths was probably the most destructive phase of central Italian history, with virtually all major settlements ravaged by one side or the other – and sometimes both. In 552 Florence fell to the hordes of the Gothic king **Totila**, whose depredations so weakened the province that less than twenty years later the **Lombards** were able to storm in, subjugating Florence to the duchy whose capital was in Pavia, though its dukes preferred to rule from Lucca.

By the end of the eighth century Charlemagne's **Franks** had taken control of much of Italy, with the administration being overseen by imperial **margraves**, again based in Lucca. These proxy rulers developed into some of the most powerful figures in the Holy Roman Empire and were instrumental in spreading Christianity even further, founding numerous religious houses. Willa, widow of the margrave Uberto, established the Badìa in Florence in 978, the first monastic foundation in the centre of the city; her son Ugo, margrave in turn, is buried in the Badìa's church.

The hold of the central authority of the Holy Roman Empire was often tenuous, with feudal grievances making the region all but ungovernable, and it was under the imperial margraves that the notion of an autonomous Tuscan entity began to emerge. In 1027 the position of margrave was passed to the **Canossa** family, who took the title of the Counts of Tuscia, as Tuscany was then called. The most influential figure produced by this dynasty was **Matilda**, daughter of the first Canossa margrave. When her father died she was abducted by the German emperor Henry III, and on her release and return to her home territory she began to take the side of the papacy in its protracted disputes with the empire. The culmination of her anti-imperialist policy came in 1077, when she obliged the Emperor Henry IV to wait in the snow outside the gates of Canossa before making obeisance to Pope Gregory VII. Later friction between the papacy, empire and Tuscan cities was assured when Matilda bequeathed all her lands to the pope, with the crucial exceptions of Florence, Siena and Lucca.

# Guelphs and Ghibellines

Though Lucca had been the titular base of the imperial margraves, Ugo and his successors had shown a degree of favouritism towards **Florence** and over the next three hundred years Florence gained pre-eminence among the cities of Tuscany, becoming especially important as a religious centre. In 1078 Countess Matilda supervised the construction of new fortifications for Florence, and in the year of her death – 1115 – granted it the status of an independent city. The new *comune* of Florence was essentially governed by a council of one hundred men, the great majority drawn from the rising merchant class. In 1125 the city's increasing dominance of the region was confirmed when it crushed the rival city of Fiesole. Fifty years later, as the population boomed with the rise of the textile industry, new walls were built around what was then one of the largest cities in Europe.

Not that the other mercantile centres of Tuscany were completely eclipsed, as their magnificent heritage of medieval buildings makes plain. **Pisa** in the tenth and eleventh centuries had become one of the peninsula's wealthiest ports and its shipping lines played a vital part in bringing the cultural influences of France, Byzantium and the Muslim world into Italy. Twelfth-century **Siena**, though racked by conflicts between the bishops and the secular authorities and between the nobility and the merchant class, was booming thanks to its cloth industries and its exploitation of a local silver mine – foundation of a banking empire that was to see the city rivalling the bankers of Venice and Florence on the international markets.

Throughout and beyond the thirteenth century Tuscany was torn by conflict between the **Ghibelline** faction and the **Guelphs**. The names of these two political alignments derive from Welf, the family name of Emperor Otto IV, and Waiblingen, the name of a castle owned by their implacable rivals, the Hohenstaufen. Though there's no clear documentation, it seems that the terms Guelph and Ghibelline entered the Italian vocabulary at the very end of the twelfth century, when supporters of Otto IV battled for control of the central peninsula with the future Frederick II, nephew of Otto and grandson of the Hohenstaufen emperor Barbarossa (1152–90). Within the first few years of Frederick II's reign (1212–50), the labels Guelph and Ghibelline had changed their meaning – the latter still referred to the allies of the Hohenstaufen, but the Guelph party was defined chiefly by its loyalty to the papacy, thus reviving the battle lines drawn up during the reign of Matilda.

To muddy the waters yet further, when Charles of Anjou conquered Naples in 1266, alliance with the anti-imperial French became another component of Guelphism, and a loose Guelph alliance soon stretched from Paris to Naples, substantially funded by the bankers of Tuscany.

Ghibelline/Guelph divisions approximately corresponded to a split between the feudal **nobility** and the rising **business classes**, but this is only the broadest of generalizations. By the beginning of the thirteenth century the major cities of Tuscany were becoming increasingly self-sufficient and intercity strife was soon a commonplace of medieval life. In this climate, affiliations with the empire and the papacy were often struck on the basis that "my enemy's enemy is my friend", and allegiances changed at baffling speed; if, for instance, the Guelphs gained the ascendancy in a particular town, its neighbours might switch to the Ghibelline camp to maintain their rivalry. Nonetheless, certain patterns did emerge from the confusion: Florence and Lucca were generally Guelph strongholds, while Pisa, Arezzo, Prato, Pistoia and Siena tended to side with the empire.

As a final complicating factor, this was also the great age of **mercenary** armies, whose loyalties changed even more quickly than those of the towns that paid for their services. Thus **Sir John Hawkwood** – whose White Company was the most fearsome band of hoodlums on the peninsula – is known today

**C**

through the monument to him in Florence's Duomo, but early in his career was employed by Ghibelline Pisa to fight the Florentines. He was then taken on by Pope Gregory XI, whom he deserted on the grounds of underpayment, and in the end was granted a pension of 1200 florins a year by Florence, basically as a form of protection money. Even then he was often absent fighting for other cities whenever a fat purse was waved in his direction.

# Medieval Florence before the Medici

In this period of superpower manoeuvring and shifting economic structures, city governments in Tuscany were volatile. The administration of Siena, for example, was carried out by various combinations of councils and governors and in 1368 its constitution was redrawn no fewer than four times. However, Florence provides perhaps the best illustration of the turbulence of Tuscan politics in the late Middle Ages.

In 1207 the city's governing council was replaced by the **Podestà**, an executive official who was traditionally a non-Florentine, in a semi-autocratic form of government that was common throughout the region. It was around this time, too, that the first **arti** (guilds) were formed to promote the interests of the traders and bankers, a constituency of ever-increasing power. Then in 1215 Florence was riven by a feud that was typical of the internecine violence of central Italy at this period. On Easter Sunday one **Buondelmonte de' Buondelmonti**, on his way to his wedding, was stabbed to death at the foot of the Ponte Vecchio by a member of the Amidei clan, in revenge for breaking his engagement to a young woman of that family. The prosecution of the murderers and their allies polarized the city into those who supported the *comune* – which regarded itself as the protector of the commercial city against imperial ambitions – and the followers of the Amidei, who seem to have politicized their personal grievances by aligning themselves against the *comune* and with the emperor.

These Ghibellines eventually enlisted the help of Emperor Frederick II to oust the Guelphs in 1248, but within two years they had been displaced by the Guelph-backed regime of the **Primo Popolo**, a quasi-democratic government drawn from the mercantile class. The *Primo Popolo* was in turn displaced in 1260, when the Florentine army marched on Siena to demand the surrender of some exiles who were hiding out in the city. Though greatly outnumbered, the Sienese army and its Ghibelline allies overwhelmed the aggressors at **Montaperti**, after which the Sienese were prevented from razing Florence only by the intervention of Farinata degli Uberti, head of the Ghibelline exiles.

By the 1280s the balance had again moved back in favour of Florence, where the Guelphs were back in control – after the intervention of Charles of Anjou – through the **Secondo Popolo**, a regime run by the *Arti Maggiori* (Great Guilds). It was this second bourgeois administration that definitively shifted the fulcrum of power in Florence towards its bankers, merchants and manufacturers – whereas in Siena, the second richest city in Tuscany, the feudal families retained a stranglehold for far longer. Agitation from the landed nobility of the countryside around Florence had been a constant fact of life until the *Secondo Popolo*, which in 1293 passed a programme of political reforms known as the *Ordinamenti della Giustizia*, excluding the nobility from government and investing power in the **Signoria**, a council drawn from the *Arti Maggiori*.

Strife between the virulently anti-imperial "Black" and more conciliatory "White" factions within the Guelph camp marked the start of the fourteenth century in Florence, with many of the Whites – Dante among them – being exiled in 1302. Worse disarray was to come. In 1325 the army of Lucca under **Castruccio Castracani** defeated the Florentines and was about to overwhelm the city when the death of their leader took the momentum out of the campaign. Then in 1339 the Bardi and Peruzzi banks – Florence's largest – both collapsed, mainly owing to the bad debts of Edward III of England. The ultimate catastrophe came in 1348, when the **Black Death** destroyed as many as half the city's population.

However, even though the epidemic hit Florence so badly that it was generally referred to as the Florentine Plague, its effects were equally devastating throughout the region, and did nothing to reverse the economic – and thus political – supremacy of the city. Florence had subsumed Pistoia in 1329 and gained Prato in the 1350s. In 1406 it took control of Pisa and thus gained a long-coveted sea port, and five years later Cortona became part of its territory. From this time on, despite the survival of Sienese independence into the sixteenth century, the history of Tuscany increasingly becomes the history of Florence.

# The early Medici

A crucial episode in the liberation of Florence from the influence of the papacy was the so-called **War of the Eight Saints** in 1375–78, which brought Florence into direct territorial conflict with Pope Gregory XI. This not only signalled the dissolution of the old Guelph alliance, but had immense repercussions for the internal politics of Florence. The increased taxation and other economic hardships of the war provoked an uprising of the industrial day-labourers, the **Ciompi**, on whom the wool and cloth factories depended. Their short-lived revolt resulted in the formation of three new guilds and direct representation for the workers for the first time. However, the prospect of increased proletarian presence in the machinery of state provoked a consolidation of the city's oligarchs, and in 1382 an alliance of the city's Guelph party and the **Popolo Grasso** (the wealthiest merchants) took control of the *Signoria* away from the guilds, a situation that lasted for four decades.

Not all of Florence's most prosperous citizens aligned themselves with the *Popolo Grasso*, and the foremost of the well-off mavericks were the **Medici**, a family from the agricultural Mugello region whose fortune had been made by the banking prowess of Giovanni Bicci de' Medici. The political rise of his son, **Cosimo de' Medici**, was to some extent due to his family's sympathies with the *Popolo Minuto*, as the members of the disenfranchised lesser guilds were known. With the increase in public discontent at the autocratic rule of the *Signoria* – where the Albizzi clan were the dominant force – Cosimo came to be seen as the figurehead of the more democratically inclined sector of the upper class. In 1431 the authorities imprisoned him in the tower of the Palazzo Vecchio and two years later, as Florence became embroiled in a futile and domestically unpopular war against Lucca, they sent him into exile. He was away for only a year. In 1434, after a session of the *Parlamento* – a general council called in times of emergency – it was decided to invite him to return. Having secured the military support of the Sforza family of Milan, Cosimo became the

# DESCENDANTS OF COSIMO IL VECCHIO

```
----------        = illegitimate child
----------  ?     = possible illegitimate child
    ↓             = minor branches
```

**Piero il Gottoso** = Lucrezia Tornabuoni
(1416–69)

Maria = Leopetto Rossi
↓

**Piero** = Alfonsina Orsini    **Giovanni**, Pope Leo X    Giuliano, Duke of Nemours = Philiberte of Savoy
(1471–1503)    (1475–1521)    (1478–1516)

? 

**Lorenzo**, Duke of Urbino = Madeleine de la Tour d'Auvergne    Clarice = Filippo Strozzi    Ippolito
(1492–1519)

Catherine = Henry II of France
(1519–89)

Francis II = Mary,    Elizabetta = Philip II of Spain    Claude = Henry,    Francis, Duke of Alençon
Queen of Scots                          Duke of Lorraine

Christine of Lorraine = **Ferdinando I**
(see chart on next page)

pre-eminent figure in the city's political life, a position he maintained for more than three decades.

Cosimo il Vecchio – as he came to be known – rarely held office himself, preferring to exercise power through backstage manipulation and adroit investment. His extreme generosity to charities and religious foundations in Florence was no doubt motivated in part by genuine piety, but clearly did no harm as

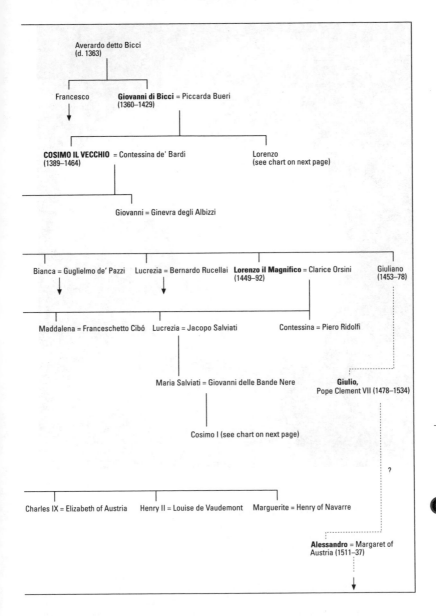

Averardo detto Bicci
(d. 1363)

Francesco     **Giovanni di Bicci** = Piccarda Bueri
              (1360–1429)

**COSIMO IL VECCHIO** = Contessina de' Bardi          Lorenzo
(1389–1464)                                           (see chart on next page)

Giovanni = Ginevra degli Albizzi

Bianca = Guglielmo de' Pazzi    Lucrezia = Bernardo Rucellai    **Lorenzo il Magnifico** = Clarice Orsini    Giuliano
                                                                (1449–92)                                    (1453–78)

Maddalena = Franceschetto Cibó    Lucrezia = Jacopo Salviati          Contessina = Piero Ridolfi

Maria Salviati = Giovanni delle Bande Nere          **Giulio,**
                                                    Pope Clement VII (1478–1534)

Cosimo I (see chart on next page)

?

Charles IX = Elizabeth of Austria    Henry II = Louise de Vaudemont    Marguerite = Henry of Navarre

**Alessandro** = Margaret of
Austria (1511–37)

a public relations exercise – even if it didn't impress the contemporary who recorded that his munificence was due to the fact that "he knew his money had not been over-well acquired".

Dante, Boccaccio and Giotto in the first half of the fourteenth century had established the literary and artistic ascendancy of Florence, laying the foundations of Italian humanism with their emphasis on the importance of the

△ Cosimo il Vecchio by Agnolo Bronzino, Galleria degli Uffizi

vernacular and the dignity of humanity. Florence's reputation as the most inno-vative cultural centre in Europe was strengthened during the fifteenth century, to a large extent through Medici patronage. Cosimo commissioned work from Donatello, Michelozzo and a host of other Florentine artists, and took advantage of the 1439 Council of Florence – a conference of the Catholic and Eastern churches – to foster scholars who were familiar with the literatures of the ancient world. His grandson **Lorenzo il Magnifico** (who succeeded Piero il Gottoso, the Gouty) continued this literary patronage, promoting the study of the classics in the Platonic academy that used to meet at the Medici villas. Other Medici were to fund projects by Botticelli, Michelangelo, Pontormo – in fact, most of the seminal figures of the Florentine Renaissance.

Lorenzo il Magnifico's status as the de facto ruler of Florence was even more secure than that of Cosimo il Vecchio, but it did meet one stiff chal-lenge. While many of Florence's financial dynasties were content to advise and support the Medici, others – notably the mighty Strozzi clan – were resentful of the power now wielded by their fellow businessmen. In 1478 one of these disgruntled families, the Pazzi, conspired with Pope Sixtus IV, who had been riled by Lorenzo's attempt to break the papal monopoly of alum mining. This **Pazzi Conspiracy** resulted in an assault on Lorenzo and his brother Giuliano during Mass in the Duomo; Lorenzo was badly injured and Giuliano murdered, an outcome that only increased the esteem in which Lorenzo was held. Now that the plot had failed, Sixtus joined forces with the ferocious King Ferrante of Naples to launch a war on Florence, and excommunicated Lorenzo into the bargain. Taking his life in his hands, Lorenzo left Florence to persuade Ferrante to leave the alliance, a mission he somehow accomplished successfully, to the jubilation of the city.

## The Wars of Italy

Before Lorenzo's death in 1492 the Medici bank failed, and in 1494 Lorenzo's son Piero was obliged to flee following his surrender to the invading French army of Charles VIII. This invasion was the commencement of a bloody half-century dominated by the so-called **Wars of Italy**.

After the departure of Charles's troops, Florence for a while was virtually under the control of the inspirational monk **Girolamo Savonarola**, but his career was brief. He was executed as a heretic in 1498, after which the city continued to function as a more democratic republic than that of the Medici. In 1512, however, following Florence's defeat by the Spanish and papal armies, the Medici returned, in the person of the vicious **Giuliano, Duke of Nemours**.

Giuliano's successors – his equally unattractive nephew Lorenzo, Duke of Urbino, and Giulio, illegitimate son of Lorenzo il Magnifico's brother – were in effect just the mouthpieces of Giovanni de' Medici (the Duke of Nemours' brother), who in 1519 became **Pope Leo X**. Similarly, when Giulio became **Pope Clement VII**, he was really the absentee ruler of Florence, where the family presence was maintained by the ghastly Ippolito (illegitimate son of the Duke of Nemours) and Alessandro (illegitimate son of the Duke of Urbino).

The Medici were again evicted from Florence in the wake of Charles V's pillage of Rome in 1527, Pope Clement's humiliation by the imperial army providing the spur to eject his deeply unpopular relatives. Three years later the pendulum swung the other way: after a siege by the combined papal and imperial forces, Florence capitulated and was obliged to receive Alessandro, who was proclaimed **Duke of Florence**, the first Medici to bear the title of ruler. Though the sadistic Alessandro lost no opportunity to exploit the immunity that came from his title, in the wider scheme of Italian politics he was a less powerful figure than his ancestors. Tuscany was becoming just one more piece in the vast jigsaw of the Habsburg empire, a superpower far more interventionist than the medieval empire of Frederick II could ever have been.

# The later Medici

After the assassination of Alessandro in 1537, power passed to another **Cosimo**, not a direct heir but rather a descendant of Cosimo il Vecchio's brother. The Emperor Charles V, now related to the Medici through the marriage of his daughter to Alessandro, gave his assent to the succession of this seemingly pliable young man – indeed, without Habsburg consent it would not have happened. Yet it turned out that Cosimo had the clear intention of maintaining

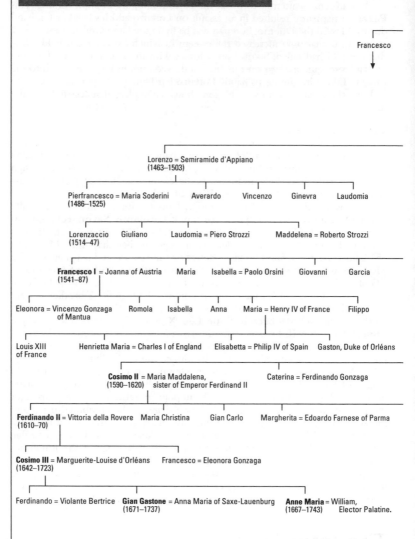

## DESCENDANTS OF LORENZO DE' MEDICI

Francesco

Lorenzo = Semiramide d'Appiano
(1463–1503)

Pierfrancesco = Maria Soderini     Averardo     Vincenzo     Ginevra     Laudomia
(1486–1525)

Lorenzaccio     Giuliano     Laudomia = Piero Strozzi     Maddelena = Roberto Strozzi
(1514–47)

**Francesco I** = Joanna of Austria     Maria     Isabella = Paolo Orsini     Giovanni     Garcia
(1541–87)

Eleonora = Vincenzo Gonzaga     Romola     Isabella     Anna     Maria = Henry IV of France     Filippo
           of Mantua

Louis XIII     Henrietta Maria = Charles I of England     Elisabetta = Philip IV of Spain     Gaston, Duke of Orléans
of France

**Cosimo II** = Maria Maddalena,                    Caterina = Ferdinando Gonzaga
(1590–1620)   sister of Emperor Ferdinand II

**Ferdinando II** = Vittoria della Rovere     Maria Christina     Gian Carlo     Margherita = Edoardo Farnese of Parma
(1610–70)

**Cosimo III** = Marguerite-Louise d'Orléans     Francesco = Eleonora Gonzaga
(1642–1723)

Ferdinando = Violante Bertrice     **Gian Gastone** = Anna Maria of Saxe-Lauenburg     **Anne Maria** = William,
                                   (1671–1737)                                          (1667–1743)   Elector Palatine.

Florence's role as the regional power-broker, and he proved immensely skilful at judging just how far he could push the city's autonomy without provoking the imperial policy-makers.

Having finally extinguished the subversive threat of the Strozzi faction at the battle of **Montemurlo**, Cosimo went on to buy the territory of Siena from the Habsburgs in 1557, giving Florence control of all of Tuscany with the

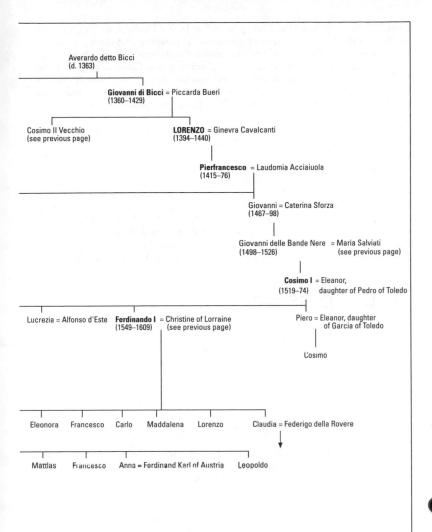

Averardo detto Bicci
(d. 1363)

Giovanni di Bicci = Piccarda Bueri
(1360–1429)

Cosimo II Vecchio
(see previous page)

LORENZO = Ginevra Cavalcanti
(1394–1440)

Pierfrancesco = Laudomia Acciaiuola
(1415–76)

Giovanni = Caterina Sforza
(1467–98)

Giovanni delle Bande Nere = Maria Salviati
(1498–1526)                  (see previous page)

Cosimo I = Eleanor,
(1519–74)   daughter of Pedro of Toledo

Lucrezia = Alfonso d'Este    Ferdinando I = Christine of Lorraine    Piero = Eleanor, daughter
                             (1549–1609)    (see previous page)              of Garcia of Toledo

Cosimo

Eleonora    Francesco    Carlo    Maddalena    Lorenzo    Claudia = Federigo della Rovere

Mattias    Francesco    Anna = Ferdinand Karl of Austria    Leopoldo

solitary exception of Lucca. Two years later Florentine hegemony in Tuscany was confirmed in the Treaty of Cateau-Cambrésis, the final act in the Wars of Italy. Soon after, though, the new Habsburg emperor, Philip II, installed a military outpost in the Orbetello area to keep Tuscany under scrutiny.

Imperial and papal approval of Cosimo's rule was sealed in 1570, when he was allowed to take the title **Cosimo I, Grand Duke of Tuscany**. In European terms Tuscany was a second-rank power, but by comparison with other states on the peninsula it was in a very comfortable position, and during Cosimo's reign there would have been little perception that Florence was drifting inexorably towards the margins of European politics. It was Cosimo who built the Uffizi, extended and overhauled the Palazzo Vecchio, installed the Medici in the Palazzo Pitti, had the magnificent Ponte Santa Trìnita constructed across the Arno and commissioned much of the public sculpture around the Piazza della Signoria.

Cosimo's descendants were to remain in power until 1737, and aspects of their rule continued the city's intellectual tradition: the Medici were among Galileo's strongest supporters, for example. Yet it was a story of almost continual if initially gentle economic decline, as bad harvests and recurrent epidemics worsened the gloom created by the shift of European trading patterns in favour of northern Europe. The half-century reign of **Ferdinando II** had scarcely begun when the market for Florence's woollen goods collapsed in the 1630s, and the city's banks simultaneously went into a terminal slump. The last two male Medici, the insanely pious **Cosimo III** and the drunken pederast **Gian Gastone** – who was seen in public only once, vomiting from the window of the state coach – were fitting symbols of the moribund Florentine state.

# To the present

Under the terms of a treaty signed by Gian Gastone's sister, Anna Maria de' Medici, Florence passed in 1737 to the **House of Lorraine**, cousins of the Austrian Habsburgs. The first Lorraine prince, the future Francis I of Austria, was a more enlightened ruler than the last Medici had been and his successors presided over a placid and generally untroubled region, doing much to improve the condition of Tuscany's agricultural land and rationalize its production methods. Austrian rule lasted until the coming of the French in 1799, an interlude that ended with the fall of **Napoleon**, who had made his sister Elisa Baciocchi Grand Duchess of Tuscany.

After this, the Lorraine dynasty was brought back, remaining in residence until the last of the line, Leopold II, consented to his own deposition in 1859. Absorbed into the new **Kingdom of Italy** in the following year, Florence became the **capital** in 1865, a position it held until 1870, when Rome – having at last become part of the otherwise united country – took over the role.

Italy's unpopular entry into World War I cost thousands of Tuscan lives, and the economic disruption that followed was exploited by the regime of Benito **Mussolini**. The corporate Fascist state of the 1920s did effect various improvements in the infrastructure of the region, but Mussolini's alliance with Hitler's Germany was a calamity. In 1943, as the Allied landing at Monte Cassino was followed by a campaign to sweep the occupying German forces out of the peninsula, Tuscany became a battlefield between the Nazis and the **partisans**. The districts around Monte Amiata and the Val d'Órcia sheltered particularly strong partisan groups, and many of the province's hill-towns had their resistance cells, as numerous well-tended war memorials testify.

Yet, as elsewhere in Italy, the loyalties of Tuscany were split, as is well illustrated by the case of Florence, an ideological centre for the resistance but also home to some of Italy's most ardent Nazi collaborators. Wartime Florence in fact produced one of the strangest paradoxes of the time: a Fascist sympathizer in charge of the British Institute and a German consul who did so much to protect suspected partisans that he was granted the freedom of the city after the war.

Although most of the major monuments of Tuscany survived the war – sometimes as a result of pacts between the two sides – there was inevitably widespread destruction. Grosseto, Pisa and Livorno were badly damaged by Allied bombing raids, while substantial parts of Florence were wrecked by the retreating German army, who bombed all the bridges except the Ponte Vecchio and blew up much of the medieval city near the banks of the Arno.

## Postwar Tuscany

Tuscany is a prosperous and conservative region that in the past has tended to return right-of-centre members of parliament. On a local level, however, **communist** and other left-wing support is high, the party's record in the war and subsequent work on land reform maintaining a loyal following. Until recently, the communists were effectively excluded from national government by the machinations of the now-defunct Christian Democrat party (which, like the old Socialist party, was undone by the corruption scandals of the early 1990s). By contrast, the communist party and newer left-wing parties projected themselves – and continue to project themselves – as the grassroots opposition to the centralization and corruption of Roman politics. It's a strategy that has been particularly successful in Tuscany, which has clung onto an image of itself as a state within the state. Since the 1970s the town halls of the region have been governed predominantly by communist-led coalitions, forming the heartland of the so-called "red belt" of central Italy.

Despite migration from the land in the 1950s and 1960s, the **economy** of Tuscany has been adroitly managed. The labour-intensive vineyards, olive groves and farms continue to provide a dependable source of income, boosted by industrial development in the Arno valley and around Livorno and Piombino. Production of textiles, leather goods and jewellery have brought money into Prato, Florence and Arezzo, while wine has brought untold prosperity to previously moribund towns such as Montalcino and Montepulciano. But **tourism** plays an uncomfortably large and ever-increasing part in balancing the books of these and other historic centres. This is a mixed blessing, sheer weight of numbers in places such as Florence, Siena and San Gimignano (and many others) overburdening an already creaking infrastructure and – worse – undermining the charm and damaging the historic and artistic treasures which attract visitors in the first place.

# A directory of artists and architects

**Agostino di Duccio** (1418–81). Born in Florence, Agostino served as a mercenary before turning to sculpture. Having possibly studied with Jacopo della Quercia, he carved the altarpiece for Modena cathedral then returned to Florence in 1442. His masterpiece is the Tempio Malatestiano in Rimini, on which Alberti and Piero della Francesca also worked. He returned to Florence briefly in the 1460s, a period during which he almost ruined the marble block that was to become Michelangelo's *David*.

**Alberti, Leon Battista** (1404–72). Born illegitimately to a Florentine exile, probably in Genoa, Alberti was educated in Padua and Bologna. One of the most complete personifications of the Renaissance ideal of universal genius, he was above all a writer and theorist: his *De Re Aedificatoria* (1452) was the first architectural treatise of the Renaissance, and he also wrote a tract on the art of painting, *Della Pittura*, dedicated to his friend Brunelleschi. His theory of harmonic proportions in musical and visual forms was first put into practice in the facade of Santa Maria Novella in Florence, while his archeological interest in classical architecture found expression in the same city's Palazzo Rucellai, his first independent project. Even more closely linked to his researches into the styles of antiquity is the miniature temple built for the Rucellai family in the church of San Pancrazio. His other buildings are in Mantua and Rimini.

**Ammannati, Bartolomeo** (1511–92). A Florentine sculptor-architect, much indebted to Michelangelo, Ammannati is best known for his additions and amendments to the Palazzo Pitti and for the graceful Ponte Santa Trìnita (though in all likelihood this was largely designed by Michelangelo). He created the fountain in the Piazza della Signoria, with some assistance from his pupil Giambologna, and the Bargello contains some of his pieces made for the Bóboli gardens.

**Andrea del Sarto** (1486–1530). The dominant artist in Florence at the time of Michelangelo and Raphael's ascendancy in Rome. His strengths are not those associated with Florentine draughtsmanship, being more Venetian in his emphasis on delicacy of colour and the primacy of light. He made his name with frescoes for two Florentine churches in the San Marco district – the Scalzo and Santissima Annunziata. For a period in the 1510s he was in France, and the received wisdom is that his talent did not develop after that. However, two of his other major works in Florence date from after his return – the *Last Supper* in San Salvi and the *Madonna del Sacco* in the cloister of the Annunziata. His major easel painting is the *Madonna of the Harpies* in the Uffizi.

**Arnolfo di Cambio** (c.1245–1302). Pupil of Nicola Pisano, with whom he worked on sculptural projects in Bologna, Siena and Perugia before going to Rome in 1277. The most important of his independent sculptures are the pieces in Florence's Museo dell'Opera del Duomo and the *Tomb of Cardinal de Braye* in San Domenico in Orvieto. The latter defined the format of wall tombs for the next century, showing the deceased lying on a coffin below the

Madonna and Child, set within an elaborate architectural framework. However, Arnolfo is best known as the architect of Florence's Duomo and Palazzo Vecchio, and various fortifications in central Tuscany, including the fortress at Poppi.

**Bandinelli, Baccio** (1493–1560). Born in Florence, Bandinelli trained as a goldsmith, sculptor and painter. He perceived himself as an equal talent to Michelangelo and to Cellini, his most vocal critic. Despite manifest shortcomings as a sculptor, he was given prestigious commissions by Cosimo I, the most conspicuous of which is the *Hercules and Cacus* outside the Palazzo Vecchio. Other pieces by him are in the Bargello.

**Beccafumi, Domenico** (1484/6– 1551). The last great Sienese painter, Beccafumi was in Rome during the painting of the Sistine chapel ceiling and Raphael's *Stanze*. He returned to Siena in 1513, when his work showed tendencies that were to become prevalent in Mannerist art – contorted poses, strong lighting, vivid artificial colouration. His decorative skill is especially evident in his illusionist frescoes in the Palazzo Pubblico and the pavement of the Duomo.

**Benedetto da Maiano** (1442–97). Florentine sculptor, best known for his portrait busts in the Bargello and the pulpit in Santa Croce.

**Botticelli, Sandro** (c.1445–1510). Possibly a pupil of Filippo Lippi, Botticelli was certainly influenced by the Pollaiuolo brothers, whose paintings of the *Virtues* he completed. The mythological paintings for which he is celebrated – including the *Birth of Venus* and *Primavera* – are distinguished by their emphasis on line rather than mass, and by their complicated symbolic meaning, a reflection on his involvement with the Neo-Platonist philosophers whom the Medici gathered about them. In the last decade of his life his lucid, slightly archaic style suffered from comparison with the more radical paintings of Michelangelo and Leonardo da Vinci, and his devotional pictures became almost clumsily didactic – a result, perhaps, of his involvement with Savonarola and his followers.

**Bronzino, Agnolo** (1503–72). The adopted son of Pontormo, Bronzino became the court painter to Cosimo I. He frescoed parts of the Palazzo Vecchio for Eleonora di Toledo, but his reputation rests on his glacially elegant portraits, whose surface brilliance makes no discrimination between the faces of the subjects and their apparel.

**Brunelleschi, Filippo** (1377– 1446). Trained as a sculptor and goldsmith, Brunelleschi abandoned this career after his failure in the competition for the Florence Baptistery doors. The main product of this period is his contribution to the St James altarpiece in Pistoia. He then devoted himself to the study of the building techniques of the classical era, travelling to Rome with Donatello in 1402. In 1417 he submitted his design for the dome of Florence's Duomo, and all his subsequent work was in that city – San Lorenzo, the Spedale degli Innocenti, Cappella Pazzi (Santa Croce) and Santo Spirito. Unlike the other great architect of this period, Alberti, his work is based on no theoretical premise, but rather on an empiricist's admiration for the buildings of Rome. And unlike Alberti, he oversaw every stage of construction, even devising machinery that would permit the raising of the innovative structures he had planned.

**Buonarroti, Michelangelo** (1475– 1564). See box on p.109.

**Buontalenti, Bernardo** (c.1536–1608). Florentine architect, who began as a military architect to the papacy. Much of his later output was for the court of the Medici – the grotto of the Bóboli gardens, the gardens of the villa at Pratolino and tableaux for court spectaculars. Less frivolous work included the Fortezza del Belvedere, the facade of Santa Trìnita, the villa Artimino and the fortifications at Livorno.

**Castagno, Andrea** (c.1421–57). The early years of Castagno's life are mysterious, and the exact year of his birth is not known. Around 1440 he painted the portraits of some executed rebels in the Bargello, a job that earned him the nickname "Andrea of the Hanged Men". In 1442 he was working in Venice, but a couple of years later he was back in Florence, creating stained glass for the Duomo and frescoes for Sant'Apollonia. His taut, sinewy style is to a large extent derived from the sculpture of his contemporary, Donatello, an affinity that is especially clear in his frescoes for Santissima Annunziata. Other major works in Florence include the series of *Famous Men and Women* in the Uffizi and the portrait of *Niccolò da Tolentino* in the Duomo – his last piece.

**Cellini, Benvenuto** (1500–71). Cellini began his career in Rome, where he fought in the siege of the city by the imperial army in 1527. His sculpture is greatly influenced by Michelangelo, as is evident in his most famous large-scale piece, the *Perseus* in the Loggia della Signoria. His other masterpiece in Florence is the heroic *Bust of Cosimo I* in the Bargello. Cellini was an even more accomplished goldsmith and jeweller, creating some exquisite pieces for Francis I, by whom he was employed in the 1530s and 1540s. He also wrote a racy *Autobiography*, a fascinating insight into the artistic world of sixteenth-century Italy and France.

**Cimabue** (c.1240–1302). Though celebrated by Dante as the foremost painter of the generation before Giotto, very little is known about Cimabue – in fact, the only work that is unquestionably by him is the mosaic in Pisa's Duomo. He is generally given credit for the softening of the hieratic Byzantine style of religious art, a tendency carried further by his putative pupil, Giotto. Some works can be attributed to him with more confidence than others; the shortlist would include *The Madonna of St Francis* in the lower church at Assisi, the *Passion* cycle in the upper church, the *Maestà* in the Uffizi, and the crucifixes in Santa Croce (Florence) and San Domenico (Arezzo).

**Daddi, Bernardo** (c.1290–1349). A pupil of Giotto, Daddi combined the solidity of his master's style with the more decorative aspects of the Sienese style. His work can be seen in the Uffizi and Santa Croce in Florence.

**Desiderio da Settignano** (c.1428–64). Desiderio continued the low relief technique pioneered by Donatello in the panel for the Orsanmichele *St George*, and carved the tomb of Carlo Marsuppini in Santa Croce, Florence. He's better known for his exquisite busts of women and children, a good selection of which are on show in the Bargello.

**Donatello** (c.1386–1466). A pupil of Ghiberti, Donatello assisted in the casting of the first set of Florence Baptistery doors in 1403, then worked for Nanni di Banco on the Duomo. His early marble *David* (Bargello) is still Gothic in its form, but a new departure is evident in his heroic *St Mark* for Orsanmichele (1411) – possibly produced after a study of the sculpture of ancient Rome. Four years later he began the intense series of prophets for the Campanile, and at the same time produced the *St George* for

Orsanmichele, the epitome of early Renaissance humanism, featuring a relief that is the very first application of rigorous perspective in Western art.

In the mid-1520s Donatello started a partnership with Michelozzo, with whom he created the tomb of Pope John XXIII in the Florence Baptistery, a refinement of the genre initiated by Arnolfo di Cambio. He went to Rome in 1431, possibly with Brunelleschi, and it was probably on his return that he made the classical bronze *David* (Bargello), one of the first nude statues of the Renaissance period. Also at this time he made the cantoria to be placed opposite the one already made by Luca della Robbia, the pulpit for Prato cathedral (with Michelozzo) and the decorations for the old sacristy in Florence's church of San Lorenzo – the parish church of his great patrons, the Medici.

After a period in Padua – where he created the first bronze equestrian statue since Roman times – he returned to Florence, where his last works show an extraordinary harshness and angularity. The main sculptures from this period are the *Judith and Holofernes* (Palazzo Vecchio), the *Magdalene* (Museo dell'Opera del Duomo) and the two bronze pulpits for San Lorenzo.

**Duccio di Buoninsegna** (c.1255–c.1318). Though occupying much the same pivotal position in the history of Sienese art as Giotto does in Florentine art, Duccio was a less revolutionary figure, refining the stately Byzantine tradition rather than subverting its conventions. One of his earliest works was ordered by Florence's church of Santa Maria Novella – the *Maestà* now in the Uffizi – but the bulk of his output is in his home city. Despite frequent ructions with the civic authorities, for refusing to do military service

among other transgressions, in 1308 he received his most prestigious assignment, the painting of a *Maestà* for Siena's Duomo. The polyptych no longer exists in its original form, but most of the panels are now in Siena's Museo dell'Opera del Duomo. This iconic image of the Madonna, with its rich use of gold and decorative colour, was to profoundly influence such painters as the Lorenzettis and Simone Martini, while the small scenes on the back of the panels reveal a less frequently acknowledged mastery of narrative painting.

**Fra' Angelico** (1387/1400–55). Born in Vicchio, Fra' Angelico joined the Dominican order in Fiesole, near his home town and later entered their monasteries in Cortona and Foligno. His first authenticated painting dates from the mid-1420s, but the first one that can be definitely dated is a *Madonna* he produced for the linen guild of Florence in 1433. Three years later the Dominicans took over the San Marco monastery in Florence, and soon after he embarked on the series of frescoes and altarpieces now displayed in the museum there. In the mid-1440s he was called to Rome to work on the Vatican, after which he worked at Orvieto, served for three years as prior of the monastery in Fiesole, and returned to Rome around 1452, where he died. For all their sophistication of technique, Fra' Angelico's paintings, with their atmosphere of tranquil piety, seem to belong to a less complex world than that inhabited by Donatello, his contemporary. His altarpieces of the Madonna and Saints – a genre known as *sacre conversazione* – were, however, extremely influential compositions.

**Fra' Bartolommeo** (c.1474–1517). Fra' Bartolommeo's earliest known work is the Raphael-influenced *Last Judgement* painted for the San Marco monastery in Florence in 1499. The following year he became a monk

CONTEXTS

C

there, then in 1504 became head of the workshop, a post previously occupied by Fra' Angelico. In 1514 he was in Rome, but according to Vasari was discouraged by Raphael's fame. The works he later produced in Florence had an influence on High Renaissance art, with their repression of elaborate backgrounds and anecdotal detail, concentrating instead on expression and gesture.

**Francesco di Giorgio Martini** (1439–1501/2). Sienese painter, sculptor and architect, whose treatise on architectural theory was circulated widely in manuscript form; Leonardo had a copy. Employed for a long period by Federico da Montefeltro – also a patron of Piero della Francesca – he probably designed the loggia for the Palazzo Ducale in Urbino and the church of San Bernardino. The church of Santa Maria degli Angeli in Siena and the Palazzo Ducale in Gubbio might be by him; the one Tuscan building that was certainly designed by him is Santa Maria del Calcinaio in Cortona, one of the finest early Renaissance structures in Italy.

**Gaddi, Taddeo** (d.1366). According to tradition, Taddeo Gaddi worked with Giotto for 24 years, and throughout his life barely wavered from the precepts of his master's style. His first major independent work is the cycle for the Cappella Baroncelli in Santa Croce, Florence. Other works by him are in Florence's Uffizi, Accademia, Bargello and Museo Horne. **Agnolo Gaddi** (d.1396), Taddeo's son, continued his father's Giottesque style; his major projects were for Santa Croce in Florence and the Duomo of Prato.

**Gentile da Fabriano** (c.1370–1427). Chief exponent of the International Gothic style in Italy, Gentile da Fabriano came to Florence in 1422, when he painted the gorgeous *Adoration of the Magi*, now in the Uffizi. In 1425 he went on to Siena and Orvieto, where the intellectual climate was perhaps more conducive to an artist of his conservative temperament; he finished his career in Rome.

**Ghiberti, Lorenzo** (1378–1455). Trained as a goldsmith, painter and sculptor, Ghiberti concentrated on the last discipline almost exclusively after winning the competition to design the doors for Florence's Baptistery. His first set of doors are to a large extent derived from Andrea Pisano's earlier Gothic panels for the building, yet his workshop was a virtual academy for the seminal figures of the early Florentine Renaissance, Donatello and Uccello among them. The commission took around twenty years to complete, during which time he also worked on the Siena Baptistery and the church of Orsanmichele in Florence, where his *Baptist* and *St Matthew* show the influence of Classical statuary. This classicism reached its peak in the second set of doors for Florence's Baptistery (the *Gates of Paradise*) – taking the innovations of Donatello's low relief carving to a new pitch of perfection. The panels occupied much of the rest of his life but in his final years he wrote his *Commentarii*, the main source of information on fourteenth-century art in Florence and Siena, and the first autobiography by an artist.

**Ghirlandaio, Domenico** (1449–94). The most accomplished fresco artist of his generation, Ghirlandaio was the teacher of Michelangelo. After a short period working on the Sistine Chapel with Botticelli, he came back to Florence, where his cycles in Santa Trìnita and Santa Maria Novella provide some of the most absorbing documentary images of the time, being filled with contemporary portraits and vivid anecdotal details.

**Giambologna** (1529–1608). Born in northern France, Giambologna – Jean de Boulogne – arrived in Italy in the mid-1550s, becoming the most influential Florentine sculptor after Michelangelo's death. Having helped Ammannati on the fountain for the Piazza della Signoria, he went on to produce a succession of pieces that typify the Mannerist predilection for sculptures with multiple viewpoints, such as the *Rape of the Sabines* (Loggia della Signoria) and the *Mercury* (Bargello). His workshop also turned out scores of reduced bronze copies of his larger works; the Bargello has an extensive collection.

**Giotto di Bondone** (1266–1337). It was with Giotto's great fresco cycles that religious art shifted from being a straightforward act of devotion to the dramatic presentation of incident. His unerring eye for the significant gesture, his ability to encapsulate moments of extreme emotion and his technical command of figure modelling and spatial depth brought him early recognition as the greatest artist of his generation – and even as late as the sixteenth century artists were studying his frescoes for their solutions to certain compositional problems. Yet, as with Cimabue, the precise attribution of work is problematic. In all probability his first major cycle was the *Life of St Francis* in the upper church at Assisi, though the extent to which his assistants carried out his designs is still disputed. The Arena chapel in Padua is certainly by him, as are large parts of the Bardi and Peruzzi chapels in Santa Croce in Florence. Of his attributed panel paintings, the Uffizi *Maestà* is the only one universally accepted.

**Gozzoli, Benozzo** (1421–97). Though a pupil of Fra' Angelico, Gozzoli was one of the more worldly artists of the fifteenth century, with a fondness for pageantry that is seen to most impressive effect in the frescoes in Florence's Palazzo Medici-Riccardi. His celebrated cycle in Pisa's Camposanto was all but destroyed in World War II; his other surviving fresco cycles include the *Life of St Francis* in Montefalco and the *Life of St Augustine* in San Gimignano.

**Guido da Siena** (active mid-thirteenth century). Guido was the founder of the Sienese school of painters, but his life is one of the most problematic areas of Siena's art history. A signed painting by him in the Palazzo Pubblico is dated 1221, but some experts think the date may have been altered, and that the work is from the 1260s or 1270s – a period when other pictures associated with him are known to have been painted.

**Leonardo da Vinci** (1452–1519). Leonardo trained as a painter under Verrocchio, and it is said that his precocious talent caused his master to abandon painting in favour of sculpture. Drawings of landscapes and drapery have survived from the 1470s, but the first completed picture is the *Annunciation* in the Uffizi. The sketch of the *Adoration of the Magi*, also in the Uffizi, dates from 1481, at which time there was no precedent for its fusion of geometric form and dynamic action. Two years later he was in the employment of Ludovico Sforza of Milan, remaining there for sixteen years. During this second phase of his career he produced the *Lady with the Ermine* (Kraków), the fresco of the *Last Supper* and – probably – the two versions of *The Virgin of the Rocks*, the fullest demonstrations to date of his so-called sfumato, a blurring of tones from light to dark. Innumerable scientific studies and military projects engaged him at this time, and he also made a massive clay model for an equestrian statue of Francesco Sforza – never completed, like so many of his schemes. When the French took Milan in 1499 Leonardo returned to Florence, where he devoted much of his time to anatomical research. It was during this second Florentine period that he was commissioned to paint a fresco of the *Battle of Anghiari* in the main hall of the Palazzo Ducale, where his detested rival Michelangelo was also set to work. Only a fragment of the fresco was completed, and the innovative technique that Leonardo had employed resulted in its speedy disintegration. His cartoons for the *Madonna and Child with St Anne* (Louvre and National Gallery, London) also date from this period, as does the most famous of all his paintings, the Louvre's *Mona Lisa*, the portrait of the wife of a Florentine merchant. In 1506 he went back to Milan, thence to Rome and finally, in 1517, to France. Again, military and scientific work occupied much of this last period – the only painting to have survived is the *St John*, also in the Louvre.

**Lippi, Filippo** (c.1406–69). In 1421 Filippo Lippi was placed in the monastery of the Carmine in Florence, just at the time Masaccio was beginning work on the Cappella Brancacci there. His early works all bear the stamp of Masaccio, but by the 1530s he was becoming interested in the representation of movement and a more luxuriant surface detail. The frescoes in the cathedral at Prato, executed in the 1550s, show his highly personal, almost hedonistic vision, as do his panel paintings of wistful Madonnas in patrician interiors or soft landscapes – many of them executed for the Medici. His last work, the *Life of the Virgin* fresco cycle in Spoleto, was probably largely executed by assistants.

**Filippino Lippi** (1457/8–1504) completed his father's work in Spoleto – aged about 12 – then travelled to Florence, where his first major commission was the completion of Masaccio's frescoes in Santa Maria del Carmine (c.1484). At

around this time he also painted the *Vision of St Bernard* for the Badìa, which shows an affinity with Botticelli, with whom he is known to have worked. His later researches in Rome led him to develop a self-consciously antique style – seen at its most ambitious in Santa Maria Novella.

**Lorenzetti, Ambrogio** (active 1319–47). Though Sienese, Ambrogio spent part of the 1320s and 1330s in Florence, where he would have witnessed the decoration of Santa Croce by Giotto and his pupils. He's best known for the *Allegory of Good and Bad Government* in the Palazzo Pubblico, which shows painting being used for a secular, didactic purpose for the first time, and is one of the first instances of a landscape being used as an integral part of a composition rather than as a mere backdrop. The Uffizi *Presentation of the Virgin* highlights the difference between Ambrogio's inventive complexity and the comparative simplicity of his brother's style (see below).

**Lorenzetti, Pietro** (active 1306–48). Brother of Ambrogio, Pietro Lorenzetti was possibly a pupil of Duccio's in Siena. His first authenticated work is the altarpiece in Arezzo's Pieve di Santa Maria (1320); others include frescoes in Assisi's lower church, in which the impact of Giotto is particularly noticeable, and the *Birth of the Virgin* in Siena's Museo dell'Opera del Duomo, one of the best demonstrations of his skill as a narrative painter. It's probable that both the Lorenzettis died during the Black Death.

**Lorenzo Monaco** (1372–1425). A Sienese artist, Lorenzo Monaco joined the Camaldolese monastery in Florence, for which he painted the *Coronation of the Virgin*, now in the Uffizi. This and his other earlier works are fairly conventional

Sienese-style altarpieces, with two-dimensional figures on gold backgrounds. However, his late *Adoration of the Magi* (Uffizi), with its fastidious detailing and landscape backdrop, anticipates the arrival of Gentile da Fabriano and fully fledged International Gothic.

**Maitini, Lorenzo** (c.1270–1330). Sienese architect and sculptor, Maitini was the only local artist to challenge the supremacy of the Pisani. In 1310 he was made supervisor of Orvieto's Duomo, for which he designed the biblical panels of the facade – though it's not certain how much of the carving was actually by Maitini. Virtually nothing else about him is known.

**Martini, Simone** (c.1284–1344). The most important Sienese painter, Simone Martini was a pupil of Duccio but equally influenced by Giovanni Pisano's sculpture and the carvings of French Gothic artists. He began his career by painting a fresco counterpart of Duccio's *Maestà* in the city's Palazzo Pubblico (1315). Soon after he was employed by Robert of Anjou, King of Naples, and there developed a sinuous, graceful and courtly style. In the late 1320s he was back in Siena, where he probably produced the portrait of Guidoriccio da Fogliano – though some experts doubt its authenticity. At some point he went to Assisi, where he painted a cycle of *The Life of St Martin* in the lower church. In 1333 he produced a sumptuous *Annunciation* for the Siena Duomo; now in the Uffizi, this is the quintessential fourteenth-century Sienese painting, with its immaculately crafted gold surfaces and emphasis on fluid outline and bright colouration. In 1340 Martini travelled to the papal court of Avignon, where he spent the rest of his life. It was at Avignon that he formed a friendship with Petrarch, for whom he illustrated a magnificent copy of Virgil's poetry.

**Masaccio** (1401–28). Born just outside Florence, Tommaso di ser Giovanni di Mone Cassai – universally known as Masaccio – entered the city's painters' guild in 1422. His first large commission was an altarpiece for the Carmelites of Pisa (the central panel is now in the National Gallery in London), which shows a massive grandeur at odds with the International Gothic style then being promulgated in Florence by Gentile da Fabriano. His masterpieces – the *Trinity* fresco in Santa Maria Novella and the fresco cycle in Santa Maria del Carmine – were produced in the last three years of his life, the latter being painted in collaboration with Masolino. With the architecture of Brunelleschi and the sculpture of Donatello, the Carmine frescoes are the most important achievements of the early Renaissance.

**Maso di Banco** (active 1340s). Maso was perhaps the most inventive of Giotto's acolytes, and his reputation depends chiefly on the cycle of the *Life of St Sylvester* in Santa Croce, Florence.

**Masolino da Panicale** (1383–1447). Masolino was employed in Ghiberti's workshop for the production of the first set of Baptistery doors, and the semi-Gothic early style of Ghiberti conditioned much of his subsequent work. His other great influence was the younger Masaccio, with whom he worked on the Brancacci chapel.

**Michelangelo** - see box on p.109.

**Michelozzo di Bartolommeo** (1396–1472). Born in Florence, Michelozzo worked in Ghiberti's studio and collaborated with Donatello before turning exclusively to architecture. His main patrons were the Medici, for whom he altered the villa at Careggi and built the Palazzo Medici, which set a prototype for patrician mansions in the city, with its rusticated lower storey, smooth upper facade, overhanging cornice and inner courtyard. He later designed the Villa Medici at Fiesole for the family, and for Cosimo de' Medici he added the light and airy library to the monastery of San Marco. In the Alberti-influenced tribune for the church of Santissima Annunziata, Michelozzo produced the first centrally planned church design to be built in the Renaissance period.

**Mino da Fiesole** (1429–84). Florentine sculptor, perhaps a pupil of Desiderio da Settignano, Mino is known chiefly for his tombs and portrait busts; there are examples of the former in Fiesole's Duomo and the Badìa in Florence, and of the latter in the Bargello.

**Nanni di Banco** (c.1384–1421). A Florentine sculptor who began his career as an assistant to his father on the Florence Duomo, Nanni was an exact contemporary of Donatello, with whom he shared some early commissions: Donatello's first *David* was ordered at the same time as an *Isaiah* from Nanni. The finest works produced in his short life are his niche sculptures at Orsanmichele (especially the *Four Saints*) and the relief above the Duomo's Porta della Mandorla.

**Orcagna, Andrea** (c.1308–68). Architect-sculptor-painter, Orcagna was a dominant figure in the period following the death of Giotto, whose emphasis on spatial depth he rejected – as shown in his only authenticated panel painting, the Strozzi altarpiece in Santa Maria Novella. Damaged frescoes can be seen in Santa Croce and Santo Spirito, but Florence's principal work by Orcagna is the massive tabernacle in Orsanmichele. Orcagna's brothers Nardo and Jacopo di Cione were the most influential painters in Florence at the close of the fourteenth century; the

frescoes in the Strozzi chapel are by Nardo.

**Perugino** (1445/50–1523). Born Pietro di Cristoforo Vannucci in Città della Pieve, Perugino was the greatest Umbrian artist. Possibly a pupil of Piero della Francesca, he later trained in Florence in the workshop of Andrea Verrocchio, studying alongside Leonardo da Vinci. By 1480 his reputation was such that he was invited to paint in the Sistine Chapel, filling the east wall with his distinctive gently melancholic figures; today only one of Perugino's original three panels remains. In 1500 he executed his greatest work in Umbria, a fresco cycle commissioned by the bankers' guild of Perugia for their Collegio di Cambio. This was probably the first occasion on which he was assisted by his pupil Raphael – and the moment his own career began to wane. Vasari claimed that he was "a man of little or no religion, who could never bring himself to believe in the immortality of the soul" and the production-line altarpieces that his workshop later turned out were often lacking in genuine passion. Yet he was still amongst the most influential of the Renaissance painters, the catalyst for Raphael and mentor for a host of Umbrian artists. In Tuscany he is best seen in the Uffizi and in the church of Santa Maria Maddalena dei Pazzi.

**Piero della Francesca** (1410/20–92). Piero was born in Borgo Sansepolcro, on the border of Tuscany and Umbria. In the late 1430s he was in Florence, working with Domenico Veneziano, and his later work shows the influence of such Florentine contemporaries as Castagno and Uccello, as well as the impact of Masaccio's frescoes. The exact chronology of his career is contentious, but much of his working life was spent in his native town, for which he produced the *Madonna della Misericordia* and the *Resurrection*, both now in the local Museo Civico. Other patrons included Sigismondo Malatesta of Rimini and Federico da Montefeltro of Urbino, of whom there's a portrait by Piero in the Uffizi. In the 1450s he was in Arezzo, working on the fresco cycle in the church of San Francesco, the only frescoes in Tuscany that can bear comparison with the Masaccio cycle in Florence. He seems to have stopped painting completely in the early 1470s, perhaps to concentrate on his vastly influential treatises on perspective and geometry, but more likely because of failing eyesight.

**Piero di Cosimo** (c.1462–1521). One of the more enigmatic figures of the High Renaissance, Piero di Cosimo shared Leonardo's scholarly interest in the natural world, but turned his knowledge to the production of allusive mythological paintings. There are pictures by him in the Uffizi, Palazzo Pitti, Museo degli Innocenti and Museo Horne.

**Pietro da Cortona** (1596–1669). Painter-architect, born Pietro Berrettini, who with Bernini was the guiding force of Roman Baroque. The style was introduced to Florence by Pietro's ceiling frescoes in the Palazzo Pitti. His last painting is in his home town.

**Pinturicchio** (1454–1513). Born Bernardino di Betto in Perugia, Pinturicchio was taught by Perugino, with whom he collaborated on the painting of the Sistine Chapel. His rich palette earned him his nickname, as well as Vasari's condemnation for superficiality. Most of his work is in Rome but his last commission, one of his most ambitious projects, was his *Life of Pius II* for the Libreria Piccòlomini in Siena.

**Pisano, Andrea** (c.1290–1348). Nothing is known of Andrea Pisano's life until 1330, when he was given the commission to make a new set of doors for the Florence Baptistery.

He then succeeded Giotto as master mason of the Campanile; the set of reliefs he produced for it are the only other works definitely by him (now in the Museo dell'Opera del Duomo). In 1347 he became the supervisor of Orvieto's Duomo, a job later held by his sculptor son, Nino.

**Pisano, Nicola** (c.1220–84). Born somewhere in the southern Italian kingdom of the Emperor Frederick II, Nicola Pisano was the first great classicizing sculptor in pre-Renaissance Italy; the pulpit in Pisa's Baptistery (1260), his first masterpiece, shows clearly the influence of Roman figures. Five years later he produced the pulpit for the Duomo in Siena, with the assistance of his son Giovanni (c.1248–1314) and Arnolfo di Cambio. Father and son again worked together on the Fonte Gaia in Perugia, which was Nicola's last major project. Giovanni's more turbulent Gothic-influenced style is seen in two other pulpits, for San Andrea in Pistoia and for the Pisa Duomo. The Museo dell'Opera del Duomo in Siena has some fine large-scale figures by Giovanni, while its counterpart in Pisa contains a large collection of work by both the Pisani.

**Pollaiuolo, Antonio del** (c.1432–98) and **Piero del** (c.1441–96). Though their Florence workshop turned out engravings, jewellery and embroideries, the Pollaiuolo brothers were known mainly for their advances in oil-painting technique and for their anatomical researches, which bore fruit in paintings and small-scale bronze sculptures. The influences of Donatello and Castagno (Piero's teacher) are evident in their dramatic, often violent sculptural work, which is especially well represented in the Bargello. The Uffizi's collection of paintings suggests that Antonio was by far the more skilled artist.

△ Portrait of Michelangelo by Giuliano Bugiardini

**Pontormo, Jacopo** (1494–1556). Born near Empoli, Pontormo studied under Andrea del Sarto in Florence in the early 1510s. His friendship with Rosso Fiorentino was crucial in the evolution of the hyper-refined Mannerist aesthetic. His early independent works include the frescoes in the atrium of Santissima Annunziata in Florence, showing an edgy quality quite unlike that of his master, who also frescoed this part of the church. In the 1520s he was hired by the Medici to decorate part of their villa at Poggio a Caiano, after which he executed a *Passion* cycle for the Certosa, to the south of the city. His masterpiece in Florence is the *Deposition* in Santa Felìcita (1525), unprecedented in its lurid colour scheme but showing some indebtedness to Michelangelo's figures. The major project of his later years, a fresco cycle in San Lorenzo,

Florence, has been totally destroyed. Other pieces by him are to be seen in the Uffizi and at Carmignano and Sansepolcro.

**Quercia, Jacopo della** (1374–1438). A Sienese contemporary of Donatello and Ghiberti, della Quercia entered the competition for the Florence Baptistery doors which Ghiberti won in 1401. The first known work by him is the tomb of Ilaria del Carretto in Lucca's Duomo. His next major commission was a fountain for Siena's main square, a piece now reassembled in the loggia of the Palazzo Pubblico; before that was finished (1419) he had begun work on a set of reliefs for Siena's Baptistery, a project to which Ghiberti and Donatello also contributed. From 1425 he expended much of his energy on reliefs for San Petronio in Bologna – so much so, that the Sienese authorities ordered him to return some of the money he had been paid for the Baptistery job.

**Raphael** - see Sanzio, Raffaelo

**Robbia, Luca della** (1400–82). Luca began as a sculptor in conventional materials, his earliest achievement being the marble *cantoria* (choir gallery) now in the Museo dell'Opera del Duomo in Florence, typifying the cheerful tone of most of his work. Thirty years later he made the sacristy doors for this city's Duomo, but by then he had devised a technique for applying durable potter's glaze to clay sculpture and most of his energies were given to the art of glazed terracotta. His distinctive blue, white and yellow compositions are seen at their best in the Pazzi chapel in Santa Croce, the Bargello, and at Impruneta, just outside Florence. The best work of his nephew, Andrea della Robbia (1435–1525), who continued the lucrative terracotta business, is at the Spedale degli Innocenti in Florence and at the monastery of La Verna.

Giovanni della Robbia (1469–1529), son of Andrea, is best known for the frieze of the Ceppo in Pistoia.

**Rossellino, Bernardo** (1409–64). An architect-sculptor, Rossellino worked with Alberti and carried out his plans for the Palazzo Rucellai in Florence. His major architectural commission was Pius II's new town of Pienza. As a sculptor he's best known for the monument to Leonardo Bruni in Santa Croce – a derivative of Donatello's tomb of John XXIII in the Baptistery. His brother and pupil Antonio (1427–79) produced the tomb of the Cardinal of Portugal in Florence's San Miniato al Monte, and a number of excellent portrait busts (Bargello).

**Rosso Fiorentino** (1494–1540). Like Pontormo, Rosso Fiorentino was a pupil of Andrea del Sarto, but went on to develop a far more aggressive, acidic style than his colleague and friend. His early *Deposition* in Volterra (1521) and the roughly contemporaneous *Moses Defending the Daughters of Jethro* (Uffizi) are typical of his extreme foreshortening and tense deployment of figures. After a period in Rome and Venice, he eventually went to France, where with Primaticcio he developed the distinctive Mannerist art of the Fontainebleau school.

**Sangallo, Antonio da, the Elder** (1455–1534). A Florence-born architect, Antonio da Sangallo the Elder produced just one major building, but one of the most influential of his period – San Biagio in Montepulciano, based on Bramante's plan for St Peter's in Rome. His nephew, Antonio the Younger (1485–1546), was also born in Florence but did most of his work in Rome, where he began his career as assistant first to Bramante then to Peruzzi. He went on to design the Palazzo Farnese, the most spectacular Roman palace of its time. In Tuscany his most important building is the Fortezza da Basso in Florence.

**Sangallo, Giuliano da** (1445–1516), sculptor, architect and military engineer, was the brother of Antonio the Elder. A follower of Brunelleschi, he produced a number of buildings in and around Florence – the Villa Medici at Poggio a Caiano, Santa Maria delle Carceri in Prato (the first Renaissance church to have a Greek-cross plan) and the Palazzo Strozzi in Florence, the most ambitious palace of the century.

**Sanzio, Raffaelo (Raphael)** (1483–1520). With Leonardo and Michelangelo, Raphael forms the triumvirate whose works define the essence of the High Renaissance. Born in Urbino, he joined Perugino's workshop some time around 1494 and within five years was receiving commissions independently of his master. From 1505 to 1508 he was in Florence, where he absorbed the compositional and tonal innovations of Leonardo; many of the pictures he produced at that time are now in the Palazzo Pitti. From Florence he went to Rome, where Pope Julius II set him to work on the papal apartments (the Stanze). Michelangelo's Sistine ceiling was largely instrumental in modulating Raphael's style from its earlier lyrical grace into something more monumental, but all the works from this more rugged later period are in Rome.

**Sassetta** (c.1392–1450). Sassetta was basically a conventional Sienese painter, though his work does show the influence of International Gothic. Works by him are on show in Siena, Assisi and the Uffizi.

**Signorelli, Luca** (1450–1523). Though a pupil of Piero della Francesca, Signorelli is more indebted to the muscular drama of the Pollaiuolo brothers and the gestural vocabulary developed by Donatello. In the early 1480s he was probably working on the Sistine Chapel with Perugino and Botticelli, but his most important commission came in 1499, when he was hired to complete the cycle begun by Fra' Angelico in Orvieto's Duomo. The emphasis on the nude figure in his *Last Judgement* was to greatly affect Michelangelo. Shortly after finishing this cycle he went to Rome but the competition from Raphael and Michelangelo drove him back to his native Cortona, where he set up a highly proficient workshop. Works are to be seen in Cortona, Arezzo, Monte Oliveto, Perugia, Sansepolcro, and in the Uffizi and Museo Horne in Florence.

**Spinello Aretino** (active 1370s–1410). Probably born in Arezzo, Spinello studied in Florence, possibly under Agnolo Gaddi. He harks back to the monumental aspects of Giotto's style – thus paradoxically paving the way for the most radical painter of the next generation, Masaccio. His main works are in Florence's church of San Miniato al Monte, and Santa Caterina d'Antella, just to the south of the city.

**Uccello, Paolo** (1396–1475). After training in Ghiberti's workshop, Uccello went to Venice, where he worked on mosaics for the Basilica di San Marco. He returned to Florence in 1431 and five years later was contracted to paint the commemorative portrait of Sir John Hawkwood in the Duomo. This trompe l'oeil painting is the first evidence of his interest in the problems of perspective and foreshortening, a subject that was later to obsess him. After an interlude in Padua, he painted the frescoes for the cloister of Santa Maria Novella (c.1445), in which his systematic but non-naturalistic use of perspective is seen at its most extreme. In the following decade he painted the three-scene sequence *Battle of San Romano* (Louvre, London National Gallery and Uffizi) for the Medici – his most ambitious non-fresco paintings, and similarly notable for their strange use of fore-shortening.

**Vasari, Giorgio** (1511–74). Born in Arezzo, Vasari trained with Luca Signorelli and Andrea del Sarto. He became the leading artistic impresario of his day, working for the papacy in Rome and for the Medici in Florence, where he supervised (and partly executed) the redecoration of the Palazzo Vecchio. His own house in Arezzo is perhaps the most impressive display of his limited pictorial talents. He also designed the Uffizi gallery and oversaw a number of other architectural projects, including the completion of the massive Madonna dell'Umiltà in Pistoia. He is now chiefly famous for his Tuscan-biased *Lives of the Most Excellent Painters, Sculptors and Architects*, which charted the rebirth of the fine arts with Giotto and the process of refinement that culminated with Michelangelo.

**Veneziano, Domenico** (1404–61). Despite the name, Domenico Veneziano was probably born in Florence, though his preoccupation with the way in which colour alters in different light conditions is more of a Venetian concern. From 1439 to 1445 he was working on a fresco cycle in Florence with Piero della Francesca, a work that has now perished. Only a dozen surviving works can be attributed to him with any degree of certainty and only two signed pieces by him are left – one of them is the central panel of the so-called *St Lucy Altar* in the Uffizi.

**Verrocchio, Andrea del** (c.1435–88). A Florentine painter, sculptor and goldsmith, Verrocchio was possibly a pupil of Donatello and certainly his successor as the city's leading sculptor. A highly accomplished, if sometimes over-facile, craftsman, he ran one of Florence's busiest workshops, whose employees included the young Leonardo da Vinci. In Florence his work can be seen in the Uffizi, Bargello, San Lorenzo, Santo Spirito, Orsanmichele and Museo dell'Opera del Duomo.

# Books

Most of the books recommended below are currently in print, and those that aren't (indicated by the abbreviation "o/p") shouldn't be too difficult to track down on websites such as ⓦwww.abebooks.com or ⓦwww.alibris.com. Wherever a book is in print, the UK publisher is given first in each listing, followed by the publisher in the US, unless the title is available in one country only, in which case we have specified the country concerned. If the same publisher produces the book in the UK and US, the publisher is simply named once. The 🛪 symbol signifies titles that are especially recommended.

## Travel books and journals

**Charles Dickens** *Pictures from Italy* (Penguin). The classic mid-nineteenth-century Grand Tour, recording the sights of Emilia, Tuscany, Rome and Naples in measured and incisive prose.

**Wolfgang Goethe** *Italian Journey* (Penguin). Revealing for what it says about the tastes of the time – Roman antiquities taking precedence over the Renaissance.

**Edward Hutton** *Florence*; *Country Walks About Florence*; *The Valley of the Arno*; *A Wayfarer in Unknown Tuscany*; *Siena and Southern Tuscany*; *Cities of Umbria*; *Assisi and Umbria Revisited*; *The Cosmati* (all o/p). A Tuscan resident from the 1930s to 1960s, Hutton was nothing if not prolific. Some of his prose adds a new shade to purple, but his books, between them, cover almost every inch of Tuscany and Umbria, and are packed with assiduous background on the art and history.

**Henry James** *Italian Hours* (Penguin). Urbane travel pieces from the young James; perceptive about particular monuments and works of art, superb on the different atmospheres of the great Italian cities.

**Mary McCarthy** *The Stones of Florence* (Penguin, o/p; Harvest). Written in the mid-1960s, *Stones* is a mix of high-class reporting on the contemporary city and anecdotal detail on its history – one of the few accounts that doesn't read as if it's been written in a library.

**H.V. Morton** *A Traveller in Italy* (Methuen; Da Capo). Morton's leisurely and amiable books were written in the 1930s (long before modern tourism got into its stride), and their nostalgic charm has a lot to do with their enduring popularity. But this title – recently reissued – is also packed with learned details and marvellously evocative descriptions.

**Tobias Smollett** *Travels through France and Italy* (Oxford University Press, o/p). One of the funniest travel journals ever written – the apotheosis of Little Englandism, calling on an unmatched vocabulary of disgust at all things foreign.

C

# History and society

## Italy: general history

**Harry Hearder** *Italy: A Short History* (Cambridge University Press). The best one-volume survey of the country from prehistory to the present.

**Giuliano Procacci** *History of the Italian People* (Penguin; Harper &

Row, o/p). A comprehensive if indigestibly dense history of the peninsula, charting the development of Italy as a nation state and giving a context for the story of Tuscany.

## The late-medieval period

**Frances Stonor Saunders** *Hawkwood: Diabolical Englishman* (Faber). Fascinating study of the rapacious mercenary captain whose private army terrorized vast tracts of Italy in the late fourteeenth century,

in the wake of the miseries of the Black Death. More than an excellent biography, this book is a vivid reconstruction of a hellish period of Italian history.

## The Renaissance: general history

**Jacob Burckhardt** *The Civilization of the Renaissance in Italy* (Penguin). A pioneering nineteenth-century classic of Renaissance scholarship – the book that did more than any other to form our image of the period.

**Mary Hollingsworth** *Patronage in Renaissance Italy* (Johns Hopkins University Press, o/p). The first comprehensive English-language study of the relationship between artist and patron in quattrocento

Italy's city-states. A salutary corrective to the mythology of self-inspired Renaissance genius.

**George Holmes** *Florence, Rome and the Origins of the Renaissance* (Oxford University Press). Magnificent – and costly – portrait of the world of Dante and Giotto, with especially compelling sections on the impact of St Francis and the role of the papacy in the political and cultural life of central Italy.

## Florence

**Gene A. Brucker** *Renaissance Florence* (University of California Press). Concentrating on the years 1380–1450, this brilliant study of Florence at its cultural zenith uses masses of archival material to fill in the social, economic and political background to its artistic achievements.

**Eric Cochrane** *Florence in the Forgotten Centuries 1527–1800* (University

of Chicago Press, o/p). Massively erudite account of the twilight centuries of Florence; intimidating in its detail, it's unrivalled in its coverage of the years when the city's scientists were more famous than its painters.

**J.R. Hale** *Florence and the Medici* (Weidenfeld & Nicolson, UK). Scholarly yet lively, this covers the full span of the Medici story from the foundation of the family fortune to the calamitous eighteenth century. Vivid in its re-creation of the various personalities involved, it also presents a fascinating picture of the evolution of the mechanics of power in the Florentine state.

**Christopher Hibbert** *The House of Medici: Its Rise and Fall* (Perennial). More anecdotal than Hale's book, this is a gripping read, chock-full of heroic successes and squalid failures.

**Christopher Hibbert** *Florence: The Biography of a City* (Penguin; Norton, o/p). Yet another excellent Hibbert production, packed with illuminating anecdotes and fascinating illustrations – unlike most books on the city, it's as interesting on the political history as on the artistic achievements, and doesn't grind to a standstill with the fall of the Medici.

**Michael Levey** *Florence: A Portrait* (Pimlico; Harvard). An often illuminating analysis of the city's history, and its artistic history in particular, with snippets and details missed by other accounts.

**Luaro Martines** *April Blood: Florence and the Plot Against the Medici* (Pimlico; Oxford University Press). A thorough and engrossing account of the most notorious conspiracy in Florentine history.

**Paul Strathern** *The Medici: Godfathers of the Renaissance* (Pimlico, UK). Like Hibbert's book, this is a pacy and well-researched narrative of Florence's most famous family, but gives a little more space to the various luminaries (Michelangelo, Galileo etc) who were drawn into their orbit.

## Siena

**Edmund G. Gardner** *The Story of Siena*. Published in Dent's "Medieval Towns" series in the 1920s, this pocket encyclopedia contains lots of anecdote and historical detail you won't find elsewhere.

**Judith Hook** *Siena: A City and Its History* (Hamish Hamilton, o/p – but available in Siena). This superb study of the city and its art concentrates on the medieval heyday but also takes the story through to the present, and includes a good analytical section on the Palio.

## Contemporary Italy

**Luigi Barzini** *The Italians* (Penguin; Atheneum). Published in 1964, Barzini's study is packed with fascinating material, much of which remains valid.

🏃 **Paul Ginsborg** *Italy and Its Discontents* (Penguin; Palgrave). If you want to understand contemporary Italy's baffling mixture of dynamism and ideological sterility, this book – lucidly argued and formidably well-informed – is an essential read. There is no better book on the subject.

**Tobias Jones** *The Dark Heart of Italy* (Faber; North Point Press). Written during a three-year period in Parma, and comprising essays dealing with aspects of modern Italian society, from the legal and political systems to the media and football. Bewildered and fascinated at every turn, Jones reveals a culture in which evasiveness and ethical malleability are as significant as the much-celebrated virtues of vivacity, charm and sophistication – a culture exemplified above all by the character of Silvio

Berlusconi, in effect the owner of the Italian state. An affectionate but clear-eyed corrective to the sentimental-izing claptrap perpetrated by so many English and American expats.

**Charles Richards** *The New Italians* (Penguin; Michael Joseph, o/p). An affectionate and very well-informed survey of modern Italy, with plenty of vivid anecdotes that illustrate the

tensions within a culture that is at once deeply traditional yet at the same time enthralled by the trappings of modernity.

**Frederic Spotts & Theodor Wieser** *Italy: A Difficult Democracy: A Survey of Italian Politics* (Cambridge University Press). Authoritative and highly read-able account of religion, social history and economics in postwar Italy.

# Art and architecture

**Charles Avery** *Florentine Renais-sance Sculpture* (John Murray, o/p). Dependable introduction to the milieu of Donatello and Michelangelo.

**Michael Baxandall** *Painting and Experience in Fifteenth-Century Italy* (Oxford University Press). Invaluable analysis, concen-trating on the way in which the art of the period would have been perceived at the time.

**Vincent Cronin** *The Florentine Renaissance* and *The Flowering of the Renaissance* (Pimlico, UK, o/p). Concise and engaging narrative of Italian art's golden years – the first volume covers the fifteenth century, the second switches the focus to sixteenth-century Rome and Venice.

**Rona Goffen** *Renaissance Rivals* (Yale University Press). It's a truism that the cultural history of Renaissance Italy is to a large extent a history of competition – between artists, between individual patrons and between the various city-states. However, Rona Goffen's masterly book, published in 2003, is revela-tory in its analysis of the depth and the complexity of the antagonisms involved in the production of high art in this period. Concen-trating above all on the work of Michelangelo, Leonardo, Raphael

and Titian, and making incisive use of a wealth of documentation, from poetry to legal contracts, she illu-minates a world in which painters, sculptors and architects were cease-lessly endeavouring to supersede their contemporary rivals and the exemplars of the ancient world.

**Richard Goy** *Florence: the City and Its Architecture* (Phaidon). Published in 2002, this book presents a fresh approach to a subject about which you might think there's noth-ing new to say. Instead of writing a doggedly sequential history, Goy has constructed a book that uses multiple perspectives to illuminate the archi-tecture of Florence: the first section summarizes the city's development up to the unification of Italy; part two looks at the influence of the two chief "nuclei of power" – the Church and the State; part three analyzes the fabric of the city according to build-ing type (*palazzi*, churches, forti-fications etc); and the final section looks at the changes that Florence has undergone in the last century and a half. Encompassing everything from the Baptistery to the football stadium, and magnificently illustrated, this is a clear first choice.

**J.R. Hale** (ed.) *Concise Encyclopaedia of the Italian Renaissance* (Thames & Hudson, o/p in UK).

Exemplary reference book, many of whose summaries are as informative as essays twice their length; covers individual artists, movements, cities, philosophical concepts, the lot.

🏃 **Frederick Hartt & David Wilkins** *History of Italian Renaissance Art* (Prentice Hall). If one book on this vast subject can be said to be indispensable, this is it. In view of its comprehensiveness and the range of its illustrations, it's a bargain.

**Michael Levey** *Early Renaissance* (Penguin, o/p). Precise and fluently written account from a former director of the National Gallery, and well illustrated; probably the best introduction to the subject. Levey's *High Renaissance* (Penguin, o/p) continues the story in the same style.

**Anna Maria Massinelli and Filippo Tuena** *Treasures of the Medici* (Rizzoli; Vendome). Illustrated inventory of the Medici family's collection of jewellery, vases and other *objets d'art*, published to celebrate the 500th anniversary of the death of Lorenzo il Magnifico, perhaps the clan's most compulsive collector. Not the first book to buy for your Florentine library, but definitive in its field.

**Peter Murray** *The Architecture of the Italian Renaissance* (Thames & Hudson; Schocken). Begins with Romanesque buildings and finishes with Palladio – useful both as a gazetteer of the main monuments and as a synopsis of the underlying concepts.

**Diana Norman** *Painting in Late Medieval and Renaissance Siena* (Yale University Press). First published in 2003, this concise and well-illustrated book explicates the evolution of Sienese art from the thirteenth century to the middle of the sixteenth, finishing with the work of Beccafumi, the last Sienese painter of any magnitude.

**John Shearman** *Mannerism* (Penguin, o/p). The self-conscious art of sixteenth-century Mannerism is one of the most complex topics of Renaissance studies; Shearman's brief discussion analyzes the main currents, and never succumbs to oversimplification or pedantry.

🏃 **Giorgio Vasari** *Lives of the Artists* (Penguin). This two-volume abridgement is the fullest available translation of Vasari's classic (and highly tendentious) work on his predecessors and contemporaries. Includes essays on Giotto, Brunelleschi, Leonardo and Michelangelo. The first real work of art history, and still among the most revealing books on Italian Renaissance art. Oxford University Press publishes a newer and briefer one-volume selection.

## Individual artists

**James A. Ackerman** *The Architecture of Michelangelo* (University of Chicago). A concise, scholarly and highly engaging survey, which will make you see Michelangelo's architecture with fresh eyes.

**Charles Avery** *Donatello: An Introduction* (Murray, o/p; Icon, o/p). A perfectly serviceable book that does exactly what its title suggests, but there is a gap in the market for a more substantial English-language study of this seminal figure of the Renaissance.

**Charles Avery** *Giambologna* (Phaidon). This is the best survey of the career of the pre-eminent sculptor of the Mannerist period – an artist who can be seen as the successor of Michelangelo and precursor of Bernini. Though a little dogged in its approach – a synopsis, followed by thematic chapters devoted to "Monumental statues", "Religious sculpture", "Marble fountains" etc – Avery's book is admirably comprehensive (every single sculpture is covered) and beautifully illustrated, with plenty of detailed close-ups of the major pieces and fascinating examples of the clay models that Giambologna created while sketching out his ideas.

**Umberto Baldini and Ornella Casazza** *The Brancacci Chapel* (Thames & Hudson, o/p; Abrams, o/p). Written by the chief restorers of the Brancacci cycle of frescoes by Masaccio, Masolino and Filippino Lippi, this luscious book is illustrated with magnificent life-sized reproductions of the freshly cleaned masterpieces.

**Luciano Bellosi** *Duccio: The Maestà* (Thames and Hudson). Published in 1999, this superb production aims to present "a very direct experience of Duccio di Buoninsegna's masterpiece", and it does just that, with page after page of the highest-quality details from the greatest of all Sienese paintings. The analytical essay that precedes the reproductions is a useful introduction to the work, but essentially this is a book to contemplate rather than to read.

**Kenneth Clark** *Leonardo da Vinci* (Penguin). Old-fashioned in its reverential connoisseurship, but still highly recommended.

**Bruce Cole** *Giotto and Florentine Painting 1280–1375* (HarperCollins, o/p). Excellent introduction to the art of Giotto and his immediate successors.

**Ludwig Goldscheider** *Michelangelo: Paintings, Sculpture, Architecture* (Phaidon). Virtually all monochrome reproductions, but an extremely good pictorial survey of Michelangelo's output, covering everything except the drawings.

**Anthony Grafton** *Leon Battista Alberti* (Penguin; Harvard University Press). A fascinating study of one of the central figures of the Renaissance, Grafton's book illuminates every aspect of Alberti's astonishingly versatile career, which encompassed not just the visual arts and architecture, but also music, law, science and literature. Invaluable, not just as a portrait of an amazing man, but as an introduction to the whole culture of quattrocento Italy.

**James Hall** *Michelangelo and the Reinvention of the Human Body* (Chatto & Windus; Farrar, Straus & Giroux). A provocative and frequently brilliant study of Michelangelo, arguing for the essential modernity of Michelangelo's unprecedented emphasis on the male nude. Not all of Hall's observations are wholly convincing, but on almost every page there's an insight that will make you look afresh.

**William Hood** *Fra Angelico at San Marco* (Yale University Press). Maintaining this imprint's reputation for elegantly produced, scholarly yet accessible art books, Hood's socio-aesthetic study of the panel paintings and frescoes of Fra' Angelico is unsurpassed in its scope. A book to read after you've made your first acquaintance with the pictures.

**Anthony Hughes** *Michelangelo* (Phaidon). This is one of the first titles in Phaidon's "Art & Ideas" series, a project which aims to present well-illustrated overviews of the work of individual artists and art movements, written by scholars but in a style that's accessible to all. *Michelangelo* is a superb advertisement for the series, giving a clear narrative while delineating the social and cultural milieu, and explaining clearly the key issues of style, technique and intepretation.

**Martin Kemp** *Leonardo* (Oxford University Press). Kemp is one of the world's leading Leonardo scholars, but he wears his learning lightly in this brief study, which is primarily concerned with revealing the intellectual preoccupations that unite the artist's multifarious creations.

**Ross King** *Brunelleschi's Dome* (Penguin). The tale of one of the most remarkable feats of engineering in European history – the design and construction of the dome of Florence's cathedral. King is good on the social and intellectual atmosphere, and has a thriller-writer's sense of pace.

**Marilyn Aronberg Lavin** *Piero della Francesca* (Phaidon). Another title in Phaidon's "Art & Ideas" project, this is the best English-language introduction to this most elusive of major Renaissance artists. Marilyn Aronberg Lavin is perhaps the world's leading authority on the subject, but this overview is perfectly pitched for the general reader, and benefits from having been published after the restoration of the Arezzo cycle, so its illustrations are uniquely accurate.

🏃 **Charles Nicholl** *Leonardo: The Flights of the Mind* (Penguin). Leonardo left more than 7000 pages of manuscript notes, and Nicholl's dazzling biography is founded on an intensive study of these largely unpublished writings. The result is a book which is both a highly persuasive portrait of this elusive genius,

and a compendious reconstruction of the milieu in which he worked.

**Jeffrey Ruda** *Fra Filippo Lippi* (Phaidon). First published in 1993, Ruda's monograph is a fine achievement, combining a biographical study of the most wayward of early Renaissance masters with a consistently illuminating analysis of the paintings, which are reproduced in gorgeous large-format colour plates. The paperback edition is an abridged version of the hardback (the catalogue of Lippi's output is reduced to a list of key works), but it's as thorough as any lay reader could want, and astonishingly inexpensive for a production of this quality.

**John White** *Duccio: Tuscan Art and the Mediaeval Workshop* (Thames & Hudson, o/p). The fullest study of the Sienese master available in English, concentrating on his art in the context of medieval workshop practices.

**Alison Wright** *The Pollaiuolo Brothers: the Arts of Florence and Rome* (Yale University Press). As painters, sculptors and goldsmiths, the Pollaiuolo brothers ran one of the busiest workshops in fifteenth-century Florence. Wright's book is a thorough and superbly illustrated study of the business of art production, as well as giving an unimprovable guide to the brothers' highly varied and innovative output.

# Literature

**Dante Alighieri** *The Divine Comedy* (Oxford University Press, 3 vols). No work in any other language bears comparison with Dante's poetic exegesis of the moral scheme of God's creation: in late medieval Italy it was venerated both as a book of almost scriptural authority and as the ultimate refinement of the vernacular Tuscan language. There are numerous

translations; the Oxford University Press version is in prose, but it has the advantage of presenting the original text opposite the English, and has exemplary notes.

**Ludovico Ariosto** *Orlando Furioso* (Penguin). Barbara Reynolds has done a fine job in this two-volume verse translation of Italy's chivalric epic, set in Charlemagne's Europe. Oxford University Press produces a one-volume prose translation.

**Giovanni Boccaccio** *The Decameron* (Penguin). Set in the plague-racked Florence of 1348, Boccaccio's assembly of one hundred short stories is a fascinating social record as well as a constantly diverting and often smutty comedy.

**Benvenuto Cellini** *Autobiography* (Penguin). Shamelessly egocentric record of the travails and triumphs of the sculptor and goldsmith's career; one of the freshest literary productions of its time. Oxford University Press also publishes an excellent translation, under the title *My Life*.

**Niccolo Machiavelli** *The Prince* (Oxford University Press). A treatise on statecraft which actually did less to form the political thought of Italy than it did to form foreigners' perceptions of the country; yet there was far more to Machiavelli than the *Realpolitik* of *The Prince*, as is shown by the selection of writings included in Viking's superb anthology, *The Portable Machiavelli*.

**Petrarch (Francesco Petrarca)** *Selections from the Canzoniere* (Oxford University Press). Often described as the first modern poet, by virtue of his preoccupation with worldly fame and secular love, Petrarch wrote some of the Italian language's greatest lyrics. This slim selection at least hints at what is lost in translation.

**Leonardo da Vinci** *Notebooks* (Oxford University Press). Miscellany of speculation and observation from the universal genius of Renaissance Italy; essential to any understanding of the man.

# Language

# Language

# Language

The ability to speak English confers prestige in Italy, and there's often no shortage of people willing to show off their knowledge, particularly in the main cities and resorts. However, in more remote areas you may find no one speaks English at all.

## Pronunciation

Wherever you are, it's a good idea to master at least a little Italian, a task made easier by the fact that your halting efforts will often be rewarded by smiles and genuine surprise. In any case, it's one of the easiest European languages to learn, especially if you already have a smattering of French or Spanish, both of which are extremely similar grammatically.

Easiest of all is the **pronunciation**, since every word is spoken exactly as it's written, and usually enunciated with exaggerated, open-mouthed clarity. The only difficulties you're likely to encounter are the few **consonants** that are different from English:

**c** before e or i is pronounced as in **ch**urch, while **ch** before the same vowel is hard, as in **c**at.

**sci** or **sce** are pronouced as in **sh**eet and **sh**elter respectively. The same goes with **g** – soft before e or i, as in **g**eranium; hard when followed by h, as in **g**arlic.

**gn** has the ni sound of our o**ni**on.

**gl** in Italian is softened to something like li in English, as in stal**li**on.

**h** is not aspirated, as in **h**onour.

When **speaking** to strangers, the third person is the polite form (ie *Lei* instead of *Tu* for "you"); using the second person is a mark of disrespect or stupidity. It's also worth remembering that Italians don't use "please" and "thank you" half as much as we do: it's all implied in the tone, though if you're in any doubt, err on the polite side.

All Italian words are **stressed** on the penultimate syllable unless an **accent** (´ or `) denotes otherwise, although accents are often left out in practice. Note that the ending –ia or –ie counts as two syllables, hence trattoria is stressed on the i. Generally, in the text we've put accents in whenever it isn't immediately obvious how a word should be pronounced – though you shouldn't assume that this is how you'll see the words written in Italian. For example, in *Maríttima*, the accent is on the first i, but on Italian maps it's often written Marittima.

## Italian words and phrases

### Numbers

| uno | 1 | quattro | 4 |
| due | 2 | cinque | 5 |
| tre | 3 | sei | 6 |

| | | | |
|---|---|---|---|
| sette | 7 | trenta | 30 |
| otto | 8 | quaranta | 40 |
| nove | 9 | cinquanta | 50 |
| dieci | 10 | sessanta | 60 |
| úndici | 11 | settanta | 70 |
| dódici | 12 | ottanta | 80 |
| trédici | 13 | novanta | 90 |
| quattórdici | 14 | cento | 100 |
| quíndici | 15 | centuno | 101 |
| sédici | 16 | centodieci | 110 |
| diciassette | 17 | duecento | 200 |
| diciotto | 18 | cinquecento | 500 |
| diciannove | 19 | mille | 1000 |
| venti | 20 | cinquemila | 5000 |
| ventuno | 21 | diecimila | 10,000 |
| ventidue | 22 | cinquanta mila | 50,000 |

## Basics

| | | | |
|---|---|---|---|
| Buongiorno | Good morning | Oggi | Today |
| Buona sera | Good afternoon/ evening | Domani | Tomorrow |
| | | Dopodomani | Day after tomorrow |
| Buona notte | Good night | Ieri | Yesterday |
| Ciao (informal; to phrases above) | Hello/goodbye strangers use | Adesso | Now |
| | | Più tardi | Later |
| Arrivederci | Goodbye (formal) | Aspetta! | Wait a minute! |
| Sì | Yes | di mattina | In the morning |
| No | No | nel pomeriggio | In the afternoon |
| Per favore | Please | di sera | In the evening |
| Grázie (molte/ grazie mille) | Thank you (very much) | Qui/La | Here (there) |
| | | Buono/Cattivo | Good/bad |
| Prego | You're welcome | Grande/Píccolo | Big/small |
| Va bene | Alright/that's OK | Económico/Caro | Cheap/expensive |
| Come stai/sta? (informal/formal) | How are you? | Presto/Ritardo | Early/late |
| | | Caldo/Freddo | Hot/cold |
| Bene | I'm fine | Vicino/Lontano | Near/far |
| Parla inglese? | Do you speak English? | Velocemente/ Lentamente | Quickly/slowly |
| Non ho capito | I don't understand | | |
| Non lo so | I don't know | Piano | Slowly/quietly |
| Mi scusi/Prego | Excuse me | Con/Senza | With/without |
| Permesso | Excuse me (in a crowd) | Più/Meno | More/less |
| Mi dispiace | sorry | Basta | Enough, no more |
| Sono qui in vacanza | I'm here on holiday | Signor . . . | Mr . . . |
| Sono inglese/ scozzese/ gallese/ irlandese | I'm English/ Scottish/ Welsh/ Irish | Signora . . . | Mrs . . . |
| | | Signorina . . . | Miss . . . |
| | | (il Signor, la Signora, la Signorina when speaking about someone else) | |
| Abito a . . . | I live in . . . | | |

## Driving

| | | | |
|---|---|---|---|
| Sempre diritto | Go straight ahead | Rallentare | Slow down |
| Gira a destra/sinistra | Turn to the right/left | Strada chiusa/ guasta | Road closed/ up |
| Parcheggio | Parking | | |
| Divieto di sosta/ Sosta vietata | No parking | Vietato il transito | No through road |
| | | Vietato il sorpasso | No overtaking |
| Senso único | One-way street | Incrocio | Crossroads |
| Senso vietato | No entry | Limite di Velocità | Speed limit |

## Some signs

| | | | |
|---|---|---|---|
| Entrata/Uscita | Entrance/exit | Affitasi | To let |
| Ingresso líbero | Free entrance | Binario | Platform |
| Signori/Signore | Gentlemen/ladies | Cassa | Cash desk |
| Bagno | WC | Avanti | Go/walk |
| Libero/Occupato | Vacant/engaged | Alt | Stop/halt |
| Aperto/Chiuso | Open/closed | Dogana | Customs |
| Arrivi/Partenze | Arrivals/departures | Non toccare | Do not touch |
| Chiuso per restauro | Closed for restoration | Perícolo | Danger |
| Chiuso per ferie | Closed for holidays | Attenzione | Beware |
| Tirare/Spingere | Pull/push | Pronto soccorso | First aid |
| Guasto | Out of order | Suonare il campanello | Ring the bell |
| Acqua potabile | Drinking water | Vietato fumare | No smoking |

## Accommodation

| | | | |
|---|---|---|---|
| Albergo | Hotel | Ha niente che costa di meno? | Do you have anything cheaper? |
| C'è un albergo qui vicino? | Is there a hotel nearby? | | |
| | | Pensione completa/ mezza pensione | Full/half board |
| Ha una camera ... | Do you have a room ... | | |
| per una/due/ tre person(a/e) | for one/two/ three people | Posso vedere la camera? | Can I see the room? |
| per una/due/tre nott(e/i) | for one/two/three nights | La prendo | I'll take it |
| | | Vorrei prenotare una camera | I'd like to book a room |
| per una/due settiman(a/e) | for one/two weeks | | |
| | | Ho una prenotazione | I have a booking |
| con un letto matrimoniale | with a double bed | Possiamo fare il campeggio qui? | Can we camp here? |
| con una doccia/ una vasca | with a shower/bath | C'è un camping qui vicino | Is there a campsite nearby? |
| con una terrazza acqua calda/freddo | with a balcony hot/cold water | | |
| | | Tenda | Tent |
| Quanto costa? | How much is it? | Cabina | Cabin |
| È caro | It's expensive | Ostello per la gioventù | Youth hostel |
| È compresa la prima colazione? | Is breakfast included? | | |
| | | una camera singola | Single room |
| | | una camera doppia | Double room |

LANGUAGE | Italian words and phrases

353

| | | | |
|---|---|---|---|
| una camera a due letti | Room with twin beds | ho una prenotazione | I have a reservation |
| una camera con bagno | Room with private bathroom | potrei guardare un'altra camera? | Could I see another room? |
| avete camere libere | Do you have rooms free? | il facchino | Porte |
| | | ascensore | Lift |
| | | la chiave | Key |

## Questions and directions

| | | | |
|---|---|---|---|
| Dove? (Dov'è/ Dove sono) | Where? (where is/are) | Mi può dare un passaggio a . . . ? | Can you give me a lift to . . . ? |
| Quando? | When? | Mi può dire di scendere alla fermata giusta? | Can you tell me when to get off? |
| Cosa? (Cos'è?) | What? (what is it?) | | |
| Quanto/Quanti? | How much/many? | A che ora apre? | What time does it open? |
| Perchè? | Why? | | |
| È/C'è (È/C'è . . . ?) | It is/there is (is it/is there . . . ?) | A che ora chiude? | What time does it close? |
| Che ora è/Che ore | What time is it? | Quanto costa? (Quanto costano?) | How much does it cost ( . . . do they cost?) |
| Come arrivo a . . . ? | How do I get to . . . ? | Come si chiama in italiano? | What's it called in Italian? |
| Quant'è lontano a . . . ? | How far is it to . . . ? | | |

## Travelling

| | | | |
|---|---|---|---|
| Aeroplano | Aeroplane | A che ora parte? | What time does it leave? |
| Porto | Port | Quando parte il prossimo pullman/ treno/traghetto per . . . ? | When is the next bus/ train/ferry to . . . ? |
| Bicicletta | Bicycle | | |
| Traghetto | Ferry | | |
| Stazione ferroviaria | Railway station | Devo cambiare? | Do I have to change? |
| Autobus/pullman | Bus | Da dove parte? | Where does it leave from? |
| Autostop | Hitchhiking | | |
| Nave | Ship | Da quale binario parte? | What platform does it leave from? |
| Autostazione | Bus station | | |
| Aliscafo | Hydrofoil | Quanti chilometri sono? | How many kilometres is it? |
| Taxi | Taxi | | |
| Macchina | Car | Quanto ci vuole? | How long does it take? |
| A piedi | On foot | Que número di autobus per . . . ? | What number bus is it to . . . ? |
| Treno | Train | | |
| Un biglietto a . . . | A ticket to . . . | Dov'è la strada a . . . ? | Where's the road to . . . ? |
| Solo andata/ andata e ritorno | One-way/return | | |
| Posso prenotare un posto? | Can I book a seat? | La prossima fermata, per favore | Next stop please |

# Italian menu reader

## Meals and courses

| la colazione | breakfast | zuppe/minestre | soups |
|---|---|---|---|
| pranzo | lunch | secondi | main courses |
| cena | evening meal | contorni | vegetables |
| antipasti | starters | dolci | desserts |
| primi | first courses | menù degustazione | tasting menu |

## General terms

| il cameriere | waiter | maionese | mayonnaise |
|---|---|---|---|
| il menù/la lista | menu | marmellata | jam (jelly) |
| la lista dei vini | wine list | olio | oil |
| un coltello | knife | olive | olives |
| una forchetta | fork | pane | bread |
| un cucchiaio | spoon | pane integrale | wholemeal bread |
| senza carne | without meat | panino | bread roll/sandwich |
| coperto | cover charge | panna | cream |
| servizio | service charge | patatine | crisps (potato chips) |
| aceto | vinegar | patatine fritte | chips (french fries) |
| aglio | garlic | pepe | pepper |
| biscotti | biscuits | pizzetta | small cheese and tomato pizza |
| burro | butter | | |
| caramelle | sweets | riso | rice |
| cioccolato | chocolate | sale | salt |
| focaccia | oven-baked snack | uova | eggs |
| frittata | omelette | zucchero | sugar |
| grissini | breadsticks | | |

## Cooking terms

| affumicato | smoked | al Marsala | cooked with Marsala wine |
|---|---|---|---|
| arrosto | roast | Milanese | fried in egg and breadcrumbs |
| ben cotto | well done | | |
| bollito/lesso | boiled | pizzaiola | cooked with tomato sauce |
| brasata | cooked in wine | | |
| cotto | cooked (not raw) | al puntino | medium (steak) |
| crudo | raw | ripieno | stuffed |
| al dente | firm (not overcooked) | al sangue | rare (steak) |
| aí ferri | grilled without oil | allo spiedo | on the spit |
| fritto | fried | surgelato | frozen |
| grattuggiato | grated | umido | steamed/stewed |
| alla griglia | grilled | | |

L

355

## Pizzas

| | | | |
|---|---|---|---|
| calzone | folded pizza with cheese, ham and tomato | | fresh (**funghi freschi**) |
| capricciosa | literally "capricious"; topped with whatever they've got in the kitchen, usually including baby artichoke, ham and egg | margherita | cheese and tomato |
| | | marinara | tomato, anchovy and olive oil |
| | | napo/napoletana | tomato |
| | | quattro formaggi | "four cheeses", usually including mozzarella, fontina and gruyère |
| cardinale | ham and olives | quattro stagioni | "four seasons"; the toppings split into four separate sections, usually including ham, green pepper, onion, egg etc |
| frutta di mare | seafood; usually mussels, prawns and clams | | |
| funghi | mushrooms; the tinned sliced variety, unless it specifies | | |

## Antipasti

| | | | |
|---|---|---|---|
| antipasto misto | mixed cold meats and cheese | melanzane in parmigiana | aubergine in tomato and Parmesan cheese |
| caponata | mixed aubergine, olives, tomatoes | peperonata | green and red peppers stewed in olive oil |
| caprese | tomato and mozzarella salad | pinzimonio | raw seasonal vegetable in olive oil, with salt and pepper |
| crostini | mixed canapés | | |
| crostini di milza | minced spleen on pieces of toast | pomodori ripieni | stuffed tomatoes |
| donzele/donzelline | fried dough balls | prosciutto | ham |
| fettuna/bruschetta | garlic toast with olive oil | prosciutto di cinghiale | cured wild boar ham |
| finocchiona | pork sausage flavoured with fennel | salame toscano | pork sausage with pepper and cubes of fat |
| insalata di mare | seafood salad | | |
| insalata di riso | rice salad | salsicce | pork or wild boar sausage |
| insalata russa | Russian salad (diced vegetables in mayonnaise) | | |

## Primi

| **Soups** | | carabaccia | onion soup |
|---|---|---|---|
| | | garmugia | soup made with fava beans, peas, artichokes, asparagus and bacon |
| acquacotta | onion soup served with toast and poached egg | | |
| brodo | clear broth | | |

| minestra di farro | wheat and bean soup |
| minestrina | any light soup |
| minestrone | thick vegetable soup |
| minestrone alla fiorentina | haricot bean soup with red cabbage, tomatoes, onions and herbs |
| pappa al pomodoro | tomato soup thickened with bread |
| pasta fagioli | pasta soup with beans |
| pastini in brodo | pasta pieces in clear broth |
| ribollita | winter vegetable soup, based on beans and thickened with bread |
| stracciatella | broth with egg |
| zuppa di fagioli | bean soup |

| penne | smaller pieces of rigatoni |
| penne strasciate | quill-shaped pasta in meat sauce |
| rigatoni | large, grooved tubular pasta |
| risotto | cooked rice dish, with sauce |
| risotto nero | rice cooked with cuttlefish (in its own ink) |
| spaghettini | thin spaghetti |
| tagliatelle | pasta ribbons (another word for **fettuccine**) |
| tortellini | small rings of pasta stuffed with meat or cheese |
| vermicelli | "little worms" (very thin spaghetti) |

## Pasta

| cannelloni | large tubes of pasta, stuffed |
| farfalle | literally "butterfly"-shaped pasta |
| fettuccine | narrow pasta ribbons |
| gnocchi | small potato and dough dumplings |
| gnocchi di ricotta | dumplings filled with ricotta and spinach |
| maccheroni | tubular spaghetti |
| pappardelle | wide, short noodles, often served with hare sauce (**con lepre**) |
| pasta al forno | pasta baked with minced meat, eggs, tomato and cheese |
| pasta alla carrettiera | pasta with tomato, garlic, pepper, parsley and chilli |

## Pasta sauce (salsa)

| arrabbiata | spicy tomato sauce with chillies |
| bolognese | tomato and meat |
| burro | butter |
| carbonara | cream, ham and beaten egg |
| funghi | mushrooms |
| matriciana | tomato and cubed pork |
| panna | cream |
| parmigiano | Parmesan cheese |
| peperoncino | olive oil, garlic and fresh chillies |
| pesto | green basil and garlic sauce |
| pomodoro | tomato sauce |
| ragù | meat sauce |
| vongole | clam and tomato sauce |

## Secondi

## Meat (carne)

| agnello | lamb |
| bistecca | steak |
| cervello | brain |
| cinghiale | wild boar |
| coniglio | rabbit |

| costolette | chops |
| cotolette | cutlets |
| fagiaon | pheasant |
| faraona | guinea fowl |
| fegatini | chicken livers |
| fegato | liver |

| involtini | meat slices, rolled and stuffed |
| lepre | hare |
| lingua | tongue |
| maiale | pork |
| manzo | beef |
| mortadella | salami-type cured meat |
| osso buco | shin of veal |
| pernice | partridge |
| pancetta | bacon |
| pollo | chicken |
| polpette | meatballs |
| rognoni | kidneys |
| salsiccia | sausage |
| saltimbocca | veal with ham |
| spezzatino | stew |
| tacchino | turkey |
| trippa | tripe |
| vitello | veal |

## Fish (pesce) and shellfish (crostacei)

| acciughe | anchovies |
| anguilla | eel |
| aragosta | lobster |
| baccalà | dried salted cod |
| calamari | squid |
| céfalo | mullet |
| cozze | mussels |
| dentice | dentex |
| gamberetti | shrimps |
| gámberi | prawns |
| granchio | crab |
| merluzzo | cod |
| ostriche | oysters |
| pescespada | swordfish |
| polpo | octopus |
| sarde | sardines |
| sgombro | mackerel |
| sogliola | sole |
| tonno | tuna |
| triglie | red mullet |
| trota | trout |
| vóngole | clams |

## Tuscan specialities

| arista | roast pork loin with garlic and rosemary |
| asparagi alla fiorentina | asparagus with butter, fried egg and cheese |
| baccalà alla livornese | salt cod with garlic, tomatoes and parsley |
| bistecca alla fiorentina | thick grilled T-bone steak |
| cibreo | chicken liver and egg stew |
| cieche alla pisana | small eels cooked with sage and tomatoes, served with Parmesan |
| lombatina | veal chop |
| peposo | peppered beef stew |
| pollo alla diavola/ al mattone | chicken flattened with a brick, grilled with herbs |
| scottiglia | stew of veal, game and poultry, cooked with white wine and tomatoes |
| spiedini di maiale | skewered spiced cubes of pork loin and liver, with bread and bay leaves |
| tonno con fagioli | tuna with white beans and raw onion |
| trigile alla livornese | red mullet cooked with tomatoes, garlic and parsley |
| trippa alla fiorentina | tripe in tomato sauce, served with Parmesan |

# Vegetables (contorni) and salad (insalata)

| asparagi | asparagus | carciofini | artichoke hearts |
| basílico | basil | carotte | carrots |
| capperi | capers | cavolfiori | cauliflower |
| carciofi | artichokes | cávolo | cabbage |

| cetriolo | cucumber | insalata mista | mixed salad |
| cipolla | onion | insalata verde | green salad |
| fagioli all'olio | white beans served with olive oil | melanzane | aubergine |
| | | origano | oregano |
| fagioli all'uccelletto | white beans cooked with tomatoes, garlic and sage | patate | potatoes |
| | | peperoni | peppers |
| | | piselli | peas |
| fagiolini | green beans | pomodori | tomatoes |
| finocchio | fennel | radicchio | chicory |
| frittata di carciofi | fried artichoke flan | spinaci | spinach |
| funghi | mushrooms | zucchini | courgettes |

## Sweets (dolci), fruit (frutta), cheese (formaggi) and nuts (noce)

| amaretti | macaroons | meringa | frozen meringue with whipped cream and chocolate |
| ananas | pineapple | | |
| anguria/coccómero | watermelon | | |
| arance | oranges | mozzarella | bland soft white cheese used on pizzas |
| banane | bananas | | |
| brigidini | anise wafer biscuits | | |
| buccellato | anise raisin cake | necci | chestnut-flour crêpes |
| cacchi | persimmons | nespole | medlars |
| cantucci/cantuccini | small almond biscuits, served with Vinsanto wine | panforte | hard fruit, nut and spice cake |
| | | parmigiano | Parmesan cheese |
| castagnaccio | unleavened chestnut-flour cake containing raisins, walnuts and rosemary | pecorino | strong hard sheep's cheese |
| | | pere | pears |
| | | pesche | peaches |
| cenci | fried dough dusted with powdered sugar | pignoli | pine nuts |
| | | provolone | strong hard cheese |
| ciliegie | cherries | ricciarelli | marzipan almond biscuits |
| fichi | figs | | |
| fichi d'India | prickly pears | ricotta | soft white sheep's cheese |
| fontina | Northern Italian cooking cheese | | |
| fragole | strawberries | schiacciata alla fiorentina | orange-flavoured cake covered with powdered sugar, eaten at carnival time |
| frittelle di riso | rice fritters | | |
| gelato | ice cream | | |
| gorgonzola | a soft blue cheese | | |
| limone | lemon | schiacciata con l'uva | grape- and sugar-covered bread dessert |
| macedonia | fruit salad | | |
| mandorle | almonds | | |
| mele | apples | torta | cake, tart |
| melone | melon | uva | grapes |

LANGUAGE | Italian menu reader

**L**

359

| zabaglione | dessert made with eggs, sugar and Marsala wine | zuccotto | sponge cake filled with chocolate and whipped cream |
| | | zuppa inglese | trifle |

## Drinking essentials

| aperitivo | pre-dinner drink | caffè | coffee |
| digestivo | after-dinner drink | cioccolata calda | hot chocolate |
| vino rosso | red wine | frappé | milkshake made with ice cream |
| vino bianco | white wine | | |
| vino rosato | rosé wine | frullato | milkshake |
| spumante | sparkling wine | ghiaccio | ice |
| secco | dry | granita | iced drink with coffee or fruit |
| dolce | sweet | | |
| birra | beer | latte | milk |
| litro | litre | limonate | lemonade |
| mezzo | half-litre | selz | soda water |
| quarto | quarter-litre | spremuta | fresh fruit juice |
| Salute! | Cheers! (toast) | succo di frutta | concentrated fruit juice with sugar |
| acqua minerale | mineral water | | |
| aranciata | orangeade | tazza | cup |
| bicchiere | glass | tè | tea |
| bottiglia | bottle | tonico | tonic water |

# Glossary of artistic and architectural terms

**AMBO** A kind of simple pulpit, popular in Italian medieval churches.

**ANFITEATRO** Amphitheatre.

**APSE** Semicircular recess at the altar, usually eastern, end of a church.

**ARCHITRAVE** The lowest part of the entablature.

**ATRIUM** Inner courtyard.

**BADÌA** Abbey.

**BALDACCHINO** A canopy on columns, usually placed over the altar in a church.

**BALUARDO** Bastion.

**BASILICA** Originally a Roman administrative building, adapted for early churches; distinguished by lack of transepts.

**BATTISTERO** Baptistery.

**BELVEDERE** A terrace or lookout point.

**BORGO** Medieval suburb or hamlet.

**CALDARIUM** The steam room of a Roman bath.

**CAMPANILE** Bell-tower, sometimes detached, usually of a church.

**CAMPO** Square.

**CAMPOSANTO** Cemetery.

**CANTORIA** Choir loft.

**CAPITAL** Top of a column.

**CAPPELLA** Chapel.

**CASTELLO** Castle.

**CENACOLO** Last Supper.

**CHANCEL** Part of a church containing the altar.

**CHIESA** Church.

**CHIOSTRO** Cloister.

**CIBORIUM** Another word for baldacchino.

**COLLEGIATA** Church just below the hierarchy of a cathedral.

**CONTRADA** Ancient quarter of a town.

**CORTILE** Galleried courtyard or cloister.

**CORNICE** The top section of a classical facade.

**CRYPT** Burial place in a church, usually under the choir.

**CUPOLA** Dome.

**CYCLOPEAN WALLS** Fortifications built of huge, rough stone blocks.

**DIPTYCH** Twin-panelled painting.

**DUOMO/CATTEDRALE** Cathedral.

**ENTABLATURE** The section above the capital on a classical building, below the cornice.

**EX-VOTO** Artefact designed in thanksgiving to a saint. The adjective is ex-votive.

**FONTE** Fountainhouse.

**FORTEZZA** Fortress.

**FRESCO** Wall-painting technique in which the artist applies paint to wet plaster for a more permanent finish.

**GONFALONI** Painted flags or standards.

**INTARSIA** Inlaid stone or wood.

**LOGGIA** Roofed gallery or balcony.

**LUNETTE** Semicircular space in vault or ceiling.

**MAESTÀ** Madonna and Child enthroned.

**MATRONEUM** Women's gallery in early church.

**MUNICIPIO** Town hall.

**NARTHEX** Vestibule of a church.

**NAVE** Central space in a church, usually flanked by aisles.

**PALAZZO** Palace, mansion, or block of flats.

PALAZZO DEL PODESTÀ Magistrate's palace.

PALAZZO DEL POPOLO, PALAZZO PUBBLICO, PALAZZO COMUNALE Town hall.

PANTOCRATOR An image of Christ, usually portrayed in the act of blessing.

PIANO NOBILE Main floor of a palace, usually the first.

PIETÀ Image of the Virgin mourning the dead Christ.

PIETRA DURA Hard or semiprecious stones used for decorative inlay.

PIEVE Parish church.

PINACOTECA Picture gallery.

POLYPTYCH Painting on several joined panels.

PORTA Gate.

PORTICO Covered entrance to a building.

PREDELLA Small panel below the main scenes of an altarpiece.

PUTTI Cherubs.

RELIQUARY Receptacle for a saint's relics, usually bones. Often highly decorated.

ROCCA Castle.

SALA DEI PRIORI Council chamber.

SANTUARIO Sanctuary or chancel.

SGRAFFITO Decorative technique whereby a layer of plaster is scratched to form a pattern.

SINOPIA Sketch for a fresco, applied to the wall.

STUCCO Plaster made from water, lime, sand and powdered marble, used for decorative work.

TEATRO Theatre.

TEMPIO Temple.

THERMAE Baths, usually elaborate buildings in Roman villas.

TONDO Round painting or relief.

TORRE Tower.

TRIPTYCH Painting on three joined panels.

TROMPE L'OEIL Work of art that deceives the viewer by tricks of perspective.

# Glossary of Italian words and acronyms

## Italian words

**ALTO** Upper.

**AUTOSTAZIONE** Bus station.

**AUTOSTRADA** Motorway.

**BASSO** (or **SCALO**) Lower.

**BIBLIOTECA** Library.

**CENTRO** Centre.

**CENTRO STORICO** Historic centre.

**COMUNE** An administrative area; also the local council or town hall.

**CORSO** Avenue or boulevard.

**ENTRATA** Entrance.

**FESTA** Festival, holiday.

**FIUME** River.

**GIARDINO** Garden; **GIARDINO BOTANICO** (or **ORTO BOTANICO**), botanical garden.

**MERCATO** Market.

**MUSEO** Museum.

**OSPEDALE** Hospital.

**PAESE** Place, area or village.

**PALIO** Horse race (most famously in Siena).

**PARCO** Park.

**PASSEGGIATA** The customary early evening walk – sometimes applied to a promenade.

**PIANO** Plain.

**PIAZZA** Square.

**QUESTURA** Main police station.

**SENSO UNICO** One-way street.

**SOTTOPASSAGIO** Subway.

**STAZIONE** Station.

**STRADA** Road.

**USCITA** Exit.

**VIA** Road (always used with name, eg Via Roma).

## Acronyms

**ACI** Automobile Club d'Italia.

**APT** Azienda Provinciale di Turismo.

**EPT** Ente Provinciale di Turismo (provincial tourist office); see also **APT** and **AAST**.

**IVA** Imposta Valore Aggiunto (VAT).

**RAI** The Italian state TV and radio network.

**SS** Strada Statale; equivalent to a British "A" road, eg SS18.

# Travel store

TRAVEL

# & MORE

Visit us online

# www.roughguides.com

Information on over 25,000 destinations around the world

- **Read** Rough Guides' trusted travel info

- **Share** journals, photos and travel advice with other readers

- Get exclusive Rough Guide **discounts** and travel deals

- Earn membership points every time you contribute to the

  **Rough Guide community** and get free books, flights and trips

- Browse thousands of **CD reviews** and artists in our music area

# ONLINE

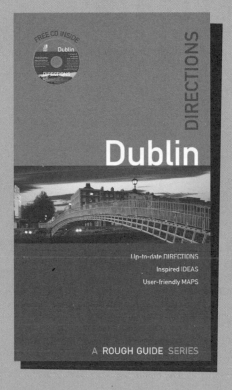

Rough Guide Maps, printed on waterproof and rip-proof Polyart™ paper, offer an unbeatable combination of practicality, clarity of design and amazing value.

## CITY MAPS

Amsterdam ·Athens · Barcelona · Berlin · Boston · Brussels · Chicago · Dublin Florence & Siena · Frankfurt · Hong Kong · Lisbon · London · Los Angeles Madrid · Marrakesh · Miami · New York · Paris · Prague · Rome · San Francisco Toronto · Venice · Washington DC and more...

US$8.99        Can$13.99        £4.99

## COUNTRY & REGIONAL MAPS

Algarve · Andalucía · Argentina · Australia · Baja California · Brittany · Crete Croatia · Cuba · Cyprus · Czech Republic · Dominican Republic · Dubai · Egypt · Greece · Guatemala & Belize · Iceland · Ireland · Kenya · Mexico · Morocco · New Zealand · Northern Spain · Peru · Portugal · Sicily · South Africa · South India · Sri Lanka · Tenerife · Thailand · Trinidad & Tobago · Tuscany · Yucatán Peninsula · and more...

US$9.99        Can$13.99        £5.99

# MAPS

# NOTES

TRAVEL STORE

ROUGH
GUIDES

# Small print and

# Index

# A Rough Guide to Rough Guides

Published in 1982, the first Rough Guide – to Greece – was a student scheme that became a publishing phenomenon. Mark Ellingham, a recent graduate in English from Bristol University, had been travelling in Greece the previous summer and couldn't find the right guidebook. With a small group of friends he wrote his own guide, combining a highly contemporary, journalistic style with a thoroughly practical approach to travellers' needs.

The immediate success of the book spawned a series that rapidly covered dozens of destinations. And, in addition to impecunious backpackers, Rough Guides soon acquired a much broader and older readership that relished the guides' wit and inquisitiveness as much as their enthusiastic, critical approach and value-for-money ethos.

These days, Rough Guides include recommendations from shoestring to luxury and cover more than two hundred destinations around the globe, including almost every country in the Americas and Europe, more than half of Africa, and most of Asia and Australasia. Our ever-growing team of authors and photographers is spread all over the world, particularly in Europe, the USA and Australia.

In the early 1990s, Rough Guides branched out of travel, with the publication of Rough Guides to World Music, Classical Music and the Internet. All three have become benchmark titles in their fields, spearheading the publication of a wide range of books under the Rough Guide name.

Including the travel series, Rough Guides now number more than 350 titles, covering: phrasebooks, waterproof maps, music guides from Opera to Heavy Metal, reference works as diverse as Conspiracy Theories and Shakespeare, and popular culture books from iPods to Poker. Rough Guides also produce a series of more than 120 World Music CDs in partnership with World Music Network.

Visit www.roughguides.com to see our latest publications.

Rough Guide travel images are available for commercial licensing at www.roughguidespictures.com.

## Rough Guide credits

**Text editor**: Ruth Blackmore
**Layout**: Amit Verma
**Cartography**: Maxine Repath and Rajesh Mishra
**Picture editor**: Harriet Mills
**Production**: Katherine Owers
**Proofreader**: Diane Margolis
**Cover design**: Chloë Roberts
**Photographer**: James McConnachie
**Editorial**: **London** Kate Berens, Claire Saunders, Geoff Howard, Polly Thomas, Richard Lim, Clifton Wilkinson, Alison Murchie, Karoline Densley, Andy Turner, Ella O'Donnell, Keith Drew, Edward Aves, Nikki Birrell, Helen Marsden, Alice Park, Sarah Eno, Joe Staines, Duncan Clark, Peter Buckley, Matthew Milton, Tracy Hopkins; **New York** Andrew Rosenberg, Richard Koss, Steven Horak, AnneLise Sorensen, Amy Hegarty, Hunter Slaton, April Isaacs
**Design & Pictures**: **London** Simon Bracken, Dan May, Diana Jarvis, Mark Thomas, Jj Luck; **Delhi** Madhulita Mohapatra, Umesh Aggarwal, Ajay Verma, Jessica Subramanian, Ankur Guha

**Production**: Julia Bovis, Sophie Hewat
**Cartography**: **London** Ed Wright, Katie Lloyd-Jones; **Delhi** Manish Chandra, Rajesh Chhibber, Jai Prakash Mishra, Ashutosh Bharti, Animesh Pathak, Jasbir Sandhu, Karobi Gogoi
**Online**: **New York** Jennifer Gold, Suzanne Welles, Kristin Mingrone; **Delhi** Manik Chauhan, Narender Kumar, Shekhar Jha, Rakesh Kumar, Lalit K. Sharma, Chhandita Chakravarty
**Marketing and publicity**: **London** Richard Trillo, Niki Hanmer, David Wearn, Demelza Dallow, Louise Maher; **New York** Geoff Colquitt, Megan Kennedy, Katy Ball; **Delhi** Reem Khokhar
**Custom publishing and foreign rights**: Philippa Hopkins
**Manager India**: Punita Singh
**Series editor**: Mark Ellingham
**Reference director**: Andrew Lockett
**PA to Managing and Publishing directors**: Megan McIntyre
**Publishing director**: Martin Dunford
**Managing director**: Kevin Fitzgerald

## Publishing information

This first edition published March 2006 by
**Rough Guides Ltd**
80 Strand, London WC2R 0RL
345 Hudson St, 4th Floor,
New York, NY 10014, USA
14 Local Shopping Centre, Panchsheel Park,
New Delhi 110017, India
**Distributed by the Penguin Group**
Penguin Books Ltd
80 Strand, London WC2R 0RL
Penguin Putnam, Inc
375 Hudson Street, NY 10014, USA
Penguin Group (Australia)
250 Camberwell Road, Camberwoll
Victoria 3124, Australia
Penguin Books Canada Ltd
10 Alcorn Avenue, Toronto, Ontario
M4V 1E4 Canada
Penguin Group (New Zealand)
Cnr Rosedale and Airborne Roads,
Albany, Auckland, New Zealand

Typeset in Bembo and Helvetica to an original design by Henry Iles
Printed and bound in China.
© Jonathan Buckley and Tim Jepson
No part of this book may be reproduced in any form without permission from the publisher except for the quotation of brief passages in reviews.
384pp includes index
A catalogue record for this book is available from the British Library.
ISBN-13: 978-1-84353-590-4
ISBN-10: 1-84353-590-4
The publishers and authors have done their best to ensure the accuracy and currency of all the information in **The Rough Guide to Florence and Siena**; however, they can accept no responsibility for any loss, injury or inconvenience sustained by any traveller as a result of information or advice contained in the Guide.
1   3   5   7   9   8   6   4   2

## Help us update

We've gone to a lot of effort to ensure that the first edition of **The Rough Guide to Florence and Siena** is accurate and up to date. However, things change – places get "discovered", opening hours are notoriously fickle, restaurants and rooms raise prices or lower standards. If you feel we've got it wrong or left something out, we'd like to know, and if you can remember the address, the price, the time, the phone number, so much the better.

We'll credit all contributions, and send a copy of the next edition (or any other Rough Guide if you prefer) for the best letters. Everyone who writes to us and isn't already a subscriber will receive a copy of our full-colour thrice-yearly newsletter. Please mark letters: **"Rough Guide Florence and Siena Update"** and send to: Rough Guides, 80 Strand, London WC2R 0RL, or Rough Guides, 4th Floor, 345 Hudson St, New York, NY 10014. Or send an email to **mail@roughguides.com**.

Have your questions answered and tell others about your trip at **www.roughguides.atinfopop.com**.

# Acknowledgements

**Charles:** a great many thanks to Monica Griesbach, who generously solved accommodation problems (and Kate Crowe, who introduced us), Miriam Hurley for her great commments, time and assistance, Peter and Jean Hoare for babysitting and comments, Jason Waite for help, Sara Watkinson for visiting, and of course Caroline and Molly Hebbert for everything.

**Tim** would like to thank Duncan and Amanda Baird, Marella Caracciolo, Michael Sheridan and Yasmin Sethna.

## Photo credits

All photos © Rough Guides except the following:

**Cover**
Front cover: Michelangelo's *David*, Accademia, Florence © Alamy.
Inside back cover: The Palio, Siena © roughguidespictures.com.
Back cover: Tuscan countryside near Siena © Alamy.

**Full page**
Duccio's *Maestà* in Museo dell'Opera dell Duomo, Siena © Rough Guides, with thanks to Opera Della Metropolitana, Siena.

**Introduction**
View across the Arno bridge, Florence © Nico Tondini/CuboImages srl/Alamy.

**Things not to miss**
01 Botticelli, Sandro (1445–1510): *Spring*. Florence, Galleria degli Uffizi © 1991, Photo Scala, Florence – courtesy of the Ministero Beni e Att. Culturali.
02 Siena Campo during Palio © Rough Guides, with thanks to the Comune di Siena & APT Siena.
03 Michelangelo (1475–1564): *Prisoner known as Atlas*. Florence, Accademia © 2004, Photo Scala, Florence – courtesy of the Ministero Beni e Att. Culturali.
05 Sala del Pellegrinaio, Ospedale di Santa Maria della Scala © Rough Guides, with thanks to Musei di Santa Maria della Scala.
08 Giotto (1266–1336): *Scenes from Life of Saint Francis: Death of the Saint* – detail. Santa Croce (Cappella Bardi) © 1990 Photo Scala, Florence/Fondo Edifici di Culto – Min. dell'Interno.
14 Museo dell Opera del Duomo © Rough Guides, with thanks to Opera Della Metropolitana.
15 Masaccio (1401–1428): *Expulsion from Paradise* (detail). Galleria degli Uffizi, Florence © 1990 Photo Scala, Florence/Fondo Edifici di Culto – Min. dell'Interno.
17 *Madonna and Child with Saints, Doctors of the Church and Angels* by Ambrogio Lorenzetti (1285–c.1348) Pinacoteca Nazionale, Siena © 1990 Photo Scala, Florence – courtesy of the Ministero Beni e Att. Culturali.
19 Siena Palio racing © Rough Guides, with thanks to the Comune di Siena & APT Siena.
22 Titian (1477/89-1576): *The Magdalen*. Florence, Galleria Palatina © 1990, Photo Scala, Florence – courtesy of the Ministero Beni e Att. Culturali.
24 Martini's Guidoriccio da Fogliano fresco, Museo Civico © Rough Guides, with thanks to the Museo Civico, Siena.

**Black and whites**
p.105 *St. Dominic Sending Forth the Hounds and St. Peter Martyr Casting Down the Heretics* from the Spanish Chapel, c.1365 (fresco) (detail) by Andrea di Bonaiuto (Andrea da Firenze) (fl.1343–77). Santa Maria Novella, Florence © Bridgeman Art Library.
p.114 Michelangelo (1475–1564): Tomb of Lorenzo, Duke of Urbino. Florence, Medici Chapels © 1992, Photo Scala, Florence – courtesy of the Ministero Beni e Att. Culturali.
p.158 *La Velata* (Woman with a Veil) by Raphael (1483–1520). Galleria Palatina, Florence © 1990 Photo Scala, Florence – courtesy of the Ministero Beni e Att. Culturali.
p.242 Siena Duomo facade © Kristiane Adelt/age fotostock/®www.superstock.co.uk.
p.254 Detail from original Fonte Gaia, Ospedale di Santa Maria della Scala © Rough Guides, with thanks to the Musei di Santa Maria della Scala, Siena.
p.295 *Grand Hotel Continental*, "Salone delle Feste" ballroom © Park Hotel Siena & Grand Hotel Continental.
p.320 Bronzino, Agnolo (School): Portrait of Cosimo the Elder. Florence, Galleria Palatina © 1990 Photo Scala, Florence – courtesy of the Ministero Beni e Att. Culturali.
p.336 Bugiardini, Giuliano (1476–1555): Portrait of Michelangelo Wearing a Turban. Florence, Casa Buonarroti. © 1990, Photo Scala, Florence.

**Colour insert: Food**
Vegetable market, Florence © John Heseltine/Italian Archive.
Vineyard Greve in Chianti, Tuscany © Jon Arnold Images/Alamy.

**Colour insert: Palio**
All photographs © Rough Guides, with thanks to the Comune di Siena & APT Siena.

# Index

Entries relating to Florence are marked (F); entries for Siena are marked (S).

INDEX

381

# Map symbols

maps are listed in the full index using coloured text

| | | | |
|---|---|---|---|
| ═══ | Major road | ✡ | Synagogue |
| ═══ | Minor road | ★ | Bus stop |
| ▬▬▬ | Pedestrianized street | ⚊ | Campsite |
| ⊞⊞⊞ | Steps | ⓘ | Tourist office |
| - - - - - | Path | ⊠ | Post office |
| ▬▬▬ | Railway line | 🅿 | Parking |
| ─── | River | 🅃 | Toilets |
| ▄▄▄▄ | Wall | ⊞ | Church |
| ⊠—⊠ | Gate | ▬ | Building |
| ◉ | Accommodation | ⬭ | Stadium |
| ✈ | Airport | ▨ | Park |
| ▲ | Mountain peak | ⊞ | Cemetery |

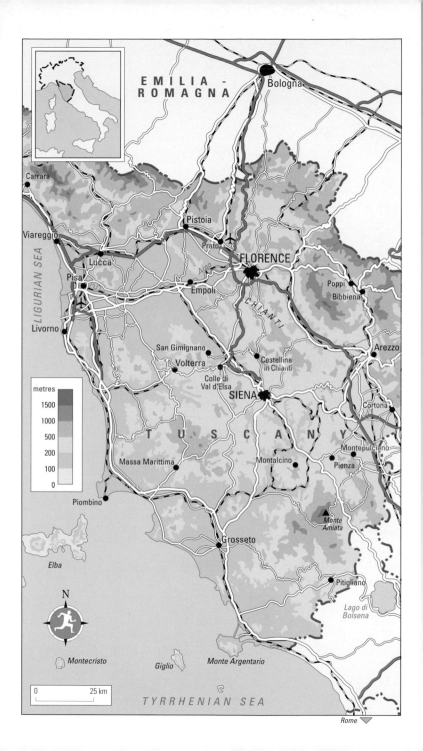

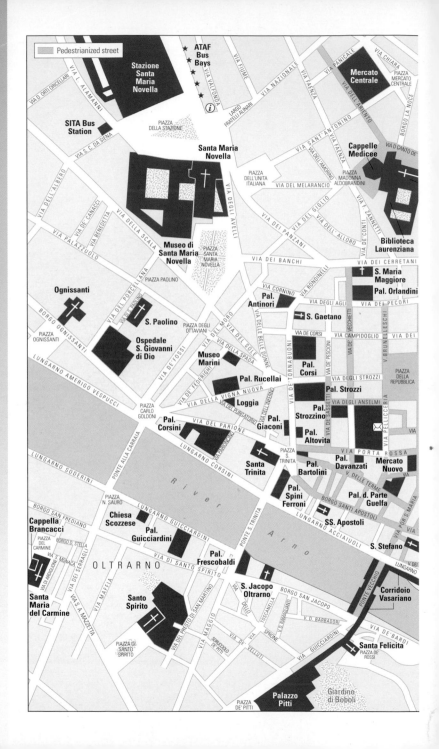

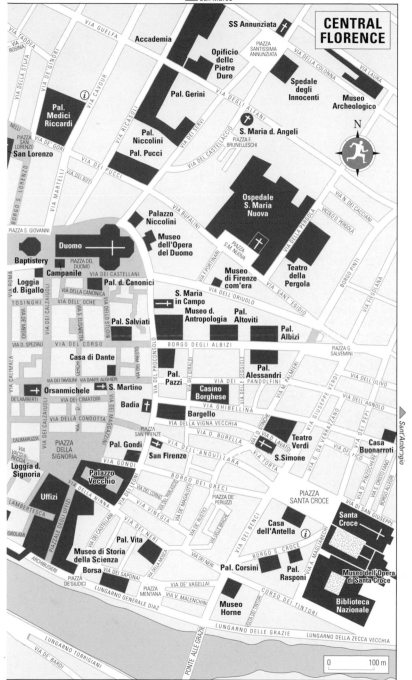

CENTRAL FLORENCE

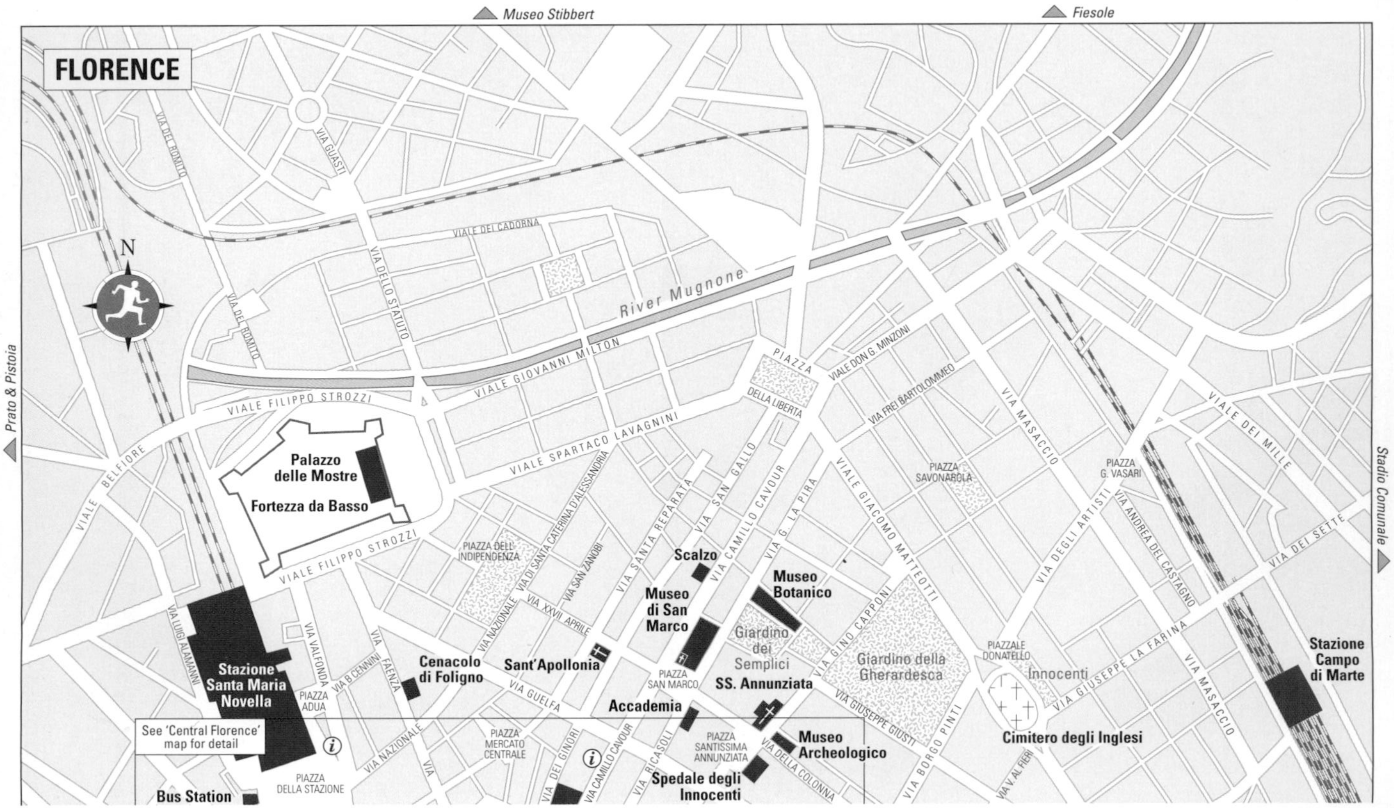

Museo Stibbert
Fiesole
FLORENCE
Prato & Pistoia
Stadio Comunale
N
River Mugnone
Palazzo delle Mostre
Fortezza da Basso
Stazione Santa Maria Novella
Bus Station
See 'Central Florence' map for detail
Cenacolo di Foligno
Sant'Apollonia
Scalzo
Museo di San Marco
Museo Botanico
Giardino dei Semplici
SS. Annunziata
Accademia
Museo Archeologico
Spedale degli Innocenti
Giardino della Gherardesca
Innocenti
Cimitero degli Inglesi
Stazione Campo di Marte
VIA DEL ROMITO
VIA GUASTI
VIALE DEI CADORNA
VIA DELLO STATUTO
VIALE GIOVANNI MILTON
VIALE FILIPPO STROZZI
VIALE BELFIORE
VIALE SPARTACO LAVAGNINI
PIAZZA DELLA LIBERTA
VIALE DON G. MINZONI
VIA FREI BARTOLOMMEO
VIA MASACCIO
PIAZZA SAVONAROLA
PIAZZA G. VASARI
VIALE DEI MILLE
VIA DEI SETTE
VIA DEGLI ARTISTI
VIA ANDREA DEL CASTAGNO
VIALE GIACOMO MATTEOTTI
VIA G. LA PIRA
VIA CAMILLO CAVOUR
VIA SAN GALLO
VIA SANTA REPARATA
VIA DI SANTA CATERINA D'ALESSANDRIA
VIA SAN ZANOBI
PIAZZA DELL' INDIPENDENZA
VIA XXVII APRILE
VIA NAZIONALE
VIA LUIGI ALAMANNI
VIA VALFONDA
VIA B. CENNINI
VIA FAENZA
PIAZZA ADUA
PIAZZA DELLA STAZIONE
VIA GUELFA
PIAZZA SAN MARCO
PIAZZA MERCATO CENTRALE
VIA DEI GINORI
VIA RICASOLI
PIAZZA SANTISSIMA ANNUNZIATA
VIA DELLA COLONNA
VIA GINO CAPPONI
VIA GIUSEPPE GIUSTI
VIA BORGO PINTI
PIAZZALE DONATELLO
VIA GIUSEPPE LA FARINA
VIA V. AL FIERI
VIA

△ S. Salvi

200 m

0

River Arno

Santa Maria dei Pazzi
Santa Maria Maddalena dei Pazzi
Synagogue
S. Ambrogio
Mercato Sant'Ambrogio

PIAZZA G. OBERDAN
VIA FRA PAOLO SARPI
VIA DEI GHIBELLINA
VIA VINCENZO GIOBERTI
VIA DEI PILASTRI
VIA DELL'AGNOLO
VIA FRA GIOVANNI ANGELICO
VIALE BERNARDO SEGNI
VIALE GIUSEPPE MAZZINI
VIALE ANTONIO GRAMSCI
VIA NICCOLINI
PIAZZA MASSIMO D'AZEGLIO
PIAZZA CESARE BECCARIA
VIALE GIOVANNI AMENDOLA
VIA PIETRAPIANA BORGO LA CROCE
VIA DEI MACCI
VIA GHIBELLINA
VIA DELLA MATTONAIA
VIA DELL'ORIUOLO
VIA DEI PILASTRI

LUNG. D. TEMPIO
VIALE DELLA GIOVINE ITALIA
VIA DELLA VECCHIA
PONTE SAN NICCOLÒ
PIAZZA FRANCESCO FERRUCCI
VIALE MICHELANGELO
VIA GIAMPAOLO ORSINI
VIA CARLO GOLDONI SALUTATI

LUNGARNO BENVENUTO CELLINI
Camping Michelangiolo
PIAZZALE MICHELANGELO
San Salvatore al Monte
San Miniato al Monte
VIALE MICHELANGELO
VIALE GALILEO GALILEI

Pal. Medici Riccardi
Cappelle Medicee
San Lorenzo
Museo dell'Opera del Duomo
Ospedale S. Maria Nuova
Duomo
Baptistery
Campanile
Casa Buonarroti
Santa Croce
Museo Horne
Badia Fiorentina
Bargello
Osanmichele
Palazzo Vecchio
Uffizi
Pal. Strozzi
Pal. Rucellai
Palazzo Davanzati
Santa Trinita
Santa Maria Novella
Ognissanti
Santo Spirito
Santa Felicita
Palazzo Pitti
La Specola
Giardino di Boboli
Forte di Belvedere
Museo Bardini
San Niccolò
Cappella Brancacci
Santa Maria del Carmine
Porta Romana

OLTRARNO

VIA CAVOUR
VIA MARTELLI
PIAZZA DELL'UNITÀ D'ITALIA
VIA PANZANI
PIAZZA S. MARIA MAGGIORE
PIAZZA SANTA MARIA NOVELLA
VIA DELLA SCALA
VIA PALAZZUOLO
LUNGARNO AMERIGO VESPUCCI
BORGO OGNISSANTI
PONTE ALLA CARRAIA
VIA DEI FOSSI
VIA DEI TORNABUONI
VIA DELLA VIGNA NUOVA
PIAZZA ANTINORI
BORGO SS. APOSTOLI
LUNG. CORSINI
PONTE S. TRINITA
PONTE VECCHIO
BORGO SAN JACOPO
VIA DELLE TERME
VIA PELLICCERIA
PIAZZA DELLA REPUBBLICA
VIA DEI CALZAIUOLI
VIA ROMA
PIAZZA DEL DUOMO
VIA DEL CORSO
VIA DEL PROCONSOLO
PIAZZA SAN FIRENZE
PIAZZA DELLA SIGNORIA
VIA DEI GONDI
VIA DEI BENCI
VIA DE' SERVI
PIAZZA SAVONAROLA
PIAZZA SALVEMINI
PIAZZA DEI CIOMPI
VIA DEI MALCONTENTI
VIA DELL'OSTE
VIA DEI GIRALOMO
BORGO D'GLI ALBIZI
VIA STUFA
VIA DELL'ALFANI
PIAZZA SANTA CROCE
VIA GIUSEPPE VERDI
VIA DEL GIGLIO
LUNG. DELLE GRAZIE
PONTE ALLE GRAZIE
COSTA DI S. GIORGIO
VIA DE' BARDI
LUNGARNO TORRIGIANI
VIA DI BELVEDERE
VIA DI SAN LEONARDO
LUNGARNO SERRISTORI
LUNGARNO GIUSEPPE POGGI
VIA DI POGGI
VIA DI SAN NICCOLÒ
VIA DE' MAGGIO
VIA GUICCIARDINI
VIA DEI SERRAGLI
VIA SANTA MONACA
VIA DI SANTO SPIRITO
VIA DI SANT'AGOSTINO
VIA SANT'AGOSTINO
PIAZZA SANTO SPIRITO
VIA ROMANA
VIA MAZZETTA
VIA DI SAN FREDIANO
PIAZZA CASTELLO
PIAZZA DEL CARMINE
BORGO SAN FREDIANO
VIA DELLA CHIESA

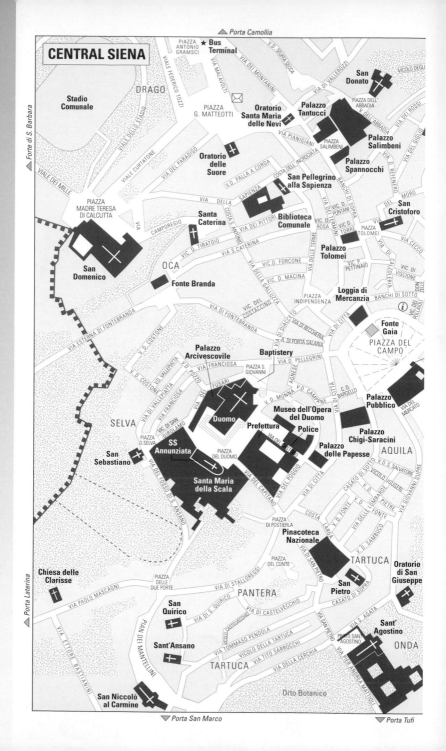